THE ORIGINS OF THE SECOND WORLD WAR:
AN INTERNATIONAL PERSPECTIVE

The Origins of the Second World War: An International Perspective

Edited by Frank McDonough

continuum

Continuum International Publishing Group

The Tower Building   80 Maiden Lane

11 York Road   Suite 704

London SE1 7NX   New York NY 1003

www.continuumbooks.com

First published 2011

British Library Cataloguing-in-Publication Data
A catalogue record for this book is available from the British Library

ISBN: HB: 978-1-4411-6443-8
PB: 978-1-4411-8593-8

Library of Congress Cataloging-in-Publication Data
A catalog record for this book is available from the Library of Congress

Typeset by Fakenham Prepress Solutions, Fakenham, Norfolk NR21 8NN
Printed and bound in India

Contents

Contributors

Editor

Frank McDonough is leading authority on Anglo-German relations in the period 1905 to 1945. He is Professor of International History at Liverpool John Moores University. His many books include *Neville Chamberlain, Appeasement and the British Road to War*, *The Conservative Party and Anglo-German Relations, 1905–1914* and *The Holocaust*. His most recent book was *Sophie Scholl: The Woman Who Defied Hitler*, which was a *London Evening Standard* 'Book of the Year' 2009.

Contributors (in alphabetical order)

Anthony Adamthwaite is a leading authority on twentieth century international history. He is Professor of History at the University of California at Berkeley. He has published on a number of aspects of international relations, including *France and the Coming of the Second World War, 1936–1939*; *The Making of the Second World War*; *The Lost Peace: International Relations in Europe 1918–1939*; *Grandeur and Misery: France's bid for power in Europe, 1914–1940*.

Peter Bierl, a graduate of at the Ludwig-Maximilians-University in Munich, is a freelance journalist who works for *Süddeutsche Zeitung* in Munich and the weekly *Jungle World* in Berlin. He has also published several books, including *Alle Macht den Räten – Rosa Luxemburg: Rätedemokratie und Sozialismus*.

Richard Bosworth is a scholar of Italian history and Mussolini. He is a Professor of History at Reading University and the University of Western Australia. He has written over twenty books, including *Mussolini's Italy: Life under the Dictatorship 1915–1945*, *Italy and the Wider World 1860–1960 and Italian Fascism: History, Memory and Representation*.

John Charmley is an expert on Neville Chamberlain and the author of a controversial biography of Winston Churchill. He is Professor of Modern History at the University of East Anglia, UK. He received acclaim for his study *Chamberlain and the Lost Peace*, which argued a strong revisionist case. He is the author of many other works, including *Churchill's Grand Alliance*

1940–1957, A History of Conservative Politics and *Splendid Isolation? Britain and the Balance of Power, 1871–1914.*

Robert Citino is currently Professor at University of North Texas, US. He has written many critically acclaimed books, most notably *The Path To Blitzkrieg: Doctrine and Training in the German Army 1920–39* and *Quest for Decisive Victory: From Stalemate to Blitzkrieg in Europe 1899–1940.* He has won numerous awards for his books and his teaching.

Patrick O. Cohrs is a specialist on the role of the USA in international affairs during the inter-war years. He is Associate Professor of History at Yale University. His recent study, *The Unfinished Peace After World War I: America, Britain and the Stabilisation of Europe 1919–1932,* was critically acclaimed.

David Dutton is an authority on British foreign policy in the twentieth century and one of Britain's leading political biographers. He was Professor of History at Liverpool University until his retirement in 2010. He has written a number of acclaimed biographies, including titles on Neville Chamberlain, Austen Chamberlain, Sir John Simon and Sir Anthony Eden.

Conan Fischer is a Professor in the School of History at the University of St Andrews. His expertise focuses on inter-war Germany and Franco-German relations during the same period. His more recent publications include *The Rise of the Nazis, The Ruhr Crisis, 1923–1924, and Europe between Democracy and Dictatorship, 1900–1945.*

Jürgen Förster is an expert on German foreign policy and military strategy during the Nazi era. He is a Adjunct Professor of History at the Albert-Ludwig University of Freiburg. He has made contributions to the ground-breaking multi-volume *Germany and the Second World War* and his books include *Stalingrad: Risse im Bündis, 1942–1943.*

T.G. Fraser is a specialist in contemporary international history with a special interest in the Arab–Israeli Conflict. He is currently Emeritus Professor of History and Honorary Professor of Conflict Research at the University of Ulster. His books include *The USA and the Middle East since World War 2, The Arab–Israeli Conflict,* and, with Andrew Mango and Robert McNamara, *The Makers of the Modern Middle East.*

Milan Hauner is an historian of Czechoslovakia and on twentieth-century transnational history. He is an Honorary Fellow at the University of Wisconsin-Madison. Among his publications are *India in Axis Strategy, Hitler – A Chronology of His Life and Time* and a critical reconstruction of *Edvard Beneš' Memoirs 1938–45* in three volumes.

Baroness Ruth Henig is an authority on the League of Nations. She has written numerous books and articles, including *The Origins of the First World War*. She was awarded a CBE in 2000 and was made a life peer in June 2004.

Haruo Iguchi is an expert on Japan's role in the origins of the Asia Pacific War. He is currently Professor in International History at Nagoya University. He has written extensively on Japanese diplomacy and politics, international history and US–Japanese relations.

Talbot Imlay's specialism is British and French strategy during the late 1930s. He is Associate Professor at the history department at the Université Laval, Canada. Among his recent highly acclaimed books is *Facing the Second World War: Strategy, Politics and Economics in Britain and France, 1938–1940*.

Manfred Jonas is an authority on the policy of 'isolationism' during the Roosevelt era. He is the John Bigelow Emeritus Professor of History at Union College, New York, US. He is the author or editor of six books, including *Isolationism in America, 1935–1941* and *American Foreign Relations in the 20th Century*.

Efraim Karsh is an expert on European neutrality and Middle Eastern Affairs. He is currently Professor of Mediterranean Studies at King's College, London. He has held posts at Harvard, the Sorbonne, Columbia, Helsinki and Tel Aviv. His many books include *The Gulf Conflict 1990–1991: Diplomacy and War in the New World Order*.

Mark Levene's specialism is modern Jewish history and the causes and consequences of genocide. He is Reader in History at the University of Southampton, UK. He is the author of a major two-volume study of genocide: *The Meaning of Genocide: Genocide in the Age of the Nation State* and *The Rise of the West and the Coming of Genocide*.

Lars Lüdicke is an historian of German foreign policy in the Nazi era. He gained his PhD at the University of Potsdam under the supervision of Professor Klaus Hildebrand. He has produced many books and articles on German foreign policy between 1933 and 1945 including an important study of Constantin von Neurath, the German Foreign Minister.

Enrique Moradiellos is an authority on the international implications of the Spanish Civil War. He is a Professor of History at the University of Extremadura, Spain. His many books in Spanish include *Nuetraliadad Benávola* and he has made contributions to many edited volumes on Spain's role in the international politics of the 1930s.

Richard J. Overy is one of the leading experts on the Second World War and is Professor of History at the University of Exeter, UK. In 2001 he was awarded the Samuel Elliot Morrison Prize of the Society for Military History for his contribution to the history of warfare. He has written twenty-five books, including *The Origins of the Second World War*, *Interrogations: Inside the Minds of the Nazi Elite* and *The Dictators: Hitler's Germany and Stalin's Russia*, which won the Wolfson Prize in 2005.

Anita Prazmowska is a scholar of Polish foreign policy between 1918 and 1945. She is a Professor of History at the London School of Economics. Her books include *Poland: A Modern History*, *Britain and Poland 1939–1943: The Betrayed Ally* and *Britain, Poland and the Eastern Front, 1939*.

Kevin Quinlan received his Ph.D. in History from the University of Cambridge. His doctoral thesis focused on the inter-war history of MI5. He currently works as an analyst for the Department of the Navy in Washington, DC.

Jeffrey Record is currently a Professor at US Air Force War College in Montgomery, US. He has extensive experience on Capitol Hill serving, most notably, as a Professional Staff member of the Senate Armed Services Committee. He is the author of several books, including *Dark Victory: America's Second War against Iraq*.

Geoffrey Roberts is an internationally recognised authority on Soviet foreign policy, Stalin's war leadership and the early history of the cold war. He is Professor and Head of the School of History at University College Cork, Ireland. His many books include: *The Unholy Alliance: Stalin's Pact with Hitler*, *The Soviet Union and the Origins of the Second World War*, *The Soviet Union in World Politics, 1945–1991*, *Victory at Stalingrad: The Battle That Changed History*, and *Stalin's Wars: From World War to Cold War, 1939–1953*.

Alan Sharp is an authority on the Paris Peace Settlement of 1919 and British foreign policy during the inter-war period. He is Emeritus Professor of History at the University of Ulster. He has written numerous books and articles on international history, most notably *The Versailles Settlement: Peacemaking after the First World War 1919–1923*.

M.G. Sheftall is an expert on militarism and national identity in modern Japan. He is currently Associate Professor at Shizuoka University, Japan. He published *Blossoms in the Wind: Human Legacies of the Kamikaze* in 2005 and has contributed chapters on Japanese kamikaze warfare for numerous scholarly volumes.

Calder Walton received a Ph.D. in History from the University of Cambridge, after which he held a Junior Research Fellowship also at Cambridge, and was a research assistant on Professor Christopher Andrew's unprecedented authorized history of MI5, published by Penguin in 2009. Calder is currently completing a book about British intelligence and the end of the British empire, and is training to become a Barrister.

Piotr S. Wandycz is one of the leading experts on Poland's role in interwar European diplomacy. He is now Bradford Durfee Professor Emeritus at Yale University and the former President of the Polish Institute of Arts & Sciences of America. He is the author of 18 books and over 400 articles. He has been awarded four honorary doctorates, most notably from the Sorbonne in Paris.

Neville Wylie is professor of contemporary history at the University of Nottingham, UK, and currently Dean of the Faculty of Arts & Social Sciences at Nottingham's campus in Malaysia. He is co-editor of *Contemporary European History*; his most recent book, *Barbed Wire Diplomacy. Britain, Germany and the Politics of Prisoners of War, 1939–1945*, appeared in 2010.

Marco Wyss is a Senior Research Fellow at the Centre for Security Studies, ETH Zurich. He recently completed a doctoral thesis at the Universities of Nottingham and Neuchâtel on Anglo-Swiss relations during the early Cold War. He is the author of *Un Suisse au service de la SS: Dr. Franz Riedweg*.

Robert J. Young is an historian of French foreign policy during the inter-war period. He is Professor of History at the University of Winnipeg, Canada. He has written numerous books and articles in his research area, including *In Command of France: French Foreign Policy and Military Planning, 1933–1940* and *France and the Origins of the Second World War*.

Introduction

Frank McDonough

In an article published in *National Interest* in 1989 Francis Fukuyama confidently predicted the end of history: 'that is, the end point of mankind's
ideological evolution and the universalization of Western liberal democracy as
the final form of human government'.[1] The fall of the Berlin Wall, the collapse
of communism and the end of the Cold War all seemed to confirm Fukuyama's
prophecy. Yet the crashing of three hijacked jets into the twin towers of New
York's World Trade Center and the Pentagon in Washington in September
2001, subsequent protracted wars in Iraq and Afghanistan and a banking crisis
comparable to the Wall Street Crash serve to demonstrate that history is very
much alive and kicking in the twenty-first century.

In the discourse of modern-day international relations the causes and
consequences of the Second World War are still current. 'Auschwitz' and
'Hiroshima' are words that evoke this 'century of violence'. Any politician who
mentions 'appeasement' is derided. No one wants to be cast in the role of
Neville Chamberlain. George W. Bush, US President from 2000 to 2008, called
Iran, Iraq and North Korea the 'Axis of Evil' – an obvious reference to the Axis
powers of the 1930s. Words like 'war crimes' and 'genocide' occur regularly in
debates on present-day conflicts. This is therefore an opportune moment to
offer a wide-ranging re-assessment of the international crisis that led to the
bloodiest global conflict in human history.

What we now call the Second World War is generally thought to have started
with the German attack on Poland on 1 September 1939. In fact, that did not
start a 'world war', only a limited conflict involving five European powers:
Germany, Poland, France, Britain and the Soviet Union. It was really a five-week
German–Polish War. Poland's Western allies stayed on the sidelines. Hitler and
Stalin then shared the spoils as part of a secret bargain struck during negotiations for the infamous Nazi–Soviet Pact signed on 23 August 1939. The Western
European war that began in the spring of 1940 was primarily a Franco-German
War, leading to a German occupation of Paris and preceded by a humiliating,
if miraculous, British evacuation at Dunkirk. The war in Europe only escalated
into a protracted struggle following the massive German attack on the Soviet
Union in June 1941. The African theatre of war primarily involved Britain
defending its imperial possessions against Italian forces, helped by a limited
number of German tank units. In Asia, Japan and China had been at war since
1937. The Japanese decision to attack the American naval fleet at Pearl Harbor
on 7 December 1941 marked a further escalation of the conflict. Four days later,
Hitler declared war on the USA. This is the point at which we can really talk
of a 'world' war, though even that claim needs refinement. It is more precise to

define the Second World War as a series of major and minor regional conflicts occurring on a global scale. Each had distinctive causes and characteristics.

An earlier European war that began in 1914 had also expanded to involve all the main protagonists who later participated in the Second World War and the potential connections between the two twentieth-century global conflicts have exercised scholars ever since. Some would argue that there was a 'European Civil War' going on in the first half of the 'century of violence'. There were many developments to which the 1914–18 war made a significant contribution: the fall of the Romanovs and the triumph of Bolshevism in the Russian Revolution of 1917; the crisis of Italian liberal parliamentarianism and the rise of Mussolini and Fascism in 1922; the economic disruption that culminated in the 1929 Wall Street Crash and the Great Depression, which combined with disgruntled nationalism to bring Hitler and the Nazis to power in Germany in 1933; and a number of disappointed or discontented powers seeking opportunities to overturn the post-war order.

It has long been my belief that this seminal event of the twentieth century can only be fully understood through international collaboration. This project brings together a team of leading historians and international relations experts to offer new insights based on cutting-edge research. The specially commissioned chapters that follow form the widest-ranging international perspective on the origins of the Second World War ever attempted in a single volume.

Any meaningful understanding of the origins of the war must begin with an assessment of the Paris peace settlements of 1919. Historians have generally viewed them as a failed compromise between the idealism of Woodrow Wilson, the US President, and the hard-headed realism of the victorious European powers: Britain, France, and Italy. The central objective was to prevent another war by imposing restrictions on the defeated powers. The Treaty of Versailles, which dealt with Germany, was signed on 28 June 1919.[2] For the iconoclastic British historian A.J.P Taylor a second war between Germany and Britain and France over Versailles was implicit from the moment that treaty was signed. [3] Alan Sharp acknowledges the strong contemporary and subsequent condemnations of Versailles, but suggests in a nuanced account that we should take more account of the enormous pressure under which the peacemakers deliberated, which made the conclusion of any treaties a remarkable feat. Sharp claims that if blame is assigned fairly, then it should be spread between those who concluded the settlement and subsequent leaders who had ample opportunity to rectify its alleged deficiencies between 1919 and 1939. Sharp points to three key reasons why this did not happen: America's renunciation of responsibility for executing treaties that its representatives in Paris had crucial roles in drafting; deep Anglo-French divisions of policy that persisted throughout the inter-war period; and Germany's refusal to accept the military verdict of the First World War.

The Paris Peace Conference also gave birth to the League of Nations. The League, based in neutral Geneva, was pledged to 'respect and preserve against external aggression all the members' and to take action against any aggressor via economic sanctions and if they failed through 'collective military action'. The League of Nations has been branded as a failure by most historians. Ruth Henig explains that while in the short term it could not fulfil the ambitious goals of its founders, largely because of the non-cooperation of the USA and the Soviet Union and then by the military challenges of Japan, Italy and Germany, the League was an important foundation for the flowering of international collaboration and was an important influence in the development of global multilateral cooperation.[4]

The three powers that effectively destroyed the world order established at Paris were Japan, Italy and Germany. All three had fascist or extreme nationalist regimes. They were perceived to be 'have-not' powers unhappy with the post-war world order. During the 1930s they increased military expenditure and engaged in foreign policies that flouted the authority of the League of Nations. Their determination to upset the status quo made a fundamental contribution to the outbreak of war. Yet each of these powers felt it had legitimate grievances that could only be rectified by force. It was their determination to act in this way that produced the trigger points that led to the Second World War and a great weight of historical research has been devoted to trying to explain why they acted as they did, including a number of chapters in this volume.

Japan embarked on a series of conflicts with China, the USA and the British Empire.[5] M.G. Sheftall's chapter on Imperial Era Japanese military ideology argues that it was distorted reactions to perceived Western cultural threats during the period of rapid industrialization after the mid-nineteenth century that found their ultimate expression in the ideological extremes of Japanese militarism, with dire consequences for tens of millions of lives in Asia. Sheftall claims that 'bugs' in Japan's 'cultural software' eventually manifested themselves in irrational decision making by Japanese political and military leaders and encouraged a popular wave of public support for wars that culminated in disaster and occupation. In a complementary chapter, Harao Iguchi, using new evidence from Japanese archives, concentrates on why Japan went to war with the USA in 1941. He points out that the Japanese Empire from 1937 to 1941 depended heavily on US capital and technology for its aggression against China and explores the possibility of whether war between the USA and Japan was inevitable once the US placed an embargo on oil supplies in 1941, or whether it might have been postponed if Japanese diplomats in Washington had been able to influence Tokyo to halt its planned attack because the tide appeared to be turning against Hitler in the war against the Soviet Union.[6]

Italy's history during the inter-war years was marked by the elevation of Benito Mussolini in 1922. The *Duce* was the first European leader to dispense with multi-party democracy and set up a fascist dictatorship. In 1935, Italy undermined the peace settlement by invading Abyssinia (modern-day Ethiopia) in October, then intervened in the Spanish Civil War after July 1936 and invaded Albania in 1939. At other times, Mussolini was a paradoxical character.

He acted as a 'peace broker' during the Czech crisis of 1938 and when war broke out in September 1939 opted for neutrality. Only after France was effectively defeated in 1940 did Italy join Hitler's 'Axis of Evil' with Japan.[7] Richard Bosworth's survey of Italian foreign policy seeks to answer the great question of what drove the disastrous course of Italian policy: was it the ideology of fascism with its unapologetic dynamism and violence? Or was Italy, as the 'least of the great powers', an 'unsatisfied' nation that opportunistically looked for advantage during the international crises of the 1930s?

The appointment of Adolf Hitler as German Chancellor on 30 January 1933 initiated an increasingly unstable period in international relations. Precisely what objectives the Nazi dictator was pursuing in foreign policy has been at the centre of ceaseless wrangling among historians.[8] Two key points of discussion have revolved around the questions of whether Hitler was pursuing a consistent programme – a 'timetable of aggression' – or whether he was merely an unprincipled opportunist. Lars Lüdicke explores these questions by evaluating the latest German thinking on the role of Hitler's foreign policy in the origins of the war.

One of the key aspects of this debate is whether Hitler's foreign policy after 1933 marks a sharp discontinuity with the German past. The view that war occurred in 1939 because Germany could not be reconciled to the new world order after 1918 remains the dominant explanation. The signing of the Locarno Treaties of 1925 represented a return of Germany to diplomatic equality. For a brief period, it seemed the 'German problem' might be solved. The constructive partnership between Gustav Stresemann, the German Foreign Minister, and his French counterpart Aristide Briand was a well-meaning attempt to bring a constructive relationship between Berlin and Paris after years of bitter conflict. The untimely death of Stresemann in 1929 – so the traditional argument runs – put an end to this 'Locarno honeymoon' and paved the way to an increasingly belligerent stance by his successor, Julius Curtius, which was then accelerated by Hitler. Conan Fischer, utilizing new archival evidence, looks at German–French relations in the crucial period 1929 to 1932, demonstrating that Curtius and senior officials in the German foreign office never abandoned the search for reconciliation with France and maintained an open and constructive dialogue with French ministers well into 1932. Fischer also points out that the German response to Briand's European Union plan was much more positive than has hitherto been appreciated.[9]

The German army was, of course, the bedrock of German preparations for war. The traditional picture of the *Wehrmacht* that overwhelmed Western Europe between 1939 and 1940 obscures the fact that its forerunner, the *Reichswehr* of the Weimar Republic, was restricted to 100,000 men. The German military historian Jürgen Förster offers fresh insights as to why Hitler's authoritarian and militaristic Führer state became so much more popular than the political and military leadership of the two Weimar Presidents Friedrich Ebert and Paul von Hindenburg. Förster also emphasizes that Hitler and the

loyal military took pains to create 'political soldiers' who combined professionalism with a commitment to Nazi ideology. The question of why the German
people were prepared to march with Hitler and his Nazis into an aggressive war
is also explored.[10]

The type of war Hitler planned has been a key part of the historical debate. It
is often assumed the German army planned to fight short, lightning wars causing
maximum damage to the enemy, but avoiding a long and costly war of attrition.
This debate has centred on the economic preparation that underpinned the so
called '*Blitzkrieg* strategy'[11] Robert Citino questions whether the rapid series of
German victories between 1939 and 1941 were due to the creation of a new,
mechanized form of 'shock and awe' warfare and demonstrates that *Blitzkrieg*
was not a revolutionary new form of warfare at all, but dated back to Frederick
the Great. Thought to have died in the static trench warfare on the Western
Front in the First World War, Citino shows this distinctive and swift 'German
way of war' was simply made immeasurably more effective by new military
technologies like tanks, aircraft and radio.[12]

Alongside the German role in the origins of the war there is a mountain
of books devoted to Neville Chamberlain's pursuit of a peaceful arrangement
that would satisfy Hitler's grievances while safeguarding Britain's interests. It
was called 'Appeasement'. In practice, it meant accepting a series of German
revisions of the Versailles Treaty that progressively strengthened Germany's
strategic position and failed to prevent war.[13] In the famous 1940 British
polemic *Guilty Men*, a number of left-wing writers depicted appeasement as an
ill-thought-out and immoral policy. David Dutton considers the validity of this
charge when applied to three of Chamberlain's closest colleagues in government:
Sir John Simon, Sir Samuel Hoare and Lord Halifax.[14] Each served as Foreign
Secretary in the National Government, all were at the heart of the foreign policy
process during the 1930s and they came together in Chamberlain's inner circle
as appeasement reached its climax in 1938. Dutton systematically examines
the dilemmas they faced, the similarity or otherwise of their policies to those
Chamberlain espoused, their responsibility for the drift towards war and above
all the concept of 'guilt' as applied to their respective performances in office.[15]

When British government records on foreign policy were opened to public
scrutiny in 1967, the way was open to rehabilitate Neville Chamberlain's
shattered reputation. The revisionists emphasized that Chamberlain had
appeased the dictators because Britain did not possess sufficient military or
economic strength to deter or prevent Germany from achieving a revision
of the Treaty of Versailles. Instead, he hoped high level negotiations might
persuade Hitler to resolve his grievances without resort to force. This approach
was accompanied by increases in defence spending designed to stop Hitler,
if he proved unappeasable.[16] John Charmley, the leading and most thought-
provoking 'revisionist', argues that not only has Sir Winston Churchill's negative
view of Chamberlain shaped the public and the historical debate, but it has also
allowed a new critical framework to emerge that has enabled the Churchillian

consensus to reassert itself among historians, led by the late R.A.C. Parker, who have adapted the central revisionist arguments to create yet another critical assessment.

This 'post-revisionist' interpretation combines key elements of the orthodox and revisionist positions. It argues that Chamberlain believed in appeasement so passionately that he dismissed all possible alternatives and made errors that ensured that Britain and France were in a weak strategic position when war broke out. I have become associated with the 'post-revisionist' perspective ever since my book *Neville Chamberlain, Appeasement and the British Road to War* was published.[17] My contribution here is to offer a reassessment of Chamberlain's pursuit of appeasement by suggesting the 'Guilty Men–Churchillian', 'revisionist' and 'post-revisionist' positions have now served their usefulness, and that future discussion and research should be focused on whether appeasement was a viable policy and to examine whether alterative policies existed that would have worked better and allowed Britain to enter the war in a more favourable strategic position than was the case in 1939.

Jeffrey Record, who has acted as a leading US foreign policy adviser, explains that the 'lessons' of the Munich conference have informed almost every threatened or actual use of force by the USA since the Second World War. He shows that repeated presidential invocations of the Munich analogy have been used to inflate foreign policy threats, demonize dictators and rally public opinion for military action. He argues that the use of appeasement in US foreign policy debates ignores the singularity of the threat posed by Hitler and the unique circumstances that encouraged Anglo-French appeasement of Nazi Germany until 1939. He concludes that Hitler's aims in Europe lay beyond the imagination of the statesmen who appeased him and practically no one, including Churchill, recognized that Hitler was undeterrable.

The 'missing dimension' of British foreign policy in the 1930s is unquestionably the role of the intelligence services.[18] The need for accurate secret information became vital to policy makers, but British intelligence in the 1930s remained the preserve of upper-class amateurs working on a shoestring budget. MI5 was so ill prepared for the outbreak of war that none of its officers even knew the name of the *Abwehr*, the German intelligence service. In an enlightening chapter, Calder Walton and Kevin Quinlan examine the complex relationship between British intelligence and policy making in the 1930s. They show how Chamberlain received mixed messages. SIS information provided to Chamberlain nearly always endorsed his policy position.[19] MI5's attempt to warn about Germany's determined military planning for war was consistently ignored or downplayed by Chamberlain. They conclude that the story of the intelligence services and British foreign policy in the late 1930s is one of missed opportunities: of government officials failing to listen to intelligence information they did not want to hear or which ran counter to their already agreed line.

Inter-war French foreign policy suffered a string of failures, most notably the inability to enforce German reparations payments, the failure to prevent the rise of Hitler or avert his subsequent moves into the Rhineland, Austria, Czechoslovakia, Poland and eventually Paris.[20] But while these failures are incontestable, is it really appropriate to place all the blame on the governments of the Third Republic? Robert Young looks at how British foreign and military policy influenced French decision making, notably the effect of Britain's refusal to honour the guarantee of French security it had initially promised during the Paris Peace Conference. For much of the 1920s Young shows that British governments and public alike mistook the French fear of invasion as evidence of French military ambition. This led France to seek other allies to insure against future German aggression. Conversely, in the 1930s, Young argues that French foreign policy became increasingly passive – an adjustment that was inspired by Britain's increasing movement towards the policy of appeasement. Not for the first time, the width of the Channel proved far greater in the mind than in miles.

Talbot Imlay also suggests that without a full evaluation of French foreign and military policy the story of appeasement is incomplete.[21] Yet he suggests that France was a major actor in its own right and exerted a far greater influence on British policy than has generally been acknowledged in many Anglo-centric interpretations. He believes the very term 'appeasement' inadequately captures the varied ways in which Britain and France responded to the growing possibility of war and argues that as the crisis became acute British and French policies in the strategic, political and economic realms were neither coherent nor coordinated.

With attention focused on how all these principal power-brokers behaved, we tend to lose sight of powers that opted for neutrality before and during the Second World War. Recent studies of the neutral powers have depicted them as adopting the 'posture of an ostrich' in the face of the Fascist challenge, of failing to support the League of Nations, pandering to Germany's economic needs and failing to offer sanctuary to refugees from Nazi oppression.[22] Neville Wylie and Marco Wyss examine the plight of that archetypal neutral power – Switzerland – and its response to the Italo-Abyssinian War of 1935–6. They explore the pressures faced by the political and business elites in Switzerland, explain how these events challenged many of the basic assumptions governing Swiss thinking on neutrality and led to discussions about how Switzerland could maintain its neutrality and survive yet another European conflagration. Wylie and Wyss explain that the Abyssinian crisis exposed the dangers of supporting a system of collective security whose political interests were increasingly at odds with those of Switzerland's great power neighbours, Germany and Italy, and gave rise to a conception of Swiss neutrality that become increasingly narrow and self-interested as the international crisis intensified.

In a complementary chapter, Efraim Karsh explores how the European neutral powers coped after the outbreak of the Second World War, concluding that a policy combining credible deterrence with skilful exploitation of the belligerents' weaknesses can ensure the successful preservation of neutrality, even during the most total and comprehensive war. By contrast, an insufficient awareness on the part of the neutral power of the maelstrom of events and a failure to find the most sensible reaction both politically and diplomatically to them will most probably result in the collapse of political neutrality.[23]

Spain was another major European neutral power. Yet the most bloody European conflict in the 1930s – the Spanish Civil War – took place within its borders. It began in February 1936 when Nationalists in Spain, led by General Franco, refused to accept the election victory of a 'Popular Front' coalition composed of republicans, socialists and communists.[24] This domestic conflict soon developed into a European civil war in miniature: a genuine 'cockpit' of the coming struggle. Germany and Italy gave military support to Franco's forces, whilst the USSR offered limited assistance to the elected government. In a speech on 26 July 1936, Hitler explained that if there had not been the danger of communism overwhelming Europe, he 'would not have intervened'.[25] Mussolini committed his military forces to the conflict to stop the 'Bolshevik menace'.[26] Yet Germany and Italy both recognized the strategic benefits, especially in the naval balance of power in the Mediterranean, and the weakening of the French strategic position that would result from a grateful Nationalist regime gaining power. The Soviet Union hoped to persuade Britain and France to back the 'Popular Front' and thereby strengthen the policy of collective security, but both countries opted for non-intervention. Stanley Baldwin, the British Prime Minister, felt that 'on no account' should Britain or France enter the civil war 'on the side of the Russians'.[27]

The leading Spanish historian Enrique Moradiellos explains what a pivotal moment the Spanish conflict was in the events that led to war by arguing that the uneven intervention and non-intervention of European powers played a crucial role in the course and the final outcome of the civil war. Without the diplomatic and military support from Germany and Italy it is not possible to understand the unconditional victory achieved by the military insurgents led by General Franco. Moradiellos concludes that without the all-out embargo imposed by the Non-Intervention Pact, it is highly unlikely the Republican 'Popular Front' government would have suffered such a brutal and devastating defeat. During the Second World War Franco maintained Spanish neutrality while not hiding where his sympathies lay and the great bulk of Spain's trade aided the Axis powers.[28]

One region that tends to be ignored in most traditional accounts of the origins of the Second World War is the Middle East.[29] Yet as the diplomatic situation in Europe rapidly deteriorated, the importance of this region, especially for the security of the British Empire, came sharply into focus. Britain's crucial lines of communication ran through the region, not least the Suez Canal. T.G. Fraser shows how the issue of Palestine came near to the top of the British political agenda in the late 1930s, as Britain tried to reconcile the pledges made to Arabs and Jews for separate homelands during and after the First World War. These promises were not fulfilled, leaving a stalemate in Jewish–Arab relations. By

1939, Britain had abandoned a policy of partitioning Palestine into Arab and Jewish zones, which was regarded by Jews as an act of betrayal.

The promise of a Jewish homeland in Palestine was one solution offered for the 'Jewish Question' at a time when the Nazis were already waging a war against the Jews inside Germany that eventually led to an attempt to annihilate European Jewry during the Second World War. Mark Levene shows that the 'Jewish Question' was of much greater significance in the countdown to war in Europe in 1939 than is generally appreciated. He contends that the origins of the 'international Jewish conspiracy' motif, a staple feature of Nazi anti-Semitic propaganda, owes much more to a wider European belief that bubbled to the surface during the First World War and its aftermath. Levene concludes that while the Western allies sought to row back from any explicit reference to the Zionist conspiracy myth in the inter-war period, the geo-political interplay between the democracies and the Nazis in the late 1930s continued to betray a deeper and disturbing psycho-cultural pattern of anti-Semitism that was common to all European political elites and would find its deadly apotheosis once the war began.[30]

Multi-ethnic division was most accentuated in Central and Eastern Europe and it was this region Hitler designated as the epicentre of his 'Greater German Reich'. It was here where the key disputes that eventually led to the outbreak of war in Europe occurred. Yet Czech and Polish interpretations of these events are rarely integrated in British, US and French narratives.[31] This volume redresses this imbalance. Drawing on unique access to Beneš's private papers, Milan Hauner looks at the Munich crisis through Czech eyes. He shows how Eduard Beneš, the Czech leader, decided to remain passive in his contest over the Sudeten issue with Hitler's regime. Hauner points out that while one may understand and sympathise with the Czech leader's deep disgust of Hitler, his refusal to negotiate directly with him meant that the Czechs had to rely on British mediators who were sympathetic to German demands and French politicians who were willing to follow the British lead. This reduced Beneš's own position to one of three choices: war, plebiscite or transfer. In the end, he chose the option of transfer.

The seventieth anniversary of the outbreak of the Second World War has intensified discussions about the role played by Poland. The German attack on Poland was preceded by a long-drawn-out propaganda campaign focused on the port city of Danzig. British and French ministers saw the Polish–German dispute over this relatively unimportant town as a dubious reason to start a European war. Indeed, in 1919 Lloyd George had posed that very question to Clemenceau – would France make war for Danzig? The bigger issue was Hitler's attempt to settle the matter by force. This final crisis on the road to war is usually examined from the perspective of the major powers.[32] In this study, two leading experts on Polish foreign policy, Piotr Wandycz and Anita Prazmowska, delve deep into Polish motivations. Wandycz examines the evolution of Polish foreign policy between 1918 and 1939, seeking to explain and contextualize the difficulties faced by Polish ministers as they attempted to find a viable means of dealing with Germany, France, the Soviet Union and Britain. He shows that Poland was willing to negotiate with Germany during the Danzig crisis, but was unwilling to be browbeaten into a humiliating surrender and become a de facto vassal of the Third Reich. The Poles chose to fight rather than suffer such a humiliating fate. Anita Prazmowska focuses attention on how the German–Polish dispute over Danzig ultimately led to the outbreak of war. For most of the 1930s both states had appreciated the need for some form of diplomatic accommodation, most visibly demonstrated by the 1934 German–Polish non-aggression pact. The key turning point was the Munich agreement, which led to the dismemberment of Czechoslovakia. From that point onwards Hitler's policies towards Poland changed from seeking some stability in diplomatic relations towards subordinating Poland to German demands. The end game over Danzig can be dated, according to Prazmowska, to the autumn of 1938 when Joachim von Ribbentrop, the German Foreign Minister, demanded the city be returned to the Reich. The new element in this situation from March 1939 onwards was the French and British guarantee to uphold Polish independence. The willingness of the British government to try and find a negotiated settlement might have solved the crisis, but Prazmowska believes this was hampered by a failure by the Polish government to reveal to British ministers the true extent of conflict between the Polish state and the Danzig authorities and by Hitler's determination to use the Danzig issue as pretext for his pre-planned attack on Poland. In these circumstances, a negotiated settlement was never a realistic proposition.

The two major powers that did not join the Second World War until 1941 – the Soviet Union and the USA – emerged from it as global superpowers. During the Cold War era, the Soviet Union was 'the black hole of diplomatic history of the 1930s'. But recently, new archives have opened up leading to a more detailed understanding of Soviet motivations.[33] Some historians argue that Stalin's foreign policy was initially determined to uphold the principles of collective security to deter German aggression and only moved towards the signing of the Molotov–Ribbentrop pact because British and French attempts to appease Hitler gave grounds for suspicions in Moscow that Anglo-French policy was content as long as Hitler marched east, a fear that seemed justified when the Western allies delayed signing a triple alliance to deter Hitler in the summer of 1939.[34] However, this 'collective-security' approach has been viewed on the opposite side of the debate as giving a much too sympathetic interpretation of Soviet foreign policy.[35] Some German historians have contended that Soviet foreign policy desired a restoration of the close Soviet–German cooperation that emerged after 1918 and was cemented by the Treaty of Rapallo in 1922.

Geoff Roberts, who has examined the recently opened Soviet archives, claims that recent revisionist claims of Stalin being a key instigator of the Second World War are wide of the mark. Roberts shows in this study that the Soviet dictator was convinced by August 1939 that war between Germany and Poland was inevitable, so the issue narrowed to whether the Soviet Union should fight alongside France, Britain and Poland or remain neutral. Stalin doubted whether Britain and France were ever serious about signing an alliance with the Soviet Union and he suspected their goal was to trap the Soviet Union into fighting a war alone against Germany, with the Western democracies offering minimal support and possibly concluding a later deal with Hitler to stay out of the European war.

The traditional view of US policy during the inter-war years focuses on the isolationism and neutrality that underpinned the policies of successive US presidents and especially of Franklin D. Roosevelt from 1933 onwards. Yet the pursuits of American policy makers between 1919 and 1941 were more complex than is often appreciated. The critical challenge for US decision makers was how to exercise and legitimate a liberal American hegemony over the international system. More profoundly, a 'Pax Americana' was only sustainable if the US took the lead in establishing new ground rules of international politics, security and economic cooperation.

Manfred Jonas traces the roots of the policy of 'isolationism' from the days of George Washington to the attack at Pearl Harbor in 1941. He concedes this policy influenced US decisions to opt out of membership of the League of Nations and enact three Neutrality Acts in the mid-1930s.[36] However, Jonas explains that by 1938 the events in Europe and Asia led to a clear view in Washington that the Axis powers posed a direct threat to the US strategic and economic interests and had to be countered by an active policy of providing aid to their enemies and stepping up US rearmament. Jonas concludes that whatever remained of the policy of isolationism was rapidly disappearing well before Japan's assault at Pearl Harbor. By then Roosevelt had decided that US policy needed to exert international leadership during the war and fashion a post-war world based on the US model.

Seeking to shed further light on the US role in the wider origins of the Second World War, Patrick Cohrs suggests the USA played a much more pivotal role in the embattled inter-war international system than is conventionally understood. He traces US policy during that period as comprising four stages. In its first two stages, it culminated in two quests to reform the international order after Versailles. First was the attempt in the 1920s by Charles E. Hughes, the US Secretary of State, to establish under the isolationist constraints of the Republican New Era a transatlantic community of ideals and a new peace system in the Far East. There followed a second initiative by Herbert Hoover to adopt a more non-committal approach to international conflicts. The third stage was reached when Hoover saw no alternative to a reversion to US unilateral action in the hope of surviving the shock waves of the 'Great Depression'. The final stage of this process began with Roosevelt's New Deal reforms. It was the economic crisis that produced the real shift towards unmitigated isolationism. As a consequence, the United States withdrew from any meaningful commitments in Europe and Asia. Cohrs contends that Roosevelt's underlying aim was to create a more stable US economy that would create the conditions for a renewed and more powerful engagement of the United States in the world order, but in the short term America's withdrawal into isolation meant it hindered real aid to the Western democracies and thereby contributed to the outbreak of the Second World War.[37]

There is a very obvious sense in which the Second World War can be seen as war growing out of economic problems. Most on the left in Europe assumed this was an 'imperialist war', provoked by an unresolved crisis in the capitalist system that had economic roots. Such views are no longer given serious attention by historians when discussing the origins of the war in 1939. The 'Capitalists' in most European countries seem to have preferred peace to war. This was no less true of appeasing businessmen in Britain than bankers in Nazi Germany. The belief that the possession of vast material resources, territory and population determined national wellbeing, guaranteed independence and made it possible to wage war effectively now seems the product of the mind-set of a particular age.[38] Since 1945, a buoyant world trading economy has rendered obsolete the view that 'living space' and indigenous raw materials are pre-requisites of economic prosperity. Germany and Japan both declined in size, but became economic giants in the post-war era and Britain and France both lost empires, but remained in the top ten world economic powers. In a major re-evaluation of the role of economic factors, Richard Overy argues that a crude Malthusian view of political survival made it seem that possession of territory and material resources was the only real security. It was this belief that directed Japan, Italy and Germany to swallow up Manchuria, Abyssinia, Czechoslovakia and Poland because they supplied additional economic resources. Britain and France tried appeasement and belated rearmament before finally embarking on war in 1939 to protect their global economic and political interests. Overy rejects the recent argument put forward by Adam Tooze that suggested that Hitler embarked on war with Poland to secure vitally needed additional economic resources and take a bold first initiative to secure 'living space' in Eastern Europe.[39] In contrast, Overy concludes that it was Hitler's political ambition to dominate Europe, not economic necessity, that drove Germany to attack Poland in 1939, but it was a sense that war could not be postponed without great economic risk that drove Britain and France to declare war on Germany two days later.

Debates and controversy are the prerequisites for progress in historical research. In a wide-ranging and thoughtful concluding chapter Anthony Adamthwaite examines what he terms the 'war between historians' on the origins of the Second World War. It is not only that such cataclysmic events demand regular reappraisal, but also because the key legacies of the conflict – nuclear weapons, genocide, ethnic cleansing and the targeting of civilians in global conflicts – still impact on the world we live in today. Adamthwaite concludes that the academic debate has now reached a 'post revisionist phase' with the focus on stock taking and finding common ground rather than continuing to make revisionist and counter-revisionist claims. He now urges historians to reach out beyond academia to a wider public audience by striving for accessibility in their writing and attempting to move beyond the narrow parameters of older disputes.

This book attempts to rise to that challenge.

Notes

1 F. Fukuyama, 'The End of History', *National Interest* vol. 16 (1989), pp. 3–4.
2 D. Andelman, *A Shattered Peace: Versailles 1919 and the Price We Pay Today*. London, 2008; A. Adamthwaite, *The Lost Peace: International Relations, 1918–1939*. London, 1980; J.M. Keynes, *The Economic Consequences of the Peace*. London, 1919.
3 A.J.P. Taylor, *The Origins of the Second World War*. London, 1961, p.267
4 For recent assessments see M. MacMillan, *Peacemakers: The Paris Peace Conference of 1919 and its Attempt to End War*. London, 2001; Z. Steiner, *The Lights that Failed: European International History, 1919–1933*. Oxford, 2005.
5 See J. Morley (ed.), *The Road to the Asia-Pacific War*, 4 vols. New York, 1976–84; A. Iriye, *The Origins of Second World War in the Asia-Pacific*. Harlow, 1987.
6 H. Iguchi, *Unfinished Business: Ayukawa Yoshisuke and US Relations, 1937–1941*. Cambridge, 2003.
7 R.J. Bosworth, *Explaining Auschwitz and Hiroshima: History Writing and the Second World War, 1945–1990*. London, 1994, pp. 118–41. See also D. Mack-Smith, *Mussolini's Roman Empire*. London, 1976.
8 I. Kershaw, *The Nazi Dictatorship: Problems and Perspectives of Interpretation*. London, 2000, 4th ed., pp. 134–60.
9 The most important recent work is J. Wright, *Gustav Stresemann: Weimar's Greatest Statesman*. Oxford, 2002.
10 For a detailed discussion see W. Deist, M. Messerschmidt, H-E. Volkmann and W. Wette, *Germany and the Second World War Volume 1: The Build-up of German Aggression*. Oxford, 1990.
11 This view was most forcefully put forward by A.J.P. Taylor in *The Origins of the Second World War* and elaborated by Tim Mason. See T. Mason 'The Primacy of Politics – Politics and Economics in National Socialist Germany' in H. Turner (ed.), *Nazism and the Third Reich*. New York, 1972, pp. 175–200. This was effectively challenged by Richard Overy. See R. Overy 'Hitler's War and the German Economy: A Reappraisal', *Economic History Review* vol. 35 (1982), pp. 272–91; R. Overy, 'Germany, "Domestic Crisis" and War in 1939', *Past and Present* vol. 116 (1987), pp. 138–68. More recently, Adam Tooze has attempted to revive this theme. See A. Tooze, *The Wages of Destruction: The Making and Breaking of the Nazi Economy*. London, 2006.
12 R. Citino, *The German Way of War: From the Thirty Years' War to the Third Reich*. Kansas, 2005; J. Moser, *The Blitzkrieg Myth: How Hitler and the Allies Misread the Strategic Realities of World War II*. London, 2004; R. Evans, *The Third Reich at War, 1939–1945*. London, 2008.
13 Among the many studies see R.J. Overy, *The Origins of the Second World War*. London, 1988; D.C. Watt, *How War Came: The Immediate Consequences of the Second World War, 1938–1939*. London, 1989.
14 The best biographies of Halifax, Simon and Hoare are: A. Roberts, *'The Holy Fox': A Biography of Lord Halifax*. London, 1991; D. Dutton, *Simon: A Political Life of Sir John Simon*. London, 1992; J. Cross, *Sir Samuel Hoare: A Political Biography*. London, 1977.
15 See also D. Dutton, *Neville Chamberlain*. London, 2001.
16 For a detailed examination of John Charmley's original 'revisionist' position see J. Charmley, *Chamberlain and the Lost Peace*. London, 1989. See also P. Neville, *Hitler and Appeasement: The British Attempt to Prevent the Second World War*. London, 2006, which also offers a stout defence of Chamberlain.

17 The key 'post-revisionist' studies are: R.A.C. Parker, *Chamberlain and Appeasement: British Policy and the Coming of the Second World War*. London, 1993; F. McDonough, *Neville Chamberlain, Appeasement and the British Road to War*. Manchester 1998; S. Aster, ' "Guilty Men": The Case of Neville Chamberlain' in R. Boyce and E. Robertson (eds), *Paths to War: New Essays on the Origins of the Second World War*. London, 1989, pp. 233–68.

18 C. Andrew and D. Dilks (eds), *The Missing Dimension: Governments and Intelligence Communities in the Twentieth Century*. London, 1984. For a recent critical assessment of appeasement see N. Ferguson, *The War of the World*. London, 2007, pp. 312–82.

19 For details see K. Jeffrey, *The Official History of the Secret Intelligence Service, 1909–1945*. London, 2010.

20 For a detailed study of French foreign policy see R. Young, *French Foreign Policy, 1918–1945: A Guide to Research Materials*. Wilmington, 1981; R. Young, *France and the Origins of the Second World War*. London, 1996.

21 For a good introduction into recent work on France see M. Thomas, 'Appeasement in the Late Third Republic', *Diplomacy and Statecraft* vol. 19 (2008), pp. 566–607.

22 For details see N. Wylie (ed.), *European Neutrals and Non-Belligerents During the Second World War*. Cambridge, 2002.

23 E. Karsh, *Neutrality and the Small States*. London, 1988.

24 For details see P. Preston, *The Spanish Civil War: Reaction, Revolution and Revenge*. London, 2006.

25 Quoted in H. Thomas, *The Spanish Civil War*. London, 1977, p. 35

26 D. Mack-Smith, *Mussolini's Roman Empire*. London, 1976, p. 100.

27 Quoted in G. Stone, 'The European Great Powers and the Spanish Civil War, 1936–1939', in Boyce and Robertson (eds), *Paths of War*, p. 213.

28 See E. Moradiellos, 'The Origins of British Non-Intervention in the Spanish Civil War: Anglo-Spanish Relations in Early 1936', *European History Quarterly* vol. 23 (1991), pp. 339–64.

29 T.G. Fraser, *The Arab–Israeli Conflict*. Palgrave, 1995.

30 For a more detailed examination of Mark Levene's interpretation see M. Levene, *Genocide in the Age of the Nation State*, 2 vols. London, 2005.

31 For Polish perspectives see A. Prazmowska, *Eastern Europe and the Origins of the Second World War*. Basingstoke, 2000; P. Wandycz, *The Price of Freedom: A History of East Central Europe from the Middle Ages to the Present*. London, 2001.

32 For details see P. Wandycz, 'Poland Between East and West' in G. Martel (ed.), *The Origins of the Second World War Reconsidered: The A.J.P. Taylor Debate after Twenty-Five Years*. London, 1986, pp. 187–209.

33 Boyce and Robertson (eds), *Paths of War*, p. 16.

34 See J. Haslam, *The Soviet Union and the Struggle for Collective Security in Europe, 1933–1939*. London, 1984; G. Roberts, *The Soviet Union and the Origins of the Second World War: Russo-German Relations and the Road to War, 1933–1941*. London, 1995.

35 See E. Topitsch, *Stalin's War: A Radical New Theory on the Origins of the Second World War*. London, 1987. See also N. Tolstoy, *Stalin's Secret War*. London, 1981 for a similarly critical view.

36 See M. Jonas, *Isolationism in America 1935–1941*. Ithaca, 1969; M. Jonas, *United States and Germany: A Diplomatic History*. Ithaca, 1984.

37 See P.O. Cohrs, *The Unfinished Peace after World War 1: America, Britain and the Stabilisation of Europe, 1919–1932*. Cambridge, 2008.

38 R. Overy, *The Morbid Age: Britain Between the Wars*. London, 2009.

39 See Tooze, *The Wages of Destruction, passim*.

Chapter 1

The Versailles Settlement: The Start of the Road to the Second World War?

Alan Sharp

On 3 September 1939 Britain and France declared war on Germany, initiating their second major confrontation in twenty-five years. Continuing condemnations of the Versailles settlement as the root cause of this second global conflict are readily found. 'For more than half a century, it has been widely recognized that the unfettered revenge against Germany and the Austro-Hungarian Empire that was the cornerstone of the Treaty of Versailles created the circumstances that led inevitably to World War II' claims the dust jacket of foreign correspondent David Andelman's 2008 book *A Shattered Peace: Versailles 1919 and the Price We Pay Today*. 'The final crime', according to *The Economist*'s summary of the Millennium in December 1999, 'was the Treaty of Versailles, whose harsh terms would ensure a second world war.' In 1996 the historian Jay Winter declared, 'The Peace Conference which ended the Great War was more about punishment than about peace. Perhaps inevitably, anger and retribution followed four years of bloodshed, ensuring the instability and ultimate collapse of the accords signed in the Hall of Mirrors at Versailles on 28 June 1919. The road to World War II started here.'[1]

The American diplomat George Kennan wrote in 1985:

> I think it's increasingly recognized that the Second World War was an almost unavoidable prolongation of the first one, resulting from the very silly, humiliating and punitive peace imposed on Germany after World War I. The treatment of Germany in the 1920s and early 1930s by the French and the British (here, we Americans were not involved because we had concluded a separate peace and didn't sign the Versailles Treaty) was bound to favour the emergence of precisely those extreme forces that arose in Germany in the 1930s.[2]

He had earlier blamed the Allies for not dealing directly with Russia and Germany, for their bloodsucking policies on reparations and war debts and for policies that he suggested were responsible for bringing Adolf Hitler to power.[3]

Given such formidable indictments, it is hardly surprising that many history teachers will have shared the frustrating experience of trying to direct their students to a more balanced and nuanced understanding of the thought processes, dilemmas and limitations of the peacemakers in 1919 as they confronted a truly awesome task. In essence, the stereotypical images identified by Marc Trachtenberg thirty years ago remain largely intact – a vindictive peace, concluded because the new diplomacy of the idealistic Woodrow Wilson failed to temper the cynical old methods of the balance of power and alliances, personified by France's Georges Clemenceau, with Britain's David Lloyd George interposed between them.[4]

Attempts, not least by Trachtenberg himself, to question some of these orthodoxies by utilizing the newly released documentary material that became available from the 1960s onwards have struggled against a powerful tide, and this is unsurprising because the idea of a fatally flawed settlement has a very long history.[5] From the outset, substantial numbers of its framers were deeply disappointed at the results of their labours. Harold Nicolson's familiar lament in his part-contemporary 1919 diary, part historical reflection, published in 1933 – 'We came to Paris convinced that a new order was about to be established; we left it convinced that the old order had merely fouled the new' – was a harsh verdict, but one shared by many of the British and American diplomats and expert advisers in Paris. At a meeting on 30 May 1919, to set up what became the Royal Institute of International Affairs – Chatham House – Lord Robert Cecil spoke on their behalf when he said, 'There is no single person in this room who is not disappointed with the terms we have drafted.'[6]

Their ideas were given eloquent public expression first in John Maynard Keynes's highly influential (and highly tendentious) polemic *The Economic Consequences of the Peace*, published only six months after he quit the conference in disgust in June 1919, and later in the memoirs and diaries of other participants, notably Robert Lansing's *The Peace Negotiations: A Personal Narrative*, Nicolson's *Peacemaking 1919*, Stephen Bonsal's *Unfinished Business* and James Headlam-Morley's *Memoir of the Paris Peace Conference 1919*. Archibald Wavell, the British soldier who would serve in both world wars, summed up the collective feeling of the critics when he declared: 'After the "war to end war" they seem to have been pretty successful in Paris at making a "Peace to end Peace".' Even Lloyd George suggested, within a year of leaving office, 'If I had to go to Paris again I would conclude quite a different treaty.'[7]

Keynes's brilliant and coruscating book has cast a long shadow over subsequent studies of the peace conference. His seductive reduction of the bewildering complexities of peacemaking after an unprecedentedly destructive war explained the resolution of enormously complicated global problems in terms of the personalities, interests and foibles of the three principal peacemakers (he ignored the Italian premier, Vittorio Orlando). A naïve and foolish 'old Presbyterian' (Wilson) was bamboozled by the 'Tiger' (the caustic and cynical Clemenceau) and the 'Welsh Wizard' (the elusive and quick-thinking Lloyd George) and failed to deliver the idealistic visions he had outlined in his 1918 speeches, most famously the Fourteen Points of 8 January. Instead they created a vindictive and unworkable settlement.

Given the unpalatable nature of the peace to some of the victors, it is scarcely surprising that the losers concurred with even greater conviction. German publicists and historians, often encouraged and subsidized by the special section of their Ministry of Foreign Affairs set up to contradict the conveniently assumed accusation of exclusive German war guilt that none of the treaties actually made, attacked the settlement with great vigour. A plethora of published documents (carefully chosen, edited and – if necessary – falsified) followed, first from Germany, then from other participants. Overwhelmed by the weight of this evidence the general consensus by the mid-1930s was that the First World War was an accident for which no one power was primarily accountable. This in turn undermined the credibility of a settlement assumed to be based on the premise of German responsibility.

Renewed conflict in Europe in 1939, escalating in 1941 into a new world war, incurred costs and consequences even more far reaching than the inconceivable losses, by the standards of the time, of the First World War. By 1945, Europe was a ruined continent dominated by two extra-European powers, the United States and the Soviet Union. The rapid collapse of their victorious alliance into a Cold War that would last for over forty years transformed a rift already apparent in 1919 between Eastern and Western Europe into an ideological power struggle between two super-powers divided by an iron curtain. That confrontation did freeze some of the persistent post-Versailles problems of the 1920s and 1930s, but when first the Soviet empire and then the Soviet Union itself collapsed, many of these issues re-emerged.

There can be little doubt that 1991 made 1919 relevant in a way that it had not been during the Cold War. Indeed, Eric Hobsbawm has suggested 'The national conflicts tearing the continent apart in the 1990s were the old chickens of Versailles coming home to roost.' That settlement is thus held responsible for the multi-ethnic conflicts in Europe and Asia following the collapse of the USSR, and for the Balkan problems ensuing from the demise of Yugoslavia. In the wider world, it has been blamed for its reinforcement of imperialism in Africa, Asia and Latin America and, in particular, for the nightmare of the Middle East because of the artificially constructed and sketchily defined states that it created, and the hopelessly conflicting promises made to Jews and Arabs during and after the First World War.[8]

In assessing the responsibility of the peacemakers for failing to create a lasting European order it is of paramount importance to remember that politics is the art of the possible and that, although alternative outcomes might have been desirable, they were not always within the power of those concerned to deliver, especially in the pressured and confused circumstances of the immediate post-war period. Kennan's accusation that the victors excluded Germany and Russia from the peace conference is a case in point. The peacemakers knew that their decisions in relation to these two countries would be crucial determinants of the future stability of Europe but they faced major difficulties in engaging directly with either.

In 1919 it is very hard to see how there could be any prospect of realistic negotiations with Russia since, in the midst of a series of civil wars and foreign interventions, there was no clear government with which to deal. Attempts to gather the warring factions together on Prinkipo Island in the Sea of Marmara in the hope of creating a voice for Russia failed. Lenin and the Bolsheviks were emerging as the possible victors in Russia, but the situation remained extremely uncertain and, should the Soviets win, their ideology suggested that dealing with them in any conventional framework of international relations might be problematic. There were some abortive efforts to open communications with Lenin by a young American diplomat, William Bullitt, and later by Jan Smuts through the Hungarian revolutionary leader, Bela Kun. Neither produced any tangible results and the Treaty of Versailles dealt with Russia in two brief clauses: one requiring Germany to renounce the Treaty of Brest-Litovsk and to recognize any new Russian frontiers established by the conference; and the other protecting Russia's right to possible reparations. Whilst it could not be said that this was a promising start to relations with whatever new Russia emerged from its present turmoil, the art of the possible did impose limitations.[9]

The same problem applied to Germany, but for reasons that were much more the product of the Allied perceptions of the havoc that direct negotiations with Germany might bring. From the outset, the French proposed a dictated peace but their allies were less clear about the choreography of peacemaking. If the Paris negotiations followed the precedents established after the last general European war in 1814–15 there would be a preliminary settlement between the major belligerents that would establish boundaries, compensation and specific conditions of peace. This might require an inter-allied gathering to agree the terms of such a settlement with the main enemy, Germany, and its allies. Then a wider consultation involving the former belligerents and significant neutrals would consider broader questions of international order and necessary adjustments to the system. Contemporaries tended to distinguish between the two stages by calling the first a conference and the second a congress.

No clear decisions were reached before the formal opening of proceedings on 18 January 1919 and the Paris negotiations seemed to encompass some discussions more appropriate to a congress, such as those on the League of Nations or the future regulation of international waterways, with others more pertinent to a conference, including inter-allied considerations and issues specific to a settlement with Germany. All of which seemed to confirm the prediction made by veteran French diplomat, Jules Cambon, that the whole organization of peace would be 'une improvisation'. Nonetheless the assumption, despite French reservations, was that there would be direct negotiations with the Germans. Hence the experts and diplomats set to establish the allied terms tended towards maximum demands in the expectation that this would offer room for manoeuvre and possible concessions in the eventual bargaining. It became clear very quickly that any Allied agreement on peace terms was both hard won and fragile. In 1815 Talleyrand, the representative of the then-defeated power, France, had deftly sown dissension in the ranks of the victors. The Allies were aware that it would not take a German of anything like Talleyrand's calibre to expose the fault lines in their unity and by early March 1919 it was increasingly obvious that there would be no face-to-face negotiations with the Germans. Harold Nicolson, then a young British diplomat, highlighted some of the consequences of this confusion:

> We were never for one instant given to suppose that our recommendations were absolutely final. And thus we tended to accept compromises, and even to support decisions, which we ardently hoped would not, in the last resort, be approved.[10]

The pressure of events, the perception that rapid decisions were necessary by the Big Four after two months in which little had been resolved, and the lack of negotiations with the Germans created a draft treaty that consisted of a series of decisions and demands made in isolation from each other. The final settlement was thus harsher than some of the negotiators had intended. There was, for example, no review of the totality of German border adjustments before the draft treaty was presented to German delegates on 7 May and no correlation made between such losses and Germany's ability to pay reparations. There may have been double jeopardy at times – Germany was required to deliver twenty million tons of coal to France annually for five years to compensate for the deliberate sabotage of mines in Northern France in 1918 but its surrender of the Saar for fifteen years so the French could own and work its mines was also predicated on the same coal losses. There was widespread concern in the British delegation as its members saw the complete treaty for the first time and – despite German efforts to engage in detailed written criticisms of the proposals – most of the few alterations between the draft and final treaties, in particular the provision of a plebiscite to decide the fate of Upper Silesia, came as a result of Lloyd George's attempt to allay colleagues' reservations. Many in the delegation saw these alleviations as only the first step towards greater revisions in the future.[11]

In assessing the origins of the Second World War the key indictments against Versailles must be those that suggest its terms made a new conflict inevitable. Reparations, some of the new frontiers (particularly the Polish–German border) and the general treatment of Germany would feature strongly in such a list. Yet inevitability is a concept that sits very uneasily with most historians and it must be questionable whether it is reasonable to hold the peacemakers of 1919, the last of whom left office forever in October 1922, accountable for the decisions taken by their successors, who might have followed many alternative turnings on the road that it is claimed led directly from 1919 to 1939. As Gerhard Schulz pointed out in 1967, 'There is a serious lack of logic in all verdicts passed on the peace treaty which ignore the fact that the pre-war policies could not prevent war, and which fail to appreciate the essential continuity of the pre-war period, the war, peace-time and the era of revision.'[12]

1914 clearly marked, for many who survived the ensuing cataclysm, the point at which an old world died, but its demise did not remove all of the problems that had convinced key decision-makers in Europe that the existing international structures must be recast, even if that entailed the risky stratagem of war. Indeed, beyond the destruction of Germany as an imperial and naval rival, the war resolved none of the pressing concerns facing the powers in 1914. Some states had disintegrated, compounding the dilemmas, whilst the bitter legacy of the death, destruction and human and material debris left from the fighting made the peacemakers' work all the more difficult, not least in an age where they were much more directly accountable to electorates than those facing similar tasks in earlier times.

The peacemakers had no easy task to create their new world order. They faced enormous responsibilities arising from the unprecedented and more or less simultaneous collapse of the four great empires that had dominated Eastern and Central Europe for centuries, such that, as Margaret MacMillan argued, Paris became, in the first half of 1919, the world's capital, with the huge project of restoring order to vast areas of the continent and the wider world. Yet the further the distance from Paris, the less the real authority of the conference – as the British Chief of the Imperial General Staff, Sir Henry Wilson declared, 'The root of evil is that the *Paris writ does not run*.'[13]

This problem was reflected in the paradoxical stipulation of the armistice with Germany that its troops in Eastern and Central Europe must withdraw to the German pre-war frontiers but only 'as soon as the Allies shall think the moment suitable, having regard to the internal situation of these territories'. In other words, the only tangible signs of Allied authority in these regions were German forces and, as the conference became more and more prolonged and the Allies demobilized, the situation became more precarious. Philip Kerr, Lloyd George's private secretary, wrote from Paris in July 1919

> Mr Balfour [Arthur Balfour, the British Foreign Secretary] pointed out that the Allies who six months ago possessed the greatest military power in the world were now militarily impotent to impose their will either upon their old enemies or upon the rebellious little states in Eastern Europe.[14]

Yet the peacemakers believed they should – and could – resolve the world's problems swiftly. They were driven in particular by the fear that if they did not deal with the vacuum of power in Eastern and Central Europe, that void would be filled by Bolshevism. Communist regimes in Munich and Hungary increased this concern. As American Secretary of State Robert Lansing noted on 4 April 1919, 'It is time to stop fiddling while the world is on fire, while violence and bestiality consume society. Everyone is clamouring for peace, for an immediate peace.' Wilson, in particular, was acutely aware that Lenin could offer an alternative, revolutionary, vision to his own ideal of a reformist capitalist and democratic world. His European colleagues were equally aware of the threat of increasing radicalism at home, driven in part by frustration at the halting attempts of governments to undo the massive mobilizations of men, women and resources required to fight a total war.[15]

Clemenceau was on home ground, but the other major players were isolated from their pressing domestic responsibilities, which were more likely to have a decisive influence on their future electoral fortunes than the outcomes of the peace conference. President Harry Truman later defined a statesman as a retired politician. Lloyd George had no intention of retiring, nor, at that point, did Orlando. The American constitution did not then debar Wilson from seeking a third term, whilst even the seventy-seven-year-old Clemenceau believed that a grateful French parliament should choose him by acclamation to replace his bitter rival Raymond Poincaré as President of the Republic when the latter's seven year term ended in early 1920.[16]

Each of the Four had thus to be mindful of the political repercussions of his actions – whether Wilson in terms of the perceived threat of increased Asian immigration which forced him to resist Japanese demands for a racial equality clause in the Covenant of the League, or Orlando, whose freedom of manoeuvre over the vexed issue of Italy's newly advanced claim to Fiume (Rijeka) was greatly limited by the pressure of public expectation at home. In both Britain and France the electorate expected their leaders to achieve substantial compensation from Germany towards the enormous costs they had incurred in winning the war and, in the French case in particular, the anticipated heavy burden of repairing the damage to their territory. Issues such as these were difficult and important in their own right, but they also offer insights into the complexities of peacemaking, in particular the extreme difficulties of reconciling contending principles in such a way as to offer a sense of fairness and practicality to all concerned – or, given that such an ideal outcome was probably impossible to achieve, a solution that offended most people the least.

Conforming to the art of the possible was made even more difficult by an intangible but very real consideration that affected many of the matters under discussion. Wilson's 1918 speeches, which, according to the 5 November 1918 pre-Armistice agreement with Germany, were supposed to form the principled basis of the eventual treaty, set a higher moral standard for this settlement than for previous peace negotiations. When this aspiration foundered, as it often did, on the complexities of competing national interests and practicalities, it was easy for critics to brand the settlements as hypocritical. Expectations had been raised, often far beyond the President's intentions, and many anticipated that Wilson would deliver exactly what he had said.

'Open covenants of peace, openly arrived at' proved impractical. Any negotiation risks being derailed by the premature disclosure of parts of the potential agreement before the total settlement has been reached – at any particular stage one or more parties to the discussions may appear to have made damaging concessions without achieving reciprocal benefits in exchange. Rapidly grasping this, the peacemakers kept a disappointed world press at arm's length, though each was not immune to the temptation to let slip nuggets of information to favoured correspondents in the hope of domestic political advantage.[17]

Aspiration and reality collided with particular force over the level of compensation due from the defeated to the victors, which became one of the key elements in the labelling of Versailles as immoral, vindictive and impracticable. This was a highly charged political issue. The French finance minister Louis-Lucien Klotz allegedly declared, *'L'Allemagne paiera'* – Germany will pay – and the British and French publics expected this to happen. During the British 1918 election campaign Lloyd George promised that the Germans 'must pay to the uttermost farthing, and we shall search their pockets for it', though he did qualify this by warning of potential limits on Germany's capacity to pay.[18]

Wilson had ruled out punitive contributions although he had spoken of the need for restoration of the territories invaded by the Central Powers. Even if this definition expanded to include mercantile shipping losses and damage from air and sea raids, Britain's share of any payments would be small, and Australia, which had spent more money and lost more men than Belgium, would receive nothing. The fundamental question was thus whether the Allies could legitimately require Germany to compensate them for all their costs associated with winning the war (an indemnity) or only for the repair of damage done to their civilian population (reparations). Practically it might make little difference, because, as economists like Keynes pointed out, Germany could probably not afford either, but there was a strong moral aspect to this as well.

Wartime speeches by Lloyd George and Wilson, coupled with the pre-Armistice agreement that restricted liability to 'all damage done to the civilian population of the Allies and their property by the aggression of Germany by land, by sea, and from the air' apparently ruled out an indemnity. Yet when the peace conference opened, every delegation, except that of the United States, submitted a claim for its full war costs. Clemenceau and Lloyd George, adamant that this was their right, were confronted by Wilson, who was equally determined that it was not. A crisis loomed. It was 'solved' by one of the classic short-term fixes replete with unintended consequences – Articles 231 and 232 of the treaty – which asserted the Allied moral right to full compensation from Germany (and its allies) for all their losses because Germany (and its allies) were responsible for the war, but then, for practical reasons rather than prior commitment, limited their actual claims to certain categories of civilian damage.

Controversially, these included the costs of pensions and allowances paid to servicemen and their families when Wilson acceded to the dubious argument advanced first by Lord Sumner, one of Lloyd George's contentious advisers on reparations, and then, more acceptably, by the South African Defence Minister, Jan Smuts, that service personnel were only civilians in uniform. Acknowledging its weakness, Wilson declared: 'Logic? I don't give a damn for logic, if you will excuse my French. I am going to include pensions.' He did so under the assumption that he was creating a fairer basis for the distribution of either an agreed fixed sum (which would be less than the 'real' total of Germany's liabilities) or some other limited German payment.[19]

However, the Council of Four failed to reach an agreement on figures, instead setting up a Reparation Commission to make recommendations in 1921. When it did so, in theory at least, the inclusion of pensions nearly doubled the sums asked of Germany but, equally, most of the apparent demand for £6,600,000,000 was patently 'phoney money' – window dressing to make the bill palatable to Allied public opinion but whose payment was never seriously expected. Of the three series of bonds the Germans were to issue, over £4,000,000,000 were C bonds, which could, joked the Belgian Premier Georges Theunis, be stuck 'in a drawer without bothering to lock up, for no thief would be tempted to steal them'. Germany's real debt, under the A and B bonds, was therefore about £2,500,000,000, well within the margin of British and American estimates of its capacity to pay, and less than an earlier German offer, admittedly with a number of unacceptable caveats, to pay £5,000,000,000.

The 1920s began with forceful efforts to persuade Germany to pay, culminating in the Franco-Belgian invasion of the Ruhr in 1923. The collapse of this adventure was followed by two American-led attempts to create workable reparations schedules, in the Dawes and Young Plans of 1924 and 1929 respectively. Germany finally defaulted on its reparation liabilities in 1932. It is very difficult to be precise, given all the potential complexities of accounting, but Germany probably paid about £1100 million in reparations, including deliveries in kind. Germany could do so partly because foreign investors, mostly American, lent it about £1275 million between 1924 and 1930. Hitler later refused to repay most of these loans, prompting Stephen Schuker to write of 'American "Reparations" to Germany'. Yet, as Conan Fischer graphically illustrates, this apparent net gain did not mean that ordinary German workers benefited: indeed the reverse was true, especially in the early 1920s.[20]

The debate about whether Germany could, had it chosen, have met its obligations has been fierce, but ultimately sterile. Gerald Feldman's pithy claim that 'apparently the only people who really believed that the Germans could fulfil their reparations obligations ... are some historians' is not the whole truth. This was always as much a political as an economic and financial question but those who suggested that Germany certainly might have made a stronger effort without disastrous economic effects have included Niall Ferguson, Sally Marks, Stephen Schuker and Trachtenberg, the sceptics include Barry Eichengreen, Feldman himself, David Felix and Fischer.[21] What is indisputable is that reparations bedevilled the international relations of the early 1920s.

The peacemakers faced a whole clatter of conflicting issues. The war had been very expensive – one British estimate suggested £24 billion in 1914 terms as the cost of winning it.[22] It had also been very destructive. On the Western Front alone France faced the prospect of reconstructing an area the size of Holland. If there is something shabby about the way in which the peacemakers approached the problem there is also the reality that this issue had the potential to reverse the military outcome of the war. As the American historian Sally Marks has perceptively written:

At heart, reparations were about two fundamental and closely related questions: who won the war and who would pay for it, or at least the cost of undoing the damage ... If the Allies, and especially France, had to assume reconstruction costs on top of domestic and foreign war debts, whereas Germany was left with only domestic debts, they would be the losers, and German economic dominance would be tantamount to victory. Reparations would both deny Germany that victory and spread the pain of undoing the damage done.[23]

Some of that pain might also have been alleviated had the Americans been willing to admit a link between reparations and the inter-allied debts contracted to pay for the war. Whereas the Europeans wished to interpret those debts as part of a common effort to defeat the Central Powers in which some partici- pants had paid in blood and others in cash, the Americans refused to liquidate the sums owed to them. Of some £3.7 billion of total debts, £2.96 billion was owed to the United States, mainly by the British, who had borrowed money on behalf of their less creditworthy allies. The Europeans favoured an all-round cancellation of these debts in return for reducing Germany's reparation liabil- ities but the American position was succinctly summarized by President Calvin Coolidge – 'Well, they hired the money, didn't they?' Whilst Britain, still a creditor nation in these arrangements, would have suffered a theoretical loss had the debts been cancelled, the reality was that many of its debts were bad, whereas America would have been the major loser and the political cost of making such a concession, mainly in Britain's favour, was too high. Once again the art of the possible proved a stumbling block to a more desirable outcome.[24]

No one – not even the Germans – disputed that some compensation was due, but there were no easy solutions given the weight of public expectations, no neat formula that would simultaneously lead both sides to believe they had achieved a good bargain. Instead reparations would bedevil not only relations between Germany and its former enemies, but also between the former allies, most notably Britain and France. The interpretation of Article 231 to mean exclusive German responsibility for the outbreak of war in 1914 was grist to German publicists seeking to incriminate other powers and to undermine the credibility of the treaty. Not surprisingly, they redoubled their efforts after Lloyd George claimed at the London conference of March 1921 that 'For the Allies, German responsibility for the war is fundamental. It is the basis upon which the structure of the treaty has been erected, and if that acknowledgement is repudiated or abandoned, the treaty is destroyed.'[25] Reparations became a potent weapon for discontented German nationalists whilst Keynes provided British critics with evidence of the dubious morality and practicality of the policy. The tangle of reparations and inter-allied debts contributed heavily to the economic and financial problems of the post-war period that culminated, after the brief respite provided by the Dawes and Young plans, in the social, political and economic turmoil of the Great Depression following the 1929 Wall Street Crash. It was thus not one of the most edifying or effective aspects of peacemaking, but the Allies did have a strong case against Germany, which they marred by some dubious dealings.

Across the globe Wilson (and Lloyd George) had, intentionally or otherwise, encouraged peoples who perceived themselves to be oppressed to have faith in the principle of national self-determination. Wilson's doctrine gave a great boost to existing or emerging nationalist groups who believed (without any realistic justification) that he was about to sweep aside the European colonial empires.[26] Wilson did insist, however, that Germany's former colonies be redistributed to the victors as mandates, not absolute property. In Europe the settlements would eventually reduce the number of people living in countries in which they were not the dominant nationality from sixty million in 1914 to thirty million, but each of those thirty million remained living proof that national self-determination either was not, or could not be, fully applied. Often there was an irreconcilable conflict between ethnographic, economic, military and historic considerations, coupled with incompatible aspirations.

Nowhere was this better illustrated than in Germany's bitter resentment of its new frontier with Poland, which it never accepted and which was one of its most hated aspects of the settlement. Wilson's thirteenth point had suggested:

> An independent Polish state should be erected, which should include the territories inhabited by indisputably Polish populations, which should be assured a free and secure access to the sea, and whose political and economic independence should be guaranteed by international covenant.

The definition, identity and location of 'genuinely Polish elements' or 'indisputably Polish populations' were debatable, but the big gap between the central area that most would concede was 'Polish' and the sea posed an enormous problem. Wilson's promises were contradictory: on the one hand, secure access to the Baltic, and on the other national self-determination. Danzig, the obvious port, was – equally obviously – German, and Poles were in a minority in the lands that would be needed to make a 'corridor' to Danzig, splitting East from West Prussia.[27] The compromise of Free City status for Danzig and adjustments to the corridor in Germany's favour after plebiscites would never satisfy disgruntled German nationalists. Whilst Stresemann might concede (sincerely or otherwise) at Locarno that Germany's western frontiers were now final, there was never any prospect of an eastern equivalent.[28]

Unsurprisingly, in the immediate aftermath of a bitter war, the overwhelming sense during the Paris negotiations was of a zero sum game. For the French any diminution of German strength, whether through financial penalties, restrictions on armaments or reduction of territory, represented either a potential direct gain, for example in their claims on Alsace-Lorraine, the Rhineland and Saar, or an indirect improvement if German territory and resources were ceded to Poland or Denmark.[29] In such circumstances there was little chance that national self-determination would be allowed to work in Germany's favour. It had taken a massive coalition to defeat a state with sixty-five million people, and to add a further eight million German speakers from Austria or three million from the Sudetenland to a country that despite its wartime losses still remained, along with Russia, one of the two potential continental giants, was simply never going to happen, whatever scope this might offer to those seeking to brand the settlement as hypocritical.

Here, as with the collective security of the League of Nations, the peace-makers found themselves torn between an idea that Wilson proclaimed a failure – the balance of power – and new ways of drawing the European map or reorganizing the world's international system. Their thinking, and that of those who followed them in power, was confused on both counts. The confusion was compounded in the case of the League by what seemed the electoral imperative of the need to offer public support for its new methods even though this clashed with the private conviction of most political leaders that this constituted a dangerous and unproven experiment. Yet much was expected of the League, not least that it would offer an opportunity to put right the mistakes that the peacemakers recognized would inevitably be made in the Parisian cauldron. In the absence of the United States, however, such hopes were unrealistic.

In Britain's case the ultimate revelation of the gulf between the public and private positions of its leaders came during the Abyssinian crisis of 1935 with decision-makers torn between their perception that the government needed to support the League in order to secure re-election (and, perhaps, to preserve the League and its methods) and their belief that Italy, despite its blatant aggression against a fellow member of the League, was a vital partner in keeping Adolf Hitler's resurgent Germany under control. Their policy of apparent but half-hearted backing for the League may have returned the National Government to power but alienated Italy, propelling Benito Mussolini towards an alliance with Hitler, whilst simultaneously confirming the League's irrelevance.[30]

The peacemakers have been accused of 'Balkanizing' Eastern and Central Europe, creating a series of small, squabbling states in place of the three great empires that had dominated the area for centuries. Whilst there were policy advisers who favoured the creation of smaller, national, states in place of the multi-national autocracies that Wilson and other liberals blamed for bringing about the conflict, there was still an innate conservatism amongst senior officials and politicians that preferred some continuation of the former structures, albeit with reforms. There was, for example, no clear wartime consensus either within or between the allied countries about the future of Austria-Hungary. Some favoured using the potentially suicidal weapon of encouraging internal nation-alist revolts to destroy the empire; others preferred to try to split the Central Powers and encourage an intact empire to make a separate peace.

The empire's implosion, taken together with the collapse of Russia and revolution in Germany, left the peacemakers struggling to impose order on a vast area of Europe over which they had little control. There were some desultory attempts to recreate some sort of economic bloc to replace the

Austro-Hungarian empire but these collapsed and much of the new map of Eastern and Central Europe arose less from decisions taken in Paris than from actions taken on the spot by self-created governments seeking, where it was expedient, to claim the justification of national self-determination for their ambitions, but, when necessary, willing to use force to achieve their ends. Few were satisfied with the outcomes and their continuing grievances with neighbours undermined their individual and collective chances of coping with a revived Germany or Russia – or both.[31]

It was always the French contention that it was in the east, rather than in a direct assault on France, that any German attempts to revise the new map of Europe would occur – there would be a new Sadowa before a new Sedan (a reference to a decisive Prussian victory against Austria in 1866 which preceded that against France in 1870). Reluctant to make any commitment in Europe, Britain was prepared to consider (though not to implement except in the highly ambiguous Locarno agreements) guarantees for the security of metropolitan France, but would never contemplate extending such support to the new states of Eastern Europe that the French anticipated would become the early targets of an indirect assault on themselves. Their concern (and a false hope of discovering a substitute menace to Germany's eastern frontiers in the absence of a credible Russian presence) led the French to conclude a series of alliances with states few of whom, as a despairing Quai d'Orsay assessment in 1936 declared, regarded themselves as allies of the others.[32] Anglo-French delusions were shattered by the Munich crisis. The Czechs expected France to be a provider, not a consumer, of security, whilst Britain's attempt to divide Europe into a west, in which it accepted, however reluctantly, a connection with its own security, and an east, to which its attitude was, as Austen Chamberlain declared at best 'not disinterested', came to an abrupt end when his half-brother, Neville, flew to Germany in September 1938.

Clemenceau's strategy at the peace conference straddled the twin policies of ensuring continuing Anglo-American support and more tangible assets such as border adjustments and the weakening of Germany. When, in March, Wilson and Lloyd George offered him guarantees for France's future security and Wilson conceded a fifteen-year occupation of the Rhineland to which Lloyd George reluctantly acquiesced, Clemenceau believed he had achieved success. It was illusory: American failure to ratify their guarantee released Britain from its promise and, despite leaders in both Britain and France professing to believe that an alliance between them would ensure the maintenance of peace, no such deal could be struck. Instead the central theme of the early 1920s was the Anglo-French inability to construct a coherent policy towards Germany.[33]

When the Germans suggested that they could not execute parts of the treaty, the British were generally sympathetic, whereas the French suggested that it was not that the Germans could not comply, rather that they would not. The real tragedy here was that they did not grasp the lessons of the Spa conference of July 1920 when a firm Anglo-French front forced Germany to take steps to disarm. Instead in the early 1920s Lloyd George clashed, with varying intensity, with a succession of French leaders. He got on better with Aristide Briand, the Breton with whom it was claimed he could converse in Welsh, than with the tough Lorrainer, Poincaré, but the differences between Britain and France were not personal. Rather they rested on differences of geography, history and philosophy. France did indeed have an impressive overseas empire but saw itself, inescapably, as a European power whereas Britain wished to re-emphasize its imperial and global role, and, if possible, distance itself from Europe. This idea was well expressed by Kerr, who advised Lloyd George to leave 'Europe to itself with such assistance as the League of Nations can give to it' and Smuts, who suggested to the 1921 Imperial Conference 'I would rather assume a position of independence, putting the British Empire entirely aside from all of them.'[34] Such a mindset was not conducive to good relations with France, particularly given the legacy of earlier mutual animosity, which always lurked in the background of dialogues between London and Paris.

'[W]e Americans were not involved ...' This skilful (or forgetful) release of the United States from most of the blame that he was attributing to the vengeful Europeans is not the least interesting of Kennan's perceptions. It would, of course, be easy to fault him on detail – the United States did sign the Treaty of Versailles. What its Senate failed to do, on 19 November 1919 and 19 March 1920, was to ratify the signatures of its President and other plenipotentiaries, thereby abrogating responsibility for a settlement that they, and Wilson in particular, had a huge part in shaping, often against the wishes and judgement of their European associates. This American retreat from the consequences of its decisive intervention in the war itself, and from Wilson's crucial role in the peace negotiations, left Britain and France as the main executors of a treaty that, left to their own devices, they would not have concluded and as the reluctant foster-parents to the orphaned League of Nations, the main element in Wilson's New World Order. Had the United States taken its proper share of treaty enforcement there was at least a chance that an Anglo-American partnership might have adapted the settlement to changing circumstances more successfully than the Anglo-French leaders did, though much would still have rested on the willingness of Germany to accept the military outcome of the war.

Whatever the potential miscalculations (or worse) of decision-makers in 1919 this is perhaps the crucial consideration. Would Germany have found acceptable any treaty predicated on its defeat? There were clearly a number of specific provisions that caused resentment and annoyance, but the fundamental problem was that Germany did not accept the key premises on which the Allies based their conclusions: that Germany was primarily responsible for starting the war; that it had fought that war in an unacceptable manner; and – most crucial of all – that it had lost.

Whilst there is a clear case to be made that the victors did not ease the passage of the new Weimar state, they were not assisted by the attitude of a regime that found it difficult to come to terms with defeat. This might be understandable for German citizens who were aware of victory in the east and a situation in the west where the war ended with German soldiers still occupying much of Belgium and north-eastern France and where no allied soldier had his foot on German soil. Even so the experiences of the 'turnip winter' of 1917 and the continuing privations they suffered must have raised doubts about the reality of Germany's success and their military and political leaders were certainly better informed. Nonetheless the leader of the new German government, President Ebert, told troops returning to Berlin on 11 December 1918 'No enemy has overcome you', thus reinforcing a growing myth that Germany's victorious armies had been stabbed in the back by dissident forces at home and setting the tone for later exchanges.[35]

With hindsight it could be argued that the Allies might have persisted beyond November 1918 and invaded Germany to bring the full extent of its defeat home, as would happen in 1945. The art of the possible excluded such an outcome. Among the Allied leaders only Poincaré, who felt constitutionally inhibited from pressing his opinion, and the American general John Pershing advocated a rejection of Germany's armistice request. Henry Wilson and Douglas Haig dissipated Lloyd George's early enthusiasm for continuing the struggle, mistakenly suggesting that Germany was not yet desperately in need of peace. Marshal Ferdinand Foch, the French commander-in-chief of the Allied armies on the Western Front, summed up the general mood well on 31 October: 'I am not waging war for the sake of waging war. If I obtain through the Armistice the conditions that we wish to impose upon Germany, I am satisfied. Once this object is obtained, nobody has the right to shed one more drop of blood.' The Allied perception was that the armistice encapsulated a German acknowledgement of defeat and that its terms deprived Germany of any chance of resuming the war. The latter was true: the former was not.[36]

The Versailles settlement continues to be seen, in Keynes's phrase, as a 'Carthaginian' peace.[37] Yet, unlike Carthage's fate at the hands of Rome in 146BC, Germany was palpably not destroyed by Versailles and indeed such was never the intention of any of the peacemakers. Some regretted this – after a very tough campaign in Italy against German soldiers, their health allegedly destroyed by the Allied wartime blockade and the treaty's cruelty, General Mark Clark was unsympathetic to pleas to avoid a new Carthaginian peace in 1945, wryly declaring 'Well, we don't seem to get too much trouble from those Carthaginians today.' Yet for Wilson and Lloyd George Germany was an essential element in any solution to the problems of restoring European stability and Clemenceau recognized the reality that France would continue to share a border with a powerful state.

The treaty did impose swingeing cuts on Germany's armed forces; the 4 million men of 1914 were reduced to an army and navy totalling 115,000, deprived of an air force, tanks and a general staff. There was the uncertainty of a potentially massive reparations bill. Germany did lose territory and population in 1919 – most accepted the loss of Alsace-Lorraine, but the cession of land to Poland was a bitter blow. The conventional estimates are that Germany lost 13 and 10 per cent of its territory and people respectively, but Robert Boyce argues for a reassessment. He suggests that, discounting territory conquered in the last fifty years, the non-Germans in transferred lands and the movement of Germans in those areas to Germany itself, losses of 9.4 per cent of its land and 1.8 per cent of its pre-war population would be more accurate.[38] Such calculations would, of course, be irrelevant to the perceptions of Germans who wished to perceive the settlement as wicked and unfair. To take one example, what others might see as a desirable extension of the definition of war crimes to include not simply operational infringements but the responsibility of Wilhelm II and others for political and strategic decisions, Germany saw as 'shame clauses'.

Yet paradoxically, far from being Carthaginian, the settlement left defeated Germany in a potentially stronger relative position than in 1914. Then it had been bordered by three great powers – France, Austria-Hungary and Russia. Austria-Hungary had disintegrated into two small rump states, with the remainder of its territory shared out between the Italians and Romanians and the new or revived powers of Czechoslovakia, Poland and Yugoslavia. Russia had collapsed into revolution, its future uncertain, and with Poland interposed, it no longer shared a common frontier with Germany. This left only France, its already threatened demographic strength further sapped by spending a much greater proportion of its young men to gain victory. Whereas German industry was unscathed and its debts internal, France faced the daunting expense of restoring the devastated battlefields of the Western Front and repaying loans to America and Britain.

Three important recent studies approach the 1920s from different perspectives. Zara Steiner's magisterial volume *The Lights That Failed* offers a comprehensive coverage of the League, the economic recovery and European relations, including the role of some of the smaller states whose importance is often overlooked in a story dominated by Britain, France and Germany, together with Russia and the United States. Patrick Cohrs' *The Unfinished Peace after World War I* advances the thesis that, whereas the peacemakers in Paris failed, a cooperation between the financial and economic power of the United States and Britain's political leverage created the basis for a stable European peace until scuppered by the onset of the Great Depression. Robert Boyce argues challengingly in *The Great Interwar Crisis* that the combination of economic and political crises that ultimately proved fatal to European peace should be analyzed as linked rather than coincidental occurrences. What all three accept is that it was what Steiner calls 'the hinge years' of 1929 to 1933 that created a decisive change to the world's future. The peace settlement at the end of the First World War was thus part of a much larger picture.[39]

The central problem of that peace was to create a European framework within which Germany could play a role concomitant with its resources and talents without overwhelming its neighbours. As West Germany's Foreign Minister, Hans-Dietrich Genscher, would neatly express it on the eve of German reunification in 1990, quoting Thomas Mann, 'We seek a European Germany not a German Europe.'[40] The strategy of the peacemakers, insofar as they had a coherent one, was to try to encourage a democratic Germany, conceding that it had lost the war, to accept the settlement as just. They were aware that the signature of the treaty was the beginning, not the end, of the story. If Germany made an honest attempt to execute it, became a good European neighbour and a pillar of the new international community overseen by the League of Nations, then the peacemakers recognized that the settlement might require readjustment and they were willing to make concessions. There were indeed hopeful hints and indications in the 1920s of Franco-German economic cooperation presaging post-1945 developments. The alternative was to enforce the treaty rigidly and to insist on German execution. The tragedy was that neither policy was ever pursued to the extent that it might have been effective and the early 1920s experienced an unfortunate and self-defeating combination of conciliation and coercion which eventually contributed to the outcome that neither France nor Britain desired. Foch gloomily predicted at the signature of the treaty 'This is not Peace. It is an Armistice for twenty years.'[41] He proved wrong – by sixty-seven days – but any explanation of this disaster must look beyond the faults and failures of the peacemakers alone.

Notes

1 D. Andelman *A Shattered Peace: Versailles 1919 and the Price We Pay Today*. London, 2008; *The Economist* (December 1999); Jay Winter and Blaine Baggett, *1914–1918: The Great War and the Shaping of the Twentieth Century*. London, 1996, p. 338

2 G.F. Kennan, *At a Century's Ending: Reflections 1982–1995*. London, 1996, p. 21.

3 In 1984. Ibid., p. 18.

4 See, for example, Bill Keylor's encounter recorded in W. Keylor, 'Versailles and International Diplomacy' in M. Boemeke, G. Feldman and E. Glaser (eds), *The Treaty of Versailles: A Reassessment after 75 Years*. Cambridge, 1998, pp. 469–70; M. Trachtenberg, 'Versailles after Sixty Years', *Journal of Contemporary History* vol. 17, no. 3 (July 1982), pp. 487–506.

5 For more sympathetic evaluations see M. Trachtenberg, *Reparations in World Politics: France and European Economic Diplomacy 1916–1923*. Columbia, 1980; M. Boemeke, G. Feldman and E. Glaser, 'Introduction' in Boemeke, Feldman and Glaser (eds), *The Treaty of Versailles*, pp. 11–20; Z. Steiner, 'The Treaty of Versailles Revisited' in M. Dockrill and J. Fisher (eds), *The Paris Peace Conference 1919: Peace without Victory?* Basingstoke, 2001, pp. 13–33 and *The Lights that Failed: European International History 1919–1933*. Oxford, 2005; M. Mazower 'Two Cheers for Versailles', *History Today* 49 (1999); M. MacMillan, *Peacemakers: The Paris Peace Conference of 1919 and its Attempt to End War*. London, 2001; M. Hughes and M. Seligmann, *Does Peace Lead to War: Peace Settlements and Conflict in the Modern Age*. Stroud, 2002, pp. 23–45; A. Sharp, *The Versailles Settlement: Peacemaking after the First World War, 1919–1923*. Basingstoke, 2008, 2nd ed.

6 H. Nicolson, *Peacemaking 1919*. London, 1933, p. 187; Cecil quoted by A. Lentin, *Lloyd George and the Lost Peace: From Versailles to Hitler*. Basingstoke, 2001, p. 69.

7 J.M. Keynes, *The Economic Consequences of the Peace*. London 1919; R. Lansing *The Peace Negotiations: A Personal Narrative*. Boston, 1921; S. Bonsal, *Unfinished Business*. London, 1944;

A. Headlam-Morley, R. Bryant and A. Cienciala (eds), *Sir James Headlam-Morley: A Memoir of the Paris Peace Conference 1919*. London, 1972; Wavell quoted by D. Fromkin, *A Peace to End All Peace: The Fall of the Ottoman Empire and the Creation of the Modern Middle East*. London, 2000, frontispiece; Lord Hardinge, *Old Diplomacy: The Reminiscences of Lord Hardinge of Penshurst*. London, 1947, p. 240.

8   E. Hobsbawm, *Age of Extremes: The Short Twentieth Century, 1914–1991*. London, 1994, p. 31.
9   MacMillan, *Peacemakers*, pp. 71–91.
10 Nicolson, *Peacemaking 1919*, pp. 128–9.
11 MacMillan, *Peacemakers*, pp. 469–84; A. Lentin, *Guilt at Versailles: Lloyd George and the Pre-History of Appeasement*. London, 1984, pp. 132–46.
12 G. Schulz, *Revolutions and Peace Treaties, 1917–1920*. London, 1967, 1972 translation, p. 223.
13 MacMillan, *Peacemakers*, p. 7.
14 Article XII of the armistice signed with Germany, 11 November 1918, in H.W.V. Temperley (ed.), *A History of the Peace Conference of Paris*, 6 vols. Oxford, 1920–4, vol. 1, pp. 463–4. Kerr to Lloyd George (no date, c. 23 July 1919), F89/3/11 in the Lloyd George Papers in the House of Lords Record Office (LGP).
15 Quoted by D. Perman, *The Shaping of the Czechoslovak State*. Leiden, 1962, p. 169.
16 Lloyd George to Tom Jones, 17 March 1919, F/23/4/37 LGP; David Watson, *Georges Clemenceau: France*. London, 2008, pp. 156–9.
17 See Sisley Huddlestone on a 'vital interview' with Lloyd George about the Fontainebleau Memorandum. *In My Time: An Observer's Record of War and Peace*, London, 1938, pp. 133–42.
18 Speech, Newcastle, 29 November 1918. *The Times*, 30 November 1918.
19 A. Lentin, 'Maynard Keynes and the "Bamboozlement" of Woodrow Wilson: What Really Happened at Paris? (Wilson, Lloyd George, pensions and pre-armistice agreement)', *Diplomacy and Statecraft* vol. 15, no. 4 (2004), pp. 725–63 and *The Last Political Law Lord: Lord Sumner (1859–1934)*. Newcastle, 2008, pp. 90–1.
20 The estimate of Germany's payments comes from Etienne Weill-Raynal, *Les Reparations Allemandes et la France*, 3 vols. Paris, 1947, vol. 3, pp. 769–71. Niall Ferguson, *The Pity of War*. London, 1998 suggests similar though slightly different figures on p. 417. S. Schuker, *American 'Reparations' to Germany, 1919–1933: Implications for the Third-World Debt Crisis*. Princeton, 1988, Schuker quotes Theunis, p. 46. C. Fischer 'The Human Price of Reparations', *Diplomacy and Statecraft* vol. 16, no. 3 (2005), pp. 499–514 and *The Ruhr Crisis 1923–4*. Oxford, 2003, *passim*.
21 Ferguson, *The Pity of War*, pp. 412–19; Marks, 'Smoke and Mirrors: In Smoke-Filled Rooms and the Galerie des Glaces' in Boemeke, Feldman and Glaser (eds), *The Treaty of Versailles*, pp. 337–70; Schuker, *American 'Reparations'*, *passim*; B. Eichengreen, *Golden Fetters: The Gold Standard and the Great Depression, 1919–1939*. Oxford, 1992, pp. 127–34, 139–46; G. Feldman, *The Great Disorder: Politics, Economics, and Society in the German Inflation, 1914–1924*. Oxford, 1993, pp. 309–627, 'The Reparations Debate', *Diplomacy and Statecraft* vol. 16, no. 3 (2005), pp. 487–98 and 'A Comment on the Settlement of Accounts' in Boemeke, Feldman and Glaser (eds), *The Treaty of Versailles*, pp. 441–7, the quotation is from p. 445. D. Felix, 'Reparations Reconsidered with a Vengeance', *Central European History* (June 1971), pp. 171–9; Trachtenberg, *Reparations in World Politics*, pp. 66–8. See Steiner, *The Lights that Failed*, pp. 182–255 for an excellent overview of the economic complexities of the diplomacy of the period.
22 This figure would need to be multiplied roughly seventy-five times to give a current (2011) equivalent.
23 Marks, 'Smoke and Mirrors', pp. 337–8.
24 A. Sauvy, *Histoire économique de la France entre les deux Guerres*, 2 vols. Fayard, Paris, 1965–7, vol. 1, p. 169. The United States had sequestered £85,060,000 worth of German property; B. Kent, *The Spoils of War: The Politics, Economics and Diplomacy of Reparations, 1918–1932*. Oxford, 1989, pp. 67, 76–8; A. Turner, *The Cost of War: British Policy on French War Debts, 1918–1932*. Sussex, 1998, *passim*. P. Cohrs, *The Unfinished Peace after World War I: America, Britain and the Stabilisation of Europe 1919–1932*. Cambridge, 2006, *passim*; Steiner, *The Lights that Failed*, pp. 181–255. D. Artaud calculates the comparative losses as $3 billion for Britain and $9.5 billion for America, mainly because the bulk of Britain's debts were probably irrecoverable,

whereas America's were less insecure. 'Reparations and War Debts: The Restoration of French Financial Power, 1919–1929' in R. Boyce (ed.), *French Foreign and Defence Policy, 1918–1940: The Decline and Fall of a Great Power*. London, 1998, pp. 89–106, p. 92.

25   E.L. Woodward and R. Butler (eds), *Documents on British Foreign Policy, 1919–1939*. First Series, HMSO, 1947 onwards, vol. xv, pp. 258–9.

26   E. Manela, *The Wilsonian Moment: Self-Determination and the International Origins of Anticolonial Nationalism*. Oxford, 2007.

27   D. Lloyd George, *War Memoirs*, 2 vols. London, 1938, vol. 2, p. 1514; Temperley, *A History of the Peace Conference*, vol. 1, pp. 434–5.

28   See J. Wright, *Gustav Stresemann: Weimar's Greatest Statesman*. Oxford, 2002, p. 2 and pp. 508–23 for a discussion of his sincerity and his foreign policy aims.

29   For examples see Trachtenberg, *Reparations in World Politics*; S. Schuker, *The End of French Predominance in Europe: The Financial Crisis of 1924 and the Adoption of the Dawes Plan*. Chapel Hill, 1976; J. Bariéty, *Les Relations Franco-Allemandes après la Première Guerre Mondiale: 10 Novembre 1918–10 Janvier 1925. De l'exécution à la négociation*. Paris, 1977; W.A. McDougall, *France's Rhineland Diplomacy, 1914–1924: The Last Bid for a Balance of Power in Europe*. New Jersey, 1978.

30   R. Henig, *The League of Nations*. London, 2010; A. Sharp, 'From Balance of Power to Collective Security? The League of Nations and International Diplomacy' in R. Stradling (ed.), *Crossroads of European Histories: Multiple Outlooks on Five Key Moments in the History of Europe*. Strasbourg, 2006, pp. 173–85.

31   Sharp, *The Versailles Settlement*, pp. 139–68.

32   A. Sharp and K. Jeffery, '"Après la Guerre finit, Soldat anglais partit": Anglo-French Relations 1918–1925', *Diplomacy and Statecraft* vol. 14, no. 2 (June 2003), pp. 119–38; M. Howard, *The Continental Commitment: The Dilemma of British Defence Policy in the Era of Two World Wars*. London, 1974, pp. 74–96; A. Adamthwaite, *The Making of the Second World War*. London, 1977, pp. 158–60.

33   See A. Lentin, 'Lloyd George, Clemenceau and the Elusive Anglo-French Guarantee Treaty, 1919: "A Disastrous Episode?"' and A. Sharp, 'Anglo-French Relations from Versailles to Locarno, 1919–1925: The Quest for Security' in A. Sharp and G. Stone (eds), *Anglo-French Relations in the Twentieth Century: Rivalry and Co-operation*. London, 2000, pp. 104–19, 120–38.

34   Kerr Memorandum, 2 September 1920, LGP F/27/3/39; Imperial Conference Paper E6, 24 June 1921, CAB 32/2/E7, The National Archives, Kew.

35   D. Newton, *British Policy and the Weimar Republic 1918–1919*. Oxford, 1997; H. Harmer, *Friedrich Ebert: Germany*. London, 2008, p. 67.

36   F. Foch, *The Memoirs of Marshal Foch*. Heinemann, 1931, p. 541; G. Wormser, *La République de Clemenceau*. Paris, 1961, pp. 339–41. See K. Schwabe, D. French, D. Stevenson, T. Knock and A. Sharp on 'Peace Planning and the Actualities of the Armistice' in Boemeke, Feldman and Glaser (eds), *The Treaty of Versailles*, pp. 37–144.

37   Keynes, *The Economic Consequences of Peace*, p. 33.

38   R. Boyce, *The Great Interwar Crisis and the Collapse of Globalization*. Basingstoke, 2009, pp. 53–5.

39   Steiner, *The Lights that Failed*; Cohrs, *The Unfinished Peace*; Boyce, *The Great Interwar Crisis*. See also S. Marks, *The Ebbing of European Ascendancy: An International History of the World, 1914–1945*. London, 2002, which introduces a greater sense of a world aspect to these questions and the excellent chapter by Carole Fink: 'Revisionism' in G. Martel (ed.), *A Companion to Europe, 1900–1945*. Oxford, 2006, pp. 326–40.

40   *Time*, 26 September 1990.

41   W.S. Churchill, *The Second World War: Volume I – The Gathering Storm*, 6 vols. London, 1949 ed., p. 6.

Chapter 2

The League of Nations: An Idea before its Time?

Ruth Henig

A balanced assessment of the history of the League of Nations is long overdue. Over ninety years after its establishment in 1919, it is largely written off by historians who either conclude simplistically that it was a complete failure or dismiss it as a total irrelevance in the interwar period. Margaret MacMillan's withering comment in *Peacemakers*, published in 2001, that 'only a handful of eccentric historians still bother to study the League of Nations'[1] is echoed by Brian Morton's conclusion, in his recent biography of Woodrow Wilson. He writes, 'the League stands now as a kind of noble irrelevance, little researched and not much admired'. Fortunately, in recent years two historians who are far from eccentric, Zara Steiner and Susan Pedersen, have offered more balanced and positive assessments of the League's achievements, successes and failures, and I have recently added my own analysis of its operation and its legacy.[2]

In this chapter I would like to continue the process of revision and of rehabilitation. Patently the League was unable to satisfy the exalted expectations of its founders and to prevent the outbreak of a second world war only twenty years after the end of the first, but was this a realistic aim? Given the environment in which the League operated and the obstacles it faced, what successes did it achieve? What were the main factors that undermined its effectiveness and what was the nature of the legacy it bequeathed to the world after 1945?

The League was a complex international body which offered a number of different 'avenues of escape' from war.[3] Not all of these proved as effective as its founders hoped. Some provided respite from previous conflicts rather than protection against future threats. Others were based on unrealistic or overoptimistic assessments of how states could be induced to work co-operatively together. An editorial in *The Daily News* of 3 August 1922 observed perceptively that the League was established 'to prevent a repetition of the debacle of 1914', and undoubtedly its dispute-solving procedures owed much to British assumptions about how the outbreak of the First World War might have been averted. Furthermore, its emphasis on the reduction of members' armaments to 'the lowest point consistent with national safety' was strongly influenced by the perception, articulated by Lord Grey in his memoirs, that 'great armaments lead inevitably to war ... the enormous growth of armaments in Europe, the sense of insecurity and fear caused by them – it was these that made war inevitable'.[4] Unfortunately, League mechanisms designed to deal with the circumstances believed to have triggered the outbreak of war in 1914 were unlikely to be very effective in combating more deliberate aggression. As Lord Balfour observed in 1924, 'the danger I see in the future is that some powerful nation will pursue a *realpolitik* in the future as in the past … I do not believe we have yet found, or can find, a perfect guarantee against this calamity.'5

The French government did try to equip the League to deal with such pre-meditated aggression in the future. Yet French attempts at Paris to give the League a standing army or powers to compel members to take economic or military sanctions against aggression were flatly rejected by the United States and Britain. Wilson, the US President, took a different approach. He argued that League members had the duty of guaranteeing each other's territorial integrity and political independence against external aggression to ensure the League did not operate as a mere 'debating society'. This may have seemed a workable approach to peacekeeping to an American President who had toyed with it as a way of guaranteeing stability in Central and South America, but the attempt to impose such a structure on over fifty League members during a time of manifold international problems was without doubt misconceived and unrealistic.

Not all of the League's 'avenues of escape' from war were as backward looking or potentially ineffective as the sceptics thought. The creation of a permanent international organization able to pre-empt conflict by joint action through the League Council was certainly innovative. So too was the creation of an annual League Assembly for representatives of all members, at which small and medium powers could raise issues, offer views on world developments and put pressure on the major powers. These gatherings helped to establish international 'norms' of conduct and to develop a real 'spirit of Geneva' that promoted international collaboration and compromise. Furthermore, the founding of a secretariat enabled the League to carry out a wide range of administrative, humanitarian, economic and social activities, including the protection of minority rights in sixteen European and Middle Eastern countries, the supervision of the mandates system imposed on former German colonies and Turkish possessions and the establishment of two enduring bodies: The Permanent Court of International Justice at the Hague and the International Labour Organisation.

The main problems facing the League did not stem from the provisions of the Covenant being ill conceived, backward looking, overambitious or unduly optimistic. It was the international context in which the League operated that really constrained its effectiveness, undermined its attempts to promote international stability and ultimately caused it to be sidelined in the later 1930s. It must be stressed that the impact of the First World War was far reaching and long lasting. The 'war to end all wars' had profound social, economic and political effects that impacted heavily on the inter-war period. In the short term, the damage was immediately visible. Four great empires had collapsed. There was massive financial indebtedness amongst nations. There were revolutions, serious social unrest, a devastating flu epidemic, scarred battlefields and millions of war wounded, widows and orphans. Even while the peacemakers at Paris were locked in acrimonious negotiations, turmoil and conflict was engulfing large parts of east and south-east Europe, the Middle East and Asia.

One of the most enduring legacies of the First World War was the establishment of the Bolshevik regime in Russia. Soviet leaders attacked the 'discredited' capitalism and imperialism of Western nations. The challenge of socialism after 1919 was not just confined to the Soviet Union. There were communist parties scattered throughout the globe. In Germany and Italy communism posed an internal threat to stability and social cohesion and in most capitalist countries the fear of communism was strong. The Bolshevik leaders attacked the League as an alliance of capitalist powers. They did all they could both to undermine it and to challenge its authority in the 1920s, and encouraged other radical and left-wing groups to do the same.

But a far more serious blow to the League was the failure of the USA to join.[6] This left League members trying to second guess how Washington might react in a crisis or seek to defend its interests or respond to an appeal for assistance. Just at the time when economic and financial power was shifting decisively from Europe to North America, the world's leading economic power remained outside and the League's ambition to be a truly global organization was checked at the outset. Its ability to apply sanctions or to initiate arms limitation agreements was also greatly reduced in scope.

In the absence of the Soviet Union and the USA, the League was driven by European powers. There were thirty two members at the outset, soon rising to over forty, and including China, Japan, India, Argentina and Brazil. Yet European power was in long-term decline by the 1920s. Britain and France, the two great imperial powers of the nineteenth century, were struggling to maintain their far-flung world-wide empires in the face of rising levels of nationalist fervour in Egypt, the Middle East, India and south-east Asia. The growth of Japanese political and economic power and of Chinese nationalism posed a serious threat to Western economic interests in Asia. Neither Britain nor France had the military capacity or the economic strength to prevent Japan from seeking territorial expansion on the Chinese mainland during the inter-war years.

The Western alliance between Britain, France, Italy and the USA that had won the war quickly fractured. The Italians protested at what they called the 'mutilated' peace and signed the peace treaty only under duress. Italy retained unfulfilled expansionist ambitions. Britain and France, meanwhile, strongly disagreed about whether Germany should be contained or conciliated. The resulting Treaty of Versailles was an uneasy compromise, which the French government aimed to enforce stringently, but which the British Government sought to revise in Germany's favour through a policy that soon became known as 'appeasement'. This fundamental difference of view about how to maintain European peace in the future had the effect of deadlocking the League of Nations because the territorial integrity and political independence of states that members were pledged to guarantee under article ten of the Covenant was in effect the settlement agreed to at Paris. Hence, France and her East European allies were intent on strengthening the League's role as a guarantor of the 1919 territorial settlement, and keeping Germany out of the League, while Britain, the Dominions, the Scandinavian states and the Netherlands promoted the possibility of peaceful change, to utilize the League's consultative machinery and bring Germany into the League at the earliest opportunity.

With the United States, Russia and Germany outside the League, the British government had no wish to strengthen the existing League peacekeeping machinery and the French blocked any revision of treaties or serious attempts at disarmament. The result for the League, until the mid 1920s, was complete deadlock. As Salvador de Madariaga recalled in his memoirs, 'everything went on as if, for lack of any common adversary, France and Britain had chosen the League as the arena in which to fight each other'.[7] Yet the message the two governments delivered to the voters was very different. They claimed the existence of the League would safeguard peace for the future and prevent a Second World War. This produced unrealistic expectations about the League in both countries. In Britain, the League of Nations Union boasted 200,000 members, with over half of all MPs affiliated to it. Membership soon climbed steadily to over half a million. A similar French League Society had over 120,000 members by the end of 1927 scattered throughout the country. There were similar groups in Belgium, Switzerland and other European countries, including a German pressure group called *Liga fur Volkerbund*, which advocated German membership of the League.[8] These groups pressed their governments to uphold the League Covenant and to pursue foreign policy objectives through the League by means of open diplomacy. Instead of making any attempt to educate voters on the problems and constraints the League faced, League pressure groups put out the strong message that the new organization would prevent a future war.[9]

On three occasions in the 1920s the League did meet public expectations: during the Aland Islands dispute between Sweden and Finland in 1920, dealing with hostilities between Yugoslavia and Albania in 1921, and acting effectively after the invasion of Bulgaria by Greek troops in 1925. In all these cases the League intervened decisively and resolved these disputes successfully. But this was due in large measure to the fact that the countries involved were small powers and there was unanimity among League members on the action taken.[10] The League was also given the invidious task of delimiting the frontier in Upper Silesia between Poland and Germany in 1922 after the Supreme Council failed to resolve the issue. In just six weeks a League Commission had drawn up a line of demarcation that both Poland and Germany reluctantly agreed to. The frontier was effectively administered under League supervision for the next fifteen years, even though the border remained disputed. Equally contentious was the League's role in delimiting the frontier between Turkey and Iraq, over which Britain exercised a mandate in 1924, and in awarding the oil-rich province of Mosul to Iraq. This outcome was initially challenged by Turkey, but then grudgingly accepted.

There were, however, disputes in the early 1920s that caused division and were not effectively resolved at Geneva. Fighting between Turkey and Greece in 1922 – dubbed the 'Chanak crisis' by the press – were not brought before the League, nor was the Franco-Belgian-led invasion of the Ruhr in early 1923 or the underlying failure of Germany to meet reparations payments. The League also struggled to resolve a dispute that began with the murder of an Italian official helping to delimit the Greek–Albanian frontier on behalf of the Conference of Ambassadors in 1923 and that ended with the Italian seizure of the Greek island of Corfu. The Greek government appealed to the League and to the Conference of Ambassadors for help to regain Corfu, but Mussolini was able to resist this pressure and avoid League censure. British attempts to get the dispute examined and dealt with by the League Council were thwarted by France, and a further British suggestion of a joint Anglo-French naval demonstration off the coast of Corfu to force Italian evacuation of the island was 'received coldly by the French'. Mussolini even threatened to withdraw Italy from the League if the dispute was not handed over to the Conference of Ambassadors for settlement and he got his wish.[11] Yet Italy was forced to evacuate Corfu, albeit with an assurance from Greece to pay fifty million lire, if the murderers of Tellini were not apprehended.

The Corfu crisis revealed several important constraints on the League's effectiveness. It showed that it could not operate successfully if Britain and France were divided. It further revealed that if a major power was threatened with sanctions, it retained the option to leave the organization and weaken the League's authority. Even so, the impact of over fifty nations debating the rights and wrongs of a dispute and agreeing to criticize or to take action against a member state was potentially very powerful. Neville Chamberlain's verdict in 1923 was that 'if there had been no League, Corfu would never have been evacuated'. League supporters were further heartened by the fact that League pressure had helped to bring the Corfu crisis to a peaceful solution.[12] It was more than ten years before Mussolini ran the risk of challenging the League of Nations again.

The authority of the League gained a massive boost in 1926 when Germany became a member, shortly after the signing of the Locarno agreements. In the years before 1925, France had sought unsuccessfully to buttress its security by strengthening the machinery of the League through the Draft Treaty of Mutual Assistance and the Geneva Protocol. The French also pressed the British for a military alliance, which was firmly rejected by successive British Governments. Locarno revealed both the limited extent to which the British government was prepared to assist France, and the differing roles which the two powers hoped the League would play in resolving European disputes in the future. The French wanted a strong, coercive League ready to stop any military attempt to challenge the European status quo, but the Locarno accords were very restricted geographically and flexible in operation. The frontiers of Western Europe were affirmed by France, Belgium and Germany, and further guaranteed by

Britain and Italy, and there were provisions for security against aggression and arbitration included in the settlement. But no similar guarantees were entered into in respect of Germany's disputed eastern borders and though Britain was a party to arbitration treaties covering Germany's western frontiers it would not bind itself to defend the status quo in Eastern Europe. Sir Austen Chamberlain, the British Foreign Secretary, claimed Locarno had strengthened the League by containing the important provision that Germany would join the organization, but in reality 'Locarno was widely interpreted as a green light for Germany in the east'.[13]

Even in Western Europe, Britain was simultaneously guaranteeing France against a German attack and Germany against a French attack. So the War Office could not make any concrete plans in advance concerning an outbreak of hostilities in Western Europe and did not make any plans for a 'continental commitment' in the event of a second European War. As the Chiefs of Staff told the British Foreign Office in 1926, 'so far as commitments on the Continent are concerned, the Services can only take note of them'.[14] In the words of Professor Fred Northedge, Locarno was 'totally at variance with the League system and went far to destroy it'.[15] This is a somewhat harsh verdict. But what Locarno did reaffirm was the diametrically opposed views of Britain and France towards the major functions of the League. The French government pressed for co-ordinated collective action to counter aggression, while Britain wanted the League to function as a flexible and consultative addition to more conventional diplomatic machinery.

In the years immediately after Locarno, doubts about the settlement were pushed into the background. Austen Chamberlain, Briand and Stresemann jointly received the Nobel Peace Prize for their success in reconciling national antagonisms and these three leading political figures worked together at Geneva and elsewhere to resolve a range of problems. Indeed the meetings of the Locarno powers – dubbed 'Locarno tea parties' – began to arouse resentment amongst the medium and smaller League powers as they increasingly resembled a re-incarnation of the old 'Concert of Europe'. Austen Chamberlain, however, was convinced that the unity of the Locarno powers was an essential pre-requisite both for the effective operation of the League and for ensuring the future peace of Europe, and he continued to discuss agenda items in advance of League meetings with Stresemann and Briand and to reach agreement on major issues in spite of mounting criticism.[16]

There is much debate about the immediate post-Locarno years. The 'optimists' take the view that this was a 'golden era' when Germany finally became reconciled to the Versailles peace settlement and showed a willingness to co-operate with its former enemies. This harmony, so the argument goes, was shattered by the death of Stresemann and the Wall Street crash, which led to the rise of Hitler. The 'pessimists' stress that the consensus was superficial and the problems stemming from the 1914–18 conflict had not been resolved and the status quo was not fully accepted by the German government, which still looked for a future revision of the peace settlement.

The League of Nations certainly enjoyed if not a 'golden age' then at least a new lease of life after Locarno. It began to pursue bold plans for disarmament and supported security pacts that strengthened its authority. The Soviet Union and the USA joined the disarmament discussions and toned down the antagonism they had previously displayed towards League activities. The United States agreed to a French proposal to sign an arbitration treaty modelled on Locarno, called the 'Kellogg–Briand Pact', in 1928, under which all signatories renounced war as an instrument of national policy and agreed to settle disputes through peaceful means. Yet the Pact raised as many questions as it solved. It had no enforcement mechanism and was accurately described by one American senator as an 'international kiss' and a perfunctory one at best.[17] Even its chief author Frank Kellogg, the United States Secretary of State, made it clear that in his view 'every nation alone is competent to decide whether circumstances require recourse to war in self defence', a view endorsed by the British government. Instead of bringing the US closer to Geneva, Kellogg's initiative emphasized the key differences in approach between the US and League members, and once more highlighted further divisions between Britain and France.

The eagerly awaited Commission for Disarmament, which met at Geneva from 1926 to 1930, did not make substantive progress. The representatives of all the world's great powers and six smaller ones – encompassing politicians, diplomats, expert advisors and military and naval officials – laboured in vain to find some basis of general agreement, while at the same time their governments sought to ensure that their own country's security, relative to that of their neighbours and rival states, was either enhanced or not in any way diminished.[18] The arguments, debates and frequent adjournments that ensued suggested to informed observers and peace campaigners that member states were deliberately being obstructive and refusing to live up to the lofty commitments they had undertaken as League members. The reality – much clearer now – was that the questions being considered were almost impossible for up to twenty diverse independent nations to agree on through multi-lateral negotiations. All this seems much clearer with the benefit of hindsight. As F. P. Walters recalled, the remit of the Preparatory Commission was to reach agreement on a range of issues such as 'How armaments should be defined? How could they be compared? Could offensive weapons be distinguished from those intended only for defence? … Could the total war strength of a country be limited, or only its peace establishments? Was it possible to exclude civil aviation from the calculation of air armaments? How could such factors as population, industrial resources, communications, geographical position, be reckoned in preparing an equitable scheme? Could there be regional schemes of reduction, or must reduction necessarily be planned on a world scale?' Given these difficulties, it is not surprising that agreement proved elusive.[19] It is probably worth adding that the hostility among large sections of German society towards the post-war settlement never subsided. Every concession Stresemann wrung from his Locarno colleagues gave rise to further demands.[20] Had the international situation continued to stabilize, and the global economy to improve over a number of years, this might have helped Stresemann and other centre-right German politicians to negotiate enough peaceful change to satisfy their more moderate political opponents, but this was not to be. The Wall Street Crash of 1929, which was followed by the rapid spread of a world-wide depression, brought the optimism of the late 1920s to an abrupt halt. The political consequences were even more damaging. The end of cheap United States credit, spiralling unemployment and falling commodity prices and wages fuelled the growth of support for the Nazi Party in Germany, led to ultra-nationalism in Japan and to inward-looking policies of self interest in Britain, France and the USA.

In 1931 came the first major challenge to the authority of the League of Nations when Japanese troops stationed in Manchuria embarked on an aggressive campaign of expansion directed not just against China but against their own government, which they believed to be insufficiently nationalist and patriotic. As the opening date for the much-trumpeted League Disarmament Conference drew near, the League Council was preoccupied with unfolding events in Manchuria. By the time sixty delegations converged on Geneva in early 1932 to start serious disarmament discussions, any hope of reaching meaningful agreement had disappeared. The League's failure to deal decisively with the Manchurian crisis and to conclude a Disarmament Convention did not bode well for what has become known as 'The Devil's Decade'.

The outbreak of hostilities in distant Manchuria in mid September 1931 occurred at a particularly difficult time in the development of the world economic crisis. The British government had just been forced off the gold standard and was in the midst of forming a National Government led by the ex-Labour leader Ramsay MacDonald. The European countries were locked in acrimonious discussions with the United States government about reducing or postponing reparation and war debt payments. The unfolding political and economic crisis in Germany had led Hitler's Nazi Party to become the most popular party in Germany. No wonder the crisis in Manchuria seemed less threatening in Europe at that time.

The 11,000-strong Japanese Kwantung army was stationed in Manchuria quite legitimately to guard the track and railway zones of the South Manchurian railway, under treaty rights dating back to Japan's victory against Russia in the war of 1904–5 and to agreements subsequently reached with China. The province of Manchuria was not one of the eighteen provinces of China, but was an outlying area north of the Great Wall, ruled since 1911 by a series of independent warlords. The Japanese portrayed their role there as one of establishing and maintaining order against unruly and corrupt Chinese elements and the possible spread of communist influence, a stance welcomed by Western trading companies, which operated mainly in and around Shanghai and Hong Kong. Thus on 30 September 1931 the League Council responded to a Chinese appeal to the League under Article 11 by accepting the reassurances of the Japanese delegate that Japan had no warlike intentions in Manchuria and no territorial designs, and that its troops would soon be withdrawn back to the railway zone.

Unfortunately, the Japanese government was not in control of the situation in Manchuria. It was the headstrong Kwantung army that instigated the Manchurian incident in a deliberate bid to inflame nationalist sentiment within Japan and to bring about the replacement of the civilian government by military rule. Though the military authorities in Tokyo declined at this stage to move against the government, they made it clear that they agreed with radical junior officers in the Kwantung army who asserted that weak-kneed liberal policies were responsible for inflaming the wrath of patriotic Japanese soldiers and nationalists. Within three months, assassination lists of leading politicians and business leaders were being drawn up by a range of fanatical and extremist groups competing to express their anger at public figures who they claimed had betrayed the interests of Japan or who had enriched themselves at the expense of poor farmers and peasants. In early 1932 a former Minister of Finance and a director of the Mitsui Corporation were both murdered in broad daylight in Tokyo. Not long afterwards, Prime Minister Inukai was shot dead in his official residence.[21]

Thousands of miles away in Geneva, League officials were becoming aware of the increasingly precarious position of the Japanese delegates who were representing their government at Council and Assembly meetings, but were nevertheless anxious to try to broker a negotiated and orderly settlement of the crisis. In this aim they were supported by the United States, though Washington had made it clear that US representatives would operate only under the Washington agreements of 1922 or the Kellogg–Briand Pact. In November Japan's League representatives put forward a proposal for a League Commission of Enquiry to visit China, Japan and Manchuria to observe the problems and issues of contention at first hand and to propose solutions. This course of action satisfied the League's concern to apply the provisions of article 15 to seek a peaceful solution. Behind the scenes, the League's other great powers made it clear that they had no appetite for a confrontation with Japan. France, Italy and Germany were much more concerned with events in Europe, and agreeing to provide a member each for the Commission of Enquiry was the limit of their active participation in the crisis. Sir John Simon, the British Foreign Secretary, told the Cabinet that British policy 'should be one of conciliation, with the avoidance of implied threats', while at the same time upholding the authority of the League.[22] The chairman of the Commission of Enquiry, Lord Lytton, did his best to follow this brief.

The five-member Lytton Commission spent six months in 1932 travelling around north China and Manchuria and visiting Japan in an attempt to find a settlement. Meanwhile, fierce fighting broke out in Shanghai in the first two months of the year, and the Japanese army in Manchuria completed its occupation of the whole province and helped to establish a new, nominally independent state of 'Manchukuo' with the heir to the Manchu dynasty, Pu-Yi, as its ruler. At the end of August, the Lytton Commission summarized its findings in a report to the League Council. It acknowledged legitimate grievances on both sides, but also cast strong doubt on the Japanese claim that Manchukuo had been called into existence by 'a genuine and spontaneous independence movement'. The League Council considered the Lytton Report at the end of November 1932 at a meeting of a special Assembly. By now, the Japanese delegates had made it clear that their government regarded the establishment of Manchukuo as non-negotiable and that if Japan was formally censured for her actions in Manchuria, she would leave the organization. Further League proposals to establish a largely autonomous Manchuria under Chinese sovereignty were opposed by Japan and on 27 March 1933 the Japanese government gave notice of its intention to leave the League, though it agreed to participate in the up-coming and much delayed Disarmament conference.

The League's failure to prevent Japan's occupation of Manchuria and Japan's departure from the League were serious blows, made worse by the failure of the World Economic Conference and then of the Disarmament Conference in 1933. Delegates to the Disarmament Conference were fully aware of the insurmountable problems facing them in trying to reach agreement on a multilateral Disarmament Convention, but they needed to demonstrate to their electorates that they were doing everything possible to bring about disarmament and prevent the outbreak of another war.

In the face of a resurgence of nationalism in Germany, the French government was reluctant to support further arms reductions. The British government had progressively disarmed to the absolute limits of national safety and it adopted the role at the Conference of trying to pressurize other powers, particularly France, to follow suit. The US delegation shared the British view that French military power in combination with its East European allies was a major obstacle to progress on disarmament. Concerns were also raised in the press in Britain and France as to whether Italian and Japanese delegates were serious about pursuing disarmament.

The most urgent problem was the demand from the German delegates that if the other powers failed to conclude the substantive arms limitation agreements they had signed up to at Paris in 1919, then Germany would demand the right to rearm and to acquire weapons such as tanks, warplanes and heavy artillery, which had been prohibited under the Treaty of Versailles. For the German government, the Conference offered a significant opportunity to win political concessions on rearmament on the grounds that this might halt the rise of the Nazis. German rearmament had been taking place in secret since 1928 and German delegates were well aware that the other powers would find it virtually impossible to reach agreement on levels of armament reduction, and this gave them the opportunity to denounce such failure and open the way towards full-blown rearmament.

During the latter part of 1932 the search was on for a disarmament formula that balanced the German demand for equal treatment with the French obsession with security. In December 1932, Britain, Italy, Germany and France agreed a protocol that claimed 'one of the principles that should guide the Conference on Disarmament should be the grant to Germany, and to the other disarmed powers, of equality of rights in a system which would provide security for all nations'. In response, the German government agreed to return to Geneva and to resume negotiations. The French government was still primarily concerned about the scale of German demands. Herriot told the French military chiefs of staff in October 1932 – just three months before Hitler came to power – that: 'I am convinced Germany wishes to rearm ... she is beginning a positive policy. Tomorrow it will be a policy of territorial demands with a formidable means of intimidation: her army.' Winston Churchill warned the House of Commons a month later that the Germans were not really after equality of status, but were 'looking for weapons, and when they have the weapons, believe me they will ask for the return of ... lost territories'.[23]

When Hitler came to power, worries over German rearmament intensified among the victorious European powers of 1918. Mussolini took the lead by formulating a Four Power Pact, which he hoped would bind Germany into an agreement with Britain, France and Italy to preserve peace and work for treaty revision through the League of Nations. It was duly signed in June 1933 but had no effect in restraining German ambitions. Not long afterwards Hitler led the German delegates out of the Disarmament Conference and left the League of Nations. The long-cherished dream of a successful Disarmament Conference ended in total failure. The political climate of the early 1930s made it impossible for governments to 'bridge the gap between internationalist ideals and the demands of national security'.[24] In the post-war era, international disarmament conferences learned a great deal from the world's first serious attempt at multilateral arms limitation, but at the time the failure of the Disarmament talks contributed greatly to disillusionment about the ability of the League to preserve international peace.

One bright note at Geneva was the decision of the Soviet Union to join the League in 1934. The expansionist nationalism emanating from Berlin and from Tokyo persuaded Stalin to send delegates to the League, but would it be possible for democratic Britain and France, Fascist Italy and the communist Soviet Union to work closely together to deter future military aggression? The answer was not long in coming and it was Italy that was to test the peace keeping machinery of the League to breaking point. The Italian dictator had talked grandly for some time of his aim to turn the Mediterranean Sea into 'an Italian lake', but British and French naval strength were major obstacles in the way of Italian naval expansion. A much easier target was North Africa, where it might be possible to link up the Italian protectorates of Eritrea and Somaliland to establish a more coherent and powerful north-east African empire. Mussolini made it clear to successive French leaders that he was willing to work with them to contain German expansionist aims, especially over Austria, but in return he expected a free hand to pursue Italian territorial ambitions in North Africa.

To the French government, fearful of the revival of German military power, this seemed a price worth paying. In the first week of January 1935, the French Foreign Secretary Pierre Laval visited Rome to discuss the European situation and colonial matters. He agreed to make minor territorial concessions to Italy on the fringes of Tunisia and on the Somali coast and he gave the impression that the French government would not stand in the way of an Italian protectorate over some or even all of Abyssinia [modern-day Ethiopia] provided it was achieved peacefully.[25] At the Stresa conference in April, Britain joined France and Italy in declaring all three powers would oppose the 'unilateral repudiation of treaties likely to engender the peace of Europe', but the official talks did not stray beyond European issues. This meeting was followed up by talks between France and Italy over air pacts and the possibility of army and navy co-operation. In May, the French government conclude a treaty of mutual assistance with the Soviet Union.

What Laval could not secure was a firm promise of British support against Nazi aggression, only public commitments to uphold the League Covenant and the Locarno accords. Paris wanted to augment its military pacts to deter Germany, but London was still hoping conciliatory gestures might appease Hitler and draw him back into League membership and achieve treaty revision within a negotiated framework. As British policy had to contend with Japanese nationalist ambitions in the Far East and Mussolini's ambitions in the Mediterranean area, a policy of appeasing the dictators seemed attractive. In June 1935 the British government signed the Anglo-German naval agreement, which limited German naval expansion to a limit of 35 per cent of the strength of the British navy, but recognized Germany's right to re-arm. Eliminating a possible naval race with Germany made good pragmatic sense for the British, even if the French government saw the agreement as a betrayal of the Stresa agreements. Once again, British and French policies were pulling in different directions.

Mussolini took the opportunity to exploit the division between Britain and France to seize Abyssinia in October 1935. The French government realized strong League action against Mussolini would break the Stresa front and possibly drive Mussolini into Hitler's orbit. The British government, however, was in the midst of an election campaign in which the National Government was committed to strong support for the League of Nations following the endorsement of ten million voters for sanctions against an aggressor in a Peace Ballot organized by the League of Nations Union only weeks before.[26] Sir John Simon recorded in his diary in May, 'We have warned Italy in plain terms that if it comes to a choice between Italy and the League we shall support the League.'[27]

Pierre Laval, the French Foreign Minister, tried to ensure that any League action against Mussolini would be mild with 'no provocative talk of sanctions and no wounding of Italian feelings'.[28] Samuel Hoare, the British Foreign Secretary, still hoped, as he told his Cabinet colleagues, that a settlement of the crisis could be reached that 'would not destroy Abyssinian independence but would give Italy some satisfaction'.[29] The military invasion of Abyssinia by Italy torpedoed this strategy. The League Council ruled that Italy had resorted to war against another League member in flagrant disregard of its obligations, and that sanctions had to be imposed straightaway. A Co-ordination Committee was established to liaise with member states whose responsibility it was to take the sanctions 'directly and individually', and to draw up an agreed list of measures, including an embargo on the export of arms and ammunitions to Italy, the withholding of loans and credits, the prohibition of imported goods from Italy and a ban on the export of certain key products to the offending state.

In a bid designed to head off stronger sanctions in case Mussolini became completely alienated from his Geneva colleagues, the French government increased pressure on Britain to agree to a package of proposals that would allow Italy to retain some Abyssinian territory in the east and south east and an extensive economic development zone in the south and south west under League supervision, though still nominally under Abyssinian sovereignty. This was the basis of the infamous Hoare–Laval Pact that was leaked to the press in early December and caused outrage. In Britain, the Labour Party described the clandestine arrangement as an attempt to 'reward the declared aggressor at the expense of the victim, destroy collective security and conflict with the expressed will of the country and of the Covenant'. Simon warned Stanley Baldwin, the Prime Minister. that 'this was very nearly what the Cabinet felt'.[30]

The Italian offensive, which included mustard gas attacks against both Abyssinian combatants and civilians, continued unchecked. Sir Anthony Eden, a firm supporter of the League who had replaced the discredited Hoare as British foreign secretary, was prepared by the end of February 1936 to support the imposition of oil sanctions, but the French government blocked this move. Meanwhile, the British government was trying to tempt Hitler into discussions about colonial concessions and an air pact, but these discussions came to nothing. Then suddenly, in the first week of March 1936, Hitler exploited the deep divisions between Britain, France and Italy by marching German troops into the de-militarized Rhineland, citing France's ratification of the 1935 Franco-Soviet pact as justification. This was a breach of the Treaty of Versailles and the Locarno Pact. The French government, facing an election within two months, turned to Britain for support. The British War Office, however, had already made it clear to their French counterparts that in the event of hostilities breaking out over Rhineland remilitarization they could only offer to despatch to the area two regular divisions, which would take three months to mobilize. Neville Chamberlain, the Chancellor of the Exchequer, believed that 'neither France nor England was really in a position to take effective military action'.[31]

Intense efforts to resolve the Rhineland issue now took centre stage. While the British government hoped to appease Hitler by conciliation and by negotiation, the French did not believe this was a realistic prospect, but could not risk taking action alone. Both powers agreed that every effort should now be made to obtain Mussolini's support. In July 1935 economic sanctions against Italy were abandoned. This came too late in the day to appease Mussolini. Once Abyssinia had been absorbed into Italy's empire, the Italian government announced that it would leave the League of Nations. With the outbreak of the Spanish Civil War in summer 1936, Mussolini opted – like Hitler – to support the renegade Spanish military leader General Franco. At Geneva, meanwhile, Britain, France and the Soviet Union were left to face the growing and concerted aggression of Germany, Japan and Italy as the United States moved further towards a policy of isolationism from European affairs.

The total failure of Britain and France to agree on a common approach to deal with the aggressive ambitions of Mussolini and Hitler robbed the League of any ability to maintain international peace through collective action. Divisions in the 1920s had undermined the effectiveness of the League, but the failure to protect Abyssinia against Italian aggression now destroyed its credibility completely. The League could still have been mobilized if there had been a united resolve by Britain, France and Russia to make its machinery effective. But from the outset it had been the British government that opposed the concept of a coercive League in favour of an international body that was consultative and conciliatory. By the mid-1930s even that approach was discarded in favour of 'old diplomacy', which rejected the idea of any pact with Russia until mid-1939 and hoped to conciliate Hitler by a series of concessions, which inexorably led to the signing of the Munich agreements of 1938. Before long another major European war had broken out, which it had been the League`s task to prevent.

And yet the United Nations was established after 1945 bearing 'a most embarrassing resemblance to its predecessor'.[32] It was to operate through two main bodies, a Supreme Council and a General Assembly, and to be administered by an international secretariat under an independent Secretary-General. It was to be composed of sovereign states, all of which retained jurisdiction over their domestic affairs, and to have responsibilities and agencies designed to maintain peace and to improve the general welfare of its member states. But there were four significant differences. The United Nations was created as a free-standing body, not linked to a peace treaty. Its Supreme Council was based unequivocally on its five permanent members – the USSR, the USA, Britain, France and China – working together in concert, each able to exercise a veto on any proposed action, and the inclusion of the USA and the USSR ensured that the United Nations had a global reach and power the League never enjoyed. And finally, the Supreme Council could take decisions by majority vote, which were binding on all members of the United Nations, thus ensuring that the body could take action to enforce peace, something which the French government had vainly urged in 1919 that the League should be equipped to do.

What is clear now with the benefit of hindsight is that the League was a pioneering organization that brought together 'the strands of pre-1914 international organization and wartime co-operation into a more centralised and systematic form on a global scale, thus providing a stepping stone towards the more enduring United Nations'.[33] In some areas of activity it did achieve great success, but it was severely hampered by the unstable international environment in which it had to operate, and by the absence of the USA and the USSR and by the loss of Germany, Italy and Japan as members by the mid-1930s. It was therefore driven by two great, but waning, imperial powers: Britain and France, whose leaders were fatally divided in their views on how the League could most effectively maintain international peace and on the best way to deal with military aggression. And while the League was conceived as a world-wide organization, its engine was in practice powered by declining Europe states not strong enough or willing enough to maintain peace by means of deterrence, opting instead for compromise, vacillation and conciliation.

And yet the ideals that underpinned the League – a striving for the establishment of a peaceful international community of states all agreeing to abide by a clear set of rules of conduct – remained powerful, evoked strong popular support and might have made a bigger impact with a more determined set of leaders- particularly in Britain and France. The League helped to bring into existence a 'different dynamic of international cooperation' and those who worked on its behalf began to craft a 'network of norms and agreements by which our world is regulated, if not quite governed'. It was not able to fulfil the ambitious aspirations of its founders or the exaggerated hopes of its most fervent supporters, but it was the world's first 'sustained and consequential experiment in internationalism',[34] a significant and exploratory first phase, which could not prevent the outbreak of the Second World War, but which paved the way for a second, more effective and more lasting period of international collaboration under the United Nations.

Notes

1   M. MacMillan, *Peacemakers: The Paris Peace Conference of 1919 and its Attempt to End War*. London, 2001, p. 92.
2   B. Morton, *Makers of the Modern World: Woodrow Wilson, United States of America*. Haus, 2008, p. 196. Z. Steiner, *The Lights That Failed: European International History 1919–33*. Oxford, 2005; S. Pedersen, 'Back to the League of Nations', Review Essay in *American History Review* vol. 112, no. 4 (October 2007).
3   R. Henig, *Makers of the Modern World: The League of Nations*. Haus, 2010, pp. 43–52.
4   Viscount Grey, *Twenty-Five Years 1892–1916*. London, 1925, vol. 1, pp. 91–2.
5   R. Henig (ed.) *The League of Nations*. Edinburgh, 1973, p. 10.
6   See W. Kuehl, *The United States and International Organisation to 1920*. Nashville, 1969, pp. 313–37.
7   S. de Madariaga, *Morning Without Noon*. London, 1974, p. 33.
8   Henig (ed.), *The League of Nations*, pp. 73–4.
9   D. Birn, *The League of National Union, 1918–45*, Oxford, 1981, p. 24, 48.

10 See J. Barros, *The Aland Islands Question: Its Settlement by the League of Nations*. Connecticut, 1968; J. Barros, *The League of Nations and the Great Powers: The Greek–Bulgarian Incident, 1925*. Oxford, 1970.

11 J. Barros, *The Corfu Incident of 1923: Mussolini and the League of Nations*. Princeton, 1965.

12 14 September 1923, Cecil papers, 51126.

13 S. Marks, *The Illusion of Peace: International Relations in Europe 1918–33*. Basingstoke, 1976, p. 71.

14 Quoted in M. Howard, *The Continental Commitment*. London, 1972, p. 94.

15 F. Northedge, *The League of Nations: Its Life and Times 1920–46*. Leicester, 1986, p. 97.

16 F.P. Walters, *A History of the League of Nations*. Oxford, 1952, pp. 341–7.

17 Marks, *The Illusion of Peace*, p. 100.

18 For a more detailed analysis, see D. Richardson, *The Evolution of British Disarmament Policy in the 1920s*. London, 1989.

19 Walters, *The League of Nations*, pp. 364–5.

20 R. Henig, *The Weimar Republic 1919–33*. London, 1998, pp. 43–4.

21 R. Storry, *The Double Patriots: A Study in Japanese Nationalism*. Cambridge, 1956, pp. 101–2.

22 C. Thorne, *The Limits of Foreign Policy: The West, The League and the Far Eastern Crisis of 1931–33*. Basingstoke, 1972, pp. 187–9.

23 Steiner, *The Lights That Failed*, pp. 786–92.

24 Ibid., p. 812.

25 P. Guillen, 'Franco-Italian Relations in Flux 1918–1940' in R. Bryce (ed.), *French Foreign and Defence Policy 1918–40*. London, 1998, p. 156.

26 Dame A. Livingstone, *The Peace Ballot: The Official History*. London, 1935.

27 D. Dutton, *Sir John Simon*. London, 1992, pp. 204–5.

28 Northedge, *League of Nations*, pp. 230–1.

29 Cabinet meeting, 2 October 1935. Cab 23/82.

30 Dutton, *Sir John Simon*, p. 233; Northedge, *League of Nations*, p. 242.

31 R.A.C. Parker, *Chamberlain and Appeasement*. Basingstoke, 1993, pp. 60–1.

32 Quoted in D. Armstrong, L. Lloyd and J. Redmond, *From Versailles to Maastricht: International Organisation in the 20th Century*. New York, 1996, p. 62.

33 C. Archer, *International Organisations*. London, 1992, p. 23.

34 Pedersen, 'Back to the League of Nations', *passim*.

Chapter 3

An Ideological Genealogy of Imperial Era Japanese Militarism

M.G. Sheftall

*We can understand much of human history as the struggle to achieve,
maintain, and reaffirm a collective sense of immortality under constantly
changing psychic and material conditions.*

Robert Jay Lifton[1]

On 12 November 1948 the justices of the International Military Tribunal for the Far East (IMTFE) presented to the world their official judgment on the primary issue they had addressed over two and a half years of legal proceedings: Who was to be held to account for leading Japan into a reckless fifteen-year-long campaign of military opportunism on the Asian continent and its disastrous four-year-long war on the West? Few observers were surprised by the majority opinion verdict: the twenty or so senior Japanese statesmen, soldiers and bureaucrats in the defendant's dock were found guilty (two defendants posthumously) as to the most serious charges of 'crimes against peace', judged by the *mens rea* logic of the tribunal's charter to have been members of a 'criminal militaristic clique' whose 'policies were the cause of serious world troubles, aggressive wars, and great damage to the interests of peace-loving peoples, as well as the interests of the Japanese people themselves'.[2] The judgment offered a simplistic explanatory narrative for historical posterity and contemporary public consumption – both within and outside of Japan – by which an elite cabal of morally corrupt oligarchs, beginning roughly with the invasion of Manchuria by the Japanese Kwantung Army in 1931, had plotted imperialistic world domination and duped, bullied or otherwise cajoled a docile but essentially blameless compatriot populace (and, of critical importance to the smooth implementation of policy by Japan's postwar Allied occupiers, an equally innocent Emperor Hirohito) into acceding to their nefarious plans. Thus found guilty by the tribunal only of having lacked a healthy political cynicism that might otherwise have inoculated them against bad government, the Japanese people as a whole were now free to slip into a comfortable historical amnesia by which their roles as enthusiastic supporters of aggressive wars of collective self-aggrandizement could be conveniently forgotten, allowing them instead to assume the historical mantle of victims not only of Allied bombs but also of incompetent and culturally inauthentic leadership.[3] The overall plotline was easily grasped, and its cast of variously bespectacled, mustachioed and shaven-headed 'villains' comprised a rogues' gallery of pulp literary archetypes instantly and readily recognizable by any schoolboy reading Fu Manchu comic books in 1948. Now that these 'bad guys' had been safely caught in the final reel, Nanking, Pearl Harbor, Singapore and Bataan were to be considered sufficiently avenged. Considered as rhetoric, the message of the IMTFE verdict was clear: it was time for the world to forgive Japan and move on.

In contrast with the pragmatic benefits the tribunal provided for the Japanese populace and for the smooth operation of Allied Occupation policy, it cannot be claimed that the cause of accurate historical interpretation of the war's origin was as satisfactorily served by the tribunal. This chapter will attempt to redress what I feel is one of the tribunal's most significant interpretive shortcomings, i.e. its glossing of deep-level ideological (inclusive of historical, cultural, and social) factors behind Japan's period of Imperial Era militarism. The war crimes trial interpretation of the war as having been primarily the consequence of relatively short-term and calculated Japanese imperialistic rapacity was either simplistically mistaken or cynically disingenuous in claiming the existence of such a clear-cut motive – and such a safely limited number of active agents. The political and historical phenomenon of the war is more appropriately likened to an ideological train wreck than to a consciously committed crime. Accordingly, this chapter may be considered an accident investigation of sorts. It will focus on aspects of the ideological construction of national subjectivity in post-Meiji Restoration Japan that were key factors in promoting the Imperial Era militarism that eventually led the nation to wage its disastrous and very nearly suicidal war against the West. Before proceeding, I realize that some readers not intimately familiar with social psychology theory may appreciate some further elaboration of the term 'ideological construction of national subjectivity' appearing in the preceding paragraph. Accordingly, I will consign some of our preciously limited space to an explanation of the meaning and key concepts behind this term which, in any case, is absolutely central to my argument.

Eschewing more Marxist-informed definitions of ideologies as systems of information regulation established to maintain exploitative power structures in a society, I subscribe instead to a more politically neutral, anthropological definition of ideology as 'that part of culture which is actively concerned with the establishment and defense of patterns of belief and value'.[4] By this formulation, belonging to a culture can be understood as being beholden – typically by coincidence of birth – to a certain set of 'patterns of belief and value', which in turn constitute a 'lifeworld' of knowable, experienceable and mutually interpretable human existence one inhabits with cultural compatriots.[5] The collective consciousness of sharing a lifeworld with cultural compatriots – a shared awareness of being 'the bearer(s) of a particular kind of cultural software, a configuration existing at this time and at no other ...' – is a good working definition for 'subjectivity' in the sense that the term is used in this chapter.[6]

The establishment of the abovementioned 'patterns of belief and value' – that is, the creation and maintenance of a lifeworld and its concomitant cultural worldview – is culture's primary function, providing us with cognitive tools for the navigation and interpretation of both physical and symbolic space. Specifically, this entails the provision of: first, a 'reality system' for the interpretation of value and meaning necessary for efficient interaction with cultural compatriots and environmental elements in the *physical* universe; and second, on a *symbolic* plane, 'hero-systems' in the form of culturally scripted and socially reinforced social roles and life path narratives which, if followed loyally and functioning as intended, provide us with self-esteem, i.e. a sense of valued, meaningful existence which is, in essence, a form of symbolic immortality (a culture which also has robust religious beliefs in the existence of an afterlife actually goes this one better, augmenting the effectiveness of its more secularly grounded hero-system[s] with guarantees of *literal* immortality in 'Heaven', 'Paradise', 'Valhalla', etc.).[7] Regardless of whether this culturally afforded sense of immortality is supplemented by dogmatic religious beliefs or based solely on satisfactory adherence to cultural norms and/or satisfactory/exemplary performance of social roles, this symbolic function is critically important for our psychological well-being, as it offers us significant protection against the otherwise unbearable anomie and terror that would assail us as sentient, intelligent beings conscious of our own inevitable mortality and aware of the perhaps even more disenchanting and ontologically terrifying possibility that our ostensibly 'heroic' strivings in life may be, all things said and done, essentially 'inconsequential in the cosmic scheme of things'.[8]

As history has repeatedly shown, not only in nineteenth- and twentieth-century Japan but in cultures across the globe and throughout the ages, when a worldview (and its concomitant hero-system) is threatened with desymbolization – i.e. when a culture's ability to protect its constituents from excessive existential anxiety is compromised – by encounter with an alternate, rival worldview, the result is all too often reactions of humiliation, rage and extreme irrationality among the constituents of the challenged worldview, even to the point of unwilling (or in the case of the modern suicide bomber, quite consciously willed) self-destruction in the cause of worldview defence.[9] A central concept in this chapter is that Japanese reactions to desymbolization threats of this nature (both domestic and externally generated) at several key junctures in Japan's pre-1945 modern history eventually found widespread and generally enthusiastic governmental and popular expression in the ideological extreme of Japanese militarism, with the direst eventual consequences for tens of millions of human lives.

The analysis will focus on the origins and intended functions of the subjectivity-formulating cultural software with which Japanese subjects were 'installed' during Japan's Imperial Era and during the tumultuous era of initial Japanese encounter with Western 'modernity' in the mid-nineteenth century that immediately preceded (and ultimately motivated) the formal codification and implementation of this software. I will finally demonstrate how 'bugs' in this software eventually manifested themselves not only in the irrational decision-making of Japan's political and especially military leadership, but also in enthusiastic popular support for the wars of the most aggressive phase of Japanese imperialist expansion in the early and mid-twentieth century, culminating in the nation's fateful war on the West – an experience of generation-traversing trauma from which, in many ways, modern Japanese subjectivity has yet to recover.

To begin with, it is important to appreciate the psychological compulsion behind the populist militarism of Japan's Imperial Era from the late nineteenth to mid-twentieth centuries and the collapse of ontological security suffered by Japanese society at the end of the Edo (Shogunate) Period in the mid-nineteenth century.[10] Therefore, at this point I would like to enjoin the reader to travel back in time for a moment to step into the lifeworld of an adult male resident of the Japanese archipelago one July morning in 1853. Let us further qualify our hypothetical subject as occupying a precisely 'median' position in Japanese society in terms of his socio-economic status, his education level, the scale of his lifeworld and the persuasive strength of his soon-to-collapse hero-system, i.e. the system of beliefs, values and life narrative 'stage directions' that provided him with self-esteem and ontological security.[11]

Our hypothetical subject – let us call him 'Tarō' – is a tenant farmer from the rural hinterlands on the main Japanese island of Honshu, working a rice paddy field with the rest of his family members far from Edo (Tokyo) and the comparatively cosmopolitan culture of the other major urban centers along the island's Pacific coast. Tarō is prosperous enough to put food on his family's table most of the time, but the spectre of famine after a failed crop is never far from his mind. He has lived in the same village and plied the same trade as untold generations of his ancestors, but unlike the members of the one or two samurai households in his area, he has no family name and his local Buddhist temple has kept no birth records of his forebears, so he has no way of tracing his ancestral roots beyond the ken of family oral tradition.

By centuries-old political design, force of habit and perhaps also by some degree of personal preference, Tarō's lifeworld is microcosmic – probably even smaller than that of a socio-economic counterpart on a late Medieval European farm half a millennium earlier. One significant factor in the severe constriction of his lifeworld is the fact that Tarō, his fellow inhabitants of the Japanese archipelago and nearly ten generations of their forebears have been effectively cut off from any contact with or even knowledge of the outside world for over two centuries under the feudal shogunate's brutally enforced policy of *sakoku* ('country chained shut').[12] Moreover, prevented by shogunate law from changing his hereditary occupation as a farmer or even from changing his place of residence, Tarō has never in his life travelled more than a day's walk from his village – perhaps on that occasion as a participant in a pilgrimage to a local shrine – and he has little interest in doing otherwise. In terms of his daily agenda of normal cognitive activity, the world outside the borders of his village simply does not exist.

Tarō knows there is a *daimyō* – a feudal lord – ruling over his region, and he may even have seen him in person a few times in his life, passing by on a local road in ornate procession on his way to or from his compulsory biennial period of residence in the shogunate capital of Edo. But Tarō is shrewd enough to appreciate the value of understanding the humble status of his own place in the order of things, and so has never asked any probing questions about the structure and functioning of the political system to which he pays taxes, but with which he otherwise has no contact and to which he owes no obligation beyond his adherence to its laws and his diligence as a producer and consumer of rice. He is so completely immersed in his tiny lifeworld that the concept of a 'country' or 'nation' is obscure and essentially irrelevant to him. He may have used the word *Nihon* – Japan – only a few times in his life, if at all, but he knows nothing of the shogunate regime that rules the land so named, and he may not even know of the existence of an 'emperor' living in a far off city called Kyoto. He has never seen nor even heard of war occurring in his lifetime, although he has heard frightful stories from village elders and the occasional travelling raconteur about days many generations ago, when the warring private armies of rival *daimyō* roamed far and wide across the land, taking by force what provisions they needed from the local peasantry.

While the physical aspects of Tarō's lifeworld are arduous and occasionally even grim, the ontological security of his symbolic universe is reassuringly durable. He is offered some promise of *literal* immortality by stories told by the local monks about the serene Pure Land he will inhabit after death, if he has loyally followed the teachings of *Shakasama* – the Buddha – in life. But Tarō's lifestyle and traditions comprise a hero-system that is much more important for his self-esteem and psychological well-being than the (in any case suspiciously highbrow and obscure) explanations of literal immortality offered by Buddhist monks. The stability of his symbolic lifeworld is primarily grounded not in lofty imagery of ultimate afterlife destinations, but in the comfort offered by the reassuring predictability and repetitive cycle of his daily life: working hard in his rice field; garnering the respect of his neighbours through his self-abnegating diligence and loyalty to village traditions; raising obedient children, secure in the knowledge that he is living as his forebears have lived, and that his children and their descendants will live as he has, forever and ever, in a world without end, Amen. But on this morning he cannot know that the first of a series of events has just occurred that will in short order shatter this lifeworld forever. For today is 8 July 1853 and four black-hulled U.S. Navy warships under the command of Commodore Matthew C. Perry's flotilla have just crested the horizon off of Uraga Bay near present-day Tokyo.[13]

The American-coerced 'opening of Japan' that was the eventual consequence of Perry's mission resulted in Japan's traumatized emergence from nearly two and a half centuries of self-imposed and near-total seclusion from the outside world. The resultant cultural shockwave that rocked Japanese society was first experienced in full force by the humiliated samurai elite and by other residents of the large urban concentrations on the Pacific Coast who, among Japan's population of non-samurai commoners, had the most ready access to breaking news of current events at the time, and who would be the unwilling hosts to the first arrivals of foreigners in significant numbers a year later. The resultant psychological crisis set in motion a fifteen-year-long chain of events that saw the collapse of the 265-year-old shogunate regime in 1868, after a successful revolution by lower and middle-ranked samurai, primarily hailing from the south-western provinces of the country, who had been motivated in their actions by an overwhelming sense of ontological panic compounded by disgust and indignant fury at what they saw as the shogunate's treasonous and cowardly bowing to American demands to open Japan to foreign contact.

In what is now known to history as the Meiji Restoration, these samurai (shortly to become ex-samurai) 'Founding Fathers' of modern Japan replaced the shogunate regime with a centralized national bureaucracy staffed by themselves and their former samurai clan compatriots, wielding sovereign authority through direct imperial edicts (later augmented by a national legislature and a judiciary branch) under the tutelary aegis of the young Emperor Meiji (1852–1912).[14] As the reader should now appreciate after our short excursion in the previous section into the lifeworld *pastorale* of late Edo Era Japan, the society the new Imperial regime inherited from its Shogunate predecessors was one that was still, in many senses of the term, medieval. By any measure, Japan was at this point still woefully unprepared – socially, politically, economically, culturally and militarily – to interact from anything but the most obsequious subaltern position with the dominant Western powers (*rekkyō*) that now loomed so suddenly large on the Japanese psychological landscape. Realizing they were in no position to roust the unwelcome foreigners – at least for the time being – the founders of the new regime determined that their only recourse was for them to hold their noses and accommodate and imitate the foreigners until their country became strong enough to beat the West at its own military and economic game. But before they could even begin to do that, they first had to create something called 'Japan,' and in turn to do this, they first had to create a national populace of 'Japanese'.

From the outset of the great Meiji Era nation-building project, one major obstacle to the new regime's agenda was the fact that the vast, politically disenfranchised and for all purposes functionally illiterate rural proletariat that was the overwhelmingly dominant Japanese demographic cohort of this essentially feudal society had little in the way of any shared concept of national subjectivity beyond a catalogue of vague cultural foundation myths and 'brave samurai of yore' legends passed down through oral tradition by troubadours and local wise men.[15] Like 'Tarō the ideal type tenant farmer' it is doubtful that many new 'Imperial subjects' even had a clear conception of the existence of the emperor or of the institution of the Imperial throne. But the unflagging efforts of the new regime eventually bore nation-building fruit. The new oligarchy would begin this process first through the emotionally wrenching but nevertheless politically necessary elimination of their own samurai status as an elite Japanese social class – a gesture dramatically symbolized by the government's granting in 1870 of surnames (previously a privilege only for the samurai class and other social elite) to the ninety-four per cent of the Japanese population still without family names at the time of the edict.[16] Of even more importance in creating a nation of mass national stake-holders were the long years of patient and generous national investment in educational policy and, of somewhat more sinister portent, in the creation of a national military that eventually inculcated millions of young Japanese men – with subsequent influence on Japanese society and culture as a whole – with an archly xenophobic, Social Darwinist- worldview, with a fanatic formulation of both patriotic and religious individual identity inextricably committed to the iconic institution of the Emperor, and last but not least, with a powerful new militaristic hero-system for the masses that fetishized self-sacrifice in service to the greater glory of the state.

In his 2007 monograph *Unmodern Men in the Modern World*, strategic analyst Michael J. Mazarr holds that 'From the outset, modern Japan was to some degree erected on an explosive foundation of sublimated rage'.[17] This is an excellent encapsulation of the motivational package of the ruling class of Japan's new regime, comprised as it was of former samurai whose class had never gotten over the humiliation and desymbolization anxiety of the West's – specifically America's – rude intrusion on their tidy little feudal lifeworld in 1853. Temporarily sublimating their rage in a flurry of furious nation-building activity, they would end up turning Japan into a world-class military power in fewer than thirty years. But Mazarr's observation tells only half of the story. An ideology, which after all is basically rhetoric on a huge and highly complex scale, requires a rhetor *and* an audience in order to function. If the ex-samurai Founding Fathers of the new regime were rhetors motivated by rage, what was their audience's motivation? In short, the millions of new Imperial subjects were a captive audience. As philosopher Erich Fromm has observed, 'ideas can become powerful forces, but only to the extent to which they are answers to specific human needs prominent in a given character'.[18] In Fromm's sense, the mass audience of new Imperial subjects during the early Meiji era was motivated to receive the new regime's ideological message because they were desperate for a replacement for the ontological security they also had just lost. They were primed to receive the message by a psychological condition of existential bewilderment in the wake of the sudden desymbolization of their own Edo period lifeworlds, and by the equally sudden and historically unprecedented awareness and fear on their part of a culturally alien and threatening outside world. We can say that the modern 'Japanese' were truly born as a people a generation later, when the respective motivational profiles of rulers and ruled met on middle ground; once the populace opted for stability and security over freedom, accepting as its own the regime's dark view of the world outside Japan as being a jungle ruled by the law of 'eat or be eaten', the 'single communal faith' envisioned by the Meiji oligarchs was complete.[19] Under such conditions, any nascent Japanese political movement toward liberal democracy never really had a chance.

In fairness to the ex-samurai crafters of this new Japanese lifeworld, it is perhaps unreasonable to bemoan the failure of their ranks to produce political philosophers of vision and genius who might otherwise have guided modern Japan from the outset toward a more liberal and democratic future. After all, it had been their feudal forefathers who had chosen to slam the national door on the first extended feelers of Western Enlightenment in the early 1600s and throw away the cultural key for over two centuries. Ideologically blinkered from the start, the stalwart samurai founders of the new Japan were, at best, imperfect revolutionary heroes whose collective imagination was tragically limited by the lifeworld that had moulded them – a lifeworld that, in its way, was just as tiny and constricted as that of the populace they were now determined to mould into a mass army of national stake-holding warriors (or brides and mothers of future warriors) serving at the convenience and for the greater glory of the new state. The potential extent of their vision and ambition was equally constrained by the limits of lifeworld upheaval they could reasonably their peers and new popular constituency to endure. To many early Meiji ideologues, for example, Western-style democracy appeared not as the pinnacle of civilized political freedom, but as an invitation to interminable social chaos and selfishness, while a political system of checks and balances appeared not as responsible governance, but as a blasphemous intrusion on the sacrosanct and inviolate sovereign prerogatives of the Emperor. Appreciative of such limitations but also aware of the need to get a more modern Japan up and running as soon as possible, the new leadership attempted to placate the cultural and psychological sensitivities of the new national constituents undergoing this lifeworld upheaval by reassuring them that Japanese modernization would be a culturally authentic process undertaken 'with Japanese spirit in our hearts, and Western technology in our hands' (*wakon yosai*).[20] But what may have at the time sounded like a culturally authentic plan for national modernization seems, in hindsight, more like the recipe for cultural schizophrenia it arguably turned out to be.

In an even less flattering light, the samurai founders of the New Japan can be regarded as a kind of collective Dr Frankenstein who could not resist the narcissistic temptation of trying to mould their creation in their own image. Infusing their new national project with an ersatz 'bushidō for the masses', they would keep the hero-system of their dying warrior culture on artificial life support by transforming every Japanese man into a samurai – if not necessarily in cultural refinement, then at least in the sense of the possession of a national stake-holder consciousness and identity that would make him as willing to give up his life for his Emperor as his putative forebears had been willing to sacrifice themselves for their feudal lord in some 'Golden Age' of Japanese warriorhood.

As is the wont of reactionaries in any culture, the samurai Founding Fathers of modern Japan automatically and unthinkingly assumed that their fundamental system of 'way of the warrior' beliefs and values were already the embodiment of moral perfection. As such, they must also have regarded as reassuringly culturally authentic their own ideological system of conquering and sublimating natural urges to individual autonomy through devotion to discipline, violence against external rivals and fetishized group loyalty and self-abnegation in the cause of collective aggrandizement. Moreover, and from a more politically pragmatic perspective, they clearly also felt the fundamental tenets of this moral system provided the best and quickest means to forge a powerful modern nation from the popular raw material they had to work with. An appreciation of this psychological profile of the ex-samurai ideologues who made the amazing Meiji transformation of Japanese society possible – largely through their power base of the Imperial Japanese Army (IJA) – is vital to an understanding of how and why the Imperial Era worldview and its hero-system were so effective in transforming the new nation of Japan into such a potent instrument of war. Historian Leonard Humphreys explains the ideological agenda at work during the Meiji Period as one:

> informed by a crude social Darwinism – not of the individualistic or eugenic form (this would come later) but of the collective variety. It saw Japan as an organismic whole fighting for survival in a hostile world of similarly competing entities ... In Japan this conception revived confidence in a Confucian ideal that embodied all the nation in a great family working as one to ensure the preservation of the state, its emperor, its people, and its collective values. The army sought to position itself at the forefront of this absolutely vital cause and to exhort and cajole all the people in its support. The military judgment that Japan was in a very poor position to survive in this struggle gave it added impetus to seek concerted action to enhance the defensive capabilities of the state. Lacking the resources of the other great powers, the Japanese military reached two somewhat contradictory and ultimately fatal conclusions: (1) they must seize the necessary resources to survive from already failed (Asian) neighbors, and (2) they must win in a war against materially superior enemies by preparing their soldiers with the psychological armor of an indomitable spirit.[21]

The symbolic lynchpin of this Imperial Era worldview – the careful crafting of which was indelibly marked by the influence of arch-conservative IJA figures such as ex-samurai Field Marshal Yamagata Aritomo (1838–1922) – was the notion of divinely ordained Japanese cultural infallibility manifest in the august person of the Emperor himself, from whose immortal ancestral line all Japanese were descended, regardless of social station, and to whom all owed as a sacred debt their entire existence, being, loyalty and destiny, both physical and symbolic.[22]

Proselytized with brilliant efficiency by Meiji Japan's national education system and the army, the new Imperial Era Japanese worldview embraced a hero-system that valorized self-sacrifice for the greater Japanese good as the pinnacle of symbolic immortality to which any loyal subject of the Emperor might aspire – a somewhat more earthbound and figurative Japanese equivalent to the literal afterlife immortality aspired to by believers in the 'revealed' faiths of Christianity and Islam. This was a supremely efficient ideological foundation for the mobilization of a society *in toto* for the era of industrialized total war these Meiji ideologues foresaw – not without a certain self-fulfilling prescience – as humankind's fate in the upcoming twentieth century.[23] Yasukuni Shrine in downtown Tokyo, a pilgrimage site for the exaltation of Imperial military war dead constructed at public expense in the Meiji era, is a still-extant (and since 1945 quite controversial) relic of the early stage of the Imperial Era formulation of national subjectivity around what George Mosse identifies as 'the official linkage of the cult of the fallen to manliness and national glory'.[24]

Prevented by native religious tradition and cultural pride from access to the ontological safety net of the unfalsifiable theological systems animating the worldviews of Japan's Western rivals in imperialistic competition, the Meiji ideologues instead fashioned a 'god' out of Japan itself to provide the theological mortar for the structure of their new worldview. Unfortunately for the nation's later fortunes, the new 'god' of an infallible and invincible Japan these ideologues foisted on their countrymen turned out to be hypersensitive to desymbolization threat by worldly events. Once the overwhelming majority of the populace had been effectively co-opted into this new and increasingly totalitarian formulation of subjectivity, mass public opinion tended to encounter news of any sort of national setback or perceived national slight at the hands of foreign rivals not only with patriotic indignation, but with the irrational and narcissistic rage of the religious fundamentalist confronted by an act of blasphemy. The consequences of this ideological flaw would have grievous consequences for Japanese national policy in coming decades. This was most notoriously the case among the company and field grade officer ranks of the IJA, beginning in the late 1920s, as dire domestic economic straits, ever newer internal desymbolization pressures arising from the continuing process of Japanese modernization and new worldview threats arising from Japanese geostrategic competition with rival powers pushed this military cohort and its civilian political and ideological allies to paroxysms of reactionary narcissistic rage.

By the late 1920s, the IJA – constitutionally protected from any civilian legal interference outside of budgetary allotments – had effectively positioned itself as the supreme arbiter of the symbolic aspects of Japanese subjectivity (what we might call 'Japaneseness') in every arena of public and political discourse, inclusive of national educational policy. Once Japanese discourse became thus constricted and monopolized, any public criticism of the military became first 'unpatriotic', then by the early 1930s 'treasonous', and then finally 'blasphemous' once the country had reached terminal velocity on its course toward war with the West. Any rare civilian politician, jurist or public intellectual either principled or foolish enough to raise a voice of protest against this trend was all too soon silenced through blackmail, arrest, professional ruin or co-option, or most simply and effectively, assassination.[25]

In hindsight, it may be said that the greater share of the problem of increasing fanaticism in the Japanese military – again, particularly in the IJA – can be traced to Founding Father-generation oligarchs like Yamagata forgetting to tell their protégés in succeeding generations of Japanese leadership that the mass bushidō 'every man a samurai' ideology had only been a temporary stopgap to get the new country up and running in time to hold off being overwhelmed by Western encroachment. After all, it was clear to any observer that this national goal had been achieved by the time of Japan's 1895 victory over Qing China, and certainly by the time of its geostrategic paradigm-shifting victory over Russia in 1905. Why hadn't Japan been satisfied to just rest on its military laurels after that, settling down to the peaceful business of making money and improving the living standards of its citizens? In actuality, there were a great many influential Japanese, especially during the reign of Meiji's successor, the Emperor Taishō (1912–25), who had tried to steer the nation in just such a direction. But in the end they had been shouted down (and in more than a few instances, *cut* down) by the patriots. By the early 1930s, any such voices had for all intents and purposes been silenced altogether, with a final round of mass assassinations of (comparatively) liberal Japanese political figures by fanatic young IJA officers in February 1936 putting the final nail in the coffin of prewar Japanese liberalism and thus ending the hopes of any significant public dissent against the cause of Japanese militarism.

The keystone of Japanese militarism was the symbolic notion of *kokutai* – a concept usually translated somewhat vacuously at 'national polity' (it literally means 'national body') but is best understood as a mystic embodiment of the essential unity of the Japanese people, inextricably bound up with *volkisch* ideas about the mythical divine origins of the nation, all under the august beneficence of the institution of a divine emperor and the providential protection of several millennia worth of ancestral ghosts. For the IJA, as well as for tens of millions of Emperor Meiji's subjects, the *kokutai* was not merely a source of pride and spiritual power for the nation, it *was* the lifeworld of the nation *in toto*, not only in social and political but also in theological and cosmological terms, and no means were too extreme nor sacrifice too great if deemed necessary for its survival.

While Yamagata had been ever ready to identify threats to the *kokutai* beyond Japan's shores, his ideological and political protégé, Army Minister and later Prime Minister Tanaka Gi'ichi – being as shrewd a politician as he was vigilant a soldier – had become increasingly aware in the early years of the twentieth century that sociopolitical and ideological winds were beginning to blow across the globe that could pose as much danger to the *kokutai* from within Japan as from without. Tanaka would devote the rest of his career in military and political spheres to defending the sovereignty of the nation from both forms of threat, and the multi-generational program of the dissemination of the mass bushidō hero-system he continued and intensified would be the primary means he would employ toward this end.

For Tanaka, the most serious domestic threat to the health of the *kokutai* was what he had determined to be a burgeoning class-consciousness among the Japanese people that was a natural and unavoidable development of capitalism, industrialization and the beginnings of what would in the postwar era develop into the predominant Japanese lifeworld milieu of secularized (i.e., 'disenchanted') mass consumerism. One variant of this danger was manifested in the growing disparity between 'the haves' and 'have-nots' in the country's rapidly growing urban population centres as liberal capitalism played out a domestic version of Social Darwinism, potentially leaving a door open for Bolshevist contamination of the *kokutai*, and perhaps most worryingly, from the standpoint of national unity, between an Japanese urban culture that was becoming increasingly Westernized, cosmopolitan, politically cynical and materially affluent on one hand, and on the other, a Japanese rural culture increasingly left behind in the economic dust, witnessing these changes from afar and seething in resentment.[26]

As a soldier, Tanaka was acutely aware of the damage Japanese military potential would suffer if the countryside were to be lost to political disenfranchisement, taking with it the nation's patriotic backbone and the IJA's traditional source of its most obedient soldiers. At the conclusion of the 1904 Russo-Japanese War, Tanaka – then a youngish major general on the fast-track to Imperial General Headquarters – had made the observation that he believed that the Russian defeat had been in large part due to the poor morale of its soldiers, which had in turn been exacerbated by simmering class antagonisms between the haughty, aristocratic Russian officers and their salt-of-the-earth enlisted men.[27] While, for the time being, patriotic sentiment and the fundamentally egalitarian and meritocratic ethos of the IJA rendered insignificant any poisonous class consciousness between its own officers and men, there was no guarantee that the rapid industrialization of Japanese society, Westernization, socialism and capitalism might not engender such tensions in the ranks in a not-too-distant future. Tanaka realized that, in a world where conflict would soon be characterized by 'total' wars, any rend in the nation's social fabric might prove fatal in a conflict in which victory would go to the side best able to realize 'total national mobilization.'[28]

In 1910 Tanaka, now at the Army Ministry and with the continued assistance of the superannuated Yamagata working as a behind-the-scenes mentor and political string-puller, masterminded a project to ensure that divisive class conflict would never pose a serious threat to Japan's capacity for national mobilization for war.[29] This experiment in mass social engineering, a precursor to similar projects in Italy and Germany undertaken, respectively, ten and twenty years later, was the establishment of the Zaigō Gunjin Kai (Imperial Military Reserve Association) as a semi-public agency to be run in close cooperation with the Army Ministry. Initially, the IMRA was created: to enable the quick mobilization of reserve soldiers around the country in time of national emergency; to facilitate the IJA's conscription system[30] at the local level;

and, in the rather ominous phrasing of its original charter, to 'spread militaristic thought among the population at large'.[31] But the association's true intended function – the hyper-militarization of the entire nation with an eye to apocalyptic, cataclysmic and most likely ethno-racially delineated future conflict – soon became evident. In 1915, a national federation of Youth Associations was established as an adjunct organization to the IMRA, with branches in every city neighborhood, town, village and hamlet in the country, to provide the nation's young men (and much later, in the last stages of the Second World War, young women as well) with patriotic education and realistic military training.[32] Ten years later, under the tutelage of Tanaka's ideological successor General Ugaki Kazushige, militarist indoctrination of the nation's adolescents was formalized through the establishment of a national network of Youth Training Schools (*Seinenkunrenjo*), also under IMRA direction, and even more significantly, through the institution of the IJA's Attached Officer Program (*Haizokuseido*) in which active duty IJA officers were posted to every normal elementary school (*kōtōshōgakkō*) and junior high school in the country, where these professional soldiers instructed their charges in military drill, tactics, gymnastics and a heavy dose of indoctrination in ultra-nationalistic *kokutai* ideology under the guise of 'civics'.[33]

The conscious honing of the Japanese polity into a sharpened instrument of total war was undertaken by the likes of Tanaka, Ugaki and later key military ideologues such as IJA generals Araki Sadao and Mazaki Jizaburō, who aimed to produce a populace with the spiritual and psychological stamina to sustain this hyper-mobilized status indefinitely. This hyper-mobilized status was itself to comprise the new Japanese national subjectivity. This was to be true not only in terms of the spiritual and psychological fitness of the nation's soldiers and the populace at large for the demands of modern, First World War-style attrition warfare, but just as significantly, in terms of the securing of the logistical means to wage this warfare and the ability of the Home Front to make the most efficient use of these means.

During the 1920s and 1930s, as the longing eyes the Japanese military began turning eastwards and southwards to the raw material riches of the Asian Continent and the East Indies as a means of indefinitely fueling their war machine, Japan itself would evolve beyond mere Great Power status to metamorphose ideologically into a true *gunkoku* – a 'military nation' mobilized for total war at every conceivable level of society – perhaps the first society so thoroughly organized as such since the days of ancient Sparta or the empire of Genghis Khan. All conceivable material, economic, political and spiritual preparations were made for the total war toward which Japan seemingly lurched under the blind momentum of its own ideology – a momentum that only increased as Japan's Western rivals undertook measures to protect their own geostrategic and imperialist interests by impede Japan's movement in this direction. And when the inexorable total war to roust Western influence from East Asia (and of equal importance, from the Japanese psychological landscape) finally came to pass, tens of millions of human lives would be lost as a result.

If there is any lesson to be learned from this sad eighty-year stretch of Japanese history, we may sum it up as a sobering fable about the hazards not only of basing a formulation of national subjectivity on theological precepts – which is after all a common enough political arrangement in the human experience – but far more dangerously, of tying the persuasive authority of these theological precepts, in turn, on perceptions of the ebb and flow of the fortunes of this subjectivity in real-world, real-time competition with cultural rivals. Under such subjective conditions, every military, diplomatic or economic setback Japan suffered, no matter how trivial, could be (and was usually) framed as evidence that the nation's ontological roof was in danger of caving in – imagery all too accessible for the Japanese since 1853 – and that only increased vigilance and preparedness for outwardly projected national aggression could save the day. In socio-psychological terms, this agenda can be explained as the clear circumscription and defence-at-all-costs of the boundaries of collective national identity – a normative and perennial compulsion toward vigilant awareness that there were ever barbarians at the gates of the Japanese lifeworld, threatening to sully and subvert the entire complex cultural worldview mechanism. The resultant perennially paranoid Japanese worldview was a veritable incubator for the reactionary policies that prevailed in political discourse throughout the Imperial Era, again, most tragically and fatefully from the late 1920s on.

At virtually each and every stage in the ideological development of post-Restoration and Imperial Era Japan we can see this reactionary worldview at work in the missed opportunities for alternative nation-building which, if taken in time, could have led to a less militaristic and totalitarian final product. Since the 1868 Restoration and through to the end of the Imperial Era, at virtually every fork in the road of national development manifest in a choice between a more liberal, individualist and cosmopolitan framework versus a more conservative, collectivist and parochial framework on which to construct and then maintain national subjectivity, the Japanese establishment consistently came down on the side of the latter – somehow seemingly managing at each of these junctures to also convince the populace that the culturally authentic choice had been made. Perhaps this assessment of authenticity was correct, given the cultural worldview then prevailing in Japan. In any case, it is undeniable that the result was a fundamental orientation of national subjectivity toward the preparation for and fighting of total war – a prophesied national fate with a teleological momentum that eventually became self-fulfilling.

Shortly after the Japanese attack on Pearl Harbor on 7 December 1941, British journalist and 'old Japan hand' Hugh Byas opined that the 'Japanese revulsion from Western liberalism expresses a fear, so deep that with the majority it lies in the subconscious, that [the] cherished Japanism they revere cannot live in contact with a world which values freedom more than tradition.'[34] This fundamental, subjectivity-colouring fear and revulsion of a permanent state of lifeworld desymbolization threat at the hands of the West may be said to have constituted the primary motivation behind the process that, after an eighty-year-long incubation period, led Japan to wage total war on the West. And although that war – at least in terms of its pursuit through open military belligerence – is more than six decades in the past, the rough outline and echoes of this Imperial Era formulation of national subjectivity continue to influence the basic cultural worldview of Japanese even today.

Notes

1   J. Lifton, *The Broken Connection: On Death and the Continuity of Life.* New York, 1979, p. 283.
2   R. Pritchard .and S. Zaide, *The Tokyo War Crimes Trial: The Complete Transcripts of the Proceedings of the International Military Tribunal for the Far East in Twenty-Two Volumes.* New York, 1981, vol. 1, p. 1.
3   A key conceptual element in the politically moderate postwar Japanese interpretation of the legacy of the war to which most Japanese ascribe is the psychologically comforting notion that the nation's experiment in aggressive imperialism was a brief and – most importantly – culturally inauthentic aberration from Japan's true nature as a peace-loving nation.
4   Quoted in C. Geertz, *The Interpretation of Cultures.* New York, 1973, p. 231.
5   I use 'lifeworld' as per the usage popularized by Edmund Husserl, Martin Heidegger and Jürgen Habermas.
6   J. Balkin, *Cultural Software: A Theory of Ideology.* New Haven, 1998, p. 6.
7   See Lifton, *The Broken Connection.*
8   C. Raymo, *Skeptics and True Believers.* New York, 1998, p. 110
9   This idea, in its basic form, dates at least from the writings of Thucydides, and has arguably been a component in the collective instinctual apparatus of human culture for far longer. Its most eloquent modern formulation has been promoted by the philosopher Ernest Becker and the psychologist Robert J. Lifton since the 1970s and has been supported by over two decades' worth of rigorous empirical research on 'Terror Management Theory' by social psychologists Sheldon Solomon, Tom Pyszczynski and Jeff Greenberg. Perhaps the most comprehensive exploration of this idea – and one readily accessible to social psychology specialists and general readers alike – can be found in T. Pyszczynski, S. Solomon and G. Greenberg, *In The Wake of 9/11: The Psychology of Terror.* Washington, 2003.
10 See A. Giddens, *Modernity and Self-Identity.* Cambridge, 1991.
11 For inspiring the imagery of 'life narrative stage directions', I am indebted to my reading of E. Goffman, *The Presentation of Self in Everyday Life.* London, 1990.
12 The Shogunate did allow a trickle of foreign commerce and contact throughout the period at a single location, namely, the port of Nagasaki in western Japan.
13 W. LaFeber, *The Clash: U.S.–Japanese Relations Throughout History.* New York, 1997, p. 13.
14 See D. Keene, *The Emperor of Japan: Meiji and His World, 1852–1912.* New York, 2002.
15 Andrew Gordon cites literacy figures for this rural proletariat as having possibly reached as high as half of adult males and one-third of adult females by the early 1800s. See *A Modern History of Japan: From Tokugawa Times to the Present.* New York and Oxford, 2003, p. 27. However, this is countered somewhat by historian Carol Gluck's citation of Meiji Era army draft board figures reporting that one-third of conscriptees from Osaka (the second largest city in Japan, after Tokyo) in 1893 – ostensibly after two decades of intensive compulsory national education efforts – were still functionally illiterate. See *Japan's Modern Myths: Ideology in the Late Meiji Period.* Princeton, 1985, p. 172.
16 H. Idota, 'Heimin myōji hisshō rei: Kokumin kaisei', *Nihon Hōsei Gakkai Hōseironsō* vol. 21 (1985), pp. 39–48.
17 M. Mazarr, *Unmodern Men in the Modern World.* Cambridge, 2007, p. 107.
18 E. Fromm, *Escape from Freedom.* New York, 1994, p. 279.
19 I have borrowed the term 'single communal faith' from T. Rohkrämer, *A Single Communal Faith? The German Right from Conservatism to National Socialism.* New York, 2008.

20 S. Sato, 'The Foundations of Modern Japanese Foreign Policy' in R.A. Scalapino (ed.), *The Foreign Policy of Modern Japan*. Berkeley, 1977, pp. 367–90.
21 L. Humphreys, *The Way of the Heavenly Sword: The Japanese Army in the 1920s*. Stanford, 1995, p. ix.
22 Comprehensive treatments of Yamagata's role in promoting this new ideology can be found in: E. Norman, 'Soldier and Peasant in Japan: The Origins of Conscription', *Pacific Affairs* vol. 16, no. 1 (1943), pp. 47–64; R. Smethurst, *A Social Basis for Prewar Japanese Militarism: The Army and the Rural Community*. Berkeley, 1974.
23 For a superlative portrait of this worldview at work in the mind of an influential Japanese military leader, see M. Peattie, *Ishiwara Kanji and Japan's Confrontation with the West*. Princeton, 1975.
24 G.L. Mosse, *Fallen Soldiers: Reshaping the Memory of the World Wars*. Oxford, 1990, p. 223.
25 For accessible historical accounts of the 'Young Officers Movement' era of political assassinations by military personnel and right-wing activists in the 1930s, see H. Byas, *Government by Assassination*. New York, 1942; B. Shillony, *Revolt in Japan: The Young Officers and the February 26, 1936 Incident*. Princeton, 1973.
26 Tanaka witnessed firsthand the power of Bolshevism to cause political upheaval during a pre-Russo-Japanese War period of study, at army expense, in St Petersburg. See M. Harries and S. Harries, *Soldiers of the Sun: The Rise and Fall of the Imperial Japanese Army*. New York, 1991, p. 81.
27 Smethurst, *A Social Basis for Prewar Japanese Militarism*, p. 14.
28 Ibid., p. 25.
29 Ibid.
30 The Imperial Japanese Navy was an all-volunteer force from the time of its inception until its disbandment at the end of the Second World War nearly eighty years later.
31 S. Ōe, *Kokumin Kyōiku to Guntai*. Tokyo, 1974, p. 324.
32 Smethurst, *A Social Basis for Prewar Japanese Militarism*, p. 26.
33 H. Kawano, *'Gyokusai' no Guntai, 'Seikan' no Guntai: Nichibeihei ga mita Taiheiyō Sensō*. Tokyo, 2002. pp. 32–4. For a monograph-length Japanese examination of the Attached Army Officer Program, see H. Hirahara, *Haizoku Shōkō Seido Seiritsu Shi no Kenkyū*. Tokyo, 1993.
34 Byas, *Government by Assassination*, p. 281.

Chapter 4

Italian Foreign Policy and the Road to War 1918–39: Ambitions and Delusions of the Least of the Great Powers

R.J.B. Bosworth

On 5 November 1918, one day after Italy had driven Habsburg armies to defeat at the Battle of Vittorio Veneto, the Italian ambassador in London, Marchese Guglielmo Imperiali, was dissatisfied. 'Britain', he wrote to his Foreign Minister, Sidney Sonnino, was not displaying proper appreciation of 'our triumphal, decisive victory'.[1] His disappointment was soon to be widely shared in national political circles. After all, since Italy entered the war on 24 May 1915, the country had in under four years matched all previous government spending since the Risorgimento. In battle, its armies had suffered a death toll of over 689,000, a military casualty list of 700,000 (the graphic Italian term is *mutilati*), while a further 600,000 civilians perished as a direct result of the conflict.[2] In total, the First World War brought almost three times as many Italians to the grave as did the Second. The visceral nature of events between 1915 and 1918 was destined play a massive role in subsequent Italian history, an inheritance inadequately conveyed in the reiterated conclusion by official Italy in recent times that the national victory amounted to 'the greatest triumph in our history and … the supreme proof of the political strength of the post-Risorgimento state'.[3]

In 1919, as Imperiali feared, it seemed that the war effort had been largely wasted. Not long after the guns fell silent, nationalist propagandists adapted the word 'mutilated' to define the Italian fate in the post-war era. With this usage they complained that, despite its sacrifice of blood and treasure, Italy was still treated by an ungrateful world as a lightweight power, an all but 'honorary defeated' state, a victim of the horrendous conflict rather than a victor. Many in the political class were left to rue this moral loss and to dream that a revision of an 'unjust' peace might at last open a door to real national greatness.

Meanwhile, the legacy of war blighted any prospect that the governing Liberal regime could restore Italian society to the seeming sunshine of the *belle époque*. On 23 March 1919 a disparate group, disgruntled at Liberal 'failure' and determined to impose a new order domestically and perhaps in Italy's interna-tional status and behaviour, came together in a rented room facing the Piazza San Sepolcro in central Milan and proclaimed themselves fused in a *fascio di combattimento* (returned soldiers' league). The meeting was to be glorified as the foundation of the Italian Fascist movement and the first hailing of its *Duce*, Benito Mussolini.

In the three following years, much of northern Italy, with epicentres in the newly annexed Trieste and Trentino, and in Tuscany and the Po valley (where socialist peasant unionism was strong), the Fascists strode forward as the aggressors and victors in a mini social civil war. Their campaign culminated on 28 October 1922 in the 'March on Rome', half coup and half triumph of political manipulation by Mussolini, who, during the crucial days, stayed beside the telephone in his newspaper office in Milan.[4] The conflict between the Fascists and their foes was underpinned by rival interpretations of Italy's recent war. Marxists and the more radical Catholics doubted its purpose and rejected its 'glory'. The Fascist movement was heavily staffed by ex-soldiers – the myth of Mussolini the *Duce* was nourished by heroic or spartan tales from his own posting to the front[5] – or by bourgeois and petit-bourgeois students regretful that they had been too young for war service. All pledged to 'defend' the war. When, on 3 January 1925, the Mussolini government turned into a dictatorial regime, determined to rule into the foreseeable future, Fascism began to explain that it was imposing a 'totalitarian' state on to Italy. This neologism, one with a future despite being no more than a grand-sounding tautology ('totally total'), entailed the transfer into the domestic affairs of peacetime Italy of the techniques and assumptions of 'total war'.

Notoriously flaunted among them was a contempt for the idea of perpetual peace, an exaltation of soldiering and a habitual recourse to a militant and military vocabulary. In his speech on the afternoon of 23 March 1919, Mussolini had stated 'we declare war against socialism'[6] and, then and thereafter, the Fascist cause was regularly advanced in inexorable 'battles'; its followers were summoned as loyal, armed, 'legionaries' to vast and disciplined *adunate* (musters), where the throng hailed 'victories' now and to come. Of all the regimes in interwar Europe (and, by the end of 1938, liberal democracy survived only on the continent's western fringe), the Italian was the most noisily aggressive, with its propaganda turning real in the invasion and the conquest of Abyssinia (modern-day Ethiopia) in October 1935 to May 1936, participation on the insurgent side in the Spanish Civil war (July 1936 to March 1939), the annexation of Albania (April 1939) and eventual participation in all the Second World Wars as 'first ally' of the Nazis from June 1940. On the surface, and quite a few historians accept that the truth lies there,[7] Mussolini or Fascism or both meant war. Therefore, they pronounce, once Fascism was installed in Rome, Italy's fate again to engage in battle when opportunity came was sealed.

Yet, before endorsing this conclusion, it is sensible to pause and consider the deep structures of Italian foreign policy, those born in the process of national unification in the nineteenth century, thereafter accompanying Italian life and conditioning 'decision making' by Italian politicians, whether Liberal or Fascist. All is summarized in the situation whereby Italy was 'the least of the Great Powers'.[8] From 1860 to 1945 Italy had the lowest industrial production, the shakiest banking system, the poorest energy resources and the feeblest sinews of the minerals and energy of the leading industrialized powers. For many reasons, Italy possessed the least-advanced economy of those states that assumed they formed the natural leadership of the world. It had the smallest population of any of its competitors, a situation scarcely remedied by massive emigration, notably to the Americas, from the 1880s to 1914. Furthermore, compared with Britain, France, Germany and the United States, Italy had the highest illiteracy rates and the most poorly educated, least 'modern', citizenry. It was, in sum, the Western nation whose peoples were most unreliably nationalized and where the writ of a modern state most doubtfully ran.

This formidable set of drawbacks made military failure all but certain. The Italy that, after 1870, placed its capital in Rome had been constructed more by the sacrifice of the soldiers of Napoleon III in 1859 and the victories of Prussia in 1866 and uniting Germany in 1870 than by the 6000 'Italians', killed in the Risorgimento's battles (although the exploits of Giuseppe Garibaldi, the purest 'hero' of his era, ensured that the territories of the Kingdom of Naples–Sicily, south of Rome, joined the nation). Nor did matters change after unification. At Adowa, on the border of Abyssinia, in March 1896 an Italian army lost to forces commanded by the local Emperor, Menelik II, a colonial defeat that was unique for a pre-1914 European power in that it was not avenged but rather followed by a shame-faced retreat from the area (and a postponement for the foreseeable future of national imperium there).

The impact of this internal and external weakness might have prepared Italy to pursue the path that, by the early twentieth century, was pioneered by Sweden, symbolized in its acceptance of an independent Norway in 1905 and its commitment thereafter, at least most of the time, to international amity and the avoidance of European war. Italy was not so wise or fortunate, and most Italian diplomatic historians[9] assume that it was simply impossible for a country positioned where Italy was, in what may have been the heart of Europe, to avoid participation in the conflicts of the greater powers. The record of Italy after 1945, when no longer an aspirant to greatness, may suggest otherwise. In any case, until the defeat of Fascism much was expressed in the fact that the national capital was Rome, a city possessed of a 'myth-history' grander than any other. For any Italian rulers from 1860 to 1945, avoiding the inheritance of Caesar and resultant hungry and envious thoughts of empire and glory, eternity and universality was taxing indeed.

The temptations were evident as the first decade of the twentieth century came to an end and, from 1909 to 1911, the nation celebrated its fiftieth anniversary. The prospect for the nation was symbolized in the opening in June 1911 at Rome of the grandiose Victor Emmanuel monument, grandiloquent architectural statement of the lustre that should necessarily burnish the 'Third Italy'. Positioned athwart the Capitol and Forum, the shiny white edifice shimmered with an intention to outdo the Caesars. As if in proof, despite the country's ultra moderate leadership from the canny liberal, Giovanni

Giolitti, in September 1911 Italy attacked Turkish forces in territories across the Mediterranean now annexed to Italy under their 'restored' classical Roman name of Libya. Equally, guided by the more conservative leadership of southern lawyer and landowner Antonio Salandra, and of Sonnino, in May 1915 Italy entered the First World War in an act of aggression against Austria-Hungary. In no way was Italy's First World War occasioned by its leaders 'stumbling over the brink into the boiling cauldron of war'. Rather they acted deliberately, even if doubtless charged with their own 'short-war illusion' that an Italian appearance at the front would decisively change the current battle order, delivering victory to the Allies by Christmas.

The point of any analysis of the diplomatic and military behaviour of Liberal Italy is that it plainly was not characterized by an abiding love of peace. Back in the 1859, Cavour had talked cheerfully of his willingness to 'set Europe alight' to achieve his ends and, once combat with Austria was agreed, allowed the ghost of Caesar to speak through him: 'alea jacta est; we have made history, so now we can have dinner'.[10] Aggression and ambition, if often conditioned by caution, cynicism and trepidation, were the birth rites of all governing Italian politicians well before the country fell under Fascist dictatorship.

This 'peculiarity of Italian history' was well enough evidenced during the Versailles crisis, where Sonnino and his Prime Minister, Vittorio Emanuele Orlando, became the whipping boys of the Wilsonian new diplomacy. As the diplomats of the world assembled in Paris, ambition was easy enough to locate in the highest circles in Italy. Army chief Armando Diaz hoped for full control of the Libyan hinterland (eventually to be achieved with vicious brutality under the Fascist regime), the rounding out of Italy's rule over the Horn of Africa, where since the 1880s there had been a rudimentary Italian presence in Eritrea and at Mogadishu, through the cession of British and French Somalia, and the acknowledgement of 'our *unique influence*' [sic] in Ethiopia.[11] More generically, King Victor Emmanuel III worried that the nation was 'more and more needy', beseeching his politicians to avoid the 'disillusion of our just aspirations'.[12] But the initial Italian enthusiasm about what Wilson might deliver and what he might stand for – shared by Mussolini among others – soon turned sour. Point IX of Wilson's list of fourteen, whereby 'a readjustment of the frontiers of Italy should be effected along clearly recognisable lines of nationality', scarcely requited Italian hopes. Orlando was left in Paris suddenly to deplore the nation-alism that he feared was getting out of hand back home.[13] As a recent analyst has explained, at the peace-making 'Italy's tactics were irritating, transparent and frequently inept'[14] – those, in other words, of the least of the Great Powers.

A nadir was reached on 24 April when Orlando and Sonnino walked out of the Paris talks. Their return to Rome was briefly cheered in Italy but they carried no policy options with them and less than a fortnight later were driven to announce that they would timorously go back to the French capital. Unilateralism had proved impossible for a country like Italy. By the time all the peace agreements were signed, Italy had in fact done quite well out of the war, especially given the collapse of its ancient enemy, Austria-Hungary. Moreover, certainly in the South Tyrol (or Alto Adige) and even in Trieste, Italy had achieved borders that were more strategic than a scrupulous example of 'self-determination'. But, despite alluring talk about a mandate in Georgia (Orlando naively thought it a 'promised land in so far as primary resources are concerned' and Mussolini, too, flirted with backing the nation there),[15] Italy scarcely achieved imperial advantage. Rather, it saw the gap between its modest extra-metropolitan territories and those of Britain and France yawn more widely. Even Australia won a bigger and richer 'mandate' than did Italy. As the Liberal system stumbled to its collapse, the international situation brought the country little kudos but rather enhanced the idea that, whatever had actually happened in the war, Italy was losing the peace.

In these circumstances, it is scarcely surprising that Mussolini, still combining the roles of crusading journalist and politician on the make and carelessly mixing ideology and 'realism', frequently sounded off about foreign affairs. Those who are anxious to paint Mussolini as a rogue politician from birth to death can readily enough find articles in his voluminous writings demanding that Italy seize Malta, Corsica, the Ticino and Dalmatia, befriend the IRA and push forward aggressively wherever there was opportunity on the Mediterranean littoral in order to 'defend victory' in the First World War.[16] No doubt an atmosphere and a set of long-term hopes (a more appropriate term than plans) were being fostered here; the classical idea of the *mare nostrum* was widely accepted in patriotic circles as a requirement for the 'Third Italy' well before 1922. Yet, in office, the *Duce* hastened to assure the powers, be it at home or abroad, that his government's behaviour would not be untoward. A formal letter to the Prime Ministers of Britain and France on 31 October 1922 announced that Mussolini had been nominated by the King as Prime Minister because he was 'the Representative of the ideals and ambitions [*idealità*] of [the victory at] Vittorio Veneto'. His intention now was to help safeguard the 'supreme national interests' while assisting the spread of 'peace and civilization in the world'. He was strongly committed to 'friendly solidarity with the Allied Nations' to that end.[17]

Neither his own diplomats (only one career official resigned on the Fascist assumption of authority) nor those of other countries blanched at the new administration. Elite reaction was expressed in an editorial in the London *Daily Telegraph* on 1 November 1922. Mussolini, it stated, 'is undeniably the most interesting, the most original and the most powerful man in Italy at the moment'. In so far as international diplomacy was concerned, he had in the past spouted 'dangerous words' but, the editorialist added, 'it may be confidently predicted that will change with office as indeed Mussolini's message on taking office has shown'. All would probably be well, even if, the editorial concluded portentously, 'Italy is only at the beginning of a chapter of her history that is full of the gravest possibilities'.[18] Six months later, the paper's worries had diminished. Now Italian patriots could delight at the way that Mussolini had used his power with 'remarkable wisdom and moderation'. They should 'perceive not only the purification of the public life and the ardent revival of the national spirit but also the plain fact that their country counts today for more in the councils of Europe than at any earlier period'.[19]

In these phrases, the paper was illuminating the stance of conservative circles in Britain and the rest of Europe to the Italian regime throughout the first decade of its existence. Mussolini, it was believed with relief, had dished the communists who had threatened to take over Italy. His rhetoric was on occasion extreme but, in its militancy, seemed directed at domestic consumption. Were not Italians, by definition, a people given to flamboyant gesture? Even after he officially became a dictator and announced the building of a totalitarian state (the adjective did not yet possess the sinister overtones that it now has), Mussolini seemed a colourful personality but not one who seriously imperilled the good order of post-war Europe.

True, there had been one moment of drastic action and a resultant fear that the Italians had opted for unilateral aggression abroad in a repetition there of the violence that Fascists had ruthlessly deployed to cement their power within Italy. On 27 August 1923 General Enrico Tellini, an Italian official assisting an international mission to demarcate the southern Albanian border, was murdered by 'bandits'. In Rome, the assumption was that the killers were indirect or direct agents of the Greek government, and that evening Mussolini opted for a violent response. A set of implacable Italian demands for apology and reparation was speedily drafted. Before there was any time for reasoned Greek reply, on 30 August the Italian navy was ordered to bombard and occupy the Adriatic island of Corfu, a place Mussolini announced, with apparent revisionist fanfare, that had once been part of the Venetian empire. According to a diplomatic historian who reviewed the event in the 1960s, here 'Europe was seeing a type of diplomacy which was to reach its zenith and its most cynical form in the coming decade'.[20]

At the time, Fascist party circles were excited by this 'first act of Fascist foreign policy'[21] and the event was predictably portrayed in the ever more tightly controlled Italian media as a stupendous naval and diplomatic triumph. However, international conciliation swiftly forced Italy to back down and withdraw from the island, while Mussolini's threat to abandon the League of Nations proved hollow. Thereafter, Italy dutifully served as member of many League councils and committees, until 1935 behaving little differently in Geneva from any other power. In 1928 Italy even signed the Kellogg–Briand peace pact, which renounced war as a legitimate instrument of policy, despite Mussolini dismissing it savagely as 'a vain and sterile' document, sprung from 'principles antithetical to the new Italy'.[22] Moreover, in 1923, although Mussolini himself, reported to have been 'incandescent' at Tellini's death, had initiated Italian action against Corfu, his response needs to be placed into a context of long-running Italian disputation with Greece. Ironically, this poor peasant nation was armed with as overweening a myth from classical times as was Italy

(Mussolini must have savoured his adjective as he denounced Greek guilt in 'barbarous massacre').[23] It was therefore all the more a 'Small Power' that Italy needed visibly to overmaster. Predictably, therefore, government policy during the Corfu crisis was applauded by wide sectors of the old liberal elite. Perhaps, in those days, Mussolini did not precisely work towards the Italians but he scarcely drove them where they did not want to go. In 1923, Fascist policy remained recognizably that of the least of the Great Powers.

The next year was a momentous one for Mussolini and his regime after the kidnapping and murder of moderate socialist leader Giacomo Matteotti on 10 June 1924 (either at the *Duce*'s direct behest or sponsored by his intimate henchmen) provoked months of domestic turmoil that were not resolved until Mussolini formally proclaimed a dictatorship on 3 January 1925. His speech on that occasion endorsed the Fascist movement's long record of violence. The diplomatic world watched these events in puzzlement but saw little to deplore and nothing to suggest the cutting of their ties with Italy. The authoritative *Times* in June 1924 had pronounced patronizingly that 'homicide is commoner [in Italy] ... than in most other civilized states'. Six months later, the paper was a little more troubled at the 'many and palpable evils' of Fascist mayhem, yet eager to applaud the 'unquestioned benefits' brought to Italy by 'the tyrannical but efficient hands of Signor Mussolini'.[24]

While open dictatorship settled into place within Italy, the country played a normal and what was accepted as a reasonably helpful part in the negotiation of the Locarno agreement, the key diplomatic arrangement in Europe of the decade and seeming symbol that the world war was at last fully over with Germany's resultant restoration to the comity of nations. On occasion, Mussolini complained that Britain and France did not devote enough attention to Germany's border with Austria — an *Anschluss*, the *Duce* urged, must lead to immediate war in order to prevent Germany from obtaining greater strength than it had possessed in 1914.[25] In 1925–6 there were spats between Italy and Germany over the Italianization policy that Fascist administrators were pursuing in the Alto Adige to the cost of German-speaking peasants. But no serious combat was foreseen even when, in April 1925, Paul von Hindenburg, just elected President of the Weimar Republic, greeted a delegation from Bolzano (Bözen) as 'co-nationals beyond the frontier, indissolubly bound to us'.[26] For the other powers the thought that Italy was another state potentially challenged by German demands, should revision of Versailles be attempted, may not have been unpleasing.

At this stage, the idea that Fascism would make an alliance with its enemy in the last war was still fantastical, but Italy was studiously realistic in its dealings with the USSR, even though the regime had installed itself as the enemy of communism.[27] Unlike Germany, Italy did not sponsor secret rearmament deals with the state that was so long a pariah in the European system, but instead dealt with it in severely practical mode, with trade being the key.[28] Whether or not Mussolini and his movement were already threaded with anti-Semitism may be debated, but neither now nor later was the *Duce* a fundamentalist foe of 'Judeo-Bolshevism' as Hitler was.

The most serious menace of international Fascist violence surfaced in Italy's relationship with its neighbour, Yugoslavia, as on occasion enhanced by the Italian determination to act as the protector of Albania, a role that had been taken up by the Liberals before 1914. On 2 October 1926, for example, Mussolini sent a brisk note to the Chief of General Staff, Marshal Pietro Badoglio, urging that 'there was not a minute to lose' in priming '20 divisions' to attack Yugoslavia. For the dictator, it was crucial that Italy could at a moment's notice give a lesson to the Yugoslavs, a people, he warned, who were stained by an irredeemable 'political and mental crookedness' (Mussolini was not the only Italian to harbour racial prejudice about the 'Slavs' who lived across the border, as well as, in some numbers, within Venezia Giulia).[29] Yet words were words: no military action followed.

True, the Italian government, but not Mussolini personally, gave subsidies and asylum to Croat enemies of the Yugoslav union, among them Ante Pavelić, later to be the terrorist Poglavnik of a brutal Nazi-fascist Croatian regime in wartime.[30] Other lavish funds passed to pro-Italian dissidents in Switzerland, Kosovo, Austria, Spain, Britain and other places, as well as to the Grand Mufti of Jerusalem and to such 'revisionist' Zionists as Ze'ev 'Vladimir' Jabotinsky, with some slight ensuing disruption of the political order. Yet all states have their friends and clients abroad and what is most evident in the Fascist case is their poor quality and unreliability, demonstrating that a country that was the least of the Great Powers operated in a less-rewarding and secure market than did the United States, Britain, France and Germany.

Most significant for a regime that some have viewed as viscerally ideological, Mussolini's Italy scarcely prompted the admiration that was aroused among many communists by the Soviet Union [USSR], despite its poverty, and when Stalin's actions might seem blatantly to expose what a murderous tyranny it had become. Neither signed photographs of the *Duce*, nor Rome meetings with him and other leading Fascists by English eccentrics on the right could elevate him to a globally politically significant figure. By the time a Fascist 'International' had uneasily united itself in 1934 under active and generous Italian sponsorship,[31] the boast that the Italian dictatorship was the model 'ideology of the twentieth century' and the template of 'universal fascism' was undermined from elsewhere on the Right. Adolf Hitler and his Nazi movement had taken power in Germany. At once their variant of fascism (if that is what it was) shook the European order in a fashion that had not happened during the first decade of Mussolini's power. Now, indeed, a track to the Second World War came into view, but it was opened by the dynamism of Nazi Germany, not Italy.

Before 1933 Hitler had been a petitioner at Mussolini's gate, all the more because the *Führer* was an unusual figure on the German Right in treasuring an alliance with Italy, thereby countermanding the usual German (racial) prejudice that Italians were a nation of thieves and beggars. As far as the Nazi chief was concerned, Mussolini, in his March on Rome and his firm policies thereafter, was a direct inspiration.[32] When, in October 1930, Mussolini was still peaceably endorsing the line that Fascism was 'not for export', it was Hitler who advised ingratiatingly that this limitation was only true about detail, while the 'general conceptions' of Fascism had 'international appeal'.[33] Mussolini, who, in his workaday life in Rome, met very many people, had snubbed Göring when that Nazi had come to enjoy southern fleshpots.[34] Although by the end of the 1920s a private wire connected the dictator with the Nazis through Giuseppe Renzetti, the *Duce* long favoured the *Stahlhelm* and the more respectable German Right over Hitler's party. The first meeting (the Italians stressed that it was 'absolutely unofficial' in character) between *Duce* and *Führer* did not occur until 14–15 June 1934 in (for Hitler) dreamy Venice.[35] It was only after that event, the Nazi 'Night of the Long Knives', the murder of Austrian Chancellor Engelbert Dollfuss (esteemed by Mussolini as a friend and client) and the failed German putsch in Vienna, each deplored in Rome, that Fascist Italy would turn to open aggression. What, it might be asked before reviewing that development, had been achieved in the first decade of Fascist rule to deal with Italy's structural weaknesses?

Very little is the answer. Take the economy. In January 1929, just as the negotiations with the Vatican were culminating in the signature of the Lateran Pacts and the trumpeted resolution of the 'Roman Question', Bernardino Nogara approached the dictator. Nogara was a man of many parts, having been active under Giolitti as an agent of imperial advance in Asia Minor, and there-after the key financial advisor to successive popes. By May 1940 Nogara was clear-sighted enough about coming battle and its likely result to transfer Vatican gold to the US Federal Reserve and, from 1937, the church had switched its chief investment to Wall Street blue chip stocks with rich results.[36] In 1929 Nogara was still hopeful in Fascism but, he complained, just as he had done under Giolitti,[37] what Italian industry and finance needed was government help. At home, the nation was too backward to offer entrepreneurs sufficient capital for 'initiatives beyond the national borders'. Could not something be done by the Fascist state to overcome this deficiency?[38]

Mussolini's response is not recorded. But neither then nor in the 1930s did Italy acquire the financial, industrial or even agricultural strength that would allow it to match the greater powers. True, briefly in the aftermath of the Wall Street Crash, there was boasting that the dictatorship's 'corporatism' (in reality always more a theory than a reality) had allowed it to avoid the collapse occurring elsewhere, and some celebrated international economists endorsed the view that Rome was possessed of a recipe for economic advance. But, as the 1930s wore on, it was the regime's economic failure that became more evident. Production fell, unemployment increased, wages were cut and the Fascist version of a welfare state was riddled with corruption and political favour-itism. Inevitably, with the global advance of science, some features of a modern economy did take root in Italy. However, the standard economic history of the dictatorship, contrary to the legend that its rule was effectively 'developmental', states bluntly that 'one thing is certain [amid the dubious statistics], and that is that Fascism failed to narrow the economic gap between Italy and the other industrialised powers'.[39] When, as a member of the Axis, Italy geared itself for war, the hazard of bankruptcy grew; as an expert would comment wanly, the late 1930s had become a time of 'heroic remedies' rather than of serious or credible policy.[40]

If the dilemmas of economic inferiority had not been resolved, military weakness had also not been properly addressed, despite the decade of militant propaganda. The national air force (*Regia Aeronautica*) was often in the headlines, winning speed competitions or engaging in dramatic cross-oceanic 'crusades' to the New World. However, little attempt was made to clarify how it should function in real war (and the country was left sadly deficient in air defences). The navy fostered ever more expensive battleship construction but could never really hope to match British or French forces, unless they were devastated by their international commitments beyond the Mediterranean. The Army remained a highly traditional organization. Its officers and men were better equipped to fight the last war than to deal with a new one, hindered by inadequate mechanization and armaments; no Italian tank stunned the fighting world. All in all, the situation was and remained bleak. As a recent analysis of the subject has concluded: 'Mussolini thought of wars and his soldiers, sailors and airmen planned them, but a lack of clear distinction meant that his wishes did not mesh with their designs and his choices ultimately did not square with their capabilities.'[41] Rather than a military that somehow expressed the totalitarian passion and disciplined purpose of a Fascist 'revolution', Italy once again was still equipped with the forces of the least of the great powers.

Nor, contrary to loud boasting, were Italians themselves convinced that they were fully fledged Fascists (or, indeed, Italians), permanently on the alert to 'believe, obey and fight' and to live 'one day as a lion rather than a hundred years as a sheep' (as regime propaganda bellowed). To be sure, here the historiography is divided with some commentators ready to assert that a cultural or 'anthropological' revolution was permeating Italian souls and forging them into new men and women.[42] Yet any attempt at social as distinct from cultural history, any refusal to take Fascist words at their face value, refutes this line. As the 1930s proceeded, Italians, doubtless deprived of information rival to the Fascist and often marshalled into cheering display, may have willingly granted short-term 'consent' to dictatorship. But their applause at this or that touted 'triumph' did not mean that they had abandoned familial, Catholic, local, class (most staunchly, peasant) and patron–client assumptions, longer-term loyalties that often jarred with Fascism. The limitations of the dictatorship and its failure altogether to grip its subjects' minds were destined to be nakedly displayed when Italians confronted what the regime optimistically labelled the 'test' of war.

What, then, had been the regime's chief foreign policies during the enveloping crises? The first major break in what had seemed the established line of Fascist foreign policy occurred in 1935 with the attack on Ethiopia. Both the prelude to that event and the invasion and conquest were conducted with maximum brutality and 'modernity' (including the use of contemporary chemical weapons of mass destruction), apparently winning the backing of almost all the population. Mussolini's tubby eldest son, Vittorio, with Fascist thuggery, wrote how disappointing it was that 'Ethiopian huts made out of mud and twigs gave no satisfaction to a bomber'.[43] Killing blacks brought few signs of metropolitan grief. Italians did not bother to count indigenous casualties and neither did Renzo De Felice, the author of the most detailed post-war account of the regime, although Ethiopian historians today estimate the terrible tally, during combat and under Italian rule to 1941, fell somewhere between 300,000 to 730,000 men, women and children.[44]

Yet, as Vittorio Mussolini was implying, the scene of action in 1935–6 was Africa. Beneath the swagger, the Italians, when, in May 1936, their forces drove into Addis Ababa and established colonial rule there, were not ahead but behind the times. They were doing what their betters had already done in the nineteenth century. After 1937 the dictatorship even appointed a royal prince, the Duke of Aosta, to be national viceroy in lands that Mussolini never even visited. Quickly, too, racial legislation was framed to deal with those countrymen, by no means only humble soldiers, who too obviously got close to the 'natives'. In the brief years before the sun set on the still humble Italian empire, quite a few of those in residence there (more likely to be government officials or businessmen on the make than permanent farming settlers) tried to be pukka sahibs of a kind rather than the terrible agents of modernizing Fascism. However brutal was their rule and however high its costs for the local peoples, the Italians never contemplated genocide in Ethiopia in any serious meaning of the word. They (unsuccessfully) pursued the glory, God and gold of old-fashioned European empire rather than the totalized ethnic cleansing that lay at the heart of Nazi plans genocidal for *Lebensraum*.

Before and during the Ethiopian campaign, Mussolini assumed the lead in pushing for 'total' victory, taking evident pleasure in ratchetting up outraged foreign criticism and in ignoring nervous brethren in the Fascist party or royal family or Army at home – in 1934, Badoglio did not hide his dismay at the loss of finance and military material of any colonial campaign.[45] But then, in 1911, with the great world splitting into those alliances that would fight the First World War, Giolitti had similarly ignored hostile moralizing in Britain and France, insisting on no diplomatic compromises but rather the complete seizure of Libya. Should a Fascist have been more polite than a Liberal? Furthermore, in a memorandum that he prepared in 1932, the plan to attack Ethiopia had been sketched by a career diplomat, Raffaele Guariglia, whose career spanned Liberal, Fascist and then Republican times.[46] Guariglia wrote it down on a piece of paper but the temptation to take Ethiopia and avenge the defeat at Adowa in 1896 (in 1935 Italian armies were proclaimed to have won a brilliant first victory there) was deeply inscribed into the secret hopes of most of the Italian ruling elite. Similarly, the population at large would also not renounce opportunity for gain (if that was what empire might mean). The Ethiopian war was as much Italian as it was Fascist or a Mussolinian designed form of aggression.

It was, however, not an end but a beginning. No sooner had victory been proclaimed in Africa and before the costs of governance there could be appraised, the dictatorship deliberately entered the next of 'Mussolini's wars'. Ignoring the warnings given by history and by more judicious contemporaries, the Fascist government poured men and treasure into what soon became the quicksand of a foreign Civil War that was prompted in Spain by the military's imperfect coup against the Republic on 17 July 1936. As battle dragged on, cheap promises from Francisco Franco, the *caudillo* dictator in the making, that his forces aimed to establish 'Fascist-style' government in Spain, and cheap advice from Mussolini that, nowadays, an authoritarian government must necessarily opt to be 'popular and social' and armed with a single party, a single militia and a single union[47] were all very well. But by 1 April 1939, when Franco celebrated his brutal victory over the 'Reds' in Madrid, it had become plain that Italy's structural weaknesses were rendering it again an honorary loser of war.

Back in 1934 Mussolini had been sage enough to note that any advance in Africa would need to be rapid because Nazi government in Berlin had destabilized the Europe built at Versailles. Then he had been preoccupied at a future where Italy's war potential had been diminished.[48] Now, however angrily he might deny it, the *Duce* was palpably drifting into being 'dictator minor', dragged along the dynamic and conquering course of the *Führer*, but unable to direct or control it. Much had been decided in March 1938 with the *Anschluss*, an expansion that brought German power to the Brenner frontier and cancelled Italy's chief strategic gain from the First World War. At least Hitler understood the implications when Italy offered no opposition. His effusive thanking of the *Duce* almost went too far. 'I will never forget it. Never, never, never ... I really want to thank him [Mussolini] from my heart. I will never, never forget this.'[49] What Hitler was being grateful about between the lines was that a Fascist dictatorship, whose power he still greatly overestimated, was allowing German troops, presumably under some nationalist leadership other than his own, eventually to envisage a revision of the loss of the South Tyrol and Trieste in 1919. In the meantime, hereafter, the German presence offered a polite threat that, should Italy waver in alliance, then it would experience a high and immediate cost for betrayal.

Once Germany and Austria were united, the die for Italy was cast in most foreseeable circumstances. The announcement in November 1936 that the two dictatorships were joined in an Axis, the signature a year later of the tripartite Anti-Comintern pact with Japan and Italy's withdrawal from the League of Nations (December 1937) had signalled an accelerating drift into an alliance either of those urgently committed to revision of the post-First World War treaties or into an unholy pact of aggressors. But Mussolini had long been emphatic that treaties were 'ephemeral', should the eternal interests of the nation be at play. Maybe the Axis could break? Yet, after March 1938, it was hard to imagine an advantage that could come from such a shattering. The deal with Germany could not be matched by any other.

Therefore ties were cemented between the regimes as never before. Mussolini and his brash party secretary, Achille Starace, urged regular exchanges between servants of the two regimes in many fields, with the *Duce* developing the habit of dropping the German word *Stimmung* into his conversations whenever he wanted to allege that each regime and people was possessed of the same world view. Now Italy, if probably for domestic and imperial reasons and not at direct German ordering, began to introduce draconian anti-Semitic legislation and the regime's propaganda pumped up incredible claims that the Italians were Aryan in blood. Now, too, and potentially most dangerous and humiliating, Italy began to send its own underemployed agricultural and industrial labourers to be 'guest workers' in the Reich: 37,095 in 1938, 46,411 in 1939, 98,719 in 1940 and 228,563 in 1941, every one a hostage to the flourishing of the Axis.[50] Now Mussolini solaced himself insolently writing off the Pope, the liberal democracies (the *Duce* decided that the USA was less a 'mountain' than a 'blister', despite the popular Italian knowledge drawn from emigration that the country was rich beyond the dreams of avarice) and any who might reject Nazi-fascism.[51]

Even if the attack on Albania in April 1939 was at least partially an envious response to Germany's continuing gains as most recently evidenced in their seizure of rump Czechoslovakia, the next months further tightened the Axis. On 22 May the 'Pact of Steel' seemed to entail open military partnership. Already for some time, Mussolini, his military chiefs and key officials had begun to talk gaily about war starting in '1940' or '1941' or '1942' when, they were sure, Italy would be armed and ready.[52] Maths had been one of Mussolini's worst subjects as a schoolboy and his growing fondness to declare his 'mathematical certainty' in this ostensible 'planning' precision is indeed ironical.

The irony became plain when, in August 1939, the Italians suddenly realized that their German *camerati* were determined at any cost, including world war, to crash or crash through and, without whisper to Rome, had cynically signed a deal with their ideological foes, the Soviet Union, to expedite their liquidation of Catholic and authoritarian Poland, a country with which Fascist Italy had many reasons to be friends. The story is familiar. Italy's youthful Foreign Minister, that clever yuppie Galeazzo Ciano, less a Fascist hard man than a young conservative, if one ready to sponsor murder, now suddenly back-pedalled from the German partnership rather as his Liberal predecessors had deserted the Triple Alliance in July–August 1914. In September, war started, and the 'iron-hard' Fascist dictatorship was no more than a 'non-belligerent' in it.

Eventually Italy would enter the war and do so on the Nazi side on 10 June 1940, with the Fascist dictatorship taking the same time to make up its mind as had the Liberals in the first war. Explanation varies. For some, Mussolini never for a moment intended to desert Hitler in battle and in the acquisition of booty, and had given definitive promise by March or May 1940.[53] Certainly it is a little hard to imagine the *Duce* surviving in office if staying neutral throughout the conflict (although Franco did) or joining the Allies. Yet the countering personal and ideological explanation similarly has its problems. Italy did wait a long time before committing itself. By 10 June, France was routed and, to many, the war of 1939–40 seemed over. In those circumstances, would any imaginable leader of the least of the great powers not have sought to earn a ticket to the peace conference at the sacrifice of a few thousand dead soldiers (the *Duce* himself put it that way)? At that peace, might not even Mussolini have sought to maximize Italian gain in Djibouti, Corsica, Malta and Tunis, while simultaneously seeking to limit the German victory lest those troops pour south from the Brenner? Mussolini headed a cruel and irresponsible dictatorship whose failures should not be allowed to hide its murderous aggression and tyranny. Nonetheless, a historian can legitimately conclude that, so far as foreign policy was concerned, Fascism did not altogether infringe the norms of Italian history while that nation sought to be a genuine Great Power.

Notes

1   *Documenti diplomatici Italiani* (hereafter *DDI*) 6th series, vol. I, 17 (5 November 1918), Imperiali to Sonnino.
2   M. Thompson, *The White War: Life and Death on the Italian Front 1915–1919*. London, 2008, p. 381.
3   See, for example, R. Romeo, *L'Italia unita e la prima guerra mondiale*. Bari, 1978, p. 157; C.A. Ciampi, 'Prefazione' to M.R. Stern (ed.), *1915–1918: la guerra sugli Altipiani: testimonianze di soldati al fronte*. Vicenza, 2000, pp. vii–ix.
4   For the violence involved, see G. Albanese, *La Marcia su Roma*. Bari, 2006.
5   For background, see R.J.B. Bosworth, *Mussolini* rev ed. London, 2010; cf. P. O'Brien, *Mussolini in the First World War: The Journalist, the Soldier, the Fascist*. Oxford, 2005.
6   In English, C.F. Delzell (ed.), *Mediterranean Fascism 1919–1945*. New York, 1970, p. 9.
7   In English, see R. Mallett, *Mussolini and the Origins of the Second World War, 1933–1940*. Houndmills, 2003; M. Knox, *To the Threshold of Power, 1922/33: Origins and Dynamics of the Fascist and National Socialist Dictatorships* vol. 1. Cambridge, 2007.
8   For my first statement of this matter, see R.J.B. Bosworth, *Italy: The Least of the Great Powers: Italian Foreign Policy before the First World War*. Cambridge, 1979.
9   They are in majority a patriotic and conservative crew. For introduction, see R.J.B. Bosworth, 'Italy's Historians and the Myth of Fascism' in R. Langhorne (ed.), *Diplomacy and Intelligence during the Second World War: Essays in Honour of F.H. Hinsley*. Cambridge, 1985, pp. 85–105.
10 D. Mack Smith, *Cavour*. London, 1985, pp. 153, 163.
11 *DDI* 6th series, vol. II, 63 (22 January 1919), Diaz to Orlando.
12 Ibid., II, 66 (23 January 1919), Victor Emmanuel III to Orlando.
13 R. Lansing, *The Peace Negotiations: A Personal Narrative*. London, 1921, p. 284; *DDI* 6th series, vol. II, 240 (5 February 1919), 773 (12 March 1919), both Orlando to Victor Emmanuel III.
14 M. MacMillan, *Peacemakers: The Paris Conference of 1919 and its Attempt to End War*. London, 2001, p. 301.
15 See, for example, Bosworth, *Mussolini*, p. 137; *DDI* 6th series, vol. II, 917 (22 March 1919), Orlando to Victor Emmanuel III. The king was sensibly sceptical of the idea.

16   G. Rumi, *Alle origini della politica estera fascista (1918–1923)*. Bari, 1968, p. 5. Mussolini's own works have appeared in 36 volumes, *Opera omnia*, E. and D. Susmel (eds). Florence, 1951–63, republished with 8 extra volumes Rome, 1978–80.

17   *DDI* 7th series, vol. I, 7 (31 October 1922), Mussolini to Poincaré and Bonar Law.

18   *Daily Telegraph* 1 November 1922.

19   *Daily Telegraph* 18 April 1923.

20   J. Barros, *The Corfu Incident of 1923: Mussolini and the League of Nations*. Princeton, 1965, p. 40.

21   E. Di Nolfo, *Mussolini e la politica estera Italiana 1919–1933*, Padua, 1960, p. 90.

22   *DDI* 7th series, vol. VI, 391 (8 June 1928), Mussolini to De Martino.

23   Ibid., II, 186 (28 August 1923), Mussolini to Montagna.

24   *The Times* 21 June 1924, 6 January 1925.

25   *DDI* 7th series, vol. IV, 21 (8 June 1925), Mussolini to Della Torretta and Romano Avezzana.

26   A.E. Alcock, *The History of the South Tyrol Question*. Geneva, 1970, p. 38.

27   For a paradoxical example, see Mussolini's offer to Austen Chamberlain to break relations with the USSR since the Soviet regime was 'a permanent threat not only to the social and national order of Western states, but against the very basis of human civilization', fretted by the blunt statement a month later than Italy did not intend to change its satisfactory ties with Moscow. *DDI* 7th series, vol. V, 213 (19 May 1927), Mussolini to Chiaramonte Bordonaro; 288 (23 June 1927), Mussolini to Cerruti.

28   For narrative, see G. Petracchi, *Da San Pietroburgo a Mosca: la diplomazia Italiana in Russia 1861/1941*, Rome, 1993, pp. 293–336.

29   *DDI* 7th series, vol. IV, 448 (2 October 1926), Mussolini to Badoglio.

30   For detail, see J.J. Sadkovich, *Italian Support for Croatian Separatism 1927–1937*. New York, 1987.

31   For a narration of its bathetic history, see M.A. Ledeen, *Universal Fascism: The Theory and Practice of the Fascist International, 1928–1936*. New York, 1972.

32   For further detail see Bosworth, *Mussolini*, pp. 264–71.

33   *DDI* 7th series, vol. IX, 289 (28 September 1930), Hitler to Mussolini.

34   J. Petropoulos, *Royals and the Reich: The Princes von Hessen in Nazi Germany*. Oxford, 2009, p. 121.

35   *DDI* 7th series, vol. XV, 411 (13 June 1934), Suvich to Dollfuss.

36   J.F. Pollard, *Money and the Rise of the Modern Papacy: Financing the Vatican, 1850–1950*. Cambridge, 2005, p. 187; 'The Vatican and the Wall Street Crash: Bernardino Nogara and Papal Finances in the Early 1930s', *Historical Journal* 42 (1999), p. 1091.

37   Bosworth, *Italy, the Least of the Great Powers*, pp. 353–5.

38   *DDI* 7th series, vol. VII, 188 (18 January 1929), Nogara to Mussolini.

39   V. Zamagni, *The Economic History of Italy 1860–1990*. Oxford, 1993, p. 274.

40   F. Guarneri, *Battaglie economiche fra le due guerre*, L. Zani (ed.). Bologna, 1988, p. 457.

41   J. Gooch, *Mussolini and His Generals: The Armed Forces and Fascist Foreign Policy, 1922–1940*. Cambridge, 2007, p. 521.

42   For the historiographical debates, see Bosworth, *The Italian Dictatorship: Problems and Perspectives in the Interpretation of Mussolini and Fascism*. London, 1998.

43   V. Mussolini, *Voli sulle Ambe*. Florence, 1937, p. 28.

44   A. Del Boca, *L'Africa nella coscienza degli italiani: miti, memorie, errori, sconfitte*. Bari, 1972, p. 113.

45   *DDI* 7th series, vol. XV, 219 (12 May 1934), Badoglio to De Bono.

46   Ibid., XII, 222 (26 August 1932), 223 (27 August 1932), Guariglia to Mussolini. Cf. also 393 (5 November 1932), memorandum of meeting at Ministry of Colonies.

47   *DDI* 8th series, vol. IV, 599 (23 July 1936), De Rossi to Ciano; V, 154 (4 October 1936), Mussolini to De Rossi; VII, 191 (9 August 1937), Mussolini to Viola.

48   *DDI* 7th series, vol. XV, 686 (10 August 1934), Mussolini to De Bono and others.

49   Petropoulos, *Royals and the Reich*, p. 184. Cf. Hitler's more detailed promises of forever respecting the Brenner, *DDI* 8th series, 296 (11 March 1938), Hitler to Mussolini.

50   For further details, see B. Mantelli, '*Camerati del lavoo': i lavoratori italiani emigrati nel Terzo Reich nel periodo dell'Asse 1938–1943*. Florence, 1992.

51   *DDI* 8th series, vol. VII, 523 (6 November 1937), memorandum of Mussolini–Ribbentrop talk.
52   For fine examples, see ibid., IX, 311 (15 July 1938), Pariani to Ciano; X, 344 (28 October 1938), memorandum of Mussolini–Ciano–Ribbentrop talk.
53   For this line, see M. Knox, *Mussolini Unleashed 1939–1941: Politics and Strategy in Fascist Italy's Last War*. Cambridge, 1982.

Chapter 5

The Failure of Détente? German–French Relations between Stresemann and Hitler, 1929–32[1]

Conan Fischer

France's leaders viewed the 1919 Versailles Peace Settlement with mixed feelings. It was the child of fractious inter-Allied bargaining and not a directly negotiated accord with the defeated enemy. For Paris, security from Germany was paramount, but for London and Washington eventual reconciliation with Germany played a significant role. Georges Clemenceau had extracted the best guarantees he could, short of alienating his British and American partners, but the (French) commander in chief of the Allied forces, Field Marshal Ferdinand Foch, was among the more outspoken detractors of the treaty. He boycotted the signing ceremony, lamenting that Kaiser Wilhelm had lost the war but that Clemenceau had squandered the peace.[2] All France could expect was a twenty-year ceasefire in hostilities.

The passage of time proved the Field Marshal uncannily prescient, but his prophetic powers owed as much to luck as to judgement. It was Hitler's government after 1933 that set Europe on the road to war, but in 1919 the future German dictator was merely an obscure army corporal. Rather than anticipating the Third Reich, Foch was questioning the *bona fides* of the fledgling First German (Weimar) Republic and this issue formed part of a wider debate in post-1919 France. The political right and most of the army command wrote off the new republic as nothing more than a fig-leaf masking an incorrigibly malign and revanchist Germany, whereas the left, in opposition until 1924, argued that republican Germany ('the other Germany') should be given a fair break. Each side drew on distinctive aspects of their neighbour's history: the right regarding Prussian militarism as definitive; the left looking to the philosophers, poets and composers of Enlightenment Germany. To suppress these positive forces, the left maintained, would merely play into the hands of the militarists their right-wing colleagues abhorred and feared.

During the first decade of peace no one anticipated a Nazi regime. Were the German Republic to collapse, an unwelcome restoration of the Hohenzollern monarchy seemed most likely and the victor powers were dismayed when in 1923 Gustav Stresemann's government allowed the Prussian Crown Prince to return to Germany from exile, albeit as a private citizen. Did Weimar Germany offer a substantive alternative to the bellicose regimes that preceded and followed it, or did it form part of a baleful continuity in German history that culminated with Hitler and was only finally brought to a close by the Allied victory of 1945?

The career of Gustav Stresemann has dominated much of this debate. He was leader of the centre-right liberal party, the German People's Party (DVP), and after a brief term as Chancellor during the latter half of 1923, made his mark as republican Germany's longest-serving Foreign Minister. Stresemann's work was cut short by a fatal stroke in October 1929, so complicating any evaluation of his legacy. Always a committed parliamentarian, he had nonetheless supported Germany's annexationist programme during the First World War before adopting a more conciliatory line during the early 1920s. Once in office, he fostered positive relations with Britain and the United States and, most significantly, forged a close partnership with his French counterpart, Aristide Briand (also a former annexationist).[3] Thanks to Stresemann's ability to reconcile Allied concerns with a measured degree of German revisionism, Weimar regained key elements of its national sovereignty in exchange for participation in a new European system of multilateral security guarantees.

The Locarno Treaty of 1925 stood at the heart of this process, through which Germany, France and Belgium collectively reaffirmed their mutual Versailles frontiers and also the demilitarized status of the Rhineland, with Britain and Italy serving as guarantors of this negotiated settlement. Less-robust arbitration procedures were agreed for any future disputes over Germany's eastern frontiers, so leaving open the possibility of eventual revision. In 1926 Germany joined the League of Nations, but the move attracted criticism from German nationalist circles. Stresemann was forced to steer a tortuous course between the language of international accommodation and, on occasion, a less-conciliatory tone at home in order to secure the nationalist support required to gain the two-thirds parliamentary majority that international agreements often demanded. This applied in particular to reparations, where Stresemann negotiated milder settlements in 1924 (the Dawes Plan) and 1929 (the Young Plan), but in so doing enraged the German right who refused to recognize the legitimacy of reparations at all. During the Young Plan talks in The Hague, he was able to secure the final Allied military evacuation of the southern Rhineland five years ahead of schedule. Doubtless this was intended in part to provide more moderate sections of the right with sufficient reason to support ratification of the Young Plan, but Stresemann had never made any secret of his personal desire to eliminate the more onerous provisions of the Versailles Treaty.

Not surprisingly, contemporaries were divided over where Stresemann's heart really lay. In 1927 he, Briand and the British Foreign Secretary, Sir Austen Chamberlain, received the Nobel Peace Prize for their achievements, but the prominent French diplomat and economic expert Jacques Seydoux, who had been intimately involved with the reparations question and wider dimensions of Allied-German relations, spoke for many when doubting Stresemann's sincerity. He maintained that while France was prepared to explore every avenue leading to peace, Germany regarded peace merely as one possible means to achieve supremacy on the European continent. 'An abyss', he concluded, 'separated the two conceptions.'[4] Or, as the Permanent Secretary in the French Foreign Office,

Philippe Berthelot, commented to his Prime Minister, Raymond Poincaré, the Germans when it came to rapprochement were 'probably sincere, and also insincere,' although in fairness he added that all great powers displayed a similar degree of ambivalence.[5]

Since 1945 Stresemann's biographers have disagreed profoundly over his motives and ultimate objectives, but something of a consensus has now been reached. An essentially sympathetic picture has emerged of a German patriot, but also a man who sought to accommodate German national recovery within a wider European framework, providing for mutual security and economic collaboration. He remained steadfastly committed to the process of negotiation, always mindful that any agreement had to respect the legitimate concerns of foreign counterparts as much as it advanced German interests.[6]

It was this conviction that had opened the way to collaboration with Briand. The French Foreign Minister appreciated that German consent offered a more stable and potentially enduring guarantee of his country's security than the indefinite coercion of its more populous and economically powerful neighbour. Franco-German rapprochement also soothed British concerns, with London believing that the rehabilitation of Germany offered clear economic and diplomatic advantages. Shortly before Stresemann's death Briand floated notions of some sort of European union with a Franco-German axis at its core, something the German statesman cautiously supported, although without subscribing to the anti-American and protectionist undertones of the French.

Stresemann's death is widely taken to mark the end of this short-lived era of détente, although a series of other setbacks compounded the damage. March 1930 saw the collapse of the last German government formed around the pro-Weimar parties of the centre and centre-left who were the strongest supporters of international rapprochement. In its place emerged an executive resting on Presidential power with an increasingly conservative and nationalist political profile. Like Stresemann, the new Foreign Minister, Julius Curtius, was a liberal, but, it is held, quickly adopted a less politically adept tone despite claiming the mantle of his predecessor. In international relations, tone and presentation count for a great deal. In the case of Curtius this did not work to Germany's advantage.[7] Thereafter, Carl von Schubert, the pro-Western Permanent Secretary (*Staatssekretär*) at the Foreign Office who had collaborated closely with Stresemann, was replaced in mid-1930 by the more abrasive Bernhard von Bülow, whose interests focused on the promotion of German interests in south-eastern Europe. The wider political environment was also becoming less propitious and the Nazi party breakthrough in the September 1930 Reichstag elections testified to the poisonous impact of the Great Depression on German domestic politics and further reduced parliamentary backing for any sort of international conciliation.

Peter Krüger's magisterial history of foreign policy in the Weimar Republic subscribes unreservedly to this interpretation, not least by breaking off its detailed coverage in 1929, after the first Hague Conference and the death of

Gustav Stresemann. While 506 pages are devoted to the first decade of the Republic, Krüger deals with the complex events of its final three years in an epilogue of 48 pages.[8] His verdict on these years is withering. Curtius and von Bülow are dismissed as 'committed opponents of the Locarno spirit and the Stresemann era' and the policies of Chancellor Heinrich Brüning, who also took on the foreign policy portfolio in October 1931, as opaque, often reactive.[9] Under Brüning, Krüger continues, the Foreign Office lost a measure of its traditional power and influence to rival ministries and to a Chancellor given to taking risks in the hope that 'it would turn out alright on the day (daß es gut ginge)'.[10] This brinkmanship left Berlin unresponsive to Briand's European union proposals. Germany also sought to dismantle the Young Plan and adopt an unyielding line at the 1931–2 International Disarmament Conference. This sea change in German foreign policy allegedly isolated the remaining supporters of détente in Berlin, including Karl Ritter in the Foreign Office Economic Section, who was at best ignored and saw his continued efforts to forge new multilateral economic agreements in Europe 'sabotaged'.[11] Similarly the rapprochement-minded German Ambassador to Paris, Leopold von Hoesch, is widely portrayed as something of a voice in the wilderness.[12]

Furthermore, when France honoured the earlier agreement with Stresemann and evacuated its troops from the Rhineland in June 1930 the official response in Germany bordered on the triumphal. Paris, however, viewed the early evacuation as a particularly magnanimous gesture and had anticipated a commensurate show of gratitude from Berlin. Instead, bombastic parades by the German army veterans' association, the Stahlhelm, and speeches laced with nationalist rhetoric – condemned by the British Ambassador to Berlin as a display of 'ingratitude and tactlessness' – appalled the French right.[13] Briand's personal credibility was dealt a blow, despite Curtius's retrospective effort to make amends with a private letter of thanks to the French Foreign Minister and a major public speech in which he identified 'rapprochement' and 'equal rights' as the twin pillars of German foreign policy.[14] The Nazi breakthrough in the September 1930 Reichstag elections further alarmed French opinion and led to a temporary withdrawal of French short-term credits from cash-strapped Germany, but worse was to follow during early 1931.

Once Paris had taken stock of the post-election political landscape in Germany, it came to view Brüning and his Cabinet essentially as a bulwark against the ambitions of the right-wing German National People's Party (DNVP) and the radicals of the NSDAP. There were prospects of a diplomatic thaw and with it French long-term credits to make good the haemorrhage of short-term international funds from Germany. However, in March, Curtius announced the conclusion of customs union agreement between Vienna and Berlin. Stresemann mooted an Austro-German customs union in 1927, but dismissed early action as politically inopportune.[15] Any form of Austro-German union was forbidden by the peace treaties, and Curtius' initiative was widely condemned by international opinion. It met with a robust French response in the form of a legal challenge and French counter-proposals regarding south-east European economic cooperation – the *plan constructif*.[16] The fall of the Austrian banking giant, the Creditanstalt, in May and the subsequent collapse of Austria's public finances forced Vienna to turn to Paris for help, which came with a string of political conditions, including an effective veto of the customs union. German public finances were in similarly desperate straits and although France had gold reserves and money to spare, Paris was no longer willing to offer its neighbour financial assistance without political strings attached. Berlin was unwilling to accept French aid on these terms, instead insisting that Germany be freed from the remaining provisions of the Versailles Treaty and accorded equal rights with the other great powers. Quite apart from the resulting damage to the struggling German economy, this whole affair is often taken to signify the end of Franco-German rapprochement. Among other things it dealt a massive blow to Briand's political credibility in France, arguably costing him the 1931 Presidential elections.[17] On 3 September 1931 Vienna and Berlin finally disowned the doomed customs union, which was in any case declared illegal by the International Court of Justice in The Hague two days later.

Curtius's deeper motives, however, remain less clear. David Kaiser once described the customs union as 'the centrepiece of a carefully elaborated policy of penetration of Southeastern Europe conceived principally by State Secretary Bülow and Foreign Minister Curtius',[18] but Andreas Rödder's biography offers a more sympathetic picture of Curtius. He was undoubtedly a colder, more private and detached personality than Stresemann and, as Sir Horace Rumbold, British Ambassador to Berlin, had reported to his Foreign Minister Arthur Henderson before the German September 1930 election: 'Dr Curtius has, indeed, not for a moment lost his poise, and he is also possessed of the "courage of patience," but the trouble is that he cannot make himself interesting enough, and at the moment he is being overlooked.'[19] Curtius, it seems, promoted the customs union in an ill-judged effort finally to 'make himself interesting' and also divert attention from Germany's domestic crisis. In fact the opposite occurred. Brüning distanced himself from Curtius's scheme and maintained a personal grip on the reparations question, where a fortuitous breakthrough came in June 1931. US President Herbert Hoover proposed a moratorium on international financial obligations, which included Allied war debts to America, and also reparations. Their suspension promised to remove a major burden on the German budget at a stroke and offer relief from the fiscal stringency of the depression years. Meanwhile, Bülow also tried to mend fences with France during mid-1931, leaving a marginalized Curtius to resign his office at the end of September.

Rödder is not alone in speculating that even Stresemann might have fared less well in the malign political climate of the early 1930s.[20] Curtius failed when all is said and done, but he did not, his biographer maintains, ever abandon the values and objectives of his predecessor. The gulf that separated his foreign policy from the aspirations of the German right were profound and earned him a vitriolic reception in parliament, so forcing him to play to the nationalist gallery, just as Stresemann had once done. The difference between the two lay essentially in Stresemann's capacity for squaring his policy of rapprochement with domestic nationalist feeling and Curtius's inability, in less propitious circumstances, to achieve the same.[21]

The reaction of the German Cabinet to Briand's European union plan is a case in point, affording it in Curtius's words 'a first-class funeral'.[22] However, whilst these words are widely taken to reflect the Foreign Minister's personal view, Rödder argues that he was essentially receptive to Briand's proposals, but found himself forced by the Cabinet to adopt a more reserved stance: 'The words "first-class funeral" [served] not as an expression of his own position ... but quite possibly as an ironic take on the Cabinet decision.'[23] In fact, Foreign Office records demonstrate that there was more to the Cabinet discussion than this and that Germany's response to the Briand plan should be viewed in an altogether more positive light.

Deep divisions had surfaced within the German government following the publication of Briand's proposals, which needed to be papered over at the Cabinet meeting before an essentially conciliatory response was sent to Paris on 14 July, in accordance with the Foreign Minister's original wishes. His anger, then, was arguably an immediate reaction to the tone adopted by less-supportive or hostile Cabinet colleagues rather than reflecting subsequent German policy or the quality of German–French relations. Curtius had already canvassed the views of other Ministries on 31 May. His circular regretted that Briand had afforded priority to the political rather than to the economic dimensions of European union, suspecting that Paris wished to set the frontiers of eastern and south-eastern Europe in stone. This cut across German aspirations for an eventual revision of its eastern frontier, which Stresemann had also desired. Curtius continued that Briand's vision of a political Europe could also prejudice Germany's relations with the United States and the Soviet Union, and feared that Britain would remain outwith such an organization. In other words the multilateralism of German foreign policy, which had been advocated consistently by Stresemann, now appeared threatened. Curtius added that anything that duplicated the role and undermined the effectiveness of the League of Nations should equally be avoided. However, he continued that Germany should examine and seek to flesh out the sketchier economic dimensions of Briand's proposals, involving trade, energy, the abolition of customs dues and passport formalities, and the liberalization of foreign residence laws. The eventual German response to Briand would, therefore, focus on economic rather than political affairs.[24]

Not surprisingly, the Economics Ministry replied in the greatest detail, noting that the unsuccessful 1927 World Economic Conference had regarded 'exaggerated economic nationalism and the territorial upheaval [of the Paris Peace Settlement]' as particularly damaging to European prospects.[25] The devastation now being wrought by the global economic crisis made action essential and the Ministry agreed 'with its French counterpart that efforts must be made through a "progressive liberalisation and simplification in the movement of goods, capital and people" across Europe to realize "a rational ordering of production and European trade".'[26] It warned against imposing any onerous external continental tariff to the detriment of global trade and against prejudicing the powers of the League of Nations. However, the Ministry concluded on a positive note: 'that the German government has no objections to European cooperation ... indeed in some areas regards the case as pressing, merely wishing to ensure that ... any duplication of responsibilities is averted'.[27] The Labour Ministry was similarly upbeat, noting that the International Labour Organisation (ILO) was functioning effectively and should not be undermined, but continued that 'this reservation apart I can only welcome the notion of European solidarity with regard to social policy, whether universal or between particular states, both within and outwith the ILO'.[28] It looked to collective wage bargaining on a European level, the elimination of institutional hindrances to the free movement of labour within Europe and the coordination of welfare provision between states. 'To this extent', the Ministry concluded, the Briand plan 'can be supported unreservedly in its essentials'.[29]

On 19 June Bülow opened a meeting of senior civil servants from the various Ministries to take stock of Briand's proposals.[30] He repeated that Germany 'would assume a positive stance' but that the economic dimension needed to be prioritized over the political and that the outcome should avoid undermining the League of Nations in any way.[31] Bülow insisted that the meeting confine itself to positive proposals,[32] but it quickly became apparent that while the Labour, Finance, Economics and Interior Ministries viewed the Briand plan favourably, the Reichswehr, Communications, Agricultural, Justice and Occupied Territories Ministries were either unenthusiastic or openly hostile. Midway through the discussion Bülow handed over the chair to his Deputy, Gerhard Koepke, who had been Head of the Western Desk (*Abteilung* II) since 1923.[33] Koepke was a known supporter of international reconciliation with a particular interest in Franco-German rapprochement and Bülow must have anticipated that his Deputy would bring the meeting to a positive conclusion.[34] Koepke stressed that key Ministries saw opportunities for European cooperation, and that since 'the remaining Ministries have been unable to identify such areas', proposed that the Economics Ministry and Foreign Office flesh out the details of the official German response between them.[35] No one thought to disagree.

The Cabinet meeting in essence changed little, despite Curtius's much-quoted outburst, and on 14 July Ambassador Hoesch delivered the German reply to the French Foreign Ministry on the Quai d'Orsay. Curtius had telegraphed Hoesch three days earlier, stressing that the reply 'made clear Germany's positive attitude to European cooperation and to the peaceful resolution of all European problems'.[36] The political dimensions of the Briand plan remained problematic, he continued, but that Germany was pushing the economic dimension where prospects were particularly promising.[37] The textual balance of the reply itself reflected this strategy. A page and a half was dedicated to Germany's political reservations, couched in general terms, while two and a half pages focused on the economic dimensions of Briand's proposals and stressed the urgency lent to these by the world economic crisis.[38]

If the German response offered Paris half a loaf, the British were less forthcoming and confirmed widespread French suspicions that London's heart was not really in the European project at all.[39] The influential French commentator Jules Sauerwein had observed in *Le Matin* on 7 July that Britain remained attached to its Empire rather than Europe. 'It is clear', he continued, 'that only a Franco-German entente can provide the basis for a European initiative ... Despite all the incidents and upsets, I believe that Germany will stand alongside us to rebuild Europe.'[40] The lukewarm British response merely offered passive support to a process of continental European integration, seen by some British leaders as a parallel to British–American Atlanticism.[41] As if in retrospective confirmation of this Winston Churchill published a lengthy article in the *Berliner Börsen-Courier* in January 1931, observing that Britain's attitude to European integration was 'supportive but non-committal ... [for] we operate in other milieux which are of greater material and emotional significance to us'.[42] Britain proposed that a League of Nations sub-committee look at Briand's scheme and there, during 1931, it died a lingering death.

Briand had anticipated problems from a relatively early stage and offered his German counterparts concessions. On 25 June, during discussions with Hoesch, he conceded that the conclusion of a political statute would require time whereas the economic crisis 'was particularly pressing'.[43] Indeed he could envisage replies to his memorandum that supported the notion of political integration in principle while leaving the detail to future negotiation. This would allow immediate discussion on economic collaboration. He continued that his plan had merely attempted to summarize the content of earlier discussions between himself, Stresemann and others in Geneva (at the League of Nations) rather than encapsulating a specifically French strategy. The British, he hoped, would recognize the value of participating, but he regarded the response of 'a leading continental power' as decisive to the success or failure of his project.[44]

Hoesch met again with Briand on 15 July to deliver verbally a French-language translation of the German reply. The French Minister pressed the Ambassador on Berlin's evident reluctance to underwrite the territorial status quo: 'One should be clear that Europe in its current form rests on treaties and that one would bring about the fragmentation rather than the unification of Europe by placing the problem of treaty revision on the agenda.'[45] Hoesch replied that the treaties themselves 'contained paragraphs that allowed for evolution. Accordingly, Germany was not abandoning the framework of the treaties by raising and advocating thoughts of evolution.' The German reply had only raised the issue at all, he continued, because of a perception in Berlin that France was fixated on the status quo.[46] Briand insisted that he had no objections to Germany seeking change within the framework of the existing treaties as long as such changes were not made a precondition for German participation in the process of European integration.[47] The matter appeared resolved. Briand discussed with Hoesch the other replies to his memorandum and rounded on the Italians, asking 'whether, in their desire to toy with alterations to the European status quo, the Italians had considered giving up the territorial gains they achieved in war at the cost of others'.[48] With the mood suitably lightened, Hoesch was able to report that 'All in all Briand's response to our reply was essentially positive,' helped, he continued, by their personal discussion and the verbal clarification he was able to provide.[49] Thereafter Briand saw to it that key French newspapers responded favourably to the official German reply, presenting it 'as satisfactory and an appropriate contribution to the further development of the European idea' (even if the right-wing press was less complimentary) and also that German foreign correspondents in Paris were briefed positively by the Quai d'Orsay.[50]

When the plan came up for discussion at the League of Nations during early September it was consigned to the long grass of a sub-committee (the Committee of Enquiry into the European Union). This accorded with German wishes not to prejudice the competences of the League itself, but Berlin remained committed to the principle of economic integration. In his speech to the League Curtius was uncharacteristically effusive, advocating rapid economic integration between particular states whose fundamental similarities outweighed any differences. The *Deutsche Allgemeine Zeitung* conceded that his ideas remained vague, but detected in his words 'nothing less than the thought of a Franco-German customs union and a Franco-German customs parliament'.[51] Well-informed readers would recall the important role played by the nineteenth-century German Customs Union (Zollverein) in the process of German unification; a process perhaps to be repeated on a European scale.

With the Committee of Enquiry due to meet in January 1931, the German and French governments spent the intervening months refining their respective positions. The French Prime Minister, André Tardieu, declared on 13 November that Paris would now prioritise the economic question, but added unhelpfully that European economic integration would serve as a double barrier: against Bolshevism, but also against the revision of frontiers. This may have soothed the French right but ruffled German feathers and reinforced Berlin's conviction that the Committee should not take on a life of its own, instead remaining subordinate to the League.[52] However, on 30 December, Briand assured Hoesch that Germany's position 'was more or less in accord with that of France', adding that Paris would play down the political dimension without formally abandoning it.[53] As far as the economy went the two governments agreed to assist the struggling grain producers of south-eastern Europe and settled on a strategy of prior Franco-German consultation to establish a common position before the Committee met.[54] On 13 January, Briand suggested to Hoesch that sub-committees be created to deal with economic questions, standardization of passport formalities and coordination of postal services, but reassured him 'that he did not intend to propose creating a sub-committee to deal with political questions'.[55] Differences remained over whether and when to co-opt non-League members on to the Committee, with Germany keen to involve the Soviet Union and Turkey at an early stage whilst France favoured waiting 'until the European question had moved on from the exploratory phase ... and reached some firm conclusions'.[56]

The Committee of Enquiry met on 16 January and although scheduled to last two days, remained in session for five days. Particular attention was paid to the grave economic and agricultural crisis and, after lobbying from various quarters, it was agreed to include non-League members Iceland, Turkey and the Soviet Union in future economic discussions. A sub-committee was created to draw up a constitution and organizational guidelines for the main Committee but the high water mark of the Briand plan, such as it was, had come and gone. Although Briand remained Foreign Minister, successive governments collapsed and were re-formed around him, doing nothing for the consistency of French policy, even if he remained personally satisfied with the outcome of the January meeting.[57] It is probably worth adding that Briand served in Cabinets formed around the parties of the centre-right, who merely tolerated the rapprochement schemes of France's elder statesman. Although the political left did back the essentials of his foreign policy, it was reluctant to lend support to administrations it abhorred.

All of this reduced the prospects of any far-sighted or altruistic foreign policy emanating from either Paris or Berlin. French uncertainty, British indifference and the distraction of Curtius's Austro-German customs union scheme saw the Briand plan marginalized and eventually abandoned. Despite the meeting of French and German minds during 1930 on the European question, Berlin became more strident as it complained to the League over the treatment of the German minority in Poland. Germany, it seemed, hoped to exploit the League as a tool for treaty revision, whereas the Quai d'Orsay had always regarded it as a guarantor of the status quo. Although Curtius continued to protest his commitment to Franco-German rapprochement, his efforts simultaneously to play to the nationalist gallery in the Reichstag antagonized opinion in Paris. Supporters of rapprochement with Germany tried to make the best of a bad job, but Hoesch warned in January that he had noticed in Briand's utterances 'for the first time somewhat less warmth and somewhat less trust'.[58]

However, the experience of the European union proposal was more than a flash in the pan and extraordinary developments during the latter half of 1931 (almost completely ignored by other historians) demonstrated that whatever divided the two countries, an underlying community of interests continued to offer genuine prospects of enduring détente. These developments took the form of visits by Brüning and Curtius to Paris during July and by the French Premier, Pierre Laval and Briand to Berlin in September. A parallel exchange between the Lord Mayors of the French and German capitals was designed to cement a new era of rapprochement. The Stresemann years had not witnessed such exchanges and it appeared that this low-key but practical work would culminate in far-reaching Franco-German economic integration. This, it was hoped, would offer an alternative route to European unity, through Paris and Berlin, to supplement the glacial progress on the Briand plan in Geneva.

These visits also served to mend fences damaged by the customs union adventure. Despite the tensions of the Great Depression era, the German Foreign Office consistently dedicated time and resources to the cause of Franco-German détente, as did the Quai d'Orsay. Both sides strove to overcome the poisonous legacy of the Great War on a cultural plane: through literary and artistic exchanges, educational placements and the elimination of overtly hostile material from history textbooks.[59] Private initiatives were also supported by Berlin and Paris. These included the subsidization and distribution of a cultural journal, the *Deutsch-Französische Rundschau* (penned by prominent French intellectuals for a German readership), and a French counterpart, the *Revue d'Allemagne et des Pays de Langue allemande* (in which German intellectual and cultural grandees wrote for a French readership).[60] Paris and Berlin also collaborated with the German–French Study Association (Deutsch-französöesische Studienkommission), otherwise known as the Mayrisch Committee after the name of its founder, the Luxembourg industrialist Émile Mayrisch. It was dedicated to overcoming the post-war economic fragmentation of Western Europe and attracted prominent figures from the French and German business and political world, including government ministers.[61] And almost in anticipation of post-1945 Christian Democracy, leaders of the German Catholic Centre Party (Chancellor Brüning's party) exchanged visits and ideas with a small but expanding group of French Catholic counterparts (the Popular Democrats) who had abandoned their longstanding monarchist and nationalist stance. Indeed, during his visit to Paris, Brüning left time for a private meeting with the Popular Democrats' leader, Pensions Minister Champetier de Ribes, 'in the light of their common ideological outlook'.[62]

The very organization of German Foreign Office papers concerning France speaks volumes on the structure of a complex relationship. Ten bulky folders cover '[French] political relations with Germany' during the period 1929–32 and focus on issues such as frontier revision, reparations and disarmament. Filed in chronological order, they make for depressing reading and inform the conventional historical interpretation of the period. However, the Foreign Office weeded out a mass of documentation from its original daybooks, which it filed separately, on 'Efforts to bring about German-French détente'. Eleven thick folders cover the Great Depression era and a further folder documents 'Franco-German rapprochement'. This very substantial collection offers a strikingly different perspective on German–French relations. A further nine folders cover the 1931 ministerial visits, five cultural activities, four the Mayrisch Committee and three Briand's European Memorandum, further confirming the intensity of the effort to promote Franco-German collaboration.[63]

By way of contrast, the records concerning Alsace-Lorraine demonstrate that, French claims to the contrary notwithstanding,[64] Berlin consistently sought to distance itself from the powerful Alsatian autonomist movement that had sprung up in response to ham-fisted efforts by Paris to impose the French language on its German-speaking province. The Foreign Office and Interior Ministry placed severe restrictions on academics keen to research the 1871–1918 period of German rule for fear of a negative French reaction and censored broadcasting output.[65] A particularly fierce battle erupted in Alsace over language use in Catholic-run schools – Alsace was exempted from the secular education policy of inland France. Berlin did intercede with the Vatican, which was condoning efforts by the Bishop of Strasbourg to promote the Francization of the Alsatian education system, bizarrely by importing secular Francophone teachers from elsewhere in France. However, Berlin's primary aim was to dampen growing anger in the German Catholic press over the affair which, it was feared, could complicate relations with Paris.[66] The contrast with policy towards the German minority in Poland could not have been greater.

However, the immediate catalyst for the Franco-German ministerial exchanges was provided by an Anglo-German summit, held on 5 June at Chequers. British ministers regarded Brüning as the final barrier against the reactionaries of the DNVP and the radicals of the NSDAP and heard him out with a sympathetic ear. However, London looked to Washington for any international rescue package for the German economy and as rumours circulated of a major American initiative Paris came to feel increasingly isolated. A fortnight later the French diplomat Oswald Hesnard sounded out Berlin over the Chequers visit, adding 'that he had heard it asked whether the two gentlemen [Brüning and Curtius] would now pay a visit to Paris'.[67] A delicate exchange followed over the niceties of such an arrangement: 'We Germans only go where we are invited', but that 'the Chancellor and Foreign Minister would accept an invitation to Paris as enthusiastically as they had the extremely kind invitation to Chequers'.[68] Some colourful unofficial diplomacy followed as a Paris diamond merchant, M. Ascher, a colleague in Cologne, Herr Goldschmidt, and the Convener of the Zionist Association in France, Senator Godard, tried to engineer an invitation from Laval to Brüning. A slightly bemused Hoesch concluded that 'it would be appropriate to put the affair on an official footing' and, with explicit backing from Brüning and Curtius, began to prepare the ground for the visit.[69]

The Hoover Moratorium on international financial obligations was announced on 20 June, and on 23 June Brüning responded with a broadcast to the nation. He dedicated a large part of his speech to German–French relations, which he described as particularly important, insisting that despite 'certain difficulties and obstacles ... with mutual goodwill ways and means could be found to emphasise areas of agreement and common interest'. European cooperation and positive economic relations with the New World would only be secured, he continued, when 'our two great peoples ... have overcome the moral burden of the past and turn to face the spiritual, economic, and political future together ...'[70] French press reaction varied. *Le Journal* regarded the broadcast 'as the most important announcement by a German statesman since the day on which Stresemann moved to end the "Battle of the Ruhr" and over the following days left-wing papers such as *République, Populaire* and *La Victoire* heaped praise on Brüning. *Volonté* demanded that his 'highly conciliatory and sincere proposals be reciprocated without hesitation', but the right-wing press was largely hostile. *Echo de Paris* demanded to know 'what Germany wanted', continuing that 'it was dangerous to let a man like Briand, who was so lacking in diplomatic culture and caution, sit at a table with Brüning'.[71]

The visit was mooted because difficulties had multiplied during the spring. However on 6 July Brüning promised not to divert the budgetary savings offered by Hoover's Moratorium from reparations to armaments[72] and while some members of the French Cabinet sought further reassurances from Germany, Laval and Hoesch agreed that preconditions for the visit were best avoided.[73]

When the German delegation arrived in Paris on 18 July, it was greeted with cries of 'Long live peace, long live Laval, long live France!' Hoesch judged the atmosphere 'not unfriendly'.[74] The two days of talks and meetings seemed to achieve little of substance. The official communiqué recorded that 'both sides recognised the importance of this meeting and emphasised that it marked the beginning of cooperation based on trust', economic and political, but without any further elaboration.[75] The visit did, however, lend fresh impetus to the wider process of rapprochement. Longstanding semi-official efforts to coordinate economic activity and so bring about 'a political rapprochement between the two countries' were intensified and supported by a remarkable number of politicians and business leaders,[76] although they tended to founder on a tangle of competing ambitions, institutional and personal.[77] Of greater immediate significance was the replacement of Pierre de Margerie, a diplomat of the old school, as Ambassador to Berlin by the junior Cabinet minister, André François-Poncet, who knew Germany well and had an excellent command of the language. Paris 'stressed that by appointing a Cabinet member to this important post, it wished to continue the negotiations initiated in Paris in an atmosphere of trust'[78] and François-Poncet declared that Berlin was a higher priority than his domestic political ambitions.[79] He immediately opened discussions with Hoesch over the impending French ministerial visit to Berlin.[80]

On 17 September Bülow informed Hoesch that he viewed the visit firstly as a means to achieve 'a normalisation and improvement in Franco-German relations' and secondly to develop a common German–French strategy to address the global economic crisis. This 'economic cooperation [would] simultaneously mark the beginning of wider-ranging German-French rapprochement'.[81] Bülow envisaged extensive economic cooperation, including joint Franco-German initiatives in third countries and German economic engagement in the French colonies, particularly Morocco. French officials were to prove accommodating here.[82] He counselled against discussing more sensitive problems, such as the Saarland or reparations, and hoped that Franco-German détente would also breathe fresh life into Briand's European union proposals. 'These must not merely remain on paper,' he continued, 'but be made reality through active German-French collaboration.'[83] Bülow, then, was clearly far less confrontational or anti-Western than the literature generally allows.

The agenda for the visit was finalized during a series of meetings between German and French diplomats. The realities of the Franco-German relationship precluded anything spectacular, but they agreed to announce in Berlin the creation of a Franco-German Joint Commission of senior politicians, officials and business figures to promote wide-ranging economic cooperation between the two countries and with third parties.[84] The *modus operandi* of the Joint Commission would be decided in Berlin, the practicalities of economic collaboration left to the new organization itself. The visit, Laval assured a press conference, would offer the possibility of 'active cooperation between our two great peoples' and was, therefore, 'more than a simple act of courtesy'.[85]

When the French statesmen arrived in Berlin on 27 September they were greeted by large, enthusiastic crowds, and the Nazi and Communist paramilitaries who plagued the streets of late-Weimar Berlin were nowhere to be seen. Brüning's welcome echoed his July broadcast, declaring that 'the significance of this event is best characterised by the fact that since the Congress of Berlin [1878] ... no senior French statesman had spent time in Berlin in an official capacity'. 'European peace', he continued, 'would only appear guaranteed when the two great neighbouring peoples of Germany and France had spiritually overcome their past and turned their gaze to a common future, cultural, economic and political.'[86] The official joint communiqué looked to 'a stable and trusting' Franco-German relationship before turning to the structure and purpose of the Joint Commission. Led by members of the two governments and with a permanent secretariat, it would begin its work as quickly as possible, meeting in each country in turn. The structure and development of Franco-German economic relations, including cartel arrangements and trade, formed its remit 'without ignoring the interests of third parties and the need for wider international collaboration ... The representatives of the German and French governments hope in this way to have created the basis for cooperation open to all, the first stage of a process of unification responding to the necessities of the moment.'[87] Days later Belgium asked to be included in the Commission 'given Belgium's close [economic] links with Germany and France'.[88]

Just four days before his resignation Curtius complained that the visit had achieved little of substance beyond the establishment of the Joint Commission, regretting that issues such as disarmament or reparations had remained off the agenda.[89] However, since both sides had previously agreed to avoid contentious issues, his professed disappointment was curious at best.[90] Creation of the Joint Commission had been the purpose of the visit. Berthelot for one spoke of 'an unmistakable and enormous change in the atmosphere', while a sickly Briand declared that 'in the light of his Berlin experience he would hang on as Foreign Minister for as long as his health allowed'.[91] And in fact Curtius spent his final days in office working on the internal structure of the Joint Commission, proposing among other things that the two Foreign Ministers, or their nominees, chair the meetings, that economic experts be seconded to the Commission when appropriate, that a Press Office be created and means found to finance the activities of the Commission.[92]

During October German and French politicians and diplomats busied themselves with the practicalities of the Commission. On 3 November Brüning met its German members to announce that four Sub-Commissions had been created, the first to deal with overall Franco-German economic relations (the 1927 Trade Treaty and private cartels), the second transport, the third closer integration of particular economic sectors, and the fourth Franco-German collaboration elsewhere in the world.[93] The Foreign Office Economic Section and its Director, Karl Ritter, were to preside over the German input to the Commission.[94] On 13 and 14 November Laval chaired the first meeting of the Commission in Paris, to be followed until mid-1932 by regular meetings of the parent body and its Sub-Commissions.[95]

For all this the Commission's very existence has been largely ignored by historians, arguably because its achievements fell far short of expectations and were overshadowed by the disintegration of the Weimar Republic during the latter half of 1932. By then, economic forces had already conspired against the Commission rather than offering a road to détente. During 1931, the chill winds of the Great Depression reached France. The Trade Ministry turned to protectionism to shelter its struggling domestic industries from foreign competition. Quotas were imposed on a widening range of imported goods and commodities. Meanwhile, German businesses had been starved of foreign currency since the banking crisis of summer 1931 and were less able to import than before. The result was a growing balance of trade surplus with France, leading officials in Paris and hard-pressed businessmen to consider partially rescinding the 1927 Franco-German Trade Agreement, which exempted a wide range of German products from punitive tariffs or quota restrictions. The Quai d'Orsay remained committed to rapprochement, but was unable to staunch the protectionist tide.[96] It only remained to be determined how and on what terms to impose quotas on imports from Germany.

Rather than proceeding by official diktat, it was agreed where possible to resolve issues in discussions between existing private cartel partners within the framework of the Joint Commission.[97] This was no accident, for existing Franco-German cartel agreements were perceived as a major and substantive force along the road to rapprochement.[98] German representatives therefore perceived this as a lesser evil and went along with the process, but the mediation in detail of French protectionist policy was a far cry from the almost idealistic ambitions of mid-1931, which had included a Franco-German customs union.

Not surprisingly, longstanding problems such as the armaments question filled the vacant political space and a series of incidental disasters compounded the damage. Briand died in March and Brüning was dismissed as Chancellor and Foreign Minister by President von Hindenburg in May 1932. The publication of Stresemann's memoirs, privately edited and uncensored by the German Foreign Office, contained frank expositions and correspondence that cast significant doubt on the sincerity of his relationship with Briand. Many French supporters of rapprochement felt betrayed and berated their German contacts – and relatives – over the apparent duplicity of the great Weimar statesman.[99]

Upsets had occurred in the past and had eventually been smoothed over. A centre-left coalition was elected to power in France during April, which was committed in principle to continued détente. Franz von Papen, who replaced Brüning, was a longstanding member of the Mayrisch Committee and a declared Francophile. Desperate efforts were made to breathe new life into the Joint Commission, but Papen's government was now struggling to contain Hitler's ambitions and maintain the legal process of government on any terms at all. French politics also remained fractious and the continuity that Briand's presence in a succession of governments had lent French foreign policy was sorely missed. Contrary to the impression left by most historians, an intensive and sustained effort to forge a Franco-German partnership had engaged Paris and Berlin during the crisis-wracked Depression years, but the moment had passed. It would not come again until the lessons of the Second World War had been learned.

Notes

1   I would like to thank the British Academy and the Elizabeth Barker Endowment for generously funding the archival research on which this chapter is based.
2   M. MacMillan, *Peacemakers: The Paris Conference of 1919 and its Attempt to End War*. London, 2001, p. 486.
3   J. Bariéty, 'Aristide Briand et la sécurité de la France en Europe, 1919–1932' in S. A. Schuker (ed.), *Deutschland und Frankreich. Vom Konflikt zur Aussöhnung. Die Gestaltung der westeuropäischen Sicherheit 1914–1963*. Munich, 2000, pp. 117–23.
4   Quoted in S. Jeannesson, 'L'Europe de Jacques Seydoux', *Revue Historique* CCXIX/I, p. 141.
5   Quoted in A. Adamthwaite, *Grandeur and Misery: France's Bid for Power in Europe 1914–1940*. London, 1995, p. 125.
6   The most important recent works are: C. Baechler, *Gustave Stresemann (1878–1929): De l'imperialisme à la sécurité collective*. Strasbourg, 1996; J. Wright, *Gustav Stresemann: Weimar's Greatest Statesman*. Oxford, 2002. For a brief discussion of earlier, more critical works: P. Krüger, 'Der abgebrochene Dialog: die Deutschen Reaktionen auf die Europavorstellungen Briands in 1929' in A. Fleury (ed.), *Le Plan Briand d'Union fédérale européenne*. Bern, 1998, pp. 290–1.
7   A. Rödder, *Stresemanns Erbe: Julius Curtius und die deutsche Außenpolitik 1929–1931*. Paderborn, 1996, pp. 40, 84, 221–2.
8   P. Krüger, *Die Außenpolitik der Republik von Weimar*. Darmstadt, 1985.
9   Ibid., pp. 513, 514.
10 Ibid., pp. 518–19, quote on p. 515.
11 Krüger, 'Der abgebrochene Dialog', pp. 300–1.
12 Martin Vogt, 'Die deutsche Haltung zum Briand-Plan im Sommer 1930: Hintergründe und politisches Umfeld der Europapolitik des Kabinetts Brüning' in Fleury (ed.), *Le Plan Briand*, pp. 324–5.

13 Ibid., p. 319.
14 Rödder, *Stresemanns Erbe*, pp. 108–10.
15 D. Kaiser, *Economic Diplomacy and the Origins of the Second World War: Germany, Britain, France, and Eastern Europe, 1930–1939*. Princeton, 1980, p. 27.
16 Ibid., pp. 33–4.
17 F. Knipping, *Deutschland, Frankreich und das Ende der Locarno-Ära 1928–1931*. Munich, 1987, p. 216.
18 Kaiser, *Economic Diplomacy*, p. 27.
19 Quoted in Rödder, *Stresemanns Erbe*, p. 84
20 Ibid., p. 93. See also Wright, *Gustav Stresemann*, pp. 517–18.
21 Rödder, *Stresemanns Erbe*, pp. 14–15, 27ff, 78–9.
22 Krüger, *Die Außenpolitik*, p. 529.
23 Rödder, *Stresemanns Erbe*, pp. 116–17.
24 Auswärtiges Amt, Politisches Archiv (hereafter AA), Handakten-Sammlung, Ges. Seeliger. Briand Memorandum, R105491: Auswärtiges Amt, Vbd. 1530, signed Curtius, Berlin, 31 May 1930.
25 AA, R105491, zu Vbd. 1873/30, Vertraulich! undated, p. 1.
26 Ibid., p. 2.
27 Ibid., p. 9.
28 AA, R105491, Abschrift Vbd. 1803, signed Stegerwald, Berlin, 18 June 1930.
29 Ibid., p. 9.
30 AA, Büro Reichsminister. Bund der Vereinigten Staaten von Europa. Antwort der deutschen Regierung auf das Briand-Memorandum 11.7.1930, R28630: Aufzeichnung über die Ressortbesprechung vom 19 Juni 1930 über das französische Europa-Memorandum, Berlin, 19 June 1930, D702772–9.
31 Ibid., D702772–3.
32 Ibid., D702773–4.
33 Ibid., D702776.
34 Koepke wore his heart on his sleeve in a letter to Pierre Viénot, co-founder of the Mayrisch Committee on 5 December 1932: AA, R70544, H021103.
35 Ibid., D702777.
36 AA, R28630: Abschrift. Vbd. 2061 Ang. 1, signed Curtius, Berlin, 11 July 1931, D702896.
37 Ibid., D702896–8.
38 AA, R28630: Antwort der Deutschen Regierung auf das Memorandum der Französischen Regierung vom 1. Mai 1930 über die 'Organisation einer europäischen Bundesordnung', Berlin, 11 July 1930, D702899–905.
39 Thus: Andrea Bosco, 'The British Foreign Office and the Briand Plan' in Fleury (ed.), *Plan Briand*, pp. 347–58.
40 AA, R28630: Telegramm Paris Nr.672, signed Hoesch, Paris, 7 July 1930, D702885&6.
41 Ibid., D702884–5. See also Bosco, 'British Foreign Office', p. 357.
42 AA, R28631: Winston Churchill, 'Die Vereinigten Staaten von Europa', *Berliner Börsen-Courier*, 11 January 1931.
43 AA, R28630: Telegramm Paris Nr. 626, signed Hoesch, Paris, 26 June 1930, D702828.
44 Ibid., D702828–30. Quote on D702830.
45 AA, R28630: Telegramm Paris Nr. 715, signed Hoesch, Paris, 15 July 1930, D702911.
46 Ibid.
47 Ibid.
48 Ibid., D702913.
49 Ibid.
50 AA, R28630: Telegramm Paris Nr. 719, signed Hoesch, Paris, 16 July 1930, D702917.
51 AA, R28631: 'Gefahr einer Illusion', *Deutsche Allgemeine Zeitung*, 17 September 1930.
52 AA, R28631: Abschrift. Vbd. 3679 II, signed Curtius, Berlin, 20 December 1930, D702984–9.
53 AA, R28631: Telegramm Paris Nr. 1191, signed Hoesch, Paris, 31 December 1930, D702997–8.
54 AA, R28631: Telegramm Paris Nr. 19, signed Hoesch, Paris, 6 January 1931, D703011–13 & D703052 as in note 53.

55 AA, R28631: Telegramm Paris Nr. 52, signed Hoesch, Paris, 14 January 1931, D703051–2.
56 Ibid.
57 AA, R28631: Telegramm Paris Nr. 171, signed Hoesch, Paris, 11 February 1931, D703146–7.
58 AA, Politische Beziehungen zwischen Deutschland und Frankreich, R70504: Telegramm Paris Nr. 53, signed Hoesch, Paris, 13 January 1931, K240572.
59 AA, Gegenseitige Besuche führender Staatsmänner, R70568: Aufzeichnung über kulturelle Beziehungen mit Frankreich, 24 September [1931], H026316–19; Die Deutsch-Französische Studienkommission, R70576: Aktivierung der Deutsch-Französischen Zusammenarbeit auf dem Gebiet des Auswanderungswesens und der Kulturpolitik, signed Freytag, Berlin, 5 October 1931, H027126–31; R70576: Aufzeichnung, signed Sievers, undated, H027132–6; Paris. Beziehungen Frankreichs zu Deutschland. Paris 563b: Exposition du Musee 'Guerre ou Paix' et des Livres scolaires (Bordeaux 15–30 Juin 1931).
60 AA, Die Deutsch-Französische Gesellschaft (Grautoff) und deren Veröffentlichungen, R70550–R70554. For a summary of personnel and activities: R70553: Deutsch-Französische Gesellschaft e.V., signed Grautoff, Berlin, 8 November 1929, H023496–505.
61 Relevant documentation in AA, here R70576–9.
62 AA, R70567: Telegramm Paris Nr. 779, signed Feßler, Hoesch, Paris, 18 July 1931, H025923. See also Paris 563c: Deutsche Botschaft Paris A 2521. Betr. Französische Katholiken zum Verständigungsproblem Deutschland-Frankreich, signed Kühn, Paris, 10 July 1931.
63 File references in: Politisches Archiv des Auswärtigen Amts, Findbuch Auswärtiges Amt 1920–1945 (Kent 1).
64 For example: AA, Elsass-Lothingen A, R30201b: No 311 Sénat Année 1932. Session Ordinaire, 18 March 1932. Services d'Alsace et de Lorraine, pp. 56–60.
65 Thus: AA, Politische Beziehungen Elsaß-Lothringens zu Deutschland, R71141: stv. Dir. Zu II Fr., signed v. Bülow, Berlin, 16 August 1929, L442290–2; R71141: Aufzeichnung. Zu II Fr. 2626, signed Bassenheim, Berlin, 7 November 1929, L442295–6; R71141: Abschrift III 1403/3.1., signed Prof. Dr Aurich, Prof. Dr Wolfram, Frankfurt a.M., 3 January 1930, L442326–7; R71141: II Fr 1058, signed B., Berlin, 30 April 1930, L442343–4.
66 AA, R30201a: Nr II Fr 110, signed Bülow, Berlin, 9 January 1929, E439510–17; R30201a: Deutsche Botschaft beim päpstlichen Stuhle, Nr. 11, signed Bergen, Rome, 20 January 1929, E439520–24.
67 AA, R70567: V.L.R. Reinebeck, G.A., signed Reinebeck, Berlin, 19 June 1931, H025863.
68 Ibid.
69 AA, R70567: R.M., St.S., Reichskanzlei, Aufzeichnung, unsigned, Berlin, 23 June 1931, H025864–7.
70 AA, R70567: Wolff's Telegraphisches Büro, 82. Jahrgang, Nr. 1307, Berlin, 24 June 1931.
71 AA, R70567: Ref.: LS Graf Saurma. Betrifft: das Echo der Reichskanzlerrede vom 23.VI.31 in Frankreich. Aufzeichnung. Unsigned, undated, H025885–90.
72 Rödder, Stresemanns Erbe, p. 252.
73 AA, R70567: Telegramm Paris Nr 737, signed Hoesch, Paris, 8 July 1931, H025905–8.
74 AA, R70567: Telegramm Paris, Kzl. Nr. 1132, signed Fessler – Hoesch, Paris, 18 July 1931.
75 AA, R70567: Anlage. Das Communiqué über die Deutsch-Französischen Verhandlungen. Unsigned, undated, H025933–4.
76 AA, R70567; Deutsche Botschaft A2771, signed Hoesch, Paris, 20 July 1931, HO25971–8. Quote on H025975; R70576: Telegramm Paris Nr. 809, signed Hoesch, Paris, 30 July 1931, HO26937–8.
77 Briefly here: AA, R70576: Auswärtiges Amt II Fr. 2526, signed Friedberg, Berlin, 26 August 1931, H027005–9; R70576: Deutsche Botschaft Paris A 3189, signed Forster, Paris, 5 September 1931, H027041–4.
78 AA, R70567: Signed Kordt, Berlin, 3 August 1931, H025964–5.
79 AA, Paris 563c: Dr Kurt Ihlefeld, Unterredung mit François-Poncet, Paris, 20 August 1931.
80 AA, R70576: Telegramm Paris, Nr. 813, signed Hoesch, Paris, 31 July 1931, H026944–9.
81 AA, R70567: e.o. II Fr. 2815. St. S., signed Bülow, Berlin, 17 September 1931, H026103–13. (Quote on H026103.)
82 AA, R70577: Telegramm Paris Nr. 1094, signed Hoesch, Paris, 13 October 1931, H027251–2.

83   AA, R70567: e.o. II Fr. 2815. St. S., signed Bülow, Berlin, 17 September 1931, H026103–13.
84   AA, R70568: II Fr 2840. Schnellbrief, signed [Im Auftrag] von Friedberg, Berlin, 18 September 1931, H026149–50; R70568: Telegramm Paris Nr. 970, signed Forster, Paris, 21 September 1931, H026228–32; R70568: Telegramm Paris Nr. 974, signed Forster, Paris, 22 September 1931; R70568: Telegramm Paris Nr. 978, signed Forster, Paris, 23 September 1931, H026296.
85   AA, R70568: Telegramm Paris Nr. 1008, signed Forster, Paris, 26 September 1931, H026355–6.
86   AA, R70569: Auswärtiges Amt II Fr. 3016, 28 September 1931, Aussprache des RK, HO26371–4. Quotes on H026371&2.
87   AA, R70569: 'Communiqué Officiel', Le Temps, No. 25803, 29 September 1931; 'Communiqué über den Abschluß der Deutsch-Französischen Besprechungen', Nacht-Ausgabe, Wolff's Telegraphisches Büro, 82. Jahrgang, Nr. 2048, Berlin, 28 September 1931.
88   AA, R70577: Deutsche Gesandtschaft Brüssel A 326. Betr.: Die Deutsch-Französische Wirtschaftskommission, Brussels, 9 October 1931.
89   AA, R70569: e.o. II Fr. 3062, signed Curtius, Berlin, 29 September 1931.
90   Compare with: AA, Pressestimmen zum französischen Gegenbesuch in Berlin, R70575: 'Bilan politique de la première journée d'entretiens Franco-Allemands', Le Journal, 14225, 28 September 1931; 'Die Deutsch-Französischen Tage. Warmer Empfang der französischen Staatsmänner in Berlin. Wirtschafts-Abmachungen im Vordergrund', Berliner Tageblatt, 457, 28 September 1931.
91   AA, R70569: Telegramm Bern Nr. 49, signed Adolf Müller, Bern, 2 October 1931, H026503.
92   AA, R70576: Abschrift. Auswärtiges Amt Nr. II Fr 3088, signed Curtius, Berlin, 2 October 1931.
93   AA, R70578: 'Erste Sitzung der deutschen Mitglieder des Deutsch-Französischen Wirtschaftskomitees', Wolff's Telegraphisches Büro, 82. Jahrgang, Nr 2311, Berlin, 3 November 1931.
94   Compare with Krüger, 'Der abgebrochene Dialog', pp. 299–301, where Ritter is seen as essentially excluded from European affairs by mid-1930.
95   AA, R70878: Deutsche Abteilung der Deutsch-Französischen Wirtschaftskommission, No. W.5592, signed Ritter, Berlin, 23 November 1931, H027344–6.
96   AA, R70578: Abschrift zu II Fr. 3582. Aktenvermerk, signed Ritter, Berlin, 9 November 1931, H027342–3.
97   AA, R70578: Abschrift. Auswärtiges Amt. II Fr. 3582, signed von Bülow, Berlin, 11 November 1931.
98   Clemens August Wurm, 'Internationale Kartelle und die Deutsch-Französische Beziehungen 1924–1930: Politik, Wirtschaft, Sicherheit', in Schuker (ed.), Deutschland und Frankreich, pp. 98–103.
99   For example: AA, Memoiren Stresemann, R70518: Deutsche Botschaft Paris A 2028, signed Hoesch, Paris, 13 May 1932, E684801–3; R70518: Telegramm Paris Nr. 741, signed Hoesch, Paris, 23 May 1932, E684835–6.

Chapter 6

Hitler, German Foreign Policy and the Road to War: A German Perspective

Lars Lüdicke
Translated by Peter Bierl

The Third Reich is one of the most heavily investigated areas of historical study.[1] Even experts have difficulty coping with the vast outpouring of literature on the subject. The crimes of Hitler's dictatorship are daunting and tax historians' claims to objectivity. The historiography of National Socialism has centred on a key question: how could a man like Hitler gain power and carry out such immense crimes? Various answers to that conundrum fill whole libraries and a fully satisfying answer remains elusive.[2] Immediately after the end of the war, two studies were published by Friedrich Meinecke and Ludwig Dehio that tried to explain the 'German tragedy'. Both attempted to fix Hitler's rule within the broad sweep of German history.[3] The foundation of the Institute of Contemporary History in Munich in 1950 led to a dedicated research archive being established to study Nazism.[4] Researchers then focused on the establishment of the dictatorship, the part of Hitler, the terror of the SS state, the mass murder during war time and resistance.

As early as 1941, Ernst Fraenkel emerged with his empirical study about 'Dual State', which challenged the image of a monolithic 'Führer State'. He pointed out the Janus-faced reality of the Third Reich and sketched out typical dualism of where the conventional rule of law (*herkömmlicher Normenstaat*) and a terrorist-like acting state (*terroristischer Maßnahmenstaat*) functioned alongside each other. The following year, Franz Neumann in his deeply influential book *Behemoth* delivered the first major structural analysis of the Nazi state.[5]

By the mid 1960s German historians building on these two pioneering studies had produced a number of studies confirming the chaotic nature of Hitler's rule. The result was a paradigm change in German thinking. The classic view of the primacy of Hitler and foreign policy over decision making in Nazi Germany was pushed aside by a younger generation of historians and replaced by a close examination of social history.[6] Such a widening of the debate away from the person of Hitler did produce many interesting new insights about the inner structure of the Third Reich and on whether the concept of totalitarianism was really applicable to Germany.[7] This 'polycratic model' greatly reduced Hitler's role as 'a mere executioner of proceedings that were only understandable as impersonal'.[8] Hitler was no more a protagonist who was acting autonomously, but merely presiding over 'institutional chaos'. Such a depersonalization of history seemed to discredit the popular genre of Hitler biographies, which had depicted Hitler as an all-powerful dictator following a clear plan for power, aggression and genocide.[9]

The view that Hitler's personality, ideas and strength of will drove foreign policy was advanced primarily by historians working outside Germany. The first major 'intentionalist' interpretation that became widely known was the biography of Adolf Hitler written by the British historian Alan Bullock, which was published for the first time in 1952 and became regarded as a benchmark for many years. But Bullock's main thesis was unmistakably stamped by an image of Hitler that was already shaped by Konrad Heiden, a journalist observer of the Nazi movement in the 1930s. Bullock presented the German dictator – as Heiden had done – as an opportunistic politician seeking power with a 'revengeful lust for destruction which eventually led to self-destruction'.[10] Drawing on the memoirs of the former Nazi politician and President of the Senate of Danzig, Hermann Rauschning, who migrated into exile in 1936, Bullock depicted Hitler's rule as a 'revolution of nihilism' with foreign policy aims that had no fully thought out final objective.[11]

Yet Bullock's thesis has lost credence as time has gone by.[12] A more influential study, as far as German historians are concerned, is the British historian Hugh R. Trevor-Roper's essay on 'Hitler's War Aims' in which he developed the theory of the Nazi leader following a master plan he outlined in his 1920s autobiography *Mein Kampf*. The two most persistent themes in Hitler's writings were a burning desire to gain *Lebensraum* (living space) in Eastern Europe through a war of conquest against the Soviet Union and a passionate and radical determination to find a 'Final Solution' to the 'Jewish Question'.[13] This classic 'intentionalist perspective' of a programmatic dictator with clear ideological purposes underpinning his policy was viewed by German historians as more applicable than Bullock's thesis of a power-greedy and ruthless opportunist pursuing unclear and over-ambitious aims without any real ideological zeal.

Yet one outcome of Trevor-Roper's emphasis on the radical aims of Hitler's rule led German historians to place Nazi ideology centre stage. The subject of the aims of Hitler's foreign policy assumed a great part of what became known as the intentionalist–functionalist debate. The 'intentionalists' favoured the programmatic and protagonist-centred view, underlining the leading role of Hitler, his will and his decisive influence over key events in foreign policy. The 'structuralists' proclaimed an impromptu development of policy, with no masterplan. The followers of the 'intentionalist' interpretation tried to understand a complex situation with multiple factors, with the help of social and historical concepts. The structuralists viewed the war as a result of a polycratic system of domination combined with a series of ad hoc and ill-thought-out decisions with the interaction of rival institutions and protagonists that produced a radicalization of policy, which developed out of unforeseen circumstances. By contrast, the intentionalists view Hitler's radical ideology as the decisive factor, because from the very start of his leadership as German chancellor he aimed at conquering new territory and imperial rule based on racist doctrines. They suggest the racist dogma was essential to the foreign policy of the Nazis.[14] The person, politics and the ideology of Hitler became the key point of reference because to intentionalists Hitler was the driving force of the Third Reich.

It was Eberhard Jäckel who published a pioneering work about the ideology of the dictator, which gave German research a decisive push. Trevor-Roper had only remarked briefly about Hitler's 'plan' whereas Jäckel drafted a sophisticated and detailed layout of Hitler's programme and pointed out that the Holocaust was a constituent part of the drive for *Lebensraum*. Jäckel drew not just on *Mein Kampf*, but also on a second unpublished volume that was not published in his lifetime ('Hitler's Secret Book'). Jäckel described Hitler following a 'stage-by-stage' plan in foreign policy to achieve *Lebensraum* and racial domination. This interpretation emphasized the driving force behind foreign policy was Hitler's unshakable and radical objectives.[15]

Entirely in line with this view, regarding Hitler as the most powerful force in foreign policy, was the work of Andreas Hillgruber.[16] He went even further than Jäckel (who regarded Hitler's territorial objective as conquering Eastern Europe) and deduced that a total global dominance was the ultimate aim. Hillgruber claimed Hitler first aimed to achieve supremacy all over Europe, then over the vast territory of the Soviet Union and the Middle East. The establishment of a self-sufficient empire in continental Europe – which could resist any blockade – would have served as the basis to fight successfully for global power. Hillgruber and Jäckel represent the two factions of the 'continentalists' who see Hitler as attempting European hegemony and the 'globalists' who see world domination as the final goal. Yet both highlight the conquering of living space and imposing the rule of a master-race as the centrepiece of Hitler's foreign policy.[17]

This version of Hitler's long-term aims has been disputed by the structuralists. They reject the idea of Hitler as having precise long-term aims, but rather see him as someone who responded flexibly and opportunistically to permanently changing situations to protect his popularity, prestige and the support of his followers. He was forced to integrate important elites like the leaders of the army and big business into his foreign policy objectives. Last but not least, he had to take account of pressures from state, the Nazi Party, which urged him to fulfil the promises of Nazi propaganda. In short, foreign policy success became a Hitlerian strategy to sidetrack unresolved problems of home affairs.[18]

The leading structuralist Martin Broszat argued that it was not Hitler who determined the framework of Nazi politics, but social and economic pressures beyond his control. He showed that the structure of power in the Third Reich led to an unplanned dynamic radicalization (*dynamische Radikalisierung*), which ended up in genocide and a degree of destruction in Europe never seen before. According to Broszat, Hitler's eccentric style of administration led to an inherent rat race between administrations and individuals, which developed a devastating momentum. Broszat portrayed Hitler as a man who preferred to delay decisions and was often influenced by others who were close to him and in many ways this made him a 'weak dictator'. This style of administration allowed great autonomy for other key figures and groups to put their own radical policies in motion. In this way the ideological axioms of Hitler simply became an ideological metaphor, as individuals operated radical policies they believed conformed with Hitler's radical ideological agenda. According to Broszat, the Holocaust even more than the war was not the result of a fixed precise and practical agenda, but a purposeful goal carried out by middle-ranking bureaucrats. [19]

Influenced by Broszat's interpretation, Hans Mommsen argued against any uni-dimensional interpretation of National Socialist objectives, as Hitler was not the decisive factor nor did he have any fixed ideological convictions. It was not, argued Mommsen, Hitler's ideological views that were the driving force for war and Holocaust, but a complex structure of decision-making. This structure was the result of the polycratic system of domination, which produced a cumulative radicalism that ultimately led to military aggression and genocide.[20] In other words, the structure was central, not Hitler's personality.[21] Mommsen views German foreign policy as not based on long-term planning at all, but as the result of a projection of domestic politics into foreign affairs.[22] Foreign policy was conducted in a permanent state of emergency, which was typical of Nazi rule in so many domestic areas. This kind of strategy for foreign policy sometimes caused many dynamic victories mainly through bluff, which then drove the regime to dare warfare on a continental scale, even though the armed forces were not prepared for a long war of attrition. Put this way, the foreign policy of the Nazis was domestic politics projected to the outside world and permanent action became essential to the regime – a situation that ruled out any hope of a political stabilization.[23] Triumphs in German foreign policy came to be seen by Hitler as the only way to maintain power and the popularity of a regime that was failing to fulfil domestic demands for 'guns and butter'. Mommsen, like Broszat, explains German foreign policy as resulting from complex structures and proceedings: both put Hitler's personal responsibility into perspective, without the intention to lower his guilt and responsibility. [24]

Yet the idea of Hitler as a 'weak dictator' has increasingly come under sustained attack. In a major biography published in 1973 Joachim Fest once more emphasized the decisive role of Hitler and his ideology, particularly in the realm of foreign policy. [25] Even if Fest was criticized and in some aspects even corrected, his interpretation remains deeply influential among German historians.[26] In the wake of Fest's study, a succession of new biographies about the dictator followed, partly supporting it and partly disputing it. The flood of books on the Nazi dictator became known in Germany as 'The Hitler Wave'.[27] Two were important in achieving a better understanding of the Nazi dictator. One was Brigitte Hamann's study, which looked at Hitler's early years and provided important new insights into how his ideological thinking on foreign and racial policy developed.[28] Even more important was the exceptionally well-informed and substantial biography of Hitler by the British historian Ian Kershaw. Written by an acknowledged expert of National Socialist research, the two volumes represent the results of long-term research.[29] Kershaw focused on the essence of Hitler's rule.[30] His analysis restored Hitler's monopoly of leadership in matters of foreign policy and emphasized a radical ideological programme of conquest and genocide underpinned his actions.[31]

Kershaw's view that Hitler was the decisive force in foreign policy once more confirmed a consensus on the subject, which can be traced via Trevor Roper and Hillgruber to Axel Kuhn's reconstruction of Hitler's programme of aggression and other outstanding studies, including Barbara Zehnpfennig's examination of Hitler's foreign policy ideas in *Mein Kampf* and Frank-Lothar Kroll's analysis of the role ideology played in the formulation of policy in the Third Reich.[32] Kroll's study is worthy of mention because it convincingly refuted the thesis of National Socialism as a revolution without any ideological doctrine.[33] Based on a detailed analysis of the heterogeneous ideas of Hitler, Rosenberg, Darré, Himmler and Goebbels, Kroll concluded that all major ideologues of the regime believed in and tried to realize the substance of their particular *Weltanschauung* (world-view). National Socialism, despite all minor ambiguities, did aim at a utopian and revolutionary 'regeneration of the world'.[34]

In recent times, the controversy among German historians between 'intentionalists' and 'functionalists' has long lost its previous fierceness. Increasingly, that old dispute had been overtaken by a shifting focus of research away from the structure of the state and foreign policy to that of German society.[35] The most detailed and impressive analysis about the development of domestic politics of the Third Reich can be found in the work of British historian Richard J. Evans, who published a monumental survey of the National Socialist era in three impressive volumes between 2004 and 2008. Evans even compiled research about cultural, educational and religious policy, but his description of foreign policy receives one chapter compared to seven chapters about domestic politics.[36] There are other general studies in which foreign policy takes a back seat to descriptions of the internal mode of operation of the National Socialist regime, such as Norbert Frei's work on the 'Führer State'.[37]

These studies reflect a general drift among German historians away from foreign policy, which was once the major topic of elder publications to an emphasis on life inside Germany – the favoured ground of the intentionalists.[38] Even after all these years, Klaus Hildebrand's analysis of German foreign policy from Bismarck to Hitler remains the most authoritative and comprehensive standard work on Hitler's foreign policy that has not undergone any major revision.[39] Hildebrand's analysis is a synthesis of painstaking research in archives and scientific examinations over a distinguished career. He examines eighty years of German foreign policy in a sweeping mode and against the background of developments of domestic and European politics as well as in a global context. He combines narrative passages and reflecting interpretations to a history of politics which shows leeway of decision as well as approaches of leading actors. Even in this overall view, Hildebrand emphasizes the 'primacy of politics' in the area of foreign policy. He shows that Hitler followed a stage-by-stage plan in foreign policy within a framework that allowed for improvisation and tactical flexibility as he pursued his objective of *Lebensraum* within a radical racist ideology that envisaged wars of conquest.

In 2002 Rainer F. Schmidt published a sound and descriptive survey about the foreign policy of the Third Reich, but did not present new sources or additional aspects and his conclusions followed the established insights and appraisals in the existing literature.[40] A book by Marie-Luise Recker contains an encyclopedic survey of foreign policy as well as results and trends of research, but once again offers little to shake the overwhelming orthodoxy.[41] Of more interest is Hermann Graml's book *Europe's Way to War*, which examines the basic trends of international politics in the last month before war broke out, but his conclusion that Hitler successfully forced Europe into war is hardly new.

Based on recent scientific research long-time research in archives, I have examined the Foreign Policy of the Third Reich between 1933 and 1945 extensively. My view is that the key to understanding Hitler's foreign policy is to focus extensively on the inner context of Hitler's way of thinking, to explore his political and ideological motives, and then to explore how constraints then influenced the implementation of his plans.[42] In 'Hitler's Grip on World Domination' I looked at the role of Constantin Freiherr von Neurath, the last foreign secretary of the Republic of Weimar and the first of the Third Reich. Neurath was the leading figure in the Foreign Office between 1932 and 1938. I believe Neurath – who was not a Nazi – executed a foreign policy that was determined by Hitler, but he ensured its true aims were kept secret in diplomatic discussions and thereby fooled many skilled diplomats in the major European capitals.[43]

In the past few years an independent German commission of historians, set up by Joschka Fischer in 2005, has been investigating the history of how the foreign ministry dealt with its dreadful past after being refounded in 1951 and the question of personal continuity or discontinuity after 1945. It seems quite clear that it will conclude that the foreign office as a whole and some individual diplomats have been deeply implicated in the crimes of the Third Reich.

The strategy of the commission reflects a present trend to diversify historical research in Germany. Recently there have been a whole series of works investigating different groups of perpetrators or geographic areas. Ulrich Herbert's study about Werner Best is ground breaking for the research of delinquents describing this ideologist and organizer of the *Reichssicherheitshauptamt* as typical for a special sort of young wrongdoers with an academic background who got the chance to unfurl his radical folkish and racist ideas in the bureaucratic organization of genocide.[44] This followed up Michael Wildt's study about the biographies of members of the SS technocrats who played an active role in the Holocaust.[45] Similar to this approach is the biographical analysis of twenty-five German supreme commanders of the war against the Soviet Union in which Johannes Hürter reveals how the military elite came into close collaboration in the crimes of the Third Reich.[46]

This resurgence of biography as a method is a noticeable trend in recent German historiography on foreign and racial policy. The object of research has not been from an individualistic point of view, but rather to analyze the general circumstances that stamped individuals and to contextualize the roles of key individuals in the structure, organization and history of the Nazi regime. Peter Longerich has filled a biographical gap with his impressive study about Heinrich Himmler. Other important studies were published about Werner von Blomberg, Minister of the War Department from 1933 to 1938, responsible for the upgrading of the German army, about Hjalmar Schacht, long-term Minister of the Department of Economy and President of the Reichsbank, and Hitler's chief ideologist Alfred Rosenberg.[47] Yet all these studies have confirmed rather than refuted the leading role of Hitler on foreign policy. As Ulrich von Hehl observed, research shows time and again an 'absolute dominance of the Führer over his closest paladins'.[48] Hans-Ulrich Wehler, who is completing a definitive five-volume history of National Socialism, has been accused in Germany of once more pushing Hitler back to the centre stage.[49] But there are still surprising gaps, for instance about such high-ranking protagonists as Rudolf Hess, Joachim von Ribbentrop, Martin Bormann, Wilhelm Keppler, Hans Heinrich Lammers and Roland Freisler. So there is still a lot of work for biographers to do to compile a full picture of the Nazi elite that surrounded their dictator as he pursued his foreign and racial policy. The results gained by the biographical method are illuminating, affording deepened insights into the way the National Socialist regime worked, but the danger is that understanding becomes segmented.

For all the mountain of research that has been produced on Hitler's foreign policy we are left with the conclusion that Hitler played the central role and that his 'intentions' and the 'structures' surrounding foreign policy are both indispensible analytical tools to understand fully the German road to war. The ideological contours he had mapped out in *Mein Kampf* informed that now-familiar unfolding plan of aggression, but strategic, economic and political considerations and the opportunities presented by his opponents led to deviations in the timing of the dynamic direction of his policy. We can now see that many within Germany were willing to go along with his aggression and the Western powers were willing to compromise with him. As much as historians have attempted to weave alternative interpretations, this dominant and still-plausible explanation is unlikely to be altered.

Notes

1   K. Bracher, *Die deutsche Diktatur: Entstehung-Struktur-Folgen des Nationalsozialismus*. Köln/Berlin, 1969, p. 1.
2   D. J. Peukert in I. Kershaw (ed.), *Der NS-Staat: Geschichtsinterpretationen und Kontroversen im Überblick*. Reinbek bei Hamburg, 2006, 4 Aufl., p. 4.
3   F. Meinecke, *Die deutsche Katastrophe*. Wiesbaden, 1946; L. Dehio, *Gleichgewicht oder Hegemonie: Betrachtungen über ein Grundproblem der neueren Staatengeschichte*. Krefeld, 1948.
4   U. Hehl, 'Nationalsozialistische Herrschaft' in *Enzyklopädie Deutscher Geschichte*, Bd. 39. München, 2001, 2 Aufl., p. 52.
5   E. Fraenkel, *The Dual State: A Contribution to the Theory of Dictatorship*. New York, 1941; F. Neumann, *Behemoth: The Structure and Practice of National Socialism*. Toronto, 1942.
6   H-U. Wehler, 'Geschichte der Soziologie' in H-U. Wehler (ed.), *Geschichte als Historische Hilfswissenschaft*. Frankfurt am Main, 1973, p. 26.
7   H. Mommsen, 'Nationalsozialismus' in *Sowjetsystem und demokratische Gesellschaft. Eine vergleichende Enzyklopädie*, Bd. 4. Freiburg, 1971, pp. 695–713.
8   Hehl, 'Nationalsozialistische Herrschaft', p. 58.
9   V. Ullrich, *Die schwierige Königsdisziplin* in *Die Zeit* 4 April 2007.
10 A. Bullock, *Hitler: Eine Studie über Tyrannei*. Düsseldorf, 2000, p. 795; K. Heiden, *Adolf Hitler: Eine Biographie* vol. 1, *Das Zeitalter der Verantwortungslosigkeit*. Zürich, 1936.
11 H. Rauschning, *Die Revolution des Nihilismus: Kulisse und Wirklichkeit im Dritten Reich*. Zürich, 1938.
12 Bullock, *Hitler*, p. 794.
13 H. Trevor-Roper, 'Hitlers Kriegsziele' in *Vierteljahrshefte für Zeitgeschichte* 8 (1960), pp. 121–33.
14 A. Hillgruber, *Endlich genug über Nationalsozialismus und Zweiten Weltkrieg? Forschungsstand und Literatur*. Düsseldorf, 1982, p. 65.
15 'Wie kam Hitler an die Macht?' in K. Erdmann, D. Karl and H. Schulze (eds), *Weimar: Selbstpreisgabe einer Demokratie. Eine Bilanz heute*. Düsseldorf, 1980, p. 305.
16 A. Hillgruber, *Hitlers Strategie: Politik und Kriegführung 1940–1941*. Frankfurt am Main, 1965.
17 K. Hildebrand, 'Die Geschichte der deutschen Außenpolitik (1933–1945) im Urteil der neueren Forschung: Ergebnisse, Kontroversen, Perspektiven' in K. Hildebrand, *Deutsche Außenpolitik 1933–1945: Kalkül oder Dogma?*. Stuttgart/Berlin/Köln, 1990, 5th ed., pp. 183–201.
18 H-U. Wehler, 'Sozialimperialismus' in H-U. Wehler, *Imperialismus*. Königstein, 1979, 4th edition, pp. 83–96.
19 M. Broszat, *Soziale Motivation und Führer-Bindung des Nationalsozialismus* in: *VfZ* 18 (1970), pp. 392–409; 406–9.
20 H. Mommsen, 'Nationalsozialismus oder Hitlerismus?' in M. Bosch (ed.), *Persönlichkeit und Struktur der Geschichte*. Düsseldorf, 1977, pp. 62–71.
21 Mommsen, *Nationalsozialismus*, p. 702.
22 Ibid., p. 703.
23 H. Mommsen, '*Ausnahmezustand als Herrschaftstechnik*' in M. Funke (ed.), *Hitler, Deutschland und die Mächte*. Düsseldorf, 1976, S. 30–45, hier S. 43–5.
24 Broszat in E. Jäckel and J. Rohwer (eds), *Der Mord an den Juden im Zweiten Weltkrieg. Entschlußbildung und Verwirklichung*. Frankfurt am Main, 1987, p. 211.
25 J. Fest, *Hitler: Eine Biographie*. Frankfurt am Main, 1973.
26 Hildebrand, *Das Dritte Reich*, p. 186.
27 E. Jäckel, 'Rückblick auf die sogenannte Hitler-Welle' in *Geschichte in Wissenschaft und Unterricht* 28 (1977), pp. 695–710.
28 B. Hamann, *Hitlers Wien: Lehrjahre eines Diktators*. München, 1996.
29 I. Kershaw, *Hitlers Macht: Das Profil der NS-Herrschaft*. München, 1992.
30 I. Kershaw, *Hitler: 1889–1936*. Stuttgart, 1998, p. 23.
31 K. Hildebrand, *Nichts Neues über Hitler* (forthcoming).
32 A. Kuhn, *Hitlers außenpolitisches Programm. Entstehung und Entwicklung 1919–1939*. Stuttgart, 1970. B. Zehnpfennig, *Hitlers Mein Kampf: Eine Interpretation*. München, 2000.

33 F. Kroll, *Utopie als Ideologie: Geschichtsdenken und politisches Handeln im Dritten Reich: Hitler-Rosenberg-Darré-Himmler-Goebbels*. Paderborn, 1999, Aufl. 2, p. 17.
34 Ibid. p. 101.
35 Hildebrand, *Das Dritte Reich*, p. 146.
36 R.J. Evans, *Das Dritte Reich, Bd. 2: Diktatur*. München, 2006.
37 N. Frei, *Der Führerstaat. Nationalsozialistische Herrschaft 1933 bis 1945*. München, 2002, p. 7ff.
38 J. Dülffer, *Deutsche Geschichte 1933–1945: Führerglaube und Vernichtungskrieg*. Stuttgart, 1992; L. Herbst, *Das nationalsozialistische Deutschland 1933–1945: Die Entfesselung der Gewalt. Rassismus und Krieg*. Frankfurt am Main, 1996. H-U. Thamer, *Verführung und Gewalt: Deutschland 1933–1945*. Berlin, 1986.
39 W. Baumgart in *Forschungen zur brandenburgischen und preußischen Geschichte*, Bd. 6. Berlin, 1996, pp. 136–9.
40 R. Schmidt, *Die Außenpolitik des Dritten Reiches 1933–1939*. Stuttgart, 2002.
41 M. Recker, 'Die Außenpolitik des Dritten Reiches', *Enzyklopädie Deutscher Geschichte*, Bd. 8. München, 2010.
42 L. Lüdicke, *Griff nach der Weltherrschaft: Die Außenpolitik des Dritten Reiches 1933–1945*. Berlin, 2009.
43 L. Lüdicke, *Constantin Freiherr von Neurath: Eine politische Biographie*. Phil. Diss. am Historischen Institut der Universität Potsdam.
44 U. Herbert, *Best: Biographische Studien über Radikalismus, Weltanschauung und Vernunft 1903–1989*. Bonn 1996.
45 M. Wildt, *Generation des Unbedingten: Das Führungskorps des Reichssicherheitshauptamtes*. Hamburg, 2002.
46 J. Hürter, *Hitlers Heerführer: Die Deutschen Oberbefehlshaber im Krieg gegen die Sowjetunion 1941/42*. München, 2006.
47 P. Longerich, *Heinrich Himmler: Biographie*. München, 2007; K. Schäfer, *Werner von Blomberg: Hitlers erster Feldmarschall. Eine Biografie*. Paderborn, 2007. C. Kopper, *Hjalmar Schacht: Aufstieg und Fall von Hitlers mächtigstem Bankier*. München/Wien, 2006; E. Piper, *Alfred Rosenberg: Hitlers Chefideologe*. München, 2007.
48 Hehl, 'Nationalsozialistische Herrschaft', p. 66.
49 H-U. Wehler, *Deutsche Gesellschaftsgeschichte*, 5 vols. München, 2008.

Chapter 7

Germany's Twisted Road to War, 1919–39

Jürgen Förster

At the end of his life, Othello bids farewell to the 'pomp and circumstance of glorious war'.[1] Shortly before his suicide, Adolf Hitler dictated to his secretary that he would 'die with a happy heart' being aware of the immeasurable sacrifices of the German people during the past six war years.[2] The modern consensus holds that wars are evil. Historians, however, classify the First World War as long, industrial and costly, and the Second World War as long, total and murderous. Both global wars command an enormous literature. That of the Second World War surpasses that of the 'war to end all wars'. The literature on the inter-war period in German history is immense too. Since the 'lost world war' infiltrated virtually every issue, every debate in the Weimar Republic and created enormous space for military thoughts on future warfare and national mobilization, it is surprising that the *Reichswehr* has for the most part been left out of general descriptions of Weimar Germany. Though the cross winds of arguments have for many decades gone over the path that connects 1919 with 1939, there are still enough visible marks to highlight the continuities and discontinuities of German military policy that eventually risked another European war.

The academic debate about Germany's responsibility for the Second World War is altogether different from that on its contribution to the First World War. Most historians agree that the origins of the war lay in and with Germany. It was Adolf Hitler, the Führer [of the nation] and Supreme Commander of the *Wehrmacht*, who ordered his troops to invade Poland in the early hours of 1 September 1939. However, historians still discuss why the German people, with and without uniform, were prepared to march with Hitler and his Nazis into an aggressive war and kept on fighting after the European war was followed by a world war after 1941. To be sure, Weimar's succession of crises and conflicts gave the Nazis an opening, but their public support deserves a more complex explanation because Hitler's movement 'had never before the 1930s been capable of moving from the fringe to the mainstream'.[3] The quick change from the democratic 'calamities' of the Weimar Republic to Hitler's authoritarian Führer-state between 1933 and 1938 is another point for discussion. There can be no doubt that Hitler's political and military leadership between 1934 and 1939 was much more popular than that of Friedrich Ebert or Paul von Hindenburg during the Weimar era.[4] To the range of political, economical and cultural explanations for Hitler's success I would like to highlight the importance of military factors.

The traditional picture of the *Wehrmacht* in the summer of 1939 usually obscures the fact that in January 1933 the *Reichswehr* consisted of a 100,000-man army and the 15,000-man navy permitted by the Versailles Treaty. Yet that *Reichswehr* was different from those professional armed forces that Hans von Seeckt had formed after 1921. It had crossed the treacherous marsh of military utopia, left the nadir of military powerlessness vis-à-vis a French occupation behind, accepted the republic as a fact of life, and was willing to correlate its defensive measures with German foreign policy. The most prominent exponents of that 'new course' of military policy were Wilhelm Groener, *Reichswehr* minister between 1928 and 1932, and his military aide and 'cardinal *in politicis*' Kurt von Schleicher, who later succeeded him as minister and became the last Weimar Chancellor before Hitler. The military leadership's preparedness for cooperation with civilian cabinets and ministries was qualified by its conviction in using the state for military aims and stamping out political attacks on the *Reichswehr*. This policy of conditional cooperation and renouncing secret armament was in so far successful as it resulted in getting a SPD-dominated coalition government to fund army armament and navy construction programmes as well as the Foreign Office to attend operational war games. Yet this cooperation could neither ease the tension within military policy between the *Reichswehr*'s limited capabilities of the present and far-reaching aims for the future nor its dislike for civilian rule. If the military elite was unhappy with the republic, especially the SPD-led government in Prussia, the same can be said for other strata of German society that perceived party politics as messy and unsatisfactory. So in the spring of 1930, Groener and Schleicher created a political condition that was even more favourable for their interests. It was under the chancellorship of Heinrich Brüning who was dependent on the *Reich* President's power to issue emergency decrees under Article 48 of the Weimar constitution that Groener signed the far-reaching directive of 16 April 1930 and sent it to chiefs of army and navy commands. For the first time, the *Reichswehr* was prepared to accept that the political leadership assigned the tasks to the armed forces. Moreover, Groener emphasized that 'definite prospects of success' were the precondition for employing the *Reichswehr* in battle. This 'new objectivity' in German military policy found little sympathy within the officer corps at large. Many an officer did not want to share military control and felt that Germany had the duty to defend itself against military attack, especially by Poland, even if that meant suicidal operations.[5] Some of them even went so far as to contact the Nazi Party and spread their propaganda within the barracks in Ulm. Together with the Nazis' landslide success in the national elections in September 1930, it was Hitler's oath of legality at the trial against the three insubordinate officers in Leipzig and his party's participation in the Thuringian regional government that brought about a *rapprochement* between the *Reichswehr* and the Nazi Party. Groener and Schleicher even thought they could tame Hitler and split his party as a mass militant movement into rival factions. Thus the military leadership who had done so much to stabilize the republic in 1919 helped to destroy it by underestimating Hitler's will to power and his further backing by the voters. Groener and Schleicher in Berlin as well as Werner von Blomberg and Walther von Reichenau in Königsberg knew that their military aims could not be realized without popular support. By the end of 1932, the *Reichswehr* had made some progress in the matter of state-organized 'pre-military training of young [male] people', as Groener already demanded in August 1919, but the complementary introduction of 'soldierly thinking' was still lacking in schools' policy. In addition to becoming a political player in domestic affairs, the *Reichswehr* managed to get another army armament programme (1933–8) approved by the government providing the planned twenty-one-division field army with a first issuing of weapons, equipment and ammunition as well as minimum stocks for a period of six weeks. In accord with the army programme, the navy was not only allowed to take every advantage of the possibilities the Versailles Treaty offered but also an aircraft carrier, a series of submarines and naval aviation units were put into service or organized.[6] These comprehensive armament and personnel programmes prove that the *Reichswehr*'s old intention of circumventing the military limitations of 1919 had produced some results before Hitler began to dismantle Versailles completely.[7]

While policy makers were influenced by pacifism and disarmament, German military planners developed a third approach to the defeat of 1918, namely, finding a more effective way to fight the inevitable next war. The latter made much of the inherent strength of the defensive but also sought new ways to tilt the balance back towards the offence and emphasized moral mobilization. Not surprisingly, historians have paid considerable attention to these aspects of German military history.[8] If there was one common thread running through the army manuals of 1921 and 1933, it was the equation of strategy with army operations, considering warfare as 'an art, a free creative activity resting on scientific foundations', or general statements like 'The teachings of wartime command cannot be summarized in regulations.'[9] Though mobility had become a dogma in military thinking under Hans von Seeckt, the 'blitzkrieg tactics of 1939 and 1940' did not spring directly from the army regulations published in 1921–3, as James Corum maintains.[10] Its introduction that already thought of Germany as a 'major military power' with a modern army was more meant to help the officer to skip the current, bleak realities of the *Reichswehr* and to think of a bright military future. That would entail a well-led, well-trained, well-equipped army with superior morale, supported by airpower and mechanized warfare being capable of defeating larger invading forces in the classical pattern of operational-level war making. The form had changed but not the German military spirit. Seeckt believed that a short war was the only kind that Germany could win. 'The goal remained the destruction of the enemy army in a great *Kesselschlacht*; the means remained *Bewegungskrieg*.'[11]

However, there was another strand of military thought emerging in the twenties. Both the French–Belgian occupation of the Ruhr and the Lithuanian annexation of the Memel Territory in 1923–4 had confronted the *Reichswehr* with the bitter reality that that it was not even capable of border defence, albeit preserving German sovereignty. Anger, fear, frustration and old enemy images against the French prompted Joachim von Stülpnagel, head of the Operations Section in the *Truppenamt* (army general staff), to think about the 'war of the future' as a another 'war of liberation' against the hated French. It was to be fought in the manner of a brutal *Volkskrieg* (people's war). Deviating from the official view of a small, mobile professional force concentrating on limited warfare, Stülpnagel argued for a combination of conventional and irregular warfare. If it came to an invasion of superior French or French–Polish forces on German soil, German soldiers and civilians would engage in unlimited warfare to delay the attacking forces in order to gain time, first to regroup for a battle of annihilation, second to get international support as a victim of aggression.[12] Stülpnagel's 'categorical imperative of fighting and dying for the fatherland' was not meant for the foreseeable future. Because of Germany's military impotence, his cry for the present was 'Let us arm!' secretly in pursuit of 'national discipline'.[13] Stülpnagel's vision of a primordial defensive struggle for the liberation of Germany did not become the official doctrine of the *Reichswehr*. The main problem with *Volkskrieg* was that the people were unwilling to fight, at least for the time being. It was not only Seeckt who favoured a more strictly conventional warfare of manoeuvre and who preferred to live with the current 'shameful' situation than to commit German blood to hopeless battle, risking *finis Germaniae*. Yet one thing was clear to all of them: the enemy was France. Even if Stülpnagel's radical warfare scenario had met criticism, the top brass became convinced that they could not seriously think of beginning a war without mobilizing the society in peacetime.

I will now turn to the question of how Hitler and the military took Germany to war. In doing so, I revisit some well-established debates about Hitler's own aims, the military's goals, Hitler's decision making as supreme commander and the so-called 'German way of war': *Blitzkrieg* or total war, conventional warfare or *Vernichtungskrieg*? On 30 January 1933 Hitler was appointed German Chancellor as head of a coalition government. The twenty-first and final Weimar cabinet contained only three Nazis. Hitler had been the *Reichswehr*'s choice too. But he refused to be anyone's instrument. As in 1918, there was a rush to identify the new course as a 'revolution', but this time a national one. For those of a conservative or national liberal conviction, be it in the elite groups of the *Reichswehr*, government administration or in business, the Nazis seemed to offer at last clear leadership in restoring traditional values, employment at home and the dismantling of Versailles. Lieutenant-General Ludwig Beck welcomed the Hitler's regime as 'the first great ray since 1918'.[14] A younger general staff officer, Gotthard Heinrici, was more outspoken about the end of the Weimar republic and welcomed the national government as a way 'out of the Marxist–Jewish mess'.[15] By the summer of 1933 the Nazis commanded all the resources of single party control over almost every dimension of politics, society, culture, education and leisure. The only important organization that had not been 'co-ordinated' was the *Reichswehr*. Hitler's structural and psycho-logical success was not unpopular among the military, neither at the top nor among the officers at large. General Werner von Blomberg, the new Minister and Commander of the *Reichswehr*, described the achieved totality of the party as 'fortunate'. The soldiers' main task now was 'to serve the national movement with all dedication'. Hans Meier-Welcker, a young infantry officer, optimistically compared Germany to Italy. 'We all belong to it [i.e. the totality of National Socialism], just as every Italian working for his fatherland is a Fascist today. The more comprehensive National Socialism becomes in Germany, the better it will be for all of us.'[16] Meier-Welcker could not know what Hitler's 'seizure of power' really meant for Germany and Europe, but Blomberg and his colleagues at the top certainly did. In several addresses to commanders and officers in the summer of 1933, Blomberg stressed that the new cabinet was not a normal change of government. It indeed represented a 'fundamental change in the views and will of the entire nation, and the realization of a new view of the world'. [17]

Only four days after his appointment as Chancellor, Hitler had been given the chance to address a large group of senior officers at the home of the Chief of Army Command, Kurt von Hammerstein-Equord, together with the Foreign Minister, Constantin von Neurath. The notes of that address by one of the generals present have been included in many an edition of documents dealing with the Third Reich. They have recently been confirmed by a second account from an unlikely source through which Joseph Stalin received knowledge of Hitler's long-term aggressive goals within two weeks.[18] Hitler took pains to reassure and flatter the military on which he would in time depend as the 'most important prerequisite' for the recovery of Germany's political power and to expand the German 'living space'. But before he could pursue an aggressive foreign policy the national will to defend itself had to be strengthened 'by all means'. He further told the generals that he needed the *Reichswehr* and its expertise to build up a new people's *Wehrmacht* on the basis of conscription. The unruly Storm Troopers would not pose a real threat to the military's monopoly of arms.

The *Reichswehr* for its part needed Hitler. Leaving aside Hitler's domestic aims like the 'destruction of Marxism', the military was also grateful for the priority given to rearmament and the measure of development opportunities offered to them. It required the support of the Nazi party and the resources of the whole of society to achieve mass mobilization and to maintain public morale for the war of the future. Within the course of a few weeks a loyal collaboration developed between Hitler and Blomberg. Both political players shared the belief that Germany's destiny was to become once again a great power, even if that meant another war. If Germany was to succeed, and this was a lesson learned from both the First World War and the 1918 Revolution, the government had to undertake a comprehensive armament programme (*Wiederwehrhaftmachung*) that went far beyond purely military matters. This alliance was much more popular among the officer corps at large than Groener's cooperation with the republic, be it with Ebert or Brüning.

Did Hitler in the end, then, really gain much more from the military supporting him in consolidating his authoritarian rule, even against his own followers as on 30 June 1934, than did the generals? Yes, they allowed him, after Hindenburg's death in August 1934, to become both President and Chancellor and swore an oath of loyalty to the *Führer* in person rather than to the constitution or Fatherland. But Hitler left the reigns of command to his loyal minister albeit his decisive influence on foreign policy. It was not before February 1938, when the first field marshal of the Third Reich fell from power over a personal affair, that Hitler really began to exercise the full powers as supreme commander as well. It was then that the military had become another instrument of the Führer's executive will. The central question, as Hitler had admitted on 3 February, was how Germany could rearm for war without provoking foreign intervention since the context of German sovereignty was still set by the Treaty of Versailles. As Hitler and Blomberg were determined on rearmament in its full context, they were prepared to make whatever concessions were necessary to achieve that goal. Each of the choices they made in foreign or military policy had consequences, be its impact on other powers or on the growing *Wehrmacht*. Complex processes resulted, which acquired a momentum of their own that both leaders had to direct as well as to manage.

The first diplomatic coups were the withdrawal from the disarmament conference and the League of Nations on 14 October 1933, the Non-Aggression Pact with Poland on 25 January 1934 and the Saar's return to German jurisdiction at the beginning of March 1935. Comparable coups on the military field were two bold declarations of Germany's military sovereignty in March 1935, thus making the defence limitations of Versailles obsolete – announcing the existence of an air force, the introduction of conscription to produce a peacetime army of thirty-six divisions, the signing of a bilateral naval agreement with Britain on 18 June 1935, and the reoccupation of the Rhineland in mid-March 1936. These tactical masterpieces surprised the European powers, satisfied the nation, turned public opinion in Hitler's favour and changed the structural and operational basis for Germany's military policies considerably.

As Hitler had made clear on 3 February 1933 that he did not think of risking war in the short term, the *Reichswehr*'s actual military planning did not change instantly. Yet the transition from *Reichswehr* to *Wehrmacht* was a smooth one. While marching carefully through the 'risk zone' of military impotence, Hitler and Blomberg were determined to meet every armed violation of German sovereignty with resistance. The army was ordered to fight 'for reasons of honour even when there was no prospect of success'.[19] A first, hasty step towards rearmament was made by the end of December 1933 when the army decided on a peacetime force of 21 divisions (300,000 men) by April 1938. This programme was geared to provide the basis for a wartime army of sixty-three divisions already fighting 'a defensive war on several fronts with some prospect of success'.[20] Between 1933 and 1934 there was neither an intention on Hitler's side to attack anyone nor did the Foreign Ministry fear a preventive war by France and Britain. Yet as Hitler wanted Germany to be able to 'play a more active role in important questions of international politics', he opted for an earlier deadline of the December programme, namely by April 1935. Of course, the general staff agreed with Hitler to build up a larger peacetime army as rapidly as possible, but Major-General Ludwig Beck preferred a solid depot of trained men for the future wartime army to an improvised instrument of state power.[21] Here is not the place to outline all the memoranda, considerations, studies and inter-service rivalries for choosing the right path that would eventually lead to a *Wehrmacht* capable of winning the next war. This has been well done by the late Wilhelm Deist. And it was he who noted first that there was no opposition to Hitler's rearmament goals and second that the army leadership was not able to understand the need for coordination between the organizers of material rearmament, buildup of personnel and operational planning. The fact that little thought for financial orthodoxy or the long-term health of economy was given was another reason, not Hitler's interference, that 'the whole rearmament of the army acquired the character of temporary, partial solutions', which in turn affected the quality of the *Wehrmacht*.[22] With open eyes, the general staff abandoned the principle that the officer corps had to comprise of seven per cent of the army's total strength. Michael Geyer is wrong in saying that the general staff began comprehensive preparations for war as early as the summer of 1935.[23] The basic decision to increase the army's offensive power by forming three Panzer divisions had indeed been made. But only an experimental formation with a few MK I light tanks with two machine guns was available in that year. It was the events of March 1936 that opened up new possibilities for further armament and operational planning. More men had become liable for military service, the Ruhr area with its industrial centres was no longer exposed to foreign attack, and the *Wehrmacht* had gained a much stronger defensive position along the Rhine as well as west of it between Saarbrücken and Aachen. Although they were aware of Germany's inferiority,[24] this improved situation prompted both Hitler and the army to think anew. And it was in this context that the general staff overturned the plans of summer 1935, gave its concept of fighting a defensive war on several fronts with some prospect of success a more realistic meaning. The acceleration of rearmament was quite in accordance with the introduction of a two-year period of service. In his memorandum on the second Four-Year Plan, of August 1936, Hitler again gave pride of place to rearmament, which could not be too swift. Yet he considered the plan a temporary expedient. It had to serve the goal of temporarily easing the economic problems during a transition period, and in that connection the production of arms and ammunition had absolute priority over the accumulation of foreign currency reserves and raw materials. 'The final solution', he wrote, 'lies in extending our living space, that is to say, expanding the sources of raw materials and foodstuffs of our people.' At the end of his memorandum,

Hitler set the following tasks: '1. The German army must be operational within four years. 2. The German economy must be fit for war within four years.' Nothing and nobody would be allowed to stand in the way. But Hitler would not have been Hitler if he had not put this directive into an ideological context. In its struggle for life, Germany was threatened by the 'aggressive will founded on the authoritarian ideology' of Bolshevism and world-wide Jewry. Yet because of her people, impeccable political leadership, ideology and military organization, Germany was the key to resisting this world peril. In doing so, Hitler felt he could only rely on Italy and Japan. As

> a victory of Bolshevism would not lead to a Versailles Treaty but to the final destruction, indeed to the annihilation of the German people ... All other considerations than the warding off of this danger must recede into the background as completely irrelevant ... Unless we succeed, within a very short time, to make the German *Wehrmacht* the foremost army in the world, in training, in the establishment of its formations, in equipment, and above all in spiritual education, Germany will be lost![25]

How important was Hitler's memorandum for Germany's way to war? The simple answer is that it is important because it reveals both Hitler's leadership and dynamism as well his emphasis on a solid ideological grounding for all servicemen. It is highly unlikely that the army would have embarked on its last comprehensive rearmament programme in autumn 1936 without giving much thought to its economic efficiency if it had not had Hitler's memo in its head. The programme began with the telling sentence 'In accordance with the *Führer*'s orders, a powerful army is to be created in the shortest possible time' and was presented to Field Marshal von Blomberg on 12 October 1936.[26] The views of two economically critical generals, Fritz Fromm and Kurt Liese, were only mentioned in passing. That did not mean that economical factors became less important in reality. They came to the surface and attention of the political and military leadership again in the autumn of 1937 and were the reason of their often-cited gathering in the Reich Chancellery on 5 November 1937.

The navy and the air force underwent similar expansion. Like the rearmament of the army, that of the navy also had its starting-point in the last days of the Weimar Republic, with its 'reorganization plan' of November 1932. Naval thinking was dominated by its longtime Commander in Chief, Admiral Erich Raeder (1928–43). In opposition to Groener's directive of April 1930 that the navy should focus on the Baltic, the naval leadership despised a brown-water navy and favoured oceanic cruiser warfare that would be coordinated with battle fleet action in the North Sea. Yet what he told Groener was that wishful thinking was fateful and that any armed conflict with Britain had to be avoided. Although Raeder planned to operate offensively, his grand strategy was purely defensive. He (and Hitler) saw the navy as a factor worthy of alliances and as an instrument for a future German maritime position of power. The Anglo-German naval agreement of 18 June 1935 was not considered as definitive.

The settlement of the relative strength of German and British naval forces was quite compatible with the *Kriegsmarine*'s traditional goals concealed behind the phrase of qualitative and quantitative parity with France. The agreement helped to expand its armament greatly. Yet the rapid realization of the warship programme exceeded the capacity of German shipyards but actually supported the submarine construction. The news of British construction of five battleships in December 1936 provided both the impulse for new planning and reviving the anti-British ideology on the German side. The ground was laid for an open change of course against Britain that was declared by Hitler on 5 November 1937.[27]

From the three services of the *Wehrmacht*, it was the new *Luftwaffe* (air force) that fulfilled its grand strategic role best to dampen the enthusiasm of France and her allies for an attack on Germany during its 'risk zone' of rearmament. Its planners happily noted the first signs of public concern in Britain of fear about bombing as early as the summer of 1933. When the *Luftwaffe*'s existence was made public in March 1935, the actual air force bore little similarity to one its first planner, Robert Knauss, had sketched in his memorandum of May 1933. The *Luftwaffe* possessed only 800 operational aircraft and none fulfilled the technical and tactical requirements recommended by Knauss. Yet Hitler boasted misleadingly to the British Foreign Secretary, Sir John Simon, that Germany had already achieved parity with the Royal Air Force and would soon catch up with the French. Though this statement was in accord with the *Wehrmacht*'s leadership and marked a new phase in presenting the *Luftwaffe* as *the* 'risk' service,[28] an internal study of autumn 1935 proved that air armament was completely inadequate to destroy the French air force and its Czech and Lithuanian allies. How much worse would the *Luftwaffe*'s effectiveness be in a two-front war, if a new potential enemy appeared on the planners' horizon against whom an effective air war was impossible for geographical reasons: Britain? A military confrontation with that state was indeed briefly treated in Blomberg's directive of 24 June 1937, which will be dealt with later, and estimated as 'unacceptable, even hopeless'.[29] The *Luftwaffe*'s situation did not look so dark when viewed against the white background of the Legion Condor's performance as an instrument of *Blitzkrieg* and 'heavy artillery' for the army in the Spanish Civil War.[30]

While the three services made strong efforts in armaments, the *Wehrmacht* leadership was concerned about the ideological inculcation in all soldiers of the guiding principles of the National Socialist state. On 24 May 1934, Blomberg urged all officers to make the ideal of *one* nation as an 'indissoluble community of blood and destiny' the basis of their educational work among the troops. To help them, the ministry published official guidelines 'on political issues of the day'. The reintroduction of conscription and the new military law in the spring of 1935 marked a change for education in the armed forces. They were defined as the arms-bearer of the German people and soldierly school of the nation. In obvious criticism of the old *Reichswehr*, the new *Wehrmacht* must no longer lead a life of its own, but set an example of 'German character and German nature' to the whole nation. In order to be able to fulfil their task to produce soldiers who could both handle their weapons well and were conscious of their political duties, the officers had to possess the Nazi ideology 'in spiritual unanimity, as something of their own and an inner conviction'. Needless to say that none had to be an expert in Hitler's *Weltanschauung*. What mattered in this transitional phase was not ideological indoctrination but a fusion of national pride, dedication, readiness for sacrifice, a sense of fatherland and community, and for character forming in the National Socialist spirit and the Hitler myth. Training and cohesion of the heterogeneous troops still enjoyed priority over ideological conformity. As Hitler himself declared in the autumn of 1935: 'I am not concerned that the recruits coming in turn the [*Reichswehr*] soldiers into National Socialists, but that the army turns National Socialist [recruits] into soldiers.' Legend has it that the army was Prussian, the navy imperial and only the air force was National Socialist. In reality, the three service chiefs agreed with Blomberg's ruling that those officers who were unable to reconcile themselves to Nazi ideology were to leave the armed forces.[31]

The first directive for a 'uniform war preparation of the *Wehrmacht*', which has been mentioned before, was issued by the War Minister and Commander in Chief on 24 June 1937. Blomberg's directive is interesting in two ways. First it is meant to show his leadership in overall strategic planning for a future war to the envious services, especially the army, and second it dealt with two concrete possible scenarios for war. Assuming that Germany was not facing an attack from any side and would not unleash a European war itself, Blomberg ordered the *Wehrmacht* to be constantly prepared for war, first to defend Germany at any time and second to exploit militarily any politically favourable opportunity. In his directive, he paid special attention to two probable tasks for the *Wehrmacht*. Both dealt with a war on two fronts. In reaction to a change in foreign relations, Austria, Italy and Hungary were no longer considered as German allies. 'Case Red' put the emphasis on the western theatre of war, i.e. against France, while 'Case Green' anticipated a conflict in south-east Europe, i.e. Czechoslovakia. Strategically, the war against France would be conducted defensively. 'Case Green', on the other hand, incorporated the army's idea of 'offensive defence': 'To prevent an imminent attack of a superior enemy coalition, the war in the east can commence with a surprise operation against Czechoslovakia.' Blomberg, accepting the primacy of policy, left it to Hitler to bring about favourable political and legal preconditions for such an action. There was no mention of a war against Russia.[32]

The directive of 24 June 1937 was heavily criticized from within the army's leadership. The sharpest attack was not aimed at its political and military objectives or its timing, but against the growing strategic authority of Blomberg and his small staff, the *Wehrmachtamt* under Wilhelm Keitel and Alfred Jodl. Although Beck, the Chief of Army General Staff, wanted to avoid war before Germany was fully prepared, all he could say was that the army, as Germany's most important service, should have the decisive say in advising Hitler, not only in the question of war planning and time schedules, but also in questions pertaining to the political framework of the German state. Beck continued his old struggle for grand strategic influence on Hitler and directing operations even after Hitler had assumed Blomberg's position and had put Keitel and Jodl in charge of his own military staff, the OKW (Supreme Command of the *Wehrmacht*). Both senior officers were fervent believers in the *Führer* principle and less prepared to give way to centrifugal initiatives.[33]

Just a little over four months later, Hitler overthrew Blomberg's grand strategic assumptions and set new targets for the armed forces. By the autumn of 1937, Hitler had come under pressure from various quarters. Despite the priorities set out in the 1936 Four-Year Plan and the moving ahead of the economy, there were continuing problems with the rearmament programme. All service chiefs fought for preferential treatment of their allocation demands and requested an immediate decision from the *Führer*. Hitler was also under pressure from outside since Britain had embarked on rearmament. While some advisers favoured negotiations, Hitler and others had come to the conclusion that Britain would not accept Germany's expansion to the east. Action necessarily involved deciding on a strategy which risked ending in a war with Britain on the side of France. Hitler had already indicated in conversation that the annexation of Czechoslovakia and Austria would bring Germany enormous strategic and economic gains. So on 5 November 1937, he called together the foreign minister and top military leaders to tell them of his next projected moves. The only other person present at that important meeting in Hitler's impressive chancellery was his senior Military Adjutant, Colonel Friedrich Hossbach. He took notes in his diary and later wrote them up to the 'Hossbach memorandum'.[34]

The significance of this meeting has been examined in detail many times. Hitler's statements about the vital necessity of acquiring living space in Europe were consistent with his earlier views and the Four-Year Plan memorandum. This problem could only be solved by force and never without risk. There is one important difference. Hitler did not mention the Soviet Union as the ultimate source of German living space. Yet to the dismay of the navy and air force especially, the Führer now regarded Britain as Germany's 'most dangerous enemy' and proposed to reorient German strategy appropriately. In turning to the important questions of the 'when' and 'how' of military expansion, Hitler discussed three possible cases. The first and most probable one was by 1943–5 at the latest. The first objective to improve Germany's situation was to overthrow Czechoslovakia and Austria at the same time. Given an earlier, favourable opportunity, the *Wehrmacht* should act with 'lightning speed' (*blitzartig schnell*) so that no outside power could be inclined to intervene. Hitler seemed not to be surprised being rebuffed by his senior advisers. But his audience raised objections to the practicality of what he wanted but not to the principle of conquering living space. Needless to say, Blomberg's staff translated Hitler's aggressive intentions into a new directive replacing that of 24 June 1937. 'Case Green' took precedence over 'Case Red':

> When Germany has achieved complete preparedness for war in all fields, then the military prerequisite will have been created for an offensive war against Czechoslovakia, so that the solution of the German problem of living space can be carried to a victorious conclusion even if one or another of the Great Powers intervenes against us.[35]

Three months later, Hitler began to carry out his plan and to move from preparation for war to deciding the where and when of German expansion. He politically manoeuvred to annex Austria, incorporate the Sudeten Germans and destroy Czechoslovakia, 'gambling successfully on the reluctance of Britain and France to go to war again and mesmerizing German elites and public opinion by his compulsive risk-taking'.[36] Next to the political and operational stories, there are a structural and an educational one. Having also taken the military helm into his hand after Blomberg's downfall in early February 1938, Hitler concerned himself with constructing a series of fortifications against France and Belgium, reduced *Wehrmacht* operational planning to directives for single tasks and the services' general staffs to mere instruments of his 'unalterable decision to smash Czechoslovakia . . . in the foreseeable future'.[37] Parallel to the military road to war, Hitler and the *Wehrmacht* leadership took pains in guiding the officers ideologically. The year 1938 saw many a communication, leaflet or personal address that defined the German officer as a 'political soldier', combining professionalism and ideology with an 'unswerving loyalty to the Führer's will'. As the *Wehrmacht* was an instrument of Hitler's politics, the officer corps could not allow anyone to surpass it 'in the purity and fastness of National Socialist ideology'.[38]

There may have been a difference between Hitler's view of war and that of the military in November 1937. The latter may have thought that a greater living space was to protect a German empire that would be formed by annexing Austria, destroying Czechoslovakia and revising the Versailles frontiers with Poland. But from January 1939 onwards, the officers learnt that Hitler thought in terms of racial war. Again and again, he hammered home the message that space and race were critical. Germany must expand or die. Hitler was determined to solve the problem of living space, and that effort dominated his life. He left the commanders in no doubt that a war to adjust *Lebensraum* to Germany's growing population would not be fought along traditional lines. The next conflict, he stated on 10 February 1939, would be a 'purely ideological war, i.e. consciously a people's and a racial war'. To follow him into such a war of annihilation, compliance was not enough. Hitler demanded from his *Wehrmacht* 'that even if, in my struggle for this ideology, I am abandoned by the rest of the nation in its entirety, then, more than ever, every German soldier, the entire officer corps, man by man, must stand beside me and by me'. This address must be seen against Hitler's earlier speech in the *Reichstag* on 30 January 1939, which the commanders had heard too:

Today I will once more be a prophet: if the international Jewish financiers in and outside Europe should succeed in plunging the nations once more into a world war, then the result will not be the Bolshevization of the earth and thus the victory of Jewry, but the annihilation of the Jewish race in Europe.[39]

By the end of March 1939, Hitler ordered the army to prepare for the invasion of Poland ('Case White'). Though the *Wehrmacht* had greatly gained from its actions against Austria and Czechoslovakia, in financial resources, manpower, materiel, industrial base and strategically, it was still not well prepared for a war on several fronts. Hitler himself was busy with isolating Warsaw and putting it in the wrong by rejecting his 'generous offers' to resolve the frontier problems. In contrast to the crisis over Czechoslovakia there was no opposition from the military leadership to a military conflict with Poland. 'A combination of anti-Polish feeling, confidence that victory would be easy and acceptance that Hitler's judgment about the democracies had proved right before led to an unwillingness to question his authority.'[40] In two addresses, on 23 May and 22 August 1939, Hitler explained the political situation to his most senior commanders and justified his decision to go to war. Not Danzig, but the fundamental need for living space and making food supplies secure, was the key issue in the conflict with Poland. Germany had only a temporary advantage in military equipment, organization, tactics and leadership. Time was working against the Reich, militarily and economically. In the address on 22 August Hitler reiterated what kind of war he was about to unleash against the Polish people: 'Close your hearts to pity. Act with greatest brutality. Eighty million people must obtain what is their right.' At that time, only a few senior officers in the army high command knew of the additional, murderous task of the *SS-Einsatzgruppen* following the fighting troops.[41]

At the end of their march from collapse to rebirth, the military leaders let themselves be again persuaded by their supreme political and military commander that Britain and France would not intervene. This time Germany need not fear a two-front war since Hitler had surprisingly secured the Soviet Union's neutrality via the Ribbentrop–Molotov Pact of 23 August 1939. They seem to have completely misunderstood the relationship between means and ends. Hitler's folly was that he assessed the situation of 1939 in terms of preconceived, fixed notions while ignoring any contrary signs on the side of the Western powers after March 1939. Despite his show of confidence, Hitler was unsure of his risky decision making in the last days of August 1939. He became broody and thoughtful when Mussolini told him that Italy would not take part in the war if Britain and France would intervene. Joseph Goebbels noted in his diary on 26 August: 'That is a bad blow for him.'[42]

It became worse for Hitler and his compliant generals and flag officers. Two days after the first shots to solve the Polish problem had been fired early on 1 September 1939 they also found themselves at war with the Western powers. The prospect of a European war had come much too early for the *Wehrmacht*.

While the *Luftwaffe* had claimed in early May 1939 that it was superior to any other European air force in quantity and quality of its aircraft, organization, training and command of air war even if British and French air forces should fight together,[43] the navy was less optimistic. On 3 September 1939 the Commander in Chief assessed the results of naval rearmament:

> Today the war against France and England broke out, the war which, according to the *Führer's* previous assertions, we had no need to fear before 1944. [The navy] is in no way very adequately equipped for the great struggle with Britain by autumn 1939 … The submarine arm is still much too weak to have any decisive effect on the war. The surface forces are so inferior in number and strength to those of the British fleet that, even at full strength, they can do no more than show that they know how to die gallantly and are resolved in this way to lay the foundation for a new build-up later.[44]

Once war broke out, Hitler found the public support he needed. There was little evidence of war fever, but little opposition either. Political and military leaders judged the mood of the German people more solid, better for the further war than that of 1914 and did everything to raise their 'confidence in final victory, not in peace'.[45]

Notes

1   William Shakespeare, *Othello*, Act III Scene 3.
2   B. Sax and D. Kuntz (eds), *Inside Hitler's Germany: A Documentary History of Life in the Third Reich*. Lexington, 1992, p. 512.
3   J. Wright, *Germany and the Origins of the Second World War*. Basingstoke, 2007, p. 1.
4   See J. Förster, ' "Ich bin der erste Soldat des Reiches": Adolf Hitler (1889–1945)' in S. Förster, M. Pöhlmann and D. Walter (eds), *Kriegsherren der Weltgeschichte: 22 historische Portraits*. München, 2006, pp. 341–56 and 409–10 respectively.
5   See J. Hürter, *Wilhelm Groener: Reichswehrminister am Ende der Weimarer Republik (1928–1932)*. München, 1993; W. Deist, 'The Rearmament of the Wehrmacht' in W. Deist, M. Messerschmidt, H-E. Volkmann and W. Wette, *Germany and the Second World War* vol. 1. Oxford, 1990, pp. 386–92; M. Geyer, 'German Strategy, 1914–1945' in P. Paret (ed.), *Makers of Modern Strategy from Macchiavelli to the Nuclear Age*. Princeton, 1986, pp. 561–4.
6   Deist, 'The Rearmament of the Wehrmacht', pp. 392–408.
7   The navy's secret 'fight against Versailles' between 1919 and 1935 is proudly recorded in its secret manual no. 352 (1937), BA-MA, RMD 4/352. Translated extracts can be found in Nuremberg document C-156, TWC, vol. X/1. Washington, 1951, pp. 433–65.
8   See for instance M. Strohn, *The German Army and the Defence of the Reich: Military Doctrine and the Conduct of the Defensive Battle, 1918–1939*. Cambridge, 2010; G. Groß, 'Das Dogma der Beweglichkeit. Überlegungen zur Genese der Deutschen Heerestaktik im Zeitalter der Weltkriege' in B. Thoß and H-E. Volkmann (eds), *Erster Weltkrieg, Zweiter Weltkrieg: Ein Vergleich*. Paderborn, 2002, pp. 143–66. Its European context has been studied by D. Showalter, 'Plans, Weapons, Doctrines: The Strategic Cultures of Interwar Europe' in R. Chickering and S. Förster (eds), *The Shadows of Total War: Europe, East Asia, and the United States, 1919–1945*. Cambridge, 2003, pp. 55–81; G. Jensen (ed.), *Warfare in Europe 1918–1938*. Aldershot, 2008.
9   See Jürgen Förster, 'Evolution and Development of German Doctrine 1914–45', *The Occasional* vol. 30 (September 1997), pp. 18–31.

10   J. Corum, *The Roots of Blitzkrieg: Hans von Seeckt and German Military Reform*. Lawrence, 1992, p. 199.

11   R. Citino, *The German Way of War: From the Thirty Years' War to the Third Reich*. Lawrence, 2005, p. 240, and his chapter to this volume.

12   See now G. Vardi, 'Joachim von Stülpnagel's Military Thought and Planning', *War in History* XX (2010), pp. 1–24.

13   Joachim von Stülpnagel, 'Gedanken über den Krieg der Zukunft', Military Archive, Freiburg [BA-MA], RH 2/417, pp. 8, 38 and 40 respectively

14   K-J. Müller, *Armee und Drittes Reich 1933–1939: Darstellung und Dokumentation*. Paderborn, 1989, p. 151

15   J. Hürter, *Ein deutscher General an der Ostfront: Die Briefe und Tagebücher des Gotthard Heinrici 1941/42*. Erfurt, 2001, pp. 22–3.

16   Müller, *Armee und Drittes Reich*, p. 150, letter to a comrade of 2 July 1933. See M. Knox, *To the Threshold of Power, 1922/1933: Origins and Dynamics of the Fascist and National Socialist Dictatorships* vol. 1. Cambridge, 2007, pp. 399–406.

17   See for example the address of 15 September. Published in Müller, *Armee und Drittes Reich*, p. 165.

18   One of Hammerstein's daughters! See Wright, *Germany and the Origins of the Second World War*, p. 36. For General Curt von Liebmann's account, see J. Noakes and G. Pridham (eds), *Nazism 1919–1945: A Documentary Reader* vol. 3. Exeter, 1988, pp. 628–9.

19   Directive of 31 October 1933, signed by Hammerstein, BA-MA, RH 2/25.

20   Deist, 'The Rearmament of the Wehrmacht', p. 414.

21   Ibid., pp. 415 and 417 respectively.

22   Ibid., pp. 420 and 425.

23   Geyer, 'German Strategy', p. 568.

24   See Strohn, *The German Army*, ch. 6.

25   A translation of Hitler's memorandum can be found in Sax and Kuntz (eds), *Inside Hitler's Germany*, pp. 290–4.

26   See Deist, 'The Rearmament of the Wehrmacht', pp. 443–7. The Commander in Chief assured Blomberg that a peacetime army of 830,000 men and a wartime army of 2,421,000, organized in 102 divisions, could be created by 1 October 1939. In 1914 the German wartime army had consisted of 87 divisions and 44 militia brigades with 2,147,000 men.

27   Ibid., pp. 456–67; W. Rahn, 'German Naval Strategy and Armament, 1919–39', in P. O'Brien (ed.), *Preparing for the Next War at Sea: Technology and Naval Combat in the Twentieth Century*. London 2001, pp. 109–27.

28   See Deist, 'The Rearmament of the Wehrmacht', pp. 480–91; K. Maier, 'Total War and Operational Air Warfare' in K. A. Maier, H. Rohde, B. Stegemann and H. Umbreit, *Germany and the Second World War* vol. II. Oxford, 1991, pp. 33–41; J. Corum, *The Luftwaffe: Creating the Operational Air War, 1918–1940*. Lawrence, 1997, p. 164.

29   Printed in International Military Tribunal (IMT), vol. XXXIV, pp. 732–47.

30   See K. Maier, 'The Condor Legion: An Instrument of Total War?' in Chickering and Förster (eds), *Shadows of Total War*, pp. 285–94.

31   Blomberg's directive of 30 January 1936: see J. Förster, 'Ideological Warfare in Germany 1919–1945' in R. Blank et. al., *Germany and the Second World War* vol. IX/1, Oxford, 2008, pp. 504–9 and 577.

32   IMT, vol. XXXIV, pp. 732–47.

33   See J. Förster, *Die Wehrmacht im NS-Staat. Eine strukturgeschichtliche Analyse*. München, 2nd ed. 2009, pp. 40–50.

34   See the detailed discussion on that controversial document in Wright, *Germany and the Origins of the Second World War*, pp. 102–5.

35   Pridham and Noakes (eds), *Nazism 1919–1945*, doc. 506

36   See Wright, *Germany and the Origins of the Second World War*, pp. 111–45.

37   Directive of 30 May 1938, cited partly by Pridham and Noakes (eds), *Nazism 1919–1945*, doc. 523.

38   See Förster, 'Ideological Warfare in Germany 1919–1945', pp. 516–20.

39 Pridham and Noakes (eds), *Nazism 1919–1945*, doc. 770.
40 Wright, *Germany and the Origins of the Second World War*, p. 139.
41 See A. Rossino, *Hitler Strikes Poland*. Lawrence, 2003; K-M. Mallmann, J. Böhler and J. Matthäus (eds), *Einsatzgruppen in Polen: Darstellung und Dokumentation*. Darmstadt, 2008.
42 Wright, *Germany and the Origins of the Second World War*, p. 143.
43 Maier, 'Total War', pp. 52–3.
44 E. Mawdsley, *World War Two: A New History*. Cambridge, 2009, p. 82.
45 Förster, 'Ideological Warfare in Germany 1919–1945', pp. 524–5.

The Prussian Tradition, the Myth of the Blitzkrieg and the Illusion of German Military Dominance, 1939–41

Robert M. Citino

The question of German preparations for war in the 1930s has generated an enormous literature. Essentially, the debate has been between the intentionalists ('Hitler intended to start the war all along, either from the moment he came to power or even before') and the functionalists ('war broke out for a number of interrelated reasons, including Hitler's foreign policy, the weak and divided Allied response, and the international economic crisis'). Yet Germany had been preparing for this war for a very long time – for centuries, in fact. No surprise, then, that it was the one state in Europe prepared for the outbreak of the Second World War 1939 or that the conflict opened with a run of spectacular and decisive victories. Spearheaded by it its fearsome tank (Panzer) formations, supported by a powerful air force circling overhead, the German army ran over or around every defensive position thrown in its path. The Polish army was smashed in eighteen days, although a bit more fighting was necessary to reduce Warsaw to rubble. Equally impressive had been the earlier invasions of Denmark and Norway in April 1940, which saw two enemy capitals, Oslo and Copenhagen, fall on day one to a well-coordinated combination of ground forces, seaborne landings and paratroopers. Allied formations intervening in Norway got a quick taste of the *Luftwaffe* and soon evacuated under heavy fire. May 1940 saw the great offensive in Western Europe. Here the Panzers had smashed the cream of the French and British armies, destroying the former and encouraging the latter in a humiliating evacuation at Dunkirk.

The pattern continued into 1941 with a lightning drive into the Balkans that overran Yugoslavia and Greece. When a British force arrived to help defend the latter, the Germans booted it from one position to another and eventually drove it off the mainland altogether. The British destination this time was Crete, and here they were hit by a true thunderbolt: Operation Mercury, the first all-airborne military operation in history. It quickly seized the island from its British and Commonwealth defenders, who ran away yet again, this time to Egypt. Indeed, in the opening phase of the war, it often seemed as if the evacuation had become the characteristic British military operation, and that 'BEF' stood for 'back every fortnight' or 'back every Friday'. For the British, it was a case of pack up your troubles in your old kit bag and run, run, run.

Finally, the summer of 1941 witnessed Operation Barbarossa, the German assault on the Soviet Union and the greatest undertaking in military history.

German success in the opening weeks still boggles the mind. With the Panzers ranging far and deep into Soviet terrain, the *Wehrmacht* undertook one immense encirclement after another. By December, the German juggernaut stood just thirty miles from Moscow. On the way, the *Wehrmacht* inflicted four million casualties on the Red Army, about three million of whom were prisoners. Many observers though the Soviet Union was finished. Historical analysis of these operations continues to paint them as examples of a new method of war making called *Blitzkrieg* (lightning war). Allegedly invented in the inter-war era, the strategy is supposed to have transformed warfare by mechanizing it.[1] In place of the foot soldier and the cavalry came trucks, tanks and aircraft. In place of the trench deadlock that characterized the First World War, there were now vast campaigns of breakthrough, encirclement and maneouvre.

The only trouble with this consensus is that it is largely fictitious. Even the word *Blitzkrieg* is a fiction. The German army didn't invent it. They hardly ever used it outside quotation marks. It was a term that had been kicking around international military circles in the 1930s to describe any rapid and decisive victory, in contrast to the long, horrible war of attrition that had just ended, and it first gained widespread currency in the West, in articles in *Time* and *Life* magazines, in fact. This period was a time of rethinking and experimentation for Germany, yes, but we could say the same thing for all armies of the day. The British invented the tank, after all, and were working on a radical experimental mechanized brigade as early as 1928. Likewise, if there was one army in the world that was obsessed with the possibilities of tanks, aircraft, and airborne, it was the Red Army. What distinguished the inter-war German army was that it was not trying to discover something new. Unlike its neighbours, it felt that it already had a workable war-fighting doctrine.

Since the earliest days of the German state a unique military culture had evolved. This can be called a 'German way of war'. Its birthplace was the kingdom of Prussia. Starting in the seventeenth century with Frederick William, the 'Great Elector' of Brandenburg, Prussia's rulers recognized that their small, impoverished state on the European periphery had to fight wars that were '*kurtz und vives*' (short and lively).[2] Trapped into a tight spot in the middle of Europe, surrounded by states that vastly outweighed it in manpower and resources, it could not win long and drawn-out wars of attrition. So Prussia's military solution was to find a way to fight short, sharp wars that ended in decisive battlefield victories. Its conflicts had to be 'front-loaded', unleashing a storm against the enemy, and either destroying it or bringing it to the table for negotiations.

The solution to this strategic problem was something that the Prussians called *Bewegungskrieg* – the war of movement. It was a way of war that stressed maneouvre on the operational level, not simply tactical maneuverability or a faster march rate, but the movement of large units like divisions, corps and armies. Prussian commanders and their later German descendants sought to move these formations in such a way as to strike the mass of the enemy army a sharp, annihilating blow as rapidly as possible. This might involve a surprise assault against an unprotected flank or both of them. On several notable occasions, it even resulted in entire Prussian or German armies getting into the rear of an enemy army, the dream scenario of any general schooled in the art. The desired end-state was the *Kesselschlacht*, literally, a 'cauldron battle,' more specifically, a battle of encirclement trapping the enemy on all sides prior to destroying it in a series of 'concentric operations.'

This vibrant and aggressive operational posture imposed certain requirements on German armies: firstly, an extremely high level of battlefield aggression; secondly, an officer corps that tended to launch attacks no matter what the odds. The Germans also found over the years that conducting an operational-level war of movement required a flexible system of command that left a great deal of initiative in the hands of lower-ranking commanders. It is customary today to call it *Auftragstaktik* (mission tactics): the higher commander devised an *Auftrag* (general mission) and then left the means of achieving it to the officer on the spot. It is more accurate, however, to speak, as the Germans themselves did, of the 'independence of the lower commander' (*Selbständigkeit der Unterführer*).[3] A commander's ability to size up a situation and act on his own was an equalizer for a numerically weaker army, allowing it to grasp opportunities that might be lost if it had to wait for reports and orders to climb up and down the chain of command.

It wasn't always an elegant thing to behold. Prussian–German military history is littered with lower-level commanders making untimely advances, initiating highly unfavorable, even bizarre, attacks and generally making nuisances of themselves, at least from the perspective of the high command. There were men like General Eduard von Flies, who launched one of the most senseless frontal assaults in military history at the battle of Langensalza in 1866 against a dug-in Hanoverian army that outnumbered him two to one;[4] General Karl von Steinmetz, whose impetuous command of the 1st Army in the Franco-Prussian War in 1870 almost upset the entire operational applecart;[5] and General Hermann von François, whose refusal to follow orders almost derailed the East Prussian campaign in 1914.[6] Nearly forgotten today, these events represent the active, aggressive side of the German tradition, as opposed to the more intellectual approach of a Clausewitz, Schlieffen or Moltke the Elder.

The war of movement is central to understanding just what the Germans thought they were doing in the 1930s, and in the opening years of the Second World War. It was here that the Germans saw the tank and airplane making their contribution. Characteristically, they employed these new weapons in larger units. The Panzer Division was a formation built around tanks, but also containing a full panoply of combined arms: infantry, artillery, reconnaissance, supply columns, bridging trains, all of which had their mobility raised to the level of the tank. A Panzer Division could assault and penetrate, smash through defences into the clear, pursue and destroy any defensive position or formation that tried to stop it, then reform and do it all over again. It wasn't a wonder weapon or a magic bullet, but it certainly might have looked that way if you happened to be a Polish lancer or a Belgian anti-tank gunner, or a Greek infantryman. Like all military cultures, then, the Germans had evolved a unique combination of traits. This was a 'distinctive language' spoken only by the *Wehrmacht*, as the leading German military journal of the day, the *Militär Wochenblatt*, put it.[7]

Indeed, if war was a simple contest to see who could most completely humiliate an opponent in a first encounter, then the *Wehrmacht* would have won the Second World War hands down. The Polish, Danish, Norwegian, French, Yugoslavian, Greek, British and Soviet armies all learned this lesson the hard way. The first six armies did not survive to tell the tale, nor did the states they were called upon to defend. British armies were smashed not just in France but in the next three theatres as well: North Africa, Greece and Crete. Britain only managed to survive the experience thanks to the presence of the English Channel. Likewise, the Soviet army was hammered as hard as any military in history during that first awful campaigning season. And finally, lest we forget, the US army's first meeting with the *Wehrmacht* on an obscure hunk of Tunisian rock called the Kasserine Pass proved a humbling experience too.

As all these armies learned, first encounters with the *Wehrmacht* were inherently dangerous. Case White (*Fall Weiss*), the invasion of Poland, set the tone. It bore all the marks of the Prussian–German tradition: a classic example of the *kurtz und vives* campaign, now made immeasurably more effective by mechanization. The operational plan aimed to deliver an overwhelming blow from the outset, with air raids on Polish airfields in the opening minutes and then massed Panzer assaults at multiple locations along the border. It also featured the prime Prussian characteristic of concentric operations: converging drives by widely separated forces, in this case, separated army groups belonging to General Fedor von Bock (Army Group North, containing 4th Army in Pomerania and 3rd Army in East Prussia) and General Gerd von Rundstedt (Army Group South, with three armies: 8th and 10th Armies in Silesia, and 14th Army straddled between Silesia and occupied Slovakia).[8] The battle plan called for the two army groups to smash through the Polish defensive positions along the border and catch the main body of the Polish forces in a great pincer movement (*Zangenbewegung*), with the main weight of the attack (three armies to two) borne by Army Group South.

Another hallmark of the Prussian tradition also evident in the Polish campaign was that independent-minded and highly aggressive field commanders ran things pretty much as they saw fit. Throughout the planning process, General Bock had registered unhappiness with what he saw as a subsidiary role. The unusual conformation of the border meant that Army Group North had to deploy in two separate zones divided by the Polish Corridor.[9] Its first task, therefore, would be a relatively minor one: overrunning the Polish Corridor and establishing overland communications with East Prussia. Only then could it take part in the major operation: the drive into Poland proper and destroy the Polish army. There were no such operational distractions in the south, the reason that the plan made Rundstedt's Army Group South the point of main effort or *Schwerpunkt*.

Bock deemed this secondary role insulting, and had spent the summer peppering the High Command of the Army (OKH) with plans to expand it.[10] After overrunning the Corridor, he wanted to ship his entire 4th Army from Pomerania to East Prussia, inserting it on the left of 3rd Army, and sending it on a wide sweep to the east of Warsaw. If Polish forces tried to regroup in the interior of the country, he would then be in a position to encircle them east of the capital. The chief of the OKH, General Walther von Brauchitsch, took a dim view of such a major redeployment in the midst of the fighting. He warned Bock that committing troops too far to the east of Warsaw could have serious repercussions in case of an Allied attack in the west.[11] Eventually, however, he allowed Bock's army group full freedom of action.[12] As always, the man in the field took precedence in German war making.

The campaign went like clockwork. Army Group North crossed the border before dawn on 1 September 1939. There was some hard fighting here and there, but by the end of the first day, the Germans had sealed off the southern end of the corridor, trapping two Polish infantry divisions (9th and 27th) and a cavalry brigade (Pomorska). Polish attempts to break out came to nought, with all three formations smashed in the course of the fighting and 15,000 prisoners in German hands by the third day.[13] The next day the 3rd and 4th armies linked up to the east of the Corridor. In the south, Rundstedt was swinging a far heavier bat, the full weight of the German army. It is always easy to detect the point of main effort (*Schwerpunkt*) of German operations in the Second World War: simply count the Panzer divisions. Army Group South contained four of the six then in existence, along with three of the four light divisions. Altogether, Rundstedt had three armies on line, from left to right the 8th, 10th and 14th. It was their task to destroy the mass of the Polish army by a direct thrust north east towards Warsaw. The 10th Army in the centre would form the army group spearhead, with no less than six mobile formations: two Panzer divisions, two light divisions and two motorized infantry divisions. It was, by 1939 standards, an immense concentration of force.

Not surprisingly, Rundstedt broke through almost everywhere. On the left, 8th Army reached the Prosna river on the second day of operations, slashing through the defences of the Polish Łódź Army. This was largely the work of well-drilled infantry as the 8th Army had no Panzer elements outside of the few tanks of the SS *Leibstandtarte Adolf Hitler*, at the time just a motorized infantry regiment. On the right, 14th Army, including XXII (Motorized) Corps, broke into Poland from the Jablunka Pass in the west to Novy Targ (Neumarkt) in the east. It was the centre of the army group that made the most progress. Here 10th Army blasted through the seam between the Łódź Army on its left and the Kraków Army on its right, reaching the Warthe river and then crossing it in stride. This is where the Poles got their first look at the full German mechanized package: tank columns deploying off the road at the first sign of resistance and bypassing the defenders on both flanks; heavy air attacks by Stuka dive-bombers, their screeching sirens adding a note of terror to the bombing run; rapid advances by tank columns deep into the rear that suddenly materialized into blocking positions when the Poles tried to retreat.

In concert with 14th Army to its right, the advance of 10th Army also had the benefit of working concentrically against the Kraków Army, tucked into the south-western corner of Poland. Soon its remnants were attempting to retreat into the interior, a task that in many places meant running a gauntlet of German armour that had already established itself in the rear. By 6 September 1939, Kraków had fallen to the invaders. The collapse of the Kraków Army and the Pomorze Army far to the right in the Corridor, in turn, meant disaster for the two Polish armies between them: the Łódź Army, already pressed hard by 8th Army's attacks, and, deployed deep in the section of the Polish border bulging out towards Germany, the Poznań Army under General Tadeusz Kutrzeba. Facing only German border defence units, the latter was at the moment still largely untouched by enemy action, but it was already doomed, one hundred miles from the relative safety of Warsaw, with two complete German army groups closing in behind it.

By week two, the Germans were in full throttle all across the front of both army groups. While the Germans themselves referred to the maneouvre as 'pincers', in fact, the Polish army was being pressed between two very heavy iron slabs. The first German Panzer forces reached the outskirts of Warsaw by 8 September as the armoured spearheads of 10th Army slashed across the southern Polish plain towards the capital. In the course of its headlong rush, 10th Army actually overran the Polish 'Prusy Army' while it was still in the process of assembling.[14] This was an apocalyptic moment in the history of modern military operations. Polish casualties were everywhere horrendous. The few defending formations with an open retreat path to Warsaw were desperately trying to get there, but there were gradually coming apart under unrelenting air attack. Polish command and control had broken down, and the only army still functioning as such, the only formation still intact, was the isolated Poznań Army.

In fact, it was Poznań Army's belated attempt to retreat that would bring about the climax of the campaign. As it tried desperately to slither out of the jaws clamping down on it from both right and left, it smashed into the northern (left) flank guard of the advancing German 8th Army along the Bzura river west of Warsaw on 9 September – just eight days into the campaign.[15] The 14th, 17th and 25th Infantry Divisions, along with the Podolska and Wielkopolska Cavalry Brigades, hit the overextended German 24th and 30th Infantry Divisions strung out along the river. It was half counterattack, half formless melee – the Poles were in the midst of a hurried retreat, after all. Still, the initial thrust managed to achieve surprise and made good progress at first, capturing some 1,500 German prisoners from the panic-stricken 30th Division alone. It certainly caused heartburn at German headquarters: army, army group and OKH alike.

What it could not do, however, was have lasting repercussions. Kutrzeba and his army were trying to break out, but break out to where? The attackers were isolated, without any hope of support or reinforcement. In addition, they were facing in the *Wehrmacht* a force that could stop at will, turn around, and then launch heavy attacks in a way that was not yet typical of western armies. Within a day, German reinforcements were on the way to the Bzura, including the mass of 10th Army's armoured units. Diverted instantaneously from the drive on Warsaw, they shifted their axis 180 degrees in effortless fashion. Faced with concentric attacks from all four points of the compass, the mass of the Polish attackers was soon hemmed into a shrinking pocket on the Bzura, along with remnants of Army Pomorze who had managed to escape the blows of Army Group North. Subjected to non-stop attack by the *Luftwaffe* and punished heavily by the German artillery, in a hopeless strategic situation, over 100,000 men would surrender. At this point, 10th Army's armored divisions did it again: shifting their axis of advance 180 degrees for the second time in a week, and hurrying back towards Warsaw.[16] By 19 September, Warsaw was the only spot on the map still in Polish hands, and the Germans, in fact, would speak of an 'Eighteen Days' Campaign'.[17] Surrounded and under heavy aerial bombardment, Warsaw would surrender on 27 September.

Yet if one campaign may be said to define the *Wehrmacht*'s early run of successes it was the offensive in the West in May 1940, codenamed Case Yellow (*Fall Gelb*).[18] There was much here that was reminiscent of the Polish campaign. There was the same emphasis on operational-level maneouvre leading to a rapid decision, the same jockeying for position among the generals, with Bock once again winding up playing second fiddle to Rundstedt, the same emphasis on careful, even meticulous planning to deliver a shattering blow from the outset. Historians tend to dote on the controversies within the German high command in planning Case Yellow, especially the role played by General Erich von Manstein in devising the bold move through the Ardennes and Hitler's decision to force it on the high command. What deserves much greater recognition, however, is how typical Case Yellow appears as an opening campaign within the Prussian–German tradition.

What eventually emerged from the lengthy planning process was this: Army Group B (under Bock) would invade Belgium and the Netherlands in order to attract the attention of the Allied forces in France, and perhaps lure them to the north. Once they had swallowed the bait, there would be a gigantic Panzer thrust by Army Group B (*Rundstedt*) through the difficult terrain of the Ardennes. With its dense old-growth forest, steep-banked rivers and winding roads and trails, it was hardly a place that you would think of when the phrase 'tank country' came to mind. That, of course, was precisely the point. The Panzers would likely meet little resistance in the forest, since the French and Belgians considered it unsuitable for operations by armour. Having passed through the Ardennes, the Panzers would have a single river to cross: the Meuse between Sedan and Dinant. Once over that small obstacle, there would be nothing in the way except open country all the way to the English Channel.

On 24 February 1940 Army Chief of Staff General Franz Halder issued a set of operational directives for the upcoming offensive.[19] Bock's Army Group B would contain two armies: the 18th (General Küchler) would overrun the Netherlands; the 6th (General Walter von Reichenau) would push into Belgium. It was essential that the Allies view Army Group B as the main German thrust. Thus, Bock's command included a hefty sampling of the new mobile units: a number of paratrooper and glider units, including the 7th Flieger Division and 22nd Airlanding Division; two complete Panzer corps, the XVI (General Erich Hoepner) and the XXXIX (General Rudolf Schmidt), as well a significant commitment of air power.

Still, the point of main effort (*Schwerpunkt*) lay in the south. Army Group A contained three armies: the 4th (General Günther von Kluge), 12th (General Wilhelm von List) and 16th (General Ernst Busch), plus a newly organized Panzer Group (*Panzergruppe*) under General Ewald von Kleist. All told it contained seven of Germany's ten operational Panzer divisions. The employment of Panzer Group von Kleist – three complete corps – brought German mechanized operations to a new stage of development and complexity. Since the Kleist group would have to pass through the Ardennes and then launch its attack on an exceedingly narrow front, the plan had it echeloned in some depth. The first echelon would consist of Guderian's Corps, now upgraded from its 1939 designation of 'motorized' to 'Panzer'; the second of the Panzer Corps under General Georg-Hans Reinhardt; and the Motorized Corps under General Gustav von Wietersheim. The first Flak Corps would advance between the two leading Panzer groups providing protection from any Allied air assault that might penetrate the *Luftwaffe*'s air umbrella.[20] It was the mightiest mechanized force that the military world had yet seen: 134,000 men, 41,000 vehicles, 1,250 tanks and 362 reconnaissance vehicles.

The actual operation, opening on 10 May 1940, proved to be much less troublesome than the battle over planning it. As ever, in German operational planning, there were a series of shocks to the Allied commanders early in the fighting.[21] In the Netherlands, it was the use of both airborne and airlanding troops – two complete divisions – to seize airfields, bridges over the numerous watercourses and other strategic installations.[22] In fact, the government districts of The Hague, army headquarters and Queen Wilhelmina herself were amongst the targets. Not all of these special operations went completely according to plan. A number of bridges fell to the landing forces – the Moerdijk causeway south of Rotterdam, for example. By and large, however, the jumps against the airfields were disastrous. The attempt to seize the Ockenburg, Valkenburg and Ypenburg airfields around The Hague collapsed in the face of larger-than-expected airfield garrisons and the failure of *Luftwaffe* raids to knock out Dutch anti-aircraft batteries in the area. Disaster begot disaster when the German transports arrived with the air landing troops, expecting to land at the captured fields. At Ypenburg Dutch fire destroyed eleven of the first thirteen JU-52 transport aircraft in the air. It might be argued that the shock and panic these landings caused in the Dutch command, which had to face combat outside the very walls of the capital and throughout the four corners of the land from the very first moment, might have made them worthwhile anyway. Whether shattering the Dutch was worth the loss of so many highly trained specialist troops is another question. The arrival of the mass of Küchler's 18th Army soon made it a moot point.

To the south, the Germans mounted a bold glider assault on the modern Belgian fortress of Eben Emael, at the junction of the Meuse and the Albert Canal.[23] The glider added a new dimension to operations, its silent approach being a complement to the piercing siren of the Stuka. Operation Granite involved landing a force on top of the fort itself, knocking out its guns, then forcing the surrender of the troops inside. It certainly had its share of problems. The glider carrying the commander of the operation, Lieutenant Rudolf Witzig, was one of two that released prematurely. He had his pilot glide back over the Rhine, called the nearest *Luftwaffe* headquarters, and got himself another tow plane. Meanwhile, the assault forced landed and within ten minutes had knocked out all of the guns and installations on the surface of the fort. It was an impressive debut for the hollow charge explosive, which proved effective against the armored cupolas of the Belgian guns.[24] The tiny force – just seventy-eight men – did have some problems with a Belgian garrison ten times its own size, although German morale rose considerable when a lone glider appeared over the fort, landed and disgorged the fiery Lieutenant Witzig. He and his men managed to keep the garrison bottled up until German ground forces, elements of the 4th Panzer Division (6th Army), arrived the next day.

The rest of Army Group B played its role to the hilt. The large 6th Army (five corps) entered the southern Netherlands with Hoepner's XVI Panzer Corps in the van. The plan called for a quick crossing of the 'Maastricht appendage' and then entry into the central Belgium plain west of the Meuse and Sambre. Unfortunately, the Dutch blew the Meuse bridges up before the Germans could seize them, and Hoepner's Panzers spent a whole full day immobilized in Dutch territory. On 11 May they got moving again and the next day crashed into a large French mechanized force advancing from the south. This was the Cavalry Corps of General René Prioux, containing the 2nd and 3rd Light Mechanized Divisions. In a two-day clash of armor near Gembloux, the French managed to handle the German pretty roughly, bringing them to a standstill in several places. This should not surprise us, as the French tanks, especially the medium SOMUA S-35, were in most respects superior to their German counterparts. The German captain who described the first day at Gembloux as a 'hard and bitter day' did not lie.[25] Nevertheless, the skills of the veteran and better-trained German crews eventually began to tell against a French force that was tasting combat for the first time. After a concentrated German attack managed to penetrate the front of the 3rd Light Mechanized division, Prioux ordered the Cavalry Corps to retire on 14 May 1940.

In fact, the Cavalry Corps was at Gembloux not to seek decisive battle, but merely to cover the major Allied operational maneouvre of the campaign.

The Allies were following 'Plan D', which called for the Anglo-French force to enter Belgium and take up a strong defensive position along the Dyle river.[26] Four complete armies were involved: from west to east the 7th Army, the latest version of the British Expeditionary Force, the 1st and the 9th. The advance would proceed in tandem with a wheel to the right, so that by the time they had finished their advance, the Allies would be facing nearly due east, from Belgian Monthermé in the south to the Dutch border. In March 1940, the French introduced the so-called 'Breda variant' to the plan, with 7th Army on the left extending the line up to Breda in the Netherlands.[27] This 'Dyle–Breda position', the Allies believed, would be an ideal place to meet the principal German thrust coming down on them out of the north. As the Belgians and Dutch armies retreated, they could plug themselves into it as well, no small consideration to the final shape of the plan.

Once again, as in 1914, French operational plans played ideally into German hands. Facing the German *Schwerpunkt*, an immense armored force aiming towards Sedan, was the French 2nd Army. Its task was simply to function as a hinge for the Allied swing into Belgium, and it was essentially performing what one modern authority has called 'an economy of force operation'.[28] It had low priority in manpower, in equipment and in air support. Of its five divisions, two were overage reservists, or 'series B', one was North African and one a colonial unit from Senegal.

Once the two rival deployments are understood, the actual campaign in the south is a simple story. The Panzers entered the Ardennes without incident – a snake of tanks, trucks and reconnaissance vehicles fifty miles long. The most anxious moments for the *Wehrmacht* were traffic delays. They brushed aside weak Belgian resistance in the forest itself, mainly light Belgian *Chasseurs Ardennais*, who set up a number of roadblocks and demolitions but little else. Early in the evening of 12 May – just day three of the operation – the head of the German snake emerged from the forest. It was Guderian's XIX Panzer Corps, heading towards Sedan. Rather than pause and stage a set-piece river crossing the next day, Guderian forced a crossing that evening on his own initiative. A handful of infantry in rubber assault boats, as well as a few tanks and motorcycles, managed to establish a bridgehead on the far bank. The campaign had been decided, although no one knew it yet.

The next day, the French 2nd Army took the kind of pounding that only Polish veterans could have understood. There were tanks, a huge mass of them in fact, stretching as far as the eye could see, along with heavy artillery concentrations, both 105 mm and 150 mm, and finally ceaseless screeching dive-bombing by the Stukas. Units of the French 2nd Army broke in panic even before the Germans were over the river in force, and the same thing happened to French 9th Army at the two Meuse river crossings to the north, one at Monthermé (Reinhardt's XLI Panzer Corps) and one at Dinant (Hoth's XV Panzer Corps, part of 4th Army). By the end of the day on 13 May, the Germans had torn a great gash some fifty miles wide in the French line.

This was not simply a tactical opening, but an operational one too. In the course of the next week, the three armies of Army Group A would pour through the gap. With the Panzers in the lead, and the poor infantry force-marching until it dropped, the Germans slid across the rear of the huge Allied army in Belgium. This had to be a satisfying moment for the German commanders, veterans all of the previous war. Those very place names in Flanders that had hung just tantalizingly out of reach in 1918 were falling like dominoes: Arras, Amiens, Mt Kemmel.

The Germans reached yet another milestone on 20 May 1940. Late in the day, the 2nd Panzer Division (XIX Panzer Corps) reached Abbeville at the mouth of the Somme river. It meant the destruction of the Allied army to the north, no less than a million and a half men. It was a *Kesselschlacht*, the greatest battle of encirclement in military history up to this point. During their drive across northern France, the Panzers had been nearly unmolested. The French managed a pair of counterattacks, led by the commander of the newly formed 4th Armored Division, General Charles de Gaulle. Neither his first attack at Montcornet (17 May) nor a second one at Crécy-sur-Serre (19 May) managed to halt German momentum. Neither did the single British counterstroke of the campaign, near Arras on 21 May.

What they did achieve was to give the German high command, up to and including Hitler, an attack of the shakes. Their situation maps showed an ominous picture: long, vulnerable armoured spearheads strung out on the roads, completely out of contact with their follow-on infantry divisions. Orders actually went out to Guderian to halt and allow time for the infantry to catch up. Once they had consolidated a defensive position on his flanks he could drive on. Anyone who has studied the centuries-long operational pattern of the German army could not possibly be surprised at Guderian's response. He ignored his orders and continued on, undertaking a 'reconnaissance in force' that included – no surprise – his entire XIX Panzer Corps.[29] He reached the Channel, wheeled north and kept on attacking. The time was coming, soon, when such independent action would no longer be tolerated in the *Wehrmacht*, but that time was not yet.

The campaign would end in disappointment, as is well known, with the escape of most of the British Expeditionary Force from Dunkirk. How it happened – or how the Germans allowed it to happen – has generated a historical controversy. Hitler's decision to halt the Panzers at the Dunkirk perimeter, a decision taken to reassert some control over a campaign and an officer corps that had apparently slipped out of his grasp, was the principal reason, but it goes much deeper than that. Even the most successful campaigns contain what the great Prussian sage Karl Maria von Clausewitz called 'friction': little things that go wrong, and that eventually add up to larger things. No military campaign is perfect. In Case Yellow, the Germans came, through good planning, aggressiveness and luck, about as close as you can get.

The Germans fought two more classic 'short and lively' campaigns in the Balkans in spring 1941.[30] Operation Marita, the invasion of Greece, had been in the works for months, a response to the humiliating defeat suffered by the Italian army in its invasion of Greece in late 1940. The invasion of Yugoslavia, by contrast, had been put together overnight, quite literally, as a response to a pro-Allied coup in Belgrade on the night of 26–27 March 1941. The brief time-span for conception and planning did leave a few loose ends here and there, and in fact the undertaking would take place under the nearly anonymous designation of 'Operation 25'.

It is easy to underestimate the significance of a campaign like this. After all, given its population and resource advantages, Germany should have been able to beat the Greek army, or the Yugoslav one, or both at the same time, without much difficulty. We might say the same thing about the Polish campaign in 1939, or the invasion of Denmark and Norway in 1940. Yet, those who look at the Balkan campaign and see only a great power landing a hit on two of the war's weaker sisters miss the point entirely: the *Wehrmacht*'s complete and rapid victory over the Greeks and Yugoslavs mirrors precisely the treatment it meted out in every first encounter of the war, without exception.

Let us focus for a moment on the campaign in Greece, in many ways an exemplar for the 'short and lively' war of the Prussian tradition. Here the *Wehrmacht* encountered not just another weak army of a second-rate power, as it was fighting in Yugoslavia, but a British and Commonwealth intervention as well. Operation Marita met Operation Lustre, the transfer of a British expeditionary force from North Africa to the Balkans.[31] 'Force W', as it was known, was small, just two divisions (2nd New Zealand, 6th Australian), as well as the 1st Tank Brigade (of the 2nd Armoured Division), along with a small contingent of airpower. One German commentator called it 'a drop in the ocean by the standards of continental warfare'.[32] The commander of the expedition, General Henry Maitland Wilson, was placed in a nearly impossible position, having to thrust forward a small force against an onrushing *Wehrmacht* coming at him from all directions.

The precise placement of this force was a thus a matter of crucial importance, as well as controversy within the Allied camp. Essentially, the Greek supreme commander, General Alexander Papagos, wanted the British as far north as possible. Maitland Wilson preferred to stay as far south as he could manage.[33] The plan that eventually evolved was, typically, the worst of both worlds. Force W would advance not-too-far-north, not-too-far-south to a defensive position stretching along the Vermion mountains and Aliakmon river (the 'Vermion line', it was called, rather grandiloquently, since there were no prepared works there at all).

For their part, and as always, the Germans were planning a bold operational-level stroke, using 12th Army's mechanized formations. While the infantry divisions of XXX Corps crossed the Rhodope Mountains into western Thrace, and the XVIII Mountain Corps had the unenviable task of smashing through the well-fortified Metaxas Line along the Bulgarian frontier, 2nd Panzer Division would cross into Yugoslavia towards Strumica. From here it would wheel sharply south, pass just west of Lake Doiran on the Greek–Yugoslav border, then drive as rapidly as possible on the major port of Thessaloniki. Its seizure would be a strategic blow to the Greeks, cutting off their entire 2nd Army still fighting to the east.

Simultaneously, however, there would be an even more dramatic stroke: a westward drive into southern Yugoslavia by 9th Panzer Division, *Leibstandarte Adolf Hitler* SS Motorized Infantry Regiment and the 73rd Infantry Division. These corps would drive towards the Vardar river between Skoplje and Veles, then once again wheel sharply south, passing through the Monastir Gap and crossing into central Greece from the north. This would result in a link up with the Italians and the isolation of the Greek 1st Army still fighting in Albania. Moreover, the German manoeuvre would also fatally compromise the Allied defensive position, outflanking Force W no matter what line it happened to occupy.[34]

And so it went. There was a signal moment at the start of Marita. On 6 April a *Luftwaffe* raid on the port of Piraeus scored a direct hit on the 12,000-ton ammunition ship SS *Clan Fraser*. It exploded spectacularly, triggering secondary explosions all over the harbour, destroying much of the port itself, along with twenty-seven craft docked there and a great deal of shore equipment, and shattering windows seven miles away in Athens.[35] It was a kind of calling card, announcing to Greece and to the world that the *Wehrmacht* was on the march. Within hours, German forces were across the Greek border in strength. On the far left, XXX Corps had fairly easy going, since much of the Greek force in isolated western Thrace had been evacuated when German troops first entered Bulgaria. In the center, XVIII Mountain Corps found the Metaxas Line, and the Greek soldiers defending it, to be as tough as anything they had encountered in this war. Losses were heavy here, with at least one regiment having to be pulled out of the line, but the attack on both sides of the Rupel Gorge, supported by massed artillery and non-stop attack by Stukas, finally chewed its way through the Greek wire, pillboxes and concrete bunkers.[36]

The battle for the Metaxas Line soon became a moot point, however, as 2nd Panzer Division cut through light opposition to the west and reached Thessaloniki on 9 April. In the course of its short hop south, it overran elements of the Greek 19th Division, which were just moving up into position. The Greek formation was ostensibly 'motorized', which meant in this case possessing a handful of Bren carriers and captured Italian tanks and trucks.[37] The fall of Thessaloniki made the entire Greek force to the east superfluous, and 2nd Army surrendered to the Germans on 9 April.

The *Schwerpunkt* of this campaign, however, lay with XXXX Panzer Corps (General Georg Stumme). Jumping off at 5.30 a.m. on 6 April 1941, it encountered Yugoslav forces almost immediately (elements of 5th Yugoslav Army). Brushing them aside, the mass of the corps reached its objective (the line Skoplje–Veles) the next day. Stumme's lead formations had made sixty miles in that one day, and had to perform a major river crossing of the Vardar to boot. Passing through Prilep on 8 April and Monastir on 9 April, the corps stood ready to invade Greece the next day. On 10 April, XXXX Corps crossed the border, peeled off the 9th Panzer Division to link-up with the Italians in Albania, and continued the drive to the south, towards the Greek town of Florina.[38]

It was not immediately apparent, but the drive on Florina and thence into central Greece had unhinged the entire Allied position. Not only had the maneouvre uncovered the communications of the Greek 1st Army in Albania, it had also inserted a strong mobile German force far into the rear of the original British defensive position along the 'Vermion position'. Maitland Wilson could read a map, and this news sent the entire Commonwealth force scurrying back down to the south from whence it had come, desperately trying to extricate itself from the jaws of two pursuing German pincers. Australian and New Zealand troops fought with their usual tenacity, and there was some gritty action of the rear guard variety, but on the operational level the front line moved steadily southwards. The original 'Vermion position' became the 'Aliakmon Line' (11 April) which gave way to the 'Mt Olympus position' (16 April) and then the 'Thermopylae line' (24 April), the last actually a crescent-shaped defensive position stretching across central Greece from Molos in the east to the Gulf of Corinth in the south.[39] The place names make the after-action reports read like some lost essay by Herodotus, which continues to lend the entire affair a certain epic aura that it does not at all deserve. In fact, the retreat was a nightmare, carried out under a nearly constant barrage of Stuka attacks. It had been thus in Norway and at Dunkirk, and now it was more of the same in Greece.

Making good use of the difficult terrain, the Commonwealth rear guards did hold up the Germans just long enough to allow the main body to escape, and that was no small feat. The Germans, for their part, managed to keep up the pressure only by sending light pursuit groups ahead of their main body. There certainly were not entire Panzer divisions in play during this portion of the campaign. But even the smaller pursuit groups found themselves limited by the difficulty of mountainous terrain. At one point they tried, unsuccessfully, to pass a tank column through the pass at Thermopylae: the original European tactical exercise, one might say.[40] Even the most celebrated incident of the campaign, the 26 April airdrop on to the isthmus of Corinth by two battalions of the 2nd *Fallschirmjäger* Regiment, failed to seal the deal. Indeed, it met with disaster when a lucky shot detonated charges over the canal bridge, dropping it and killing most of the German paratroopers crossing it, along with the German war correspondent filming the action.[41] It mattered not, one way or another. Most of Force W was off the mainland by this time, having already been evacuated from Rafina and Porto Rafti in Attica or from Monemvasia and Kalamata further south.

Athens fell on 27 April and the fighting was over three days later. General List's 12th Army had dismantled the Greek army and driving the British into another helter-skelter retreat, and forcing them into yet another evacuation that saved the men only at the cost of abandoning virtually all of the equipment. Nor were British manpower losses inconsiderable: 11,840 men out of the 53,000 plus who had originally embarked for Europe. In 'tossing Tommy from the continent',[42] German losses had been much heavier than in the Yugoslav campaign, yet still startlingly light overall: 1,100 killed and 4,000 wounded. By the way, the campaign in Yugoslavia cost the Germans exactly 558 casualties (151 killed, 392 wounded, 15 missing in action).

Let us now pause here to take stock. The *Wehrmacht* had enjoyed an amazing run during these two years, smashing every enemy army within reach. There is no need to romanticize any of it, however. From 1939–41, circumstances had conspired to hand the *Wehrmacht* a perfect opportunity to fight the only kind of war for which it was adequately prepared. It was not the false notion of a new kind of war, a *Blitzkrieg*, but rather *Bewegungskrieg*: a series of short, sharp campaigns within the friendly confines of Central and Eastern Europe, with its relatively short distances, temperate climate and highly developed road and rail net. When it came to operational-level maneouvre warfare under these conditions, the *Wehrmacht* had no peer, and had it continued fighting under these conditions would have won the war. Yet none of this was new in Prussian or German history, and indeed we might apply the exact same description to Prussian armies under Frederick the Great as Hitler armies between 1939 and 1941.

And yet, *Bewegungskrieg* had never been a panacea for Germany's strategic problems. For all the skill that the Germans have shown in an operational-level war of movement, they have historically shown serious and persistent weaknesses in other areas. The problem of logistics has rarely been on the front burner. A quick and decisive battlefield victory obviates the need for a deep logistics net and, in fact, in seeking the former the Germans have traditionally campaigned on what western armies would consider to be a logistical shoestring. Intelligence and counter-intelligence have been among the worst in European military history. Strategic planning – setting long-range goals in manpower allocation and industrial production – was almost entirely absent, especially in the Second World War. Above all, there was the conceptual disconnect between even the most decisive battlefield victories we have discussed and how they might serve to translate into a victorious war.

Finally, this was an army that had a definite comfort zone: the Central European heartland. By mid-1941, however, Germany's national leadership was pointing the army towards higher goals. One was the physical destruction of the Soviet Union and the maintenance of a 1,300-mile long defensive position from Archangel on the Arctic Ocean to Astrakhan on the Caspian Sea. Another was the prosecution of a logistics-heavy campaign in the vast and faraway deserts of North Africa. Both proved to be impossible tasks for an army that, historically, had been designed for far more limited encounters.

Indeed, let us end our narrative in that fateful first week of December 1941. The *Wehrmacht* had driven deep into the Soviet Union, but events were already in train that would change things forever. A highly gifted Soviet field commander was assembling massive mechanized formations in great secrecy, deploying them in a great arc in front of Moscow, and preparing them for a mighty blow against the invaders. Likewise, in the Pacific Ocean, a great Japanese carrier task force was heading east out of home waters, taking the northerly route to elude prying eyes. That fleet was about to summon the United States to its own rendezvous with destiny.

Hitler had won a war, conquering the European continent from 1939 to 1941. Germany had been well prepared to fight that war, and it had triumphed. Yet what we might loosely still call the '*Blitzkrieg*' had now come to an end. A new and much greater conflict was about to begin, one that would finally lay bare for all to see the deep inadequacies of the 'German way of war'.

Notes

1   The term '*Blitzkrieg*', usually credited to Western, specifically American, journalists, can actually be found here and there in pre-1939 professional literature. For the earliest printed use of the term that I have found, see Lieutenant Colonel Braun, 'Der strategische Überfall', *Militär-Wochenblatt* 123, no. 18 (28 October 1938), pp. 1134–6, although the sense here is that the word has been already been in use: 'Nach dem Zeitungsnachrichten hatten die diesjährigen französischen Manöver den Zweck, die Bedeutung des strategischen Überfalls – auch "Blitzkrieg" genannt – zu prüfen' (p. 1134).

2   For in-depth discussion of this point, see R. Citino, *The German Way of War: From the Thirty Years' War to the Third Reich*. Kansas, 2005; as well as R. Citino, *Death of the Wehrmacht: The German Campaigns of 1942*. Kansas, 2007.

3   Major Bigge, '*Ueber Selbstthätigkeit der Unterführer im Kriege*': *Beihefte zum Militär-Wochenblatt 1894*. Berlin, 1894, pp. 17–55; as well as General von Blume, '*Selbstthätigkeit der Führer im Kriege*': *Beihefte zum Militär-Wochenblatt 1896*. Berlin, 1896, pp. 479–534.

4   For the nearly forgotten battle of Langensalza, see G. Wawro, *The Austro-Prussian War: Austria's War with Prussia and Italy in 1866*. Cambridge, 1996, pp. 75–81. Wawro's work has largely superseded the earlier standard on the 1866 war, G. Craig, *The Battle of Königgrätz: Prussia's Victory over Austria, 1866*. Philadelphia, 1964. See also the still-useful older sources, such Oscar von Lettow-Vorbeck, *Geschichte des Krieges von 1866 in Deutschland – Volume 1: Gastein-Langensalza*. Berlin, 1896, an analysis by a General Staff officer accompanied by excellent maps. For a synthesis, see Citino, *The German Way of War*, pp. 153–60.

5   See G. Wawro, *The Franco-Prussian War*. Cambridge, 2000, which has now largely superseded the earlier standard work by M. Howard: *The Franco-Prussian War*. New York, 1962. D. Showalter's *Wars of German Unification*. London, 2004 places all three wars firmly into their historical contexts in often quite surprising ways. A. Bucholz, *Moltke and the German Wars, 1864–1871*. New York, 2001 is also indispensable. For an operational history that is firmly grounded in issues of organizational and management theory see Helmuth von Moltke, *The Franco-German War of 1870–71*. New York, 1988.

6   François deserves a military biography in English. On the Tannenberg campaign generally, the standard work is D. Showalter, *Tannenberg: Clash of Empires*. Washington, 2004. N. Stone, *The Eastern Front, 1914–1917*. London 1975 is still indispensable and so is H. Herwig, *The First World War: Germany and Austria-Hungary, 1914–1918*. London, 1997.

7   'Seitdem mit dem Ende des Winters die deutschen Waffen wieder ihre vernehmliche Sprache zu reden begonnen haben …' in *Grossdeutschlands Freiheitskrieg*, part 145; 'Die deutsche Frühjahrsoperation auf der Krim', *Militär-Wochenblatt* 126, no. 47 (22 May 1942), pp. 1345–8. The quote is from p. 1345.

8   For Case White, begin with the belated official history commissioned by the Militärgeschicht-liches Forschungsamt, *Das Deutsche Reich und Der Zweite Weltkrieg, Volume 2: Die Errichtung der Hegemonie auf dem Europäischen Kontinent*. Stuttgart, 1979 (hereafter *DRZWK*); R. Kennedy, *The German Campaign in Poland, 1939*. Washington, 1956.

9   *DRZWK*, vol. 2, p. 95.

10 For the dispute over the German operational plan, see *DRZWK*, vol. 2, pp. 92–9; Kennedy, *The German Campaign in Poland*, pp. 58–63 and 73–7.

11 Kennedy, *The German Campaign in Poland*, p. 62.

12 *DRZWK*, vol. 2, p. 96.

13 Kennedy, *The German Campaign in Poland*, p. 83.

14 *DRZWK*, vol. 2, p. 117.

15 For the battle of the Bzura, see S. Zaloga and V. Madej, *The Polish Campaign, 1939*. New York, 1991, pp. 131–8. For German primary sources, see J. Kielmansegg, *Panzer zwischen Warschau und Atlantik*. Berlin, 1941; as well as C. Kinder, *Männer der Nordmark an der Bzura*. Berlin, 1940.

16 J. Lucas, *Battle Group! German Kampfgruppen Action of World War Two*. London, 2004, pp. 10–24.

17 R. Bathe, *Der Feldzug der 18 Tage: die Chronik des polnischen Dramas*. Oldenburg, 1939.

18 For Case Yellow, the scholarly work of choice is K-H. Frieser, *The Blitzkrieg Legend: The 1940 Campaign in the West*. Annapolis, 2005. For the planning of the offensive, see the still-crucial article by H-A. Jacobsen, 'Hitlers Gedanken zur Kriegführung im Western', *Wehrwissenschaftliche Rundschau* 5, no. 10 (October 1955), pp. 433–46. See also *DRZWK*, vol. 2, pp. 233–327. The standard works in English remain J. Gunsburg, *Divided and Conquered: The French High Command and the Defeat in the West*. 1940 Westport, 1979; and especially R. Doughty, *The Breaking Point: Sedan and the Fall of France, 1940*. Hamden, 1990).

19 *DRZWK*, vol. 2, p. 254.

20 F.K. Rothbrust, *Guderian's XIXth Panzer Corps and the Battle of France*. Santa Barbara, 1990, p. 29.

21 For these '*Sonderunternehmen*' see *DRZWK*, vol. 2, pp. 259–60.

22 See D. Meyler, 'Missed Opportunities: The Ground War in Holland', *Command* 42 (March 1997), pp. 58–69.

23 See J. Mrazek, *The Fall of Eben Emael*. Novato, 1970.

24 See ibid., p. 56, for a diagram of the Hohlladung.

25 J. Gunsburg, 'The Battle of the Belgian Plain, 12–14 May 1940: The First Great Tank Battle', *Journal of Military History* 56, no. 2 (April 1992), pp. 207–44.

26 For the Dyle Plan, see Gunsburg, *Divided and Conquered*, pp. 119–46 and 265–92. See also Doughty, *The Breaking Point*, pp. 12–14. For a very useful recent sampling of French scholarly and military opinion, see C. Levisse-Touzé, *La Campagne de 1940*. Paris, 2001.

27 For the Breda variant, see Doughty, *The Breaking Point*, pp. 14–17; Gunsburg, *Divided and Conquered*, pp. 138–9.

28 Doughty, *The Breaking Point*, p. 102.

29 For the 'reconnaissance in force', see the primary source: H. Guderian, *Panzer Leader*. New York, 1957, pp. 87–8.

30 The Balkan campaign is due for a modern, multilingual, scholarly monograph. The best place to start, as always for the German army in the Second World War, is with the official history: *DRZWK*, vol. 3, pp. 417–511. In English, G. Blau, *The German Campaign in the Balkans (Spring 1941)*. Washington, 1953 has of necessity been the go-to work for a long time now, too long in fact. Part of the venerable German Report Series, it assembles the testimony of a number of German officers who took part in the campaign, but it needs to be supplemented with other sources. English-language works tend to focus on the British intervention in Greece. R. Higham, *Diary of a Disaster: British Aid to Greece 1940–1941*. Lexington, 1986 is carefully researched (the narrative is in diary form, and often goes down to the level of minutes) and nuanced in its argument. It largely superseded the previous standard account, C. Cruickshank, *Greece 1940–1941*. London, 1976, although the latter is still useful on certain details. See also C. Buckley, *Greece and Crete, 1941*. London, 1952, which has the attraction of offering a

comparative discussion of both the failed intervention in Greece and the fighting on Crete. M. Willingham, *Perilous Commitments: The Battle for Greece and Crete 1940–1941*. Staplehurst, 2005 is another perfectly serviceable and well-written popular account.

31   For the origins of 'Lustre' and 'W', see Cruickshank, *Greece 1940–1941*, pp. 105–17 as well as Higham, *Diary of a Disaster*, pp. 94–117.

32   F. Mellenthin, *Panzer Battles: A Study of the Employment of Armor in the Second World War*. New York, 1956, p. 39.

33   On this question, see also A. Papagos, *The Battle of Greece*, pp. 322–3 and pp. 325–6. (Athens: Hellenic Publishing, 1949).

34   Kurt von Tippelskirch, 'Der deutsche Balkanfeldzug 1941', *Wehrwissenschaftliche Rundschau* 5, no. 2 (February 1955), pp. 54–5.

35   Willingham, *Perilous Commitments*, pp. 73–4.

36   General Hans Tieschowitz von Tieschowa, 'Der Feldzug im Südosten', In Oberkommando der Wehrmacht, ed., *Die Wehrmacht: Um die Freiheit Europas* (Berlin: Verlag 'Die Wehrmacht,' 1941), pp. 158–9.

37   Willingham, *Perilous Commitments*, p. 74. See also Papagos, *The Battle of Greece*, pp. 355–6.

38   Blau, *The German Campaign in the Balkans*, pp. 86–7.

39   For the retreat, there is no better guide than British armored commander R. Crisp, *The Gods Were Neutral*. London, 1960, pp. 138–56.

40   Willingham, *Perilous Commitments*, pp. 90–1. For a detailed account of the Thermopylae fighting, see the New Zealand Official History, W. G. McGlymont, *To Greece*. Wellington, 1959, especially pp. 384–99.

41   J. Piekalkiewicz, *Krieg auf dem Balkan 1940–1945* (München: Sudwest Verlag, 1984), pp. 110–11

42   The title of an article by German war correspondent Gert Habedanck: 'Wir fegten den Tommy vom Kontinent' in *Die Wehrmacht: Um die Freiheit Europas*, pp. 175–85.

Chapter 9

Guilty Men? Three British Foreign Secretaries of the 1930s

David Dutton

The genesis of the myth of the 'Guilty Men' – the notion that Britain was led to the very brink of disaster in 1940 by a group of incompetent politicians within the National Government – may be dated to the publication in July of that year of a tract written by three anonymous left-wing journalists working for Beaverbrook newspapers.[1] This remarkably influential polemic made its mark, not through meticulous historical analysis, but by offering simple answers to a public desperate to understand the nation's current predicament. The generation of 1940 could not otherwise comprehend how the country they had grown up to regard as the greatest of all nations and whose empire extended to all corners of the earth could have been brought so catastrophically to its knees almost as soon as the 'real' fighting of the Second World War began. The explanation, it was argued, lay in the personal failings of a small group of men who, dominating the politics of the 1930s, had blindly ignored the ever-mounting threat posed to the country's safety by the rise of the fascist powers in continental Europe.

A short book of no more than 125 pages, cobbled together it was said over a single weekend, should perhaps have been no more than a nine-day wonder, an 'adolescent triumph' on the part of its authors, as one Conservative MP suggested, but of no lasting historiographical significance.[2] But the impact of *Guilty Men* was lasting and profound on the evolution of the historiography of British foreign policy in the 1930s for at least the next two decades, and popular perceptions of this era for much longer still. Indeed, it is necessary to question whether the epithet of 'myth' is entirely appropriate. Perhaps the most striking feature of the enormous literature on the 1930s is the failure of historians to reach anything approaching a consensus in their interpretations and analysis. Moreover, after a period in which an almost too convincing array of determinants and constraints was brought forth to explain the policy decisions which led to 'appeasement', a clear school has emerged in recent years of post-revisionists ready to reassert, in a suitably modified and more sophisticated guise, the original thesis of 1940.[3] Their starting point is that, notwithstanding the constraints under which the National Government operated, choices did still exist and the policy options chosen by the 'Guilty Men' were often the wrong ones. Perhaps then, as the longest surviving member of the trio of authors more recently wrote, 'those who wish to know what actually happened in the 1930s, how the nation was so nearly led to its doom, had better stick to rough-and-ready guides like *Guilty Men*'.[4]

The notion of the 'Guilty Men' had begun to emerge some weeks before Michael Foot, Peter Howard and Frank Owen put pen to paper. Speaking in the House of Commons at the opening of the second day of the celebrated Norwegian debate in May 1940 Herbert Morrison seemed to anticipate the later indictment contained in *Guilty Men*:

> The fact is that before the war and during the war, we have felt that the whole spirit, tempo and temperament of at least some Ministers have been wrong, inadequate and unsuitable. I am bound to refer, in particular, to the Prime Minister [Neville Chamberlain], the Chancellor of the Exchequer [John Simon] and the Secretary of State for Air [Samuel Hoare]. I cannot forget that in relation to the conduct of British foreign policy between 1931 and 1939, they were consistently and persistently wrong. I regard them as being, perhaps more than any other three men, responsible for the fact that we are involved in a war which the wise collective organisation of peace could have prevented, and just as they lacked courage, initiative, imagination, psychological understanding, liveliness and self-respect in the conduct of foreign policy, so I feel that the absence of those qualities has manifested itself in the actual conduct of the war.[5]

Morrison's attack seems to have hit its target. Chamberlain was ready to sacrifice his two colleagues in a desperate attempt to hold on to the premiership, apparently unaware that parliamentary hostility was directed as much against himself as it was against Simon and Hoare.[6] Strikingly, too, Chamberlain, Simon and Hoare occupy the first three places in the cast list with which *Guilty Men* begins.

Before long the international events of the 1930s were fitted into a seductively simple pattern in which aggression, first in the Far East, then in Africa and finally in Europe, had been accepted, indeed condoned, by the British government. It was a pattern which, critics began to argue, could and should have been broken in its early stages, making the 'Guilty Men' who had failed to stop the aggressor in his tracks when Japan invaded Manchuria in 1931 and when Italy attacked Abyssinia in 1935 just as culpable as those who had allowed Nazi Germany to embark upon its progress in Europe in the second half of the decade. Indeed, it was the failure to take action in 1931 and 1935 which gave the green light to Hitler to undo the international settlement by force, confident in the knowledge that Britain would not lift a finger to stop him. Writing in 1941, the Liberal MP Geoffrey Mander drew the conclusion that had been only implicit in Herbert Morrison's Commons speech: 'We now know', he asserted, 'that the pathway to the beaches of Dunkirk lay through the wastes of Manchuria'.[7]

Guilt, as Talleyrand once wrote, is a question of dates and the concept of the 'Guilty Men' became a convenient means by which the political left could develop its broader critique of the National Government, which took office in August 1931. That administration, it was argued, held power as a result of Ramsay MacDonald's 'great betrayal', the decision of the erstwhile Labour Prime Minister to stay in office at the head of a supposedly all-party government, which was in practice dominated by the Conservatives. It was to the misfortune of the reputations of men such as Chamberlain, Simon and Hoare that these men occupied prominent positions within that government. Chamberlain was a member throughout. Briefly Minister of Health from August to November 1931, he then served as Chancellor of the Exchequer until becoming Prime Minister in May 1937. Simon was Foreign Secretary from November 1931 until June 1935. He then became Home Secretary before succeeding Chamberlain as Chancellor in May 1937. Hoare was Secretary of State for India between August 1931 and June 1935 when he succeeded Simon as Foreign Secretary. Resigning in December of that year, he returned to government as First Lord of the Admiralty in June 1936 and was then successively Home Secretary, May 1937–September 1939, Lord Privy Seal, September 1939–April 1940 and Secretary of State for Air, April–May 1940. In this sense *Guilty Men* was something of a *party* political document. It arguably played its part in securing Labour's overwhelming victory in the General Election of 1945. During the course of the Second World War, *Guilty Men* and a succession of similar publications captured the moral high ground and succeeded in convincing a significant section of the public that the Conservatives (even though few of the leading 'Guilty Men' were by then still active in politics) could not be trusted again with the conduct of the nation's affairs.

Even so, the presentation of *Guilty Men* as a simple attack from the 'left' upon the 'right' must be significantly qualified. In the first instance it needs to be stressed that the 'Guilty Men' themselves were not really of the 'right'. The Conservatism which held sway in the 1930s was largely of the centre ground. Contrary to the complaints of the Labour party, there was more to the National Government than undiluted Toryism. Indeed, many contemporary Conservatives criticized the government for succumbing to the charms of an effete liberalism – what one called 'MacStanleyism' – when it was perfectly capable, in terms of its parliamentary strength, of pursuing a straightforward Conservative course.[8] The Tory journalist Collin Brooks noted growing dissatisfaction with the government's 'Socialist character'.[9] Winston Churchill went so far as to complain that the country lacked a Conservative Party.[10] Chamberlain, of course, came from a Liberal family, remaining throughout his life in some ways a Liberal Unionist, and never becoming a natural Tory, like his half-brother, Austen, a former Tory leader.[11] He certainly boasted a record of achievement in the realm of social reform not usually associated with the political right. Simon was never a member of the Conservative party. The Liberalism that had characterized the first three decades of his political life did not desert him overnight when he left the mainstream party in 1931. Samuel Hoare once described himself as a 'liberal amongst conservatives and a conservative amongst liberals'.[12] A member of the progressive Unionist Social Reform

Committee before 1914, his views on matters such as education and penal reform were always to the left of the majority of his party colleagues and, at the end of his life, he found himself a lone advocate for the abolition of the death penalty on the Conservative benches in the House of Lords. Lord Halifax, the third Foreign Secretary named in the cast list of *Guilty Men*, seems at first sight a typical example of aristocratic Conservatism. But the then Edward Wood had entered parliament in 1910 as a Tory for no stronger reason than that the Liberal party no longer represented those Whig values in which he believed. In 1918 he co-authored a political pamphlet which argued that the Conservative party should focus on the welfare of the country rather than the advantage of the individual. Finally, as Viceroy in the 1920s, it was his Declaration on India's future destiny as an independent state which ultimately drove Churchill from the Conservative front bench.

The *Guilty Men's* attack was also strengthened by the endorsement of the Churchillian 'right'. Churchill's history of the Second World War was published between 1948 and 1954. The first volume, *The Gathering Storm*, focused largely on the period before the outbreak of hostilities and it sold more copies than any of the succeeding tomes. The developments of the 1930s are painted in relatively simple terms as a struggle between good and evil and, if Hitler provided the epitome of evil, Churchill left his readers with few doubts that those who had failed to appreciate Hitler's evil were themselves guilty of grievous crimes. The protagonists of appeasement were presented as weak men whose cowardice was matched only by their lack of insight. Appeasement was not just wrong – it was willfully wrong. Because of his enormous prestige and authority, Churchill added respectability to the charge sheet already drawn up by Cato's *Guilty Men*. A new school of historical writing was established which was clearly not directed from the political Left. It formed the right wing of a literary pincer movement from which the 'Guilty Men' themselves had little opportunity to escape. Thus, while the Left tended to attack them for their failure to embrace the internationalism of the League of Nations and the policy of collective security, the emphasis of the Right was upon their neglect of rearmament and national defence.

The culpability of Neville Chamberlain, inevitably 'Guilty Man Number One', will be examined in subsequent chapters in this volume, but the present chapter seeks to pursue a rather different line of enquiry by exploring the culpability of three Foreign Secretaries of the 1930s for the collective failure of the government's policy. The analysis extends beyond their individual Foreign Secretaryships, for each was prominent in government for most of the 1930s. One strong point of contrast must be noted at the outset. While Simon and Hoare stand unequivocally in the dock, Lord Halifax, Foreign Secretary from February 1938 until December 1940, ranks only sixth in the list of Cato's indicted and was never subjected to a comparable degree of vilification. The fourth Foreign Secretary of the decade, Anthony Eden, is notable for his absence from Cato's list. Indeed, he was the only one of the four to enjoy a post-war political career of significance, built largely upon his credentials as an anti-appeaser and thus upon the fact that he was in no sense a 'Guilty Man'.[13]

The case against Sir John Simon is certainly a strong one. Its main elements may be conveniently summarized. It was on Simon's watch that Japan took control of the Chinese province of Manchuria. For the first time the authority of the League of Nations had been challenged by a leading power and found wanting. Simon, it is claimed, failed to give a lead to the world community, rebuffed American attempts to take a stronger line and showed unwanted sympathy for the Japanese case at Geneva. 'That was the first important act of aggression in the post-war world,' suggested one critic. 'If it had been stopped by a united League of Nations it could have had no successors.'[14] Lord Cecil of Chelwood, the doughtiest of the League's champions, was in no doubt about the connection between what happened in the Far East in 1931–3 and the outbreak of European war in 1939: 'Above all, it encouraged aggressive Powers in Europe – first in Italy and then Germany – to set at nought the barrier so laboriously erected at Geneva against aggression, and brought us step by step to the present intensely grave position.'[15] Simon is also held responsible for his failure to respond appropriately to the coming to power in Germany of Adolf Hitler. Before Simon left the Foreign Office, Hitler had denounced the disarmament clauses of Versailles and was on the verge of being rewarded by the legitimization of his naval building programme through the conclusion of the Anglo-German Naval Agreement. Having been moved from the Foreign Office, Simon emerged as one of Chamberlain's closest supporters, one of the Prime Minister's inner circle as appeasement reached its tragic climax. Meanwhile, as Chancellor of the Exchequer after 1937, Simon was held responsible for failing to provide adequate funding to finance rearmament, vainly clinging to a policy which placed a balanced economy ahead of national security. As a ministerial colleague put it, 'Simon was the *fons et origo mali* before and during the early stages of the war of the slow pace of rearmament. He would not sanction the expenditure.'[16]

Yet if the case for the prosecution seems compelling, that for the defence is not without its merits. Simon's position as a minister in the National Government must be considered. No Foreign Secretary of the 1930s could exercise the departmental autonomy in the construction of the country's diplomacy enjoyed by Edward Grey before 1914 or even by Austen Chamberlain in the 1920s. In particular, the Chancellor of the Exchequer now played a role that was virtually unknown before the First World War, a function of the way in which many of the most pressing questions facing British foreign policy makers in the early 1930s were inextricably bound up with economic and commercial considerations. A paper drawn up inside the Foreign Office shortly after Simon took up his post neatly captured the problem:

> The links in the chain fall together more or less in the following order. The monetary
> crisis leads inevitably back to the economic chaos in Europe. The economic chaos and

all attempts to deal with it involve in their turn the political question of reparations and war debts. These are linked by the United States with the question of disarmament, and the latter, in the eyes of the French government, depends upon the problem of security. The problem of security in its turn raises the question of the territorial status quo in Europe ... which brings us to the maintenance or revision of the Peace Settlement.[17]

Then, the mounting input from ministers with responsibility for the armed services and for the various parts of the Empire, together with a marked proliferation of cabinet committees, ensured that the making of British foreign policy became a more collegial activity than ever before.

The resulting weakening of the Foreign Secretary's independence was compounded by the existence of a National Government and Simon's position within it. The construction in 1931 of what was in practice a coalition created axes of loyalty, communication and power that were inevitably different from those in a single-party administration. Simon's presence within the cabinet was important, helping to maintain the reality that this was not just a Conservative government. But as the leader of no more than three dozen Liberal National MPs set against more than 400 Tories, Simon's bargaining power was always going to be limited and he certainly never held the rank of second or third within the cabinet which a Foreign Secretary can normally expect. Furthermore, while foreign affairs came to dominate the National Government's attention in its closing years, it was not for this reason that politicians from all parties had come together in 1931. The National Government owed its existence to the impact of the world economic crisis on Britain and its leading members never forgot their primary duty in this respect. It has recently been argued that 'following on its success in the early 1920s in winning control over foreign policy-making and execution, the Foreign Office largely determined the way that British governments pursued grand strategy till late 1937'.[18] Yet such a judgment takes little account of the internal dynamics of the National Government. As will be suggested below, it was not until the first months of 1939 that the Foreign Office succeeded in reclaiming primacy from the Treasury in the conduct of Britain's external policy.

Not surprisingly, much of the criticism that Simon incurred resulted less from the actual policies he presented and more from his inability to champion those policies successfully inside the government. As his junior minister, Anthony Eden, complained:

> Simon's difficulty is not so much in making up his own mind as that once he has made it up – or at least has seemed to do so (perhaps that it is the truth it is not really made up) [sic]. Anyway he will not fight for his own policy. He expects the Cabinet to find his policy for him ... Poor Simon is no fighter. Nothing will make him one.[19]

Simon did have a tendency to prevaricate. His legal mind was better at setting out all available options (and recognizing the potential difficulties attaching to each one) than at coming to a clear-cut decision. That said, he was never well placed to dominate cabinet discussions. Not then a member of the cabinet himself, Eden failed to give full weight to the difficulties which Simon was bound to encounter. Policy over the Disarmament Conference of 1932–4 was particularly difficult to determine with the service ministries and the Foreign Office often pulling in different directions. But whereas the Air Minister, Londonderry, had the ear of the Prime Minister and Hailsham, the War Secretary, carried considerable weight within the Conservative party, the Foreign Secretary had few friends upon whom he could rely. Even before entering the National Government, Simon had been something of a political loner. For most of his tenure at the Foreign Office he had to endure periodic attacks in the press and speculation, much of it inspired from within the government, about his own future. Some time before the reshuffle of June 1935, which saw his removal, he was almost universally regarded as the weak link in the government whose exclusion would most effectively refurbish its standing in the country. 'Everyone of every party', Winston Churchill told his wife, 'official and political, wants to get rid of Simon.'[20] But, unpopularity notwithstanding, were the policies he pursued so worthy of condemnation?

The key factor determining Britain's response to the Far Eastern crisis of 1931 was that, militarily speaking, the country was in no position to intervene. This was the result of decisions taken in the 1920s for which Simon bore no ministerial responsibility. When he took office defence planning was still determined by the Ten-Year Rule, which meant that no significant calls upon the country's military capacity were anticipated before the early 1940s at the earliest. Austen Chamberlain, who in time became one of Simon's sternest critics, nonetheless concluded that

> in all that concerns the physical force that it will exert in an emergency, this country is weaker in proportion to the rest of the world than at any time within my public life ... If you want your Foreign Secretary to speak with the authority that he ought to have, if you want yourselves to be masters in your own house and able to decide your own policy, you must be in a position to defend yourself, you must be in a position to fulfil your obligations and to secure the respect of others for the obligations that they owe to you.[21]

Henry Stimson, the American Secretary of State and another of Simon's detractors, admitted that 'if anyone had planned the Manchurian outbreak with a view to freedom from interference from the rest of the world, his time was well chosen'.[22] Furthermore, Britain did not have sufficient interests in the political future of Manchuria to incur grave risks on its behalf. Though the Japanese attack would come in time to be imbued with immense significance in the history (or, more accurately, the mythology) of the inter-war years, few in 1931 saw the future peace of the world bound up in that region. The Japanese invasion should not be viewed as a far-eastern anticipation of the Prague coup of 1939, still less as an earlier version of their own attack on Pearl Harbor in December 1941. The Japan of 1931, if no longer an ally of the United Kingdom, was perceived as a friendly power with which British interests demanded good relations. In all the circumstances Simon had little choice but to keep his country out of any danger of war. He sought to act through the League of Nations and his judicial mind was naturally attracted by the idea of a commission of enquiry to determine the facts of a complicated situation. Its report did indeed find that the picture was more nuanced than many later commentators were willing to concede. Even so, Simon's much-criticized speech at the League Assembly on 7 December 1932 was much less of a defence of the Japanese case than is often claimed, as even Lord Cecil, after reading a verbatim transcript of it, had to agree. [23] And while it may have suited the public image of the United States to claim that only Simon's hesitation held Britain and America back from joint action, the reality was very different. The testimony of A.L. Rowse, a later scourge of the 'Guilty Men', is revealing:

> We on the Left all thought he was to blame for our non-intervention against the Japanese in their attack on China ... We now know that nothing on earth would have induced that pacifist Quaker, President Hoover, to intervene in the Far-East, nor his Secretary of State, Stimson.[24]

Simon was probably sceptical from the outset that any positive achievements would come out of the World Disarmament Conference, not least because of the divisions of opinion inside the cabinet. 'I don't like my position,' he once complained. 'It does not seem to me fair that whatever the services want I have to defend, however impossible their position.'[25] The problem, however, was that he would almost certainly be held responsible for the conference's failure. The Foreign Secretary's position was unenviable. As a sympathetic cabinet colleague put it, 'without military strength to back his policy, and with public opinion set upon peace, he was expected somehow or other to reconcile the French demand for security with the German claim for equality of status, and to persuade more than fifty governments in Geneva to accept a plan of disarmament.'[26] Very quickly he became the *bête noire* of League enthusiasts who had entertained unrealistic expectations about the conference's chances of success.

Eden's charge that Simon missed a golden opportunity to reach agreement on arms reductions before Hitler came to power is also difficult to uphold. Even had the French been persuaded to consider the Brüning government's proposals straight away, their endorsement could only have been bought by a British commitment to French security which Simon was in no position to offer. Following Germany's withdrawal from the conference in July 1932, Simon produced a carefully worded statement, emphasizing that the disarmament clauses of the Treaty of Versailles were still in place, deprecating any attempt by Germany to rearm and expressing the hope that a fair disarmament convention could yet be negotiated.[27] This initiative won the enthusiastic endorsement of Churchill, who suggested that Simon's firm stand had 'done more to consolidate peace in Europe than any words spoken on behalf of Great Britain for some years'.[28]

It was during Simon's Foreign Secretaryship, on 30 January 1933, that Adolf Hitler became German Chancellor. There is no evidence to suggest that Simon's reaction to this development involved a fundamental re-think of British policy. This is not to argue that he was anything other than disgusted by Nazi brutality. In May, he told the cabinet that current German policy was 'definitely disquieting', with the German government giving state sanction to a militaristic attitude of mind, as well as to various forms of military training, that could only end in one way.[29] When Britain's ambassador in Berlin pointed to the abnormality of the Nazi regime and expressed his fears for the future, Simon even said that these warnings would be 'of great and permanent value to His Majesty's Government in determining their policy towards Germany'.[30] But Simon never fully understood the intrinsic connection between National Socialist ideology and German foreign policy. So Hitler was treated pragmatically, with each new development viewed on its merits. This was a fundamental mistake on Simon's part. Yet few indeed were those who drew the immediate conclusion that Hitler was different not just in degree but in kind from previous German leaders and that he should be placed unequivocally beyond the diplomatic pale. Furthermore, the evil of Hitler and his regime was a cumulative revelation and those, like Simon, who had to deal with him in the first years of the Third Reich are more easily exonerated for their misjudgments than are the men who succeeded them later in the decade when far more of the true nature of the regime had been revealed.

It took Simon some time to devise any sort of strategy to respond to the arrival of Hitler in power, the withdrawal of Germany from the League of Nations and the final collapse of the Disarmament Conference. Gradually, however, he moved away from the quest for a disarmament convention and towards a rearmament agreement which, he hoped, would at least put a ceiling to what was inevitable. This was accompanied by recognition of the need for British rearmament and an increasing willingness to seek French and Italian friendship which, he knew, might mean reviving the notion of a continental commitment. What attitude, he bluntly asked in November 1934, should Britain adopt towards German rearmament? 'If the alternative to legalising German rearmament was to prevent it, there would be everything to be said for not legalising it.' But preventing German rearmament by force had to be ruled out and the only alternative to legalization was to allow Germany to continue on her present clandestine course. In return for legalization, Germany would be required to return to the Disarmament Conference and the League.[31] If it had not been for the presence of an entirely irrational factor in the shape of the Nazi regime and its leader, this policy might have had some chance of success.

Both at the time and later Simon incurred much criticism for his meeting with Hitler in March 1935. But he seems to have been less taken in by the experience than were some of the Führer's later visitors. As he told the King before leaving for Berlin, it was unlikely that the repudiation of the Versailles disarmament terms represented the limit of Hitler's demands. Naval rearmament, the Rhineland, Memel, Danzig and the former German colonies were also likely to be on the agenda.[32] The visit itself confirmed Simon's fears.

Hitler's ambitions were 'very dangerous to peace in Europe' and the conse-quences of German policy might be 'terrible beyond conception'. 'All this is pretty hopeless', he concluded.[33] Within three months, however, Simon himself had been moved to the calmer waters of the Home Office and it would be for others to strive to resolve the problems to which he had found no answer.

By the time Neville Chamberlain became Prime Minister in May 1937, Simon, now promoted to the Exchequer, had become one of the new premier's closest and most trusted colleagues. Chamberlain and the man who was now in effect his deputy viewed the international scene through similar eyes, but it is also difficult to exonerate Simon from the charge of sycophancy. In all proba-bility this reflected the determination of a man who had spent fifteen years out of government (1916–31) to hold on to the power and status he now enjoyed. As Chancellor, Simon did not deviate from the main lines of policy established by Chamberlain. This meant regarding a strong economy as the 'fourth arm of defence', with an importance comparable to the three armed services. This would enable Britain to survive the long war which, it was believed, offered the country the best chance of victory. It was easy to present such a policy as no more than a typical example of the miserly Treasury's reluctance to spend. 'Simon spoke on these matters in the counsels of the Cabinet', declared Cato, 'and he was successful in war as in peace in carrying through the Treasury policy of ensuring that expenditure should be vigorously limited'.[34] But the Treasury was not simply making a judgement between a sound economy and military preparedness for war and opting for the former. The two were not seen as competing alternatives, but as complementary aspects of the same problem. To damage the economy with excessive defence spending before war actually came might well jeopardize the country's longer-term capacity to fight that war to a successful conclusion. That said, the policy was probably sustained for too long. By early 1939, Simon and Chamberlain were virtually isolated within the cabinet on this issue. The German menace was too pressing and Treasury control was finally abandoned. As the former Permanent Under-Secretary at the Foreign Office, Sir Robert Vansittart, remarked: 'The Treasury are always preoc-cupied with the problem of *how* we are to live five years hence and not whether we shall be alive one year hence'.[35] Finally, Simon was not always Chamberlain's puppet. It was he who led a revolt by roughly half the cabinet on the evening of 2 September 1939, convinced that Chamberlain's delay in declaring war or even issuing an ultimatum to Germany, however well motivated, was doing damage to the standing of the government and the country.

Samuel Hoare's Foreign Secretaryship lasted just six months. Yet in that time he succeeded in placing himself incontrovertibly among the ranks of the 'Guilty Men'. In conversation after the Second World War, Eden declared that Simon was the worst holder of the office of Foreign Secretary in the entire inter-war period. Two years later, however, in the privacy of his diary, he confessed that Simon was 'much to be preferred to Hoare'.[36] Others have suggested that, in the event of a German invasion, Hoare would have been ready to assume the mantle of the British Quisling.[37] When Churchill finally despatched Hoare to the Madrid Embassy in May 1940, Alexander Cadogan expressed the view that it should instead have been to a penal settlement.[38] Like Simon, then, Hoare was not a popular figure and he had no significant body of support in the House of Commons. Like Simon, too, he was regarded as excessively ambitious and, by the late 1930s, as unnecessarily subservient to the Prime Minister – 'one of the worst and most sycophantic of Neville Chamberlain's advisers' as the young Tory backbencher, Harold Macmillan, put it.[39] Even his sympathetic biographer concedes that Hoare 'had absolutely no charisma'. 'His personality was to many irritating and unattractive; while the conjunction of obvious ability and intense ambition such as he displayed is rarely a prescription for popularity.'[40] For all that, his Foreign Secretaryship began with some promise.

Hoare's promotion was the result of his perceived success as Secretary of State for India since 1931. There, he had succeeded, in the face of concerted opposition from the Conservative Right led by Churchill, in forcing the Government of India Act on to the statute book. The experience was an exhausting one. It gave Hoare, as a cabinet minister, little scope to intervene in government business outside his direct departmental responsibilities and his contributions to matters of foreign policy were comparatively rare, though in March 1934 he did criticize as premature the idea that Britain should be preparing for war with Germany.[41] By the following year, however, in the wake of Germany's explicit abrogation of the disarmament clauses of the Versailles Treaty and anticipating the line he would take during his own Foreign Secretaryship, Hoare was ready to suggest that 'the only course for us to take is to prevent any breach between ourselves and the French and the Italians'.[42] Such, indeed, were Hoare's exertions over the India Bill that he was probably unwise to go straight to the Foreign Office, at least before taking a long holiday. As it was, his arrival at his new post found pressing business awaiting, which had begun to ferment in the last months of Simon's regime. Hoare's Foreign Secretaryship has been irredeemably tainted by his handling of this one matter.

The Wal-Wal frontier incident of December 1934 was the opening shot in Italy's attempt to advertise its claim to world power status by taking over the ancient African kingdom of Abyssinia. At other times and in other circumstances it might have been easy for the British government to turn a blind eye to this adventure in Italian imperialism. Abyssinia's record on the question of slavery hardly made it an obvious candidate for British protection. Even Austen Chamberlain, who would become one of Hoare's most trenchant critics, confessed that Abyssinia was not a client for whom he would have chosen to fight a test case.[43] But, for better or for worse, Abyssinia was a member of the League of Nations and entitled to the protection by other members which that status afforded. The British government, conscious of the League's continuing high esteem in the public mind and more nervous of the voters, in what was likely to be an election year, than with hindsight it probably needed to be, never lost sight of this fundamental point. But while the League's primary purpose was to preserve the peace through collective action, that same action might in certain circumstances involve a resort of force. It was a dilemma which Hoare fully understood:

> The general feeling of the country, fully reflected in the Cabinet, can, I think, be summarised as one of determination to stick to the Covenant and of anxiety to keep out of war. You will say that these feelings are self-contradictory. At present at least, the country believes that they can be reconciled. Most people are still convinced that if we stick to the Covenant and apply collective sanctions, Italy must give in and there will be no war. You and I know that the position is not as simple as this ...[44]

The new minister, largely untutored in foreign affairs, soon came under the influence of his Permanent Under-Secretary, Robert Vansittart. The resulting harmony between the minister and his leading civil servant was by no means a consistent feature of the 1930s, but it did mean that the Foreign Office enjoyed an ascendancy in the control of overseas policy greater than at any time before the spring of 1939. Indeed, it seems fair to conclude that the policy which culminated in the notorious Hoare–Laval Pact of December 1935 was constructed as much by Vansittart as by his ministerial master – for Hoare a sad irony granted the attachment of his own name to the ill-fated agreement with the French Foreign Minister. The *News Chronicle* was quite clear in dubbing the Under-Secretary 'the man behind it all'.[45] In the present context, however, there is a second and more significant irony, for Vansittart enjoys a reputation on the right side of the key dividing line of the 1930s. Though his course was more nuanced than he later claimed, Vansittart succeeded in his unfinished autobiography, aided posthumously by the efforts of his first biographer, in projecting himself in almost Churchillian terms as a persistent but unheeded voice, warning of the Nazi menace.[46] This was an over-simplification,[47] but no classification would ever place him among the 'Guilty Men'. What he succeeded in doing in the second half of 1935 was to convert Hoare to his own analysis of the global situation. With ever-accumulating evidence of German power and the constant possibility of a renewed Japanese threat to British interests in the Far East, the last thing Britain could afford was to alienate Italy. A hostile Italy would endanger Britain's lines of communication with the Far East, end France's capacity to focus on her German frontier and remove the key barrier in the way of German ambitions towards Austria.[48] Translated into practical terms, this meant that the loss of Abyssinia was an acceptable price to pay to keep Italian friendship in a world dominated by greater issues in Europe and the Far East, notwithstanding the damage likely to be done thereby to the authority of the League.

With the new Foreign Secretary installed, the Hoare–Vansittart influence was soon apparent. On 19 June the cabinet decided that it might be possible to reach a satisfactory solution if landlocked Abyssinia were offered access to the sea at the port of Zeila in British Somaliland, in exchange for territorial concessions to Italy in the Ogaden desert.[49] This may have been appeasement of a kind, but Hoare had not lost sight of the bigger picture, warning the cabinet the following month that the threat from Germany might materialize earlier than the Chiefs of Staff had hitherto assumed.[50] In this situation it was important to ensure that the Abyssinian 'emergency did not develop to the point where the question of [the] fulfilment [of British obligations under the Covenant] arose'.[51] At the same time, political considerations made it necessary to 'follow the regular League of Nations procedure in this crisis', and Hoare himself foresaw the 'making of a first-class crisis' if Britain appeared to be repudiating the Covenant.[52] Years later Vansittart admitted that he had 'laboured under a dualism which might look like duplicity'.[53] It was an honest assessment and his words could equally have been written by Hoare.

From the point of view of the Foreign Secretary's later reputation, much damage was done by a speech he delivered at the League Assembly on 11 September. 'The League stands', he insisted, 'and my country stands with it, for the collective maintenance of the Covenant in its entirety, and particularly for steady and collective resistance to all acts of unprovoked aggression.'[54] The speech certainly owed more to Hoare's appreciation of a delicate public relations situation than to the reality of British policy and the emphasis was always likely to change once the General Election of November was safely won. More revealing was a despatch to the Paris Embassy in which the Foreign Secretary spelt out the limits of Britain's League-based policy:

> it is essential that we should play out the League hand in September. If it is then found that there is no collective basis for sanctions, that is to say in particular that the French are not prepared to give their full co-operation … the world will have to face the fact that sanctions are impracticable … It must be the League not the British Government that declares that sanctions are impracticable and the British Government must on no account lay itself open to the charge that we have not done our utmost to make them practicable.[55]

Weeks of fruitless negotiation, punctuated by the beginnings of an Italian invasion of Abyssinia on 3 October, revealed the French Government's reservations and Hoare's mind turned increasingly towards delaying the imposition of oil sanctions on Italy while he sought the basis of a negotiated settlement. Precisely how much freedom of manoeuvre he had received from the cabinet before meeting Laval in Paris on 7 December remains a matter of debate, but the often quoted cabinet minute of 2 December – that it 'was hoped that the Foreign Secretary would take a generous view of the Italian attitude' – suggests that the resulting pact was reflective of a more collective policy than many fellow ministers later cared to admit.[56] Yet it was not immediately apparent that the deal Hoare negotiated with his French opposite number, as the possible basis of an Italo-Abyssinian settlement, would be disowned by the British government, still less that it would lead to Hoare's resignation and eventually assume a prominent position in the demonology of appeasement. The pact, involving the cession of three Abyssinian provinces and the placing of a much larger area under effective Italian control as a zone of economic expansion, was endorsed by the cabinet at meetings on 9 and 10 December. The mood of the Commons on the afternoon of 10 December, however, produced a change in the cabinet's attitude the following day.[57] A week later stinging criticism, led by Austen Chamberlain, at the Conservatives' backbench foreign affairs committee sealed the Foreign Secretary's fate. Not only would the Hoare–Laval proposals have to be dropped, but Hoare – who insisted on defending his plan in parliament – would need to do so from the backbenches. The Foreign Secretary's resignation was announced on the evening of 18 December. It was an unedifying spectacle from which Hoare emerged with somewhat more honour than most of his cabinet colleagues.

In a gesture of comfort to Lady Hoare following her husband's resignation, Neville Chamberlain insisted that he was not worried about Hoare's future career and that 'in a very short time his reputation will begin to rise again'.[58] Almost certainly, there was a tacit agreement that, providing Hoare went quietly, he would soon be restored to ministerial rank. But Chamberlain's prediction about Hoare's reputation was off the mark. His standing had been permanently tarnished. Rather as with Simon and Manchuria, he stood condemned, at least on the political Left, for 'a dire betrayal of the holy grail of collective security' for which there could be no forgiveness.[59] Even Eden later claimed that 'we had reached a climacteric in the thirties; the time had come to make a stand'.[60] Yet in the bigger picture Eden surely deserved greater censure for his failure as Foreign Secretary in 1936 to take action over the Rhineland than Hoare did for Abyssinia or Simon Manchuria. The Churchillian Right had less cause for complaint, though Churchill personally was an enemy because of Hoare's position over India and his own failed attempt to uphold breach of parliamentary privilege allegations against Hoare and Lord Derby in 1934. Hoare's strategy, or perhaps Vansittart's, had been motivated by a clear recognition of the overriding threat posed by Nazi Germany. Austen Chamberlain may have helped precipitate Hoare's fall, but that did not stop him writing emphatically the following June that the 'Italo-Abyssinian dispute is a side-issue and most of us … are thinking more of the danger threatening from Germany'.[61]

Hoare played little part in the nation's affairs over the next six months, though his statement to a well-attended meeting of backbench MPs on 17 March 1936 that Britain lacked the capacity to expel Germany from the recently re-militarized Rhineland was well received.[62] Restored to the government as First Lord of the Admiralty in June, Hoare was active in securing an acceleration of the existing naval building programme, which included the construction of two new battleships once the restrictive provisions of the London Naval Treaty expired at the end of the year.[63] He also returned to the heart of the foreign policy-making process as a result of his membership of the cabinet's newly formed Foreign Policy Committee. His basic thinking had not changed. Despite rearmament, Britain would remain unprepared for war for some time to come. Policy should therefore proceed 'very quietly' and the first objective should be to remove Italy from the list of Britain's potential enemies.[64] Such ideas made it almost inevitable that he would clash with Eden, his successor at the Foreign Office, when the latter, in an attempt to enforce non-intervention in the Spanish Civil War, proposed to blockade the Spanish coast.[65]

By the time that Neville Chamberlain became Prime Minister, Hoare certainly shared the new premier's belief that the moment had come for a more pro-active exercise in appeasement than had yet been attempted. He warned Chamberlain that the Foreign Office was so biased against Germany as to endanger any prospect of European reconciliation.[66] Hoare moved easily into the Prime Minister's inner circle, unimpeded by his ministerial responsibilities as Home Secretary since Chamberlain wanted him 'for general policy'.[67] As such he was one of the small group of ministers who constructed policy as the Czechoslovakian crisis reached its climax in September 1938. Fully supportive of what Chamberlain did at Munich, a position from which he never deviated in the years ahead, Hoare nevertheless adopted a more realistic attitude than did Chamberlain about how to capitalize on this last-minute avoidance of war. He began to call for the speeding up of rearmament, urged the Foreign Policy Committee in January 1939 to accept Vansittart's intelligence information about a possible German invasion of the Netherlands and, most significantly, was among the first ministers to speak out in favour of an alliance with the Soviet Union.[68] These developments, of course, took place behind closed doors. What the public saw, by contrast, was a picture of blind over-confidence. At Chamberlain's prompting, Hoare addressed his Chelsea constituents in early March and regaled them with the prospect of a forthcoming 'golden age' of peace and prosperity – that, only days before Hitler shattered most people's remaining illusions by marching into the rump state of Czechoslovakia. Hoare's words would rank alongside 'peace for our time' and Hitler 'missing the bus' in terms of the damage they did to the reputations of the 'Guilty Men'. At the fall of Chamberlain in May 1940 he was the only one of the 'Big Four' to be excluded completely from Churchill's government, his subsequent posting as ambassador to Franco's Spain widely seen as the British equivalent of the management of a Siberian power station.

Like the two Foreign Secretaries considered above, Edward Wood, Viscount Halifax, occupied government office for most of the 1930s. He became President of the Board of Education in June 1932 before serving briefly as Secretary of State for War between June and November 1935. He then became Lord Privy Seal until May 1937 and Lord President of the Council from then until he succeeded Eden at the Foreign Office in February 1938. Yet, while listed among the 'Guilty Men', he was not seen in the same light as Simon and Hoare: he figures nowhere else in the book outside Cato's cast list despite being Foreign Secretary during the Anschluss, Munich and the Prague coup; and he was even Labour's preferred choice to succeed Chamberlain in the crisis of May 1940.

At the same time, orthodox histories of the 1930s have been in no doubt that he should be separated from Eden and placed on the wrong side of the key dividing line, Chamberlain's 'Sancho Panza, trotting faithfully beside him' in the often-quoted words of Malcolm Muggeridge.[69] This equivocal position is not altogether easy to explain. He did not become significant in the making of foreign policy until the second half of the decade. He was certainly a more popular man than either Simon or Hoare. He enjoyed good relations with the Labour party and his position in the Lords removed the suspicion that, unlike the other two, his primary motivation was personal ambition. (Yet, ironically, he came far closer to the premiership than Simon or Hoare ever did.) But perhaps the most important factor is that it is almost possible to write of two Halifaxes, separated by a dramatic opening of the eyes over the terms offered by Hitler at the Godesberg Conference on the future of Czechoslovakia in September 1938.

Halifax had little impact on overseas policy before going to the War Office in 1935. There, he soon became aware that the country was unprepared for war, but at meetings of the Committee of Imperial Defence he challenged the assertion of the Chiefs of Staff that the paramount need was to step up the pace of rearmament. Above all, this reflected his failure to grasp the enormity of the threat posed by Adolf Hitler, as evidenced by his tendency to compare the Führer with the Indian nationalist Gandhi, with whom he had dealt as Viceroy between 1926 and 1931. In the non-departmental posts of Lord Privy Seal and Lord President he was increasingly employed for foreign affairs duties, becoming in effect Eden's deputy and the government's spokesman in the Lords. He was keen to improve relations with Germany[70] and, with government approval, accepted an invitation from Reichsmarschall, Hermann Göring, to attend a hunting exhibition in Berlin in November 1937. In later years Eden presented this episode as an illustration of Chamberlain's determination to bypass the Foreign Office to pursue the policy of appeasement in defiance of his professional advisers. Halifax, however, was careful to place his own version of events on record, according to which Eden was himself instrumental in pressing Halifax to accept the German invitation.[71] At all events, when he met Hitler, it appears to have been Halifax who initiated discussion of possible revisions to Versailles which would be beneficial to Germany. Overall, the visit did nothing to open his eyes to the true nature of the Nazi regime, and on his return he told the cabinet that the Germans had no policy of immediate adventure:

> They were too busy building up their country, which was still in a state of revolution. Nevertheless, he would expect a beaver-like persistence in pressing their claims in Central Europe, but not in a form to give others cause – or probably occasion – to interfere.[72]

By the time that he became Foreign Secretary Halifax appears to have accepted what was always the most logically sound justification for appeasement – that, in the face of a potential three-front challenge to British interests, the nightmare scenario of a hostile coalition of Germany, Italy and Japan, there was an imperative necessity to seek to reduce the number of Britain's enemies:

> In spite of all the efforts of [Eden], the Prime Minister and others, we had arrived at a position which above all we had wished to avoid and in which we were faced with the possibility of three enemies at once. The conclusion which [Halifax] drew was ... that this threw an immensely heavy burden on diplomacy and that we ought to get on good terms with Germany.[73]

Chamberlain quickly saw the advantages of having Halifax at the Foreign Office, not least because the new Foreign Secretary was blessed with an infinitely calmer temperament than his predecessor. In the belief that Eden's policy towards the dictators had been fundamentally different from that of the Prime Minister, critics readily assumed that Halifax would play the role of subservient loyalist, 'a weakling who will merely be the servile instrument of an ignorant and reckless Prime Minister', as Herbert Morrison put it.[74] It is probably more accurate to suggest that, throughout early 1938, premier and Foreign Secretary worked in close harmony because they shared a belief in the need for a more active appeasement of the dictator powers than had yet been practised. Halifax was prominent in the discussions within the Foreign Policy Committee of the cabinet in March, which determined those broad outlines of British policy towards the Czechoslovakian problem that culminated in the Munich settlement six months later. In particular, he championed the idea of keeping both France and Germany guessing as to whether British support would be forthcoming in defence of Czechoslovakia, a policy designed to hold France back from any rash actions in central Europe and to encourage Germany to reach a peaceful resolution of her claims.[75] This strategy formed the basis of Chamberlain's carefully crafted statement to parliament on 24 March. By the late summer Halifax, along with Simon and Hoare, had become a member of Chamberlain's unofficial 'inner cabinet', which effectively replaced the Foreign Policy Committee as the Czech crisis reached its climax and whose very existence did much to place its members within the category of 'Guilty Men'.

The fact that Halifax was excluded from Chamberlain's party on the latter's three visits to Germany in September seemed merely to confirm the Prime Minister's ascendancy in the control of British foreign policy. But Halifax's presence in London allowed him to view the outcome of Chamberlain's negotiations more dispassionately than might otherwise have been the case. He had no difficulty in supporting the arrangements which Chamberlain brought back from Berchtesgaden.[76] After all, to have done otherwise would have been to contradict the policies which he himself had espoused since becoming Foreign Secretary. But Halifax appears to have concluded that Chamberlain had reached the limits of concession and his attitude hardened while the Prime Minister returned to Germany for his second meeting with Hitler at Bad Godesberg. In what can only have been an attempt to stiffen Chamberlain's resolve, Halifax sent a telegram for the Prime Minister in this sense on the evening of 23 September.[77] At the same time he joined with Simon and Hoare in removing British objections to the mobilization of the Czech army in the light of reports of German troop movements near the Czech border. Even so, Halifax seemed ready to support the Prime Minister when the cabinet first considered Hitler's increased demands at its meeting on 24 September.[78] By the following day, however, influenced it seems by his Permanent Under-Secretary, Alexander Cadogan, the Foreign Secretary 'plumped for refusal of Hitler's terms' and led the first significant display of cabinet opposition to Chamberlain since the latter had become Prime Minister.[79] Not surprisingly, Halifax's defection came as a 'horrible blow' to Chamberlain.[80] But it was a significant first step in changing the balance of power within Chamberlain's government – a process which, within a few months, brought about decisive modifications to British foreign policy.

In the short term Halifax was ready to support the 'compromise' deal Chamberlain brought back from his third meeting with Hitler at Munich. But the Foreign Secretary's endorsement of the notorious pact was couched in markedly different terms from those used by the Prime Minister. The settlement should not be seen, he believed, as any sort of victory. Munich represented a 'hideous choice of evils', in which 'hard terms' were imposed on Czechoslovakia, and its principal lesson was that Britain must be 'fully and rapidly equipped' to meet future crises – a conclusion Chamberlain seemed reluctant to reach.[81] In the weeks that followed Halifax championed accelerated rearmament and the establishment of a Ministry of Supply to co-ordinate the nation's efforts. It was probably a realization of the mounting threat to British national interests, rather than any sudden insight into the true nature of the Nazi regime, which propelled Halifax on his new course. It was one thing, he said, 'to allow German expansion in Central Europe, which to my mind is a normal and natural thing, but we must be able to resist German expansion in Western Europe or else our whole position is undermined'.[82] Nonetheless, the change in tone was dramatic. By the start of 1939 Halifax had been won round to the view that Britain would have to make a 'continental commitment' in the event of a future European war. By early February it was clear that policy was changing. The Director of Military Operations noted the Foreign Secretary's impact: 'We got some admirable support from Halifax, who in response to Simon's bleats on finance said he would sooner be bankrupt in peace than beaten in a war against Germany.'[83] Finally, on 22 February after lengthy ministerial discussions, the cabinet made its decision on the army's future. The Chancellor now had to concede that 'other aspects in this matter outweigh finance' and the cabinet accepted a Field Force of two mobile divisions, four regular and four Territorial Army divisions.[84] The dominating influence of the Treasury in the shaping of Britain's foreign and defence policy was at an end and Halifax had been the key influence in bringing about the change. As the perception spread that his authority was growing at the expense of that of the Prime Minister, one well-placed observer concluded that the gulf between the government and its leading critics such as Eden had been much reduced. 'Indeed, as regards Germany, the two points of view are now very near'.[85] Even Churchill was reported to be 'well pleased with H[alifax]'.[86]

All this, of course, occurred before the more public announcement of a change in policy following the Prague coup of 15 March. Again, Halifax's influence was decisive. The difference between Chamberlain's initial response – that there would be no fundamental change in British policy – and his celebrated Birmingham speech two days later in which, by pondering on the nature of Hitler's ultimate intentions, he questioned the viability of the whole policy of appeasement, seems to have resulted from the Foreign Secretary's intervention. A fortnight later it was once more Halifax who pushed a reluctant Chamberlain into issuing a guarantee of Polish independence. Though historians continue to debate whether this represented a genuine change in the substance of British foreign policy, Halifax's biographer is in no doubt: 'In the months between Munich and Prague, he was the only man in the Cabinet who had enough authority to engineer the dismantling of appeasement before the Prime Minister's very eyes. In its place he succeeded in building a new consensus for resistance'.[87] Significantly in the present context, the existence of a split between Halifax and Chamberlain was becoming sufficiently well known to be commented on in the press, a fact which may help explain the Labour party's enthusiasm for a Halifax premiership and the comparative leniency with which he was treated when *Guilty Men* was published the following year.[88]

Halifax was slower than most of the cabinet, but at least quicker than Chamberlain, to appreciate that only an alliance with the Soviet Union could give military reality to the Polish guarantee. When negotiations did begin, Halifax incurred criticism for not convincing the Russians of Britain's sincerity by leading the negotiating team in person. Like Chamberlain, and unlike Simon, he seriously misjudged the mood of the country at the beginning of September 1939, and was as much as the Prime Minister the object of the cabinet revolt which put a stop to any further delay in the British declaration of war. But he was at least adamant that there could be no negotiations with Hitler while German troops remained on Polish soil.

With backing not only from Labour, but also the majority of the Conservative party and the King, the premiership was Halifax's for the taking in the crisis of May 1940. In the event, it was Churchill who seized the initiative, welcoming a supreme challenge from which Halifax drew back, and incidentally confirming the notion of a clear dividing line between the 'Guilty Men' and their few brave critics for which objective historical analysis offers little support. Some have seen the emergence of Churchill as Prime Minister in even more elevated terms, the result of the providential intervention of God Himself.[89] Alone among the leading architects of appeasement, Halifax retained his existing office in Churchill's new War Cabinet. Entertaining serious doubts about the judgment of the new premier, he saw a key part of his role as restraining Churchill's more fanciful excesses. But the heroic phase of Halifax's career was over. As Britain faced the prospect in the early summer of 1940 of confronting Hitler almost alone, Halifax began at wonder whether the war could in fact be won and to regard peace negotiations with the Nazis as a necessary development. 'We had to face the fact', he told the War Cabinet, 'that it was not so much now a question of imposing a complete defeat upon Germany, but of safeguarding the independence of our own Empire and if possible that of France.'[90] Whether any of the resulting intense debates at the heart of the British government reached the public ear is unclear. But the popular mood, at least in left-wing circles, had turned against Halifax by mid-July, with the *Sunday Pictorial* launching an unremitting campaign against the Foreign Secretary's continuing presence in the cabinet. This probably made it simpler for Churchill to ease a reluctant Halifax out of office when the sudden death of Lord Lothian created an unexpected vacancy at the Washington embassy. The persuasive Churchill made it clear that Halifax would never live down his reputation for appeasement and that he had no future in Britain, which was true, but that a successful mission to America would allow him to return one day on the crest of a wave, which was not.[91]

Any conclusion couched in terms of the 'guilt' or 'innocence' of the three Foreign Secretaries considered here would be to accept the basic premise of 1940 – that the crisis of that year can be uniquely attributed to the mistakes and stupidity of a small group of men and that, as Churchill would later declare, 'there never was a war more easy to stop than that which ravaged the world for the next five years'.[92] Individual politicians did make a difference, but British policy makers of the inter-war era faced a dilemma which was probably beyond the capacity of even the most gifted to resolve. The desertion of the United States from the Treaty of Versailles and membership of the League of Nations left Britain as the mainstay of the international settlement of 1919. Such a task would always have taxed the country's resources to the limit. By the 1930s, in the wake of the worst financial crisis since the Great War, at the end of a decade in which Britain's military capacity had been systematically dismantled and in the face of the emergence of three major – but geographically diverse – challenges to the international status quo, those charged with the conduct of policy confronted the most unpromising foreign situation of modern times. Stanley Baldwin once railed against the excesses of those who exercised power without responsibility. British policy makers in the 1930s exercised responsibility without power.

If Simon, Hoare and Halifax failed to resolve this situation, then in one sense they are 'guilty' as charged. There were, of course, policy alternatives to those pursued, most of them thoroughly considered at the time, but the critics of the 'Guilty Men' have the inestimable advantage that their proposed courses of action were not tried and therefore never had the chance of being found wanting. Simon put the matter well, shortly before leaving the Foreign Office:

Joining hands with France and Russia and the rest in a ring round the smoking crater [Germany] will not necessarily stop the explosion ... Volcanoes are singularly unresponsive to threats and this particular volcano is only the more likely to erupt if provided with a constant succession of demonstrations that threats are not followed by anything but more threats.[93]

One of the problems for Simon, Hoare and Halifax was their ineffectiveness in speaking up in their own defence. All wrote memoirs. Simon's *Retrospect* has been described, very reasonably, as 'among the least revealing ever written'.[94] Halifax's *Fulness of Days* is, if anything, even worse. Hoare's *Nine Troubled Years* offered a reasoned apologia for Chamberlain and appeasement, but did little to refurbish his own tarnished reputation. All three volumes were constrained by the ground rules laid down by the former Cabinet Secretary, Maurice Hankey, about what could and could not be revealed of the inner workings of the British government; and each writer displayed a commendable loyalty to the memory of their dead colleague, Neville Chamberlain, which ruled out any attempt to distance themselves from the principal 'Guilty Man'.[95] Simon's, for example, said nothing of the Cabinet revolt of 2 September 1939, which he led; Halifax gave the impression that he had been completely at one with Chamberlain throughout the Czechoslovakian crisis; and Hoare passed over his own enthusiasm for a Soviet alliance as early as March 1939 in favour of explaining the reluctance of Chamberlain and others to adopt this option – 'there was ample justification ... for our doubts about the efficacy of any Russian assistance'. [96]

'Something went very wrong with us in the thirties', thought the Foreign Office official, William Strang 'and the responsibility was general and not to be attributed to individuals.'[97] Reflecting on his own fate as a 'Guilty Man', Halifax judged that 'Winston is about the only person who has an absolutely clean sheet'.[98] The point is well taken, but too kind to Churchill. The latter had appeared unwilling to 'make any special exertion in defence of the present government of China',[99] regarded the Italian invasion of Abyssinia as little more than an irritation and had no wish to see the republican government prevail in Spain. As late as 1937 he even seemed willing to give Hitler the benefit of the doubt. Many great leaders who enriched the 'story of mankind' had risen to power by 'wicked and even frightful methods' and 'so it may be with Hitler'.[100] Is this perhaps evidence leading to a guilty verdict, pardoned only as a result of good behaviour later on? In truth there was no clear dividing line between the 'Guilty Men' and their critics, unless it be that the majority of the latter were not constrained by the practicalities of actually being in government. In many instances the two 'sides' shared common ground in their diagnosis of the problem – that British interests had to be defended in a world where three aggressor powers threatened the existing international order. But how? The 'Guilty Men' made mistakes and they failed to devise a solution, but it is doubtful whether one ever really existed.

Notes

1   Cato, *Guilty Men*. London, 1940.
2   B. Evans and A. Taylor, *From Salisbury to Major: Continuity and Change in Conservative Politics*. Manchester, 1996, p. 62.
3   See, for example, R.A.C. Parker, *Chamberlain and Appeasement: British Policy and the Coming of the Second World War*. London, 1993; F. McDonough, *Neville Chamberlain, Appeasement and the British Road to War*. Manchester, 1998; N. Smart, *Neville Chamberlain*. London, 2009.
4   M. Foot, *Loyalists and Loners*. London, 1986, p. 181.
5   House of Commons Debates (hereafter HCD), vol. 360, col. 1264.
6   J. Barnes and D. Nicholson (eds), *The Empire at Bay: The Leo Amery Diaries 1929–1945*. London, 1988, pp. 610–11; University of Birmingham Special Collections [hereafter UOB], Chamberlain MSS, NC 18/1/1156, N. Chamberlain to Ida Chamberlain 11 May 1940.
7   G. Mander, *We Were Not All Wrong*. London, 1941, p. 27.
8   A play on the names of Ramsay MacDonald and Stanley Baldwin.
9   N.J. Crowson (ed.), *Fleet Street, Press Barons and Politics: The Journals of Collin Brooks 1932–1940*. London, 1998, p. 135.
10 N. Smart (ed.), *The Diaries and Letters of Robert Bernays 1932–1939*. Lampeter, 1996, p. 191.
11 UOB, Chamberlain MSS, NC 18/1/196, N. Chamberlain to Hilda Chamberlain 4 January 1919.
12 Viscount Templewood, *Ambassador on Special Mission*. London, 1946, p. 10.
13 The first Foreign Secretary of the National Government was in fact Lord Reading, but he only held office between August and November 1931. A strong case could be made for the inclusion of Eden in any list of 'Guilty Men'. See for example D. Carlton, *Anthony Eden*. London, 1981.
14 J. Strachey in *Left News* cited in R. Bassett, *Democracy and Foreign Policy*. London, 1968, p. 625.
15 Viscount Cecil, *A Great Experiment*. London, 1941, p. 236.
16 A.H. Brodrick, *Near to Greatness: A Life of Earl Winterton*. London, 1965, p. 232.
17 National Archives (hereafter NA), CAB 24/225, memorandum by O. Sargent and F. Ashton-Gwatkin 26 November 1931.
18 B.J.C. McKercher, 'National Security and Imperial Defence: British Grand Strategy and Appeasement, 1930–1939', *Diplomacy and Statecraft* vol. 19 (2008), p. 392.
19 UOB, Avon MSS, AP 20/1/12, diary 26 July 1932.
20 M. Gilbert, *Winston S. Churchill*, vol. 5, companion pt 2. London, 1981, p. 1140.
21 HCD, vol. 262, col. 1515.
22 H.L. Stimson, *The Far Eastern Crisis*. New York, 1936, p. 6.
23 Cambridge University Library (hereafter CUL), Baldwin MSS, vol. 118, fol. 46, Cecil to Baldwin 12 December 1932.
24 A.L. Rowse, *All Souls and Appeasement*. London, 1961, p. 18.
25 UOB, Avon MSS, AP 20/1/12, diary 26 July 1932.
26 Viscount Templewood, *Nine Troubled Years*. London, 1954, p. 107.
27 *Documents on British Foreign Policy* (hereafter *DBFP*), 2nd series, vol. iv, pp. 172–5.
28 *Daily Mail* 17 October 1932.
29 NA, CAB 23/76, CC 35 (33), cabinet 17 May 1933.
30 *DBFP*, 2nd series, vol. v, p. 407, Simon to Rumbold 10 July 1933.
31 Ibid., vol. xii, pp. 271–6, note by Simon 29 November 1934.
32 NA, FO 800/290, Simon to George V 18 March 1935.
33 Bodleian Library, Oxford (hereafter BLO), Simon MSS 7, diary 27 March 1935.
34 Cato, *Guilty Men*, p. 100.
35 Minute by Vansittart 11 February 1939, cited in M. Dockrill, *British Establishment Perspectives on France, 1936–40*. Basingstoke, 1999, p. 126.
36 K. Young, *The Diaries of Sir Robert Bruce Lockhart 1939–1965*. London, 1980, p. 527; UOB, Avon MSS, AP 20/1/26, undated diary entry 1948.
37 D. Dilks (ed.), *The Diaries of Sir Alexander Cadogan 1938–1945*. London, 1971, p. 287; A.J.P. Taylor, *English History 1914–1945*. London, 1965, p. 489.
38 Dilks (ed.), *Cadogan Diaries*, p. 287.

39   H. Macmillan, *Winds of Change 1914–1939*. London, 1966, p. 449.
40   J.A. Cross, *Sir Samuel Hoare: A Political Biography*. London, 1977, p. 352.
41   NA, CAB 23/78, CC10 (34), Cabinet 19 March 1934.
42   Hoare to Willingdon 29 March 1935, cited in Cross, *Sir Samuel Hoare*, p. 190.
43   HCD, vol. 307, cols 351–3.
44   NA, FO 800/295, Hoare to Sir George Clark 24 August 1935.
45   I. Colvin, *Vansittart in Office*. London, 1965, p. 92.
46   Lord Vansittart, *The Mist Procession*. London, 1958; Colvin, *Vansittart in Office*.
47   J. R. Ferris ' "Indulged in All Too Little?" Vansittart, Intelligence and Appeasement', *Diplomacy and Statecraft* vol. 6, no 1 (1995), pp. 127, 137.
48   Cross, *Sir Samuel Hoare*, p. 202.
49   Lord Avon, *Facing the Dictators*. London, 1962, p. 221.
50   NA, CAB 23/82, CC 40 (35), Cabinet 24 July 1935.
51   Ibid., CC 41 (35), Cabinet 31 July 1935.
52   NA, CAB 23/82, meeting of ministers 21 August 1935; UOB, Chamberlain MSS, NC 7/11/28/24, Hoare to Chamberlain 18 August 1935.
53   Vansittart, *The Mist Procession*, p. 522.
54   *DBFP*, 2nd series, vol. xiv, appendix iv, p. 789.
55   Ibid., p. 535, Hoare to Clark 24 August 1935.
56   NA, CAB 23/82, CC 50 (35), Cabinet 2 December 1935.
57   Ibid., CC 54 (35), Cabinet 11 December 1935.
58   CUL, Templewood MSS VIII, Chamberlain to Lady Maud Hoare 19 December 1935.
59   Cross, *Sir Samuel Hoare*, pp. 311–12.
60   Avon, *Facing the Dictators*, p. 243.
61   UOB, Chamberlain MSS, AC 41/4/43, A. Chamberlain to E. Wadsworth 24 June 1936.
62   A. Roberts, *The Holy Fox: A Biography of Lord Halifax*. London, 1991, p. 59.
63   Cross, *Hoare*, p. 270.
64   NA, CAB 23/86, CC 63 (36), Cabinet 4 November 1936.
65   Ibid., CAB 23/87, meeting of ministers 8 January 1937.
66   UOB, Chamberlain MSS, NC 7/11/30/74, Hoare to Chamberlain 17 July 1937.
67   Cross, *Sir Samuel Hoare*, p. 276.
68   NA, CAB 27/624, Foreign Policy Committee 27 March 1939.
69   M. Muggeridge, *The Thirties in Great Britain*. London, 1967, p. 289.
70   NA, CAB 23/87, CC 2 (37), Cabinet 13 January 1937.
71   Borthwick Institute, York [hereafter BIY], Halifax MSS, A4.410.3.3, note by Halifax 6 May 1946.
72   NA, CAB 23/90, CC 43 (37), Cabinet 24 November 1937.
73   Ibid., CC 49 (37), Cabinet 22 December 1937.
74   Roberts, *Holy Fox*, p. 85.
75   NA, CAB 27/623, Foreign Policy Committee 18 March 1938.
76   Ibid., CAB 23/95, CC 39 (38), Cabinet 17 September 1938.
77   *DBFP*, 3rd series, vol. 2, p. 490, Halifax to British Delegation 23 September 1938.
78   Dilks (ed.), *Cadogan Diaries*, p. 103.
79   Ibid., p. 105; P. Neville, 'Sir Alexander Cadogan and Lord Halifax's "Damascus Road" Conversion over the Godesberg Terms 1938', *Diplomacy and Statecraft* vol. 11, no. 3 (2000), pp. 81–90. Halifax's may not have been the only intervention of significance. I am grateful to Mr Chris Cooper for showing me a copy of his forthcoming article 'Hailsham's Last Hurrah: Douglas Hailsham, Appeasement and the Rejection of the Godesberg Terms, September 1938'.
80   Dilks (ed.), *Cadogan Diaries*, p. 105.
81   House of Lords Debates, vol. CX, cols 1307–8.
82   *DBFP*, 3rd series, vol. 3, p. 252, Halifax to Phipps 1 November 1938.
83   B. Bond (ed.), *Chief of Staff: The Diaries of Lieutenant-General Sir Henry Pownall, 1933–1940*. London, 1972, p. 185.
84   NA, CAB 23/97, CC 8 (39), Cabinet 22 February 1939.
85   J. Harvey (ed.), *The Diplomatic Diaries of Oliver Harvey 1937–1940*. London, 1970, p. 253.

86   Ibid., p. 258.
87   Roberts, *Holy Fox*, p. 301.
88   *The Week* 29 March 1939, cited in ibid., p. 153.
89   Lord Hailsham, cited in ibid., p. 308.
90   NA, CAB 65/13, WM (40) 139, War Cabinet 26 May 1940.
91   J. Colville, *The Fringes of Power: Downing Street Diaries 1939–1955*. London, 1985, p. 321. Monthly Censorship Reports suggested that Halifax had 'inherited' Chamberlain's unpopularity.
92   W.S. Churchill, *The Gathering Storm*. London, 1948, p. viii.
93   Churchill Archives Centre, Cambridge, Phipps MSS, PHPP 1/14, Simon to Phipps 5 April 1935.
94   N. Rose, *Vansittart: Study of a Diplomat*. London, 1978, p. 104.
95   J.F. Naylor, *A Man and an Institution*. Cambridge, 1984, p. 235.
96   Templewood, *Nine Troubled Years*, p. 343.
97   BIY, Halifax MSS, A2.278.107, Strang to Halifax 13 January 1957.
98   Halifax diary 6 June 1940, cited Roberts, *Holy Fox*, p. 243.
99   C.B. Pyper, *Chamberlain and his Critics*. Hounslow, 1962, p. 19.
100 R.R. James, *Churchill: A Study in Failure 1900–1939*. London, 1970, pp. 291–2.

Chapter 10

Neville Chamberlain and the Consequences of the Churchillian Hegemony

John Charmley

Just over twenty years ago I commented that Chamberlain's reputation, which then stood higher than it had for forty years, might yet rise higher.[1] What actually followed was a fresh spurt of criticism that effectively restored the *status quo ante*, but in place of a weak and ignorant Chamberlain there emerged a strong and ignorant one. Churchill's Chamberlain had looked at international politics through the wrong end of a municipal drain-pipe: R.A.C. Parker's version was a lineal descendant who ignored opinions that clashed with his.[2] Most of the work that has appeared over the last twenty years has taken variants on this theme and played them to an audience already attuned to it.[3] 'Revisionism' is now largely a matter of Maurice Cowling and the English-language version that is my own *Chamberlain and the Lost Peace*.[4] Robert Self's recent biography, like the introduction to his excellent edition of the *Diary Letters*, reminds us there is still more to be said on Chamberlain, but having been over-optimistic once, the present writer is naturally hesitant about the tide ever turning back in favour of revisionism.

In his volume on the influence of Churchill's *The Second World War*, David Reynolds runs through the reasons for its immense influence. To his list might be added the picture Churchill presented of the 1930s.[5] In the beginning was the word, and word was Winston's, and it has established a hegemonic position in the historiography: indeed, as is the case with such versions, it is all but impossible to think about the war and appeasement except in Churchillian tropes. This essay explores the reasons for this, its consequences, and *still* suggests an alternative reading.

The version authored by Churchill had its origin in the accusatory pages of *Guilty Men* in 1940.[6] Churchill took the polemic forged in the political heat of imminent defeat and turned it into the Authorized Version. Few historians write with Churchill's credentials. After all, he was the man who 'won the war'; the only one of the 'Big Three' to pen memoirs; and the very way in which those memoirs were constructed, six volumes filled with quotations from official sources, added to the air of authority. On almost every page Churchill broke the Official Secrets Act. Here was the voice of history, and the Churchillian version became part of the national and international consciousness. It was the bedrock for everything written about the Second World War. The message conveyed in the first volume, *The Gathering Storm*, was one attuned to the times in which it was written. Appeasement was wrong. It did not pay. Dictators should be resisted. The mistakes made in dealing with Hitler should not be repeated with Stalin. The book provided the subtext to the Cold War. That 'appeasement' was wrong became the keystone of the Atlantic Alliance and was a foundational assumption of post-war British foreign policy: from Stalin, through Nasser to Saddam Hussein. Dictators were to be resisted; those who dissented could be dismissed as 'appeasers'; no further argument was necessary as Churchill had shown conclusively that 'appeasement' was wrong.

Against this tide none could stand. With reputations terminally damaged by 'Cato' and Churchill, the 'Guilty Men' were effectively cowed. Chamberlain, of course, was dead, and his authorized biographer, Keith Feiling, was no expert in modern history and failed to make a convincing case for rehabilitation.[7] He was easily swept aside by the Churchillian *blitzkrieg*. For the rest, Lord Maugham's *The Truth About the Munich Crisis* (1954) might have aptly adopted the title of Duff Cooper's *Old Men Forget*, whilst Sam Hoare's *Nine Troubled Years* (1954) was notable only for being the first example of a sustained attempt to argue that the Munich agreement had been designed to give Britain an 'extra year' to rearm; Halifax's *Fullness of Days* (1957) merited A.J.P. Taylor's waspish description 'dullness of days'. These were the lost men, condemned to the margins of history, and unable, or unwilling, to make out a case to justify their actions. In the meantime the Churchillians, Duff Cooper, Anthony Eden and Harold Macmillan, all supported the version authorized by 'Winston'.[8] It is usual on these occasions to see A.J.P. Taylor's *The Origins of the Second World War* as the first swallow in the revisionist spring but apart from a piece of irony about Munich being the triumph for all that 'was best' in English public life, he spent little time dealing directly with Chamberlain.[9] It was only with the opening of the archives in the later 1960s that any real attempt could be made to delineate a case for Chamberlain.

Middlemas's *Diplomacy of Illusion* was the first book to use the archival evidence seriously, and whilst highly critical of Chamberlain's diplomacy, he at least began the habit of referring to the limitations on his freedom of actions.[10] The two Pauls, Schroeder and Kennedy, attempted to add some historical depth to a remarkably shallow historiography, pointing out that there was nothing new in the practice of British Prime Ministers using diplomacy to avoid war; but their plea for perspective, whilst reiterated in my own *Chamberlain and the Lost Peace*, was lost in the flood of books making use of the newly available archival sources.[11] It is some mark of the hegemony of the Churchillian version that it should have come as a revelation that Chamberlain had good reasons for the policy he followed. Yet, as the resolutely anti-appeasement diplomat Oliver Harvey put it: 'the truth is everybody was an "appeaser" of Germany at one time or another'.[12] What the documents did was to explain something none of Chamberlain's colleagues had been able to do in their memoirs – which was that in the circumstances facing it, for the Government to have adopted any other policy would have been astounding.

The arguments advanced by Schroeder and Kennedy about appeasement being part of the long-term fabric of British foreign policy are ones which a debate obsessed with the details of 1937–9 still does not accord proper weight. Chamberlain's policy did not originate with him, nor was Churchill's preferred policy in some sense 'traditional', even though, speaking to the Conservative Committee on Foreign Affairs in March 1936, he declared: 'For four hundred years the foreign policy of England has been to oppose the strongest, most aggressive, most dominating Power on the Continent, and particularly to prevent the Low Countries falling into the hands of such a Power.' He cited the defeat of Philip II, Louis XIV, Napoleon and Kaiser Wilhelm II as examples that proved his point. Creating coalitions to achieve this purpose, and thus 'preserve the liberties of Europe' was, he declared 'the wonderful unconscious tradition of British foreign policy'.[13] The only thing 'wonderful' about this is that Churchill claimed this one-sided view was the only one possible. Recent scholarship is helping us recover a Conservative 'tradition' of foreign policy into which Chamberlain fits quite easily.[14] Churchill's version of events is enshrined within a Churchillian view of what British foreign policy *should* have been, but that, in itself, is a construct. Many years ago Rab Butler commented that it was impossible for a global empire to have one 'simple traditional policy', because British interests 'and the world itself are too complicated to enable us to follow any one high road'.[15]

We can amplify the Schroeder–Kennedy thesis by tracing a line of Conservative foreign policy going back to the mid-nineteenth century, which was happy to work towards adjusting problems as they arose, rather than seeking to make grandiose gestures with regard to the 'balance of power'. A global empire had to pursue a foreign policy designed to prevent simultaneous crises in different parts of the world. No Power, however great, could cope with simultaneous threats in Europe, the Mediterranean and the Far East. The last time this had happened was the mid 1890s, and Rosebery's experiences at the hands of the Triple and Dual Alliances led British politicians such as Joe Chamberlain to complain about isolation, and others, like the Liberal Sir Edward Grey, to value the 1904 *entente* with France as a way out of it. It was Neville Chamberlain's misfortune to face a similar concatenation of crises, but he enjoyed more success in dealing with the threats from Japan, Mussolini and Hitler than is commonly admitted. Concentrating, as so many historians have, on the 'appeasement' of Germany is something Chamberlain could not do: he had three challenges to British power and never had the luxury of being able to forget about two of them. If policy towards Germany dominates the picture, then 1939 appears to mark the point at which Chamberlain failed, but if the global challenge is taken into account, the record is more mixed. Politicians make policy in a context that is not of their own devising. This has been masked by the ubiquitous tendency to write about British foreign policy in the late 1930s as though it were a peculiarity of Chamberlain's, isolated from anything which preceded or succeeded it. These Churchillian tropes have not only constructed the image of Chamberlain which has damned him in the eyes of posterity – they have effectively confined discussion of his record within the narrow limits set by ancient political polemic. It is more than time for scholarship to break out of this procrustean bed.

The notion that there was something personal about the foreign policy Britain pursued in the late 1930s should be the first victim of any revisionism. The policy of appeasement was, in Paul Schroeder's words, 'over determined'. As Baldwin told Conservative MPs in July 1936, a combination of economic necessity, previous spending cuts and a pacific public opinion made it difficult to press on with rearmament before 1934. These same factors also created problems with the pace of rearmament once it had begun. Baldwin explained that both he and Chamberlain had felt the acute danger of 'throw[ing] back the ordinary trade of the country perhaps for many years'.[16] There was also the question which hindsight has led historians to ignore, of what Hitler actually wanted. Here, Baldwin's intuition led him to pose a question ignored by many at the time and since:

> We all know the German desire, and he [Hitler] has come out with it in his book, to move East, and if he should move East I should not break my heart, but that is another thing. I do not believe she [Germany] wants to move West because West would be a difficult programme for her, and if she does it before we are ready I quite agree the picture is perfectly awful … If they come to talk we may find out the value of all the speeches he has made about peace, and peace in the West, is false …[17]

The easy assumption that Hitler's objectives lay to the West was not one Baldwin shared. But, whatever either he or Chamberlain had done, Britain would still have faced the most serious set of challenges in half a century. This was the situation awaiting Chamberlain when he became Prime Minister in May 1937.

What was it he brought to the job? The Lloyd Georgian stereotype that he had been a 'not bad Lord Mayor of Birmingham in a lean year' has latterly been replaced by the view that he brought a businesslike efficiency to the job. Here it is usual to cite Chamberlain's comment that 'Unhappily it is part of my nature that I cannot contemplate any problem without trying to find a solution to it' as though it says the last word on the matter. And yet, when he wrote these words in 1934, he went on to say: 'And so I have practically taken charge of the Defence requirements of the country.'[18] No one would accept the last comment as an accurate summary of the situation in 1934, and yet some historians have been happy to accept the former as gospel truth. Even an historian as shrewd as Alistair Parker was happy to comment that Chamberlain's letters to his sisters provided the historian with a precise account of 'the reasons for his actions', and revealed him as a man with 'no capacity for self criticism.'[19] Yet this is to ignore the family dynamic behind the letters. Neville was big brother writing to his little sisters; he was the 'least' of the Chamberlains, and yet the only one to make it to the top: of course there is no trace of self-criticism. What brother in such a family would write to his sisters in such a way?[20] The letters show Neville's need to present himself as the success his father had never thought he could be: to treat them at face value is to buy into the notion that the letters are an objective account of his motives. They are no such thing. They are an exercise in self-justification, and as such as reliable as Churchill's more public attempts to do the same thing.

If Chamberlain seems decisive, it is because he succeeded a Prime Minister who had raised procrastination into an art form. Moreover, it is not unknown for a patient and long-serving deputy to wish to make his mark by reviewing the policies of his predecessor. Such actions are not necessarily the mark of a control freak or an egotist (although they can be). After the drift of the last few years of Baldwin, it was not just sycophants like Sir John Simon who told Chamberlain that the change was refreshing.[21] One of the reasons Chamberlain had become Prime Minister was the expectation that he would provide a lead: that should not be read (as it has been so often) as a euphemism for riding roughshod over the opinions of others. Chamberlain did bring order where there had been, if not chaos, then at least uncertainty. He knew that the rearmament programme and foreign policy had to be brought into alignment, and his 'double policy of rearmament & better relations with Germany & Italy' was the only realistic option.[22] In promoting a Defence review, Chamberlain sought to set priorities for the sort of war which might break out if diplomacy should fail; in seeking to find diplomatic solutions to the problems facing the British Empire, he sought to avoid war. His 'double policy' was designed to ensure that if diplomacy failed, Britain could wage war. In this last he was successful.

With the possibility of three simultaneous challenges on a global scale, all real choices were hard. It was, of course, easy enough for those without responsibility to talk confidently of the importance of 'rearmament', but the Treasury was clear enough here: the planned increases in the armaments budget would bear heavily on Britain's economic recovery. The Service Departments were less clear. Each of them favoured a programme that provided them with what they wanted, whilst the Foreign Office was far from convinced that it would be impossible to avoid war everywhere. In this situation the policy crafted was designed to minimize the dangers: rearmament would be continued, but would be focussed on specific areas, in particular on things which would defend the home islands if the worst were to happen. This would allow the economy to stake the strain for another couple of years, during which time the diplomats could try to find a way through the gathering storm. In its own terms, this policy was far from a failure.

When war did break out in September 1939 it was with Germany alone. Britain, by contrast, had an ally, France, and a public opinion united behind the notion that the war had been unavoidable. A modern perspective allows us to understand, better perhaps than an earlier generation of historians, the toxic effects of declaring war without public support. Neither were there grounds for supposing this localized European war would be a potential disaster. Although his pact with Stalin had delivered him from the immediate threat of a two-front war, Hitler would have to be mindful of the dangers from the East. By contrast, Britain and France enjoyed the security of pre-prepared defensive positions and a parity of arms on paper. Had the British and French armies been up to the task they were meant for, then the diplomatic success of a war in which Britain faced only one enemy might have been more noticed. The complete collapse of the Anglo-French armies in the summer of 1940 created a situation where no one wished to place the blame where it belonged – with the armed forces – so government ministers became the scapegoats for a tactical and military disaster. Short of doing to the British General Staff what Stalin did to his General Staff, it is hard to see what Chamberlain could have done to avoid that military disaster in 1940.

The *Guilty Men* and *Gathering Storm* lines of argument locked the historiography into a narrow range of arguments about the rates and types of rearmament, ignoring the simple fact that given the incapacity of the Anglo-French military leaders, more armaments would simply have resulted in extra equipment being abandoned at Dunkirk. On the narrow focus, the opening of the archives was bound to throw a lifeline to those wishing to defend Chamberlain. Money was, after all, the fifth arm of defence, and going bankrupt would hardly have helped deter Hitler. Moreover, those areas in which money was spent, Spitfires and Radar, were ones that enabled Britain to withstand Germany in the late summer and early autumn of 1940: Chamberlain's decisions created Churchill's first victory. Had Churchill's defence preferences prevailed in 1937 and 1938, Britain would have been confronting Hitler's *Luftwaffe* with medium-range bombers. The narrowness of the focus of rearmament allowed Chamberlain's defenders to win back some ground from the Churchillians, but it did nothing to facilitate a broader discussion

Standing back from the usual debates, we can see that Chamberlain was the first inter-war Prime Minister to really face up to the question of what it meant for Britain to be a Great Power. In the 1870s and 1880s successive British Prime Ministers had, with the exception of Disraeli, acknowledged that when it came to continental warfare, their country was an also ran: a global power, but with armed forces configured to meet colonial and naval challenges. Participation in a war like the Franco-Prussian or Austro-Prussian war was not considered likely. With a professional army and no conscription, Britain was not prepared for such eventualities, as the experience of 1914 showed. Not until 1916 did the British Government take the action necessary to enable the country to play the European role demanded by the nature of that war; and by 1919 conscription had been abandoned as the Lloyd George government headed back to business as usual. Between then and the 1930s Britain's imperial and external policies had borne silent witness to successive government's unwillingness to undertake any serious military activities. As early as 1930 the Chief of the Imperial General Staff was warning of the country's inability to meet its commitments under the Locarno Treaty.[23] *Pace* the Churchillian black legend, the MacDonald and Baldwin Governments were perfectly happy to begin a serious rearmament programme as early as 1934. What they were not willing to do was to set priorities, so, on paper, Britain was committing herself to deal with all the threats facing her on a global scale. This was the rearmament of fantasy and Neville Chamberlain was no fantasist. Through the Simon defence review he insisted that the country establish some priorities and then that it should begin to shift its diplomacy into alignment with them. This process was bound to lead to some casualties amongst those who preferred fantasy to reality: chief amongst these was Anthony Eden.

Eden was one of Baldwin's young men, and unlike most of those upon whom the Prime Minister smiled benignly, he was promoted. As Foreign Secretary, he proved unable to see the difference between Mussolini's Italy and Hitler's Germany. Indeed, by 1937 he seemed convinced that dealing with the former was the priority. It is true that the diplomatic purdah into which his invasion of Abyssinia had plunged Mussolini had to be resolved, but to decide to do this by denying the King of Italy the title of Emperor of Abyssinia was to show the faulty sense of perspective which marred and eventually destroyed Eden's career. Chamberlain was having none of this. He cared little for Italy, but in the absence of any overtures from Germany, he saw no reason to complicate Britain's already difficult diplomatic position by pushing Italy into Hitler's arms. Nor was he willing to defer to Eden's procrastination. Finding his hand being forced, Eden flounced off into a resignation few understood. Had Churchill not disinterred him in 1940, his career would not have recovered from this error. His successor, Lord Halifax, would, after a quiet start, play a much more notable role in the story of appeasement.

The connections between the policy of 'appeasement' and British imperial policy between the wars remain to be studied in depth, but only historians who separate out the two fields could fail to notice that Halifax, Simon and Hoare had all spent serious amounts of time dealing with India. The policy they had pursued bore a generic resemblance to the one followed in Europe. In both cases nationalists were to be negotiated with until their lowest demands could be discovered and, provided they were low enough, be granted. Nehru, Gandhi and Hitler, however much the contemporary mind rejects the equation, had much in common to British Ministers between the wars. All were nationalists making trouble who needed to be dealt with. The experience of imperial policy in the decade after 1922 suggested that however fanatical the nationalists, it was usually possible to find something that would buy them off: nothing in Hitler's approach suggested that he would be any different. It was true that he behaved in a way which would have infuriated a saint, but that hardly distinguished him from other imperial nationalists. Moreover, his vocalized demands were, unlike the way he seemed to go about making them, not unreasonable. As early as 1923 the British Government had declined to back the French in the Ruhr, and neither that one nor any of its successors showed any inclination to enforce the Versailles settlement. Indeed, as the Chiefs of Staff pointed out in 1929, Britain did not even possess the power to fulfil her obligations under the treaty of Locarno. Neither in Europe nor in the Empire was British policy predicated on the use of force. It was assumed diplomacy would fill the gap. In Chamberlain's case there was actually something of a departure from this position. As one of his colleagues told the National Labour MP and diarist Harold Nicolson: 'He [Neville] ... takes a far more active interest in Foreign Affairs than Baldwin did, and ... he is very opposed to a continuance of our policy of retreat.'[24]

The revised Churchillian version of events still obscures another reading of what Chamberlain was about. The notion that rearmament was inadequate for the demands placed on it in 1940 ignores his 'double policy' – he was rearming, and for a purpose. The notion that he was in some way taken in by Hitler at Munich foreshortens our perspective and is based on selective quotations of his remarks about Hitler after the Berchtesgarten meeting. By the same methodology we can reconstruct a Churchill who was deluded about Stalin after Yalta. No doubt such games serve their purpose in the polemic which so often marks this topic, but one might hope that historians would have grown beyond such things by this stage of the debate.

Chamberlain's reaction to the murder of Chancellor Dollfuss in 1934 ought to put an end to the notion that he was blind to the nature of Nazism: 'That those beasts should have got him at last & that they should have treated him with such callous brutality makes me hate Nazi-ism and all its works with a greater loathing than ever.'[25] He approved of Mussolini's movement of troops: 'It's the only thing the Germans understand,' he wrote in a manner that any Churchillian would have approved. He rejected the (temporary) optimism of the Foreign Office, telling his sister Hilda: 'It may be true ... that the menace from Germany has perceptibly receded, but it does not seem to me to have disappeared so completely as to warrant our disregarding her altogether.' But even then, he was alive to a danger his critics have steadily ignored: 'if we are to take the necessary measures of defence against her we certainly can't afford at the same time to rebuild our battle fleet.' Britain ought, he argued, 'to be making eyes at Japan.'[26] He would pursue precisely this policy as Prime Minister, trying to ensure that Britain never had to face her three potential enemies simultaneously.

It was Chamberlain's activism that had led to the breach with Eden, and it was the same quality that led him to seek a solution to the problems arising in Czechoslovakia. The din arising from the 'Munich crisis' has tended to obscure the fact that it arose not from Chamberlain's inactivity, but from the opposite impulse. When he complained in September about how 'horrible' it was that Britain faced war because of a 'far away country' about 'which we know nothing', few thought to riposte that he had only himself to blame. Britain, after all, had no treaty obligations to Czechoslovakia, and it could hardly be argued that it was a part of any Nazi drive to the West. If it was Hitler's ambitions that precipitated a crisis over the Sudetenland, it was Chamberlain's determination to get ahead of the game that ensured that Britain would become embroiled in it.

Disheartened and discouraged as he was by the *Anchsluss*, Chamberlain was reinforced in his belief that 'force is the only argument Germany understands' and that only 'alliances which don't require meetings at Geneva' were likely to be effective: 'Heaven knows I don't want to get back to alliances but if Germany continues to behave as she has done lately she may drive us to it.'[27] Halifax, who took the view that 'the world is a strangely mixed grill of good and evil ... and for good or ill we have got to do our best to live in it and not withdraw from it into the desert because of the evil, like the ancient anchorites',[28] concurred with the notion that something must be done. That this would not be Churchill's bright idea of a 'Grand Alliance' had nothing to do with Chamberlainite ignorance and everything with its own defects.

It is a mark of the polarized nature of the current historiography that Chamberlain should have been accused simultaneously of not listening to expert advice and of listening to it too much. Those who imagine that critics cannot have it both ways must be unfamiliar with the terms on which these sorts of argument are conducted: heads Chamberlain loses; tails his critics win. The old Churchillian line that had Chamberlain obstinately refusing to listen to expert advice has latterly found itself being replaced with a more sophisticated version whereby he did listen, but only to those experts who shared his pessimism.[29] One problem with this line of argument is that it tends to fail to identify the contemporary expert opinion which offered an optimistic prognosis; the other is that it fails to note that however pessimistic some of the reports were, Chamberlain did not retreat into isolationism. Indeed, the one complaint which might fairly be levelled at him is the one seldom made – that he should have taken more care and been more isolationist in his policy.

If we take the most egregious of the Churchillian lines of criticism, that a 'Grand Alliance' would have deterred Hitler and that Chamberlain ignored the idea, its shortcomings are readily apparent. The same idea had, in fact, occurred to Chamberlain, who talked about it to Halifax and had the Chiefs of Staff look at it:

> It is a very attractive idea, indeed there is almost everything to be said for it until you come to examine its practicability. From that moment its attraction vanishes. You only have to look at the map to see that nothing that France or we could do could possibly save Czecho-Slovakia from being over-run by the Germans if they wanted to do it.[30]

There was in this nothing of false pessimism, nor yet of overriding his officials. The Foreign Office acknowledged that there was next to nothing (for which read nothing at all) which Britain or France could do to 'save Czechoslovakia from being overrun'.[31] It was all very well to argue that Britain and France ought to guarantee Czechoslovakia, but no one could explain how aid would be delivered to her in the event of a German attack: moreover, as William Strang, the head of the Central department pointed out, giving such a guarantee would be to take the final decision for war and peace out of the hands of the British Government, a consideration which might have been remembered with advantage a year later. All that could be done was to press the French and the Czechs to see what terms Hitler might come up with. The notion advanced in some quarters that it was worth running the risk of war now because Germany would be stronger in two years' time was 'not a good argument for risking disaster now.'[32]

Of course, if the French had devised any serious plans for an offensive operation across the Rhine, there was 'something' Britain could have done, provided, that is, Chamberlain had been willing to ignore British public opinion. But the French had no such plans, and one might have thought that contemporary circumstances would have demonstrated the problem with going to war without public support. Beyond that, what did the 'Grand Alliance' consist of? The Soviet Union? One of the greatest weaknesses in Alastair Parker's treatment of Appeasement is his argument that cooperation with Stalin was not properly pursued – as befitted an admirer of the political Left, he passed over the unpleasant aspects of the Soviet regime, as well as the unlikelihood of Soviet support being forthcoming on terms Britain could have accepted. He also ignored, in a splendidly Anglocentric style, the fact that for most of the countries in Central and Eastern Europe the Soviet Union was part of the problem, not the solution. Even had the USSR been in a geographical position to have helped the Czechs, it was far from certain there would have been a united Czecho-Slovak government ready to have received it. The real criticism of Chamberlain here is not that he listened pessimistically to pessimists who confirmed his pessimism, but that he intervened at all, given the difficulty of actually doing anything.

The pessimism of which some critics have accused him was neither unnatural nor as complete as some seem to think. As the man who had steered the British economy away from the abyss in 1931–2, he was painfully conscious of the problem of affording the rearmament programme. He was also well aware of the other constraints on it: a lack of skilled manpower; the cost of importing some of the material needed; the cost to the domestic economy of making goods which only the State wanted to buy when there was a consumer market for things like motor vehicles which was unfulfilled. Nor could he see 'rearmament' in the uncomplicated way Churchill spoke about it. His thoughts were informed by the latest trends in military thinking. It was certainly true that he lacked the direct military experience of Churchill or Duff Cooper, but this was not necessarily a bad thing. Cooper could not bear to give up the cavalry, whilst Churchill seemed obsessed with medium-range bombers. Chamberlain had read Liddell-Hart instead, from whom he imbibed the notion that the war of the future would be highly mobile. His rearmament preferences were designed to prepare the country for such a war, should the resources of diplomacy fail. But, as Simon reminded the Cabinet on 14 March, 'we are in the position of a runner in a race who wants to reserve his sprit for the right time, but does not know where the finishing tape is. The danger is that we might knock out our finances prematurely.'[33] Was this over pessimistic? Hardly, as the experience of

1939–40 was to show: Britain's finances were hardly robust, and they were, in the end, knocked to pieces.

Quite why Chamberlain and his government should have run this risk prematurely is hard to see, except in the light of the argument that Hitler was insatiable and unappeasable. But even with this there are two difficulties. In the first place, it was far from clear in early 1938 that Germany could not be satisfied. As Cadogan, who was by no means an optimist, wondered, was it 'even now, too late to treat the Germans as human beings?'[34] In the second place, it made assumptions about Hitler's objectives for which there was insufficient evidence. As Halifax noted, Churchill seemed to be assuming that 'When Germany has done this that and the other in Central Europe, she will in overwhelming might proceed to destroy France and ourselves. That is a conclusion which I do not believe myself to be necessarily well-founded …'[35] It is easy to dismiss this as hopelessly naïve, but it ought to be recalled that within the year Halifax had begun to fear that Hitler's ambitions were 'Napoleonic' in scope. Nor was this sentiment as self-evidently incorrect as the Churchillian paradigm suggests. There is certainly nothing in *Mein Kampf* about hostility to Britain or its Empire: quite the opposite. Hitler's objectives were certainly malign: he wanted more *lebensraum* for the Aryan race; he wanted to combat and destroy the Communist menace; and he wanted to exterminate the lesser races, especially the Jews. But Hitler's ambitions, as Baldwin and Halifax both saw, lay to the East. Of course, when it broke out in 1939, the war was between Germany and Britain and France – but that was because of actions taken by Chamberlain and his government, which made it impossible for Hitler to achieve his ambitions in the East without turning westwards first.

The first sign on the road that would lead to this situation came in May 1938 when the rumours mounted that the Nazis were mobilizing troops near the Czech border. The British Government's reaction hardly fits with the Churchillian paradigm. When the Cabinet had considered the Chiefs of Staff report on 22 March, it had acknowledged that in the event of a German attack on Czechoslovakia 'we can do nothing to prevent the dog getting the bone, and we have no means of making him give it up, except by killing him by the slow process of attrition and starvation'.[36] Alastair Parker concluded that this report 'provided a justification, not an explanation of their action', but this shows how resort to the language of polemic can vitiate the work of even the best historian.[37] His working assumption is that Chamberlain and Halifax wanted an excuse for not acting, and this blinds him to the obvious fact that, in the face of what the military experts and the diplomats recommended, Chamberlain's freedom of action was limited: he could, of course, have ignored his officials and experts, in which case the initial Churchillian criticism would have been correct; or he could have accepted their views, in which case the revised Churchillian version of him as incurable pessimist kicks in. Perhaps if there had been an official expression of optimism, Chamberlain's mood would have lightened, but no one has produced such a document. Parker dismisses Duff

Cooper's view that Chamberlain's subsequent statement 'quite clearly implied that if France went to war, we should go too', citing it as an example of his being 'outmanoeuvred by Chamberlain's superior political skills'.[38] Yet this is another example of the way in which drawing one's conclusions in advance determines a particular reading of the evidence. Cooper was far from stupid, and as a former diplomat who had worked in the Foreign Office before the Great War, he recognized the echoes of Sir Edward Grey's comments in Chamberlain's declaration that: 'Where peace and war are concerned, legal obligations are not alone involved, and, if war broke out, it would be unlikely to be confined to those who have assumed such obligations.'[39] Cooper had felt 'ill and depressed' after the Cabinet, but he recognized that the 'tone and emphasis' of the speech was 'quite different'. Without saying so definitely, he quite clearly implied that if France went to war we should do too.[40] He had gone as far as Grey had before 1914. Moreover, Chamberlain's subsequent policy indicated that the former diplomat had divined his meaning with greater accuracy than the indignant historian.

During the May crisis of 1938 British policy followed a line very familiar to students of Anglo-French relations before the First World War. During the first Moroccan crisis of 1905–6 the British had tried to prevent any precipitate action by making it clear to the French that they could not rely on unconditional support, whilst simultaneously warning the Germans not to take it for granted that if France was attacked, Britain would stand aside. Indeed the clear implication in 1905–6 was what it was in 1938: a German attack on France would drag an unwilling Britain into war.[41] Now it was Halifax who warned France that Britain would not necessarily help to defend the Czechs.[42] At the same time he reminded Ribbentrop of the speech made by Chamberlain on 24 March, in which he had declared that 'it would be quite impossible to say where it might end and what Governments might become involved'.[43] That the same speech also included news of increases in expenditure on rearmaments made the point clear enough without actually being menacing. Halifax reiterated the point to the German ambassador: 'I would beg him not to count upon this country being able to stand aside if from any precipitate action there should start a European conflagration.'[44] Chamberlain was satisfied that his firmness had averted as crisis and that the Germans had, in the end, 'decided after getting out warnings that the risks were too great'. The episode had shown him 'how utterly untrustworthy and dishonest the German Government is'.[45] The only difficulty was that, as Strang reported after visiting Prague in late May: 'we are, naturally, regarded as having committed ourselves morally at any rate to intervene if there is a European war, and nothing that we are likely to say will remove that impression'. He warned that: 'we are certainly regarded as being more deeply committed in the Czech affair than before',[46] and so it proved. As before 1914, the language of nuance was understood by the French to imply a moral commitment, and, even more importantly, it was understood in that way by many in Great Britain.

The same reasons that had prompted Britain to make the intervention it had in May drew it inexorably into the crisis which culminated at Munich in September. Having undertaken to play a role in finding a solution to the problem of the Sudetenland, Chamberlain had embarked upon a road which would lead him in exactly the direction his critics had advocated, and to the action which they so ardently advocated. When that turned out to be the road to disaster, they would blame him for not having pursued it earlier, quietly ignoring the likelihood that if he had, disaster would have struck a year earlier. It is here, above all, that the hegemonic grip of Churchillian orthodoxy holds historians and public opinion in thrall. It is a feature of a hegemonic system that it makes thinking in any other way difficult, and that it tends to drive even unorthodox thought processes back to what it has established as a 'norm'. The war was, it is assumed, inevitable. Indeed, it was also a just war against patent evil. This makes the case for it, as well as damning Chamberlain for his failing to do something about it earlier. The assumption that defeat in 1940 was in some way also the result of Chamberlainite inaction allows, by an intellectual sleight of hand imposed by the hegemonic orthodoxy, historians to ignore the elephant in the room and assume that earlier action would have had a happier result. For this, as for the assumption that Chamberlain was ignoring some mythical optimistic scenario, there is not the slightest justification. On paper in 1940 the Anglo-French armies should have been able to prevail: in practice they did not. This was not because of any defects in 'rearmament'. It was for the simple reason that the leadership of the Anglo-French forces was inferior to that of the German forces – a simple case of military failure. Once conceded, that and the argument that going to war a year earlier fall victim to the likelihood that all that would have happened was an earlier defeat. Indeed, one might go further and say that this scenario would have been accompanied by a public opinion far from united behind the idea that a war was inevitable. The consequences of that on the morrow of the sort of defeat suffered in June 1940 ought to cause even the most obstinate of Chamberlain's critics to rethink some of their assumptions.

This is not to reinstate, via the idea of the counter-factual, the tired old *canard* that Munich 'bought' Britain a year: it did, of course, but that was not its intention. It is, however, to push hard the argument advanced first in *Chamberlain and the Lost Peace* and then by Andrew Roberts in *Holy Fox* that, far from being some sort of Chamberlain puppet, Lord Halifax played a decisive role in frustrating Chamberlain's preferences and pushing British policy down the road to war. That older Conservative tradition identified by recent scholarship found its contemporary exponent in Halifax, who, in his own quiet way, became as essential to his Prime Minister as Palmerston had been a century earlier.

Too often diplomatic historians have ignored the political context within which foreign policy was constructed and conducted. The National Government elected in 1935 had benefitted from Baldwin's avuncular style, and whilst Chamberlain was a much more impressive debater than his predecessor, and could therefore arouse much more partisan enthusiasm, Baldwin himself noted that it had a bad effect elsewhere in the House: 'the Labour fellows say "We are back to the Party dog fight. The PM's speeches are A1 partisan speeches but he talks as if he were on the hustings, so can we. And there can never be a national foreign policy as long as he is there." '[47] Halifax was a much more emollient figure, and one of the results of the Munich crisis was that he not only found his own voice, but he also began to assume the position which would lead to his being widely considered the natural successor to Chamberlain in 1940. The crucial moment came on 25 September, the day following Chamberlain's return from Bad Godesberg. Chamberlain was resigned to accepting Hitler's demands, which would have involved immediate German occupation of the Sudetenland, and he commended the idea to his colleagues, who appeared to accept it. Halifax, who had felt that public (and parliamentary) opinion was hardening against such a concession, imparted his reservations to the Permanent Under-Secretary, Sir Alexander Cadogan, who encouraged him in that line of thought. After a sleepless night, Halifax wrote to Chamberlain the following morning to say that he could not support the idea of swallowing Hitler's demands: despite Chamberlain's hope that 'Night conclusions are seldom taken in the right perspective,' Halifax remained obstinate.[48] As might have been expected, he put forward his view with due diffidence, but for Parker to read the Cabinet record as a sign that Halifax's view was both 'tentative and reluctant' is another sign of the dominance of the Churchillian view.[49] Halifax was certainly reluctant to disagree openly, but there was nothing tentative in his objections, as events were to show.

Halifax could not be treated like Eden, even had he been foolish enough to have left himself open to such a fate. He was a Tory grandee, widely respected, and a man whose Christian conscience helped mark him off as a politician of rare integrity. Underneath the self-effacing aristocratic manner, there was Yorkshire grit. Like Grey in August 1914, Halifax made plain the implications of previous 'understandings'. If Hitler threatened the Czechs and war broke out, Britain would have to join in if France honoured her treaty with Czechoslovakia.[50] Of course, Halifax could not have prevailed had he not spoken for the reservations of many of his colleagues, but since Duff Cooper, Walter Elliot, Oliver Stanley and even Lord Hailsham shared his views,[51] Chamberlain found himself conceding ground. The much-vaunted dominance of the Cabinet turned out to be nothing of the sort the first time it was really tested: only Lords Maugham and Stanhope were actually in favour of accepting the Godesberg terms and recommending them to the Czechs. If the Cabinet minutes recorded such things with due caution, that was their way, it was also because no one was under any illusion as to the probable result of their action – war, and war in a given number of days. It behoves politicians to be cautious in such circumstances, and if we remove the Churchillian blinkers, it can be seen that at this point the Cabinet was quite prepared to adopt a policy that would lead to war.

That there was no war was due not to Chamberlain's obstinacy or his dominance over his Cabinet. It was down to a combination of other factors:

French unwillingness either to honour their commitment to Czechoslovakia or to be seen to be dishonouring it; Chamberlain's willingness to help them find a way out of their dilemma; Mussolini's desire to avoid a war; and the refusal of the Czechs to risk the arbitrament of war. Parker, amongst others, places much store on the British and French reluctance to bring the USSR into the crisis, but this, too, is a sign of the influence of the hegemonic orthodoxy. Yes, Chamberlain and Daladier distrusted Stalin, and perhaps it takes a romantic old left-winger not to appreciate why that was a perfectly reasonable thing to do. Not only was Stalin's regime quite as morally reprehensible as Hitler's (it is a sure sign of old-fashioned Oxonian Labourism to miss such an obvious point), but it was hard to see how it could have been any more effective than Britain and France. The Soviet Union had no border with Czechoslovakia and no reliable way of getting her troops there. It was true that had the Romanians been willing to let Soviet troops on to their soil they could have reached the Czech border, but the notion that the Iron Guard in Bucharest would have stood by and watched King Carol do such a thing is one which can flourish only within the Anglocentric paradigm of Churchillian fantasy. The little fact that the Soviets had but recently purged their General Staff seems not to have impacted on the 'if only the Soviets had been brought in' brigade. The winter war in Finland in 1940–1 showed how effective the Soviets were operating away from the defence of their own territory. The notion that their army could have reached Czechoslovakia and made a difference to the outcome of a Nazi invasion is pure speculation. It also ignores the intricacies of Czechoslovak politics and assumes that the Benes government would have been happy to make such an approach. There was no sign of their doing so.

If we turn away from fantasy diplomacy to the realities of the autumn of 1938 we see that the British were willing to go to war, however 'horrible' the thought was. However, no one else was, and that was why the crisis ended as it did. The actual agreement negotiated at Munich was rather similar to the initial proposals put to Hitler and amounted to something of a climb-down by him, something for which he would not easily forgive himself. Indeed, had Hitler actually carried out the terms on which he had agreed, there would have been a series of plebiscites to decide which areas of the Sudetenland would go to Germany. It is typical of the emotive treatment of this subject that few historians linger on these terms. The justification for such neglect may well lie in the fact of Hitler's total neglect of the terms, but that, as we shall see, had its own consequences. The terms of the agreement were not ones of surrender; the inability to insist on its implementation was an important milestone on the road to war. Roger Makins (later Lord Sherfield and an ambassador to the USA) was appointed to the commission designed to oversee the agreement and sent a graphic, and chastening, account to Halifax's deputy, Rab Butler:

> We started off with an attempt to draw a frontier in committee with a good deal of shouting and banging of the table, but negotiation, even in such a spiritual atmosphere,

is not the Nazis' strong suit, and the Ambassadors were soon presented with a twelve hour ultimatum, to which they had no choice but to agree. After the Germans had obtained all (and more) to which in the most generous assumption they were entitled, plebiscites became both unnecessary and dangerous, and would not have been of much help to the Czechs.[52]

Of course, in the light of this, it is not difficult to be critical of the Munich agreement, but it was, at least in part, Hitler's inability to keep to an agreement he had freely signed that helped convince a sceptical British public that there was no negotiating with the fellow.

Certainly Chamberlain returned from Munich thinking he had advanced the cause of world peace, just as Churchill did when he came back from Yalta. Events were to show that both men were suffering from the well-known post-conference optimism syndrome. One was damned by posterity for this. But it was, as so often, Baldwin who provided the most acute critique of Chamberlain's position. It was, Baldwin thought, unwise of Chamberlain to have talked of 'peace with honour', which was 'a most unfortunate phrase'. He still wondered whether it might not be possible to 'turn Hitler East? Napoleon broke himself against the Russians, Hitler might do the same.'[53] Unsurprisingly the Russians argued strongly that it was necessary to prevent a German advance eastwards, and they would later attribute British reluctance to form an alliance with them to a desire to push Germany in just that direction. This line surfaced in some of the post-war polemic.[54] Rab Butler, who was close to Baldwin, suspected that German policy was to: 'Infiltrate East [and] Bluster West', and saw no reason why Britain should risk a war just to save Russia.[55] Halifax himself was prepared to concede 'German predominance in Central Europe'.[56] There was much sense in this, but there was a condition – that this should be done peacefully. This was nowhere written down as policy, but since the Germans opted not to pursue their domination in a way acceptable to Britain, it was not put into practice either. The irony is, of course, that had Hitler been capable of making the sort of changes Churchill hoped he might when he came to power, then the Germans could have had economic and political dominance in Central Europe in the 1940s. But that would have meant Hitler abiding by the piece of paper he signed at Munich. This did not happen.

Chamberlain himself had realised the limits of optimism by the time the House discussed the Munich settlement in early October. Defending the continuation of the rearmament programme, he asked his fellow parliamentarians 'not to read into words used in a moment of some emotion ... more than they were intended to convey'.[57] But, as Baldwin had feared, it was the 'emotional' phrase that stuck as a description of Chamberlain's attitude. It is all too easily forgotten that in the end Chamberlain adopted the policy of his opponents. He did so reluctantly and largely under the impulsion of Halifax's perception that it simply was not possible to sit back and accept the German occupation of Prague, even though this was Chamberlain's instinct.[58] This led straight to the adoption of just the policy rejected the year before: the guarantee to Poland left the question of war or peace to other Powers. Chamberlain refused to see it that way. For him it was a gesture designed to prevent Poland from falling into Germany's orbit: for the moment 'positive' appeasement had given way to its 'negative' counterpart.[59] But the guarantee provided Halifax with the lever to push Chamberlain in the direction he felt necessary, as Butler noted shortly after Easter: 'Halifax is determined to set up a force to counter Germany and ... is going ahead singlehandedly.'[60] In Butler's view, by 'gratuitously planting ourselves in Eastern Europe', Britain had allowed Stalin to keep his options open. This, he thought, made an alliance (which he disliked) even more improbable.[61] Even during the final crisis, Butler was still hoping that the Poles could be pressed to make the necessary concessions to Hitler as part of an Anglo-German agreement.[62] But it was too late. The last European war had begun. Britain would be saved from its consequences only by the advent of a global war in 1941. But that is another story.

Notes

1   J. Charmley, *Chamberlain and the Lost Peace*. London, 1989, p. 212.
2   R.A.C. Parker, *Chamberlain and Appeasement*. Basingstoke, 1993, ch. 1.
3   D. Dutton,, *Neville Chamberlain*. London, 2001; chs 4 and 5; R. Self, *The Neville Chamberlain Diary Letters, Volume IV*. Aldershot, 2005, pp. 5–33; S. Aster, ' "Guilty Men": The Case of Neville Chamberlain' in R. Boyce and E. Robertson (eds), *Paths to War: New Essays on the Origins of the Second World War*. London, 1989, pp. 233–68; F. McDonough, *Neville Chamberlain, Appeasement and the British Road to War*. Manchester, 1991.
4   M. Cowling, *The Impact of Hitler*. Cambridge, 1975; see also, D. Dilks, ' "We Must Hope for the Best and Prepare for the Worst": The Prime Minister, the Cabinet and Hitler's Germany, 1937–39', *Proceedings of the British Academy, LXXIII* (1987).
5   D. Reynolds, *In Command of History: Churchill Fighting and Writing the Second World War*. London, 2004.
6   Cato, *Guilty Men*. London, 1940.
7   K. Feiling, *Neville Chamberlain*. London, 1946.
8   D. Cooper, *Old Men Forget*. London, 1954; Avon, Lord, *The Eden Memoirs: The Reckoning*. London, 1965; H. Macmillan, *The Winds of Change*. London, 1968.
9   A.J.P. Taylor, *Origins of the Second World War*. London, 1961.
10 K. Middlemas, *Diplomacy of Illusion*. London, 1972.
11 P. Schroeder, 'Munich and the British Tradition', *Historical Journal* 19 (1976); P. Kennedy, 'The Tradition of Appeasement in British Foreign Policy, 1865–1939' in his *Strategy and Diplomacy 1870–1945*. London, 1984.
12 J. Harvey (ed.), *The War Diaries of Oliver Harvey*. London, 1978, p. 61.
13 W. Churchill, *The Second World War, Volume I: The Gathering Storm*. London, 1974, p. 131.
14 G. Hicks, *Peace, War and Party Politics: The Conservatives and Europe, 1846–59*. Manchester, 2007.
15 Trinity College, Cambridge, R.A. Butler MSS., RAB G/9/13, Butler to Ian Black 21 April 1938.
16 P. Williamson (ed.), *Baldwin Papers*. Cambridge, 2004, p. 377.
17 Ibid., pp. 378–9.
18 Self, *The Neville Chamberlain Diary Letters*, p. 70, Neville to Ida Chamberlain 12 May 1934.
19 Parker, *Chamberlain and Appeasement*, p. 11.
20 Self, *The Neville Chamberlain Diary Letters*, p. 253, Neville to Hilda Chamberlain, 30 May 1937.
21 Ibid., p. 5 for the references.

22 Ibid., p. 264, Neville to Hilda Chamberlain 1 August 1937.
23 N. Gibbs, *Grand Strategy Volume I*. London, 1976, pp. 60–4.
24 N. Nicolson (ed.), *Harold Nicolson: Diaries and Letters 1930–1939*. London, 1966, 30 June 1937, p. 303.
25 Self, *The Neville Chamberlain Diary Letters*, p. 81, Neville to Hilda Chamberlain 28 July 1934.
26 Ibid., p. 82, Neville to Hilda Chamberlain 28 July 1934.
27 Ibid., p. 305, Neville to Hilda Chamberlain 13 March 1938.
28 National Archives, Halifax MSS. FO 800/328 Hal/38/38, Halifax to Sir Roger Lumley 21 March 1938.
29 Parker, *Chamberlain and Appeasement*, pp. 343, 347, 364. See here also the 'post-revisionist' version advanced by McDonough, *Neville Chamberlain*.
30 Self, *The Neville Chamberlain Diary Letters*, p. 307, Neville to Ida Chamberlain 20 March 1938.
31 E. Woodward (ed.). *Documents on British Foreign Policy*, 3rd series, vols I–VIII, 1946–57 (henceforth *DBFP*); *DBFP* vol. II, no. 86 from Sir Basil Newton 16 March 1938; see also D. Dilks, *The Diaries of Sir Alexander Cadogan*. London, 1971, 14 March 1938, p. 62.
32 Charmley, *Chamberlain and the Lost Peace* pp. 64–5.
33 National Archives, Cabinet Minutes, Cab. 23/92.
34 Dilks, *The Diaries of Sir Alexander Cadogan*, p. 70
35 FO 800/269, Halifax to Sir Nevile Henderson 19 March 1938.
36 Cab. 27/627, fos 35–42 for the whole report; Cab. 23/97 for the Cabinet.
37 Parker, *Chamberlain and Appeasement*, p. 138.
38 Ibid.
39 Ibid., p. 139.
40 J. Norwich, *The Duff Cooper Diaries*. London, 2005, p. 245.
41 G. Gooch and H. Temperley (eds), *British Documents on the Origins of the War, Volume III*. London, 1928, p. 99, Lansdowne to Lascelles 16 June 1905; pp. 177–8, Grey to Bertie 15 January 1906; Grey to Bertie 31 January 1906, pp. 180–2.
42 *DBFP 3/I* no. 271, Halifax to Phipps 22 May.
43 Self, *The Neville Chamberlain Diary Letters*, p. 309.
44 *DBFP* vol. I, nos 249, 250.
45 Self, *The Neville Chamberlain Diary Letters*, p. 325, Neville to Ida Chamberlain 28 May 1938.
46 *DBFP* vol. I, nos. 264, 349.
47 *Baldwin Papers*, Baldwin to Lord Davidson 11 April 1938, p. 451.
48 Dilks, *The Diaries of Sir Alexander Cadogan*, pp. 105–6.
49 Parker, *Chamberlain and Appeasement*, p. 171.
50 Cab. 23/95, 25 September 1938.
51 Norwich, *The Duff Cooper Diaries*, 24 September, pp. 263–4
52 Trinity College, Cambridge, R.A. Butler MSS. RAB G11/130, 30 October 1938. In the catalogue this is misattributed to Sir Douglas Haking and misdated to 1940, which is a shame, since it is one of the few accounts we have of the work of the commission.
53 *Baldwin papers*, note by Lord Hinchingbrooke 14 October 1938, p. 458.
54 Charmley, *Chamberlain and the Lost Peace*, p. 144 for this.
55 Butler MSS., RAB G9/120-122, speech to 'The Parlour' 30 November 1938.
56 *DBFP* vol. I, no. 184.
57 *Hansard, House of Commons* 5th series, 339, col. 551.
58 Charmley, *Chamberlain and the Lost Peace*, pp. 164–6 for the full references.
59 Self, *The Neville Chamberlain Diary Letters*, pp. 395–8, Neville to Ida Chamberlain 26 March 1939.
60 R. Butler, *The Art of the Possible*. London, 1971, p. 77.
61 Butler MSS. RAB G10/8, character sketch by Rab, c. August 1929.
62 RAB G 10/111, note by Rab on September 1939.

Chapter 11

When Instinct Clouds Judgement: Neville Chamberlain and the Pursuit of Appeasement with Nazi Germany, 1937–9

Frank McDonough

In October 1938 Neville Chamberlain returned from Munich hailed as a 'peacemaker' who had brought "peace in our time". At Heston Airport, he held aloft a piece of paper, and then read out the contents to a cheering crowd. It promised that Britain and Germany were resolved 'never to go to war with one another again'. It had been signed by Adolf Hitler, whose aggressive policy towards Czechoslovakia had brought Europe to the very edge of conflict. This memorable 'photo opportunity' was on the front of every newspaper around the world the following day. Yet six months later, German tanks motored through the icy, cobbled streets of Prague. Hitler had ripped up the Munich agreement. On 1 September 1939, the *Wehrmacht* attacked Poland. Two days later, Chamberlain finally confessed that his 'mission' to appease Hitler, which had been the primary aim of his foreign policy, had 'crashed in ruins'.[1]

Appeasement soon became a shameful word. Chamberlain neither invented the word nor the policy, but his actions are forever associated with it. No statues are erected to his memory. He remains in the popular mind that rather tall, thin Englishman, with a strange moustache who always carried an umbrella and thought Hitler could be trusted. His name is forever filed under 'Fool', just below 'Appeasement', which is logged under 'Failure'.[2] No modern leader wants to be cast in the role of Chamberlain. It is Sir Winston Churchill, who so consistently opposed a policy of compromise with Nazi Germany and who led Britain through its darkest and finest hours to eventual victory in the Second World War, who is the 'Greatest Briton' [3] Statues are erected all around the world to his memory.

It was over twenty years after the end of the war before any attempt was made to re-evaluate this skeleton in the tomb of the British national psyche. The opening of government records under the 'thirty-year rule' in 1967 helped this process along considerably. Yet as Robert Skidelsky warned in 1972: 'Official papers tend to show nothing different could possibly have been done.'[4] Nonetheless, a sprinkling of mainly British 'revisionist' historians used these newly released documents and Chamberlain's own private correspondence – made available in 1975 – to try and rehabilitate his shattered reputation. They portrayed him as a strong-willed, realistic and able politician who took detailed diplomatic, military and economic advice, which emphasized that Britain, as a declining imperial power, had neither the military nor economic means to fight Germany, Italy and Japan simultaneously. David Dilks, one of the most eloquent representatives of the 'revisionist tendency', claimed that Chamberlain 'hoped for the best' in his dealings with Hitler but 'prepared for the worst' by steadily building up Britain's under-funded defence forces.[5]

These revisionist tracts were immediately rebuffed by a number of critical accounts by such writers as Keith Middlemas, Larry Fuchser, John Ruggerio and Sydney Aster. Just when the positions of the 'critical' and 'sympathetic' within the debate were becoming entrenched in the early 1990s came a ground-breaking study by the late Alistair (R.A.C.) Parker that attempted a careful and elegant synthesis between the two extremes of orthodoxy and revisionism. Parker dubbed his approach 'counter-revisionist', but it is more precisely described as 'post-revisionist'. What was so novel about Parker's interpretation was his acceptance of much of the revisionist case. He depicted Chamberlain – in characteristically revisionist mode – as efficient and clear-sighted, but he rejected a key tautology of the revisionist position, namely, that appeasement was an 'inevitable', indeed a logical outcome of economic and military weakness and the only sensible and realistic policy available. Instead, Parker demonstrated – using the self same government documents used by the revisionists – that appeasement may have been logical, but it was not forced on Chamberlain at all by the 'climate of opinion', imperial weakness, the dire warnings of the service chiefs or his colleagues. Chamberlain chose it from a range of other alternatives and pursued it with dynamic energy mixed in with unshakable obstinacy and unwarranted confidence that ultimately stifled 'any serious chance of preventing the Second World War'.[6] My own 1998 study *Neville Chamberlain, Appeasement and the British Road to War* offered further support to the 'post-revisionist' position by showing how appeasement operated within British society, and by questioning (another revisionist shibboleth), which held that Chamberlain's pursuit of appeasement enjoyed widespread public support.

In the past decade questions of morality and honesty in the conduct of foreign affairs have moved back to the forefront of political and public debate in the aftermath of 9/11 and ongoing debates over the origins of conflicts in Iraq and Afghanistan and other issues associated with the 'War on Terror'. Denouncing appeasement is back in fashion. Chamberlain's skeleton is back in the cupboard too, even though John Charmley in this volume has pointed to a fresh way to reinvigorate the revisionist position, which does command further discussion. Eloquently summing up the history of appeasement debate in his bestselling 2007 book *The War of the World*, Niall Ferguson writes: 'Those who condemn appeasement have a stronger prima facie case'.[7]

The whole debate – on both sides – relied heavily on different interpretations of the same government documents. Yet the documents of 'high politics' ignore the broader context in which the decisions were arrived at. They don't explain the narrow terms of reference underpinning them. Discussions of the 'morality' of appeasement were a key aspect of the policy debate outside Westminster, but it never shows up in cold and calculating civil service minutes. Clearly, the debate evolved via Churchill's ability to slant the narrative against Chamberlain, then by a revisionist case built upon the view of the 'official mind' and a 'post-revisionist' interpretation that cleverly used elements of the two approaches to produce a strong revival of yet another deeply critical interpretation.

To move into the broad 'sun-lit uplands' historians should now be urged to focus on whether appeasement was ever a viable policy to deal with the Nazi threat in the first place. In other words, to ask the question: was the policy fit for the purposes it was defined to achieve? This requires an assessment, not just of the British documents, but of a wide range of sources on the context and process in which foreign policy took place and by reference to the German, Italian, Soviet, Czech and Polish positions, as this volume has done. We need to bring back into the picture a discussion of the moral and ethical framework in which it operated and ask searching questions such as: Did Chamberlain deliberately lie to colleagues, allies and the public about the danger of the Nazi threat? Did Chamberlain's actions push France into a totally defensive outlook? Did Chamberlain's decision to concentrate on appeasing the dictators alienate Stalin and pave the way for the Nazi–Soviet Pact? Was the policy adaptable enough to cope with fast-moving events? Finally, we should also consider the counter-factual 'What if?' questions too and evaluate whether a credible alternative strategy may have proved more successful, especially at crucial moments such as the Czech crisis of 1938. My focus here is on how Chamberlain's instincts clouded his political judgement on Nazi foreign policy objectives and thereby altered the course of events in the crucial period between 1937 and 1939.

There was undoubtedly a strong strategic case in favour of appeasement. Britain had much to lose in the event of another war. The armed forces were not fully prepared to meet a simultaneous threat from Germany, Italy and Japan. This situation was self-inflicted, as successive governments since 1918 had consistently opposed increased defence expenditure. Weakness naturally begets timidity. Appeasement became another means of not facing reality and opting for a strong continental commitment towards France that was necessary to deter Germany. Every expert on British foreign policy knew that if Germany attacked France, Britain had to go to war. The stronger Germany grew militarily from the mid-1930s onwards the greater was the threat to the British place in the existing world order.

The economic case bolstering appeasement appears equally powerful on the surface. The Treasury, controlled by Chamberlain between 1931 and1937, claimed all-out rearmament would damage Britain's economic recovery. It was only in 1937 that increased borrowing to finance rearmament was sanctioned in a limited form. The 'Treasury view' was supported by numerous gloomy reports contained in umpteen files in The National Archives. All emphasized that increased arms spending would push up inflation, lead to a collapse of the pound and produce a balance of payments crisis. Yet as Anthony Eden, the Foreign Secretary, stated in November 1937: 'a good financial position would be a small consolation if London were laid flat because our air force had been insufficient'.[8] The entire rearmament debate in the Cabinet was more defined by the terms of reference laid out by the Prime Minister, Cabinet, the Treasury and the Chiefs of Staff. It does show the 'logic of appeasement', but this was a carefully constructed logic: an irresistible thesis- tablets of stone. It was really a justification for the policy and not an assessment of its overall viability as a realistic war-avoidance strategy, especially when faced with a German military revival. Every British government discussion on foreign policy was predicated on the assumption of British diplomatic and military independence too. This meant ministers were always comparing the poor condition of Britain's defence forces with a combination of stronger enemies and excluding real or potential allies from their deliberations. This clever policy framework made it difficult for opponents ever to question the validity and logic of appeasement or to comtemplate breaking free from it.

As Chamberlain was a major opponent of all-out rearmament, conscription, increased power for the League of Nations, a firm military alliance with France, any attempt to bring the Soviet Union into a closer diplomatic alignment and bringing Winston Churchill into a peacetime Cabinet, this left appeasing the dictators as his preferred option. Under Chamberlain, Britain was committed to sending just two army divisions to France in the event of war. In July 1934, Stanley Baldwin warned the House of Commons: 'when you think of the defence of England you no longer think of the chalk cliffs of Dover; you think of the Rhine. That is where our frontier lies.'[9] For Chamberlain, Dover was the final frontier, and the sky over Britain was the place that Britain would try and halt a German invasion. If Chamberlain deserves any praise it must be as the architect of the 'Battle of Britain' in 1940. It might be said that never has so much been owed by so many to a man with an umbrella and the foresight to build fighter aircraft in large quantities, but we should never have been in such a precarious situation in the first place.

Another central tenet of those who supported the logic of appeasement was to argue that all-out rearmament was economically impossible. This was simply not true. Interest rates stood way below four per cent until September 1939. Increased government borrowing to support rearmament was feasible. It was the will to implement such a policy that was lacking. British government deficits in the late 1930s amounted to one per cent of GDP. As heavy industry was already struggling to recover world market share due to the 'Great Depression', rearmament to match Germany would have stimulated growth, especially in the depressed industrial regions suffering from high levels of unemployment.[10] Putting those 'genuinely seeking work' back in jobs in desolate areas previously dependent on iron, steel, shipbuilding and coal would have been socially cohesive. A fully utilised and mobilised British economy would have greatly increased tax revenues and made further financing of additional borrowing much easier. The term 'National Government' would have been enhanced. A fully rearming Britain and France, acting in unison, and matching German military spending in the late 1930s would have been a far better option than appeasement. If that strong drive to match German military spending had been supported by Churchillian rhetoric, then such rearmament would have transformed the public mood.

Instead, a vocal lobby of influential bankers in the City of London and export orientated business types peddled the view that avoiding war with Hitler made more sense than making an early decision to stop him. These 'gentlemanly capitalists' organized many Anglo-German conferences, trade meetings and cultural exchanges. Lord Mount Temple, leader of the Anglo-German Fellowship, told an audience of like-minded German businessmen: 'our public opinion is convinced that a final and clear understanding between our two peoples must be attained so that peace and stability in the world can be established'.[11] A large assortment of people clustered around 'The Establishment' caught the appeasement bug too. The 'appeasers' shared a number of views and prejudices. They were sympathetic to the point of sycophancy towards German grievances, thought French belligerence towards Germany was the central cause of tension, and they were all strongly anti-communist, which ruled out bringing the Soviet Union into a diplomatic alignment designed to deter Germany. Sir Edward Grigg, the Conservative MP, claimed, 'most Conservatives prefer the German system to the Russian because it is nationalistic in spirit and does not seek to unbalance the unity of other nations by dividing it on class lines'.[12] The League of Nations was also derided to the point of contempt during their dinner party conversations. As the Tory MP Leopold Amery put it: 'If we were victims of unprovoked aggression today we might as well call on the man in the moon as make a direct appeal to League.'[13] Many of the 'appeasers' were frequent visitors to Nazi Germany. They returned with glowing reports about the 'new Germany' while ignoring persecution of the Jews and the brutal suppression in the concentration camps.

We will, however, fatally misunderstand Chamberlain's own mission to appease Hitler if we depict him as the 'envoy' or 'puppet' of bankers, the City, the 'Cliveden Set', the eccentric Mitford sisters and the flaky Prince of Wales.[14] Chamberlain's approach to appeasement was very personal and deeply instinctive. Chamberlain was a politician of the gut feeling and he approached all policy issues in this way. Nor should we view Chamberlain as a 'peace lover' of the pacifist variety either. He never ruled out war as an instrument of policy. After all, declaring war became policy choice in September 1939- though he was never that enthusiastic about waging war until his resignation in May 1940. To get really to the heart of Chamberlain's conduct of foreign policy, it must be appreciated that his biggest wish was to avoid another world war. This had become part of his DNA by the late 1930s. His own beloved cousin Norman had fallen in the 'Great War' This personal bereavement was always on his mind. When Chamberlain said 'war wins nothing, cures nothing and ends nothing' his voice resonated a tone of heartfelt honesty and deep emotion.[15] To avoid war, Chamberlain sacrificed many democratic and moral principles that in other circumstances he would have defended vigorously. In doing this, Chamberlain was led time and time again by his emotional instincts. Horace Wilson, a close confidante, describes Chamberlain's chief aim very succinctly: 'our policy was never designed to postpone war, or enable us to enter it more united. The aim of appeasement was to avoid war altogether, for all time.'[16]

When Chamberlain became Prime Minister it was no secret that appeasing the dictators would be his chief aim. His instinct told that he had special negotiating skills that would make a real difference to the dangerous international situation. He believed that all that was required to relieve tension in Europe was to 'sit down at a table with the Germans and run through all their complaints with a pencil'. Lord Strang, a Foreign Office official, remembers that Chamberlain had a 'naïve confidence in his own judgement and powers of persuasion, which most of the foreign office thought was misplaced'.[17] His single-minded pursuit of appeasement made him hostile and intolerant towards anyone who disagreed with him. In spite of his comic-book popular image as a weak politician outwitted by Hitler, it must be emphasized that few British Prime Ministers, with the exception of Gladstone, Thatcher, and Blair have ever pursued a policy with such dogged determination or dominated the Cabinet with such supreme managerial skill. The minutes of the Cabinet and the various government committees Chamberlain chaired between 1937 and 1940 reveal this conclusively. It's easy to be seduced by these documents, but we must remember that Chamberlain had gathered around him in government men who generally agreed with his views and followed his instincts. 'If nine times out of ten he had his way', Sir Samuel Hoare later recalled, 'it was because it was also the Cabinet's way.'[18] This was not the whole truth. The Cabinet agreed with him because those in key positions remained in office because Chamberlain knew he could rely on their support.

This explains why he conducted foreign policy in conjunction with a very narrow and trusted 'inner group' of advisers including Sir Horace Wilson, who became his 'unofficial' diplomatic envoy; Sir Joseph Ball, who ran the Downing Street press office, and R.A. 'Rab' Butler, his Parliamentary Under-Secretary on Foreign Affairs. The three key figures already examined by David Dutton – Simon, Hoare and Halifax – were all mostly reliable. Sir Warren Fisher offered energetic support from the Treasury. Sir Nevile Henderson, the British Ambassador in Berlin, proved another great supporter of the settlement of German grievances in Hitler's favour. 'It was an international misfortune', Anthony Eden remembered, 'that we should have been represented at this time [in Berlin] by a man who, so far from warning the Nazis, was constantly making excuses for them.'[19] Chamberlain liked the brittle armour that comes from being surrounded by 'yes men'. For a man who believed he couldn't be wrong, quiet agreement was what he demanded of his colleagues. So he derided, marginalized and ignored anyone who disagreed with his policy stance. This was not the personality of a really confident individual, more that of an insecure individual with an ego like an eggshell who only felt comfortable pushing his own agenda and dismissing opponents with a frustrated shrug and dismissive rhetoric.

Any assessment of the viability of the policy of appeasement as a peacekeeping policy must devote the greatest amount of attention to the period that led to the signing of the Munich Agreement of 1938. The crisis over Czechoslovakia erupted after two sensational events captured headlines of newspapers around the world. In February 1938 Sir Anthony Eden, the Foreign Secretary, resigned, citing 'fundamental differences' with Chamberlain over a number of policy issues, most notably, the usefulness of Anglo-American friendship, the slow pace of rearmament and the desire of the Prime Minister to build bridges with the erratic Italian dictator Mussolini. Eden's departure freed Chamberlain from an unwelcome and irritating critic whom he had marginalized, ignored and undermined for several months previously. Chamberlain did not throw Eden out, but he was gently guiding him towards the door. 'Anthony was always against negotiations with the dictators,' he commented only days after his departure.[20] Chamberlain was soon professing great happiness in having in Lord Halifax 'a steady unruffled Foreign Secretary who never causes me any worry'.[21]

Just as one political barrier in the way of appeasement in his own Cabinet was out of the way, he faced another when news broke of what he called the 'very disheartening and discouraging German take over in Austria'.[22] On 14 March 1938 Churchill, another constant source of irritation, suggested that the only sensible policy to deal with the obvious German threat to European peace was a 'Grand Alliance' of mutual defence based on the Covenant of the League of Nations.[23] Chamberlain's instincts told him such a scheme would inevitably lead to a European war and so rejected it. By now, Chamberlain had already made up his mind that Czechoslovakia needed to be sacrificed to avoid war. The fact that it was one of the few remaining democracies in Eastern Europe was of minor concern. A policy of letting matters take their own course was quickly ruled out as two alliances seemingly protected Czech independence. It was these diplomatic agreements that held out the real prospect of a European war. The first was the Franco-Czech alliance of 1925. The second – and more worrying – was a complex pact of mutual assistance between Czechoslovakia, France and the Soviet Union, signed in 1935. The terms laid out that in the event of a German attack on the Czechs France would intervene. Once French troops were engaged, the Red Army would be obliged to join in the military assistance of Czechoslovakia.

The obvious pretext for Hitler's highly predictable assault on Czech independence – and every uninterested observer knew it – was the three million German speakers living in the Czech horseshoe-shaped frontier with Germany called the Sudetenland. Chamberlain did not know that Hitler had generously funded the pro-Nazi Sudeten German Party, led by ex-schoolteacher

Konrad Henlein, and orchestrated him to push forward seemingly legitimate demands for 'self-determination', as if that was all Hitler wanted. Chamberlain not only accepted that German-speaking minorities should be granted self-determination, but he was sure Hitler would inevitably dominate the small states of eastern Europe anyway and so he ruled out the use of force to prevent such changes, provided Germany did not use force to achieve its objectives.[24]

During the next six months, Chamberlain worked tirelessly to ensure Hitler's demands were met and the existing agreements protecting the Czechs were abandoned. In March 1938, the Cabinet discussed British policy. 'You only have to look at the map', Chamberlain told his sister on 20 March 1938, 'to see that nothing we or France could do could possibly save Czechoslovakia from being overrun by the Germans if they wanted to do it.'[25] To bolster his position at the Cabinet meeting, the Prime Minister asked the Chiefs of Staff to produce a report on the 'military implications' of a German attack on Czechoslovakia, but asked them to exclude military support from the Soviet Union from their calculations. This narrow frame of reference – so typical of much of the foreign policy advice that informed Cabinet discussions under Chamberlain – produced the desired outcome. The report concluded that the *Wehrmacht* would defeat Czech forces in weeks, Czech territory would only be liberated by a long and bloody European war, and there was then no guarantee that the Sudeten area would be returned anyway.[26] The Czech army, which was a modern, well-equipped and well-disciplined force, was reduced to a simple pushover without any reference being made to the fighting force and equipment available to the German army or to the overall balance of military strength that might be ranged against Germany in the event that France and the Soviet Union honoured their existing agreements. Using the 'objective' verdict of the Chiefs of Staff, Chamberlain had little difficulty in getting the Cabinet to accept the seemingly irrefutable view that the Czech state was indefensible. The bigger strategic and diplomatic picture was never brought into the discussion.

This decision to abandon Czechoslovakia started the anxiety-riddled period that culminated with the signing of the Munich Agreement. In the summer of 1938, Chamberlain commissioned Lord Runciman to broker a negotiated settlement. As Henlein was already under instructions from Hitler always to, *Oliver*-like, 'ask for more', this was impossible. The Czech government complied with every Sudeten grievance only to find another one suddenly appearing. Then Henderson started sending gloomy and surprisingly accurate reports from Berlin indicating that Germany was preparing military action against Czechoslovakia, with mid-September the likely invasion date. On 18 August 1938 Ewald von Kleist-Schmenzin, an emissary of Ludwig Beck, the Chief of the Army General Staff who was planning a coup against Hitler, arrived in London to warn the British government that Hitler did have firm plans to invade Czechoslovakia. He even suggested that Hitler would be forced into a humiliating climb down if Britain and France stood firm. Churchill met him, but Chamberlain would not and dismissed his advice out of hand, even though it was true.[27] Intelligence reports conveyed by the Foreign Office pointed to an exact invasion date of 19 or 20 September 1938.[28]

Chamberlain decided the time had come to take his own unilateral action. Without consulting the Cabinet, the French or the Czech governments, he came up with 'Plan Z', a high-profile personal visit to Hitler in Germany. No British Prime Minister had ever intervened in a major diplomatic crisis in such a personal way. The only ministers told of the plan were the loyal triumvirate: Halifax, Simon and Hoare. Sir Alexander Cadogan, the Permanent Secretary at the Foreign Office, and Horace Wilson were also let in on the secret. On 14 September 1938 Chamberlain told the Cabinet that his plan 'would appeal to the Hitlerian mentality' and 'might be agreeable to his vanity'.[29] Even the pliant Hoare felt the visit carried a 'great political risk'. When Franklin D. Roosevelt, the US President, was told, he commented: 'If a Chief of Police makes a deal with leading gangsters and the deal results in no more hold ups, the Chief of Police will be called a great man, but if the gangster do not live up to their word, the Chief of Police will go to jail.'[30] Winston Churchill thought the visit was the 'stupidest thing' the Prime Minister had ever suggested.[31] Foreign Office officials had long warned against high-level personal contact by a British Prime Minister with the Nazi leader, as it was thought such a personal meeting would inevitably show that Britain did not want to fight a war on account of Czechoslovakia or for that matter on behalf of any small state in Eastern Europe. The Foreign Office much preferred to 'keep Hitler guessing' about British intentions.

The three private meetings between Chamberlain and Hitler in September 1938 – often passed off as just another part of the narrative arc of the Czech crisis – are absolutely crucial to a full understanding the viability of Chamberlain's pursuit of the policy of appeasement. On 15 September, Chamberlain's twin-engined plane took off from Heston Airport bound for Munich, the 'citadel of National Socialism'. He decided to be his own Foreign Secretary for the trip and left Halifax behind. The first time Chamberlain and Hitler met was at Berchtesgaden ('The Berghof'), the Bavarian mountain retreat of the Nazi dictator. Hitler's interpreter Paul Schmidt was the only other person who witnessed this first encounter. Chamberlain proposed that each side should explain what it wanted. Hitler said bluntly that he, 'did not care whether there is a world war or not', over his key demand of incorporating the Sudetenland in the Reich. Chamberlain, who had no authority to accept a transfer of territory, made a monumental error by stating that he 'didn't care two hoots whether the Sudeten Germans were in the Reich or out of it'. He was here raising no objections to Hitler seizing territory to which Germany had no legitimate claim. This was hardly 'keeping him guessing'. All the Nazi dictator needed to do was to arrange the transfer of territory within a negotiated framework. Chamberlain next promised to return to London to gain acceptance of Hitler's demands from the Cabinet, the Czechs and the French. Hitler promised to delay settling the matter by military force while Chamberlain effectively acted as his emissary. This was no concession, as the date set for the German attack was set for 1

October. In his notes on the first meeting, Chamberlain thought he had 'gained the trust of Hitler',[32] and believed he was 'a man who could be relied upon when he had given his word'.[33] Hitler later described the Chamberlain as a cowardly 'little worm' whom he felt had no intention to use force to stop him.[34] Given the unguarded way Chamberlain had acted in his presence during this first encounter, this was not an unreasonable assumption to make.

Chamberlain gave only a very partial account to the Cabinet on 17 September of what had transpired in his meeting with Hitler. He never even mentioned Hitler's uncompromising and bullying tone or his determination to settle the matter by force of arms. Instead, Chamberlain pointed out that only a 'peaceful transfer' of the Sudentenland to Germany would prevent war.[35] The next day he met Daladier, the French Prime Minister, and informed him that Hitler had agreed to carry out the transfer in an 'orderly fashion', knowing full well the Nazi dictator had made no such promise. In other words, he lied to Britain's key ally at a critical moment. Daladier strongly opposed applying the principle of 'self-determination' to the Sudeten case, as he felt this would encourage Hitler to press further territorial claims. Chamberlain then suggested that the only way to settle the crisis was for the Sudentenland to be transferred to the Reich as Hitler suggested. Daladier accepted this solution, but only after Chamberlain gave a firm promise that Britain would join in a fresh guarantee of the remainder of Czech territory. This became publicly known as 'Anglo-French plan'. In reality, it was Hitler's demand made palatable by being uttered from Chamberlain's lips. The Czech government was told to accept the Anglo-French plan or 'you're on your own'. It was quite literally a *Godfather*-like offer they could not refuse.

Chamberlain made a second visit to Germany on 22 September 1938, firmly believing that all of Hitler's requirements had been fulfilled. Halifax told him prior to the meeting that British public opinion had reached the 'limit of concessions'.[36] The two leaders met this time at the Hotel Dreesen in the Rhineland town of Bad Godesberg. Schmidt and Chamberlain both took notes. Chamberlain recounted the events of the past week to Hitler. As he finished, he sat back in his chair with a satisfied expression as if to say – as Schmidt put it – 'haven't I worked splendidly [on your behalf] in the past five days'.[37] Hitler now realized just how far Chamberlain was prepared to go to avoid war, so naturally, like any good poker player, he upped his demands, even though he held a weak hand. Hitler's demands were incredibly harsh. Czech troops, police and state officials had to leave the German-speaking area immediately. Any Czech citizen refusing to accept the transfer would be relieved of his property and allowed to keep just a suitcase of belongings as he acclimatized to his new refugee status and moved eastward on foot to what remained of Czechoslovakia.

Chamberlain told Hitler that he had already taken 'his political life in his hands' to gain acceptance of Hitler's Berchtesgaden demands, but was certain 'public opinion' would not accept what became known as 'the Godesburg Memorandum'. Chamberlain once again emphasized that he had no personal interest whatsoever in the fate of Czechoslovakia or its people, a position that hardly made his pledge to guarantee the revised borders of the Czech state seem very convincing to Hitler. Recognizing it was politically impossible to gain acceptance of Hitler's much harsher terms, Chamberlain adjourned the talks. The next day he informed the Nazi dictator that he was prepared to 'submit Hitler's demands to the Czechs', but did not indicate whether he found them personally objectionable.[38] On the evening of 23 September, Chamberlain met Hitler once more, but the Nazi dictator was unwilling to modify his position at all. According to Schmidt, Chamberlain left the firm impression on Hitler that he would still try and accommodate Hitler's wishes if this were possible.

On 24 September the Cabinet met three times. Some ministers felt the price now being demanded to avoid war was morally unacceptable. Chamberlain told his colleagues that he had established 'an influence over Herr Hitler' and believed he would 'not go back on his word'. Then he tried to claim there was little 'substantive difference' between the Anglo-French plan and the Godesburg Memorandum. Indeed, the case Chamberlain put forward amounted to a complete capitulation to Nazi demands once again. His instincts told him this was the only course of action. The final Cabinet meeting of the day adjourned without a final decision being reached.[39]

The next day the Cabinet met twice more. Halifax, deeply troubled by the moral implications of accepting the Godesburg Memorandum, had endured a 'sleepless night'. A week before, he had believed the Berchtesgaden demands were the only logical way to avoid war, but events at Godesburg had convinced him of the 'immorality of yielding to force'. Hitler was dictating terms as 'if he had already won a war'. The 'disorderly' nature of the transfer being demanded was – in Halifax's view – 'morally unacceptable'. Chamberlain scribbled a note to his colleague, which stated, 'your complete change of view since I saw you last night is a horrible blow to me', and implied he 'preferred to resignation to declaring war'.[40] Most of the Cabinet sided with Halifax. For the first time, the Cabinet had set a limit on Chamberlain's desire to avoid war.[41]

French leaders arrived in Downing Street on 25 September to increase Chamberlain's political isolation. Daladier rejected the Godesburg proposals out of hand by stating that Hitler had to accept the original Anglo-French plan or face war. The Czech government described the proposals as a 'de facto ultimatum' usually presented to a nation defeated in war. Chamberlain asked the Cabinet to let him send a letter to Hitler to be delivered by Wilson proposing a conference to settle the crisis. Cabinet members agreed on the strict condition that Wilson tell Hitler that if he rejected a negotiated settlement, the Czechs would fight, France would fight and Britain would stand by the French. Chamberlain asked the Cabinet to agree that the final threat be given verbally, after Hitler had digested his own more conciliatory letter.[42] On 26 September, Wilson told Hitler that the Godesburg Memorandum had been rejected. Only a conference could settle the issue peacefully. In reply, Hitler said the Czechs had to accept the Godesberg proposals before he would even consider compromising his terms. At this point, Wilson should have issued the stern warning demanded by the Cabinet, but he did not. Why? Because Chamberlain told Wilson to delay the warning until the next day and only deliver it 'in sorrow'. Wilson did finally tell Hitler that Britain would 'support France', but unwisely promised Hitler to 'try and make those Czechs sensible' as he left the room, which once more indicated that British support for the Czechs was still wafer thin.[43]

Faced with a united stand by Britain, France and Czechoslovakia, the German Chiefs of Staff pressed home to Hitler how unprepared the German armed forces were for war. The really decisive figure in pulling Hitler back from the brink of war in 1938 was not Chamberlain or Mussolini, but Herman Göring, the leader of the *Luftwaffe*, who was the chief architect of the Munich conference. We now know that Göring drafted the terms of the agreement in consultation with Weizäcker at the German Foreign Office. When this draft was presented to Hitler on 28 September, it was presented as the work of Mussolini- who had been given details of Göring's peace plan and supported it as the Italians were not prepared for war either.[44]

The strong public, political and international condemnation of the Godesburg Memorandum was really a lost opportunity to start a two-front war. The forces available to Germany in 1938 were never as favourable as British ministers, supported by their bungling military and intelligence advisers, had predicted. The German Chiefs of Staff were as pessimistic as their British counterparts. Hitler's ability to talk a good fight spread the alarm, but he had been bluffing all along, in the hope of warning off Britain and France from supporting Czechoslovakia. Chamberlain's mad dash to avoid war led him to bargain away a modern Czech army of thirty-seven well-equipped divisions at a time when the British Army only had two divisions ready for action. The Czech army was in a far better position to fight the *Wehrmacht* than the Polish army was a year later. What is more, Chamberlain sacrificed the huge Skoda armaments factory, which greatly enhanced German's rearmament programme and greatly worsened the strategic position of Poland. In 1938, the output of the Skoda works equalled all of Britain's armaments factories put together. On a diplomatic level, Chamberlain had sidelined the Soviet Union during the crisis. This left an impression in Moscow that British policy was content as long as Hitler moved east. Even if the Red Army had not supported the Czechs militarily in 1938, the Soviet navy could have assisted in a naval blockade in the Baltic, thereby denying Hitler valuable iron ore supplies from Norway. On the Western front, France could have launched sixty well-equipped divisions against a German army in 1938, with only eight poorly equipped German divisions in defence. The French air force outnumbered the *Luftwaffe* by a ratio of four to three, and those figures excluded additional air force support of Britain and Czechoslovakia.

The economic position was far more favourable to the Western Allies in 1938 than in 1939. France and Britain had large dollar deposits in the USA, whereas Germany's foreign currency and gold reserves were rapidly running out in

1938. There was no economic advantage for Britain to delay war by a further year. A greater outflow of capital, currency and gold from London followed Munich, as investors expected that war was coming, and there was a headlong move on bonds held in Europe by British investors. This is yet another sign that the City saw war as more likely, in spite of the settlement and the spin doctoring by Chamberlain that accompanied it.

We also know that The *Luftwaffe*'s capacity to bomb British cities was merely a figment of the British Chiefs of Staff's imagination. No serious German study of the *Luftwaffe* fighting strength in 1938 has unearthed any plans to bomb Britain whatsoever. Only twenty-four fully equipped German divisions, out of a total of fifty, were even ready for the attack on Czechoslovakia. There was a severe ammunition shortage in the German army at that time too. Only five Panzer units were ready for action in 1938. Naval preparations were practically non-existent. The German armed forces had only a four-month supply of petrol and no reserve forces to draw on in September 1938. By occupying the Sudetenland without a fight, the Germans acquired 1.5 million rifles, 750 aircraft, 600 tanks and 2,000 artillery weapons. In sum, the British and French government leaders and their Chiefs of Staff totally misread how much the balance of power was loaded in their favour in 1938.[45]

Nor can it be convincingly argued that Chamberlain's policy of appeasing Hitler enjoyed widespread popular support. A high level of news management, media management and outright censorship was employed to promote this idea. BBC radio coverage of the Czech crisis was severely restricted. In March 1938 Halifax asked the BBC to use great sensitivity when reporting news about Hitler and Mussolini. In July, the Foreign Office gained the agreement to vet the scripts of a programme called *The Past Week*, presented by Harold Nicolson, when he started to discuss the Czech crisis. On 5 September Nicolson agreed not to talk about the crisis after pressure from the Foreign Office.[46] BBC radio listeners were given hardly any details about what took place in the meetings between Hitler and Chamberlain. Cinema newsreels offered an equally sanitized and Chamberlain led presentation of events. In reality, public opinion was moving against appeasement, especially when details of the Godesberg talks emerged. According the Duff Cooper, 'we were being advised on all sides to do the same thing: to make plain to Germany that we would fight'.[47]

The social research organization Mass Observation, founded in 1937, set out to uncover the views of 'ordinary people' during the Czech crisis through sample surveys, diaries and interviews. A majority of those interviewed said they had little knowledge of the issues. This was blamed on the high level of government secrecy surrounding them. A total of 71 per cent thought Chamberlain's first visit to meet Hitler was 'a good thing', but when news emerged of the Godesberg proposals 44 per cent per cent were 'indignant' and just 18 per cent were 'pro-Chamberlain'. Once the public had clear and accurate information about Hitler's bullying tactics they swiftly turned against the whole idea of appeasing him. A further MO poll showed that 93 per cent of respondents did not believe

Hitler when he said he had 'no more territorial demands in Europe'.[48] A diary entry by a middle-class housewife in Glasgow on 24 September states: 'My knowledge of the crisis comes from the wireless [radio], for I never miss the bulletins'.[49] A month later, she noted that most of the people in the office she worked for had a 'hostile reception' to the Munich Agreement.[50] An eighty-year-old women in Ilford, Essex, recorded in her diary on 1 October 1938 that though 'thankful that the cloud of horror had lifted ... I cannot rejoice'.[51] A middle-aged housewife from Barrow took soundings in her neighbourhood about the reaction to the Munich Agreement. A schoolteacher neighbour of hers commented, 'we will have war ... in another year'. Her next-door neighbour talked of British 'betrayal and weakness' and the writer noticed generally that, 'there was not the joyful feeling abroad I had expected'.[52] It seems likely that if Chamberlain had chosen to reveal how aggressively Hitler had acted during his face-to-face meetings with him, then a public drive to 'stop Hitler' would have proved far more popular than the policy of appeasement. There was a powerful and growing sense of unease about the morality of appeasement that really took hold as the Czech crisis developed and moved sharply in an anti-appeasement direction thereafter.

Post-Munich, Hitler made a complete mockery of Chamberlain's hope for lasting peace. He first of all announced a greatly accelerated programme of German rearmament, which included a pledge to reach parity with the Royal Navy in submarines and plans for increased spending on the army and the *Luftwaffe*. In several speeches Hitler denounced 'umbrella-carrying politicians' who interfered in the settlement of future German grievances – an obvious reference to Chamberlain's shuttle diplomacy. Hitler depicted Munich as the victory of 'German brute force' and promised to apply such force in the future.[53] In November 1938, came news of the horrific brutality of *Kristallnacht*, the most violent night of destruction launched against the Jewish community in Nazi Germany. In January 1939 Hitler promised the 'extermination of the Jewish race in Europe' in the event of a Second World War in the Reichstag. Roosevelt now admitted to 'great shame' in having originally given support for the policy of appeasement. The moral legitimacy for appeasing Hitler was ripped into shreds well before Hitler marched into Prague.[54]

It has often been claimed that Chamberlain 'hoped for the best, but prepared for the worst' after Munich.[55] The evidence suggests otherwise. Increasing armament in preparation for an inevitable war was never uppermost in Chamberlain's mind. On 22 October 1938 Chamberlain told his sister Ida: 'A lot of people seem to me to be losing their heads and talking and thinking as though Munich made more instead of less imminent'.[56] 'The only thing I care about', he commented on 4 December 1938, 'is to carry out the policy I believe, indeed know to be right'.[57] When the War Office urged him to create six army divisions to aid France in the event of war, he rejected the proposal, and agreed new spending for anti-aircraft weaponry. In August 1939 Britain still had only two fully equipped army divisions to send to France in the event of war.

In October 1938, Chamberlain was still arguing that 'the burden of armament might break our backs'. The pressure to increase arms expenditure came from the service chiefs, the Cabinet, his political critics and a growing section of public opinion. Yet Chamberlain went on 'hoping' for an agreement with Hitler and Mussolini to 'stop the armament race'.[58] On 31 October, Chamberlain told the Cabinet his policy remained 'appeasement', with the chief aim of 'establishing relations with the [fascist] Dictator Powers which will lead to a settlement in Europe and to a sense of stability'. What Chamberlain wanted was 'more support for my policy, and not a strengthening of those who don't believe in it'.[59] For this reason, he resisted Churchill's demand to create a Ministry of Supply. When Halifax suggested Chamberlain create a government of 'national unity' shortly after Munich, including Churchill and Eden, Chamberlain said such a move would 'wreck the policy with which I am identified with and would soon make my position intolerable'.[60]

Chamberlain even went on offering economic concessions to Germany long after Munich. Montagu Norman, the Governor of the Bank of England, went to Berlin to discuss a possible British loan to Germany after Munich. British exports of raw materials to Germany continued, even though the Foreign Office pointed out that most of this continuing trade helped boost the German arms industry. While the US government imposed a punitive tariff on German imports after Prague, the British government imposed no similar sanctions. In November 1938, the Board of Trade advised the Federation of British Industry to open negotiations with its German equivalent to explore new trade agreements and hold an 'industrial Locarno', in Dusseldorf in March 1939, attended by forty British firms and trade associations. In January 1939, the Board of Trade helped to negotiate an Anglo-German coal cartel. In February 1939 the Duke of Saxe-Coburg, speaking at a dinner of the Anglo-German Fellowship, referred to the 'very good progress being made in Anglo-German trade negotiations'.[61] The Dusseldorf trade convention opened on the morning of 15 March 1939 – the same day German tanks motored through the streets of Prague. Amazingly, the FBI went ahead with the conference on the grounds that 'political difficulties have nothing to do with industrialists'.[62] On the eve of the Second World War, there were 133 separate trade agreements between British and German business groups, and a great many of those were signed after Munich. [63]

Even after the occupation of Prague, Chamberlain sanctioned a number of secret conversations with leading Nazis on economic matters. From Berlin, Henderson kept telling Chamberlain economic help might preserve peace. On four separate occasions in June and July 1939, Horace Wilson held discussions with Dr Helmut Wohltat, a close adviser to Göring, in London. Wilson emphasized the willingness of Britain to cooperate with Germany in the economic sphere. Robert Hudson, apparently acting on his own initiative, also met Wohltat on 20 July 1939. He offered Germany 'a big loan' in return for political discussions and rearmament agreements. These discussions had Chamberlain's blessing, but to his utter dismay Hudson told the *Daily Express* that he 'planned

[a] peace loan to Germany', which caused Chamberlain to comment that it was now impossible to enter into any conversations with the Germans.[64]

The real problem for Chamberlain after the German march into Prague was that the policy of appeasement had lost all credibility. Munich was turned in six short months from a public relations triumph into a symbol of national humiliation. Chamberlain was now forced into a further series of equally hasty and muddled decisions that simply made matters worse. The first was the ill-judged guarantee to Poland, announced on 31 March 1939. This had been pressed on him by Halifax, as rumours abounded that Hitler was about to attack Poland, Romania and Greece. Soon Chamberlain came to love the Polish guarantee. During the Czech crisis, Polish diplomats had told Ribbentrop, the German Foreign Minister, that a blank refusal to allow the Red Army passage though Polish territory had ensured there was no hope of Czechoslovakia being saved.[65] What is more, French ministers had long mistrusted Polish intentions. They felt Colonel Beck, the Polish Foreign Minister, was slippery and as likely to reach an accommodation with Nazi Germany as with the Western powers. With Beck in charge of Polish foreign policy, Chamberlain thought there was a decent chance of settling the Danzig question without provoking a general war. The guarantee of Poland created a tangled and over-complicated diplomatic situation which made gaining an alliance with the Soviet Union without Polish agreement impossible. As the Poles refused Soviet help, this made it easier for Stalin not to give it. When the Soviet Union proposed a triple alliance between Britain, France and themselves in April 1939 they were turned down flat by the British government. Chamberlain opposed an alliance with the Soviet Union because he believed it would antagonize Hitler, alienate Poland and make war more inevitable. Chamberlain never contemplated flying to meet Stalin and rejected generous offers by Churchill and Eden to lead the negotiations. It was not until August 1939 that British and French military delegations arrived in Moscow to conduct negotiations and by that time the endless delay had already done its damage.

This lack of urgency in the Anglo-Soviet negotiations and the low profile attached to them was yet another monumental error of judgement by Chamberlain. With Britain seemingly disinterested, the question for Stalin became a simple one: why fight a war to save anti-Soviet Poland and thereby start a Nazi–Soviet war? When Hitler offered Stalin a non-aggression pact in August, it seemed a logical solution. The seeds of this situation were sown during the Czech crisis, when Chamberlain sidelined the Soviet Union and were cemented by the lack of urgency he demonstrated after Prague.

No wonder Hitler expected Chamberlain to engineer a 'second Munich' over Danzig. By August 1939 Hitler had already factored into his plans the probability that the Western powers might declare war, but he thought they were unlikely to launch any offensive operations in the West in the swift time it took the *Wehrmacht* to dispose of Poland. Hitler thought Chamberlain was bluffing in 1939 when he said Britain would stand by Poland. It was the strength of anti-Hitler opinion in Britain and France that made it impossible for Chamberlain to bring about a 'second Munich' and it was never a serious option. The sacrifice of Czechoslovakia to the cause of appeasing Hitler was in fact the last chance for appeasement. Few people in Britain or France could stomach a second humiliating climb down in the face of Hitler's aggression. Chamberlain's carefully constructed and seemingly irresistible case in favour of appeasement finally collapsed under the weight of Hitler's drive to re-draw the map of Europe by force.

Chamberlain's instinctive decision to go 'all out' to appease Hitler was a project fraught with danger; a flawed and ill-judged crisis management strategy in which Chamberlain's desire for peace led him into a serious of errors that culminated in the outbreak of war. Chamberlain's actions helped Germany increase its ability to wage war. It sidelined the idea that British policy needed to have clear moral and ethical principles. For these reasons, Chamberlain's personality must always play a central part in the explanation of why British policy took the course it did between 1937 and 1939.

Chamberlain's pursuit of appeasement operated in its purest form during the Czech crisis. The decision to meet Hitler was a monumental blunder. His desperation to satisfy Hitler's demands gave the Nazi dictator a very clear impression that Britain would not go to war to stop him gaining territory at the expense of small powers. We must not forget that Chamberlain was even prepared to accept the brutal Godesberg Memorandum. The decision to obtain Hitler's signature on the so called 'Anglo-German declaration' was yet another major error, as it gave a misleading impression about Hitler's real intentions, which Chamberlain knew were purely aggressive and uncompromising.

Chamberlain was never buying time for an inevitable struggle either. The way he conducted the 'Phoney War' from September 1939 to May 1940 shows that he wished to avoid war and if it came about to stay on the defensive for as long as he could. Yet Chamberlain – whose mind was not easily dislodged from a fixed position – went on believing, even on his death bed, that 'there is nothing more or anything different, that I could have done and that would have been more successful'.[66] The truth is an all-out drive for rearmament, a stronger commitment to France and a solid anti-Fascist alliance would have been much more successful. The real opportunity was lost in September 1938 when the balance of forces were heavily stacked against the Nazi regime. If war had broken out as a result of a German attack on Czechoslovakia in 1938, this would have forced Hitler's regime to face a military and economic combination that would ultimately have shortened the conflict.

The time has surely come to recognize that appeasement was not a viable policy to deal with the threat to world peace posed by Hitler's openly militaristic regime. The alternative Churchillian policy of standing up to Hitler could have been adopted by bringing Churchill into the Cabinet well before September 1939. After Prague, the door was open to create a united anti-Hitler stance, but once again Chamberlain muddled on with the ill-thought-out guarantee to

Poland. It is a tragedy that Chamberlain stayed on as Prime Minister, after the humiliation of Prague, in March 1939. Chamberlain was certainly a man of his time, but he was also a man led by instincts that clouded his judgement and led to muddled decisions that abandoned small nations, encouraged French weakness, fuelled Stalin's suspicion, marginalized Churchill and ultimately took Britain into war that could have been avoided or begun on much more favourable terms.

Notes

1   BBC Radio news broadcast, 3 September 1939.
2   Critical accounts include: J. Wheeler-Bennett, *Munich: Prologue to Tragedy*. London, 1948; K. Middlemass, *The Diplomacy of Illusion: The British Government and Germany, 1937–1939*. London, 1971; L. Fuchser, *Neville Chamberlain and Appeasement: A Study in the Politics of History*. London, 1982; R.J.Q. Adams, *British Politics and Foreign Policy in the Age of Appeasement in the 1930s*. Stanford, 1993; R.A.C. Parker, *Chamberlain and Appeasement: British Policy and the Coming of the Second World War*. London, 1993; F. McDonough, *Neville Chamberlain, Appeasement and the British Road to War*. Manchester, 1998; D. Dutton, *Neville Chamberlain*. London, 2001. For a recent blistering attack on Chamberlain's conduct of appeasement see: N. Ferguson, *The War of the World*. London, 2007, pp. 312–82. For another equally critical account see: N. Smart, *Neville Chamberlain*. London, 2009.
3   In a BBC TV poll in 2003 Churchill was voted by the public as the 'Greatest Briton' in history. In 1999, an EEC poll proclaimed Churchill 'Man of the Century'.
4   R. Skilelsky, 'Going to War with Germany: Between Revisionism and Orthodoxy', *Encounter* vol. 39 (1972), pp. 56–62.
5   For sympathetic portrayals see: D. Dilks, '"We must Hope for the Best and Prepare for the Worst": The Prime, the Cabinet and Hitler's Germany, 1937-1939', *Proceedings of the British Academy* vol. 73 (1987), pp. 309–52; J. Charmley, *Chamberlain and the Lost Peace*. London, 1990; G. Stewart, *Burying Ceesar: Churchill, Chamberlain and the Battle for the Tory Party*. London, 1999; P. Neville, *Hitler and Appeasement: The British Attempt to Prevent the Second World War*. London, 2006; R. Self, *Neville Chamberlain*. London, 2006.
6   Parker, *Chamberlain and Appeasement*, p. 347.
7   Ferguson, *The War of the World*, p.318.
8   Lord Avon, *Facing the Dictators*. London, 1962, p. 493.
9   House of Commons Debates, 30 July 1934, 5th series, col. 2339.
10 Ferguson, *The War of the World*, pp. 325–30.
11 Broadlands Papers, Lord Mount Temple Papers 81/1, Berlin speech 11 January 1936.
12 E. Grigg, *Britain Looks at Germany*. London, 1938, p. 14.
13 House of Commons Debates, 5th series, 11 March 1935, col. 100.
14 Most left-wing opinion portrayed Chamberlain in this manner at the time and in memoirs.
15 A. Bryant, *In Search of Peace*. London, 1939, p. 98.
16 Quoted in M. Gilbert, 'Horace Wilson: Man of Munich?', *History Today* vol. 32 (1982), p. 6
17 Lord Strang, *Britain in World Affairs*. London, 1961, p. 321.
18 Viscount Templewood, *Nine Troubled Years*. London, 1954, p. 375.
19 Avon, *Facing the Dictators*, p. 511.
20 Neville Chamberlain Papers, Birmingham University Library. 1/17/9, Neville Chamberlain to Ivy Chamberlain 3 March 1938 (hereafter NC).
21 Parker, *Chamberlain and Appeasement*, p. 124.
22 NC 18/1/1041, Neville Chamberlain to Hilda Chamberlain 13 March 1938.
23 W. Churchill, *Arms and the Covenant*, collected edition. London, 1975, p. 451.
24 NC 18/1/1030, Neville Chamberlain to Ida Chamberlain 26 November 1937.

25   NC 18/1/1042, Neville Chamberlain to Ida Chamberlain 20 March 1939.
26   National Archives (hereafter NA), Cab. 27, 'Military Implications of German Aggression against Czechoslovakia', report by Chiefs of Staff Sub-Committee March 1938.
27   Neville Chamberlain to Lord Halifax 19 August 1938. Quoted in E. Woodward and R. Butler (eds), *Documents on British Foreign Policy, 1933–1939* (hereafter *DBFP*) 3rd series, vol. 2. London, 1949, p. 686.
28   The actual date set out in the German Invasion Plan was 1 October 1938.
29   NA- CAB 23/95/37 (38), Cabinet Meeting 14 September 1938.
30   Quoted in Dutton, *Neville Chamberlain*, p. 48.
31   J. Harvey (ed.), *The Diplomatic Diaries of Oliver Harvey, 1937–1940*. London, 1970, p. 180.
32   *DBFP* vol. 2, no. 895, 'Notes of Mr. Chamberlain of his conversation with Herr Hitler at Berchtesgaden', 15 September 1938.
33   NC 18/1/1069, Neville Chamberlain to Ida Chamberlain 19 September 1939.
34   In his speech to the Generals on 22 August 1938 Hitler said 'Our enemies are little worms. I saw them at Munich.'
35   NA-CAB 23/95/37 (38), Cabinet meeting 17 September 1938.
36   *DBFP* vol. 2, p. 490.
37   P. Schmidt, *Hitler's Interpreter*. London, 1952, p. 96.
38   *DBFP* vol.2, pp. 464–6.
39   NA- CAB 23/95/37 (38), Cabinet meetings 24 September 1938.
40   A. Roberts, *The Holy Fox: The Biography of Lord Halifax*. London, 1991, pp. 116–18.
41   NA-23/95/37 (38), Cabinet meetings 25 September 1938.
42   Ibid.
43   See Gilbert, *Horace Wilson*, pp. 6–9.
44   R.J. Evans, *Third Reich in Power*. London, 2006, pp. 673–4.
45   For a detailed examination see: W. Murray, *The Change in the European Balance of Power, 1938–1939*. Princeton, 1984.
46   For details see A. Adamthwaite, 'The British Government and the Media, 1937–1939', *Journal of Contemporary History* vol. 18 (1983), pp. 281–97.
47   Quoted in Ferguson, *The War of the World*, p. 354.
48   T. Harrison and S. Freeman, *Britain by Mass Observation*. London, 1985, pp. 49–53. See also C. Madge and T. Harrison, *Britain by Mass Observation*. London, 1939.
49   Mass Observation Archive, Diary of Miss French 24–25 September 1938 (hereafter MO).
50   Ibid., 16 October 1938.
51   MO, Diary of Mrs Arnold 1 October 1938.
52   MO, Diary of Miss Bromley 1 October 1938.
53   P. Kennedy 'Appeasement' in G. Martel (ed.), *The Origins of the Second World War Reconsidered: The AJP Taylor Debate after Twenty-Five Years*. London, 1986, p. 147.
54   J. Blum (ed.), *From the Morgenthau Diaries: Years of Urgency, 1938–1941*. Boston, 1965, p. 49.
55   See Dilks, 'We Must Hope for the Best and Prepare for the Worst'.
56   NC 18//1/1074, Neville Chamberlain to Ida Chamberlain 22 October 1938.
57   NC 18/1/1078, Neville Chamberlain to Ida Chamberlain 4 December 1938.
58   *The Times* 4 October 1938.
59   CAB 23/95/37 (38), Cabinet meeting 31 October 1938.
60   Parker, *Chamberlain and Appeasement*, p. 185
61   Ibid., pp. 195–6.
62   Modern Record Centre, University of Warwick. Federation of British Industry Papers S/Walker/14, Lockock to Walker 15 March 1939.
63   S. Newton, 'Appeasement as an Industrial Strategy, 1938–1941, *Contemporary Record* (1995), p. 496. See also S. Newton, *Profits of Peace: The Political Economy of Anglo-German Appeasement*. Oxford, 1996.
64   For the Hudson article see *Daily Express* 24 July 1938.
65   For details see *Polish Review* vol. 44, no. 2 (2009), pp. 343–62.
66   Parker, *Chamberlain and Appeasement*, p. 1.

Chapter 12

Missed Opportunities? Intelligence and the British Road to War

Kevin Quinlan and Calder Walton

Sir Ian Kershaw's claim that the Second World War was 'more inevitable than most' may be true, but this was not the consensus in Whitehall in the years leading up to the German attack on Poland on 1 September 1939.[1] There was considerable dissent among Britain's civilian intelligence services and top policy-makers regarding Hitler's intentions. So the outbreak of war caught Britain's intelligence community off-guard. This had much to do with slim resources. Between the two world wars, the three civilian British intelligence services – Government Code and Cypher School (GC&CS – signals intelligence), the Secret Intelligence Service (SIS – intelligence overseas) and the Security Service (MI5 – domestic and imperial intelligence) – developed haphazardly. They mostly focused on immediate threats and especially the 'subversive' activities of the Soviet Union. A shift in priorities toward the 'German menace' in the mid-1930s further stretched finite resources.

External pressures required security officials to rethink the process of intelligence analysis. As the international situation worsened, the need for accurate intelligence became vital to policy makers. Yet the pace of events outpaced reforms. This meant there was little integrated intelligence to inform the politicians even when they were disposed to consider it. GC&CS provided little intelligence of consequence on the situation in Central Europe. Most of SIS's assessments fell within the camp of appeasers, while MI5's information had little impact at all on policymakers. MI5 was so ill prepared for the outbreak of war that none of its key officers knew either the name of the German intelligence service, the *Abwehr*, or the name of its head, Admiral Canaris. As we shall see, the role of British intelligence in the origins of the Second World War was one of missed opportunities for the politicians and the intelligence services.

British intelligence was a very informal activity before the Second World War. In the interwar period, intelligence – both as organization and practice – was highly personalized. Sir Vernon Kell, first director of MI5, and Sir Mansfield Cumming, the first chief of SIS ('C'), virtually built their organizations from a staff of one. And while Britain may boast the world's longest continuously operating intelligence services, in 1939 these services were just thirty years old. MI5 still operated under its first director and SIS under its second chief (Admiral Sir Hugh 'Quex' Sinclair, who became 'C' after Cumming died in 1923). The conduct of intelligence reflected this personal, pragmatic and essential amateur culture: recruitment was informal and training was on the job.

New recruits came by word of mouth, and often by way of upper-class gentlemen's club connections. Both SIS and MI5 had a strong contingent of former colonial police officers. Both services were slow to recruit graduates, let alone the Cambridge graduates they became infamous for. In fact, because of the recruitment of the 'Cambridge Spies' by the Soviets in 1939, there were more graduates of British universities working for Soviet intelligence than British. Although MI5 recruited female Oxbridge graduates as secretaries during the First World War, its first Oxbridge officer recruit, Sir Dick White, did not join until 1935.[2] Many senior officers rejected what they considered the 'effete intellectualism' of university types. The irascible Claude Dansey, SIS veteran and Deputy Chief during the Second World War, was fond of saying 'I would never willingly employ a university man.'[3] He later wrote, 'I have less fear of Bolshies and Fascists than I have of some pedantic but vocal University Professor.'[4]

Officers did not receive the methodical training that became the norm after the Second World War. Cumming had referred to espionage as 'capital sport',[5] and little emphasis was given to what is today called 'tradecraft'. White later described his training as 'risibly perfunctory'.[6] Interwar SIS officer Leslie Nicholson (later writing under the pseudonym John Whitwell) recalled that before he took up his first post in Prague nobody 'gave me any tips on how to be a spy, how to make contact with, and worm vital information out of, unsuspecting experts'.[7]

The Second World War changed all this. The rapid increase in recruits required an 'industrial' solution to training and recruitment. MI5 essentially broke down in 1940, unable to cope with the onslaught of increasing staff. The demands of war was the catalyst that forced a systematic approach to intelligence collection and management. It resulted, for example, in the development of training courses and the production of syllabi on the principles of tradecraft for Britain's wartime sabotage organization, the Special Operations Executive (SOE).[8] It also emphasized the importance of coordinating analytic bodies, such as the Joint Intelligence Committee (JIC). In other words, the path from amateurs to professionals in the first half of twentieth-century intelligence was also the one from apprenticeship to manual, from adventurism to committee.[9]

Even the study of the intelligence history in the UK has long remained the realm of amateurs. Until relatively recently it was the 'missing dimension' of twentieth-century history.[10] And even where intelligence has influenced the historiography of the Second World War – indeed what history of that period would now be complete without an account of Bletchley Park or Enigma? – relatively few histories of the pre-war period discuss intelligence in a meaningful way. In Piers Brendon's massive study of the 1930s, for example, MI5 and SIS receive but one mention apiece.[11] Roy Hattersley's recent account of interwar Britain even tells the story of the Zinoviev Letter without so much as mentioning the role of intelligence services.[12] There was another reason why the role of intelligence remained an untold story. Up to the 1990s, intelligence archives were unavailable. With little official documentation, 'intelligence history' took on a somewhat eccentric role. Historians attempting to study Britain's intelligence services were placed in the extraordinary position of researching a subject that did not officially exist.

Consequently, 'insider accounts' and memoirs account for the majority of the literature. They have provided insight into processes long shielded by the Official Secrets Act – such as Sir John Masterman's *The Double-Cross System* – but have equally provided a useful medium for disgruntled former officers and conspiracy theorists, as was the case with Peter Wright's tell-all memoir *Spycatcher*.[13] The study of intelligence gained firm foundations when the government commissioned two historians, Professor M.R.D. Foot and Sir F.H. Hinsley, to write official histories of British intelligence operations during the Second World War. Foot's account of SOE in France, first published in 1966, remains a classic.[14] 'Harry' Hinsley's monumental *British Intelligence during the Second World War*, published in four volumes between 1979 and 1990, is the gold standard of official intelligence history.[15]

The study of British intelligence has benefited greatly from the recent declassification of intelligence files. Following from the Security Service Act 1989 and the Intelligence Services Act 1994, which finally gave the security and intelligence services statutory footing, MI5 and the Government Communications Headquarters (GCHQ, successor to GC&CS) have begun to release files from their archives. MI5 has to date declassified some 4,000 files up to 1957, and GCHQ has transferred nearly all of its wartime records to the National Archives at Kew in London.[16] SIS, however, refuses to release any of the records from its own archives, contending that the secrecy of its past sources and methods is crucial to its current operational success.

MI5's decision in 2002 to open its archives for outside scrutiny was a landmark event. It was the first time any intelligence service sanctioned an authorized account of its history. The product, *The Defence of the Realm*, by historian Christopher Andrew, was released in late 2009 to mark MI5's centenary. SIS has followed suit with an authorized history by Keith Jeffery, which covers the period of 1909–49.[17] It remains the case that we know most, and can therefore write with much greater certainty, about MI5 than we can its fellow services. In sum, the present is an extraordinary time to research the history of British intelligence. Recently declassified documents have revised our understanding of British governance and diplomacy, making intelligence history one of the most dynamic fields of research in historical studies today.

Before the Second World War, departmental interests dominated intelligence collection in Britain. Intelligence 'failures' – inaccurate assessments, incorrect predictions, false alarms – often reflected a central weakness of the British intelligence architecture: the absence of a unifying analytical and assessment function. No such permanent body existed in Britain until the formation of the

Joint Intelligence Committee (JIC) in 1936, and it was not until 1940 that the intelligence services began to act with any real sense of communal purpose. The term 'intelligence community' did not appear until the early Cold War.[18] This too was a function of the haphazard development of pre-Second World War British intelligence. Departmental concerns dominated collection priorities during and through the First World War, but the formation of GC&CS in 1919 from MI1(b) (military signals intelligence) and Room 40 (navy signals intelligence) was the first step towards creating intelligence services of inter-departmental pertinence.

Until recently, the history of early British cryptanalysis was generally limited to Room 40, the naval bureau of cryptanalysis.[19] Relatively little has been written on the contribution of the military to SIGINT during the First World War and the interwar period.[20] Historian John Ferris has noted that MI1(b) is 'the worst documented of British intelligence agencies between 1900 and 1945'.[21] Recent literature, however, has begun to highlight the importance of MI8 (cable censorship) and MI1(b).[22] Peter Freeman, the late historian of GCHQ, has shown that military SIGINT played just as significant a role in the formation of GC&CS as Room 40 did.[23]

For bureaucratic reasons, GC&CS (the amalgamation of Room 40 and MI1(b)) was situated in the Admiralty after its formation in 1919, though it moved to the Foreign Office in 1922 (as did SIS in 1921). Despite the move, they both served multiple departments. A.G. Denniston described GC&CS as 'an adopted child of the Foreign Office with no family rights, and the poor relation of the SIS, whose peacetime activities left little cash to spare'.[24] GC&CS's officially recognized function was to 'to advise as to the security of codes and cyphers used by all Government departments and to assist in their provision', but secret instructions also ordered it 'to study the methods of cypher communications used by foreign powers'.[25] Room 40 has received more discussion, but MI1(b) 'brought the larger dowry in staff and technical experience' to GC&CS, contributing a larger proportion of both senior and junior officers. Whereas it was generally thought in 1919 that military and naval radio intercepts would consume GC&CS's future time and energy, GC&CS primarily focused on deciphering diplomatic telegrams sent over international cables, MI1(b)'s area of expertise. A sample of GC&CS's decryption output between November 1919 and January 1920 also shows that the countries covered by MI1(b) during the war accounted for over fifty per cent of GC&CS's output, whereas countries covered by Room 40 only accounted for about fifteen per cent.[26] Based on this correlation it could be could be argued that MI1(b)'s analysts were not only greater in number than Room 40's, but were also more productive.

Yet such a conclusion overlooks the strategic significance of some intercepts over others. From 1919–33, Soviet Russia was thought to pose the greatest threat to the British security, and the greatest cryptanalytic work against Soviet Russia came from the remnants of Room 40, not MI1(b). The Bolsheviks did not maintain the same high level of communications security (COMSEC) practiced by their Tsarist predecessors. Despite the security of Tsarist codes, the Bolsheviks discontinued their use and instead relied on inferior systems. Russia also suffered the loss of a number of Tsarist cryptographers after the 1917 Revolution. Ernst Fetterlein, for example, emigrated to the UK and led Britain's cryptographic assault against Soviet Russia with considerable effect.[27] During the critical initial phases of 1920's Anglo-Soviet trade negotiations, which paved the way for formal diplomatic relations, it has been concluded that 'the single most important source available to the British Government was the Soviet diplomatic traffic decrypted by Fetterlein and his assistants at GC&CS'.[28]

Between 1917 and 1927, the British had unfettered access to Soviet communiqués, a substantial achievement considering GC&CS employed a mere thirty officers at that time (in the 1930s the number increased only by ten).[29] Of the major nations occupying GC&CS's focus (Soviet Union, Germany, France, and Japan) the Soviet decrypts proved the most important as they produced the 'only real operational intelligence'.[30] But access was short lived. In 1927 the Metropolitan Police Special Branch (MPSB) raided the All Russian Cooperative Society (Arcos), a Comintern front organization, based on erroneous intelligence received from SIS that indicated the illegal possession of British signals training manual. In the ensuing diplomatic row, the British government broke off relations with the Soviets. When the incriminating document was not found, London sought to justify its actions by producing intercepts testifying to Soviet subversive activities, which prompted the Soviets to switch to unbreakable one time pads (OTPs).[31]

In the 1930 British cryptographers regained some footing when they opened an oblique route to Soviet communications. John Tiltman, together with Dillwyn 'Dilly' Knox, a Room 40 alumnus, broke the Comintern's radio traffic. The decrypts, codenamed 'MASK', gave insight into Comintern and national communist parties' activities during the period 1930–7.[32] Tiltman is said to have 'all but invented the modern science of deciphering British diplomatic and military intercepts', no doubt accounting for why he was GC&CS's chief codebreaker and deputy to A.G. Denniston. He later served as Deputy Head of GCHQ, and earned a place in the US National Security Agency's Hall of Honour as well.[33] Fetterlein and Knox also went on to play distinguished roles at Bletchley Park during the Second World War.

Where British politicians squandered success against the Soviets, cryptographers continued to enjoy intermittent access to Japanese communications. The man primarily responsible for breaking Japanese codes, Ernest Hobart-Hampden, had joined GC&CS after thirty years' diplomatic service in the Far East and spoke Japanese. Despite being 'virtually alone' in deciphering Japanese traffic, it has been claimed that up until 1931, 'no big conference was held in Washington, London or Geneva in which he did not contribute all the view so the Japanese government and of their too verbose representatives'.[34]

Understanding Japanese intentions was important to devising security strategy for British interests in the Far East.[35] GC&CS had more success than many European countries against Japanese traffic. Access to Japanese traffic in some ways compensated for cryptographic deficiencies in Central Europe. In 1936, Germany and Japan signed the Anti-Comintern Pact, which Italy joined a year later, to form the nucleus of the Axis powers. In 1937, London was anxious to discover what secret protocols the Pact contained, and whether it was a defensive alliance. Over the following year, however, decrypts revealed Japanese reluctance to join an alliance that might bring her into conflict with Britain or the United States, thus providing British diplomats with a wedge to keep Japan temporarily disengaged from an offensive agreement (although it agreed to one against the USSR). German intentions were also revealed. On 14 September 1938 GC&CS distributed a Japanese report containing the outline of Germany's proposed military alliance with Japan.[36] And although Japan continued to waver, it informed policymakers about Germany's aggressive intentions in an area of strategic interest weeks before the Munich Agreement. Many years later, Denniston proudly recorded:

> To sum up the cryptographic effort of 20 years on diplomatic traffic: we started in 1919 at the period of bow-and-arrow methods, i.e., alphabetic books; we followed the various development of security measures adopted in every country; we reached 1939 with full knowledge of all the methods evolved, and with the ability to read all diplomatic communications of all powers except those which had been forced, like Germany and Russia, to adopt OTP.[37]

In another passage, Denniston claimed the Germans 'had moved to machine encipherment, or those with contiguous European land boundaries who could use landlines to ensure cipher security'.[38] This made it difficult for the intelligence services to find out detail on German foreign and defence policy. Despite the remarkable achievements of British SIGINT, especially given its small staff and budget, GC&CS's contribution to British European diplomacy decreased as the likelihood of war increased in the late 1930s. GC&CS intercepts of Central Eastern European communications hardly existed at a time when it was of paramount importance.

We only need to look at the insight gained subsequent to breaking the ENIGMA code to imagine the insights that the decrypts (codenamed ULTRA) might have provided British policy makers.[39] Among other contributions, the codebreakers at Bletchley Park provided MI5 with advanced warning of German *Abwehr* agents' despatch to Britain and the successful building of the Double-Cross System, the greatest wartime deception in modern history. However, ULTRA did not come on stream until May 1940. This means that the overall value of GC&CS's role in an analysis of intelligence in the origins of the Second World War is minimized.

The history of SIS remains the most opaque of the agencies under consideration. Most of its inter-war activity focussed on the Soviet Union. Much of SIS's reputation for James Bond derring-do came from some genuinely sensational operations undertaken against Soviet Russia.[40] Colourful person-alities dominated these early operations, and the informal nature of intelligence organization and production during the inter-war period meant that individual personalities took on a greater role than they would have done under a highly professionalized, bureaucratized structure. Indeed the role of intelligence generally, both as analysis and organization, depended significantly on the relationships of intelligence chiefs with their responsible ministers and under-secretaries in Whitehall.[41] MI5's Kell, described by some peers as 'short-sighted and timorous',[42] struggled to command the attention garnered in Whitehall by SIS's Sinclair, which in part explains how Sinclair almost succeeded in taking over MI5 in the 1920s. But 'intelligence as charisma' sometimes had perni-cious effects. Nowhere is this more clear than the case of Sir Robert Vansittart, Permanent Under-Secretary at the Foreign Office from 1930–8. He was an avid consumer of intelligence and a critic of appeasement. He stood out against a culture where 'a large level of suspicion remained endemic among some FO officials regarding "secret reporting"'.[43] Sir Maurice Hankey, the powerful Cabinet Secretary, justified Vansittart's move to the powerless role of 'Chief Diplomatic Adviser' in 1938 because the latter paid 'too much attention to the press of all countries and to S[ecret] S[ervice] information – useful pointers in both cases, but bad guides'. This unsystematic appraisal of intelligence led many to disregard Vansittart's many warnings as crying wolf, and his personality in some ways undermined his position.[44] This opened the way for competing interpretations, including those of SIS, whose recommendations fitted within a policy of appeasement.[45]

The Soviet Union remained SIS's priority even while the German threat increased. SIS enjoyed some success in penetrating communist organizations, particularly in Europe and East Asia, but a heavy focus on Soviet activity distracted it from appreciating the emerging threat posed by Germany, Italy and Japan. The transitional period during the realignment of British defence and intelligence priorities especially taxed already stretched resources. SIS's staff consisted of only about twenty officers.[46] Given its small budget and manpower, SIS was incapable of offering comprehensive coverage of developments as wide ranging as communism in the Far East to civil unrest in Brazil, from civil war in Spain to ship movements along Dutch–Scandinavian sea lanes.[47]

Germany's rearmament brought new demands on the small agency. In 1934, a defence requirements committee (DRC) consisting of the three chiefs of staff, Sir Warren Fisher, head of the Treasury, Hankey and Vansittart, identified Germany as the 'ultimate potential enemy'.[48] The First World War had engen-dered the notion that arms production itself led to war. This notion continued to inform British policymakers, and it was thought that Britain's own pace of rearmament might have a causal effect on German rearmament. Policymakers did not want to stoke German arms production.[49] So initially the debate centred on whether Britain ought to rearm; later the question was at what rate.[50] One half of the answer was ideological, but the second half was contingent upon an assessment of German rearmament. Uncertainty surrounding the pace of German rearmament therefore placed British armed services among SIS's most demanding, but least satisfied, customers. The absence of a coordinating body to screen and priorities requirements left SIS stations abroad inundated. Consequently SIS acted

> more as a postbox than as a filter between the customer departments and the field, with the result that many [Armed] Service demands were passed, often verbatim, to [SIS] Representatives who had no possible chance of satisfying them and were, in fact, already drowning in a welter of previous requirements.[51]

The question of Nazi air power generated vigorous debate. With the British still considered rulers of the sea, in 1934, Prime Minister Baldwin insisted that no country would be allowed to surpass British air parity either, as only air power would expose London and the industrial Midlands to attack. The novelty of air power at the time should not be overlooked. Years later, Harold MacMillan wrote, 'We thought of air warfare in 1938 rather as people think of nuclear warfare today.'[52] Thus it raised enormous concern in March 1935 when Hitler brazenly announced that the *Luftwaffe* had reached parity with the RAF, officially killing the pretence of Versailles. Nazi Germany now superseded the Soviet Union in SIS's 'order of priorities'.[53] Yet the new burdens placed on SIS did not meet with a commensurate increase in funding.[54] By 1935, Sinclair complained that SIS's total budget had been so starved that the cost of running it merely equalled the cost of maintaining one destroyer in Home Waters.[55]

The armed services, and the air ministry in particular, complained about SIS's inadequate coverage of Germany's air production.[56] Despite the constraints placed upon it, SIS began to address the issue as early as 1934. The Industrial Intelligence Centre (IIC), headed by Major Desmond Morton (a former MI5 officer), started to fill the gap. The IIC traced its beginnings to the Economic Section of SIS (Section VI), but was formally established in 1931 to study the vulnerabilities of foreign nations' industries and to monitor armaments production through 'the continuous study of raw materials, machinery etc'.[57] Until the eve of war, the air intelligence staff and the IIC produced divergent estimates of German air strength. Discrepancies invited investigations from the other services and the Foreign Office, leading to acrimony among them all.

Vansittart challenged the RAF's intelligence estimates with information received from his own 'private intelligence agency'. His most valuable agent, Group Captain Malcolm Grahame Christie, the former British air attaché in Berlin (1927–30), enjoyed access to several important German sources, among them *Luftwaffe* commander Herman Göring. While Vansittart described Christie as 'the best judge of Germany we shall ever get', air intelligence greeted his much higher estimates of German air capacity with scepticism.[58] The hostility between the services and the Foreign Office inhibited an accurate – let alone consensual – appreciation of German production and capability.

Inconclusive and conflicting information thus gave room for predictions based on preconceived notions of 'Teutonic' efficiency, misguided 'mirror imaging' and official German statements and propaganda.[59]

Yet Sinclair was aware of SIS's own deficiencies. He attempted to compensate by forming other semi-autonomous organizations. In 1936 he set up 'Z Section' under Claude Dansey. Operating separately from SIS proper, it gathered intelligence on Germany and Italy through business contacts, émigrés and exiles.[60] A similar section was set up within SIS to penetrate Germany and Italy, recruiting individuals from business, journalism and academia. It primarily collected economic intelligence with the help of secretive organizations such as the British Industrial Secret Service (BISS), run by now-legendary W.S. Stephenson,[61] who had a large network of business contacts (in part informed, as it transpired, but SIS representatives).[62] Accounts are patchy, but the existence of these groups testifies to the importance placed upon economic intelligence to SIS's collection against Germany and to the role casual businessman played as intermediaries in SIS collection methods.

An accurate assessment of SIS's political reporting on Nazi Germany is impossible due to restricted access to SIS files. Even the archives themselves may not reveal much, as many of the files were kept overseas in Stations and hastily destroyed in the face of rapid German advances (which in itself is perhaps an indication of SIS's state of readiness).[63] By most accounts, SIS's performance was inconsistent.[64] This was due, again, to resource constraints, but also to difficulties inherent to intelligence collection in 'police states'. Just as overt intelligence collection became more difficult for the Foreign Office, so too did covert collection by SIS.[65] The arrest of SIS's representative in Austria in 1938 exemplified the problems it faced.[66] Further disruptions came with the German occupation of Prague and, most damagingly, the *Abwehr*'s penetration of and exposure of SIS's Amsterdam station, leading to both public humiliation and the arrest of two senior officers.[67]

However, German aggressive designs in Central and Eastern Europe opened new channels of intelligence. From 1936, SIS received summaries from Czech intelligence containing information provided by an *Abwehr* officer in Prague ('A-54'), including the Nazi order of battle. By 1939, the Czechs and SIS jointly ran Paul Thümmel, and his intelligence included advance warning of Germany's major plans and incursions against Czechoslovakia from 1937–9 and notice of the attack on Poland from the spring of 1939.[68] Based on this record, and despite inadequacies in other fields, after the Munich Agreement in 1938, Sir Alexander Cadogan, the new Permanent Under Secretary at the Foreign Office defended SIS against critics such the arch-appeaser Sir Nevile Henderson, the British Ambassador to Germany, who complained that intelligence only looked to undermine a settlement with Germany. Cadogan commented: '[SIS] did warn us of the September crisis, and they did *not* give any colour to the ridiculous optimism that prevailed up to the rape of Czechoslovakia, of which our [Foreign Office] reports did not give us more warning.'[69]

If SIS's tactical record was mixed, its strategic record was worse. One authority has written that SIS's role was the collection and dissemination of intelligence, not the analysis of it.[70] This being the case, historians have highlighted an exception that illustrates SIS's assessment of Nazi Germany and its endorsement of appeasement.[71] The 18 September 1938 report 'What Should We Do?', authored by SIS's Head of Political Intelligence Major Malcolm Woollcombe (and approved by Sinclair), recommended that Britain should pressure Czechoslovakia to cede to German demands and peacefully relinquish the Sudetenland. It predicted that Germany would likely go on to absorb Sudetenland and 'probably all of Czechoslovakia' in due course anyway.[72] In coercing Czechoslovakia, it was argued, Britain could address Germany's perceived injustices before the latter sought to resolve them by force. The move would afford international community time to register 'what *really legitimate* grievances Germany has and what surgical operations are necessary to rectify them' with the minimal amount of provocation. It was thought that an attempt to corner Germany would only justify a retaliation. The report suggested that Britain ought to ensure *'that Germany's style is "cramped", but with minimum of provocation'.*[73] Although its assessment of Nazi Germany lay in stark contrast to MI5, SIS was not alone in the belief that Germany expressed legitimate grievances. Many politicians sympathized with Germany's claim to Sudetenland, and furthermore contended that the Central European troubles lay outside British interests.[74]

SIS successfully forecasted German actions toward Czechoslovakia. This is noteworthy achievement when Hitler's decision-making was more mysterious than secret, and frequently occurred at the last minute, as with the reoccupation of the Rhineland in March 1936 and the *Anschluss* in March 1938.[75] Reports on Operation 'Green' (the codename for the invasion of Czechoslovakia) had arrived in London in early July 1938.[76] But prior to the Munich Crisis, it was generally understood that Germany was on the warpath.[77] The question in September 1938 remained what to do about it. SIS's long-term strategy included a 'permanent defensive alliance' with France and concessions to Japan, among others. Yet the mere idea of a diplomatic strategy to contain Hitler – let alone a long-term one – underscored how little SIS understood the extent of Hitler's ambitions. It aligned SIS within the broader policy of appeasement pursued by Chamberlain.[78]

False alarms of Axis aggression permeated Whitehall in late 1938 and early 1939. SIS had judged that after Czechoslovakia, Hitler would next strike to the East.[79] In January reports from the diplomatic corps insisted that the *Luftwaffe* would attempt a 'knock out' blow against London, a fear which 'bore very heavily' on Air Staff, [80] and was reinforced by reports from SIS and Vansittart. The same month, new reports lit up Whitehall with intelligence suggesting Germany would strike against Holland. The reports, likely the result of disinformation, led to 'threat fatigue' and called into question the overall value of intelligence to policymaking. Nonetheless, the false alarms had important consequences in that they convinced Cabinet members that British security was tied to the security of the continent.[81] It is a great irony that bad intelligence seemed to affect policy more than accurate intelligence, which tends to suggest such information was being used to further particular ways of dealing with the threat from Germany and Italy.

Vansittart argued that giving into demands would only encourage Hitler to ask for more and reinforce the German view that Britain was weak. Some of the intelligence supporting Vansittart's views came from MI5. Indeed MI5, in contrast to SIS, had consistently provided reports urging a hard line against Hitler from as early as 1936. MI5's sources painted a dark picture about attempts to appease Hitler. Probably its best asset was Wolfgang zu Putlitz, a young diplomat in Germany's London embassy. MI5 recruited Jona 'Klop' Ustinov ('U35'), a German journalist and father of the famous actor Peter Ustinov, to handle Putlitz. Ustinov's case officer was John 'Jack' Curry, a veteran Indian police officer who on joining MI5 in 1934 was among the first to investigate the radical right-wing British Union of Fascists (BUF). A June 1936 report written by Curry and submitted by Kell to the Committee of Imperial Defence (CID) is representative of the intelligence Putlitz provided on German strategic intentions:

> No reliance can be placed on any treaty which has been signed, or may be signed by Germany or Italy; any obligation which they have undertaken is liable to be repudiated without warning if it stands in the way of what their dictators consider at any moment to be the vital interest of their nation.[82]

On the heels of the Rhineland's reoccupation, MI5 had received clear indications that a strategy of appeasement would not work (even before Chamberlain had become Prime Minister).

Putlitz continued to provide intelligence regarding German policy through his connections with the German ambassador posted to London, Joachim von Ribbentrop. At the time, he reported Ribbentrop's increasing hostility towards Britain.[83] In February 1938, with Ribbentrop recalled to Germany to serve as Foreign Minister, MI5 submitted a valuable intelligence summary on the intentions to Nazi Germany to the Foreign Office. It stated that the German army will in future be an obedient instrument of Nazi foreign policy. Under Ribbentrop this foreign policy will be an aggressive policy. Its first aim – Austria – has been partly achieved ... Austria falls to [Hitler] like a ripe fruit. After consolidating the position in Austria the next step will be Czechoslovakia.[84] Moreover, Putlitz repeatedly insisted that Britain's policy of appeasement would fail: 'Britain was letting the trump cards fall out of her hands. If she had adopted, or even now adopted a firm attitude and threatened war, Hitler would not succeed in this kind of bluff. The German army was not yet ready for major war.'[85] There are indications this was true. The French had insisted Germany was 'bluffing', but was only willing to back Czechoslovakia with British support. Indeed Hitler had frequently said he would only take Czechoslovakia if the French and British did not stand firm.[86]

The summary report, forwarded to Chamberlain, did not have the effect that Putlitz or MI5 hoped. It might be argued that they were lost in the deluge of reports reaching policymakers, but the message was not. Two days before Chamberlain told the Cabinet of 'Plan Z', his secret plan to visit Hitler personally to diffuse the Czechoslovak crisis, Theodor Kordt, the German chargé d'affaires and one of Vansittart's sources, personally contacted senior policymakers to convey the futility of the visit and of appeasement. In secret meetings at 10 Downing Street, Kordt told both Sir Horace Wilson (a close Chamberlain advisor) and Lord Halifax (Foreign Secretary) that Hitler had already firmly decided on aggression. He was dismissed, as was Vansittart when he approached the Cabinet to reiterate Kordt's message several days later.[87]

Following the Munich fiasco – and Chamberlain's humiliating claim to have secured 'peace in our time' – MI5 submitted a report on 7 November 1938, read by both Cadogan and Halifax, that drew attention to its record of consistent and accurate forecasts of German aims based on intelligence provided by its sources. The report described in unambiguous terms the unlimited scope of Hitler's aims:

> It is apparent that Hitler's policy is essentially a dynamic one, and the question is – What direction will it take next? If the information in the [report], which has proved generally reliable and accurate in the past, is to be believed, Germany is at the beginning of a 'Napoleonic era' and her rulers contemplate a great extension of German power.[88]

Thus MI5's understanding of Europe's future alignment differed radically from SIS's. In MI5's reading, Hitler's goals could not be blunted by diplomatic containment, and his actions were not merely motivated by local grievances such as 'self-determination', as he had claimed during the Czech crisis.

MI5 went to extraordinary lengths to grab Chamberlain's attention. Of the interwar period, it has been observed that 'British decision makers sometimes focused more on determining whether a statesman was a gentleman than on indicators of his policy'.[89] Chamberlain was certainly of this ilk, as were others before him. In 1923, for example, Lord Curzon had been driven to collapse when GC&CS intercepts revealed to him that French leaders were conniving to convince Baldwin to have him replaced as Foreign Secretary. 'I had not realised that diplomacy was such a dirty game,' Curzon despaired.[90] Like Curzon, Chamberlain took personal slights to heart. To ensure its summary report received attention, MI5 took the extraordinary step of including a transcript (provided by Putlitz) of insulting references to Chamberlain made by Hitler. Curry reported that Hitler's description of Chamberlain of an '*arschloch*', which Halifax had received, underlined three times, and passed on to the Prime Minister, made a 'considerable impression'.[91] But even if the documents caused offence, the intelligence contained within the documents, though accurate, appears to have been largely disregarded.[92] Remarkably, in February 1939

Chamberlain still managed to insist, 'All the information I get seems to point the direction of peace.'[93] Only one month later Hitler abrogated the Munich Agreement and German troops occupied Prague.

In spite of the growing German threat, British intelligence services continued to operate under severe financial restraints. MI5 suffered more than the other services. It found itself under threat from a short-lived Directorate of Intelligence, led by former MPSB head Sir Basil Thomson, and by SIS, both of which attempted to absorb MI5 into a conglomerated intelligence service.[94] As late as 1938, MI5 still only consisted of thirty officers.[95] In 1937, only four officers had responsibility for investigating all of German espionage and fascism in the UK.[96] It has been claimed that no 'adequate preparations had been made in 1938–1939 to foresee and face the conditions of the war as it developed and this, in turn, was due to lack of funds'.[97] MI5's rapidly expanding remit after Munich did not coincide with a cohesive, comprehensive plan for dealing with the expansion of the service. Thus at the beginning of the war MI5 found itself 'in a state of confusion which at times amounted to chaos'.[98] A dearth of resources undoubtedly hindered MI5's ability to cope with the onslaught of intelligence it received, much of it a tragically reminiscent of false German agent 'sightings' during the First World War. The situation, however, was also at least in part attributable to a lack of strategic leadership, which ultimately led Winston Churchill to sack MI5's first and longest-serving head, Sir Vernon Kell, in 1940.

So where MI5 may have had a good grasp on Hitler's direction in Europe, it had a feeble grasp on pro-Axis activities in the UK. John Curry, later MI5's in-house historian whose account of MI5 written in 1945 laid plain the Service's failures, starkly described MI5's failures on the outbreak of war in the following terms:

> In 1939 we had no adequate knowledge of the German organisations which it was the function of the Security Service to guard against either in this wider field of the 'Fifth Column' or in the narrower one of military espionage and purely material sabotage. We had in fact no definite knowledge whether there was any organised connection between the German Secret Service and Nazi sympathisers in this country, whether of British or alien nationality.[99]

The British intelligence community's lack of knowledge regarding the intentions and capabilities of the Axis Powers brought MI5 to near-total collapse in the summer of 1940. There is little doubt that shoestring budgets hampered intelligence services throughout the inter-war period. This meant that the history of the interwar intelligence services was largely one of putting out fires. During the initial phases of the Second World War, the fire was one the intelligence services could not extinguish. In this respect, scale mattered. The overwhelming amount of information received brought into relief deeper, more systemic flaws in British intelligence.

Information management is a central feature of an intelligence enterprise. MI5's 'Central Registry' was remarkably sophisticated for its time and served as the backbone of its operations.[100] But in 1940, when erroneous reports of 'Fifth Column' subversives flooded MI5, its system collapsed. The problems of intelligence management and evaluation on an inter-departmental basis existed on a larger scale still. The external threat of war forced upon policymakers and intelligence practitioners alike the need for improved coordination and assessment.

A solution had begun to emerge with the creation of the JIC in 1936, though it made no significant impact on policy until 1940. Its emergence occurred in fits and starts. As one of the official historians of British intelligence has observed:

> On the face of it, the idea of drawing intelligence contributions from departments and inter-departmental agencies and putting them together seems so sensible, if not obvious, that it must cause surprise that it was evolved over so long a period and with such difficulty.[101]

During the interwar period there was no formal procedure for analyzing intelligence or reporting it to members of government. There was no notion of an intelligence 'product' or a community-wide 'assessment'. Strategic assessments using inter-departmental intelligence only developed in response to the urgency of war. During the pre-war period, the inter-departmental collation or assessment of intelligence was virtually absent. For much of that time, ministers were their own analysts, and they rejected good and bad information as they wished. Prior to that point, little mechanism existed for evaluating intelligence: there was no sieve to separate the gems from the silt.

A slew of misleading intelligence reports in late 1938 and early 1939 instigated a battle within Whitehall between the Foreign Office and the Chiefs of Staff, both refusing to cede ground on what each considered its exclusive intelligence prerogative. Only a belated and begrudging realization that the German threat required a combined appreciation of political and military intelligence allowed the JIC to assume what remained its essential duty throughout the war: 'the assessment and coordination of intelligence received from abroad with the object of ensuring that any Government action which might have to be taken should be based on the most suitable and carefully coordinated information available'.[102] But it was of no practical service to politicians on the eve of war.

Winston Churchill's career-long interest in intelligence, and the renewed emphasis he gave to coordination and collaboration when he came to power, had dramatic effects on the role intelligence would play during the Second World War.[103] Churchill had perhaps more experience with intelligence than any Prime Minister up to that point.[104] Like Vansittart, his conviction about the German menace was married to a conviction about the power of intelligence and he, like Vansittart, had been privy to secret sources from his earlier time in government through the 'wilderness' years.

Any conclusion about the relationship between British intelligence and policy making in the origins of the Second World War must, on the one hand, take into account the informal nature of intelligence at the time, and on the other, focus on the mentality and personality of policymakers. It remains to be answered, for example, what intelligence – if any – would have convinced Chamberlain to adopt a different track in the run-up to the Munich Crisis. It is nearly impossible to account systematically for how policymakers such as Chamberlain incorporated intelligence into policymaking. SIS at times provided sound tactical intelligence, but what little of their strategic assessments exists in the public domain situates SIS squarely in the camp of endorsing Chamberlain's position. From some quarters, such as MI5, the message was consistent and clear: reports that did attempt to counsel policymakers on Germany's determined expansionism seem to have fallen on deaf ears. This, then, is a story of missed opportunities and failures; of government officials failing listen to intelligence that they did not want to hear or which ran counter to their agreed line.

When war came, Britain found itself only half ready, at best. Policymakers scrambled to make use of intelligence as quickly as the intelligence services themselves scrambled to acquire the resources and manpower necessary to compensate for their deficiencies. The remarkable point is that humiliating 'intelligence failures' for Britain before the war were followed by unprecedented intelligence successes during the war itself.

Notes

1   Sir Ian Kershaw, 'The End of Europe's Second Thirty Years' War', Ramsay Murray Lecture, University of Cambridge, 6 May 2005.
2   White later became Director General of MI5 then Chief of SIS, the only person to date to hold both positions.
3   Quoted in P. Knightley, *Philby: The Life and Views of the K.G.B. Masterspy*. London, 2003, p. 97.
4   Quoted in C. Andrew, *Her Majesty's Secret Service: The Making of the British Intelligence Community*. New York, 1986, p. 357.
5   Ibid., *Her Majesty's Secret Service*, p. 76.
6   T. Bower, *The Perfect English Spy: Sir Dick White and the Secret War, 1935–90*. London, 1995, pp. 26–7.
7   J. Whitwell, *British Agent*. London, 1996.
8   e.g. NA KV4/172 SOE Course at Beaulieu 1945; HS 7/55–56 Lecture Folder STS 103, parts 1 and 2 (respectively), published as D. Rigdan (ed.), *SOE Syllabus: Lessons in Ungentlemanly Warfare, World War II* (National Archives, hereafter NA).
9   K. Quinlan, *Human Intelligence Tradecraft and Agent Operations in Britain, 1919–1940* (PhD dissertation, University of Cambridge, 2008), p. 310.
10 C. Andrew and D. Dilks (eds), *The Missing Dimension: Governments and Intelligence Communities in the Twentieth Century*. London, 1984
11 P. Brendon, *The Dark Valley: A Panorama of the 1930s*. London, 2001, pp. 612, 619
12 R. Hattersley, *Borrowed Time: The Story of Britain Between the Wars*. London, 2007.
13 J.C. Masterman, *The Double-Cross System in the War of 1939 to 1945*. New Haven, 1972; P. Wright, *Spycatcher: The Candid Autobiography of a Senior Intelligence Officer*. New York, 1987.
14 M.R.D. Foot, *S.O.E. in France: An Account of the British Special Operations Executive, 1940–1944*. London, 1966

15 F.H. Hinsley et al., *British Intelligence in the Second World War*, 4 vols. London, 1979–90.
16 NA, 'The Security Service at The National Archives', 'Intelligence Records'.
17 Keith Jeffery, *The Official History of the Secret Intelligence Service 1909–1945*. London, 2010.
18 See F. Johnson, *Defence by Committee: The British Committee of Imperial Defence, 1885–1959*. Oxford, 1960.
19 See, e.g., P. Beesly, *Room 40: British Naval Intelligence 1914–18*. London, 1982; R. Denniston, *Thirty Secret Years: A.G. Denniston's Work in Signals Intelligence 1914–1944*. Clifton-upon-Teme, 2007.
20 One exception is J. Ferris (ed.), *British Army and Signals Intelligence During the First World War*. Stroud, 1992.
21 J. Ferris, 'The Road to Bletchley Park: The British Experience with Signals Intelligence, 1892-1945', *Intelligence and National Security* 17 (2002), pp. 53–84.
22 As with MI5, these services underwent various name changes. Cable Censorship was initially called MO5(d) in 1914, then MO8(d) in 1915, and finally MI8 in 1916. Army cryptanalysis similarly changed titles: MO5(e) became MO6(b) in 1915 and was renamed MI1(b) in 1916.
23 P. Freeman, 'MI1(b) and the Origins of British Diplomatic Cryptanalysis', *Intelligence and National Security* 22 (2007), pp. 206–28.
24 Denniston, *Thirty Secret Years*, p. 94.
25 NA HW 43/1 The History of British SIGINT, 1914–1945, Vol. I, 'British SIGINT, 1914-1942' (by Frank Birch), p. 17.
26 Freeman, 'MI1(b) and the Origins of British Diplomatic Cryptanalysis', pp. 221–2.
27 Denniston, *Thirty Secret Years*, p. 101.
28 Andrew, *Secret Service*, p. 262.
29 Denniston, *Thirty Secret Years*, p. 95.
30 Ibid., p. 101.
31 Andrew, *Secret Service*, pp. 331–2.
32 MASK intercepts can be found in the NA HW17 series (Moscow–London exchanges at HW17/16–22). See also Nigel West, *MASK: MI5's Penetration of the Communist Party of Great Britain*. London, 2005.
33 Denniston, *Thirty Secret Years*, p. 69.
34 Ibid., pp. 101–2.
35 Anthony Best, *British Intelligence and the Japanese Challenge in Asia*. Basingstoke, 2002.
36 D. Dilks, 'Appeasement and "Intelligence' in D. Dilks (ed.), *Retreat from Power: Studies in Britain's Foreign Policy of the Twentieth Century, Vol. I: 1906–1939*. London, 1981, pp. 139–9.
37 Denniston, *Thirty Secret Years*, p. 103.
38 Ibid., p. 88
39 Hinsley, *British Intelligence in the Second World War*, vol. 1, p. 55.
40 Andrew, *Secret Service*, ch. 6; A. Judd, *The Quest for C: Mansfield Cumming and the Founding of the Secret Service*. London, 2000); P. Dukes, *The Story of "ST 25": Adventure and Romance in the Secret Intelligence Service in Red Russia*. London, 1939.
41 e.g. J. Ferris, '"Indulged in All Too Little"?: Vansittart, Intelligence, and Appeasement', *Diplomacy and Statecraft* 6:1 (1995), pp. 122–75, p. 126.
42 Andrew, *Secret Service*, p. 230
43 G. Bennett, 'The Secret Service Committee, 1919–1931' in *The Records of the Permanent Undersecretary's Department: Liaison between the Foreign Office and British Secret Intelligence, 1873–1939*. London, 2005, pp. 42–53.
44 Quoted in J. Ferris, '"Now that Milk is Spilt": Appeasement and the Archive on Intelligence', *Diplomacy and Statecraft* 19: 3 (2008), pp. 527–65.
45 D. Dilks, 'Flashes of Intelligence: The Foreign Office, The SIS and Security Before the Second World War' in Andrew and Dilks (eds), *The Missing Dimension*, pp. 101–25.
46 Andrew, *Secret Service*, p. 343.
47 G. Bennett, *Churchill's Man of Mystery: Desmond Morton and the World of Intelligence*. London, 2006, p. 191.
48 W. Wark, 'British Intelligence on the German Air Force and Aircraft Industry, 1933–1939', *The Historical Journal* 25: 3 (1982), pp. 627–48.

49 K. Neilson, *Britain, Soviet Russia and the Collapse of the Versailles Order, 1919–1939*. Cambridge, 2006, p. 13.
50 A.J.P. Taylor, *English History, 1914–1945*. Oxford, 1966, pp. 412–15.
51 Bennett, *Churchill's Man of Mystery*, p. 192.
52 Andrew, *Secret Service*, p. 400.
53 C. Andrew, *The Defence of the Realm: The Authorized History of MI5*. London, 2009, p. 195.
54 Hinsley, *British Intelligence in the Second World War*, vol. 1, p. 49.
55 Ibid., p. 51.
56 Bennett, *Churchill's Man of Mystery*, p. 192
57 W.K. Wark, 'British Military and Economic Intelligence: Assessments of Nazi Germany Before the Second World War' in Andrew and Dilks (eds.), *The Missing Dimension*, pp. 78–100.
58 Wark, 'British Intelligence on the German Air Force', p. 636.
59 W.K. Wark, *The Ultimate Enemy: British Intelligence and Nazi Germany, 1933–1939*. Ithaca, 1985, p. 228.
60 Bennett, *Churchill's Man of Mystery*, p. 192.
61 Stevenson, *A Man Called Intrepid; Bill MacDonald, The True Intrepid*. Guilford, 2000, *passim*.
62 Bennett, *Churchill's Man of Mystery*, pp. 193–4.
63 Information obtained under the Chatham House Rule, which stipulates that information obtained may be cited but the speaker's name may not be disclosed.
64 Bennett, *Churchill's Man of Mystery*, pp. 196–9.
65 F.H. Hinsley, *British Intelligence in the Second World War*. Cambridge, 1993, p. 10.
66 Andrew, *Secret Service*, p. 395.
67 Ibid., pp. 434–9.
68 Hinsley, *British Intelligence in the Second World War*, vol. 1, p. 58.
69 Bennett, 'The Secret Service Committee, 1919–1931', p. 67.
70 Bennett, *Churchill's Man of Mystery*, p. 199.
71 e.g. Dilks, 'Flashes of Intelligence'; Andrew, *The Defence of Realm*.
72 Dilks, 'Flashes of Intelligence', p. 118.
73 Andrew, *Secret Service*, pp. 398–9.
74 R.J. Overy, *The Origins of the Second World War*. London, 1998, pp. 27–8.
75 Dilks, 'Appeasement and "Intelligence"', p. 139.
76 Andrew, *Secret Service*, p. 395.
77 Dilks, 'Appeasement and "Intelligence"', p. 148.
78 Dilks, 'Flashes of Intelligence', p. 118.
79 Bennett, *Churchill's Man of Mystery*, p. 198.
80 Wark, 'British Intelligence on the German Air Force', p. 627.
81 Andrew, *Secret Service*, pp. 414–15.
82 Andrew, *The Defence of the Realm*, p. 198.
83 J. Curry, *The Security Service 1908–1945: The Official History* (with an introduction by Christopher Andrew). Kew, 1999, p. 117.
84 Curry, *The Security Service*, p. 119.
85 Andrew, *The Defence of the Realm*, p. 200;
86 Taylor, *English History*, p. 425 (n).
87 Andrew, *The Defence of the Realm*, pp. 201–2.
88 Ibid. *The Defence of the Realm*, p. 205.
89 Ferris, '"Now that Milk is Spilt"', p. 554.
90 C. Andrew, 'The British Secret Service and Anglo-Soviet Relations in the 1920s Part I: From the Trade Negotiations to the Zinoviev Letter', *The Historical Journal* 20: 3 (1977), pp. 673–706.
91 Andrew, *The Defence of the Realm*, p.205
92 Curry later wrote that the obscenity 'read with our report as a whole, had contributed materially – if only as a minor factor – towards Mr Chamberlain's reformulation of policy including the introduction of conscription in 1939'.
93 Andrew, *The Defence of the Realm*, p. 207.
94 The Secret Service Committee met in 1919, 1921, 1922, 1925, 1927 and 1931.
95 Curry, *The Security Service*, p. 142.

96 NA KV4/127 'Security Service Organization, 1918–1939'.
97 Curry, *The Security Service*, p. 145.
98 Ibid., p. 145.
99 Curry, *The Security Service*, p. 148.
100 Andrew, *The Defence of the Realm*, pp. 48–9.
101 Edward Thomas, 'The Evolution of the JIC System Up to and During World War II' in C. Andrew and J. Noakes (eds), *Intelligence and International Relations 1900–1945*. Exeter, 1987, p. 220.
102 Ibid, p. 226.
103 Hinsley, *British Intelligence in the Second World War*, vol. 1, p. 106.
104 *See* D. Stafford, *Churchill and Secret Service*. London, 2001.

Chapter 13

Appeasement: A Critical Evaluation Seventy Years On

Jeffrey Record

Some seem to believe that we should negotiate with the terrorists and radicals, as if some ingenious argument will persuade them they have been wrong all along. We have an obligation to call this what it is – the false comfort of appeasement, which has been repeatedly discredited by history.

President George W. Bush, Jerusalem 15 May 2008[1]

During the more than the six decades separating the end of the Second World War and the election of President Barack Obama, every American president except Jimmy Carter routinely invoked the Munich analogy as a means of inflating overseas national security threats and demonizing dictators. Presidents and their spokesman have not only believed the analogy but used it to mobilize public opinion for war.[2] After all, if the enemy really is another Hitler, then the use of force becomes mandatory. More recently, neo-conservatives and their allies in government have branded as appeasers all proponents of non-violent conflict resolution with hostile dictatorships. For them, to appease is to be naïve, cowardly and soft on the threat *du jour*, be it terrorism, a rogue state or a rising great power. It is to be a Neville Chamberlain rather than a Winston Churchill.

The Munich analogy informed every major threatened or actual U.S. use of force during the Cold War and was invoked during the decisions to attack Iraq in 1991 and 2003. For President Harry S. Truman, the analogy dictated intervention in Korea: 'Communism was acting in Korea just as Hitler and the Japanese had acted ten, fifteen, twenty years earlier.'[3] A year after the Korean War ended, President Dwight D. Eisenhower, citing the 'domino effects' of a Communist victory in French Indochina on the rest of south-east Asia, invoked Munich in an appeal for Anglo-American military action: 'we failed to halt Hirohito, Mussolini, and Hitler by not acting in unity and in time … May it not be that [we] have learned something from that lesson?'[4] President John F. Kennedy invoked the Munich analogy during the Cuban Missile Crisis, warning that the '1930s taught us a clear lesson: aggressive conduct, if allowed to go unchecked, ultimately leads to war'.[5]

Munich indisputably propelled the United States into Vietnam. President Lyndon B. Johnson told his Secretary of Defense, Robert McNamara, that if the United States pulled out of Vietnam 'the dominoes would fall and a part of the world would go Communist'.[6] Johnson later told historian Doris

Kearns that 'everything I knew about history told me that if I got out of Vietnam and let Ho Chi Minh run through the streets of Saigon, then I'd be doing exactly what [Neville] Chamberlain did ... I'd be giving a fat reward to aggression.'[7] President Ronald Reagan saw in the Soviet Union a replay of the challenges the democracies faced in the 1930s and invoked Munich to justify a major U.S. military build-up as well as intervention in Grenada and possible intervention in Nicaragua. 'One of the greatest tragedies of this century', he said in a 1983 speech, 'was that it was only after the balance of power was allowed to erode and a ruthless adversary, Adolf Hitler, deliberately weighed the risks and decided to strike that the importance of a strong defense was realized.'[8] Similarly, George W. Bush saw in Saddam Hussein an Arab Hitler whose aggression against Kuwait, if unchecked, would lead to further aggression in the Persian Gulf. In announcing the dispatch of U.S. forces to Saudi Arabia in response to Saddam Hussein's conquest of Kuwait, he declared, 'if history teaches us anything, it is that we must resist aggression or it will destroy our freedoms. Appeasement does not work. As was the case in the 1930s, we see in Saddam Hussein an aggressive dictator threatening his neighbors.'[9]

In the run-up to the U.S. invasion of Iraq in 2003, war proponents claimed that war with Iraq was unavoidable, citing once more the lessons of Munich. As Richard Perle, the influential Chairman of the Pentagon's Defense Policy Board, said in an August 2002 interview:

> [An] action to remove Saddam Hussein could precipitate the very thing we are most anxious to prevent: his use of chemical and biological weapons. But the danger that springs from his capabilities will only grow as he expands his arsenal. A preemptive strike against Hitler at the time of Munich would have meant an immediate war, as opposed to the one that came later. Later was much worse.[10]

In that same month Secretary of Defense Donald Rumsfeld, in a television interview, opined, 'think of all the countries that said, 'well, we don't have enough evidence. *Mein Kampf* had already been written. Hitler had indicated what he intended to do. Maybe he won't attack us ... Well, there are millions of dead because of [those] miscalculations.' Later, Rumsfeld added, 'maybe Winston Churchill was right. Maybe that lone voice expressing concern about what was happening was right.'[11] President George W. Bush, in his 'ultimatum' speech of 17 March 2003 to Saddam Hussein, pointedly noted that in 'the twentieth century, some chose to appease murderous dictators, whose threats were allowed to grow into genocide and war'.[12]

Unfortunately, invocations of the Munich analogy almost invariably mislead because they distort the true nature of appeasement, ignore the extreme rarity of the Nazi German threat and falsely suggest that Britain and France could have readily stopped Hitler before 1939. Additionally, the Munich analogy reinforces the presidential tendency since 1945 to overstate threats for the purpose of rallying public and congressional support, and overstated threats encourage resort to force in circumstances where non-use of force might better serve long-term U.S. security interests. Threats that are in fact limited – as was Baathist Iraq after the 9/11 attacks – tend to be portrayed in Manichaean terms, thus skewing the policy choice toward military action, including preventive war with all its attendant risks and penalties. If the 1930s reveal the danger of underestimating a security threat, the post-Second World War decades and post-9/11 years contain examples of the danger of overestimating a national security threat.

Appeasement, which became a politically charged term only after the Second World War, actually means 'to pacify, quiet, or satisfy, especially by giving in to the demands of', according the *Webster's New World Dictionary and Thesaurus*, which goes on to list the following synonyms for the noun, including 'amends, settlement, reparation, conciliation' and 'compromise'.[13] Stephen Rock defines appeasement as simply 'the policy of reducing tensions with one's adversary by removing the causes of conflict and disagreement',[14] a definition echoed by political scientists Gordon Craig and Alexander George: 'the reduction of tension between [two states] by the methodical removal of the principal causes of conflict and disagreement between them'.[15] Thus Richard Nixon was guilty of 'appeasing' Communist China in 1972 by embracing Beijing's one-China policy, and Ronald Reagan was guilty of 'appeasing' the Soviet Union in 1987 by resolving tensions with Moscow over actual and planned deployments of intermediate range nuclear forces in Europe.

Unfortunately, Anglo-French behaviour toward Nazi Germany gave appeasement such a bad name that the term is no longer usable except as a political pejorative. Before Munich, however, observes historian Paul Kennedy, 'the policy of settling international … quarrels by admitting and satisfying grievances through rational negotiation and compromise, thereby avoiding the resort to an armed conflict which would be expensive, bloody, and possibly very dangerous' was generally viewed as 'constructive, positive, and honorable'.[16] Five years after the Second World War, Winston Churchill, the great anti-appeaser of Hitler, declared that 'Appeasement in itself may be good or bad according to the circumstances. Appeasement from weakness and fear is alike futile and fatal … Appeasement from strength is magnanimous and noble, and might be the surest and only path to world peace.'[17]

An oft-cited case of successful appeasement from strength is Great Britain's resolution of disputes with the United States from 1896 to1903.[18] By the 1890s the number and power of Britain's enemies were growing. Britain had no great power allies and faced rising challenges from Germany and Russia on top of continuing tensions with France and the United States. Tensions with an industrially expanding and increasingly bellicose Germany became especially acute when Berlin decided to challenge British naval supremacy in European waters in the early twentieth century. Accordingly, Britain decided to reduce the potential demands on its military power by resolving outstanding disputes with the United

States and France. With respect to the United States, it agreed to American demands that Britain explicitly accept the Monroe Doctrine; submit British Guiana's border dispute with Venezuela to international arbitration; agree to U.S. construction, operation and fortification of an inter-oceanic canal through Central America; and settle an Alaskan–Canadian border dispute in America's favour. None of these concessions involved vital British security interests, which in fact were advanced by transforming the world's greatest industrial power from a potential enemy into a friend and later indispensable ally

Use of the Munich analogy not only twists the meaning of appeasement: it also ignores the extraordinary unique nature of the Nazi German threat. Though the analogy's power to persuade is undeniable, Nazi Germany remains without equal as a state threat. Genuinely Hitlerian security threats to the United States have not been replicated since 1945. The scope of Hitler's nihilism, recklessness, military power and territorial–racial ambitions posed a mortal threat to Western civilization, and there was nothing inevitable about his ultimate defeat. No other authoritarian or totalitarian regime ever employed such a powerful military instrument in such an aggressive manner on behalf of such a monstrous agenda. Hitler was simultaneously unappeasable and undeterrable – a rare combination that made war the only means, short of *coup d'état* or assassination, of bringing him down. He understood that he could not achieve his international ambitions without war, and no territorial or political concessions the democracies might offer him could have satisfied him.

Stalin, whose vast crimes were reserved largely for his associates and the peoples of the Soviet Union, had great military power, but was cautious and patient. He did not push Moscow's territorial ambitions much beyond the lines gained by Soviet forces at the close of the Second World War. He was, unlike Hitler, deterrable and deterred. Mao Zedong, also a domestic political monster, was less cautious, but militarily weak. The Korean War taught him the limits of China's power, and he was eventually double-contained by the United States and the Soviet Union. There was also Mao's repeated provocation of domestic political turmoil and disastrous economic experiments, which blocked China's journey toward great power status by condemning the country to poverty and military backwardness.

Ho Chi Minh and Saddam Hussein were minor threats when compared to Stalin and Mao. Ho's ambitions were limited, and his fighting power local, whereas Saddam was never in a position to overthrow U.S. military domination of the Persian Gulf. Saddam may have been bloody-minded and ruthless, but his power always fell far short of his ambitions. And if Ho was undeterrable in his quest for a reunified Vietnam under Communist auspices (a fact that escaped proponents of U.S. military intervention), Saddam proved vulnerable to credible deterrence. Unlike Hitler, he preferred surrender and captivity to suicide. Though during the 1980s Saddam used chemical weapons against helpless Kurdish villagers and Iranian infantry, he refrained from using them against Israel and U.S. forces during the Gulf War because he understood that to do so would invite Iraq's destruction. Kim Jong-il and his regime can wreak great damage on South Korea, but there is no reason to believe that Pyongyang would do so unless attacked by the United States. Mutual deterrence has prevailed for almost six decades on the Korean Peninsula, and the George W. Bush administration, despite a lot of bellicose talk early on, sought a diplomatic termination of Pyongyang's nuclear weapons programme that inevitably would have involved mutual concessions.

Seventy years on, it is easy to forget the strategic and political contexts of British and French policies toward Nazi Germany from 1933 to 1939. The sources of appeasement were multiple and mutually reinforcing. The first was the calamitous bloodletting of 1914–18, memories of which were still fresh. Of the over sixty million Europeans who had fought in the war, seven million had died and another twenty-one million had been disabled or seriously wounded. Over four million women had lost husbands and eight million children had lost fathers.[19] Most British and French leaders reasonably assumed that no head of a major European state would be willing to thrust the continent into another such war. They assumed that another all-out war in Europe would be a catastrophe for all involved – and they were right.

It is virtually impossible to underestimate the influence of the slaughter of the 'Great War' on official and public opinion in Europe in the inter-war years. The war had an especially profound impact on opinion in the primary appeasing country, Great Britain, where vivid memories of the lost comrades and loved ones and the special horrors of trench warfare bred an electorate of which significant segments were either pacifist or unwilling to contemplate the use of force outside the authority of the collective security framework of the League of Nations. In the case of Neville Chamberlain, who became prime minister in May1937 and whose name has become synonymous with appeasement, there was simply an inability to imagine that any European statesman, even Hitler, could or would wish to risk a repetition of the Great War. P.M.H. Bell points out that most British and French statesmen had come to regard the Great War 'as a calamity, involving human, material, and financial losses which should not again be incurred short of utmost necessity'. They also represented territorially satisfied powers 'anxious to preserve the status quo; but they also wanted peace and quiet. They would eventually fight in self-defence … but their optimism about the outcome of war was at a low ebb, and their belief in war as an instrument of policy was weak'.[20] In contrast, Hitler viewed war as unavoidable in achieving his foreign policy objectives, and he was quite confident that Germany would prevail in any war he chose to start.

French and especially British leaders also assumed that Hitler's intentions in Europe were limited. They believed that 'Nazism was a temporary extremist aberration caused by the lingering inequities of Versailles', and that if they removed those inequities, 'addressing them in point by point and in good faith … the Germans would quiet down'.[21] Even after the war, the British historian A.J.P. Taylor sought to prove that Hitler was a 'normal' European leader practicing the opportunism of *realpolitik* on behalf of liberating Germany from the shackles of the 'vindictive' Versailles Treaty and restoring Germany to a political status commensurate with its population and industrial power. 'Hitler was no more wicked and unscrupulous than many other contemporary statesmen.' Hitler's ideology consisted of nothing but 'day-dreams', and Hitler ended up in Russia because 'his judgement was corrupted by easy victories', not because he really believed it was Germany's racial destiny to carve out massive *lebensraum* (living space) in the Slavic East.[22]

Taylor's thesis was never convincing and has been thoroughly discredited by subsequent analysis.[23] The thesis could never account for Nazi behaviour in Europe or the Holocaust; more generally, it wilfully ignored the power of ideas in international politics. Much of Hitler's foreign policy *was* rooted in the foreign policies of Imperial Germany and the Weimar Republic, but Hitler's racial and territorial objectives in Europe, to say nothing of his profound craving for war, lay beyond the boundaries of pre-Nazi German foreign policy. Hitler's ideology defined the scope of his territorial ambitions in Europe, especially in the East. To be sure, he was a supreme opportunist and sought to revise Versailles in so far as it held Germany down militarily and 'imprisoned' much of the German nation outside the German state. Revisionism, however, was but an enabling precondition for action on a much larger agenda of racial conquest and enslavement.

This dimension of Hitler and his ambitions eluded proponents of appeasement as much as it did Taylor himself. It was easy to dismiss Hitler's tirades on race and *lebensraum* as fodder for domestic political consumption. The highly respected economist Dr Hjalmar Schacht, a traditional conservative who was sacked by Hitler as Reichsbank President in 1939 for opposing Germany's unbridled rearmament and who was arrested and jailed in the wake of the 20 July 1944 attempt on Hitler's life, told an interviewer after the war that in the early 1930s 'No one took [Hitler's] anti-Semitism seriously. We thought it was a political propaganda issue and would be forgotten once he got into power.'[24] Taken at face value, Hitler's vision of an Aryan empire stretching to the Urals was nothing short of fantastic: it would require the conquest of Eastern Europe, destruction of the Soviet Union and 'ethnic cleansing on a grotesque scale' – objectives beyond Germany's strengths and unacceptable to the upholders of the European balance of power.[25]

Chamberlain believed that Hitler's ambitions were limited to Germanic Europe and that the German dictator could be satisfied by territorial concessions. He believed that Hitler, like Bismarck before him, understood the limits of German power, and that he could not possibly want to plunge his country and the rest of Europe into another general war. Moreover, by the mid-1930s many British leaders had come to regard German grievances against the Versailles Treaty as legitimate. They certainly opposed risking war to enforce a treaty they believed to have been a mistake in the first place, and they felt it was inevitable that Hitler would rearm and cast off other Versailles restrictions on Germany.

Robert Jervis has observed that the uniqueness of the threat Hitler posed was not widely understood at the time. 'Nazi Germany was seen as a difficult state, but not as a wildly abnormal one. Indeed, observers lacked a readily available intellectual category into which Germany as we now see it could have been fit … It is sensible to require extraordinary evidence before one reaches an implausible conclusion.'[26]

Even had British and French leaders grasped the true nature and aims of the Nazi regime and Hitler's strategic ambitions, it is far from clear what they could have done to stop him militarily. France had a large and well-equipped army, but it was an army unwilling of undertaking offensive action against Germany. The French General Staff, determined to avoid the horrendous blood losses of 1914–18, alarmed by France's growing industrial and demographic inferiority to Germany and shackled by a parliamentary-imposed one-year term of service for conscripts, embraced a rigid defensive military doctrine and a reserve mobilization-dependent army that precluded offensive military action into German territory.[27] The French would await a German attack behind the Maginot Line, a formidable string of fortifications that conserved French manpower, while mobilizing the full strength of their army. The peacetime French army was, in fact, little more than a skeleton on which the wartime force mobilized. It lacked a standing mobile strike force. France's military posture thus not only left it up to Hitler to decide when and under what circumstances to initiate another Franco-German War, but also stripped France's alliances with Czechoslovakia and other Eastern European states of any credibility.

The British were in no better shape. Though safer from the German menace than France, Britain in the 1930s staggered under a multiplicity of military obligations that far exceeded its capacity to act upon them. The First World War had greatly weakened Britain's financial power though she inherited even greater imperial obligations as a result of the war's destruction of the German and Turkish empires. During the 1930s, Britain still controlled a quarter of the world, but with less than ten percent of its manufacturing strength and war production potential.[28] Yet as the decade progressed, Britain faced a mushrooming German threat in Europe, a rising Japanese threat in the Far East and a significant Italian threat in the Mediterranean, the latter threatening Britain's vital imperial line of communication to India via the Suez Canal. Small wonder that in 1935 the Committee of Imperial Defence (CID) warned that

> we cannot foresee the time when our defence forces will be strong enough to safeguard our territory, trade and vital interests against Germany, Italy and Japan simultaneously. We cannot, therefore, exaggerate the importance … of any political action that can be taken to reduce the numbers of our potential enemies or to gain the support of potential allies.[29]

The call to reduce the numbers of Britain's potential enemies was a call to appease Germany or Italy or Japan in order to free up military resources to deal with those who remained unappeased. It was a call that was hardly unreasonable especially as the German and Japanese threats worsened during the three years separating the CID's assessment and the Czech crisis of 1938.

Even in Europe, Britain was not in a position to project military power its military power on to the continent. The Royal Navy was preoccupied with the Italian and Japanese threats; the Royal Air Force was in the middle of rearming (largely with defensive fighter aircraft); and the army had no defined strategic role outside of home and imperial defence. Not until February 1939 did Chamberlain authorize a continental commitment in the form of two divisions within twenty-one days of the beginning of hostilities, with another two to follow within sixty-five days – drops in the bucket compared to a fully mobilized French army and a rapidly expanding German army.[30]

Nor was Britain prepared, in the crucial years before the infamous Munich Conference of September 1938, and willing to enter a military alliance with France. This refusal was critical because it drove the French, who suffered fewer illusions about German intentions in Europe, to embrace appeasement. Why? Because the French rightly believed that they could not wage war against Germany with any hope of success except in alliance with Britain. France's strategic dependence on Britain and its derivative diplomatic strategy of waiting for Britain to recognize the mortal danger effectively gave the British veto power over French policy toward Germany, a veto Chamberlain was more than willing to exercise. But the French understood that 'the basic military equation in western Europe remained a France of 40 million confronted by 75 million Germans and 40 million Italians' dictated 'cooperation in appeasement until the policy succeeded or until the British themselves woke up to its futility'.[31]

A dread of strategic bombing and a misjudgement of the real Nazi air threat further encouraged appeasement. Both governments and publics in Britain and France were gripped by a generic dread of mass air attacks on cities, and governments fell victim to a massive German deception campaign about the size and nature of the Nazi air threat. Prime Minster Stanley Baldwin's famously remarked in 1932, 'There is no power on earth that can protect its people from being bombed ... The bomber will always get through.' This view was gospel to British and American air power advocates from the early 1920s on, and was widespread among the British public throughout the 1930s. The misperception of the German threat stemmed from failure to appreciate, especially in Britain, that German air power was being developed mainly to provide tactical air support to the German army, not to conduct strategic bombing operations, and from German success in duping, among others, the chief of the French air staff, General Joseph Vuillemin, the American aviator turned pro-Nazi defeatist, Charles A. Lindberg and future British prime minister Winston Churchill (a persistent purveyor of inflated estimates of German air strength during the 1930s) into believing that German air power was seemingly irresistible. On the eve of the Munich Conference, Lindberg's widely reported view was that 'Germany now has the means of destroying London, Paris, and Praha [Prague] if she wishes to do so. England and France together do not have enough modern planes for effective defense.'[32] The historian P.M.H. Bell believes that 'Munich was a victory for the terror which the Germans inspired by displaying the Luftwaffe with panache, and letting their opponents' nerves do the rest.'[33]

Distrust of the Soviet Union and fear of communism also promoted appeasement, an alternative to which was the formation of the kind of grand alliance that defeated Germany in the First World War. Such an alliance, however, was never more than a theoretical possibility until Hitler invaded the Soviet Union in June 1941 and declared war on the United States later in the year. For the United States, domestic politics precluded war or military alliance with threatened states in Europe as voluntary policy choices. But this was not the case for the Soviet Union, which Hitler both reviled and targeted for German racial expansion. Stalin clearly understood Nazi Germany for the deadly threat that it was, but he also greatly mistrusted Britain and France as potential allies against Hitler, and in the end he chose to sign a non-aggression pact with Hitler rather than enter an alliance with Britain and France. The profoundly anti-communist government of Neville Chamberlain was never really serious about a military pact with the Soviet Union anyway. It distrusted Stalin and harboured understandable doubts about the Soviet Union's value as an ally against Hitler, especially after Stalin's decimation of the Red Army's officer corps. Large percentages of British and French voters also regarded communism as a greater threat than Nazism. Indeed, in neither country was there significant public support for the use of force against Hitler until after the German dictator seized the non-Germanic portions of Czechoslovakia on 15 March 1939. Stalin also had good reason to distrust Britain and France, especially after they had bowed to Hitler's demands against Czechoslovakia at Munich. Anglo-French appeasement of Nazi Germany and an undeclared war with Japan in the Far East persuaded Stalin to cut his own deal with Hitler, who in August 1939 had much to offer Stalin, including extensive territorial concessions east of the Vistula river, that Britain and France could not. The inescapable conclusion is that an alliance between communist Russia and the great capitalist democracies against Hitler was never in the cards short of the desperation imposed by war, a conclusion bolstered the grand alliance's disintegration in 1945.

Michael Bess convincingly argues that at Munich in 1938 'the policy of appeasement underwent a qualitative change: from an intelligent and morally defensible policy of addressing reasonable German grievances, to a dishonorable and self-defeating policy of caving in to the grossly unfair demands of a bully'.[34] Until September 1938, Hitler's moves in Europe addressed legitimate German objections to the inequities of the Versailles Treaty. Hitler's refusal to accept Germany's permanent disarmament while Europe's other great powers remained armed, his reassertion of full German sovereignty over the Rhineland via its military reoccupation in March 1936 and his uncontested occupation of the Germanic rump state of Austria in March 1938 were all peaceful and consistent with the principle of national self-determination.

In contrast, his demand that Czechoslovakia be dismembered or he would take that country by force was a demand pregnant with political and strategic dangers for both Britain and France. Czechoslovakia was not only Eastern Europe's sole democracy; it was also well armed, having a good army, strong fortifications along its mountainous border with Germany, and Eastern Europe's largest armaments industry. Perhaps most significant of all, Czechoslovakia, unlike Austria, was a treaty ally of France. Thus when the British and the French forced the Czech government to capitulate to Hitler's demand that Czechoslovakia cede to Germany the Sudetenland – those areas of Czechoslovakia adjacent to the German border in which the majority of inhabitants were Germans – they infamously sacrificed a democracy and (for France) an ally to Nazi Germany in a manner that could not fail to encourage Hitler (and Stalin) to believe that neither the British nor the French would resist further German seizures of territory in the East. Munich was a moral and strategic disaster for Britain and France. Writing about Munich after the war, Churchill observed, 'for almost twenty years [Czech] President [Edward] Benes had been a faithful ally and almost vassal of France … If ever there was a case of solemn obligation, it was here and now … It was a portent of doom when a French government failed to keep the word of France.'[35] Even French Premier Edouard Daladier felt ashamed at Munich but believed France could not defy a Neville Chamberlain determined to offer up Czechoslovakia on the altar of appeasement. Daladier understood – even if Chamberlain did not – the strategic and moral consequences of selling out the Czechs. 'I am not proud. No I am not proud,' he told the French delegation. 'The Czechs are our allies, and we have obligations to them. What I have just done betrays them … [but] what can I do if I have no one behind me?'[36]

The question, however, still remains: what could Britain and France have done to save Czechoslovakia? Gerhard L. Weinberg has wisely cautioned against ignoring 'the enormous significance of the circumstances in which military action is considered and the perceptions of such action at the time both by those who have to make the decision and by the segments of the public that will have to bear the burdens of any war'. With respect to Munich, he concludes, 'it is surprising that in the crisis over Czechoslovakia there was any serious consideration of going to war at all in Britain or France.'[37] The French rightly believed they were too weak to act without British support, and Chamberlain was simply not willing to go to war over Czechoslovakia. The sole exception was *if* Hitler attacked Czechoslovakia and *if* France then chose to honour her alliance commitment to the Czechs – a message that a Chamberlain emissary, Sir Horace Wilson, conveyed to Hitler at Munich with evident deterrent effect.[38] But Hitler, though threatening war, did not attack, and France was not willing to commit absent assurance of a British commitment. In any event, neither France nor Britain was geographically positioned to provide direct military assistance to Czechoslovakia, and, as we have seen, French military doctrine and force structure precluded an attack into Germany in response to a German invasion of Czechoslovakia. The simple – and for Czechoslovakia – unpleasant fact was that Britain or France could do little to keep Hitler from grabbing all of Czechoslovakia, except to force the Czechs into giving up some Czech territory in the hope of saving the rest. And this is what Chamberlain and Daladier did. '[N]o military pressure we can exact by sea, or land or in the air can prevent Germany either from invading and overrunning Bohemia of inflicting a decisive defeat on the Czechoslovakian army,' concluded a March 1938 British Chiefs of Staff assessment of the implications of a German attack on Czechoslovakia. 'If politically it is deemed necessary to restore Czechoslovakia's lost integrity, this aim will entail war with Germany, and her defeat may mean a long struggle. In short, we can do nothing to prevent the dog getting the bone, and we have no means of making him give it up, except by killing him by a slow process of attrition and starvation.'[39]

Ironically, while Chamberlain regarded Munich as a success, Hitler saw it as a defeat. He used the alleged persecution of the German community in Czechoslovakia as a pretext for the conquest of *all* of Czechoslovakia. He had not foreseen Chamberlain's willingness to accept the peaceful transfer of the Sudetenland to Germany. Chamberlain had wrecked his plans. 'The most disappointed man of Munich was Adolf Hitler,' contends J.W. Wheeler-Bennett, author of an early work on the Munich Conference. 'Chamberlain and Daladier had made so wholesale a surrender of Czechoslovakia that even Adolph Hitler could not find an excuse to go to war.'[40] On his return to Berlin from Munich, Hitler told Hjalmar Schacht, 'That fellow [Chamberlain] has spoiled my entry into Prague.'[41] After the war Paul O. Schmidt, who was Hitler's interpreter and who was constantly at Hitler's side during the Nazi leader's discussions with Chamberlain, recounted Hitler's disgust at Chamberlain's popularity among ordinary Germans. 'It was definitely Chamberlain who was the idol of the German people at Munich – not Hitler. The German masses gave flowers to Chamberlain. One could see on their faces that they thanked Chamberlain for saving the peace of Europe despite Hitler.' As for the latter, 'Hitler didn't like this show at all. He feared it would give the impression that the German people were pacifists, which, of course, would be unpardonable in the eyes of the Nazis.'[42] Of the British Prime Minister's performance at Munich, Richard Overy writes, 'It is easy to see why Chamberlain saw Munich as a victory ... From a position of military weakness and inferiority, with no firm allies, and an array of diplomatic imponderables, Chamberlain had almost single-handedly averted war between Germany and Czechoslovakia and compelled Hitler, for the last time, to work within the Western framework [of negotiated territorial disputes].'[43]

Critics of Anglo-French appeasement of Hitler properly recognize that appeasement failed because Hitler's ambitions in Europe reached far beyond what the appeasers were prepared to give. But the critics' assumption that Hitler could have been deterred from attempting the subjugation of Europe by an early show of force or the formation of a grand alliance to stop him reflects a misreading of Hitler and the Nazi German threat.[44] The early adoption of a policy of firmness and deterrence would have altered Hitler's tactical calculations: witness Hitler's decision at Munich to postpone his invasion of Czechoslovakia. But there is no reason to believe such a policy would have caused Hitler to change his strategic goals. Hitler's tactical opportunism did not encompass a willingness to discard his commitment to creating a German racial empire stretching to the Ural Mountains.

Historian Ernest R. May has observed that if the appeasers had illusions about Hitler, so too did many 'anti-appeasers' who 'had their own illusions which were almost equally distant from reality. They believed that Hitler could be deterred by the threat of war. Few suspected that Hitler *wanted* war.'[45] Thus Churchill was wrong when he claimed in 1946 that '[t]here was never a war in all history easier to prevent by timely action than the one that has just desolated the globe. It could have been prevented without the firing of a single shot.'[46] Hitler had wanted war no later than 1943, and he believed that Germany would be powerful enough to defeat any combination of opposing states by then. War was thus inevitable as long as Hitler remained in power. Successful deterrence would have required a Hitler not only willing to check his ambitions in Europe but also fearful of the consequences of war with the Soviet Union – i.e. a Hitler who recognized the limits of Germany power. But this was not the Hitler that was. The real Hitler recognized no curbs on his ambitions for Germany, scorned Soviet military power and did not hesitate to declare war on the United States even as Nazi military fortunes in Russia were beginning to sag.

Hitler's undeterrability renders moot much discussion about 'what might have been'. Would, for example, a credible Anglo-French alliance with the Soviet Union (Churchill's favoured course of action) have deterred Hitler from seeking to enslave the Slavic *untermensch* in the East? Hitler was ideologically propelled to invade the Soviet Union, for which he had both racial and military contempt, and he proceeded to do so in June 1941 notwithstanding an unfinished and expanding war with Britain in the West and the growing difficulties of his Italian ally in the Mediterranean. In reality there was, as we have seen, slim prospect of a credible Anglo-French-Soviet alliance in the 1930s, given Stalin's suspicions of capitalist Britain and France and the extreme hostility of much British and French political opinion to Bolshevism and the Soviet pariah state. Moreover, the Soviet Union's lack of a common border with Germany blocked Moscow from projecting its military power against Germany except through Poland and Czechoslovakia.

The fact that Hitler could be neither deterred nor appeased meant that war could have been avoided only via Hitler's death or removal from power, options that before the war were not considered by London or Paris and only briefly weighed by some German military leaders in 1938. (Democratic Britain and France were not in the business of sponsoring assassinations of European heads of state.) Beyond Hitler's departure from power, only a preventive war that crippled German military power, collapsed the Nazi regime, or both could have averted the Second World War. Yet Britain in the 1930s had no capacity to project decisive military power on to the continent, much less deep into Germany, and France, though in possession of a very large army, had adopted a purely defensive strategy. In neither country was there any public or parliamentary support for a preventive war against Germany: even Churchill rejected preventive war in favour of deterrence through the creation of a grand coalition of anti-Nazi states (and if Hitler nonetheless decided on war, then at least Britain would have locked in powerful allies).

Thus when the neo-conservative critics of appeasement speak about how Hitler could and should have been stopped before 1939, as did Richard Perle in urging a U.S. invasion of Iraq, they mean forcible regime change of the kind the United States launched against Saddam Hussein in 2003. But it is here that the neo-conservatives and others who believe in the continuing validity of the Munich analogy enter the fantasy realm of historical counter-factualism. For Britain and France in the 1930s, a decisive preventive war against Nazi Germany was morally unacceptable, politically impossible and militarily infeasible. One wonders what Richard Perle had in mind when he spoke of a 'preemptive strike against Hitler at the time of Munich'?

Neville Chamberlain *did* horribly misread Hitler, but the current neo-conservative indictment of Chamberlain falsely assumes that the option of preventive war against Germany was as readily available to London and Paris in 1938 as it was to the United States against Iraq in 2003. The truth of the matter is that Europe boarded the train toward general war the moment Hitler took power in Germany, and that nothing short of his death or removal from power – outcomes that lay beyond the democracies' ability to effect – could have stopped it.

Of course, any German government of the 1930s would have pursued rectification of the Versailles Treaty injustices, but even a government of traditional conservative nationalists of the kind that Hitler discarded on his road to war (precisely because they opposed his reckless policies) would have respected the limits of German power and the unacceptability to Britain and France of a German-dominated Europe. They would have been happy to recover lost territory in Poland, even to see Poland disappear – but not at the cost of general war for which Germany was ill prepared.

Many retrospective observers believe they now know what Britain and France *should* have done in the 1930s because we all know that the Second World War and the Holocaust were the consequences of appeasement. However, today's *should* runs afoul of yesterday's *could not* and *would not*. Hindsight is *not* 20-20 vision: it refracts past events through the lens of what followed. David Potter has shrewdly observed that hindsight is 'the historian's chief asset *and* his main liability'.[47] Robert J. Young notes, in his examination of France and the origins of the Second World War, that 'the problem with hindsight is that it is illuminated more by the present than the past'.[48] British and French statesmen in the 1930s did not know they were on the road to general war – on the contrary, they were seeking to avoid war. How differently would Munich now be seen had it not been followed by war and genocide?

It is time to retire Hitler and 'appeasement' from the American national security debate. This does not mean the United States should negotiate with any and all enemies or that it should refrain from using force against all threats that are not Hitlerian in scope. The United States is a great power with occasionally threatened interests whose protection sometimes requires threatened or actual use of force. What it does mean is that continued employment of the Munich analogy to portray threats – an analogy that, unnecessarily and disastrously, promoted the use of force in Vietnam and Iraq – impedes sound strategic thinking about foreign threats to national security and proper responses to them.

Notes

1 George W. Bush, speech to the Israeli Knesset, 15 May 2008, quoted in S. Stoleberg and J. Rutenberg, 'Bush Assails "Appeasement", Touching Off Political Storm', *New York Times* 16 May 2008.
2 See J. Record, *Making War, Thinking History: Munich, Vietnam, and Presidential Uses of Force from Korea to Kosovo*. Annapolis, 2002; and 'The Use and Abuse of History: Munich, Vietnam, and Iraq', *Survival* (Spring 2007), pp. 163–80.
3 Harry S. Truman, *Memoirs: Years of Trial and Hope, 1946–1952*, vol. 2. New York, 1956, p. 335.
4 Eisenhower letter to Winston Churchill, 1954, excerpted in R. MacMahon (ed.), *Major Problems in the History of the Vietnam War*. Lexington, 1995, 2nd ed., p. 373.
5 T. Sorenson, *Kennedy*. New York, 1965, p. 703.
6 M. Beschloss (ed.), *Taking Charge: The Johnson White House Tapes, 1963–1964*. New York, 1997, p. 428.
7 D. Kearns, *Lyndon Johnson and the American Dream*. New York, 1976, p. 252.
8 Radio address to the nation on defence spending, 19 February 1983, in R. Reagan, *Public Papers of Presidents of the United States: Ronald Reagan, 1983*, vol. 1, p. 258.
9 Address to the nation announcing the deployment of United States armed forces to Saudi Arabia, 8 August 1990, in George Bush, *Public Papers of the Presidents of the United States: George Bush, 1990*, vol. 2, p. 1108.
10 *Washington Post* 11 November 2002.
11 *Toronto Star* 2 September 2002.
12 'President Bush's Address to the Nation', *Washington Post* 18 March 2003.
13 *Webster's New World Dictionary and Thesaurus*. New York, 2002, 2nd ed., pp. 27–8.
14 S. Rock, *Appeasement in International Politics*. Lexington, 2000, pp. 25–47.
15 G. Craig and A. George, *Force and Statecraft: Diplomatic Problems of Our Time*. New York, 1990, 2nd ed., p. 250.
16 P. Kennedy, *The Rise and Fall of the Great Powers: Economic Change and Military Conflict from 1500 to 2000*. New York, 1987, pp. 16, 39.
17 D. Kagan, *On the Origins of War and the Preservation of Peace*. New York, 1995, pp. 317–18.
18 Rock, *Appeasement in International Politics*, p. 12.
19 F. McDonough, *The Origins of the First and Second World Wars*. New York, 1997, p. 43.
20 P.M.H. Bell, *The Origins of the Second World War in Europe*. London, 1997, 2nd ed., p. 11.
21 M. Bess, *Choices Under Fire: Moral Dimensions of World War II*. New York, 2006, p. 69.
22 A.J.P. Taylor, *The Origins of the Second World War*. London, 1961, pp. 68–72. Also see pp. 105–9.
23 See G. Martel (ed.), *The Origins of the Second World War Reconsidered: A.J.P. Taylor and the Historians*. London, 1999, 2nd ed.
24 Quoted in L. Goldensohn, ed. and introduced by R. Gellately, *The Nuremberg Interviews: An America Psychiatrist's Conversations with Defendants and Witnesses*. New York, 2004, pp. 223–4.

25   R.J. Overy, 'Misjudging Hitler: A.J.P. Taylor and the Third Reich', in Martel (ed.), *The Origins of the Second World War Reconsidered*, p. 95.

26   R. Jervis, 'Political Science Perspectives' in R. Boyce and J. Maiolo, *The Origins of World War II: The Debate Continues*. New York, 2003, pp. 220–1.

27   See R. Doughty, *The Seeds of Disaster: The Development of French Army Doctrine 1919–1939*. Hamden, 1984, pp. 1–40.

28   Kennedy, *The Rise and Fall of the Great Powers*, p. 320.

29   Committee of Imperial Defence, Annual Review by the Chiefs of Staff Subcommittee, quoted in J. Dunabin, 'The British Military Establishment and the Policy of Appeasement' in W. Mommsen and L. Kettenecker (eds), *The Fascist Challenge and the Policy of Appeasement*. London, 1983, p. 176.

30   See W. Murray, *The Change in the European Balance of Power, 1938–1939: The Path to Ruin*. Princeton, 1984, pp. 276–8.

31   M. Thomas, 'France and the Czechoslovak Crisis', *Diplomacy and Statecraft* (July/November 1999), p. 49.

32   T. Taylor, *Munich: The Price of Peace*. New York, 1979, p. 849.

33   Bell, *The Origins of the Second World War in Europe*, p. 216.

34   Bess, *Choices Under Fire*, p. 72.

35   W. Churchill, *The Gathering Storm*. Boston, 1948, p. 302.

36   B. F. Martin, *France in 1938*. Baton Rouge, 2005, pp. 158–9.

37   G.L. Weinberg, 'Reflections on Munich After 60 Years', *Diplomacy and Statecraft* (July/November 1999), p. 8.

38   See J. Record, *The Specter of Munich: Reconsidering the Lessons of Appeasing Hitler*. Washington, 2006, pp. 42–4.

39   Taylor, *Munich*, p. 631.

40   J. Wheeler-Bennett, *Munich: Prologue to a Tragedy*. New York, 1948, p. 331.

41   Ibid., p. 331.

42   Goldensohn, *Nuremberg Interviews*, pp. 57–8.

43   Richard J. Overy, *The Road to War*. London, 1999, p. 103.

44   Record, *The Specter of Munich*, especially pp. 15–24, 67–72.

45   E. May, *Knowing One's Enemies: Intelligence Assessment Before Two World Wars*. Princeton, 1984, p. 520.

46   J. Snell (ed.), *The Outbreak of the Second World War: Design or Blunder?* London, 1962, p. vii.

47   D. Potter, *The Impending Crisis: 1848–1861*. New York, 1976, p. 145

48   R.J. Young, *France and the Origins of the Second World War*. New York, 1996, p. 108.

Chapter 14

A Very English Channel: Britain and French Appeasement

Robert J. Young

Years ago I examined France's entrance into the Second World War in a book that employed considerations of economics, domestic and international politics, ideology and popular psychology. It argued that French citizens were divided over which risks were greatest to national security, and that from the fractures inflicted by those rival certainties a debilitating national ambivalence had emerged.[1] Reaction was mixed. Some thought that it furthered our understanding of inter-war France; others that better statesmen would have overcome the domestic fault lines and averted the catastrophic defeat of 1940. The book made little of 'appeasement', a word with more resonance in Britain than in France. That arch appeaser Neville Chamberlain has inspired many interpretations, whether they emphasize his idealism and horror of war, his concern about the nation's armaments and the related fear of depleting the Treasury prematurely, or his sustained misreading of Hitler and the intellectual arrogance that caused him to do so.[2]

Edouard Daladier, French Prime Minister between 1938 and 1940, has attracted less attention.[3] He is commonly portrayed as a weak man at the head of a divided cabinet and country, a weary Sancho Panza to Chamberlain, resigned rather than committed to the appeasement of Germany. National Defence Minister between 1936 and 1940, he would be tarred by the spectacular military collapse, an event so unexpected that the easiest explanations came first. Despite the deaths of 120,000 French soldiers in May–June 1940, such sudden defeat had to mean marginal resistance, poor military preparation, poor civilian oversight and a population riddled by apathy if not corruption and treason.[4] Hence the links between Chamberlain's determination to appease Hitler, Daladier's determination to acquiesce, their joint failure to prevent war and the French failure to withstand the German onslaught.

Much of this warrants fresh review. France was somehow complicit in war's outbreak not by bellicosity but by passivity or, rephrased, by its failure as victim. And that re-invokes the word 'appeasement'. In the 1920s, the word had been praise-worthy. In France, *apaisement* meant reconciling domestic differences to break political stalemates and reconciling international differences to ensure security. Only in the Hitler years did it turn toxic. Re-labeled by contemporary, then historical, critics as a euphemism for blindness if not cowardice, it has come to represent Anglo-French indifference to the fate of strangers in central Europe: Austrians, Czechs or Slovaks, Jews or Gentiles. And because the French had been only disingenuous appeasers, because their collapse was so sudden, and because that suddenness implied moral infirmity, their guilt has somehow emerged greater than that of Chamberlain's government.

Why is not mysterious. Shrewdly assembled, the events of 1933–9 can easily be turned into an indictment of the Third Republic. In March 1935, Germany extended its violations of the peace treaty it had signed in 1919 by reintroducing conscription and announcing the existence of an air force. In 1936 it violated the provisions of a demilitarized Rhineland. Two years later it absorbed Austria, by so doing preparing for the dismantling of the Czechoslovak state, a French ally. By the spring of 1939 it was clear that Poland, another ally, was Hitler's next target. All of this contravened the terms of the Paris Peace Conference two decades earlier. Yet successive French governments had only acquiesced as Hitler grew more menacing. There was no call to arms, no threat of sanctions. Concessions to avoid war had come to appear more sensible and prudent than risking war by refusing them.

French appeasement had changed its complexion. No longer a synonym for premeditated conciliation, a strategy to resolve differences, it was now inspired by desperation. That, at least, has been a recurring theme within the historiographical debate; and it has the merit of helping us anticipate – though after the fact – the collapse of 1940. Weakness as prologue to humiliation. But if we have lightly sketched the meaning of appeasement and its evolution, nothing has been said of its origins. What explains France's escalating passivity its resigned responses to Hitler's challenges? The answer may be found as surely in the rich soil of Britain as in the fields of France.

The seed was sewn in the spring of 1919. French Premier Georges Clemenceau, supported by President Raymond Poincaré and the allied commander, Marshal Ferdinand Foch, resolved to protect France against a German revival. Mindful of the costs associated with the German invasion of 1914, the government had two objectives. One was reparation for the damages to the country's infrastructure and its civilian population, especially the tens of thousands left widowed and orphaned.[5] The other was insurance against a repeat cataclysm. To that end, all envisaged permanent allied control of the strategic Rhine bridgeheads, while some dreamt of a semi-autonomous Rhenish state carved out of Germany. In short, they were already convinced that, once recovered, the Germans would seek revenge – unless the defences they faced were too formidable or the penalties they risked too forbidding.

Britain's Prime Minister, David Lloyd George, and the American President, Woodrow Wilson, had other convictions. Excising German territory for the sake of French security, or contemplating a permanent foreign presence on German soil, would be counter-productive. Either would entrench German hostility and make another war more likely. To avert catastrophe they offered Clemenceau something in return for a concession on the Rhineland. Together they would defend France against future aggression – although Lloyd George quickly made Britain's commitment contingent upon congressional approval of Wilson's pledge.[6] The deal died within a year. Wilson's guarantee treaty was rejected in Washington, physically lost in a congressional office, mentally lost in the controversy over his insistence on saddling the treaty with the body eventually known as the League of Nations.[7] With it went the British guarantee. The French had exchanged a secure hold on the Rhineland for promises that proved chimerical.

The collapse of those guarantees proved symptomatic of the disarray in the post-war Anglo-French 'alliance'. Indeed, the tensions that had arisen during the conference only multiplied. London and Paris quarreled over whether Germany was honouring its reparations and disarmament obligations. They quarreled over the Near East, adopting opposite sides over Turk and Greek interests at the Straits, theatre command issues, the Armenians, the fate of Syria and Mesopotamian oil. They quarreled over the balance of power in Eastern Europe, appropriate responses to the Bolsheviks and their civil war opponents, the cartographic contours of Upper Silesia and the already threatening geopolitical mire of German–Czech–Polish relations.[8]

Even before France's parliament ratified the Versailles treaty, the semi-official *Le Temps* claimed British sympathy for Germany's straightened financial condition owed much to the disappearance of German sea-power. 'Suspicion of British policy ... is now prevalent,' the ambassador reported from Paris, while his French counterpart remarked on the exceptional intensity of Anglo-French disagreements.[9] In March 1920, the former *rapporteur* on the German treaty warned of an 'alliance crisis'. America had not ratified the Versailles treaty and the solemn pledge to French security had disappeared. Conversely, the deputy added, France's closest 'ally' in Europe – Britain – had reduced its commitments by one, and added the bonus of a vanished German naval threat. 'What did England get? Gentlemen, England got her security.'[10]

Such was the context within twelve months of the completed peace treaty. America had forsaken it. Germany seemed determined to violate it. And with the German navy *hors de combat*, its air force banned, its army size-restricted to the defence of its own borders and Anglo-German commercial relations recovering, Britain had freed itself of a momentary commitment to defend France. True, others were more receptive. A Franco-Belgian accord initiated a series between France and other countries whose security depended on the 1919 settlement. That such accords surfaced in the dual wakes of Anglo-American broken promises and intense Anglo-French differences was hardly surprising. Indeed, even while the Franco-Belgian negotiations were underway, another nasty *contretemps* erupted. In April 1920, German domestic unrest prompted the Weimar government to send more troops into the Ruhr valley than the treaty permitted. Paris and Brussels responded with military occupations of Frankfurt and Darmstadt – to which London responded with outrage.[11] Recalling Germany's latest violations of her disarmament and reparations obligations, Premier Alexandre Millerand asked pointedly when England would show impatience. 'When would it say to Germany: enough? If it won't say so, then France must.'[12]

But candour produced no harmony, a condition confirmed by heated exchanges at conferences in San Remo, Brussels and Spa. Lloyd George worried that Germany would be destabilized by too stringent treaty enforcement, especially future incursions on German soil. Millerand worried about German dilatory tactics and 'lies'. That discordance, together with unresolved differences over Eastern Europe, the Near East mandates and oil, generated what the London embassy called 'a spectacle of extraordinary incoherence', a spectacle lit up by Lloyd George's incendiary reference to the French as 'Shylocks'.[13] And while he also stressed the durability of the Anglo-French alliance, that assurance sounded hollow to the French knowing what they had forfeited on the Rhine in 1919. From Paris, it seemed that Britain intended to recapture its pre-war 'splendid isolation'. An exchange in the House of Commons on 16 November 1920 confirmed that the government regarded the failed American pledge with relief and declined to reaffirm its own.[14] By then the French government, fully aware of British detachment, was negotiating a security accord with Poland, the newest recruit for an eventual defence of France. In the third week of February 1921 those two countries concluded a mutual assistance agreement and a supplementary military convention.

Given the host of Franco-British aggravations, the Franco-Polish alliance proved but another irritant, especially as an Upper Silesian crisis erupted in the spring of 1921. Seen from London, the French were unreasonably hostile to Germany's regional interests and sympathetic to those of Warsaw. Seen from Paris, British opinion had been deliberately turned against the Poles and the British Foreign Secretary, Lord Curzon, driven by personal 'hatred' for Poland. Indeed, he even threatened the break-up of what he occasionally did call the French 'alliance', a threat Ambassador Saint-Aulaire considered 'puerile' but which his ministry took more seriously.[15] Lloyd George also threatened. By siding with Poland, France was not only 'absolutely wrong' but risked creating an eastern Alsace-Lorraine – a development certain to delay a new guarantee of French security.[16] In response, one Quai d'Orsay official observed:

> By instinct England maintains the policy she has always pursued across the ages … which consists of opposing the number one power on the continent, in combination with number two. France now appears to her as the first power, and therefore it is natural to oppose us in concert with Germany, and thus to claim the role of willing mediator.

That strategy, he added, meant not only discouraging France from forceful responses to German treaty violations, but actively encouraging enough friction to impede Franco-German efforts at economic collaboration.[17]

Further proof of Anglo-French *malaise* came three months later at the Washington Naval Disarmament Conference. In a dispatch home, Lord Balfour, head of the British delegation, summarized the latest French complaints: exclusion from the opening negotiations during which British, American and Japanese delegates awarded France an inferior ratio of capital ships; Anglo-American pressure to reduce French land armaments, despite his own admission that France 'has not been given secure frontiers, in the absence of which guarantees had been promised, but not given'; and Anglo-American pressure to reduce the French air force. As for French plans for a significant submarine fleet – a force of some import to Britain – it was obvious to Balfour, if spectacularly misleading to anyone better informed, that submarines 'represented a far greater threat to our security than did our capital ships to an almost *self-supporting country* like France [author's emphasis]'.[18] In short, given the theoretically disarmed condition of Germany, the most direct threat to Britain's security came from France, whether by air or under-seas, while the greatest indirect threat to Europe's peace was from impulsive acts by France, the continent's largest land force. Indeed, British opinion had become so hostile, the French ambassador reported in January 1922, that 'we are almost unanimously regarded as the worst enemy of England and of humanity'.[19]

The French found this mystifying, given their unwavering commitment to restoring the war-time alliance. They had already reduced their military service from three years to two, and were approaching the goal of eighteen months – all at a time when England betrayed unlimited patience for German treaty violations. At Washington, France reluctantly agreed to a capital ship tonnage that was half her original target – a tonnage negotiated in her absence and without acknowledgement that there had been no capital ship construction since 1914 and that her metropolitan and colonial coastal perimeters equaled those of the United States.[20] Reworded, despite the aborted guarantees of 1919, France was expected to accelerate her disarmament on land and to accept key naval and air concessions. Indeed, the subject of those guarantees kept resurfacing. Aristide Briand purposely recalled them in November 1921, as did Albert Sarraut in December. Unless other governments pledged assistance to France, 'they have no right to impose limits on our armaments'.[21]

While the basic issue of security guarantees remained intractable, by early 1922 some differences of detail had developed. In December 1921, while reaffirming France's fidelity to the current *mésentente cordiale*, Ambassador Saint-Aulaire grew aggressive. The old guarantee of unilateral assistance now seemed 'unacceptable, even humiliating'. *Reciprocal* pledges would be more consistent with France's national honour by liberating her from the robes of mendicant. They would also remind both countries that either might fall first victim of aggression. Moreover, the original wording of '*unprovoked* aggression' needed rethinking – partly because the idea that France would ever provoke conflict was offensive in itself, and partly because the phrase under-estimated German capacity for duplicity. Troubling too was the earlier expression '*direct* aggression', for Germany would never repeat the mistake of 1914 by attacking France directly. An attack on a weaker opponent was far more probable, for instance France's principal post-1919 ally, Poland. That eventuality, he noted, had not been foreseen in the original guarantee of 1919.[22]

That *démarche* pleased a British government rhetorically committed to France as an ally, but intent on avoiding alliance. Now, the French themselves had raised the spectre of a war triggered by their commitments to Eastern Europe. Curzon and Lloyd George reacted quickly. The trouble spots of Eastern Europe, the Prime Minister told Briand at Cannes, made such a revised guarantee too risky. This observation was endorsed by one Foreign Office historian. Precedent permitted guarantees against aggression on the Rhine or through Belgium, but military assistance to Eastern Europe would be a dangerous innovation. That, at least, was 'one reason why it is impossible now to satisfy the demands of our French allies.'[23]

Whatever the other reasons, 1922 saw little improvement in Anglo-French relations, and no progress on security guarantees, unilateral or reciprocal. Curzon found some of the French ideas dangerously 'ambiguous' and calculated 'to frighten the Germans'. He even accused Paris of inspiring an Anglophobic press campaign of 'deliberate misrepresentations' and of accusing Britain of France's own double-dealing – namely searching for an 'excuse' for moving apart. As for Balfour, fresh from Washington, he had a list of obstacles to a new security pact, all 'largely owing to the attitude of the French Government'.[24] The French countered with two strategies. Saint-Aulaire kept reminding Whitehall of the price France had paid in 1919 for the British guarantee – 'without getting it' – and kept pushing for a new pact. His minister, Raymond Poincaré, feigned indifference. Attempts to invigorate an old pledge in fresh language had only produced 'mystification'. Since Britain had no choice but to intervene in the event of an attack on Belgium or France, he was 'absolutely indifferent as to whether there was a pact or not'.[25]

In fact, nothing could disguise the tensions within the 'alliance', one prime source of which was Germany's ongoing violations of her reparations obligations. In December 1922 a Foreign Office official predicted that France was 'going to upset our applecart' by forceful action. That presentiment was shared by Sir John Bradbury, Britain's principal delegate on the International Reparations Commission, who had 'an underlying feeling' that he and his French counterpart were 'traveling towards a breaking-point'.[26] He was right. In January the Commission ruled Germany in violation of her commitments and a Franco-Belgian military force moved into the Ruhr to force the resumption of payments. Bradbury refrained from supporting the ruling, and his government condemned the action. Unsurprisingly, in Britain and America the most reliably anti-French presses resumed their condemnation of French pig-headedness, militarism and imperialism.

The Ruhr crisis of 1923 is sufficiently known to permit brevity.[27] It represented the most independent French action of the inter-war period against German violation of the Treaty of Versailles, and it was roundly attacked in Britain. At least it was until June 1924, when 'the joyous tidings' arrived that

Premier Poincaré had been replaced by the apparently more conciliatory Edouard Herriot, whose administration soon agreed to withdraw French troops.[28] Before departing, however, Poincaré had done one more thing to irritate the British government. Vilified as obdurate and reckless – largely for ignoring British counsels of restraint – he had compounded his Ruhr offence by assuming another commitment in Eastern Europe, though one calculated to further the security of France. In January 1924, through an exchange of letters with the Czech Premier Edouard Benes, he had concluded the Franco-Czechoslovak Treaty of alliance and friendship. As with the Belgian and Polish accords, this treaty provided for ongoing contact between general staffs and for the preparation of 'concerted plans to stave off an aggression against one of the two countries by a common enemy'.[29]

But there was no comparable movement on the Anglo-French front. Throughout 1924 attention shifted from the elusive bilateral accord to a less familiar, if equally elusive, multilateral security protocol under the League of Nations. For a time some thought a British pledge to France might be resurrected within this broader convention, but that too proved unworkable. By the spring of 1926, Whitehall was exasperated by French attempts to keep the idea alive – long after it 'had been publicly, if not peremptorily, rejected by His Majesty's Government'.[30] In its place, it had agreed to the multilateral Locarno accords of October 1925, the key feature of which was an Anglo-Italian guarantee of the Franco-German–Belgian borders. Though a lesser version of the defunct pledge of 1919 (because it denied a unique relationship with France) the undertaking of 1925 was as far as the British government would ever commit to the defence of France until the eve of the next war. In that sense the breakthrough was limited, for it was seen in London as 'the end of a problem, rather than the beginning of a military commitment'.[31] Certainly it did not dissuade France from extending its circle of anti-revisionist friends in Eastern Europe, including Romania by a treaty of June 1926 and Yugoslavia in November 1927.

It is fair to say, however, that the Anglo-French crisis precipitated by the Ruhr occupation did recede with the more conciliatory approaches pursued between 1924 and 1930, first by Herriot and subsequently by Aristide Briand. Until then, London had commonly cast the French Republic as the villain of the post-war era: too rigid about enforcing reparations, too ready to use force, and for a country with Europe's largest army and air force, too disposed to exaggerate the German danger and too little inclined to disarm. Mindful of Anglo-French tensions, Herriot had struggled to make French policy more compatible with the expectations of France's most important wartime partner. It was, one might say, the real beginning of French appeasement policy in the pleasing sense of that word, although Herriot, like his predecessors, really would have preferred an alliance with teeth, and although Briand fretted that while 'appeasement' made sense, the French frontier defences were 'almost negligible'.[32]

On the surface, conciliatory rhetoric prevailed, but surface lustre betrayed more gilt than gold. The Weimar government continued its surreptitious rearmament, despite international monitoring efforts, and the French government invested millions in a frontier defence network – proof that suspicions of German perfidy still flourished. Nor was all well between Gauls and Britons. Even a reputed Francophile like Sir Austen Chamberlain was attuned to difference. The 'Latin mind', he conceded, 'was more logical than ours, and was inclined to always press arguments ... to their logical conclusion. It was our nature', he added, 'to shun these logical conclusions' in favour of what he called a 'middle course'.[33] By late 1929 the embassy in Paris acknowledged that Britain was seen to be resuming its habit of acting independently, 'apart from France'. And before the end of 1930 the Committee of Imperial Defence was studying how Britain could apply economic pressures on *France* in the event of war.[34]

Admittedly, this was a conventional exercise in contingency planning, applied even to a presumed ally. Friendships fluctuated in international politics, but the island's security remained dependent on the Channel's air and sea space. In a curious way, however, that appreciation reflected all that had happened since 1919. British analysts reckoned that the next war would never start with a French attack on Germany. By 1930, French military strategy was based on the principle of a two-stage war, the first of which would be defensive in character: fixed fortifications backed up by mobile land and air units. The second, delayed by as long as two years, would mark the launch of a massive war-winning offensive. No thought was given to a quick victory. Rather, the commitment was to a long war of attrition in which off-field economic and financial resources would prove as critical as guns and ammunition. The reasoning derived both from on-going calculations of Franco-German resource differentials and from the near-miss experience of the First World War. Drawing from that experience, France could only win such a conflict if allies had sufficient time to contribute manpower, material and especially money.

Demographically, France's population was increasing by less than a million births annually, compared to nearly two million German births. By 1922, the number of French births versus deaths was in the order of 70,000, compared to a German figure of 500,000, a differential that helped explain France's comparative population deficit of 23 million.[35] There were other vulnerabilities, all of them obvious to the authors of the 1930 report, even if they exploded Balfour's notion of a 'self-supporting' France. Ironically, for a nation that foresaw victory only at the end of a long war, France had to import virtually all of her oil, rubber, nickel, copper, manganese and cotton, and most of her lead, pyrites and coke – raw materials on which her automotive, armaments, aircraft and shipbuilding industries depended, to say nothing of the metallurgical industries (iron ore, pig iron, steel) so heavily concentrated near the German border. Moreover, just under two-thirds of those imports – including oil – were carried in foreign ships, a dependency almost as great when it came to revenue-generating exports.[36] Given such constraints, successive governments refused to risk war without advance assurance that they could access the resources of Britain and her Empire. Only then could advantage be taken of Germany's own critical resource deficits – iron ore, rubber, oil, bauxite, copper and nickel – deficits, which made her vulnerable to a war of attrition waged by a coalition of economically and financially superior allies. This die had been cast by the mid-1920s, on the eve of decisions to invest a fortune in frontier fortifications, and it had been cast partly in response to the blood-letting offensives of the previous war, and partly from an appreciation of what material resources were needed to wage a successful, protracted war.

The 1930s did nothing to alter French security concerns, beginning as they did with a global Depression and the advent of Adolf Hitler to power. While the reparations issue lost much of its sting, thanks to more forgiving payment schedules and President Hoover's moratorium on allied debt repayments, the thorny matter of international disarmament remained. For years preceding the Disarmament Conference of 1932 there had been intense debate between those who saw disarmament as prologue to security and those who saw security guarantees as prologue to disarmament. The Anglo-Americans – with water between them and any European aggressor – backed the first formula. The French backed the second, thereby nourishing Anglo-Saxon prejudices that Paris was the capital of recalcitrance. What was needed, one American Francophile complained, was a book on how France had been betrayed by the breaking of the 'solemn covenant' of 1919.[37]

The disarmament issue thus reinforced notions that France was blind to the consequences of keeping Germany 'down'. British Prime Minister Ramsay MacDonald, whose preferred word for the French was 'self-centered', held them responsible for the stalemate.[38] Sir Robert Vansittart, Permanent Under-Secretary in the Foreign Office and at heart a Francophile, also railed against French governments that had lived 'in a totally unreal world of judicial technicality' and were thus 'greatly responsible for the advent of Hitlerism'.[39] As if on cue, in October 1933 Hitler announced Germany's withdrawal from the Conference, allegedly because of French stonewalling. Predictably, some London observers recharged their disenchantment with France and their sympathy for Germany, despite War Office reports on German arms violations, a Foreign Office admission that German strength was 'more than twice the Treaty figure' and an embassy description of French behaviour as 'pacifist, not militarist, born of fear not of pride'. Ambassador Tyrrell insisted that France had 'persevered in the disarmament discussions' had conceded the principle of arms equality with Germany, and had only taken 'a firm stand … after Germany … left the conference'.[40]

Six months later, in April 1934, the French government of Gaston Doumergue took another stand. Since 1920, France had cut military service by two-thirds, the number of divisions by half and the number of standing effectives by a quarter.[41] It had no desire to kill the Conference, but until collective security guarantees were in place it could not commit to further reductions. In the interim, it would explore new security pacts with countries anxious about German re-armament. While some Whitehall quarters resumed their grumbling, condemning French intransigence, others were more insightful. From Paris, Ronald Campbell insisted that France had acted in 'the complete absence of the militarist spirit'. The problem was that Great Britain 'is never likely to offer the only form of security which would be of any real avail ... I think that France ... has ceased to look to us for any immediate help, and that ... she is returning to a consciousness of her own strength and of the support which her allies can afford her'.[42]

In fact, Campbell had anticipated new French efforts to recruit Russian assistance and to construct a Franco-Italian rapprochement. It fell to Pierre Laval to complete negotiations for a mutual assistance pact with the USSR early in 1935 and for a virtual alliance with Italy – one that included provisions for immediate staff talks. These initiatives, one British analyst acknowledged, demonstrated that Germany's accelerating potential for aggression was forcing France to abandon the practice of 'reducing her strength annually' and to intensify her search for allies – even if it meant upsetting London by fashioning a system 'independent of Great Britain'.[43] As Orme Sargent remarked, the French were turning to Russia 'having failed to obtain any further guarantee [of] "security" from us' and fully aware that 'such an alliance would shock and offend Great Britain'. Since it was still 'out of the question' that Britain would promise military co-operation, London's only option to prevent such an alliance was by exercising 'judicious pressure'.[44]

Although the War Office still thought the French were exaggerating German land strength, and while Foreign Secretary Sir John Simon still promoted 'appeasement in Europe', by mid-1934 the Air Ministry was alive to a German air threat. An assault on London now seemed thinkable, a civilian target softer than French fortifications, mention of which reminded air analysts that without French assistance 'this country might find herself at a desperate disadvantage in a single-handed war with Germany'.[45] Nevertheless, in early 1935 Stanley Baldwin's government reacted cautiously to French proposals for a multilateral air defence pact and flatly rejected proposals for staff talks. While the Prime Minister himself dreamt of a future when 'I should not have to meet French statesmen any more', others had deeper concerns.[46] Some still feared that any pact would contain the seed of 'direct alliance' and that talks would multiply into plans for an entire 'defensive zone, and the protection of this zone, and on and on'. Some even ventured that if such an air pact proved but a disguised attempt to pressure Germany, Britain should 'threaten' France and then approach Germany 'to see what terms we could get'.[47]

Such thinking found new expression. The turning point was the spring of 1935 when Hitler announced the return to conscription and the rebirth of the *Luftwaffe*. In response, London promptly began negotiating limits on the growth of the German navy. Determined 'to avoid publicity', on 28 March Simon instructed that nothing be said to the Russians 'about our intention to hold naval conversations with the Germans'. Not until 13 June did he tell Corbin about the imminence of a treaty and – in a spectacular blend of candour and dishonesty – he claimed that 'on no account did we wish to appear to be making a separate treaty'. No one was fooled. Two days later, Secretary-General Alexis Léger responded 'with great frankness'. Hopes of an agreement limiting land weapons had been dashed by the bilateral Anglo-German naval agreement, for it was clear that France had been 'sacrificed on the altar of British egoism'. Premier Laval, too, claimed the accord had left 'a deplorable impression' in France. 'Why', he asked, 'should not other Powers now deal separately with Germany?'[48]

Anglo-French tensions were clearly worsening even before a crisis in East Africa erupted. Angered by recent Gallic criticism, some Foreign Office officials thought the French needed disciplining. Ralph Wigram warned against being 'too tender on the French', especially given their 'unfair' attacks on Britain, and he mused about threatening them with a separate Anglo-German air pact. Vansittart, who still regarded France as 'our chief eventual support', advised 'playing on the French fundamental desire not to alienate *us*, rather than by taking a line which might alienate *them*'. For his part, Foreign Secretary Sir Samuel Hoare was fascinated by Laval's 'cunning peasant mind', a forgivable condition had it not reminded him of Lloyd George 'with his incessant desire to ... deal behind everyone else's back'.[49]

But once the Ethiopian conflict erupted, Anglo-French relations suffered further. With Britain's Mediterranean interests threatened by Italy's campaign against Ethiopia, British apprehensions about French reliability rose in perfect tandem with renewed enthusiasm for France as potential ally – including her ability to bomb northern Italy.[50] Conversely, French military officials wanted to strengthen their 'alliance' with Italy and recommended 'strict neutrality' in the event of war. Although British aid was essential to a long war with Germany, Italy could provide immediate assistance against an attack across the Rhine – a geographic reference accompanied by explicit reference to the broken British pledge of 1919. Sixteen years after the still-born British guarantee, that grievance remained: Clemenceau had made concessions on the Rhine, but England 'had not kept its promise'.[51] Their colleagues in naval headquarters also urged the government to avoid this 'conflit Italo-Britannique', while Premier Laval acknowledged the 'deep malaise' between Paris and London.[52]

London officials agreed. Long offended by perceived French truculence, they were now worried by its absence – a worry fed by rumours of a budding Franco-German rapprochement and by the admission that 'it is clearly in France's interests ... to reduce her commitments and gradually abandon her position as leader and guarantor of the anti-German bloc in Europe'. Still, it was a qualified admission, for a caveat added that 'we do expect to be kept informed' – an expectation reflecting an old belief that France was largely responsible for post-war turbulence. Because she had been 'foolishly anti-revisionist ... we lost one opportunity after another of coming to terms with Germany', an opinion endorsed by Vansittart, who recalled French 'feebleness and duplicity' and their lack of 'guts either to repudiate or act up to the League'.[53] New rumours from

Paris fanned the flames. One suggested that Laval would settle with Germany, then delight in announcing the agreement as a retort to the Anglo-German naval deal. The truth was, Wigram ventured, Laval was 'not merely a crook but a clever crook' who knew 'how to look after the interest of France extremely well'.[54]

Ultimately that meant pursuing the elusive alliance with Britain. Again and again, French military and civilian leaders returned to the *mésentente* from which they could not risk escape. General Maxime Weygand, army Chief of Staff, believed co-operation with England was indispensable. The Premier agreed, as did members of his cabinet and the *Haut Comité Militaire*. In December 1935, at the height of Anglo-Italian tension, Laval publicly affirmed that France stood with Britain. Anglo-French cooperation was essential to European security.[55] Nevertheless, anxious not to gut the anti-German potential of the 'alliance' with Italy, the government rejected thoughts of strikes against Italian territory. Indeed, sniffed one British official, the French seemed determined 'to avoid any action which would entail retaliatory measures against France itself'. For its part, while the Baldwin government thought it prudent to continue naval talks with the French, it still rejected French feelers about air or army staff conversations.[56] France was to be kept within its grasp, but at arm's length.

Were further proof needed, it came early in March 1936 when Hitler sent troops into the demilitarized Rhineland. Overshadowing the action's legal significance, however, were its strategic implications. If occupation led to the installation of German fortifications, France's ability to pressure Hitler would be compromised. As General Maurice Gamelin forecast, Rhenish fortifications could seal the fate of France's allies in Eastern Europe – a prospect which some in London found pleasing.[57] Less appealing was the observation that a remilitarized Rhineland could support an attack in the west, possibly against Belgium. Unless Britain were to join in the latter's defence, Gamelin mused, France might abandon its plan to rescue that kingdom in favour of defending its own frontier. In which case, 'Belgium would be the biggest loser, England second, and France only third.'[58]

Yet not even this spectre inspired new thoughts in London. The staff talks that followed the German coup – talks partly induced by French musings about Belgian vulnerability – proved a sham.[59] The British Chiefs of Staff judged the talks 'of little practical value' other than to expose the 'extreme weakness of France'. Accordingly, 'Staff conversations should cease.'[60] One official complained the failure was due to the inability 'to get anything positive out of the French'. Another clucked at 'the old selfish French military interest in using Belgium as a fighting ground for the protection of France', while another insisted that Britain was actually 'entitled ... to exercise a definite control over [French] policy in the East of Europe'. Even sympathizers admitted that 'our French friends are really difficult to understand.'[61]

While the Rhineland affair forced Britain to re-commit to the Locarno accords and through them to the defence of France, the commitment lacked conviction. Though the French refusal to act militarily in March 1936 did come as a relief to London, it also fanned doubts about the readiness of their armed forces and the inner strength of their leadership. Far from proving militarist and imperialist – original sins at the creation of 1919 – they now appeared passive and compliant. Indeed, Neville Chamberlain judged them predisposed 'by a phenomenon of Nature' to collapse under pressure.[62] So it is that the Rhineland 'crisis' is often seen as a turning point. Not only was it, allegedly, the last time that Hitler could have been stopped without a major war, but it demonstrated that French appeasement had changed its stripes. No longer a Locarno-like concept based on positive initiatives, it had become conflict avoidance by inertia.

Why was obvious. Since 1919 French governments had agreed that the only kind of war France could win was a long war of attrition. Therein lay Clemenceau's decision to swap Rhineland for Anglo-American guarantees. Thereafter, British governments understood the concept, understood Britain's primacy within that concept, and therefore French dependence on her and her Empire. They knew that sixty per cent of French imports came by ship, that nearly seventy-five per cent of French imports and exports were carried in foreign flagged ships and that forty-five per cent of those vessels were British owned. They knew that they supplied nearly a third of France's coal and coke imports; that British India provided a third of her manganese requirements and virtually all of her jute; that two-thirds of her crude rubber and forty per cent of her tin came from British Malaya and that over half of her raw wool came from Australia and New Zealand.[63] That is why Vansittart said the French had to realize that they needed Britain more than Britain needed France. Such was the state of mind that prevailed between the Rhineland episode and those of Austria and Czechoslovakia in 1938. In that interim, the British government did little to reaffirm its commitment to French security, and less toward joint planning.

Denied of assured support from London, the French Republic faced other intractable problems. One of them was Belgium. In March 1936, rattled by the revival of its German neighbour, the Belgian government announced its return to the pre-1914 policy of neutrality. Since 1920 years of joint planning had projected the prompt arrival of French troops to shore up Belgian defences against a German attack, not out of emotional kinship with the Belgians, but to avoid another war on French soil.[64] The March announcement compromised that strategy, for it raised the possibility that Belgium would not call for assistance in time to halt a German advance. Such an eventuality would leave France vulnerable along the northern stretches of their common frontier where her fixed defences were least developed.

The loss of a Western ally was aggravated by one in the south. The Franco-Italian accord had been regarded by the French high command as a veritable alliance. Italy's military strength – especially on sea and in the air – together with her proximity to France-associated Yugoslavia represented a potential barrier to Germany's south-eastward expansion. But that too proved ephemeral. The short-lived Stresa front – a potential coalition of France, Italy and Britain – had dissolved during 1935–6 with Mussolini's invasion of Ethiopia and armed intervention in the Spanish Civil War. Both actions were condemned by a succession of left-of-centre Popular Front regimes in Paris that governed between 1936 and 1938. Fascist Italy gravitated toward Germany's embrace, a trajectory detected by French intelligence as early as June 1936. Henceforth, Rome regarded France as a likely adversary and was effectively in Hitler's camp.[65]

Unsurprisingly, the French government began to reconsider the viability of Soviet support. The pact of mutual assistance was intact, the Red Army and Air Forces were large and the country's resource base immense. Stalin's regime had pushed for staff talks and coordinated planning, but had done so while carefully extolling collective security through the League of Nations. Distrust, however, inspired by ideological difference and some ugly realities of Soviet domestic practice, left French diplomats and strategists on edge. Given Moscow's long indulgence in anti-capitalist rhetoric and its perceived efforts to undermine capitalist regimes world-wide, it required considerable leaps of faith to accept at face value Soviet paeans to the collective security of *all* League members. Even on the military front there were doubts about the fighting capacity of Soviet forces, which – thanks to political purges – had lost a high percentage of their senior officer corps. Hence some regarded the Red Army as '*une belle façade*' and predicted its contribution in a war to be 'almost zero'.[66] Whether these were ideology-informed assessments or impartial observations confirmed by ideology, out of the brume floated the greatest spectre of them all – a fear that by urging resistance to Fascism, Stalin desired an internecine capitalist war from which he would remain aloof until it was time to destroy the exhausted victor. Thus, however alarmed they were by Germany's resurgence, French statesmen were wary – perhaps wrongly – of embracing the Russian bear.[67]

Wary, too, was the British government about embracing France through new staff talks. Not until late 1938 – following the Czech crisis – was there a shift in thinking. Until then there were three constants. Firstly, expanded conversations risked alienating Germany and/or Italy and entrapping Britain in France's web of Eastern alliances. In February 1938 the Admiralty said 'no' to more staff talks. In June, the Air Staff proscribed the use of 'ally' and 'allied' in conversations with the French. In November the Foreign Office learned that while no progress had been made toward joint naval 'dispositions and operations', it was 'doubtful' that progress mattered. Secondly, as for a land expedition to the continent, detailed planning had been avoided for fear it 'would commit us to a part in the French plan'. The Royal Air force agreed, preferring no conversations beyond the service attachés, and wishing no increase in contact lest it 'let us in for more definite commitments than we ought ... to accept'.[68] Thirdly, all were clear on what was expected of France, including the positioning of her battleships, cruisers and submarines to contain the Italian navy, the deployment of her destroyers in the Channel and the Atlantic ports and, possibly, the assumption of 'a larger responsibility in the Mediterranean' if the situation in the Far East required a strengthening of British forces there, although, it seemed advisable not to raise that possibility with the French for the time being.[69]

Not that France could be left to its own devices for, as Lord Halifax put it during the Czech crisis, 'most of our ills during the past twenty years must be ascribed to excessive deference to French policy'. Now, there was only one way out of the dilemma created by France's commitment to Czechoslovakia. The Czechs, with French help, had to 'realize the necessity of making drastic concessions to the German minority'. That way Hitler might be satisfied, there would be no attack and France would be off the hook. And lest the French failed to realize the gravity of the situation, he cautioned them in March, April, May and twice in September 1938 that they could not count on Britain to go to war for the Czechs – although on the latter occasion he finally did warn Berlin that should conflict occur, 'Britain could not stand aside'.[70] As for Britain's own security, the influential Sir Maurice Hankey urged the government to press for an extension of French fortifications between Lille and the sea. 'We do not want the German Army making a dash for the Channel Ports.'[71]

Mostly, however, British approaches were not case specific. In the most elemental sense, they simply wanted to ensure that the French Republic would act in Britain's best interests. It is in that context that some actually argued for more cooperation with France, because it would help 'influence those features of her policy which are objectionable, and thus achieve what we desire'. As another wrote, 'if we can keep them persuaded of our frankness, we are more likely to be able to keep them [on] ... the straight path'.[72] After the sobering, near-war experience of the autumn, however, such optimism was wearing thin. In a remarkable minute of 17 October 1938, Orme Sargent reflected on past and future:

> Till now we have always claimed and indeed exercised the right to intervene actively in the problems of Europe ... whenever we felt it desirable to do so. For this purpose we have collaborated with the French – or to put it crudely we have used the French army and the French system of alliances as one of the instruments with which to exert our authority on the continent ... [W]e have used France as a shield, behind which we have maintained ourselves in Europe since our disarmament.

Now, he continued, 'with France more or less isolated and without continental allies her Europe policy is likely to be...passive rather than active'. And that could mean two things. Britain might be reprieved from the nagging issue of staff talks and the thornier one of an expeditionary force, but in the event of confrontation with Germany or Italy 'we will do well not to make our calculations on the assumption ... [of] French support'.[73]

Indeed, there was evidence that French compliance was not inexhaustible. Long before the Munich crisis of September 1938 Ambassador Corbin had defended French attempts to 'create a core of resistance' in Eastern Europe. Failure to do so, he observed, meant the Western democracies would simply watch the smaller countries gravitate toward the Rome–Berlin Axis. Foreign Minister Yvon Delbos agreed. If France allowed the destruction of Czechoslovakia, she would forfeit her status as a first-class power.[74] In March 1938 Corbin had urged a joint warning to Hitler to let Czechoslovakia be, hoping that this might prevent France from being 'dragged into war' for the sake of the Czechs. In April Premier Daladier had urged resistance, emphasizing that continued conquests in Eastern Europe would deliver all the raw materials Hitler needed to undermine Western assumptions about a long war. Because, ultimately, he acquiesced to an 'ally' indispensable to that strategy, commentators have often overlooked his sustained resistance to Neville Chamberlain, his insistence that Czech concessions be kept 'reasonable', his argument for warning that the west would not tolerate 'the dismemberment' of Czechoslovakia or the violation of the 'rights of independent peoples'.[75]

But resistance proved futile. For the following five months the British government badgered the French to pressure the Czechs. Without sufficient concessions to the Sudeten Germans inside Czechoslovakia, an unappeased Hitler would unleash the Wehrmacht, France would be honour-bound to intervene and a general war would result. Sir Eric Phipps, Britain's ambassador in Paris, was pleased to think that Daladier and Foreign Minister Georges Bonnet had lost their nerve – a condition which he had nurtured – and dismissed any Frenchmen inclined to risk war as 'corrupt' members of a 'mad and criminal war party'.[76] He was wrong, too, about Daladier, who was visibly angry when he learned on 14 September that Chamberlain would meet Hitler the following day, the more so because he himself had declined a similar opportunity without a British representative being present.[77] And that anger endured, with Daladier resisting Chamberlain's belief that appeasement would end the threat of war, with him insisting – against British objections – that a redefined Czech state should have as its birthright an Anglo-French guarantee of safety, and with him demanding serious Anglo-French staff talks.[78] But en route to the final September crisis at Munich, where the Czech state was auctioned off as the price of peace, the Premier accepted the status of backseat passenger in a vehicle driven by Chamberlain.[79]

Unlike Chamberlain's smiling return, Daladier's was sullen. He dismissed his cheering compatriots as fools. They appeared to care little for the Czechs, for France's honour or the humiliation he had endured as the fourth man at Hitler's table. Stung by this public display of French weakness, he resolved to fight. Not only was French rearmament accelerated, but there would be a more robust approach toward Britain.[80] Within two weeks of Munich, French intelligence began warning of German designs on Belgium and Holland and adding ominously that France might stand aside – a threat partly endorsed by Orme Sargent, who anticipated 'a definite isolationist tinge' in French policy, and by Halifax, who feared France might turn 'defeatist'.[81] Those Paris-generated rumours of German action in the West continued from November 1938 to

April 1939, rumours projecting land operations against the Low Countries and sea and air attacks on Britain.[82] Indeed, by the end of 1938, a bizarre argument had erupted over which country Hitler had chosen to be his first victim. Despite efforts to heighten British anxieties, the French claimed pride of place for themselves. Not to be outdone, even as victim, Chamberlain insisted that Britain was Hitler's primary target. Still, there was no meeting of minds. In December his Cabinet refused to extend the scope of staff talks with France, lest any extension 'involve us in a definite commitment...'[83] That, Vansittart argued, was a mistake.

> This is how the French see things. They fight on land, where casualties will be greatest, while we are on the sea and in the air, where casualties will be lighter. They are given responsibility for the Western Mediterranean, while we look after our interests in the Far East. And we concentrate on aerial fighters to protect ourselves rather than on bombers that could act in the land campaign. So they are bitter.[84]

Some remained unmoved. As late as 6 February 1939, the British Chiefs of Staff were arguing that closer contacts 'might provoke precipitate action' from Hitler. But others were less certain. On that very day, Chamberlain assured parliament that 'any threat to the vital interests of France ... must evoke the immediate co-operation of the United Kingdom', and one week later, in a reiteration of Anglo-French solidarity, his government committed itself to an Allied war effort should Germany attack Holland or Switzerland.[85]

The stakes rose with German action against the rump Czech state on 15 March 1939. The British government now sought to convince the French that it had relocated its backbone. It 'was now a question of checking German aggression, whether against France, or Great Britain, or Holland, or Switzerland, or Romania, or Poland, or Yugoslavia, or wherever it might be'. And a week after that stunning assurance, the government proposed a joint guarantee of Polish and Romanian security.[86]

The rediscovery of British resolve came as sequel to post-Munich hardening in Paris, not as prologue. Daladier was sick of appeasement in any language. Anglo-French diplomatic exchanges in those six months testify to his intentions. Let the British finally confront the threat of an attack in the West, whether against the Lowlands or themselves. Let them wonder whether France would defend Belgium and Holland. Emphasize that 'French military authorities do not consider that France is now in a position to defend herself ... without military assistance from the United Kingdom'. Insist that 'if we do not resist now ... Herr Hitler will obtain world dominion'.[87] Ensure that Chamberlain finally understands that his strategy of saving the peace through French concessions to Mussolini are doomed to failure. Italy was already in the German camp and only saw France as 'a rich uncle who is taking too long to die'.[88] Conversely, underscore the fact that the Franco-Soviet pact remains a constant in French foreign policy, that Russia has a role to play 'in this work of mutual assistance' and that negotiations with Moscow have to be expedited.[89] It is in the light of such declarations – each communicated by the embassy in Paris – that Ambassador Corbin in London attributed to French leadership the stiffening of British policy.[90]

However one assigns credit for this post-Munich resolve, the fact was that there had been a change of heart since Hitler's two-step conquest of Czechoslovakia. The guarantee to Poland was in place, rearmament was at full speed, and both the scope and the level of Anglo-French staff talks were being extended. By mid-May 1939 conversations were underway about the defence of 'Allied territory' in the Far East, Middle East and Africa. In June 1939 Britain's Joint-Planning Sub-Committee proclaimed the following: 'It is upon France that the main burden of defence in the west against both Germany and Italy will fall. If France fails, it would be impossible to bring the war to a satisfactory conclusion. Furthermore, in the Mediterranean, the Atlantic and the Far East, France is our chief ally.'[91]

There was less certainty about Stalin's Russia, a state of mind which explained why British negotiators – heedless of French complaints – pursued the conversations with 'great slowness' and a determination to avoid precise commitments. Such wariness, reflective of a lingering ideological distrust of the Communists, proved to be central to the tortuous unfolding of the Anglo-French-Soviet conversations of August 1939 and, on 23 August, behind a cynical bargain between Hitler and Stalin. One week later Germany attacked Poland and Britain and France were at war. This was not without irony: the guarantee that Britain had withdrawn from France in 1919 – lest it contribute uncertainly to war – had been revived in the form of their joint guarantee to a war that was certain.

Thus ended the second edition of French appeasement, an edition featuring inertia, acquiescence and un-reimbursed concessions. It was not laudable, and it comprised a string of French failures: to extract German reparations and preserve a demilitarized Rhineland, to keep Germany disarmed and her neighbours safe. Failures they were, each leading to the second greatest, the failure to preserve peace. And when one adds the greatest – namely the collapse of 1940 – little wonder that 'appeasement' has acquired the ugliness of a four-letter word, or that the Third Republic has laboured ever since under the rhetorical burdens of 'hapless', 'incompetent', 'gutless' and 'defeatist'.

This study has approached French appeasement from a less-familiar direction. Few of the 'facts' recorded here will be reckoned 'new' by veterans of the British and French archives or those conversant with recent literature. Even interpretively, this paper has had worthy predecessors.[92] What is different is the way the data have been contextualized: partly by framing French appeasement of the 1930s within the entire sweep of post-1919 Anglo-French relations, and partly by emphasizing the indelible mark of the broken pledge of 1919. Unless the 'facts' are wrong, or appear unfairly marshaled, there are grounds for wondering what French leadership could have done to prevent the return of war or to prepare diplomatically for waging it. Fewer are the grounds for wondering why they behaved as they did. They simply could not face another Franco-German war without the potentially war-winning resources of Britain and her Empire.

No one then or since has ever accused Edouard Daladier of being too aggressive or – recalling complaints from the 1920s – too obstructionist. On the contrary, he and Georges Bonnet have been routinely pilloried for being weak and compliant, the very qualities that have given French 'appeasement' a bad name. As for the soldiers who advised them, the corps of professionals slurred in the 1920s by the epithet 'militarist' – what had become of them? Since Hitler's advent, their chief sin was said to be indecisiveness, a quality befitting the runts of litters sired by war-time commanders like Ferdinand Foch or Joseph Joffre. Such shifts in caricature – from implacably aggressive to implacably passive – are difficult to explain without weighing the obvious. Viewed from the Thames, the French could never get it quite right, which is to say that in the eyes of British administrations, France was really at the heart of the 'German problem' – a perspective that has earned a hallowed place in much inter-war historiography.[93] Too rigid when Britain urged flexibility, too compliant when she urged firmness, the French were accused of exaggerating national security concerns by governments at a distance that steadfastly refused to allay those concerns. On the contrary, those accusers – American as well as British – contributed to a stream of willfully unfair portraits of the French as *provocateurs* on reparations, *imposteurs* on disarmament, *défauteurs* on debts and, depending on moment and mood, either *trop durs* or *trop mous* on the overall German threat.

Speaking of fairness, all governments are entrusted to defend the interests of their constituency. The British government is not faulted here for being single-minded in the pursuit of its interests. But by persisting in its refusal to assuage French security concerns, that persistence ultimately compromised Britain's own national interests. Certainly many have concluded that British appeasement policy, especially in the 1930s, at the very least misled Hitler and thus inadvertently encouraged his expansionist ambitions. It might also be said that Britain's limitless patience toward German treaty violations in the 1920s actually provoked independent, if counter-productive, French actions in Rhineland and Ruhr. And in the 1930s the British backlash against previous French actions, together with Chamberlain's ramped-up appeasement policy and the iron imperatives of a long-war strategy, all encouraged French acquiescence – a response that proved tragically ineffectual in the face of the dictators. The intention here is not to exonerate France for its inter-war role by blaming Britain. Both became victims of a war they had sought by different means to prevent. But neither is it fair to ask the French to carry more than their share of responsibility for the breakdown of the 1919 peace settlement and the return of war twenty years later.

Notes

1   R. Young, *France and the Origins of the Second World War*. London, 1996.

2   Recent examples include J. Charmley, *Chamberlain and the Lost Peace*. Chicago, 1989; R. Cockett, *Twilight of Truth: Chamberlain, Appeasement and the Manipulation of the Press*. London, 1989; D. Dutton, *Neville Chamberlain*. London, 2001; E. Goldstein, 'Neville Chamberlain, the British Official Mind and the Munich Crisis', *Diplomacy and Statecraft* 10, no. 2 (1999), pp. 276–92; R.A.C. Parker, *Chamberlain and Appeasement*. New York, 1993; F. McDonough, *Neville Chamberlain, Appeasement and the British Road to War*. Manchester, 1998.

3   Notably Elisabeth du Réau, *Edouard Daladier, 1884-1970*. Paris, 1993.

4   Young, *France and the Origins of the Second World War*, p. 145; M. Alexander, 'After Dunkirk: The French Army's Performance against "Case Red", 25 May to 25 June 1940', *War in History*, 14 (2007), pp. 219–64.

5   R. Young, 'Out of the Ashes: The American Press and France's Postwar Recovery in the 1920s', *Historical Reflections* vol. 28, no. 1 (Spring 2002), pp. 51–72.

6   Chamber of Deputies, *Archives Nationales* (hereafter AN) C7773; Louis Barthou, *Le Traité de Paix*. Bibliothèque Charpentier, 1919; K. Morgan, 'Lloyd George and Clemenceau' in A. Capet (ed.), *Britain, France and the Entente Cordiale Since 1904*. London, 2006, pp. 28–40.

7   See W. Keylor, 'France's Futile Quest for American Military Protection, 1919–22' in M. Petricioli (ed.), *Une Occasion Manquée? 1922*. Bern, 1995, pp. 61–80; 'The Rise and Demise of the Franco-American Guarantee Pact, 1919–1921' in *Proceedings, Western Society for French History* vol. 15 (1988), pp. 367–77; A. Lentin, 'Lloyd George, Clemenceau and the Elusive Anglo-French Guarantee Treaty' in A. Sharp and G. Stone (eds), *Anglo-French Relations in the Twentieth Century*. New York, 2000, pp. 104–19.

8   See J. Bariéty, 'Le projet de pacte Franco-Britannique, 1920–1922', *Revue d'Histoire Moderne et Contemporaine (RHMC)* no. 193 (September 1999), p. 89.

9   Grahame (Paris) to Curzon 30 August 1919, *British Documents on Foreign Affairs* (hereafter *BDOFA*) 2, F. Europe, vol. 16, p. 36; 10 September, ibid., pp. 45–6; Cambon to Paris 29 February 1920, *Documents Diplomatiques Français* (hereafter *DDF*), 1920, vol. 1, no. 185, p. 267.

10 *Journal Officiel*, Deputies, Debates, 25 March 1920, p. 716.

11 R. Gibson, *Best of Enemies: Anglo-French Relations Since the Norman Conquest*. London, 1995, pp. 248–50.

12 French Note, 9 April 1920, *DDF*, 1920, vol. 1, no. 357, pp. 502–4; Chantal Metzger, 'L'Allemagne un danger pour la France en 1920?' *RHMC* no. 193 (September 1999), pp. 5–22.

13 Lloyd George–Millerand talks, *DDF*, 1920, vol. 1, no. 382, pp. 534–40; Memo (de Fleuriau) 26 July 1920, ibid., vol. 2, no. 251, pp. 317–24.

14 De Fleuriau to Paris 20 October 1920, ibid.,1920, vol. 3, no. 85, p. 123; Louis Barthou, 'Quelques raisons internationales de la nécessité de l'Union nationale', *Les Annales* 24 October 1920; Leygues to Cambon (London) 25 October 1920, *DDF*, 1920, vol. 3, no. 115, pp. 168–9; *Le Figaro* 17 November 1920; *Le Temps* 18 November 1920.

15 Saint-Aulaire to Paris, 14 May 1921, *DDF*, 1921, vol. 1, no. 382, pp. 605–6; 24 May, ibid., no. 411, pp. 650 1; Berthelot to London, 26 July, ibid., vol. 2, no. 63, pp. 96–8.

16 Note (Berthelot), 7 August 1921, *DDF*, 1921, vol. 2, no. 86, pp. 142–3.

17 Note (Seydoux), 1 August 1921, *DDF*, 1921, vol. 2, no. 76, pp. 122–8.

18 Balfour to Curzon, 1 December 1921, *BDOFA*, 2, C. North America, vol. 9, p. 25; 17 December, ibid., pp. 68–9; 28 December, ibid., pp. 83–5; A. Barros, 'Disarmament as a Weapon', *Journal of Strategic Studies* vol. 29, no. 2 (April 2006), pp. 301–22.

19 Saint-Aulaire to Briand, 4 January 1922, *DDF*, 1922, vol. 1, no. 12, p. 23; E. Goldstein, 'The Evolution of British Strategy for the Washington Conference, 1921–1922' in E. Goldstein and J. Maurer (eds), *Naval Rivalry, East Asian Stability and the Road to Pearl Harbour*. London, 1994, pp. 8–10.

20 Elise Jusserand to Helen Garfield, 10 January 1922, Library of Congress, James Garfield Papers, Box 115. See also my *An American by Degrees: The Extraordinary Lives of French Ambassador Jules Jusserand*. Montreal, 2009.

21 Unidentified press clipping, 21 November 1921, *Ministère des Affaires Etrangères* (hereafter MAE) Nantes, Ambassade (Washington), 652, '*Conférence de Washington*'; Balfour to Curzon, 17 December 1921, *BDOFA*, 2, C. North America, vol. 9, pp. 68–9.

22 Saint-Aulaire to Briand 14 December 1921, *DDF*, 1921, vol. 2, no. 454, pp. 719–31.

23 Note (Seydoux), 26 December 1921, *DDF*, 1921, vol. 2, no. 486, pp. 780–2; Résumé, 8 January 1922, ibid., 1922, vol. 1, no. 26, pp. 52–4; Hardinge to Curzon 13 January 1922, *DBOFA*, 2, F. Europe, vol. 17, pp. 1–2; 'Memorandum', 17 January 1922, *DBOFA*, 2, F. Europe, vol. 17, pp. 13–18.

24 Curzon to Hardinge 28 January 1922, *DBOFA*, 2, F. Europe, vol. 17, pp. 20–3; 21 February, ibid., p. 26; Balfour to Hardinge 13 June, ibid., p. 29.

25 Saint-Aulaire to Poincaré 19 March 1922, *DDF*, 1922, vol. 1, no. 212, p. 379; Hardinge to Balfour 16 June 1922, *DBOFA*, 2, F. Europe, vol. 17, p. 30. For these discussions, see Alan Sharp, 'Anglo-French Relations from Versailles to Locarno, 1919–1925' in Sharp and Stone (eds), *Anglo-French Relations*, pp. 126–8.

26 Minute (Wigram) on Hardinge, National Archives, Kew (hereafter NA), F0371, 7486, C14431/99/18; Bradbury letter of 13 October, sent 23 October, Treasury to F0, ibid., C14509/99/18.

27 See E. O'Riordan, *Britain and the Ruhr Crisis*. London, 2001; C. Fischer, *The Ruhr Crisis, 1923–1924*. Oxford, 2003.

28 Sir Eric Phipps subsequently recalled 'the incredibly foolish mistakes' of Poincaré's successors. Phipps (Paris) to Chamberlain 16 September 1926, *DBOFA*, 2, F. Europe, vol. 18, p. 169.

29 P. Wandycz, *The Twilight of French Eastern Alliances 1926–36*. Princeton, 1988, p. 484.

30 Chamberlain to Crewe (Paris), 28 May 1926, *DBOFA*, 2, J. League of Nations, vol. 3, pp. 217–18; See Peter Jackson, 'France and the Problems of Security and International Disarmament', *Journal of Strategic Studies* 29, no. 2 (April 2006), pp. 247–80.

31 R. and I. Tombs, *That Sweet Enemy*. New York, 2007, p. 519.

32 Phipps to Chamberlain 15 December 1926, *DBOFA*, 2, F. Europe, vol. 18, p. 174.

33 Chamberlain to Crewe, 4 June 1925, *DBOFA*, 2, J. League of Nations, vol. 1, pp. 1–3. For his distrust of Germany, see D. Dutton, *Austen Chamberlain*. New Brunswick, 1987, pp. 248, 264.

34 Report on France (1929), 9 January 1930, *BDOFA*, 2, F. Europe, vol. 19, pp. 191–4; CID (Plans) August 1930, NA, Cab 47, 4, 9737, 64 pp.

35 Louis Barthou, 'Les Espérances Françaises', *Revue Hebdomadaire* (February 1924), pp. 131–58.

36 Committee of Imperial Defence(hereafter CID) August 1930, NA, Cab 47, 4, 9737, p. 11; R. Young, 'La Guerre de Longue Durée' in A. Preston (ed.), *General Staffs and Diplomacy Before the Second World War*. London, 1978, pp. 41–64.

37 *New York Times* article by Edwin L. James, reported by Jules Henry 16 September 1930, MAE, Series B, 358, pp. 257–8; William Guthrie to Jusserand 18 February 1932, MAE, Jusserand Papers, AP/093/91/Guthrie, pp. 296–300.

38 M. Pereboom, *Democracies at the Turning Point*. New York, 1995, pp. 72, 109, 177. See also C. Kitching, 'The Search for Disarmament' in Sharp and Stone (eds), *Anglo-French Relations*, pp. 158–79.

39 Minute (Vansittart) on Campbell to F0, NA, F0371, 16712, C10759/285/18. See also C. J. Kitching, *Britain and the Geneva Disarmament Conference*. London, 2001.

40 War Office to F0 9 August 1933, NA, F0371, 16708, C7930/245/18; Minute (Wigram) 11 November, ibid., 16710, C9893/245/18; Tyrrell to F0 19 August, ibid., 17290, W9367/1/17; Tyrrell to F0 12 January 1934, ibid., 17660, C317/317/17.

41 Memorandum (Ambassador Corbin) 17 March 1934, *Service Historique de l'Armée de Terre* (hereafter SHAT), 2N19, dr. 2.

42 Campbell to F0 30 April 1934, *Documents on British Foreign Policy* (hereafter DBFP), 2nd series, vol. 6, no. 415, pp. 681–2.

43 Major Reeve to Wigram 30 May 1935, NA, F0371, 19943, C4413/55/18; Clerk to F0 20 June 1934, *DBFP*, 2nd series, vol. 6, no. 463, p. 765.

44 Memorandum by Sargent 28 January 1935, NA, F0371, 18825, C962/55/18. For earlier Paris–Moscow contacts, see David Watson, 'The Franco-Soviet Negotiations of 1924–27' in G. Johnson (ed.), *Locarno Revisited*. London, 2004, pp. 108–20.

45   Simon to Phipps (Berlin) 12 March 1935, NA, F0371, 18829, C1995/55/18; Director of Military Intelligence to F0 5 July 1934, NA, WO 190/262; Memo (Chief of Air Staff) 11 July, NA, Cab 53/24. Chiefs of Staff, 344.

46   N. Rostow, *Anglo-French Relations, 1934–36*. London, 1984, p. 247.

47   Paris Embassy to F0 25 January 1935, NA, F0371, 18824, C655/55/18; 'Notes ...' 1 February 1935, ibid., 18825, C972/55/18.

48   Simon to Eden 28 March 1935, NA, F0371, 18832, C2598/55/18; Simon to Clerk (Paris) 1 April, ibid., 18833, C2797/55/18; Memorandum (Simon) 13 June, ibid., 18846, C4746/55/18; Clerk to F0, ibid., C4725/55/18; Clerk 21 June, ibid., C4902/55/18. See also P.M.H. Bell, *France and Britain, 1900–1940*. London, 1996, pp. 184–90.

49   Minute (Wigram) on Clerk to F0, 8 July 1935, NA, F0371, 18793, C5313/33/17; minute (Vansittart) on Clerk to F0, 29 July, ibid., 18849, C5700/55/18; Hoare to Wigram, 14 September, NA, F0800, 295-Hoare Papers.

50   See Minutes, 11 September 1935, Sub-Committee on Defence Policy, NA, F0371, 19198, J4971/386//1; Instructions to Air Delegation, 7 December, NA, Cab 21, FA/G/13, 420. See also K. Neilson, 'The Defence Requirements Sub-Committee, British Strategic Foreign Policy, Neville Chamberlain and the Path to Appeasement', *English Historical Review* vol. 118, no. 477 (June 2003), pp. 651–84.

51   2e Bureau notes of 9 September 1935, *SHAT*, 5N 579, d.3; 2 October, *SHAT*, 7N 2520; 8 October, ibid.

52   Naval Command note 21 October 1925, *Service Historique de la Marine* (hereafter SHM) 1BB8, 602, #5; Laval to Rome embassy, 9 November, AN, Daladier Papers, 1DA6, Dr4, sdr a.; R. Ulrich-Pier, 'Un modèle réduit des relations Franco-Britanniques: l'année 1935', *Relations Internationales* no.117 (Spring 2004), pp. 55–69.

53   Minute (Sargent) on Phipps to F0, 25 October 1935, NA, F0371, 18816, C7266/7/18; minute (Wigram) on Clerk, 7 November, ibid., 18816, C7465/7/18; minute (Vansittart) on Clerk, 19 November, ibid., 18794, C7717/33/17.

54   Clerk to F0, 25 November 1935, ibid., C7853/33/17; minute (Wigram) on Clerk, 10 December, ibid.,19168, J9145/1/1.

55   Study commission report, 14 April 1934, *DDF*, 1e, 6, no. 93, pp. 220–37; Campbell to F0, 30 April 1934, *DBFP* 2nd series, vol. 6, no. 416, p. 685; Clerk to Simon, 14 June, ibid., no. 455, p. 754; minutes of *Haut Comité Militaire*, SHAT, 2N19, dr.3; *Journal Officiel*, Deputies, 17 December 1935, pp. 2647, 2801. See also R. Davis, 'Le Débat sur l' "Appeasement"', *RHMC* 45 (October–December 1998), pp. 822–36.

56   Air Vice-Marshal Courtney to F0, 10 January 1936, NA, F0371, 20159, J515/15/1; Minutes of 14 January, Sub-Committee on Defence Policy and Requirements, ibid.

57   *Haut Comité Militaire*, 18 January 1936, SHM, 1BB8 602, d9; Memorandum by Lord Cranborne, 17 March 1936, NA, F0800-Cranborne, 296.

58   Clerk to Eden 21 March 1936, NA, F0371, 19896, C2203/4/18; and 31 October, ibid., 19872, C7762/172/17.

59   Flandin to the Chamber of Deputies 20 March 1936, *Journal Officiel*, pp. 1063–5; Yvon Delbos, 4 December, ibid., p. 3328.

60   Chiefs of Staff Sub-Committee, 1 April 1936, NA, Cab 53/27, and of 21 July, F0371, 19919, C5356/4/18, and 29 October, Cab 24, Confidential Print, 296 (36), 265; Minute (Naval Director, Plans) on attaché (Paris) to Admiralty, ADM, 116/3379.

61   Minute (Eden) on Clerk to F0, 8 June 1936, NA, F0371, 19877, C4140/3511/17; Ovey (Brussels) to F0, ibid., 19913, C7115/4/18; minute (Sargent) 29 January 1937, ibid., 21136, R501/26/67; D. Dutton, *Anthony Eden*, London, 1997, pp. 68–9.

62   Dutton, *Neville Chamberlain*, p.165.

63   Industrial Intelligence Centre 16 January 1939, NA, F0371, 22916. pp. 28, 40, 45.

64   Marshal Pétain to the *Conseil Supérieur de la Guerre*, 17 December 1926: 'la défense de la frontière du Nord consiste donc seulement à chercher une ligne d'arrêt en Belgique'. AN, Daladier Papers, 4DA1, dr 2, sdr-a/.

65   2e Bureau reports, 12 June 1936, *SHAT*, 7N 2521; 2 October, ibid., 7N 2927, d.1; April 1937, ibid., 7N2350.

66   Schweissguth Mémento 8 October 1936, AN 351, Schweissguth Papers, AP3 dr.10.
67   For a more sanguine reading of Soviet policy see M. Carley, *1939: The Alliance that Never Was.* Chicago, 1999.
68   Cabinet Conclusions, 16 February 1938, NA, F0371, 21653, C1206/37/18; Director of Operations Intelligence to Colyer (Paris), 15 June, NA, Air 2/2952-55; Col. F.B. Webb (CID) to Strang, 18 November, NA, F0371, 21592, C14287/13/17.
69   Webb (CID) to Strang (FO), NA, F0371, 21592, C14613/13/17.
70   M. Dockrill, *British Establishment Perspectives on France, 1936–40.* London, 1999, p. 14. Halifax to Phipps, 23 March 1938, *DBFP* 3rd series, vol. 1, no. 108, pp. 85–8; 11 April, ibid., no. 135, pp. 140–3; 22 May, ibid., no. 271, pp. 346–7; 9 September, ibid., vol. 2, no. 814, pp. 275–7; 12 September, ibid., no. 843, p. 303; Halifax to Kirkpatrick (Berlin), 9 September, ibid., no. 815, p. 278.
71   Hankey to Chamberlain 28 April 1938, NA, Cab 21, 554, 14/5/13.
72   Naval attaché (Paris) to FO, 26 October 1937, NA, F0371, 20687, C7348/18/17; Campbell (Paris) to Sargent 11 August 1938, ibid., 21592, C8578/13/17.
73   Minute (Sargent) on Phipps to Halifax, 12 October 1938, NA, F0371, 21612, C12161/1050/17.
74   Record of Conversation with Corbin 5 February 1937, NA, F0371, 21136, R838/26/67; Memorandum on Eden-Delbos talk 15 May 1937, ibid., 20702, C3620/532/62.
75   Corbin to FO, 3 March 1938, NA, F0371, 22313, R2095/137/3; 'Munich' by Edouard Daladier, AN, Daladier Papers, 2DA1 Dr5, p.41; Anglo-French Conversations 28–29 April, *DBFP* 3rd series, vol. 1, no. 164, pp. 214–31.
76   Phipps to Halifax 24 September 1938, *DBFP* 3rd series, vol. 2, no. 1076, p. 510; Phipps to Chamberlain 30 September, Churchill Archives Centre, Sir Eric Phipps Papers, 1, 3/1; J. Herman, *The Paris Embassy of Sir Eric Phipps.* Brighton, 1998.
77   Phipps to Halifax 14 September 1938, *DBFP* 3rd series, vol. 2, no. 883, p. 329.
78   R. Young, 'A.J.P. Taylor and the Problem with France' in G. Martel (ed.), *The Origins of the Second World War Reconsidered.* London, 1999, p. 105.
79   See M. Thomas, 'France and the Czechoslovak Crisis' in I. Lukes and E. Goldstein (eds), *The Munich Crisis, 1938: Prelude to World War II.* London, 1999, pp. 122–59; E. Goldstein, 'Neville Chamberlain and the Munich Crisis' in ibid., pp. 276–92. For Daladier as appeaser see G. Stone, 'From Entente to Alliance: Anglo-French Relations, 1935–1939' in Sharp and Stone (eds), *Anglo-French Relations,* pp. 191–9 and A. Adamthwaite, *Grandeur and Misery.* London, 1995, pp. 208–23.
80   Philippe Garraud, 'La politique Française de réarmament de 1936 à 1940', *Guerres mondiales et conflits contemporains* no. 220 (2005), pp. 97–113.
81   Phipps to Halifax 12 October 1938, NA, F0371, 21785, C12144/11169/18, including Sargent's minute of 21 October; Halifax to Phipps 1 November, Phipps Papers, I, 1/21.
82   Minutes of air talks 16 November 1938, NA, Air 2/3081; Enclosure from military attaché, Phipps to Halifax 30 December, *DBFP* 3ed series, vol. 3, no. 509, pp. 556–7; 7 January 1939, NA, F0371, 22922, C345/281/17; 29 January, *DBFP* 3rd series, vol. 4, no. 51, pp. 49–50; see also French note, undated but between February and April, *'Conditions générales d'une offensive allemande',* NA, Air 9/95.
83   Anglo-French Conversations 24 November 1938, *DBFP,* 3rd series, vol. 3, no. 325, pp. 285–311; Minutes of CID meeting, 1 December, NA, F0371, 21597, C15514/36/17.
84   Minute (Vansittart) to Halifax, 19 December 1938, NA, F0371, 22922, C358/281/17.
85   Chiefs of Staff Sub-Committee, 6 February 1939, NA, F0371, 22922, C1545/28/17; Phipps to Halifax, 14 February, ibid., C1930/28/17.
86   Halifax's comments, 21 March 1939, Anglo-French Conversations, *DBFP* 3rd series, vol. 4, no. 458, pp. 422–7; Corbin to Bonnet 28 March, *DDF,* 2e, vol. 15, no. 176, pp. 241–2. See also Peter Jackson, 'France and the Guarantee to Romania', *Intelligence and National Security* vol. 10, no. 2 (April 1995), pp. 242–72.
87   Strang to CID, 12 January 1939, NA, Cab 21, 555, 14/15/18; Phipps to Halifax, 18 March, NA, F0371, 22912, C3377/90/17.
88   Chamberlain's pressure on France to appease Italy extended from mid-March to the end of May 1939. See in particular the Anglo-French meeting 20 May 1939, AN, Daladier Papers, 2DA6, Dr3.

89   Phipps to Halifax 11 May 1939, NA, F0371, 22912, C6995/90/17; Corbin to Halifax 16 May, *DBFP* 3rd series, vol. 5, no. 531, pp. 569–70; Bonnet to Corbin 6 and 19 July, AN, Daladier Papers, 2DA6, Dr5; and Bonnet to Halifax 19 July, ibid.

90   Corbin to Bonnet 4 April 1939, *DDF*, 2e, vol. 15, no. 253, pp. 378–85. For France's post-Munich adjustments see T. Imlay, *Facing the Second World War*. Oxford, 2003; and P. Jackson, *France and the Nazi Menace*. Oxford, 2000.

91   Note by Ismay 12 May 1939, NA, ADM 116/3767; 'Relative Strategical Importance of Countries', 22 June, NA, CAB 54/6.

92   See R. Boyce, *British Capitalism at the Crossroads 1919–1932*. Cambridge, 1987; R. Boyce, *The Great Interwar Crisis and the Collapse of Globalization*. London, 2009; J. Cairns, 'A Nation of Shopkeepers in Search of Suitable France, 1919–40', *American Historical Review* vol. 79, no. 3 (June 1974), pp. 710–43; P. Finney (ed.), *The Origins of the Second World War*. London, 1997, p. 17; M. Thomas, *Britain, France and Appeasement: Anglo-French Relations in the Popular Front Era*. Oxford, 1996.

93   Speaking of characterization, see Jean Guiffan, *Histoire de l'anglophobie en France*. Paris, 2004; Marc Vion, *Perfide Albion! Douce Angleterre?* Saint-Cyr-sur-Loire, 2002.

Chapter 15

Politics, Strategy and Economics: A Comparative Analysis of British and French 'Appeasement'

Talbot Imlay

As previous chapters have already shown, few subjects in 20th-century international history have been more closely examined than the policy of appeasement. This chapter seeks not to overturn this familiar story, but rather to suggest that it is incomplete – that it omits important aspects of what happened. It does so in two principal ways. One is by examining France as well as Britain. Although a considerable specialist literature exists on French policy during the 1930s, appeasement is still too often treated as simply a British or Anglo-German affair.[1] The neglect of France is unfortunate, not only because the latter was a major actor in its own right, but also because at times it exerted considerable influence on British policy. The second way this chapter seeks to complicate the familiar story of appeasement is by considering and comparing several aspects of British and French policy: strategic, political and economic. As will be shown here, British and French responses to the international crises were not always co-ordinated or coherent.

Although no consensual definition of the term exists, for the purposes of this examination strategy encompasses the way in which countries conceive of waging and winning a war. In the French case, the strategy for a war in Europe centered on the principle of a long conflict – *'une guerre de longue durée'*.[2] Drawing lessons from 1914–18, French planners assumed that neither side would be able to achieve a rapid victory in a future conflict. This meant that the French would avoid costly and futile offensives at the beginning of the war. Instead, they would husband their strength by remaining on the defensive behind fixed fortifications. Given France's demographic and industrial inferiority *vis-à-vis* Germany, the need for allies was self-evident, which in the first instance meant Britain. French planners judged Britain's economic, industrial, financial and eventually military strength to be essential for victory in a lengthy war. At the same time, at the start of a war Britain would help to wear Germany down by waging economic warfare, principally by blockade. But while indispensable, a British alliance alone was not enough. Throughout the inter-war period the French also sought allies in Eastern Europe who, much as Russia had done during 1914–17, would constitute a second (eastern) military front against Germany. In addition to forcing the Germans to disperse their military power, thereby avoiding its concentration in the West against France, an eastern front would help contain the growth of Germany's political and economic influence in the resource-rich region of Eastern and Central Europe. By limiting Germany's access to these resources (oil, metals, agriculture, etc.), the French hoped to reduce significantly Germany's ability to sustain a lengthy war.[3]

A fundamental strategic problem for the French was that the simultaneous pursuit of a British alliance and an eastern front proved self-defeating for much of the 1930s. Although a variety of reasons prompted French decision makers to 'appease' Germany after 1933, prominent among them was the absence of British support for a firmer policy.[4] For the French, appeasement constituted in part a stratagem to win over the British by demonstrating the ultimate futility of negotiating with Germany. But if so, the price was heavy: the undermining of a potential eastern front. Because French planners excluded the option of a genuine military alliance with the Soviet Union on ideological grounds, this left the smaller states of Eastern Europe to act as the chief buffer against German aggression. During the 1920s, France had developed political and military ties with Romania, Yugoslavia, Poland and Czechoslovakia, forming a grouping known as the Little Entente. If the grouping was always less coherent than its moniker suggested, the course of events during the 1930s further helped to dissolve it into its component parts. In particular, Germany's remilitarization of the Rhineland in 1936, followed by the *Anschluss* with Austria in 1939 and then Munich, sapped confidence in France's ability and willingness to defend its Eastern European allies. By the end of 1938, with what remained of Czechoslovakia at Berlin's mercy and with Poland, Romania and Yugoslavia united only in their mistrust of Paris, France possessed no reliable ally in Eastern Europe. An eastern front against Germany was a chimera.[5]

It was at this moment that British policy began to shift. Partly under pressure from the French, who manipulated fears in London that the Germans might launch a sudden offensive in Western Europe and that France might retreat inwards, leaving Germany free to wreak havoc throughout Europe, the British offered a firm military commitment to Paris in early February 1938. Soon afterwards, the British added meat to the bones of this budding Anglo-French alliance by introducing conscription, a move viewed in Paris as evidence that the British had finally accepted a 'continental commitment' – the need to send a sizeable army to Europe in a war.[6] Yet while certainly welcome, a British alliance was no substitute for a second front in Eastern Europe. Nor was Poland, which quickly emerged as Germany's next intended victim. French and British planners rightly placed little stock in Poland's ability to repel a German attack on its own. Since Paris and London possessed neither the intention nor the means to offer direct military help to the Poles, let alone of embarking on meaningful offensive operations in the West to relief pressure on the Polish army, the French had to look elsewhere for an eastern front. And given the lack of alternatives, this could only mean the Soviet Union. Accordingly, by spring 1939, French political and military leaders all agreed on the need for a Soviet alliance. Some, such as Foreign Minister Georges Bonnet, reasoned in diplomatic terms of deterring Germany, while others, notably General Maurice Gamelin, France's military chief, thought more in terms of creating a militarily viable eastern front. But whatever the precise calculation, French strategy during the spring and summer of 1939 focused increasingly on creating an eastern front centered on the Soviet Union. As Premier Édouard Daladier confided in July to the staff officer in charge of the French delegation to the military talks in Moscow: 'Hitler would hesitate [to] wage a two-front war – if he provokes one, it is very likely that he would lose it – thus make every effort [on your part] – considerable stake in an agreement with the USSR.'[7]

The pursuit of a Soviet alliance, however, would prove frustrating. One problem was Poland's reluctance to ally with Moscow, a reluctance rooted in profound suspicions of Soviet aims. But Warsaw's reservations did not unduly impress the French, who, convinced that Moscow must be won over whatever the price, were more than willing to sign a deal over the heads of the Poles. The real difficulty came from the Soviet side. Although scholarly debate continues on Soviet policy in the spring–summer of 1939, and is explored in a later chapter, it seems clear that Stalin recognized his strong bargaining position vis-à-vis the French (and British) and fully intended to profit from it.[8] Whatever might have been the situation earlier, the Soviets had no need to be accommodating – hence Moscow's hard-bargaining tactics. Still more to the point, once Germany entered the race for a Soviet alliance, French hopes for a deal with Moscow all but vanished. This was not so much because, in a liberal democratic regime, a French government could not easily acquiesce to Soviet demands, particularly for territorial expansion into Eastern Europe. Desperate as they were, the French appeared willing to offer a great deal to Moscow.[9] Germany, however, could provide the one thing that France could not: peace. If, as seemed increasingly likely, Germany invaded Poland, an anti-German alliance with France meant a Soviet–German war in Eastern Europe. Indeed, for the French, this was the whole point of an eastern front. For the Soviets, by contrast, an agreement with Germany bought them time, not to mention a sizeable amount of real estate. That Stalin jumped at this agreement is hardly surprising. But that the French convinced themselves that the Soviets could be won over underscores France's desperate strategic situation in 1939. Put simply, the French faced an imminent war with Germany without an eastern front – that is to say, without a central element of their long-war strategy.

Whereas French strategy focused on a future war against Germany, the aim of British strategy for much of the 1930s was to avoid a European war. The burdens of a global empire had much to do with this: it was facing simultaneous challenges from Japan in the Far East, Fascist Italy in the Mediterranean and Nazi Germany in Europe. British planners feared that the outbreak of war in one region would encourage opportunistic action at Britain's expense in the others. But perhaps no less important were the bitter recollections of trench warfare in 1914–18, which, as Michael Howard observed, fuelled the belief that 'never again' should a large British army be sent to the continent.[10] For the

Chiefs of Staff, this dangerous situation dictated diplomatic efforts to reduce the number of Britain's potential enemies. Fully sharing a repugnance for European warfare, Chamberlain as Prime Minister chose to concentrate on coming to agreement with Germany and, to a lesser extent, with Italy. But this repugnance did not influence British diplomacy alone – it also helped to shape the composition of the country's military forces. Under the rubric of 'limited liability', the priority in rearmament during much of the 1930s went to the navy, whose task it was to safeguard the seaways to and from the British isles and to impose a blockade on the enemy. Next came the air force: operating mainly from British bases, the RAF's bomber force would provide a deterrent while its fighter force (and, more generally, Britain's developing air defence system) would protect British cities and industries from enemy attack. Equally important, in the event of a European war, the bomber force in theory offered an offensive weapon, thereby eliminating the need for an expeditionary force. Last in line came the army, which was deliberately starved of resources.[11] During the Czechs crisis, Chamberlain could honestly (and conveniently) tell the French that in a war Britain could send no more than two under-equipped divisions and one hundred and twenty aircraft to the continent – a contribution the French military attaché soon afterwards aptly described as 'miniscule'.[12]

The growing likelihood of war, however, quickly revealed the hollowness of British strategic thinking. The idea that the British alone could determine the nature and extent of their military contribution to a common war effort assumed that future allies would need Britain more than Britain needed them. Yet this was not necessarily the case with France, whose army would be indispensable to the British in a European war. Thus as the evidence of Nazi Germany's continued territorial ambitions mounted in the wake of Munich, the British found themselves forced to reaffirm their alliance with the French. Interestingly, British army staff officers contributed to this process by intriguing with their French counterparts to exaggerate fears of a German attack in the West. Recognizing that Britain would have to despatch a sizeable army to the continent, these officers sought to overturn 'limited liability' by driving home to their political superiors the indispensability of France. Only by committing Britain more solidly to a French alliance, the army staff now argued, could the government be sure that France would actively resist further German expansion in Europe. This stratagem scored a notable success in April 1939 with the introduction of conscription – and, by implication, the promise of an expanded BEF.[13] But if British staff officers succeeded in undermining the principles of 'limited liability', the task of expanding the British army and preparing it for continental warfare would require considerable time. In the meantime, if war came sooner rather than later, the British would initially have little to offer their French ally.

The BEF's miniscule size ensured that Britain would be the junior partner in the developing Anglo-French alliance, particularly when it came to strategy. To some extent, this subordination mattered little: during staff talks in 1939 British and French planners agreed on the need to refrain from offensive operations against Germany during the opening stages of the war and, more generally, on the broad contours of a long-war strategy aimed at gradually wearing Germany down. Only much later, at some unspecified future date, the Allies would take the offensive and win the war. Yet Britain's status as a junior partner also meant that it was vulnerable to French influence in the strategic realm. More to the point, this vulnerability quickly became apparent over the issue of relations with Moscow. Profoundly mistrustful of the Soviets, Chamberlain recoiled at the prospect of an alliance with Moscow. Nevertheless, he was forced to seek an agreement, largely under pressure from the Chiefs of Staff, who were themselves increasingly convinced by French arguments concerning an eastern front. To be sure, the British never pursued the Soviets with the same desperation as the French, yet equally noteworthy is the distance that British policy travelled after Munich from rejecting any co-operation with Moscow to admitting the potential value of a Soviet alliance, and thus of the need to make concessions. Equally significant, British planners began to share French doubts about the soundness of the long-war strategy and its principle that time was an ally. One reason was a sharpening awareness of Britain's own long-term weaknesses, most notably in financial terms; but another reason was the ambiguity surrounding assessments of Germany's purported political and economic vulnerabilities. Here, moreover, eastern-front thinking played an important role. To British as well as French planners, the claim that the Germans could not sustain a long war depended in large part on denying Germany access to external resources, whether these be raw materials, manufactured goods (including military equipment) or manpower. Yet if the Germans succeeded in extending their hold over Central and Eastern Europe, either alone or in collaboration with the Soviets, Germany might grow stronger rather than weaker over time. And with the Nazi–Soviet Pact in August 1939 this fearful scenario suddenly became very real.

At the beginning of the war Anglo-French strategy was in shambles. Having ruled out a short war, Britain and France would wage a long war; yet without an eastern front, their prospects in a such war appeared increasingly dubious. The result would be a dangerous radicalization of military planning as French and British planners desperately sought some means to strike a decisive blow against Germany before it became too powerful.[14]

In assessing French and British responses to the growing possibility of war, developments in the domestic political realm are no less important than those in the strategic realm. Most obviously, whatever the policy chosen, each government required the backing of solid parliamentary majorities. Without such backing, they lacked both the authority and legitimacy to pursue their policy choice with the confidence and determination needed for success. However, the domestic realm also merits study because developments there would help to shape the meaning of the coming war as well as the stakes involved for each country. In France, the growing possibility of a European war polarized domestic politics, preventing the construction of a reliable parliamentary majority in favour of opposing Nazi Germany, if necessary by war. Although not without its limits, conceiving of French politics at the time in the traditional terms of right and left is useful, for it reflects the self-understanding of most politicians and parties. Excluding the extreme (fascist) right, whose political influence before 1940 historians have arguably exaggerated, what can be called the conservative right comprised a number of parties and groupings of which the most important were the *Gauche démocratique*, the *Alliance démocratique* and the *Fédération républicaine*, which together won 127 of 610 seats in the 1936 legislative elections. To be sure, this conservative right was far from a cohesive bloc because personal rivalries as well as conflicting socio-economic interests often divided the different groupings. Yet the Popular Front's electoral victory in 1936 provided an important source of unity, as all members of the Conservative right agreed on the need to counter the socialist-communist menace. This fear of the left, moreover, influenced positions on foreign policy. If a traditional anti-Germanism continued to manifest itself within the conservative right, the conviction that another European war would be a disaster for France increasingly took precedence. The prospect of human and material losses on anything like the scale of 1914–18 would not only be a tragedy on their own, but would also spell the end of France as a great and imperial power. More worrisome still, the only beneficiary of another European war would be the left inside France, whether in the form of revolution or in that of a slower, but ultimately no less dangerous, process of socialist advances in the political, economic and social realms. What William Irvine has aptly termed the 'war-revolution nexus' – the belief that war would lead to the overturning of the existing order – meant that the conservative right generally supported attempts to avoid war.[15] Accordingly, with few exceptions, its members welcomed Munich. Afterwards, moreover, more than a few voices on the right floated the idea of offering a 'free hand' to Germany in Eastern Europe in return for the promise to leave France alone.

The situation on the French left was more complicated. The creation of the Popular Front alliance in 1935–6 had brought together the centre-left and left, but divisions quickly re-emerged after the electoral victory in 1936. While domestic policies provided an important cause of friction, so too increasingly did international issues, not least the question of how to respond to the possibility of war. Following the Comintern, the French communist party (PCF) called for a policy of resistance to fascism at home and abroad – a policy that France would pursue in close alliance with the Soviet Union. In October 1938, the PCF distinguished itself as the sole political party to vote against the Munich accords. The PCF's partners in the Popular Front, however, did not welcome this strenuous advocacy of resistance. The socialist party (SFIO), caught between its pacifist traditions and its support for a peaceful and just international order in which victims of aggression could expect protection, appeared uncertain about what to do. In the end, party leaders chose to endorse the Munich accords as a necessary evil, leaving undecided the question of what to do if and when Hitler embarked on further expansion. But if the SFIO possessed the most seats of any party in the French Parliament, the radicals (Radical Socialist Party) constituted the single most important party due to its position in the middle of the political spectrum, allowing it to ally with the left or the right depending on the political situation. Having joined with the socialists and communists to form the Popular Front in 1935–6, by 1938 the pendulum within the party had swung back as a growing number of radicals sought an alliance with the conservative right. For prominent radicals such as Georges Bonnet, France's pro-Munich Foreign Minister, a significant advantage of such an alliance was the support it would provide for his policy of rapprochement with Nazi Germany. The challenge for Édouard Daladier, the leader of the radical party and from April 1938 the French premier, was to forge a political alliance with the conservative right without necessarily adopting its foreign policy.

French domestic politics rapidly evolved in the wake of Munich. The conservative right overwhelmingly approved of Bonnet's appeasement of Nazi Germany and would likely have accepted a tacit agreement with Hitler, giving him a 'free hand' in Eastern Europe – an agreement Bonnet appears to have unsuccessfully sought.[16] But even leaving aside the issue of the questionable worth of Hitler's promises, it does not appear that the Nazi leader was prepared to offer the assurances that Bonnet would need to sell such a policy at home. In any case, Nazi Germany's continued aggressive posture, together with Britain's hardening position, left Bonnet and the right little choice but to rally behind Daladier's self-described 'policy of firmness' towards Germany (and Italy). At the same time, however, the right only agreed to Daladier's policy in the hope of deterring Germany: it interpreted firmness as a means of preventing war and not as a prelude to waging war. In its embrace of deterrence, the conservative right even accepted the government's pursuit of a Soviet alliance, refraining from criticizing a move it would have violently condemned six months earlier. With the radicals now allied with the conservative right, Daladier emphasized the deterrent aspects of his policy, most visibly by keeping his detested rival Bonnet at the Quai d'Orsay; but he also sought to allay the right's fears by implementing an anti-labour policy designed to weaken the 'revolution-war nexus'. On the left, meanwhile, the PCF continued to champion a policy of resistance in alliance with the Soviets, denouncing any sign of hesitation on the government's part in the face of Moscow's mounting demands. But perhaps the most important development was the deepening of divisions within the SFIO. During 1939, the party effectively split into two, with one half grouped around Léon Blum, the parliamentary leader, who accepted the need to oppose Nazi Germany by war if necessary, and the other half grouped around Paul Faure, the party's chairman, who believed that war was the greatest evil that must be prevented at all costs. Since neither side was prepared to back down, infighting paralyzed the SFIO as divisions cut through regional federations and as well as local sections.[17] This paralysis of France's largest party had serious implications. With the radicals allied to a conservative right that refused to accept the necessity of war, no parliamentary majority existed in September 1939 in favour of a lengthy and difficult struggle against Nazi Germany.

Unlike in France, the growing possibility of war had a centripetal effect on British politics, resulting in greater overall unity. That this would be the case was not self-evident beforehand. During 1937–8, the Conservatives, by far the largest party in parliament, appeared to be firmly united behind appeasement. Chamberlain exercised something close to dictatorial control not only over his party but also over British policy in general, thanks to the Conservative's massive parliamentary majority. Nowhere was this control more evident, moreover, than in foreign policy. While historians have pointed to many factors to explain the choice of appeasement, Chamberlain's role is clearly central: he closely identified with the policy, making support for appeasement a question of confidence in his leadership. One result is that he faced limited opposition from within his party over Munich. Prominent doubters, such as Winston Churchill and Anthony Eden, were clearly isolated voices. Immediately after-wards, Chamberlain considered exploiting public relief at the avoidance of war by calling a general election in which the fundamental issue would be his foreign policy. Although in the end he decided against this course, due partly to inauspicious by-election results in the autumn of 1938, the Conservatives launched a publicity campaign that featured Chamberlain as the saviour of peace. If this decision can be seen as evidence of Chamberlain's over-weaning confidence in his abilities, the campaign had the effect of reinforcing the associ-ation of appeasement with the Prime Minister in the public's mind. Unwittingly, Chamberlain became hostage to the success of appeasement – success that depended far more on Hitler's intentions than on Chamberlain's hopes. Any discrediting of appeasement, in other words, would necessarily undermine the Prime Minister's political position.

If Chamberlain could count on strong Conservative support, the opposite was the case with the Labour Party. In fact, Chamberlain and Labour leaders loathed one another. But Labour's opposition to Chamberlain stemmed from more than personal animosity. Increasingly important as a factor was Labour's growing unhappiness with appeasement. To be sure, the influence of Labour's pacifist and anti-military traditions could still be felt. An internal party memorandum in April 1938, for example, argued against encouraging the Czechs to resist German demands on the grounds that this might provoke an unwanted war.[18] But such arguments quickly became marginal within the Labour party. Here, moreover, the Czech crisis played a significant role. As the crisis developed during the summer of 1938, Labour leaders sided more and more with the Czechs, framing the issue as one of a dictator state (Germany) unjustly bullying a smaller and weaker democratic one (Czechoslovakia). Britain and France, Labour leaders intoned, should stand up to Germany. Deterrence thinking – the belief that Germany, if confronted, would ultimately give way – certainly factored into Labour's stance. But so too did an emerging rejection of Nazi Germany on political-moral grounds. For Labour, Nazi

Germany had placed itself beyond the pale of civilized countries both by its persecution of innocent people at home, not least socialists and trade unionists, and by its expansionist warmongering abroad. Put differently, Labour was coming to view Nazi Germany as a mortal and even existential threat that must be stopped – if necessary by armed force. Thus, though Labour leaders joined the Conservatives in breathing a collective sigh of relief at the announcement of the Munich accords, this represented little more than a fleeting moment of doubt. The more important point is that during 1938 Labour's foreign policy was moving in the opposite direction from that of Chamberlain and the Conservatives.

Following Munich, Labour's hostility to Nazi Germany only grew stronger as evidence of Nazi barbarity multiplied both at home and abroad. With the Prague coup in April 1939 any lingering doubts about the futility of appeasement vanished as Labour leaders fully accepted the possibility of war. One sign was Labour's acquiescence to conscription. Previously, Labour had strongly denounced military conscription, viewing it as a prelude to industrial conscription and to the loss of trade union power that this entailed. Yet by the spring of 1939 the need to prepare Britain for war took precedence; the party thus merely sought amendments to the government's proposed conscription bill rather than rejecting it outright. Similarly, Labour leaders very strongly endorsed the pursuit of a Soviet alliance, repeatedly pressing the government to make concessions. If a deterrent element was present, Labour leaders also thought strategically about war – about what would be needed to wage a successful war against Germany. Meanwhile, Chamberlain emerged considerably weakened from the 'failure' of appeasement. Pressure to adopt a firmer policy came not only from the opposition but from his own party, compelling the Prime Minister, for example, to negotiate with Moscow for an alliance. But Chamberlain's domestic problems went deeper than this. As war clouds quickly gathered in the summer of 1939, there was increasing talk inside and outside of Parliament concerning the need for a coalition government made up of Conservatives, Labour and the rump Liberal party. Fuelling this talk, moreover, was the suspicion that Chamberlain lacked the ability to lead the country in a crisis, partly because of his poor relations with the opposition and partly because of persistent doubts about his commitment to a firm line against Germany – doubts evident even among Conservatives. For now Chamberlain could dismiss calls to enlarge his government, most notably by the inclusion of Churchill, a dissident Conservative who was far less anathema to Labour. But if war came he would clearly be forced to do so. All this underscores a significant point: unlike in France, the growing possibility of war drove the parties together rather than apart. Indeed, by the summer of 1939 it is possible to detect the contours of the coalition government that would direct Britain from May 1940.

In considering French and British responses to the possibility of war, the final realm to be examined is the economic. Whatever their doubts about the long-war strategy, French and British planners assumed that economic strength would play an important, if not decisive, role in a European war. Various elements make up a country's economic strength, such as its productive capacity, financial system and access to domestic and foreign resources of various kinds. But one element that has received relatively little attention is what might be called a country's political-economic organization.[19] The key question here concerns the relationship between the state and non-state actors in economic matters. Scholars have convincingly shown that France and Britain both undertook significant rearmament efforts beginning in the mid-1930s.[20] Although debate continues on whether a greater effort was possible, the question is not simply to what extent the two countries rearmed, but also how they did so. In addition to affecting armaments production, the organization of the economy influenced the ability of the French and British governments to mobilize their societies behind a war effort.

In France, one must begin with the Popular Front. On the heels of 1936 elections, a strike-wave broke out across the country that ended with the Matignon Accords: a state-brokered agreement between employers and trade unions that improved pay and other conditions for workers, while also notably enhancing the political influence of organized labour. Indeed, following the accords trade union leaders could aspire to an equal role with employers in determining firm and industrial matters. These ambitions are significant because organized labour, together with the SFIO, advocated what was often referred to at the time as economic planning. While sometimes vague on details, planning nevertheless did foresee an activist role for state authorities in regulating employer–worker relations as well as economic activities more generally. Thus in 1935 the *Confédération Général du Travail* (CGT), the principal umbrella group of French trade unions, endorsed an economic 'plan' calling for immediate measures, including a forty-hour work week, an ambitious public works programme and controls on prices and profits, as well as more 'structural reforms' such as the nationalization of key economic sectors (finance, credit, insurance) and industries (transport and energy).[21] The CGT envisaged the plan as providing the basis for a tripartite structure of economic direction in which organized labour, employers and government authorities would each have a say in major decisions. As rearmament expanded, the CGT incorporated the latter into its economic programme. What was needed, a CGT publication argued in 1938, was 'a method, a discipline imposed on everyone ... a veritable plan for production and defence'.[22] The Popular Front and its economic programme, however, encountered considerable resistance from employers. Although forced to accept the Matignon Accords, the principal employer's organization, the *Confédération générale de patronat Français* (CGFP), strove from the beginning to undo the accords and, more generally, to roll back organized labour's newly won influence. Not surprisingly the CGFP, together with industry-specific employer organizations, favoured an economy organized along *laissez-faire* lines in which industrialists would be free to decide matters as they deemed best. In addition to excluding trade union influence at the firm, industry and national levels, this economic organization implied a much reduced role for the state.

With French labour and industry divided, the choice of economic organization lay with the government. Here, the decisive moment came in the summer and autumn of 1938. Initially, the Daladier government had sought a compromise between the two groups and the two approaches to economic organization. In the wake of Munich, however, the French premier came down clearly on the side of employers, a decision that must be seen in the context of his efforts to ally the radicals with the conservative right. The premier signalled his decision by appointing Paul Reynaud as Finance Minister. If one aim of Reynaud's programme of economic liberalism was to catalyze France's ailing economy, it was also designed to provoke a clash with organized labour, which it duly did. With socialist support, the CGT called a one-day general strike at the end of November that the police brutally suppressed.[23] The immediate result was an employer offensive against the Matignon gains: with the trade unions greatly weakened, workers deemed 'difficult' by employers were fired while those remaining worked longer hours for less pay. But the repercussions of this employer victory and trade union defeat extended well beyond its immediate effects on workers. With the government effectively allied with employers, state authorities took a back seat in terms of rearmament, leaving industrialists free to organize the overall effort. While Daladier's choice did provide a short-term spark, it proved counter-productive in the longer-term. The conversion of a peacetime to wartime economy would be hampered by the lack of directing and co-ordinating authorities in a host of areas, including the allocation of scarce manpower and raw materials. Although industrial leaders promised to provide this authority, they largely failed to do so, with damaging results for French production in 1939–40. No less important, perhaps, the exclusion of organized labour from any political influence as well as the disproportionate burden placed on workers destroyed any hopes of creating a united social front. Not only was labour alienated, but this very alienation fuelled the fears of industrial and political leaders that revolution stalked the home front. The choice of economic organization, in short, reinforced the war–revolution nexus for the right.[24]

In Britain political–economic developments followed a different course from those in France. As in the domestic political realm, moreover, it was far from inevitable beforehand that they would do so. Much like their French counterparts, British trade unionists advocated economic planning, which they defined in terms of a tripartite management (with employers and state authorities) of economic and industrial affairs. In contrasting planning with economic liberalism, organized labour underscored its preference for a more interventionist economic approach. 'So long as private enterprise continues to control industry in this country with profit making as it main objective', the Trades Union Congress (TUC), the principal umbrella group of British trade unionists, declared as early as 1931, 'so long will the present chaos and inefficiency continue to endanger our trade and prosperity.[25] Initially, TUC leaders hesitated to incorporate Britain's rearmament effort into its campaign for planning, largely because of opposition to industrial conscription. Among the trade unions most opposed to industrial conscription, moreover, was the Amalgamated Engineering Union (AEU), many of whose members were engaged in rearmament work. Yet at the same time, both the AEU and the TUC increasingly criticized the government's appeasement policy on moral as well as practical grounds. Tension thus existed between a desire to oppose Nazi Germany on the one hand and an unwillingness to equip Britain with the economic tools needed to do so on the other.

Employers, meanwhile, fully backed the government's position that rearmament should not interfere with normal business activity – a position summed up in the phrase 'business as usual'. In concrete terms this meant that economic and industrial matters would be left to industry to decide, with organized labour excluded and the government's input reduced to a minimum. In 1937 a leading industrial group thus defined its main task as 'trying to prevent national and international idealists from running Industry by Acts of Parliament'.[26] If the belief that government interference was economically inefficient offered one reason for clinging to 'business as usual', the desire to avoid empowering organized labour and, in the political realm, the Labour Party constituted another and important motive. Industrial organizations and the Conservative government both recognized that a more planned and directed economic effort would require the co-operation of organized labour – co-operation that would require political concessions. As the head of the Engineering Employers' Federation (EEF), a prominent industrial organization, remarked in 1937, any changes to current industrial practices 'involved important political considerations' that 'would have to be bought from the Unions at considerable price'.[27]

The spring of 1938, however, proved to be a turning point in the political–economic realm in Britain. Following Germany's *Anschluss* with Austria the government decided to accelerate the existing rearmament programme without abandoning 'business as usual'. Recognizing that this would require the co-operation of trade unionists and industrialists, Chamberlain instructed government ministers to consult with both groups but to offer nothing concrete in return for their help. Yet one unintended effect of this decision was to encourage direct negotiations between organized labour and industry, which soon assumed a dynamic of their own, helping to push the government well beyond where it wanted to go. Industrialists began to revise their earlier hostility to working with trade unionists as they came to view the latter more as a potential ally than foe, not least in the struggle against intrusive government meddling. Yet British industrialists also showed themselves to be less opposed than their French counterparts to a greater measure of government regulation. The mounting demands of rearmament, moreover, had much to with this: as bottlenecks in the supply of manpower and various materials became apparent, a growing number of industrialists were prepared to admit the merits of what one of them described as an element of 'central control and conscription of capital, facilities, and labour'. Reflecting this trend, towards the end of 1938 the EEF concluded that it was becoming 'necessary to subordinate industrial considerations to national considerations'.[28] Meanwhile, on the other side of the political–economic fence, the trade unions also proved more forthcoming, particularly in regards to industrial conscription. Although resistance to this measure within organized labour remained strong throughout 1938, by early 1939 trade union leaders tacitly accepted the need for industrial conscription. If a desire to extract political concessions from both industry and the government factored into their calculations, so too did the belief that the threatening inter-national situation demanded it. Significantly, even the militant AEU agreed, with the national leadership forbidding local branches to unleash strike action in opposition to military conscription. More generally, on the eve of war in August 1939 EEF and AEU representatives signed a far-reaching agreement in which trade unionists accepted a reduction of work-related privileges in return for greater tripartite management of industry.

Growing co-operation between organized labour and industry was important for several reasons. First and foremost, it placed Britain on a political–economic path that differed significantly from the French one. Whereas the French opted for a *laissez-faire* approach, effectively leaving the task of organizing the country's emerging war economy to industrialists, the British developed a more directed or co-ordinated approach in which industry, labour and the state co-operated with one another on economic and industrial policy. Much of this difference, moreover, can be attributed to the contrasting role of organized labour and its political allies on the left. In France, labour and the left were excluded from any say in political and economic decisions, allowing an alliance of the political right and industry to impose its views. In Britain, by comparison, during the run-up to war the influence of organized labour and the Labour Party rapidly expanded, providing both with the opportunity to help shape Britain's economic and industrial effort. The result is that Britain's emerging war economy would be better equipped to meet the needs of a long war, which, notwithstanding the doubts of British (and French) planners, is the type of conflict that beckoned. Although the immediate effects on armaments production of Britain's choice of political–economic approach are difficult to gauge, a more co-ordinated system for the allocation of increasingly scarce labour and materials, for example, contributed to reducing bottlenecks in the short and long term.[29] No less important, however, were the political consequences. Put simply, the British went to war more united and therefore more confident than the French. Unlike in France, doubts about the political reliability of organized labour (the war–revolution nexus) were notable by their absence.

Several points emerge from this analysis. First and foremost, appeasement is too blunt a concept to encompass British (and French) responses to the growing prospect of war during the late 1930s. Appeasement focuses attention too narrowly on diplomatic events and on the views of individual policy makers, most notably the figure of Chamberlain. A good deal occurred that political leaders did not fully grasp and could not fully control. A second point is that British and French responses not only differed in many respects, but also do not fit easily into an account that emphasizes the growing (if belated) recognition that war with Nazi Germany was unavoidable. Thus in the strategic realm, while British and French thinking about an upcoming war converged, most notably in regards to the value of an eastern front, this convergence meant that Britain and France went to war with serious doubts about the viability of a long-war strategy. Confidence, in other words, was in short supply. Meanwhile, divergence was more in evidence in both the political and economic realms. The threat of a European war had a disintegrating effect on French politics, with the result that in September 1939 no solid majority existed in parliament in favour of a war against Nazi Germany. In Britain, by contrast, the run-up to war had a unifying effect on politics at the expense of Chamberlain's hold on power, laying the roots for the later wartime coalition under Churchill. Finally, in the economic realm, the French adopted a laissez-faire approach to organizing their emerging war economy, which would prove inadequate to the task, whereas the British felt their ways towards a more directed and co-ordinated approach that would better equip them for the long war ahead.

All told, then, the British responded better to the prospect of war than the French. But just as importantly, the responses in both Britain and France cannot be attributed simply to the wisdom and foresight or to the blindness and mistakes of a handful of political leaders.

Notes

1   For good introductions into the work on France, see M. Thomas, 'Appeasement in the Late Third Republic', *Diplomacy and Statecraft* 19 (2008), pp. 566–607; and P. Jackson, 'Post-War Politics and the Historiography of French Strategy and Diplomacy Before the Second World War', *History Compass* 4 (2006), pp. 870–905.

2   R. Young, '"La Guerre de Longue Durée": Some Reflections on French Strategy and Diplomacy in the 1930s' in A. Preston (ed.), *General Staffs and Diplomacy before the Second World War*. London, 1978, pp. 41–64; and idem, *In Command of France: French Foreign Policy and Military Planning, 1933–1940*. Cambridge, MA, 1978. Nicole Jordan has challenged the argument that French war planning was based on a lengthy war but her case requires one to set aside a mountain of evidence to the contrary. See her *The Popular Front and Central Europe: The Dilemmas of French Impotence, 1918–1940*. Cambridge, 1992. For one aspect of France's long-war planning, see T. Imlay, 'Preparing for Total War: Industrial and Economic Preparations for War in France between the Two World Wars', *War in History* 15 (2008), pp. 43–71.

3   For a recent statement of the importance of Eastern Europe (and an eastern front) to French inter-war planning, see R. Boyce, *The Great Interwar Crisis and the Collapse of Globalization*. Basingstoke, 2009, pp. 48–55.

4   Indispensable here is M. Thomas, *Britain, France and Appeasement: Anglo-French Relations in the Popular Front Era*. Oxford, 1996. Also see P. Jackson, *France and the Nazi Menace: Intelligence and Policy Making, 1933–1939*. Oxford, 2000; and Jean-Baptiste Duroselle, *La décadence, 1932–1939*. Paris, 1985.

5   On French relations with Eastern Europe, see P. Wandyz, *France and her Eastern Allies, 1919-1925*. Minneapolis, 1962; and *The Twilight of French Eastern Alliances, 1926-1936: French-Czechoslovak-Polish Relations from Locarno to the Remilitarization of the Rhineland*. Princeton, 1988.

6   On French manipulation, see P. Jackson and J. Maiolo, 'Strategic Intelligence, Counter-Intelligence and Alliance Diplomacy in Anglo-French Relations before the Second World War', *Militärgeschichtliche Zeitschrift* 65 (2006), pp. 417–61; and T. Imlay, 'The Paris Connection: Britain, France and the Making of the Anglo-French Alliance, 1938–1939' in W. Philpott and M. Alexander (eds), *Anglo-French Relations between the Wars, 1919-1940*. London, 2002, pp. 92–120.

7   Archives Nationales, Paris (hereafter AN), Papiers Edouard Daladier, 496/AP/11 2DA4, dr6 sdrc, 'Pour l'entretien avec Doumenc', ms notes, 29 July 1939.

8   For Soviet policy, compare M. Carley, *1939: The Alliance that Never Was and the Coming of World War II*. Chicago, 1999

9   Bonnet was prepared to offer the Curzon line as the Soviet Union's western border. See AN, Papiers Edouard Daladier, 496/AP/13 2DA6 Dr3, 'Extrait des notes personnelles du Ministre des Affaires Étrangères', 26 May 1939.

10 M. Howard, *The Continental Commitment: The Dilemma of British Defence Policy in the Era of the Two World Wars*. London, 1972.

11 N. Gibbs, *Grand Strategy* vol. 1, *Rearmament Policy*. London, 1976. For the British army, see D. French, *Raising Hitler's Army: The British Army and the War Against Germany, 1919-1945*. Oxford, 2000, pp. 1–183; and B. Bond, *British Military Policy between the Two World Wars*. Oxford, 1980. For the air force, see M. Smith, *British Air Strategy between the Wars*. Oxford, 1984; and J. Ferris, 'Fighter Defence before Fighter Command: The Rise of Strategic Air Defence in Great Britain, 1917–1934', *Journal of Military History* 63 (1999), pp. 845–84. For the navy, see C. Bell, *The Royal Navy, Seapower and Strategy between the Wars*. London, 2000.

12 Service historique de l'Armée de terre, Vincennes, 7N 2815, 'Étude sur la participation de l'Angleterre dans l'éventualité d'une action commune franco-britannique en cas de guerre', 167/S, Général Lelong 9 November 1938.

13 See D. Hucker, 'Franco-British Relations and the Problem of Conscription in Britain, 1939-1939', *Contemporary European History* 17 (2008), pp. 437–56; and P. Dennis, *Decision by Default: Peacetime Conscription and British Defence, 1919–39*. Durham, NC, 1972.

14 For the radicalization of Anglo-French strategy, see T. Imlay, *Facing the Second World War: Strategy, Politics, and Economics in Britain and France 1938–1940*. Oxford, 2003, pp. 17–127; and idem, 'A Reassessment of Anglo-French Strategy during the Phony War, 1939–1940', *English Historical Review* 119 (2004), pp. 333–72.

15 W. Irvine, *French Conservatism in Crisis: The Republican Federation of France in the 1930s*. Baton Rouge, 1979. But also see K. Passmore, *From Liberalism to Fascism: The Right in a French Province, 1928-1929*. Cambridge, 1997, who stresses divisions among the right.

16 On Bonnet, see H. Bellstedt, *Apaisement oder Krieg: Frankreichs Außenminister Georges Bonnet und die deutsch-französische Erklärung vom 6. Dezember 1938*. Bonn, 1993; and A. Adamthwaite, *France and the Coming of the Second World War*. London, 1977. .

17 In May 1939 Vincent Auriol, an SFIO deputy at the time, confided to a friend his 'anguish' at the party's situation and lamented the 'impotence to which we have condemned ourselves by our divisions'. See AN, Papiers Édouard Depreux, 456/AP/4-1, Auriol to Depreux 13 May 1939.

18 Archives of the British Labour Party (Harvester microfiche), Part 1, fiche 239, 'Guarantees to Czechoslovakia: In Relation to Spain', Advisory Committee on International Question, April 1938.

19 Important exceptions include K. Middlemas, *Politics in Industrial Society: The Experience of the British System since 1911*. London, 1979; H. Chapman, *State Capitalism and Working-Class Radicalism in the French Aircraft Industry*. Berkeley, 1991; and R. Frankenstein, *Le prix du réarmement Français (1935–1939)*. Paris, 1982.

20 G.C. Peden, *British Rearmament and the Treasury, 1932-1939*. Edinburgh, 1979; and Frankenstein, *Le prix du réarmement Français*.

21 For the CGT, see Jean-François Biard, *Le Socialisme devant ses choix: La naissance de l'idée du plan*. Paris, 1985, pp. 1–142.

22   Institut d'histoire sociale-CGT, Paris, 'Le Plan de la C.G.T pour la sécurité du pays', undated but 1938.

23   Still valuable is G. Bourdé, *La défaite du Front Populaire*. Paris, 1977. On Reynaud, see T. Imlay, 'Paul Reynaud and France's Response to Nazi Germany, 1938–1940', *French Historical Studies* 26 (2003), pp. 498–538.

24   For France's emerging war economy, see J. Crémieux-Brilhac, *Les Français de l'An 40* vol. II, *Ouvriers et Soldats*. Paris, 1990; M. Margairaz, *L'Etat, les finances et l'économie: Histoire d'une conversion, 1932–1952*. Paris, 1991, vol. 1; and T. Imlay, 'Mind the Gap: The Perception and Reality of Communist Sabotage of French War Production during the Phony War, 1939–40', *Past and Present* 189 (2005), pp. 179–224.

25   University of Warwick, Modern Records Centre (hereafter MRC), Trades Union Congress Archive, MSS 292/560.1/20, TUC Economic Committee, 'Short Statement on Economic Policy', Econ. C 7/2, 25 March 1931.

26   MRC, British Employers Confederation Archive, MSS 100/B/3/2/C204, Part 4, 'Notes for Sir David Owen', 28 May 1937.

27   The National Archives, Kew, LAB 8/213, Arthur Ramsay (EEF) to Phillips (Min. of Labour), 28 July 1937, and accompanying memorandum.

28   For the industrialist, see Churchill College Archives, Cambridge University, Viscount Weir Papers, 19/8, 'Note for talk of Tuesday, 15th March [1938] with S. of S. and Defence Minister', undated. For the EEF, see MRC, Electrical Engineering Federation Archive, MSS 237/1/1/36, Management Board minutes, 24 November 1938.

29   For more on this point, see T. Imlay, 'Democracy and War: Political Change, Industrial Relations, and Economic Preparations for War in France and Britain up to 1940', *Journal of Modern History* 79 (2007), pp. 1–47.

Chapter 16

Neutrality 'de jour': Switzerland and the Italo-Abyssinian War of 1935–6

Neville Wylie and Marco Wyss

Any historian given the task of reviewing events of over seventy years ago would be well advised to remember that 'hindsight' can be a fickle friend. True, retrospective studies on the origins of the Second World War such as ours can benefit from the sense of detachment we now have on the heated debates of the time. We can peruse the once-secret government papers and peer into the minds of the chief protagonists by reading their diaries and private correspondence. We can also draw on the findings of earlier scholars and pose fresh questions on the material and offer new insights. Difficulties arise, however, when we seek – consciously or unconsciously – to apply our own value system on the past; judging the utterances, attitudes and actions of those caught up in the maelstrom of events on the basis of contemporary ethical standards. Recent writing on the role of the neutral states has suffered particularly badly in this regard. With attention focused on the principal power brokers in Berlin, Paris, Moscow, Rome and London, it is not always easy to explain – far less understand – why the neutrals behaved in the way they did. Why did Europe's small democracies adopt the 'posture of an ostrich' in the face of the Nazi challenge? Why did they so readily abandon the option of collective security offered by the League of Nations when their own military defences were so palpably deficient? How can we account for the neutrals' willingness to pamper Germany's financial needs once the war began, other than by questioning the moral integrity of those involved; and how else can we explain their collective failure to offer sanctuary to the millions of luckless souls who fell victim to Hitler's racial excesses?

We cannot hope to answer all of these questions. What we can do, though, is show how 'neutral' statesmen of the 1930s sought to wrestle with the issues as they saw them, and shed light on some of the attitudes that underpinned their actions. To do so, we will address ourselves to the question of Swiss policy during and after the Italo-Abyssinian war of 1935–6. We do so partly to draw attention to the way this seminal event in the road to war in September 1939 was viewed by Swiss policy makers, but also with an eye to illuminating some of the pressures acting on the Swiss political and business elite, and exploring how the events in the Horn of Africa upset Swiss foreign political strategy and challenged some of the basic assumptions governing Swiss thinking at the time.

If it took Hitler's occupation of Prague in March 1939 finally to convince Berne of the irreconcilability of Germany's territorial ambitions on the continent, the events of 1935–6 were decisive in changing Swiss perceptions of the international environment and prompting serious discussion on the kind of measures – both internal and external – that would be required if Switzerland was to survive another European-wide conflagration.

The conflict in the Horn of Africa, lasting from 3 October 1935 until 5 May 1936, has rightly been seen as a key moment in the politics of the interwar era. By penalizing Italy for waging a war of aggression, the British and French governments irreparably compromised their standing in Rome, and set back any chance they once entertained of wooing the irascible Italian dictator away from Hitler's side. The significance of these events is all the more momentous given the fact that before Italy's unprovoked attack on Abyssinia, the prospects for peace on Anglo-French terms had looked surprisingly good. At the Stresa conference in April 1935 Mussolini had not only pledged to uphold the Locarno accord of 1925, upon which the post-war territorial settlement in Western Europe hinged, but also work towards maintaining Austrian independence – a policy he had inaugurated the previous year when he dispatched four divisions to the Italo-Austrian border in response to the attempted Nazi *coup d'état* and murder of the Austrian Chancellor Engelbert Dollfuss. It was this putative Italo–French–British alignment that was thrown into jeopardy by Mussolini's expansionist policies in East Africa.[1] The belated attempt by the Western powers to salvage something from the 'Stresa front', by offering to negotiate an end to the war on Italy's terms, resulted in a fiasco. When details of the 'Hoare–Laval pact' reached public attention in December 1935, the full extent of the West's moral bankruptcy and political confusion was laid bare. Never again could Paris and London claim to hold the moral high ground in international politics. In Rome, meanwhile, Mussolini felt sufficiently piqued by Western 'treachery' over Italy's claims in Abyssinia to justify turning a blind eye to German reoccupation of the Rhineland. No longer was he willing to act so readily as Europe's 'lightening conductor' between the revisionists and status quo powers. As Reynolds Salerno argues, 'after 1936, there would only be fleeting opportunities to draw Italy out of Germany's orbit and no chance whatsoever of Italy's siding with the Western powers against the Nazis'. 'What is often dismissed as "the Abyssinian diversion"', he concludes, 'actually started the chain of events that brought Italy into armed conflict with Britain and France in June 1940.'[2]

If the Italo-Abyssinian war dented Anglo-French prestige and fanned Mussolini's ambitions, its keenest impact was felt in Geneva, where the events dealt a shattering blow to the standing of the League of Nations. Already weakened by the collapse of the disarmament talks earlier in the decade and dithering in the face of Japanese aggression in the Far East, the League's failure to deal with Italy's blatant violation of the Covenant effectively ended its claim to play a major role in international politics. Indeed, so damaged was the League's status in the eyes of its members that by the time of the Munich crisis in 1938 it had been relegated to the margins of political debate. This need not have been the case. Few of those who attended the Assembly meetings over the summer of 1935 had any doubt that the coming months would determine whether the League was ultimately, as the Irish premier put it, 'worthy to survive'.[3] The near unanimity that greeted the initial vote of censure against Italy was unprecedented. 'No great international dispute', notes the League's historian, F.P. Walters, 'has ever been the subject of a clearer verdict.'[4] The set of sanctions proposed by the League was one of the most comprehensive packages of economic and financial measures ever put in place in peacetime. The sale of arms, military equipment and items of strategic importance to Italy were embargoed and government and private loans or credit advances were withheld from Italian companies. Member states were even called upon to suspend all imports from Italy, in the hope of denying Rome the foreign exchange needed to fund its war.[5] As with all sanctions regimes, the measures were far from water-tight – the absence of oil from the list of embargoed goods was a noticeable (and deliberate) loophole – but it was the League's palpable failure to maintain a common front on the sanctions issue that exposed the fundamental lack of common purpose lying at the heart of the League experiment. The debacle surrounding the sanctions regime against Italy – a policy famously derided by Neville Chamberlain as the 'very midsummer of madness' – heralded the end of 'collective security' as a workable concept and forced states to look elsewhere for the security and political needs.

As Italy's northern neighbour, the Swiss could hardly be expected to view the events in East Africa with equanimity.[6] Abyssinia was thousands of miles away, but Italy's invasion triggered a series of problems that bore directly on two central elements of Swiss foreign policy. The first, and most obvious, was Berne's relations with Mussolini's regime in Rome. Although no one talked in terms of overt patronage, there is little doubt that by the early 1930s Swiss policy makers had become accustomed to look towards Italy as Switzerland's sponsor at the high table of international politics. As the least domineering of Switzerland's neighbours, Italy had historically engendered less fear amongst the Swiss bourgeois political, commercial and financial elite than France or Germany. This tendency only increased after Hitler's ascension to power removed the last vestigial restraints on Germany's revisionist ambitions on the continent. Indeed, for the Swiss foreign minister, Giuseppe Motta, maintaining Italian support became the *sine qua non* of Swiss foreign policy and the principal element in guiding Swiss relations with Germany. 'Our policy towards Italy', he candidly informed Switzerland's minister in Berlin in October 1933, 'has dictated our policy with regard to Germany.'[7] This was never an easy task, given Mussolini's impetuousness and abrasive character. Nonetheless, Rome's adhesion to the 'Stresa Front' in April 1935 gave heart to those like Motta who held the belief that fascism could be 'tamed' and Mussolini brought round to playing a constructive role in European politics.

If, in retrospect, Swiss assumptions about Italian benevolence might strike us as naive, it should be remembered that Swiss reading of Italian statements and actions was inevitably coloured by the close cultural and social ties that existed between the two countries. These ties were at their most intense amongst Switzerland's 250,000 Italian speakers, the majority of who, like Motta, hailed from the canton of Ticino. But pro-Italian sentiments were also common in Switzerland's other Catholic cantons, and resonated with particular force in Motta's Catholic Conservative party, a party which, though losing out to its Free-Thinking (*Freisinnig*, or radical) and Liberal rivals in the 'Sonderbund War' of 1847, nevertheless remained a potent political force. It particularly benefited from the 'cantonal' voice in the Swiss parliament. The second chamber, the Council of Estates, was composed of representatives from each canton, and so although relatively sparsely populated, the smaller but numerous Catholic cantons could compete with their larger and more prosperous Protestant neighbours.[8] Mussolini's corporate fascist model attracted little genuine appeal in Switzerland: even in the extreme right, preferences lay more with Hitler's 'folkish' ideas of a German bastion against eastern bolshevism.[9] Nevertheless, certain elements of Mussolini's political programme struck a chord north of the Alps, especially after his concordat with the Vatican in 1929 anaesthetized opposition from the Catholic church. For a country that led the world in the manufacture of clocks, the Swiss could not but help admire Mussolini's claim to making the Italian railways run to schedule, but it was his robust handling of organized labour that earned him his greatest plaudits. Ever since the army had been called out on to the streets to deal with Switzerland's incipient revolutionary 'moment' in 1918, the bourgeois political elite had set their sights on combating socialism and curbing Moscow's 'insidious' influence over Swiss political life. That this coloured thinking over Switzerland's external relations can be seen from the decision of the National Council in 1923 to refrain from expressing its condolences to the Italian parliament over the death of Matteotti at the hands of fascist thugs.[10] No effort was made to restore relations with the Soviet Union after diplomats had been withdrawn in 1918. Indeed, Swiss politicians rarely passed over the opportunity to preach of the dangers of the 'Bolshevik bogey'. Motta openly spoke out against trying to wed 'fire and water' in opening the League to Soviet delegates in September 1934, and placed Switzerland in a minority of three – with Portugal and the Netherlands – in voting against Soviet membership. All moves to rekindle Swiss–Soviet political relations thereafter were resolutely quashed by the influential Foreign Minister.[11]

Swiss neurosis with all things 'red' promoted the three bourgeois political parties – the Catholic Conservative, Agricultural and Free-Thinking parties – to bury their historic antagonisms and find common cause in trying to reverse the mounting electoral gains of the Swiss Socialist party and denying them a seat on the Federal Council, Switzerland's seven-man political executive.[12] This tactic became increasingly problematic after the 1935 elections made the socialists the largest single party in the National Council. Nevertheless, when a Federal Council seat fell vacant in late 1938, the bourgeois phalanx again held firm to block the socialists' path. Motta even went so far as to suggest that the election of a socialist councillor would be viewed as a provocation in Berlin. (It was not until December 1943, five years later, that the socialists finally secured a seat on the Federal Council.[13]) If fascism never took a firm hold in Swiss political discourse, the major bourgeois parties all adhered to what might be considered reactionary conservatism.[14] Central to the beliefs circulating at the time was the conviction that in the turbulent era of mass politics, Switzerland's future could only be secured by calling a halt to the march of liberalism and reviving the country's own distinctive traditions and agrarian values. It is worth noting that in 1935 a referendum was put to the country, which, had it secured a majority, would have seen a re-organization of the constitution along corporatist lines and the creation of the position of 'Landammann', possessing considerable executive authority. In the Federal Council, the Catholic conservative Philipp Etter emerged as the leading advocate for social and political reform, and the most likely candidate for the post of Landammann had the referendum attracted enough support. The right's foremost ideologue, the historian Gonzague de Reynold, made no secret of his admiration for the corporatist, authoritarian models found in Salazar's Portugal and Mussolini's Italy, even if he did not consider them entirely appropriate for his homeland.[15] His widely read Conscience de la Suisse of 1938, which bore the provocative subtitle 'Notes to these gentlemen in Berne', left little doubt as to the frailties, as he saw it, of Switzerland's current political system.

Thus, despite its outwardly placid appearance, by the middle years of the 1930s Switzerland echoed to many of the same political and social debates found elsewhere across Western Europe. The tempo and rancour of political discourse might be milder, and mercifully confined to legitimate arenas of expression, but with the Depression hitting Switzerland late – delaying the first signs of recovery until the end of 1936 – tensions between organized labour and an alliance of capital and the bourgeois political establishment inevitably sharpened Swiss political life and coloured the reading of events abroad its borders. Elite attitudes towards Mussolini's political programme were markedly less critical therefore than one might expect.[16] Henri Guisan, a protestant from Canton Vaud, who, as Commander-in-Chief of the Swiss army after 1939 came to embody Swiss determination to resist foreign invaders, typified those who succumbed to Mussolini's charm. In a letter sent to the federal military department after attending Italian army manoeuvres in 1934, Guisan wrote, 'The merit of this man [Mussolini], of this genius, is to have been able to discipline all forces of the nation; to have unified them in a single current, and to exploit this current exclusively for the grandeur of his country.'[17] Such views were widely held amongst members of the influential Swiss Association for Cultural and Economic Relations with Italy (Associazione svizzera per i rapporti culturali ed economici con l'Italia), founded in June 1937 to promote Italo-Swiss exchanges, and were present in the eulogy given by the University of Lausanne the same year when it bestowed an honorary degree on the Italian dictator. It was not just political pragmatism, then, that made Berne wary of upsetting its southern neighbour. Mussolini's domestic political ambitions were widely admired, and few in Berne felt that his forays into foreign affairs were sufficiently disagreeable to warrant withdrawing their support for his regime. On the contrary, as Dario Gerardi, the most recent historian to have dealt with Italo-Swiss relations observes, 'Mussolini's regime in fact exercised a very great seductive influence over the Swiss bourgeoisie and the majority of the Swiss political elite of the time, who saw fascism a remedy to bolshevism.'[18]

The second pillar of Swiss foreign policy to be tested by the Abyssinian conflict was Switzerland's association with the League. Switzerland counted amongst the first countries to join the League, when a narrow majority of the population and cantons voted in favour of Swiss adherence in 1920.[19] The organization had acknowledged Switzerland's neutral status at a conference held in London earlier in the year, when it agreed to allow Berne to opt out of League-sponsored military operations. Nevertheless, this was 'differential' neutrality, not 'integral'. Berne was still expected to follow League rulings over measures that fell short of outright war, in particular the application of economic and financial sanctions. With the League headquartered in Geneva, the Swiss could scarcely ignore the institution, and having vigorously campaigned for Swiss membership in 1920, Motta went on to develop Switzerland's profile in Geneva and promote Swiss interests through the League channels. Though certainly not blind to the League's many faults, he clearly admired its ambitions as 'a great liberal and democratic institution'.[20]

Switzerland's association with the League, however, never sat comfortably in Switzerland partly on account of its connection with the punitive Versailles settlement and partly because of its impact on Swiss neutrality and political independence. Within a year of Swiss entry, various opposition movements drawn from the civil service, professions, business and military circles coalesced to form an 'Association for an independent Switzerland' (*Volksbund für eine unabhängige Schweiz*). Criticism of the League continued to fester throughout the 1920s, and naturally grew the following decade after Berlin's withdrawal accentuated the institution's Western, Anglo-French orientation. Motta himself was all too aware of the danger posed to Swiss interests: on the day Hitler took Germany out of the League, he pointedly remarked that Switzerland's continued active engagement with the League depended 'on the condition that the League does not assume the figure of states grouped against Germany'.[21] It was precisely this fear that prompted Motta to block Soviet membership eleven months later and justified the close police surveillance of the Soviet mission and its delegates in the following years.[22] What was true for Germany, was, of course, equally so for Italy. Mussolini's behaviour in Geneva occasionally struck Swiss onlookers as unbecoming, but it was not until the invasion of Abyssinia that Italian interests clashed head on with the League. French, and particularly British, efforts to corral the League into imposing draconian sanctions on Rome in support of the Abyssinians thus posed Swiss policy makers with an acute dilemma and threatened to upset the equilibrium upon which Berne had staked its League policy over the previous half-decade.

This, then, was the conundrum facing Swiss officials over the winter of 1935–6. Given the circumstances, it was always going to be difficult for Berne to square the circle, far less come up with a solution that did not privilege its relations with Italy above those with the League. Such preferences were, however, encouraged by the widespread sense of cultural antipathy towards the Abyssinians. For most Swiss, Abyssinia was a far-off place of which they knew little. In the Swiss case, however, this ambivalence was underscored by a reluctance to acknowledge Abyssinian claims to sovereign equality. Berne had spoken out against Addis Ababa's accession to the League in 1923 on the grounds that, as large swathes of the country were still prone to banditry, the imperial government fell short of the level of development expected from a member of the international community. The presence of an Abyssinian delegation in Geneva did little to change Swiss thinking, and Berne showed little interest in developing closer relations. It was not until 1933 that the two sides finally signed a treaty of friendship and commerce. Abyssinia opened a consulate-general in Zurich in December the following year, but the Swiss pointedly declined to reciprocate the gesture. When forced to take sides in the summer of 1935, then, Swiss instincts led in only one direction. 'One can now see how thoughtless it was for the League of Nations to admit Ethiopia,' Max Huber, one of Motta's legal advisers, noted when news of Italy's attack came through. Abyssinia was, he dryly remarked, 'a country which does not deserve other nations risking a war to protect it'.[23] Switzerland's minister in Rome, Georges Wagnière, was particularly prone to this kind of cultural chauvinism, happily accepting Italian claims that in invading Abyssinia Rome was merely shouldering the 'white man's burden' and bringing civilization to this backward corner of East Africa. Far from sympathizing with the victims of Great Power aggression, Swiss officials tended to look at the Abyssinian affair as an irritant, and deplored the fact that their painstaking work in building relations with Mussolini's regime in Rome could be thrown into disarray by the anguished appeals of a state that was scarcely worthy of the name. The prevailing opinion was probably best summed up by one National Councillor who claimed that 'if it were necessary to give up neutrality, it would be easier to do so in support of Italy, cradle of our Latin and Western civilisation, rather than in support of Ethiopia, a nation of savages'.[24]

How then did Berne manage the 'problem' thrown up by Italy's act of naked aggression against Abyssinia? As Italian violation of the Covenant could scarcely be denied, the Swiss delegation in Geneva was instructed to 'tacitly associate' itself with the findings of the League Council and affirm Switzerland's readiness to fulfil its 'duty of solidarity with the other Members of the League of Nations'.[25] This was, however, as far as the Swiss were prepared to go. In Berne, officials lost little time in working out how best to distance themselves from the Assembly's resolution, and dilute the scope and severity of the proposed sanctions. For historians, Berne's reaction to the League's proposals is of interest not merely for what it tells us about the sanctions debate, but also for the role of neutrality in Swiss thinking. Swiss actions clearly illustrate how the Swiss viewed their position in the international community, and how the concept of neutrality came to be seen less as an end in itself, but rather as a means to achieving a desired political outcome: in this case, ameliorating Swiss relations with its southern neighbour. What is particularly striking about Berne's initial response to the crisis is how little neutrality figured in their deliberations. Neutrality was so central to Swiss political vocabulary that most officials were habituated into using the language of neutrality. But, in the Federal Political Department's first statement on the crisis, presented to the Federal Council on 8 October, it was Switzerland's status as a *small* power, not as a *neutral* one, that marked its approach to the crisis. 'If a state is strong', the memorandum noted,

> it could act with a certain ease; if it is weak it is forced to appear much more prudent ... We could show our solidarity with the League's cause by associating ourselves with certain coercive measures, but it would be impossible for us to go as far in the sanctions as could go, in some circumstances, powerfully armed states like Great Britain and France, or weaker states, which are, however, geographically sufficiently remote from Italy that their actions towards that country do not have fatal consequences for them.[26]

The principal theme running through the Federal Political Department's memorandum was that as a small state Switzerland should not be required to shoulder responsibility for upholding international peace and security – even if this responsibility was being undertaken as part of a collective activity. Two issues in particular dominated Swiss thinking. The first concerned the economic implications of the proposed measures. As Wagnière irritably noted, Switzerland was being asked to behave in the same way as Haiti or Liberia, countries with no expatriate communities in Italy and no commercial or financial interests to speak of.[27] The fact that under a Finnish initiative, the League was obliged to assist vulnerable states whose economies were unduly affected by the League's collective security measures, brought the Swiss little comfort. The Swiss and Italian economies were simply too intertwined to be prized apart at the whim of the League Council. The Swiss were particularly aggrieved by what they saw as the bluntness of the measures proposed. With Swiss trade in Italy estimated to be worth some 60–70 million Swiss Francs and providing employment for over 10,000 workers, the Swiss had a lot to lose. Walter Stucki, Director of the Commercial Division in the Department of Public Economy, who master-minded the technical aspects of Switzerland's correspondence with the League, was especially moved on this point. Why was it necessary, he asked in an impassioned letter to Wagnière on 21 October, 'in order to rob the Italians of a currency surplus ... to reduce reciprocal trade to zero, to bring centuries old economic relations to a complete standstill, and deny thousands of workers of their daily bread, not only in Italy, but also particularly in Switzerland?'[28]

Even more central to Swiss concerns in the first week of the war, however, was the fear that economic sanctions were merely a prelude to armed conflict.

The Swiss were not the only people to have these concerns. The entire policies of the British and French governments were driven by the desire to avoid war, but even before the crisis broke, the British chiefs of staff believed that the imposition of economic sanctions 'would almost invariably lead to war with Italy'.[29] Thereafter, the danger of provoking the *Duce* into a 'mad dog act' was rarely absent from official discussions. The certainty of Swiss pronouncements on the issue is nevertheless striking. 'It is possible', Motta wrote, 'that an initial, purely economic, action could in the end quickly escalate into an armed conflict'. But, he went on, although

> the solidarity principle is at the core of the League of Nations ... it should not be pushed to the extent of demanding that some states sacrifice their existence in service of the common cause. There is a difference between assistance and sacrifice, which in politics one cannot lose sight of. The rule 'pacta sunt servanda' is absolute, but not to the extent to condemn a country to ruin and death.[30]

The fact that some suspected London of deliberately engineering a conflict with Rome by insisting on the total embargo of Italian exports only went to inflame these fears.

Swiss anxieties were strengthened by the fact that should armed conflict break out, it could be Swiss territory – namely the canton of Ticino – that might end up in the firing line. Over the last decade, Mussolini had become adept at playing the irredentist card when it suited. Though support for succession amongst Swiss–Italians was low, the Ticino 'issue' had been a constant source of concern for Swiss policy makers. Indeed, some officials positively welcomed Italian territorial ambitions in Africa in the belief that it would deflect Italian attention from pickings closer to home. 'I wish our press wouldn't fuss too much over Ethiopian liberties,' Wagnière told Motta a month before the invasion. 'We have, for reasons I need not dwell on, a great interest in seeing Italy develop its colonial empire and create its own concerns overseas.'[31] In reality, Italian posturing over Ticino was not as dangerous as Berne feared. When Italian military planners looked northward, their attention was directed not so much on the tempting prizes offered in the Ticino, but rather on the infinitely more pressing problem of how to defend northern Italy from a possible German attack through the Swiss Confederation.[32] Intriguingly, although all were thoroughly alarmed by the prospect of a war breaking out in the wake of the sanctions regime, only one of the Federal Councillors believed that the 'threat' to Ticino warranted Switzerland throwing its weight behind the League. The bulk of opinion, both in the Council and in the parliament at large, saw Switzerland's economic and political salvation lying in a policy of appeasement.[33]

For the Swiss, then, the Abyssinian war was not just a challenge to their country's foreign political interests, but a threat to its economic and even national survival. It was this context that framed internal discussions on the place neutrality should play in Swiss policy. The options were by no means cut and dry. Expert opinion was divided on the weight of Switzerland's commitments to the League and the room for manoeuvre it could realistically claim.[34] On the issue of arms and munitions exports, a coherent and law-based argument was, at least, to hand. By emphasizing the military nature of the Italo-Abyssinian conflict, and the likelihood of a wider conflagration, Berne could plausibly invoke the Hague Rules of War of 1907, which conveniently insisted that neutrals maintained equilibrium in any trading relations with belligerent states. Recent practice on this issue left some room for manoeuvre: Berne had embargoed arms sales to China and Japan in 1932, but had, after a fashion, followed League rulings in 1934 in permitting Bolivia access to Swiss armaments in its dispute with Paraguay.[35] Though Berne's appeal to 'Hague law' saved it from openly siding against Italy, its specious reading of its legal obligations won it few admirers in Geneva. When Motta sought to justify Swiss policy on the arms embargo his words were greeted with a chorus of rebuke from across Assembly floor and brought Swiss standing in the institution to an all-time low.

Evading the other elements of the sanctions regime required even greater dexterity. Motta's Federal Political Department would dearly liked to have renegotiated Switzerland's entire position in the League, but as time scarcely allowed for this, the Swiss delegation was instead instructed to base Switzerland's case on a mixture of political expediency – emphasizing Switzerland's special position as a neighbour of the offending regime – and a maximum reading of Switzerland's traditional neutral rights. Early drafts of Switzerland's presentation to the League were amended to remove '*military* neutrality' whenever reference was made to 'the status of our neutrality'. The term 'Swiss–Italians' was replaced with '*région de langue italienne*', to emphasize the overlapping nature of social and cultural life across Switzerland's borders. Appeals to 'economic neutrality' were naturally problematic given the basis of Switzerland's association with the League, so Switzerland's economic interests in Italy were deftly submerged under a broader discussion of the political, social and cultural ties between the two countries. Thus, while Berne was happy to receive whatever assurances of support the League could provide to ease its financial and economic plight, it repeatedly stressed that nothing could be done to rectify the sanctions' wider ramifications on Swiss interests. 'How could [member] states make up for the political, intellectual and moral damage, which would result from breaking off all economic relations between the Italian speaking parts of Switzerland and Italy?'[36] Instead of ending Swiss trade with Italy, Berne merely promised to maintain trade at pre-war levels (so-called '*courant normal*') and offered to limit Italian access to foreign exchange by bringing its trade deficit with Italy into balance. Instead of cancelling credits, Swiss exporters were offered guarantees against non-payment by Italian purchasers, and a special Italo-Swiss clearing agreement was concluded in December 1935.[37]

At one level, Berne's attempt to distance itself from the League's collective security action, though detrimental to its standing in Western eyes, must be judged a success. That it accomplished this feat can in part be explained by the 'fortuitous' direction of League discussions on the issue of oil. The decision to omit oil from the list of embargoed goods left the sanctions regime so emascu-lated that few could claim that Switzerland's inglorious behaviour was critical to the fate of the League initiative. Nevertheless, the manner in which Berne chose to apply its regulations leaves little doubt over where Swiss interests lay. Even before Berne's prohibition on the transfer of arms to the belligerents came into force on 28 October, officials did all they could to avoid incurring Italian displeasure. When Motta caught wind of Italian concerns over Swissair's sale of old Fokker aircraft to the Abyssinians in early 1935, he immediately inter-vened to have the company back out of the deal and offer the planes to Italian buyers. Pressure was also brought to bear on Swiss arms companies. In August 1935 one, the *Schweizerische Industriegesellschaft Neuhausen* (SIG) agreed to conform to the Federal Council's decision that arms sales to Abyssinia were 'undesirable until further notice'. There was less success with the anti-aircraft gun manufacturer, Oerlikon, which pushed through a consignment of weapons and munitions to Abyssinia shortly before the sanctions came into force. The fact that the sales did not contravene any law and that Oerlikon's owner, Emil Bührle, was Abyssinia's honorary Consul-General in Zurich, did not prevent Motta from roundly criticizing the company for endangering Swiss interests.[38] Questions have long been asked over Berne's influence on the International Committee of the Red Cross's role in the conflict. The ICRC's historian, Rainer Baudendistel, found no evidence of direct pressure on the committee; however, as the ICRC's president, Max Huber, had assisted Motta in crafting Switzerland's legal response to the sanctions regime, there is little doubt that the committee was fully cognizant of Berne's position. The committee's reluctance to raise Italy's use of chemical weapons in its conversations with Rome, and later decision to withhold its delegates' reports from the League investigators, tasked with exploring the matter, was in perfect alignment with Motta's foreign policy. It was exactly the same position that the committee would adopt in October 1942, in deciding against speaking out publicly against the abuse of human rights in Hitler's death camps.[39]

The impact of the Italo-Abyssinian war on Swiss foreign and domestic policy was profound. At its most obvious, the gruelling experience was decisive in convincing Swiss policy makers of the need to burnish Switzerland's neutral credentials and ultimately bring a close to its awkward experiment in 'differ-ential neutrality' under the League. Although Berne finally renegotiated its position in the League in May 1938, abandoning its residual obligations towards collective security, a renewed determination to 'go it alone' was already evident in mid-1936. 'For a small country', the Swiss delegate told his colleagues in the League, 'the application of Article 16 [on economic sanctions] may be a matter of life or death ... in a weakened League, we have no choice but to recover that full neutrality from which we only departed in 1920 in the hope that the League would become truly universal'.[40] In May 1936, the month armed Abyssinian resistance finally ended, the Swiss took the lead in pressing for an early lifting of the economic embargo. When the Dutch foreign minister, de Graeff, asked that same month for representatives of the former neutrals to meet – as they had habitually done during the disarmament talks at the start of the decade – to discuss the Italo-Abyssinian issue and the future of the League of Nations, the federal authorities were initially sceptical of the value of such an exercise. In the end, Motta only agreed to attend the meeting 'for reasons of courtesy'.[41] Berne showed little interest in making common cause with the members of the neutral club over subsequent years and stood aside from all joint declarations made by the group in support of neutral rights and the independence of small powers.[42]

Whether Berne's wager on Italy ultimately proved beneficial is open to doubt. Mussolini certainly appeared to have appreciated Motta's 'courage' during the crisis. Although the Italian press continued to give vent to irredentist claims over the Ticino, relations between the two countries gradually stabilized. The sanctions affair intensified economic and financial relations between the two countries, even if Swiss companies were denied the business opportunities in Abyssinia many had hoped to see emerge from Berne's pro-Italian position during the sanctions debates, and its early recognition of Italian suzerainty in the region in December 1936.[43] Until his retirement from public life in 1939, Motta held to the conviction that Swiss interests were best served by appeasing the Italian regime. Notwithstanding Italy's departure from the League and increasing open support for German revisionism, no one in Rome wished to see German influence in Switzerland expand. Motta's successor, Marcel Pilet-Golaz, who as Federal Councillor for Transport during the Abyssinian crisis was intimately involved in the economic debates of the time, shared this outlook. Mussolini's declaration of non-belligerency in September 1939 seemed initially to confirm the wisdom of this policy. But when Swiss independence was ultimately put to the test in May–June 1940, it is questionable whether Mussolini's patronage counted for much. Swiss appeals for support went unanswered. Indeed, the return of Berne's emissary – Gonzague de Reynold – empty handed from a meeting with the *Duce* in early June so dispirited the Federal Council that Britain's minister was left to assume that 'an agreement to the German demands even affecting Swiss neutrality is possible at any moment'. Italy obligingly left its ports open to Swiss commerce after June 1940, but its ability to act as a counterweight to German power and speak for Swiss interests in Berlin from this date was minimal.[44]

Perhaps the most interesting repercussion of the Italo-Abyssinian war lay in its impact on attitudes within Switzerland. For the Swiss socialist party, which had consistently spoken in favour of the League during the crisis, the chilling prospect of war breaking out on the continent forced a rethink in their policy towards Swiss military re-armament. Henceforth, the annual military budget was voted through parliament with only minor amendments. The Socialists also gave their blessing to Berne's programme of 'spiritual national defence'. Hesitantly begun in early 1935, these initiatives had been spearheaded by Philippe Etter's Interior Department and aimed at strengthening Swiss resilience in the face of the political and cultural claims of Switzerland's neighbours. Naturally, Etter's initiatives – especially his *Kulturbotschaft* in November 1938 – reflected his traditional, conservative views on the need for a return to core Swiss values.[45] But the issue of what it meant to be Swiss was inevitably sharpened by the League's confrontation with Italy and the concerns it raised over the loyalties of Switzerland's Italian-speaking population. In a meeting on 10 December, Mussolini had taunted Wagnière with the remark that just as its Italian-speaking population had prevented Berne from applying sanctions against Italy, 'so too, you could never apply sanctions against Germany, with your three million Swiss–Germans'. Wagnière's retort – 'The Swiss are Swiss above all else, whatever language they speak' – may have satisfied the *Duce*, but the minister was only too aware of Switzerland's vulnerability in this area.[46] Three weeks earlier he had railed against the practice of some Swiss watch firms who 'deck themselves out in English names – as if we don't have enough languages in Switzerland – [and thereby] oblige watch boutiques to put in the window displays of their stores the following [English] description "made completely in Switzerland" etc'. 'Would it not be advisable', Wagnière pointedly asked his superiors, 'to bring to the attention of the chambers of commerce the inconvenience of this ridiculous custom.'[47]

It was under the influence of such reports that the federal government redoubled its efforts to revive a sense of Swiss solidarity and patriotism in the final years of peace. The programme of 'spiritual national defence' saw renewed emphasis placed on the confederation's founding 'myths' – most notably the story of Wilhelm Tell – and on its unique linguistic roots, with Romansch elevated to the status of Switzerland's fourth 'official' national language in 1938. The return to 'integral' neutrality that same year played a central part in the process, but the pinnacle of Switzerland's 'spiritual' reawakening came the following summer with the unveiling of a hugely popular National Exhibition in Zurich, where Swiss inventions, traditions, art, literature and institutions were all on prominent display. The impact that these initiatives had on the Swiss population remains a matter of scholarly debate. However, to outsiders, the changes in Swiss outlook were unmistakable.[48] Arriving in Basle from Germany in March 1936, the scholar–journalist Elizabeth Wiskemann found the cut and thrust of Swiss public debate invigorating, but was disappointed at the depth of Swiss insularity. The 'percentage of genuinely cosmopolitan, or even Continentally minded people', she recalled, was

> probably smaller than in any of the major European countries. The sentiments which prevail in Switzerland are small-scale provincialism ... and the fierce nationalism of a small country with virtually no language of its own. As this nationalism involves the Swiss in being oddly aggressive about the defence of their neutrality, which they have elevated into providing their national mystique, it seems a little absurd to an outsider at first.[49]

Four years later, in the midst of the 'Phoney War', Britain's new Minister to Berne, David Kelly, encountered a similar scene. He was surprised to find one federal councillor firm in the belief that Britain was still at war with the Boers:

> The Swiss appear to be (and their survival is probably due to it) a hard headed and practical race, who are not desperately interested in the rights and wrongs of a war which they detest. The majority of them have long ago calculated that while a Nazi victory would not at all suit their interests, it is up to them to keep as much trade going in all directions as they can get away with.[50]

Recent studies of Switzerland's wartime conduct suggest that the outlook Kelly observed in early 1940 continued to dominate Swiss decision making for the remainder of the war.[51]

Elizabeth Wiskemann's sojourn in Switzerland was the final leg of a journey that had taken her through Western, Central and Eastern Europe in search of material for her book on contemporary European political and international relations. The first edition of the book, inopportunely entitled *Undeclared War*, reached British bookshops shortly after Hitler's invasion of Poland. Although she later claimed to regret the title, 'undeclared war' perfectly captured the tension that enveloped European political life in the final years of peace. For the Swiss, as we have seen, this period of undeclared war began four years earlier when the country's leadership was forced to confront the very real possibility of conflict returning to their borders. Not only did the Italo-Abyssinian war bring Europe perilously close to the brink of war, but it also upset the European political order that had been forged at Locarno a decade earlier. For the Swiss, the episode challenged the basic tenets of Swiss foreign policy and threw into sharp relief the dangers of associating with a system of collective security whose political interests were increasingly at odds with those of Switzerland's great power neighbours. It was not merely Switzerland's basic political preferences that were amplified by the course of events over 1935 and 1936, but the social, cultural, historical and linguistic bonds that tied Switzerland into a political landscape dominated by its German and Italian neighbours. The crisis narrowed Switzerland's political horizons, both abroad and at home, and gave rise to a conception of Swiss neutrality that was increasingly narrow in scope and exclusive in its application.

Notes

1 See E.M. Robertson, *Mussolini as Empire Builder: Europe and Africa 1932–1936*. London, 1977, pp. 114–18; George W. Baer, *The Coming of the Italian–Ethiopian War*. Cambridge, 1967, *passim*.

2 R. Salerno, *Vital Crossroads: Mediterranean Origins of the Second World War, 1935–1940*. Ithaca, 2002, pp. 13, 213. For a similar view, see B. Sullivan, '"Where One Man, and Only One Man, Led": Italy's Path from Non-Alignment to Non-Belligerency to War, 1937–1940' in N.

Wylie (ed.), *European Neutrals and Non-Belligerents during the Second World War*. Cambridge, 2002, pp. 119–49.

3   Éamon de Valera to the League Assembly, September 1935, cited in M. O'Driscoll, *Ireland, Germany and the Nazis: Politics and Diplomacy, 1919–1939*. Dublin, 2004, p. 180.

4   F.P. Walters, *A History of the League of Nations*. London, 1952, p. 653.

5   For a full description see J. Ross, *Neutrality and International Sanctions: Sweden, Switzerland and Collective Security*. New York/Westport, 1989, pp. 50–2. F. Hardie, *The Abyssinian Crisis*. London, 1974, *passim*.

6   See M. Cerutti, 'L'élaboration de la politique officielle de la Suisse dans l'affaire des sanctions contre l'Italie fasciste', *Itinera* vol. 7 (1987), pp. 76–90.

7   G. Motta (Berne) to P. Dinichert (Berlin) 14 October 1933, *Documents Diplomatiques Suisses* (hereafter *DDS*) vol. 10. Berne, 1988, Doc. 341, pp. 850–1.

8   For the Swiss political system in the 1930s, see E. Wiskemann, *Undeclared War*. London, 1939, pp. 262–77. By 1930 41 per cent of the Swiss population were Catholics. See also William E. Rappard, *The Government of Switzerland*. New York, 1936.

9   See M. Wyss, *Un Suisse au service de la SS: Franz Riedweg (1907–2005)*. Neuchâtel, 2010; R. Scheck, 'Swiss Funding for the Early Nazi Movement: Motivation, Context, and Continuities', *Journal of Modern History* vol. 71/4 (1999), pp. 793–813.

10 D. Gerardi, *La Suisse et l'Italie, 1923–1950: Commerce, Finance et Réseaux*. Neuchâtel, 2007, p. 46.

11 G. Motta, 'Switzerland's Protest', *New York Times* 23 September 1934. See C. Gehrig-Staube, *Beziehungslose Zeiten: Das schweizerisch-sowjetisch Verhältnis zwischen Abbruch und Wiederaufnahme der Beziehungen (1918–1946) aufgrund schweizerischer Akten*. Zurich, 1997.

12 See W. Gautschi, *Der Landesstreik 1918*. Zurich, 1968; M. Caillat, M. Cerutti, J. Fayet and S. Roulin (eds), *Histoire(s) de l'anticommunisme en Suisse: Geschichte(n) des Antikommunismus in der Schweiz*. Zurich, 2009; H. Meier, 'The Swiss National Strike of November 1918' in H. Schmitt (ed.), *Neutral Europe between War and Revolution, 1917–1923*. Charlottesville, 1988, pp. 66–86.

13 See K. Kobach, *The Referendum: Direct Democracy in Switzerland*. Dartmouth, 1993, pp. 16–41; Wiskemann, *Undeclared War*, p. 296.

14 See Hans U. Jost, *Die reaktionäre Avantgarde. Die Geburt der neuen Rechten in der Schweiz um 1900*. Zurich, 1992; and U. Altermatt, 'Conservatisms in Switzerland: A Study of Anti-Modernism', *Journal of Contemporary History* vol. 14 (1979), pp. 581–610.

15 See A. Mattioli, *Zwischen Demokratie und totalitärer Diktatur: Gonzague de Reynold und die Tradition der autoritären Rechten in der Schweiz*. Zurich, 1994; and de Reynold's *Portugal: Gestern – Heute*. Leipzig, 1938; French original, Paris 1936; and *Conscience de la Suisse: Billets à ces Messieurs de Berne*. Neuchâtel, 1938.

16 See D. Bourgeois, *Business helvétique et Troisième Reich: Milieux d'affaires, politique étrangère, antisémitisme*. Lausanne, 1998, pp. 51–5.

17 Col. H. Guisan to Federal Military Department, 15 October 1934. *DDS* vol. 11, Doc. 71, pp. 236–40.

18 Gerardi, *La Suisse et l'Italie*, p. 49.

19 See E. Bonjour, *Geschichte der schweizerischen Neutralität*. Basle, 1971, vol. 2, pp. 315–43.

20 G. Motta (Berne) to G. Wagnière (Rome), 21 November 1933, *DDS* vol. 10, Doc. 358, p. 881.

21 G. Motta (Berne) to P. Dinichert (Berlin), 14 October 1933, *DDS*, vol. 10, Doc. 341, pp. 850–1.

22 'Notice sur la reconnaissance de l'URSS et la neutralité Suisse' by H. Frölicher (Federal Political Department, Berne), 30 May 1936, *DDS*, vol. 11, Doc. 242, p. 719.

23 Minutes of meeting in Federal Political Department, 3 October 1935, *DDS*, vol. 11, Doc. 152, p. 461.

24 Cited in Ross, *Neutrality and International Sanctions*, p. 110.

25 *League of Nations Official Journal*, Special Supplements no. 138, p. 106, cited in *ibid.*, p. 92.

26 Memo, 'Le conflit italo-éthiopien et les sanctions', Federal Political Department, 7 October 1935, *DDS*, vol. 11, Doc. 154, p. 473.

27 Wagnière cited in Bourgeois, *Business helvétique et Troisième Reich*, p. 53.

28 W. Stucki (Director of the Commercial Division, Department of Public Economy, Berne) to G. Wagnière (Rome), 21 October 1935, *DDS*, vol. 11, Doc. 160, p. 492. See also Stucki's letter to Swiss legations in Paris, Brussels, Stockholm, Madrid, Bucharest and Prague, 7 December 1935, *DDS*, vol. 11. Doc. 192, pp. 582–5.

29 Cited in A. Marder, 'The Royal Navy and the Ethiopian Crisis of 1935–36', *American Historical Review* vol. 75/5 (1970), pp. 1327–56 (1327). By September, the Admiralty thought the danger 'possible, though not probable'.

30 Federal Political Department, 'Proposition', 7 October 1935, *DDS*, vol. 11, Doc. 154, pp. 471–7.

31 G. Wagnière (Rome) to G. Motta (Berne), 10 July 1935, *DDS*, vol. 11, Doc. 136, p. 422.

32 H. Senn, *Erhaltung und Verstärkung der Verteidigungsbereitschaft zwischen den beiden Weltkriegen.* Der schweizerische Generalstab/L'état-major général Suisse, Band VI. Basle, 1991, pp. 66–74.

33 See E. Laur (Director of the Swiss Union of Peasants) to W. Stucki (Berne), 24 October 1935, *DDS*, vol. 11, Doc. 164, pp. 505–7.

34 See 'Summary of discussion which took place in the Federal Political Department on 3 October 1935 on the subject of the Italo-Ethiopian conflict', *DDS*, vol. 11, Doc. 152, pp. 458–68.

35 See Federal Council reply of 9 July 1932 to question from National Councillor Müri of 6 June 1932, *DDS*, vol. 10, Doc. 111, p. 242.

36 See Federal Council deliberations on 28 October, *DDS*, vol. 11, Doc. 172, pp. 527–9. G. Motta (Berne) to J. Avenol (Secretary Geneva, League of Nations, Geneva), 28 October 1935, *DDS*, vol. 11, Doc. 172/2, pp. 530–1.

37 For details, see Ross, *Neutrality and International Sanctions*, pp. 98–108.

38 R. Baudendistel, *Between Bombs and Good Intentions: The Red Cross and the Italo-Ethiopian War, 1935–1936.* London, 2006, pp. 9–10. E. Buehrle (Oerlikon) to H. Obrecht (Federal Councillor for Public Economy, Berne), 26 October 1935, *DDS*, vol. 11, Doc. 169, pp. 519–21.

39 Baudendistel, *Between Bombs and Good Intentions*, pp. 261–302. J-C. Favez, *The Red Cross and the Holocaust.* Cambridge, 1999, pp. 72–81, N. Wylie, 'The Sound of Silence: The History of the International Committee of the Red Cross as Past and Present', *Diplomacy and Statecraft* vol. 13/4 (2001), pp. 186–204.

40 C. Gorgé, Swiss Delegate to the League Assembly, cited in N. Orvik, *The Decline of Neutrality 1914-1941.* London, 1971, 2nd ed., p. 181.

41 P. Bonna (Federal Political Department, Berne) to Swiss legations and consulates in Caracus, Dublin, Montreal and Shanghai, 13 May 1936, *DDS*, vol. 11, Doc. 230/1, pp. 690–2 (691).

42 See Orvik, *The Decline of Neutrality*, pp. 177–94.

43 For these issues, see Gerardi, *La Suisse et l'Italie*, pp. 61–72; and *idem.*, 'L'apport de la Suisse à l'économie de guerre italienne. Quelques réflexions autour d'un bilan chiffré, 1936–1943' in V. Groebner, S. Guex and J. Tanner (eds), *Kriegswirtschaft und Wirtschaftskriege.* Zurich, 2008, pp. 255–70. Benedikt Heuser, *Netzwerke, Projekte und Geschäfte: Aspekte der schweizerisch-italienischen Finanzbeziehungen 1936–1943.* Zurich, 2001. Germany secured preferential access to Italian colonial possessions through an accord on 10 December 1936.

44 David V. Kelly (British Minister, Berne) to Foreign Office, 16 June 1940. The National Archives, London, FO371/24530 C6684. For Switzerland's economic position in 1940, see K. Urner, *Let's Swallow Switzerland: Hitler's Plans against the Swiss Confederation.* New York, 2001.

45 For an exploration of the various roots of Swiss nationalism, see O. Zimmer, ' "A Unique Fusion of the Natural and the Man-Made": The Trajectory of Swiss Nationalism, 1933–1939', *Journal of Contemporary History* vol. 39/5 (2004), pp. 5–24.

46 G. Wagnière (Rome) to G. Motta (Berne), 11 December 1935, *DDS*, vol. 11, Doc. 194, pp. 587–90 (589).

47 G. Wagnière (Rome) to G. Motta (Berne), 16 November 1935, cited in N. Wylie, *Britain, Switzerland and the Second World War.* Oxford, 2003, p. 68.

48 See J. Mooser, ' "Spiritual National Defence" in the 1930s: Swiss Political Culture Between the Wars' in G. Kreis (ed.), *Switzerland and the Second World War.* London, 2000, pp. 236–60.

49 Wiskemann, *The Europe I Saw.* London, 1968, p. 132.

50 David V. Kelly (British Minister, Berne) to E.H. Carr (Foreign Office), 16 January 1940. The National Archives, London, FO371/24537 C958.

51 See *inter alia*, Independent Commission of Experts Switzerland – Second World War, *Switzerland, National Socialism and the Second World War.* Berne, 2002; and N. Wylie 'Switzerland: A Neutral of Distinction?' in Neville Wylie (ed.), *European Neutrals and Non-Belligerents during the Second World War.* Cambridge, 2002, pp. 331–54.

Chapter 17

The European Neutrals and the Second World War

Efraim Karsh

Like most members of the international community, the European neutrals hailed the creation of the League of Nations as a fitting substitute to the power politics of the nineteenth century and their culmination in the First World War. Implacably opposed to the use of force for the advancement of foreign policy goals and totally committed to nonparticipation in armed conflicts, they could not but welcome the first attempt to banish war from the international scene and to establish 'a better world' on the basis of collective security, though this concept was no less antithetical to the idea of neutrality than the phenomenon it sought to eliminate, seeking as it did to incorporate the entire international community into a collective effort and frowning on outsiders and fence-sitters. In the words of Article 16 of the League's covenant:

> Should any Member of the League resort to war in disregard of its covenants under Articles 12, 13, or 15, it shall *ipso facto* be deemed to have committed an act of war against all other Members of the League, which hereby undertake immediately to subject it to the severance of all trade or financial relations, the prohibition of all intercourse between their nationals and the nationals of the covenant-breaking State, and the prevention of all financial, commercial and personal intercourse between the nationals of the covenant-breaking State and the nationals of any other State, whether a Member of the League or not. It shall be the duty of the Council in such case to recommend to the several governments concerned what effective military, naval, or air force the Members of the League shall severely contribute to the armed forces to be used to protect the covenant of the League.[1]

Had the League comprised all members of the international community as envisaged by its founders, and had it applied the system of sanctions in the letter and spirit of its covenant, there might have well been a significant reduction in the pervasiveness of war and a corresponding diminution in the prevalence of neutrality. Yet notwithstanding the risk to their national strategy, and in sharp contrast to the Great Powers' lukewarm attitude to the newly established world organization (the United States was never a member while the Soviet Union, Germany and Japan participated only at various stages), the small states willingly subordinated their neutrality to the principle of collective security, joining the League and accepting its covenant without any preconditions or reservations (with the exception of Switzerland, which joined only after being absolved of the obligation to participate in military sanctions). Even when the organization imposed economic sanctions on Italy following its invasion of Ethiopia, all neutrals (apart from Switzerland) unhesitatingly joined these measures, thus indicating the great faith they placed in the principle of collective security. Small wonder, then, that these states were profoundly disappointed when the sanctions failed to have the desired effect.

They were not alone. The Ethiopian episode brought home to the entire world that the system of collective security that had been so laboriously created did not, in the final analysis, provide an adequate basis for the management of international relations; that the League had never been a truly international but only a multinational body; and that it was not guided by a sincere spirit of universalism but was a cover for the continuation of the old power politics by other means.

This painful disillusionment led to the sudden resurrection of traditional neutrality to an even greater extent than before the First World War: while in October 1935 nearly all the League's member states participated in the anti-Italian sanctions, some eight months later, on 1 July 1936, three days before the organization abandoned the sanctions, seven of the traditional neutrals – Switzerland, Denmark, Finland, Holland, Spain, Sweden and Norway – issued a joint declaration cancelling indirectly their commitment to observe Article 16 of the League's covenant.[2] This was followed in March 1937 by a Dutch declaration that Article 16 did not oblige the League's members to participate in sanctions that could endanger their vital interests, and eight months later the Swedish foreign minister went a step further by asserting that the article had no legal force whatsoever. An identical announcement was made in January 1938 by the representatives of Sweden, Switzerland and Holland and in July 1938 the neutral states' dissociation from Article 16 culminated in the Copenhagen Declaration (issued by Belgium, Denmark, Finland, Holland, Luxembourg, Norway and Sweden), which determined that this article was not legally binding.[3]

The reversion of the small states to their policy of traditional neutrality was far from enthusiastic. Notwithstanding their realization that both the idea of collective security and the League of Nations itself were bankrupt, they found it psychologically and emotionally difficult to disavow the dream to which they had subscribed for nearly two decades. Indeed, alongside its repudiation of Article 16, the Copenhagen Declaration pledged to continue to operate within the framework of the League.

This, however, was easier said than done. As the continent was set ablaze, the European neutrals found themselves on their own, with each forced to adjust to its unique set of circumstances. Having won its independence a mere twenty years earlier, Finland was suddenly pitted against its former imperial master, which, despite its August 1939 non-aggression treaty with Germany (the Ribbentrop–Molotov Pact) and the attendant territorial gains, was anxious to secure its northern flank from possible attacks.

For Russia, Finland had always represented the northward extension of its land frontier by some 720 miles, thus removing the threat posed by imperial Sweden. Finland's strategic importance was significantly enhanced at the beginning of the eighteenth century by the establishment of St Petersburg as the Russian capital and the subsequent shift of the seat of Russian political power from Moscow to the north. One of the more enduring themes in Russian strategic thinking for centuries had therefore been the belief in the necessity of establishing some control, however tenuous, over Finland so as to prevent it from becoming a springboard for an attack on Russia.

Although these fears were considerably alleviated following Finland's 1809 annexation to Russia, they were by no means dispelled. In the early twentieth century, the Russian Imperial General Staff feared that in the event of a Russo-German war, Sweden would join Germany and attempt to regain Finland, and the attainment of Finnish independence in 1917 only served to rekindle Russia's traditional fears, which peaked in the late 1930s as German power became evermore threatening.[4]

For its part Finland had been painfully aware, from its very inception, that its buffer-state position left it only two viable alternatives in coping with the Soviet threat: to develop 'good neighbourly relations' with Moscow or to seek the friendship and protection of those powers that pursued an anti-Soviet line. Finland chose the second option, seeking German backing and support vis-à-vis its large neighbour, associating with the Soviet Union's western neighbours, particularly the Baltic states, and playing an active role in the League of Nations in the hope that its collective security system would deter future Soviet aggression.

Finland's disillusionment with the League and the restoration of neutrality as the cornerstone of its foreign policy was received most favourably by the Soviets. Not only did they cease, however briefly, to view Finland through the prism of their long historic insecurity, but they apparently came to consider it a potential ally. Refusing to take Finnish neutrality literally, they seemed to believe that Helsinki had at last come back to its senses and drawn the only conclusion possible in view of its geographical position, namely, to dissociate itself from Germany and lean toward the Soviet side. Perhaps the best proof of this perception was the initiation of secret talks (in April 1938) aimed at bringing about a bilateral agreement that would prevent Finland's transformation into a base for a German attack.

During these negotiations, which lasted for a year, Moscow's demands were quite restrained and it was prepared to pay a handsome reward for their attainment. If Helsinki felt unable to sign a secret defence pact, the Finnish delegation was told, the Soviets would be satisfied with a written declaration that Finland would ward off a possible German attack and accept Soviet aid to this end. In the territorial sphere, the Soviets asked to lease some islands in the Gulf of Finland for a period of thirty years, to be used as observation points for the protection of the naval routes to Leningrad (formerly St Petersburg). In return, they offered to guarantee Finland's territorial integrity within its present boundaries, to assist it militarily in case of need, to sign a trade agreement favourable to Finland and to lease it territories in eastern Karelia in exchange for the requested islands. Significantly, the Soviets took great care to emphasize that their offer of military aid did not mean the dispatch of troops to Finland, or any territorial concessions, but rather the procurement of arms and military equipment and the defence of Finland's territorial waters. Yet, although the Soviets agreed to drop some of their territorial demands in the course of the negotiations, and notwithstanding the loose nature of the association they sought to establish, the Finnish government rejected their proposals and the talks came to an inconclusive end in April 1939.[5]

Finland's uncompromising position appears to have been caused by a fundamental misperception both of its own geo-strategic position and the Soviet sense of vulnerability. Whereas the Soviet Union saw Finland as part of the Baltic zone separating itself from Germany, Finland considered itself part of the Scandinavian neutrality system.[6] While Finland's dissociation from Germany and its more forthcoming approach toward Moscow were intended to dispel Soviet distrust as much as to strengthen Finnish neutrality, by no means did they indicate any intention to be incorporated into the Baltic buffer zone. The government's main fear was that acceptance of the Soviet demands would be interpreted as deviation from the system of Scandinavian neutrality to the extent of effective identification with the Soviet Union. This view proved to be misconceived, and before long Finland realized that neutrality did not constitute a viable foreign policy course for a buffer state in a world conflict: six months after the interruption of bilateral talks, the Soviet Union approached Finland once more with territorial demands, this time after it had obtained German recognition of its interests in the eastern part of the Baltic.

On 5 October 1939 the Finnish government received a Soviet invitation to send a delegation to Moscow to discuss 'concrete political questions'. Four days later a Finnish delegation arrived in the Soviet capital and on 12 October talks between the two parties commenced. Unlike their lenient negotiating style in the 1938–9 discussions, the Soviet demands this time were onerous. These included the leasing of the Hanko Peninsula for a period of thirty years for the establishment of a naval base; the ceding of the islands in the Gulf of Finland; the removal further north of the Soviet–Finnish border on the Karelian Isthmus, which at the time was only twenty miles from the suburbs of Leningrad, and the demolition of Finnish fortifications in this area; as well as the addition of a clause to the Treaty of Non-Aggression of 1932, whereby neither of the contracting parties could join any other state or alliance that was directly or indirectly aimed at either of them. In return, Moscow was prepared to cede a district in Soviet Karelia, twice as large as the combined area of the territories to be ceded by Finland.[7]

It was evident to the Finns that, in addition to the legal breach of their sovereignty, the new Soviet demands had far-reaching implications for their national security. The demand for Hanko and large parts of Karelia would create a dangerous gap in Finland's coastal defence and establish a bridgehead aimed at the country's most vital part. Worse, if the Karelia fortifications were to be destroyed, Finland would lose the ability to defend itself. Therefore it was unanimously agreed that acceptance of all of the Soviet demands was out of the question. Nevertheless, the government differed over the extent to which Finland could, and should, make concessions. While the hardliners, Foreign Minister Elias Erkko in particular, maintained that Finland should zealously guard its national interests, others, such as Marshall Gustav Carl Mannerheim, the country's foremost military authority, and Juho Kusti Paasikivi, head of the negotiations team in Moscow and Finland's future President (1946–56), deemed it necessary to reach an agreement with the Soviet Union that would include some territorial concessions.

In the end, the hardliners prevailed and the Finnish delegation was instructed to reject the demands for a bilateral defence treaty and the leasing of military bases on Finnish soil. The only real concession Finland was prepared to make was the withdrawal by some miles of the frontier line in Karelia. This approach was undoubtedly more flexible and forthcoming than the one displayed during the previous negotiations, but by now it was anachronistic. What would have satisfied the Soviets in April 1939 was simply not good enough in the autumn. And so it was that, after another round of talks in which the Finns offered further concessions, on 13 November the delegation returned empty handed to Helsinki. A fortnight later the Soviets invaded Finland in strength.

If Finland's neutrality was largely the casualty of its unfortunate geo-political location, Norway was the victim of the precarious balance of power between the belligerents, which generated a jockeying for position that culminated in the violation of Norwegian neutrality – paradoxically, by the power that had the greater interest in its preservation.

Berlin was the principal beneficiary of Norwegian neutrality mainly due to its contribution to the uninterrupted transport of Swedish iron ore to Germany. In the summer the Germans could transport the ore via the Baltic Sea, but during the winter months (December to April) the Baltic's waters are frozen, which necessitated the transportation of this vital natural resource by train to the Norwegian port of Narvik, and thence by ship, inside Norway's territorial waters, to Germany. This nautical route (codenamed by the British the 'Leeds') allowed the Germans to breach the naval blockade against them.

These advantages did not evade the British eyes. From the very beginning of the war Winston Churchill, then First Lord of the Admiralty, pressured his government to mine the Leeds and force the German ore-carriers into the open sea where they could be intercepted. Churchill was opposed by the Foreign Minister, Lord Halifax, who feared that violating Norwegian neutrality would antagonize the other neutrals, first and foremost the United States. He also argued that the reduction, if not cessation, of Swedish iron exports to Germany could be achieved by peaceful means, namely through an Anglo-Swedish trade agreement, at the time in the process of being drawn up.[8]

This position prevailed throughout 1939 and it was only upon the realization that the trade agreement (signed in December 1939) had failed to terminate iron supplies to Germany that Churchill's approach began to win supporters. On 6 January 1940 the Allies attempted to test the anticipated Swedish and Norwegian response to the mining of the Leeds by protesting the sinking of British merchant ships in Norwegian waters and warning of a response in kind, only to draw an angry Swedish and Norwegian retort. Also, the question of aiding Finland against the Soviet attack came to the fore and Britain feared lest a strong pressure on Norway would prompt the latter to prevent the Allies from transporting such aid.

The Leeds mining operation thus remained an open issue until 28 March 1940 when the Allied Supreme War Council decided to carry it out, four days after the issuance of a warning to the Norwegian and Swedish governments. In tandem with the operation the Allies planned to land troops in four Norwegian ports as well as to seize control of the Swedish iron mines in order to prevent an immediate German reaction, which they assessed was bound to come.[9]

On 5 April 1940 the Allies delivered their communiqué to the governments of Norway and Sweden. Explaining that they could no longer allow the course of the war to be influenced by 'benefits' granted by both countries to Germany, and were therefore taking the necessary preventive steps, the communiqué contained no hint of the intention to mine the Leeds. But on 9 April, a day after the mining operation commenced, the Nazis invaded Norway and forestalled its completion.

While Germany was the principal beneficiary from the Norwegian neutrality, or perhaps because of it, at the beginning of the war Norway was not a matter of high priority for Hitler. The Führer believed – and expressed this view on several occasions – that Norway and Sweden would not depart from their neutrality and would be prepared to defend it by force against Allied violations, which he deemed to be highly unlikely.[10]

The heads of the German navy were the first to make the case for violating Norwegian neutrality. As early as 10 October 1939 the Commander of the navy, Admiral Erich Raeder, emphasized the necessity of obtaining naval bases in Norway and warned of the adverse consequences of a British conquest of the country. Hitler promised to consider the proposal, but until December gave the idea little further attention.[11]

Undeterred, Raeder continued to mobilize support for his view, and quickly won over the Nazi ideologue Alfred Rosenberg, who supported the conquest of the Scandinavian countries and the establishment of a 'Nordic Empire' under Nazi leadership. On 11 December Rosenberg introduced Raeder to Vidkun Quisling, leader of the Norwegian Fascist party, with whom he had been in contact since 1933 and who warned Raeder that the British were about to land in Norway, proposing to forestall this eventuality by giving Germany the bases it required. Quisling even offered his followers as a 'fifth column' in the conquest of Norway, claiming that such a 'coup' would receive the blessing of army officers with whom he had been in touch, and that the king would acquiesce in this *fait accompli*.[12]

The following day, on 12 December, Raeder met with Hitler, reported to him on his conversation with Quisling and again attempted to persuade the Führer – with the aid of data and impressions gleaned from the Norwegian collaborator – to support the plan to occupy Norway. Taking a new tack, Raeder emphasized the real danger of an impending British landing in Norway, describing at length the detrimental ramifications of such a move on the general progress of the war. By contrast, he argued that Norway could now be conquered more easily by Germany owing to the 'internal coup' mounted by Quisling and his followers.

This time Hitler was more attentive. As he listened to Raeder, he exclaimed that the conquest of Norway by Britain would be intolerable from Germany's standpoint. He also responded favourably to Raeder's proposal that the German general staff be permitted to collaborate with Quisling in preparing the invasion plans, either by peaceful means (i.e. the Norwegian government asking for a German intervention) or by force. Yet he refrained from taking a final decision on the issue before meeting Quisling in person and gaining a first-hand impression of him. This he did on 14 and 18 December, and while there is no official record of these encounters, it appears that Hitler was duly impressed, for already after the first meeting he ordered the general staff to draw plans for the conquest of Norway in collaboration with Quisling.[13]

A British raid on a German auxiliary ship in Norwegian waters on the night of 16–17 February 1940 was apparently the final straw for Hitler by highlighting London's readiness to violate Norwegian neutrality at will. According to a reliable German source, Hitler was furious after the incident and on 1 March issued the first operational command for *Wasaraibung*, as the invasion was codenamed. This afforded yet another glimpse into the Führer's essentially defensive perception of the operation – as a pre-emptive step aimed at both forestalling any attempt to disrupt the Swedish iron supplies to Germany and improving the German navy's position *vis-à-vis* its British adversary. As for the question of Norwegian neutrality, Hitler simply ordered that the entire operation be presented as geared to defending this policy. Two days later, on 3 March, Hitler decided that Operation Wasaraibung would precede the offensive in the West.[14]

By now Raeder was rapidly losing heart and on 14 March he asked Hitler to reconsider the operation's necessity, recommending that the offensive against France precedes the conquest of Norway. He even expressed the fear that the German invasion would generate a British presence in Narvik. However, confronted with Hitler's resolve regarding the rapid execution of the Norwegian invasion, Raeder reverted to his earlier position and in a meeting with the Führer on 26 March argued that while there was no immediate threat of a British landing in Norway, the danger was nevertheless very real and had to be dealt with. In view of the fact that after mid-April the Scandinavian nights would become significantly shorter, thus sharply hindering the operation, Raeder recommended moving at an early date. He proposed 7 April. Hitler, while concurring in principle, did not yet issue specific orders regarding the exact date.

Meanwhile the German naval attaché in Oslo reported that Norwegian anti-aircraft units had received permission to open fire on aircraft penetrating the country's airspace without awaiting orders from superior ranks. This aroused German fears of a leak in their operational plans and spurred Hitler to fix an invasion date: 9 April 1940.[15]

Just as the failure to adjust their policies to their geopolitical circumstances led to the collapse of the Finnish and Norwegian neutrality, so the success of Sweden, Spain, Switzerland and Ireland in attaining this very objective owed much to their skilful policies. True, a measure of this success can be attributed to the elements of luck and much more comfortable geostrategic location; yet it is doubtful whether these environmental factors would have sufficed on their own to safeguard neutrality, unless exploited to the full by each of the four successful neutrals.

Take the case of Switzerland, which found itself from the onset of hostilities buffered between Germany and Italy, and from the fall of France in the spring of 1940 totally surrounded by them. Though permanent neutrality, requiring complete and unqualified impartiality vis-à-vis the warring parties in any given conflict and abstention from any steps that might harm one of them in any way, had constituted the cornerstone of Swiss national strategy since at least the Congress of Vienna (1815), where the Great Powers undertook to guarantee this status, and though Switzerland's basic sympathy lay with the Allies rather than with the Axis, President Marcel Pilet Golaz desperately sought to appease Germany. He looked for an excuse to break diplomatic relations with Britain; cancelled the prohibition on the distribution of Nazi papers in Switzerland; dispatched politicians to Germany to discuss ways and means of enhancing co-operation between the two states; met with the leader of the Swiss Nazi party; leaked information to the Vichy government concerning the anti-Nazi tendencies of some of its Swiss embassy personnel, leading to their removal; and sought to limit League of Nations activities in Switzerland, home to the world organization's headquarters, so as to avoid the German wrath.[16]

These political moves were accompanied by a long string of economic and military concessions that ran counter to neutrality's letter and spirit. Thus, for example, in a trade agreement signed on 9 August 1940, Switzerland undertook to enlarge its exports of vital goods for the German war effort and to transfer to Germany all military equipment orders placed previously by France, Norway and Britain, including a British order of aluminium that was pending at the time. In addition, Switzerland granted Germany 150 million Swiss Francs in credit and accepted control measures, which effectively gave Germany a veto over the export of all goods deemed to contribute to the Allied war effort. In

February 1941 the Swiss moved even closer to Germany by enlarging its credit line to 317 million Swiss Francs, and several months later to 350 million.[17]

In the military sphere, in June 1940 Switzerland permitted the passage of trains carrying military equipment from Germany to Italy. This was admittedly a single incident that lasted but a fleeting moment. However, given the context of the violation, one cannot help but recall, with a measure of irony, Switzerland's adamant refusal some twenty years earlier to allow the League of Nations to transfer forces through its territory – at peacetime and for peaceful purposes (i.e. to supervise a referendum over a disputed territory between Poland and Lithuania).[18]

Sweden went much further in enabling the use of its territory for the German war effort, and for three full years (July 1940 to August 1943) permitted regular transfer of German troops and equipment from Norway across Swedish soil to Germany. This activity took place within the framework of an agreement concluded on 8 July 1940 and was presented by the Swedish government as involving only force replacements by keeping a strict quantitative parity between those entering and leaving. Yet within a couple of months the capacity of the agreement was expanded: notes exchanged on 14 September determined that the frequency of troop-train movements through Sweden would be increased, and the troops – defined as 'soldiers on leave' – would be permitted to bear arms (not allowed by the original agreement). This was greatly beneficial to the Germans, for the transport of troops and war material by land across Sweden saved them from the danger of British attacks on the high seas.

During the first half year of the agreement approximately 130,000 German troops were replaced in Norway and the German force there was considerably strengthened in equipment and other supplies.[19] In addition, the Swedish authorities occasionally permitted the Germans to transport forces on an ad hoc basis through their territory. In 1940, for example, an SS battalion was transported to Norway, and in July 1941, a month after the German invasion of the Soviet Union (Operation Barbarossa), Sweden granted significant assistance to the Axis war effort by allowing the transfer of a fully armed German division across its territory from Norway to Finland, which sought to regain its losses to the Soviets by joining the German attack.[20]

Interestingly enough, Sweden not only enabled the movement of German forces through its territory, in violation of its neutral obligations, but also exerted itself to ensure the success of these transfers. Having learned, immediately after the signing of the transfer agreement, of British intention to bomb the German trains, the Swedes reinforced their air defence units in potential danger areas and even considered suspending the standard procedure of firing warning shots near foreign aircraft penetrating Swedish airspace prior to firing directly at them.[21] In other words, Sweden was prepared to use force to defend the violator of its neutrality against the power seeking to prevent this violation.

This, to be sure, did not prevent Sweden, and all the more so Switzerland, from accompanying their concessions with a military build-up aimed at signalling to the belligerents that the cost of violating their neutrality would far exceed its potential gains. Thus the Swedish government announced general conscription in April 1940, quickly expanding its armed forces from 85,000 to 400,000. Simultaneously a Swedish military delegation was sent to Berlin to impress upon the Germans that Sweden was resolved to defend its soil against any aggression.[22]

Switzerland went to far greater lengths in building its deterrent image. Upon the outbreak of hostilities, the Swiss Army Commander, General Henri Guisan, ordered the drawing of a comprehensive plan for the country's overall defence, both in terms of training and accelerated build-up of the forces, and with regard to the construction and expansion of the fortification network along the country's northern border.[23]

This process gained momentum with the German victories in the West. Following the invasion of Denmark and Norway (9 April 1940), Switzerland declared general conscription and the population was urged to oppose any invader; local auxiliary units were set up to deal with parachuted infiltrators and fifth column saboteurs, and security was intensified at bridges, tunnels and other strategic sites. In May 1940, during the fighting on the French front, Guisan concluded that the Swiss army, with its current deployment and defensive doctrine, was ill prepared to fulfil its mission of blocking a German attack. He accordingly began drawing an alternative plan that would better accomplish this goal: only limited military forces would remain on the northern border – primarily for intelligence, observation and early warning operations – while the main bulk of the Swiss army would be grouped in a kind of fortified citadel to be built in the southern part of the country, in the Alps. Those industrial plants and strategic points that were considered so vital to the Germans as to constitute the motive for invading Switzerland were to be destroyed the moment the invasion began.

In July 1940, with the strong backing of his Defence Minister, Rudolf Minger, Guisan succeeded in obtaining government approval for his plan and commenced implementing it at an accelerated pace. Realizing that this national effort would not be effective without rallying the entire Swiss population behind it, on 25 July Guisan gathered his senior officers and urged them to prepare to defend Swiss independence even if this meant abandoning cities and villages and withdrawing to the mountains. He then asked them to disseminate his call throughout the army, from which it was relayed to the entire Swiss population. Guisan's speech was also intended to signal to the Germans that the Swiss army was totally committed to fighting any invader, even at the price of destroying major sections of the country's infrastructure.[24]

Despite domestic difficulties and constraints (primarily on the part of President Pilet Golaz who, as we have seen, held out for nearly exclusive reliance on appeasement), by the end of 1941 the construction of the fortifications had been completed: the army had been readied to contain a land offensive and was well protected from aerial attack. The St Gothard and Simplon passes through which German supplies were reaching Italy, along with over 1,000 strategic industrial plants throughout Switzerland, were mined and prepared for immediate demolition, and a special task force numbering some 16,000 troops was established with responsibility for carrying out this 'scorched earth' policy the moment an invasion began.

The effectiveness of Guisan's strategy may be inferred from the following incident. In late 1942 or early 1943 Switzerland was temporarily in danger of an invasion, as the German setbacks in Stalingrad and Cyrenaica and the Allied landing in North Africa forced Hitler to explore ways of immediately strengthening the Italian front, one of which involved the occupation of Switzerland. Since Hitler did not know how far Guisan was prepared to go in defending the country, he sent a senior general to meet with Guisan. At the encounter, in March 1943, the Swiss Supreme Commander made it clear to his German counterpart that Switzerland would defend its independence against all aggressors, come what may – though in the circumstances it was clear to both parties who the potential aggressor was. Upon receiving this message, Hitler abandoned the idea of invading Switzerland, having apparently realized that such an invasion would cost Germany dearly in both equipment and manpower and would bring about the destruction of the very strategic installation coveted by Germany.

Not every state can rely on a defensive strategy: in the absence of sufficient resources the neutral state can hardly hope to create an appropriate deterrence *vis-à-vis* the belligerents and is forced to rely on its political and diplomatic skills to advance the preservation of its independence and sovereignty. The policies of Ireland, and all the more so Spain, offer a typical example of this strategy.

Anxious to maintain rigorous neutrality, Ireland found it virtually impossible to adopt a deterrent policy owing to its gnawing military weakness. True, the government did try at the outbreak of the war to consolidate its defences: universal conscription was enforced and a 100,000-strong local security force was set up for observation and reconnaissance tasks; fortifications were erected at strategic sites; and central cities, including Dublin, were placed under military rule. Yet these steps impressed neither of the belligerents, and it is doubtful whether they played any role at all in safeguarding Irish neutrality. In the words of President Franklin Delano Roosevelt:

> If he [Irish Prime Minister Éamon de Valera] would only come out of the clouds and quit talking about the quarter of a million Irishmen ready to fight if they had the weapons, we would all have higher regard for him. Personally I do not believe there are more than one thousand trained soldiers in the whole of the Free State. Even they are probably efficient only in the use of rifles and shotguns.[25]

Not that de Valera himself had any illusions about Ireland's deterrent capabilities. Keenly aware that the primary threat to Irish neutrality emanated from Britain and the United States, he sought to prevent them from applying strong pressures on Ireland – possibly even invading its territory – by exploiting democracy's 'Achilles' heel': an influential constituency of voters.

Irish neutrality had some deleterious effects on the Allies: it kept them from using its ports for military purposes, thus significantly damaging their war effort. In the Anglo-Irish 1921 agreement, which provided for Ireland's independence and institutionalized its future relations with its former imperial master, the two governments pledged that in times of war their coastal defence would be carried out by the British navy. To this end Britain was permitted to retain naval bases at the Irish ports of Cobh, Lough Swilly and Berehaven. Seventeen years later, in April 1938, the two governments signed a second agreement stipulating the transfer of these ports to Irish control. This concession aroused considerable controversy in England, with its opponents, led by Churchill, warning that were Ireland to adopt a neutral policy in a future war, Britain would be denied access to these ports.[26]

This is indeed what happened. Ireland's declaration of neutrality prevented the British fleet from using its ports and denied it key fuelling stations from which it could set out to hunt German U-boats and protect the Atlantic convoys en route to Britain. This problem was significantly compounded by the fall of France and the loss of its northern ports. Consequently, following Churchill's assumption of the premiership in May 1940, Ireland came under intense pressure to allow the use of its ports for military purposes. By way of forestalling these pressures, the Irish government focused most of its efforts on the US domestic scene in an attempt to rally the administration, and the public at large, behind its refusal to allow the military use of its ports. Nor was the government deterred from pressuring President Roosevelt through the powerful Irish lobby in the US.

No sooner had Churchill come to power than de Valera directed an unofficial appeal to Roosevelt via the US Ambassador to Dublin, David Grey, requesting that the administration declare the Irish status quo vital to American interests.[27] At the same time he sought to exploit Roosevelt's dependence on the Irish–American vote in the 1940 elections campaign by urging the Irish Americans to pressure the administration – through Irish senators and Irish influence over the media – so as to advance Dublin's political goals.[28]

On the face of it, these pressures produced no results as the administration declined the request to recognize the 'Irish status quo'.[29] Yet notwithstanding the US's complete identification with Britain's war goals and its desire to see a British victory over Germany, for most of 1940 the administration persistently evaded London's repeated appeals to pressure Ireland. Thus, for example, in May 1940 Churchill asked Roosevelt to dispatch an American flotilla to visit Irish ports and to remain there for an extended period of time. Not only would such a visit have reduced the danger, preoccupying Britain at the time, of German paratroopers landing in Ireland, but it would have also underscored the importance attached to these ports by the US. Roosevelt, nevertheless, failed to acquiesce in Churchill's request. He promised to give it a serious consideration, but the matter was unceremoniously dropped.[30]

Even after the November 1940 US presidential elections, when the critical weight of the Irish lobby was significantly diminished, de Valera persisted in his attempts to use the lobby's leverage over the administration. In early 1941, for example, he asked sympathetic parties in the US to assist in obtaining weapons and wheat for Ireland. He also worked to mobilize the Irish–American community for campaigning against violations of Irish neutrality by 'any party whatsoever' and for deflecting the administration's pressure on senior Irish personage to support British use of the Irish ports. De Valera went so far as to threaten administration officials with a serious deterioration in Anglo-Irish relations should the pressure on Dublin intensify.[31]

By 1941, however, this policy was meeting with less success. The deeper the US involvement in the war became, the greater its pressure on Ireland regarding the use of the ports. Thus, in March and April 1941 the US made the provision of military aid to Ireland dependent on the latter's readiness to support the British war effort. Later, in December 1941, Washington informed Ireland that any aid received by the Allies from any country would hasten the victory over the Nazis, adding the wish that the Irish government and people would know how to fulfil their obligations in the current situation. In any event, by 1943 the Irish ports had lost much of their importance for the Allied war effort, and pressures in effect ceased.[32]

Spain's wartime experience differed from the Irish in several crucial respects, not least since its political and diplomatic manoeuvres were mainly directed against the belligerent that posed the lesser threat to its neutrality in an attempt to exploit its vulnerabilities for extracting (primarily economic) gains. Not only did the country's internal weakness fail to undermine its relations with the belligerents, but its absolute ruler, General Francisco Franco, succeeded in turning this liability into an asset, using it, on the one hand, for deflecting German pressure to join the war, and, on the other, for obtaining economic benefits for Spain. At the same time that he told Hitler that Spain's commercial relations with the Allies were beneficial for Germany since they would improve the Spanish economy and thereby increase the chances of its joining the war, Franco was laboriously persuading the Allies that favourable trade relations between them and Spain would reduce the probability of Spanish participation in the war on the Axis side. This arguments worked with both belligerents, and over a long period enabled Spain to attain its national goals – first and foremost, the rehabilitation of its economy – while simultaneously paying what Churchill called 'small change' to the warring sides.

Thus, during the three years from June 1940 to October 1943, in which Spain officially deviated from its neutral policy to the point of becoming a mere 'non-belligerent', Franco succeeded in preventing the exercise of heavy Allied pressure on Spain, and even in obtaining most of the economic benefits he required. This success owed much to the complexity of Allied interest in Spain. On the one hand, the Allies were well aware that Spain's dire economic situation, the famine in particular, constituted the principal and possibly the only reason for remaining outside the war, and that by supplying its needs in foodstuffs they were likely to increase the probability of its joining the war on Germany's side. On the other hand, withholding economic aid from Spain might alienate it from the Allies to the point of driving it into the arms of the Axis. Finding themselves between the hammer and the anvil, the Allies had to tread a delicate middle path in their aid policy toward Spain: they had to maintain its dependency on them and cultivate Spain's interest in retaining this dependency while at the same time disallowing the country to rehabilitate itself as much as to enter the war against them.

Franco exploited this predicament to the fullest, especially in the autumn of 1940, when he realized that Germany would not meet Spain's critical economic needs. Adopting a classical 'stick and carrot' policy in his dealings with the Allies, he sought to reinforce the impression that Spain was on the verge of entering the war on the one hand, while on the other taking great care to avoid straining relations, especially with the US, which was more insistent than Britain on a quid pro quo for its economic aid. Thus, for example, Franco downplayed the significance of his declaration of non-belligerency, defining it as an expression of national sympathy, and vowing that it involved no departure from Spain's policy of neutrality.[33]

Franco's efforts were handsomely rewarded. From the summer of 1940 to early 1941, Spain concluded a string of economic agreements with Britain: in July 1940 an agreement covering £728,000; in December 1940 an additional agreement for a British loan of £2.5 million; this was followed in January 1941 by a deal for the sale to Spain of 75,000 tons of grain from British stores in Argentina and North America; and the following month an additional British loan was made available. Britain also enabled Spain to pass goods through its naval blockade on a larger scale than that allowed to other neutrals. Spain, for its part, undertook not to transfer any goods and raw materials received from Britain to the Axis powers.

Allied attempts to conciliate Spain peaked in the second half of 1942 as their landing in North Africa (Operation Torch) approached. Cognizant of the area's centrality in Spain's national aspirations, the Allies feared that active Spanish opposition, whether directly or indirectly (e.g. permitting German troops passage through Spanish territory) could jeopardize the operation, which was heavily dependent on Gibraltar. Accordingly, in late 1942 they went to great lengths to ease Spanish concerns over their North African operations, indicating that co-operation on its part would be economically profitable. On 30 July 1942 the US agreed to raise its annual fuel supply to Spain to 492,000 tons (60 per cent of Spain's annual consumption), and in October Britain expressed its readiness to supply finished products and raw materials (fuel, flour, cotton and rubber). The Allies also commenced massive purchases of raw materials and industrial products from Spain as part of their economic war against Germany, thus contributing significantly to the rehabilitation of the Spanish economy.[34]

As the war tilted in the Allies' favour, it was the Reich's turn to pay for Spain's continued neutrality. Thus, for example, in November 1943 Franco obtained German agreement to sell 100,000 tons of grain (an extraordinary quantity for the states to negotiate, even when their relations had been at their zenith) by threatening that unless Spain received this large shipment its ability to resist Allied pressure would be seriously compromised.

Spain's improved bargaining position *vis-à-vis* Germany was similarly underscored by their dispute over the terms of payment for a December 1942 agreement for the supply of German weapons, chemicals and iron products in return for Spanish pledge to oppose an Allied invasion of its territory. In the payment negotiations, which lasted for the first half of 1943, the Germans demanded 341 million Deutschmarks for the goods and raw materials, but were eventually forced to back down and accept the Spanish price tag of 216 million Deutschmarks.[35]

Franco's considerable skill in manipulating the belligerents' weaknesses reached its peak in late 1943 when he rejected repeated American demands to cease exporting strategic materials to Germany, which would have caused Spain substantial financial losses (the value of wolfram exports to Germany skyrocketed from 2.1 million gold pesos in 1940 to 200 million in 1944, with total Spanish exports to Germany in 1945 reaching 877 million gold pesos). Besides, Franco reasoned that if he ceased exporting strategic materials to Germany, the Allies would feel free to terminate their 'preventive purchases' from Spain, which would lead to the country losing its two primary sources of foreign currency income. The Spanish dictator also hoped that by rejecting the American demands he could rely on Britain to persuade its ally to soften its position, which is indeed what happened. So much so that in April 1944 Churchill warned Roosevelt, in a personal note, that unless a compromise was worked out with Spain, Britain would sign a separate 'peace' with that country and would supply it with the fuel it needed (but was embargoed by the US).[36] The threat had the desired effect. The United States backed down and in May 1944 the Allies reached a mutually satisfactory compromise with Spain on the issue of strategic exports to Germany.

'Neutral states are without an active foreign policy at all', a renowned scholar of international affairs once quipped: 'their hope is to lie low and escape notice.'[37] The historical experience of the small European neutrals in the Second World War, the severest trial ever of neutral parties, would seem to disprove this assertion. If anything it shows that an initiative and enterprising policy, especially one that combines credible deterrence with skilful exploitation of the belligerents' weaknesses and is sufficiently attentive to the vicissitudes of the conflict, can ensure the successful preservation of neutrality even in the most total and comprehensive war, at times in the face of great adversity and international isolation. By contrast, insufficient environmental awareness on the part of the neutral, as expressed in reliance upon the wrong operative component or, alternatively, failure to find the optimal political and diplomatic combination, will most probably result in the collapse of neutrality.

Notes

1 F.P. Walters, *A History of the League of Nations*. Oxford, 1965, p. 51.
2 N. Orvik, *The Decline of Neutrality*. London, 1971, pp. 177–8.
3 H. Morgenthau, 'The Resurrection of Neutrality in Europe', *American Political Science Review* vol. 33 (1939), pp. 473–86; B. Skottsberg-Ahman, 'Scandinavian Foreign Policy: Past and Present' in H. Friis (ed.), *Scandinavia between East and West*. New York, 1950, pp. 255–307.
4 K.J. Holsti, 'Strategy and Techniques of Influence in Soviet–Finnish Relations', *Western Political Quarterly* vol. 17 (1964), p. 65.
5 For a detailed discussion of the Finnish–Soviet negotiations, see: Finnish Ministry for Foreign Affairs, *The Development of Finnish-Soviet Relations*. Helsinki, 1940; V. Tanner, *The Winter War*. Stanford, 1957; Max Jakobson, *The Diplomacy of the Winter War*. Cambridge, MS, 1961; G.C. Mannerheim, *Memoirs*. London, 1953.
6 See, for example, *Documents on British Foreign Policy 1919–1939* London, 1953, 3rd series, vol. 6, pp. 50, 54–5, 161, 217–18.
7 J. Degras (ed.), *Soviet Documents on Foreign Policy*. London, 1953, vol. 3, pp. 382–4.
8 T.K. Derry, *The Campaign in Norway*. London, 1950, p. 11.
9 R. Macleod and D. Kelly (eds), *The Ironside Diaries, 1937–1940*. London, 1962, pp. 237–8.
10 International Military Tribunal, *Nazi Conspiracy and Aggression*. Washington, 1964, vol. 3, p. 585, vol. 4, p. 509 (hereinafter *NCA*).
11 Ibid., vol. 11, pp. 891–2.
12 A. Martienssen, *Hitler and his Admirals*. New York, 1948, p. 47.
13 United States Department of State, *Documents on German Foreign Policy, Series D: 1937–1945*. Washington, 1949–57, vol. 8, pp. 519–21 (hereinafter *DGFP*); *NCA*, vol. 6, p. 892.
14 *NCA*, vol. 9, p. 389; *DGFP*, vol. 8, pp. 331–3.
15 Martienssen, *Hitler and his Admirals*, pp. 53–4; *DGFP*, vol. 9, pp. 35–6.
16 J. Kimche, *Spying for Peace: General Guisan and Swiss Neutrality*. London, 1961, pp. 45, 65–6; *DGFP*, vol. 8, pp. 394–5, 495–6.
17 *DGFP*, vol. 11, pp. 231–2; W.N. Medlicott, *The Economic Blockade*. London, 1952, vol. 1, p. 588; C. Howard, 'Switzerland, 1939–1946' in A. and V. Toynbee (eds), *Survey of International Affairs: The War and the Neutrals, 1939–1946*. London, 1956, p. 217.
18 Kimche, *Spying for Peace*, p. 42.
19 For the text of the agreement see: *DGFP*, vol. 10, pp. 158–9. See also: A.H. Hicks, 'Sweden', in Toynbee and Toynbee (eds), *Survey of International Affairs*, p. 184.
20 W. Carlgren, *Swedish Foreign Policy during the Second World War*. London, 1977, p. 84.
21 *DGFP*, vol. 10, p. 157.
22 Ibid., vol. 9, pp. 208–9; Carlgren, *Swedish Foreign Policy*, p. 60.
23 Guisan was appointed to his post on 31 August 1939, a day before the outbreak of the war. According to the Swiss constitution, an army commander at the rank of general is appointed only at times of emergency and serves only for the duration of emergency.
24 Howard, 'Switzerland, 1969–1946', pp. 209–12.
25 C. Hull, *Memoirs*. New York, 1948, vol. 2, p. 1355.
26 W. Churchill, *The Second World War*. Boston, 1948, vol. 1, pp. 428–9; Lord Chatfield, *It Might Happen Again*. London, 1942, pp. 126–7.
27 United States Government Printing Office, *Foreign Relations of the United States – 1940*. Washington, 1958, vol. 3, p. 160 (hereinafter *FRUS*).
28 *DGFP*, vol. 10, pp. 379–80.
29 *FRUS* 1940, vol. 3, p. 174; 1941, vol. 3, p. 215; *DGFP*, vol. 11, p. 883.
30 F. Lowewenheim, H. Langley and M. Jonas (eds), *Roosevelt and Churchill: Their Secret Wartime Correspondence*. New York, 1975, pp. 95–6.
31 *FRUS* 1940, vol. 3, p. 174; 1941, vol. 3, p. 215; *DGFP*, vol. 11, p. 883.
32 Hull, *Memoirs*, pp. 1353–4; *FRUS* 1941, vol. 3, p. 252. 0
33 S. Hoare, *Ambassador on Special Mission*. London, 1946, p. 48.
34 Ibid., p. 63; H. Feis, *The Spanish Story: Franco and the Nations at War*. New York, 1966, p. 177.

35   Feis, *The Spanish Story*, pp. 207–12.
36   B. Crozier, *Franco: A Biographical Study*. London, 1967, p. 385.
37   M. Wight, *Power Politics*. Harmondsworth, 1979, p. 160.

Chapter 18

The International Dimensions of the Spanish Civil War

Enrique Moradiellos

The civil war that ravaged Spain between 17 July 1936 and 1 April 1939 had internal origins and domestic causes. Its immediate roots lay in the severe Spanish social tensions and violent political polarization during a profound economic crisis. Nevertheless, the war contained a crucial international and European dimension which would be decisive for its course and final outcome. Contrary to popular opinion, this European dimension did not arise from the participation of foreign powers in bringing about the tragedy. It is a fallacy to suggest that Moscow orchestrated a Communist conspiracy to foster first a social revolution and then establish a soviet regime in Spain – the military insurgents who rebelled against a constitutional government claimed they had launched a pre-emptive strike against this Soviet menace. On the contrary, the Soviet Union menaced by the Nazi threat consistently restrained the revolutionary zeal of the Spanish Communist Party and were aghast at news of the insurrection.[1] Nor had the rebel officers obtained prior tacit support and even encouragement from Fascist Italy and Nazi Germany. There were exploratory contacts by the rebel leaders both in Rome and Berlin (particularly Italian links with the Falange Party in the first months of 1936), but they produced vague results. The timing and partial success of the uprising took both fascist powers by surprise.[2]

There were two fundamental reasons for the Spanish conflict's European and international dimensions: an essential analogy and a historic synchronicity between the crisis that led to the Spanish conflagration and the general European crisis of the 1930s. These also explain the passionate debate that convulsed contemporary European public opinion and the rapid internationalization of the conflict. The Spanish Civil War had an immense impact abroad, attracting the backing or the hostility of the diverse social classes, political ideologies and state powers of the fractured European continent.

The inter-war year crisis reflected the profound impact of the First World War upon the foundations of the traditional liberal and capitalist order. There were three alternative socio-political projects that might tackle the challenges created by the huge war effort and subsequent devastation: the inter-class reformist–democratic project; the authoritarian or totalitarian reactionary alternative; and the labour-based revolutionary proposal. These three political

'Rs' (Reform, Reaction and Revolution) became the protagonists in state form of a silent and spasmodic 'European civil war'. In all the continental countries, especially after the destructive impact of the Great Depression of 1929, the three political alternatives were present to a greater or lesser degree of intensity according to the respective level of socio-professional modernization and economic development. One of the other competing models triumphed following different episodes of violence and tension: Bolshevism in Russia after the Russian Civil War of 1917–20 and consolidation of the Soviet Union; Fascism in Italy in 1922; a military dictatorship in Portugal in 1926 – the *Estado Novo* of Oliveira Salazar; Nation Socialism and Hitler and the collapse of the democratic Weimar Republic in Germany; and the advent of mass suffrage parliamentary democracy in Great Britain and France.

Spain experienced a similar re-adjustment with the crisis of the liberal monarchy, which began in the summer of 1917; the establishment of the military dictatorship of General Miguel Primo de Rivera in September 1923; and the fall of the monarchy of King Alfonso XIII and the peaceful establishment of the Second Republic in April 1931. During the democratic experience of the Republic (1931–6), none of the three competing socio-political projects proved strong enough to impose itself upon the others and achieve a stabilization of the existing tensions. By 1936 there was virtual deadlock between the fragmented democratic–reformist alternative (in power during the first two years, 1931–3), the counter-reformist and reactionary response (in power during the following two years, 1933–5) and the recurring emergence of a revolutionary alternative (articulated by Anarcho-Syndicalism rather than orthodox Communism). They were powerful enough to disestablish the other alternatives but not to supplant them.[3]

It was this balance of forces that differentiated the Spanish crisis within the general European crisis. Unlike other continental countries, Spain reached an unstable deadlock between the reformist project and its reactionary counter-model so that stabilization based on the definitive imposition of one of these projects proved impossible, and neither was able to contain the revolutionary forces. This was illustrated by the vital electoral contest of February 1936. A Popular Front coalition won by a narrow majority, but their defeated opponents resorted to military force to try to reverse the situation. Due to historical traditions and recent experiences, within the armed forces there was little sympathy for the revolutionary proposals but overwhelming support for the reactionary alternative *vis-à-vis* those backing a reformist option. The factors that identified the specific Spanish crisis with the generic European crisis and attracted European sympathizers to each warring faction in Spain were reinforced because simultaneously with the civil war (1936–9) the European international relations system experienced, after 1936, a process of irretrievable crisis leading to the outbreak of the Second World War.

This crisis of the European order originated in the frailty of the international relations system after the Allied victory in November 1918. The symbol of this system was the League of Nations. The profound economic crisis of late 1929 destroyed its precarious stability since it engendered severe imbalances in inter-state relations and in the socio-political internal dynamics of various European and extra-European powers.[4] The new counter-revolutionary, totalitarian regimes in Italy and Germany posed the main threat to the existing international order. The revisionist plans of Fascist Italy (in the Mediterranean and North Africa) and Nazi Germany (in Central and Eastern Europe as a prelude to further world aims) were in direct contrast to the interests of the two principal powers that benefited from and guaranteed the existing status quo: the democratic regimes of France and Great Britain. Both countries were apprehensive about Nazi and Fascist imperial irredentism but they considered a hostile combination of both dictatorships very improbable because there was, in principle, a clear antagonism between their respective foreign policies. The German aim to annex Austria and to achieve hegemony in the Balkans clashed with the Italian aspiration to guarantee Austrian independence as a 'cushion state' in the north and to exercise a *de facto* protectorate over the Balkans. Franco-British fears of a problematic Italo-German agreement were eclipsed by another fundamental concern: the Soviet Union's replacement of Russia after the triumph of the Bolshevik Revolution in October 1917. Its social revolutionary and anti-capitalist nature and rising influence through Communist parties in other states provoked strong reactions in the British and French governing circles whether they were conservative, liberal, social democratic or labour. Elites in both countries were convinced that another European war would only unleash new social revolutions and extend communism and this deep conviction was not totally destroyed by the perceptible moderation of Soviet diplomacy after the crucial year of 1933.

Indeed, Stalin's dictatorship had generated a remarkable change in Soviet foreign policy after the Nazi regime came to power with its declared programme of anti-Communist expansion towards Eastern Europe. Until this moment and through the Comintern, the Soviet leaders had pushed for a programme of global revolution that would bring the revolutionary regime out of its isolation and facilitate the difficult process of the 'construction of socialism within one country' through industrialization and agrarian collectivization. Once this hope had been destroyed, the Soviet Union's strategic vulnerability and military unpreparedness were aggravated by the almost simultaneous emergence of a Japanese threat in East Asia and a German threat in Central Europe. These threats to both of its remote and exposed frontiers forced Stalin to withdraw his support for world revolution and search for a diplomatic and military understanding with the democratic powers to contain the German threat and also avoid the nightmare of a giant coalition of capitalist states against the USSR. From 1934 when the Soviet Union joined the League of Nations its new foreign policy was based upon the defence of collective security and the status quo. This was accompanied by a new Communist strategy favouring the establishment of Popular Front governments across Europe defending democracy and opposing fascism. A Franco-Soviet treaty, signed in May 1935, prescribed mutual assistance in the case of third-party aggression and reflected the USSR's new political orientation and their mutual concerns about a revived German challenge.

The Japanese occupation in 1931 of the Chinese province of Manchuria struck the first blow to the precarious international system. Two years later, Hitler withdrew Germany from the League and initiated an intense rearmament programme. In 1935, it was Mussolini who challenged the policy of collective security by invading Abyssinia and resisting economic sanctions imposed by the League against Italy. Finally, in March 1936, Hitler seized the opportunity of the crisis over Abyssinia and ordered the remilitarization of the Rhineland, the strategic province bordering France that had been demilitarized not only in 1919, but, more significantly, by the freely negotiated 1925 Locarno agreements.

None of these unilateral revisionist acts was contained effectively by either France or Britain. Both still hoped to avoid a new armed confrontation and to modify Italian and German ambitions within the European and international arenas. Accordingly, British leaders, followed by the French authorities with varying degrees of enthusiasm, initiated the so-called 'appeasement policy' towards the two dictatorships. This policy was essentially an emergency diplomatic strategy designed to avoid another war by means of explicit negotiation (or implicit acceptance) of 'reasonable' changes within the territorial status quo (especially in all of Eastern Europe), which would substantially satisfy the Italo-German revisionism without endangering vital Franco-British interests.[5]

The core of this appeasement policy was based upon the conviction that the two democracies did not possess sufficient military strength on the one hand or human or economic resources on the other to enter into a possible conflict with the three revisionist powers simultaneously. Their economic weakness resulted from the severe economic crisis, a weakness that affected France much more than Britain, giving the latter a dominant position in the Entente. Secondly, France and Britain feared they would be militarily vulnerable in the event of a simultaneous conflict with Japan in the Far East, Germany in Europe and Italy in the Mediterranean. The 'Great War' had already demonstrated the intense difficulty of containing Germany's war effort on one front without allies. Thirdly, the diplomatic situation of the 1930s was unfavourable. Unlike the 1914–18 period, Britain and France could not rely on the vital support of the USA (which had withdrawn into isolation) or of Russia (now a dangerous country because of its social doctrines, suspect political motives and uncertain military strength). The fourth and last reason was the political frailty of both states as regards the expectation of war: a pacifist public opinion sought to avoid wherever possible and at whatever cost another human bloodbath such as that of the Great War.

Thus on the eve of the outbreak of the Spanish Civil War, the symptoms of disintegration of the system of inter-European relations were already evident. In this international context, on 17 July 1936, a powerful military insurrection against the Popular Front Republican government began in Spanish Morocco, extending in the following days to the rest of Spain. The rebellion failed in the most populated and developed regions of Spain (including the capital, Madrid) because of the army's own internal divisions and the prompt intervention of working-class militias. This unexpected setback left the insurgents needing to conquer the area controlled by the Republican government, while the latter set about preparing for defence despite the serious damage to its military capabilities by the vast defection amongst its armed and security forces. The partial failure of the military uprising made civil war inevitable.

Both sides realized that the conversion of a coup into a war created a vital and logistical problem given the balance in the geographical division of Spain and the existing frailty of the domestic arms industry. Both knew they lacked the necessary military means to wage war for a considerable length of time. On 19 July 1936 both the Republican government and General Francisco Franco, commander of the rebel forces in Morocco, sought aid from those European powers likely to offer reliable support for their cause.

The Republic secretly requested that France – where a Popular Front government led by the socialist Léon Blum had taken power a month earlier – send aeroplanes and ammunition to crush the uprising. Franco sent personal emissaries to Rome and Berlin to obtain aircraft and arms to transport his experienced troops to Seville, thereby enabling them to begin the march on Madrid, whose conquest was necessary to secure international recognition. These simultaneous pleas for foreign aid indicate both sides' explicit awareness of the international dimensions of the Spanish conflict and a deliberate attempt to plunge it into the severe tensions that fragmented Europe in the late 1930s. In effect, both requests initiated a rapid internationalization of the civil war.[6]

Franco's first appeals to Germany and Italy failed but on 25 July, after receiving two personal emissaries sent by Franco from Morocco, Hitler decided to send twenty transport planes and six fighter planes secretly with their crews and technical personnel. Two days later, after repeated appeals conveyed through the Italian consul in Tangier, Mussolini also decided to send twelve transport planes secretly and to back the insurgents' position in Majorca. The decision of both dictators to intervene in support of Franco (taken without mutual consultation) reflected the very similar political and strategic considerations of their respective plans for European expansion. Above all, if the dispatch of modest and covert aid favoured the triumph of the military insurrection, this would allow for a low-cost and low-risk adjustment of the balance of forces in the western Mediterranean, depriving France of a dependable ally on her southern flank and ensuring an allied or at least a neutral regime in the Iberian Peninsula. Both Hitler and Mussolini sought to reassure the British and French governments and public opinions that they were providing disinterested support to an anti-communist counter-revolution. This line of reasoning appeared to be borne out by the social revolution unleashed in the Republican rearguard during the first months of the war as a by-product of the coup. The primacy of geo-political considerations was made explicit in Hitler's secret

instructions to his first diplomatic representative in Franco's Spain, the retired
General Wilhelm Faupel, four months after the outbreak of the war:

> His (Hitler's) exclusive object was that, after the end of the war, Spanish foreign policy
> would neither be influenced by Paris or London nor by Moscow and consequently in
> the inevitable and definite conflict over the reordering of Europe, Spain would not be
> found on the side of Germany's enemies, but if possible on that of its friends.[7]

From then on, the combined Italo-German military, diplomatic and financial
support would be the foundation of the insurgents' war effort. It would prove
far more important than the logistic aid lent by the Portuguese dictatorship of
Salazar and the ideological backing rendered by the Catholic world and the
Vatican. During the entire war, nearly 80,000 Italian soldiers (forming part of
the so-called *Corpo Truppe Voluntarie*) and some 19,000 German troops (the
so-called Condor Legion) took a prominent part in nearly all the battlefields on
Franco's side.[8]

The unexpected prolongation of the war and the Italo-German commitment
to a Franco victory reinforced their original motives for intervention with other
secondary factors: Germany's aims of ensuring the supply of Spanish steel and
pyrites (essential to its accelerated rearmament programme); the transformation of the Spanish war into a military laboratory where the German and
Italian armed forces could try out techniques and acquire war experience for
the future; and the use of the conflict to accentuate the differences between the
French and British governments and to polarize the public opinion within both
countries. Yet these new factors never eclipsed the central geo-political motive
that had from the start prompted the Italo-German decision to intervene on
Franco's behalf. In late December 1936, the German ambassador in Rome
emphasized why Italy's interests were more deeply engaged than Germany's
in the conflict, not least because of its location in the Mediterranean, an area
reserved for Italian imperialism:

> The interests of Germany and Italy in the Spanish troubles coincide to the extent that
> both countries are seeking to prevent a victory of Bolshevism in Spain or Catalonia.
> However, while Germany is not pursuing any immediate diplomatic interests in Spain
> beyond this, the efforts of Rome undoubtedly extend towards having Spain fall in
> line with its Mediterranean policy, or at least toward preventing political cooperation
> between Spain on the one hand and France and/or England on the other.[9]

In contrast to Franco's success in his international negotiations, the Republic
suffered only disappointments. In France Blum's initial reaction was to aid
the Republic for obvious political and strategic motives: it was an ideologically similar regime whose friendliness and potential collaboration was vital
to guarantee the security of France's southern border in the Pyrenees and of
the communications with its colonies in North Africa (where one third of the

French army was based). But a profound domestic crisis ensued due to the open hostility of the French right-wing parties, of Catholic public opinion and of very influential sectors of the civil and military administration. All opposed the delivery of weapons to Spain's Republican government and instead favoured a policy of neutrality for two essential reasons: firstly, their antagonism towards the perceived emergence of revolutionary symptoms within the Spanish Republic that could be potentially contagious and reminded them of the spectre of the critical days experienced in France in June 1936; secondly, their fear that military involvement in Spain could trigger a European conflict in which France could find herself alone, without any allies, against the combined might of Germany and Italy.[10] Even the President of the French Republic, Albert Lebrun, warned Blum sternly: 'What is being planned, this delivery of arms to Spain, may mean war or revolution in France.'[11]

Together with the very tense domestic situation, Blum had to take into account another decisive factor: the attitude of strict neutrality adopted, from the start, by its vital ally in Europe, the Conservative-dominated British National government. The British Cabinet shared the French right's hostility towards the revolutionary symptoms within the Spanish Republic and was bent on 'a policy of appeasement' towards Italy and Germany in the belief that, with some small revisions of the continent's territorial status quo, the nightmare of a European conflagration could be avoided. Stanley Baldwin, the British Prime Minister instructed the Foreign Secretary, Anthony Eden, to follow a policy of absolute neutrality, whilst implying benevolence towards the military insurrection: 'I told Eden yesterday that on no account, French or other [Italy or Germany?], must you bring us into the fight on the side of the Russians.'[12] The British governing classes believed that the hypothetical risks caused by a Nationalist victory in Spain heavily dependent on Italo-German aid could always be countered by two crucial available means: the power and lure of sterling (key for the economic reconstruction of Spain after the war) and the might of the Royal Navy (key to protect or blockade the Spanish coast). Thus, while for the British the military victory of the insurgents presented no major threats, the alternative appeared surrounded by all sorts of perils: 'the alternative to Franco is communism tempered by anarchy' (in the words of a Foreign Office analyst). A classified minute from Sir Samuel Hoare, First Lord of the Admiralty, left no doubts about the political and strategic reasons for preferring the triumph of the insurgents' cause in Spain:

> For the present it seems clear that we should continue our existing policy of neutrality ... When I speak of 'neutrality' I mean strict neutrality, that is to say, a situation in which the Russians neither officially nor unofficially give help to the Communists. On no account must we do anything to bolster up Communism in Spain, particularly when it is remembered that Communism in Portugal, to which it would probably spread and particularly to Lisbon, would be a great danger to the British Empire.[13]

Faced with this double domestic and external opposition, Blum abandoned his initial decision and instead on 25 July 1936 announced French neutrality in the Spanish conflict, hoping to preserve the governmental coalition, prevent the mobilization of the Right and safeguard collaboration with his British ally. In early August 1936, the French government suggested a diplomatic solution to confine the Spanish war within its territory and restrict its domestic and international impact: a Non-Intervention Agreement with an arms embargo against both Spanish warring factions. Initially Blum's proposal of non-intervention was seen as the lesser evil. Years later his cabinet secretary would note the basic objective was 'to prevent others from doing what we were incapable of accomplishing'.[14] In other words, since France was in no position to come to the aid of the Spanish Republic, it would, at the very least, avoid Italy and Germany's continuous help to Franco until the opportunity emerged to promote some kind of armistice or international mediation to end the conflict. A year later, Louis de Brouckère, President of the Socialist International and Blum's close collaborator, confided to the President of the Spanish Republic, Manuel Azaña, the impossibility of adopting a different policy:

> Last year, on his return from Spain [De Brouckère had visited the country in early August 1936], he arrived in Paris when the non intervention policy was implemented. He spoke about the matter with Blum one afternoon. Blum was unable to take any other course. If he had given arms to Spain, the civil war in France would have erupted soon after. Blum told him that he did not have the security of the armed forces. The General Staff was opposed to supporting Spain. Opinion would have turned against Blum, accusing him of answering to Moscow. England would not have supported him in case of a foreign conflict. De Brouckère speaks of a 'fear of England' as one of the motives for the particular policy.[15]

The French proposal of introducing a collective arms embargo in Spain was a resounding diplomatic success. By late August 1936 all the European governments (including Italy, Germany, Portugal and the Soviet Union) subscribed to the Non-Intervention Agreement and agreed to participate in a Non-Intervention Committee established in London to supervise its application. However, it was merely a rhetorical success. Behind the façade of the agreement and the committee, the fascist powers continued systematically and in co-ordination to deliver their crucial aid to General Franco while the Republic had no access to vital military supplies from France and Britain (or other European countries).

The Western democracies' retreat before the joint surge of the newly formed 'Italo-German Axis' could be clearly perceived in the workings of the Non-Intervention Committee in London. After its inaugural meeting, the German representative sent a confidential report to Berlin emphasizing correctly the lack of a genuine Franco-British determination to stop intervention in Spain and the delaying and elusive nature of the Committee:

Today's meeting left the impression that with France and England, the two powers principally interested in the committee, it is not so much a question of taking actual steps immediately as of pacifying the aroused feelings of the Leftist parties in both countries by the very establishment of such a committee. In particular during my conversation today with [Sir Robert] Vansittart [Permanent Under-Secretary of the Foreign Office] in regard to another matter, I had the feeling that the British Government hoped to ease the domestic political situation for the French Premier by the establishment of the committee.[16]

The obvious inability of the Non-Intervention Committee to stop Axis aid to General Franco established an asymmetric structure of support that was clearly very favourable to the insurgents' cause and highly harmful to the defensive capability of the Republic. Only Mexico, presided over by Lázaro Cárdenas, endorsed openly the Spanish Republican government, but was unable to counter the combined effects of Italo-German intervention and the reluctance of the Western democracies and the United States (which had seconded the attitude of the Franco-British Entente with its own policy of neutrality).[17] Furthermore, Mexican support was effectively nullified by the open logistical aid provided by the Portuguese dictatorship and the propagandistic and moral backing offered by the Vatican and international Catholicism to the insurgents. In fact, it is significant that the only genuine number of foreign volunteers fighting with Franco's troops was the contingent of 700 Irish Catholics, led by General Eoin O'Duffy.[18] The Spanish rebels also included a detachment of foreign volunteers who could hardly be reconciled with the idea of a Christian crusade and nearly 70,000 indigenous forces were recruited amongst Moroccan mercenaries in the Spanish Protectorate.[19] Sympathy for the Republic within popular and intellectual circles in the Western world did not produce many military supplies but it was a different story when it came to the recruitment of international volunteers and the provision of humanitarian aid.[20]

Faced with the Republic's apparently imminent military collapse, Soviet policy changed radically in September 1936. Initially, the Kremlin maintained a prudent attitude of 'platonic sympathy' towards the Republic to avoid damaging its rapprochement with France and Great Britain. It subscribed to the Non-Intervention Agreement. The instructions given in early September by Maxim Litvinov, the Soviet Commissar of Foreign Affairs, to Marcel Rosenberg, the Ambassador in Madrid (who officially presented his credential letters on 31 August 1936) stated the reasons for the initial cautious Soviet approach:

Before your departure, we discussed several times the question of possible aid to the Spanish government but we reached the conclusion that it is impossible to send any aid from here. It is imperative to explain to our friends the limits of our possibilities due to the long distance, the lack of the calibres for the rifles and cartridges that Spain needs, and the danger that the rebels could intercept the deliveries. Moreover, our help would provide Germany and Italy with a pretext for a full-scale intervention and thus the supply of the insurgents to dimensions such that we would never be able to match … We are aware that the insurgents are now receiving help from their friends abroad, but it has to be done covertly and so the amount is relatively small. Nevertheless, if it could be shown that, contrary to the principles of non-intervention, military aid is rendered to the insurgents, we could then modify our position as well as put pressure on the French government which naturally has more possibilities to offer support than all the other European states put together.[21]

When the collective embargo failed to prevent foreign intervention the Soviets modified their position. On 14 September 1936 Stalin decided to confront the Axis in Spain to test the viability of his strategy of collaboration with the Western democracies and support for collective security to counter the threat of Nazi expansionism. Months after that crucial decision, a report to Moscow from the deputy leader of the Soviet military mission in Spain drew the following conclusions:

A victory for the fascists in Spain may create the conditions for strengthening the aggressiveness of all fascist states – first and foremost, Hitlerite Germany – thus extraordinarily deepening the danger of war in Europe, especially of an attack by Germany on Czechoslovakia and other democratic countries and a counterrevolutionary war against the USSR.[22]

From then on, by helping to establish the International Brigades as well as by directly delivering weapons, the Soviet Union provided the central foundation for the stubborn Republican resistance. It also constituted its main means of financial support (through the mobilization of the assets obtained by the purchase of seventy-five per cent of the gold reserves from the Bank of Spain to meet the costs of war requirements).[23] At least 35,000 foreign volunteers fought in the International Brigades. The Soviet military mission in Spain involved up to 2,082 personnel.[24] However, from the start, Soviet assistance was a provisional means to avoid the imminent Republican defeat and to fill the temporary vacuum until the hypothetical delivery of military aid by the Western democracies; a condition *sine qua non* to obtain victory. Around this desired or feared eventuality (the intervention of the Western democracies), the parallel and antagonistic foreign policies of both warring sides were taking shape.

General Franco deployed all his diplomatic and propagandistic resources to preserve the Non-Intervention Agreement. He was aware that his victory over his poorly supplied enemy depended on the Western democracies' abandonment of the Republic without affecting his own capacity to receive Italo-German military aid. This fact was recognized close to victory by a leading member of the Nationalist diplomatic corps:

In connection to the so-called 'Spanish Problem', the guiding principle of all the European Governments has been to avoid a European war out of its international repercussions. In turn, our principal and almost exclusive task was to localize the war in Spanish territory, avoiding in this way by all means an international war out of which we would have little to gain and much to lose. At the same time, however, we had to ensure that we would still be able to obtain the aid we needed from our foreign friends while ensuring at all costs that our enemy received no aid or at least that this aid was minimal.[25]

In contrast, the Republic's diplomacy, while embracing Soviet aid as a sort of 'shipwreck's table', concentrated its ultimately futile efforts on achieving the support of the Western democracies and ending the Non-Intervention embargo – an embargo that effectively applied only against the Republican government and had been fatal to its war effort. In the meantime, as Dr Juan Negrín (the Republican Prime Minister from May 1937) suggested, it was only possible to resist until the outbreak of war between the Axis and the Western democracies or to ensure the best conditions in a negotiated surrender.

> Although I have to show optimism in public, I do not believe we can gain anything of practical value out of the meeting of the League of Nations [Dr Negrín was attending the Annual Assembly in September 1937]. Germany, Italy and Portugal will brazenly continue to help Franco and the Republic will last as long as the Russians want us to last, since our defence depends on the armaments they send us. Only if the inevitable encounter of Germany with Russia and the Western Powers occurs, would we have the possibility of winning. However, if this does not happen, we will only be able to fight to achieve an honourable peace.[26]

To Negrín's chagrin and Franco's good fortune, the Western democracies never reversed their attitude. They always subordinated the 'Spanish Problem' to the fundamental objectives of appeasement followed by Britain and assumed by France (despite occasionally turning a blind eye to the smuggling of weapons through the Catalan border). In July 1937, the French Foreign Minister confessed confidentially and with resignation the following bitter truth to the American Ambassador in Paris:

> As far as he could foresee the future, the position adopted by France will depend entirely on the position of England. France will not go to war against Germany and Italy. That will be the position of France towards the Spanish affair. If England chooses to stand firmly by the side of France against Germany and Italy, France will act. If England continues to hold aloof France will not be able to act. France can never be caught in the position of having the Soviet Union as her only ally ... The British in his opinion would like to see Franco's victory provided they could feel sure that this triumph would not mean Fascist domination of the Mediterranean. They were trying to get sufficient assurances from Mussolini and Franco to convince themselves that Franco's victory would not endanger their imperial routes through the Mediterranean.[27]

In the critical summer of 1937 after the capture of Bilbao by Franco's troops following the bombing of Guernica, the precarious military stalemate achieved by the arrival of Soviet aid began to break down irretrievably in favour of the Nationalists. Facing some insurmountable obstacles (amongst others the huge geographical distances, the efficient Francoist and Italian naval blockade and the unpredictable state of the Franco-Spanish border), the intermittent deliveries of Soviet military supplies never matched the quantity or the quality of those provided by the Axis powers to Franco. From the beginning of the Nationalist campaign against the Republican northern territory (April 1937) until the triumphal offensive against Catalonia (December 1938), the Republic suffered a slow but gradual and continuous defeat before the superior forces of General Franco. The sporadic moments of military and political hope aroused by international condemnation of incidents such as the April 1937 bombing of Guernica or Franco-British reactions against the indiscriminate Italian naval campaign in the Mediterranean in September 1937 never altered the tide of events.

The persistent refusal of the Western democracies to come to their rescue massively affected the military and internal politics of the Republican camp. Indeed, the hazards in procuring military and humanitarian supplies resulted in a heavy moral and material toll at the front and at the rear that made more difficult the already arduous task of reconstructing the state and establishing some war objectives shared by the population and the Republican political forces. In contrast, the Nationalist camp, assured of international support, could accomplish its aims, unaffected either by military setbacks or by seeing the efficiency of its war efforts undermined by the spectre of famine and misery or internal ideological squabbling in the rear. Soviet motives and purposes in delivering military and diplomatic aid to the Republic clashed with the firm attitude of the Western democracies. As the Soviet Ambassador in London explained in November 1936:

> The Soviet Government's admitted sympathy towards the Government in Spain was not due to its desire to set up a Communist regime in that country ... And the Soviet Government's purpose in attempting to assist the Spanish Government was far more immediate ... The Soviet Government was convinced that if General Franco were to win the encouragement given to Germany and Italy would be such as to bring nearer the day when another active aggression would be committed – this time perhaps in Central or Eastern Europe. That was a state of affairs that Russia wished at all costs to avoid and that was her main reason for wishing the Spanish Government to succeed in its civil strife.[28]

Nevertheless, neither such Soviet explanations nor growing concerns about the Italo-German influence over Franco were enough to change the mind of the British authorities whilst they possessed two fundamental resources to mitigate any potential worries about the future of Spain: the power of the pound and the dissuasive might of the Royal Navy. A leading official in the Foreign Office expressed that position clearly in late July 1937:

> I believe that we are far too inclined to assume that General Franco must be regarded as an inevitable danger to us. If for the time being he shows certain hostility towards us, this is largely the result of the present conjunction of circumstances ... But there are other and far more enduring considerations which must lead him, in the long run, towards friendship with England. There is the fact that we want nothing from him. We do not intend to take advantage of his current grave position to extract from him embarrassing concessions. There is the fact that we are the richest country in Europe, and have indeed in the past played far the greatest part in financing the development of Spain. There is the fact that we have the greatest fleet in the world, well placed alternatively to blockade or assist in the protection of his coasts. Finally, there is the fact of our long friendship with Portugal. All these are considerations that must be constantly in his mind ... We are aware that he is not too happy with his Italian allies and probably is not too enthusiastic with Germany. A Spain under Franco is not necessarily a weakness to the British Empire. But it rests with us to take the first step, if the foundation of future friendship is to be well and truly laid.[29]

The German–Czech crisis that brought Europe close to the outbreak of a general war in September 1938 proved the critical moment in the international abandonment of the Republic. The signing of the Munich Agreement revealed that there would be no conflict due to Czechoslovakia, and even less because of Spain. Its outcome was not only the break-up of Czechoslovakia but also the practical ending of the 'Spanish problem' as a source of international tension. While Franco's decision to proclaim his neutrality during the Sudetenland crisis had soothed the last Anglo-French fears, the behaviour of the Western democracies delivered a lethal blow to the Republic's hopes of receiving their crucial support. From then on, the virtual implosion of the Republic facilitated the advance of the Nationalist troops that culminated with their total and unconditional victory on 1 April 1939.

There is no doubt that the international context of the Spanish Civil war played a crucial and direct role both in the course and final outcome of the conflict. Foreign factors bestowed obvious advantages or imposed substantial harm upon each of the warring factions. They were vital to their respective war efforts, to the strengthening of their state apparatus, to the mobilization of their economic resources and to the consolidation of civilian morale in the rear. Without the constant military aid and diplomatic and financial support from Germany and Italy, it is impossible to understand the total and unconditional victory achieved by Franco. At the same time, without the fatal impact on its military capability of the arms embargo imposed by the Non-Intervention and the attitudes of the Western democracies, it is highly unlikely that the Republic would have suffered such a brutal and devastating defeat. In this respect, the assessment put forward by the British military attaché in Spain is highly revealing:

It has become almost superfluous to recapitulate the reasons (for Franco's victory). They are, firstly, the material superiority throughout the war of the Nationalist forces on land and in the air, and, secondly, the qualitative superiority of all their cadres up to nine months or possibly a year ago ... This material inferiority (of the Republican forces) is not only quantitative but qualitative as well ... However impartial and benevolent the aims of the Non-Intervention Agreement, its repercussions on the armament problem of the Republican forces have been, to say the least of it, unfortunate and, no doubt, hardly what they were intended to be. The material aid of Russia, Mexico and Czechoslovakia (to the Republic) has never equalled in quantity or quality that of Germany and Italy (to Franco). Other nations, whatever their sympathies, have been restrained by the attitude of Great Britain.[30]

If it is unquestionable that the international context was crucial for the outcome of the Spanish Civil War, it is also true that the influence of this military struggle on the European crisis of the second half of the 1930s was limited and minimized by the partial success of the collective Non-Intervention policy. The Spanish conflict would not be the catalyst of a general European conflict that broke out later and for different reasons. Nonetheless it had three grave consequences of huge significance: the definitive sealing of the Italo-German Axis based on an anti-democratic rather than anti-communist stance; the weakening and paralyzing division of the Franco-British Entente and of its respective public opinions; and the shift of the Soviet Union towards a progressively isolationist position.

In this context, the Spanish war can be regarded as the prologue and preface to the Second World War (especially from June 1941, when a great alliance against the Axis took shape). Although first and foremost a Spanish Civil War, it was also a European civil war in miniature: a genuine 'European cockpit'. Two well-informed and different leading politicians such as Anthony Eden and Joachim von Ribbentrop had already perceived with absolute precision in late 1936 that 'a European war on small scale was getting under way in Spain'.[31] It is extremely curious that each of their governments acted accordingly, but in a totally different way.

Notes

1 H. Southworth, *El mito de la Cruzada de Franco*. Barcelona, 1986, proved many years ago the lack of any truth about Soviet revolutionary plans to seize power in Spain. Southworth also analyzed how such a myth was fundamental in providing political legitimacy to the military rebellion. After the opening of the Soviet archives in 1990, authors such as M. Bizcarrondo and A. Elorza, *Queridos camaradas: La Internacional Comunista y España*. Barcelona, 1999, p. 283 and Á. Viñas, *La soledad de la República: El abandono de las democracias y el viraje hacia la Unión Soviética*. Barcelona, 2006, have revealed the initial uneasiness in the Kremlin.
2 The thesis of Italo-German intervention in the origins of the conflict has been rejected by the works of Á. Viñas, *Franco, Hitler y el estallido de la guerra civil*. Madrid, 2001; and I. Saz, *Mussolini contra la Segunda República*. Valencia, 1986.

3   For a synthetic view of the origins and course of the Spanish crisis, see: J. Linz, 'From Great Hopes to Civil War: The Breakdown of Democracy in Spain' in J.J. Linz and A. Stepan (eds), *The Breakdown of Democratic Regimes*. Baltimore, Johns Hopkins, 1978, pp. 142–215; P. Preston, *A Concise History of the Spanish Civil War*. London, 1996; H. Graham, *The Spanish Civil War*. Oxford, OUP, 2005. .

4   For a useful survey of this period, see A. Adamthwaite, *The Lost Peace: International Relations in Europe, 1918–1939*. London, 1980; W. Keylor, *The Twentieth Century: An International History*. Oxford, 1984; and P.M.H. Bell, *The Origins of the Second World War in Europe*. London, 1993. A recent and good summary can be found in R.J. Overy, *The Inter-War Crisis, 1919–1939*. London, 2009.

5   On the foundations of the policy of Franco-British appeasement see: A. Adamthwaite, *France and the Coming of the Second World War*. London, 1977; J. Duroselle, *Politique étrangère de la France: La décadence, 1932–1939*. Paris, 1979; R.A.C. Parker, *Chamberlain and Appeasement: British Policy and the Coming of the Second World War*. London, 1994; G. Schmidt, *The Politics and Economics of Appeasement: British Foreign Policy in the 1930s*. Leamington Spa, 1984.

6   A good and classical summary of the process can be found in A.J. Toynbee, *Survey of International Affairs: 1937. Vol. II: The International Repercussions of the War in Spain (1936–1937)*. London, 1937. For a more recent evaluation see E. Moradiellos, *El reñidero de Europa: Las dimensiones internacionales de la guerra civil Española*. Barcelona, 2001.

7   Quoted in D. Smyth, 'Reflex Reaction: Germany and the Onset of the Spanish Civil War' in P. Preston (ed.), *Revolution and War in Spain, 1931–1939*. London, 1984, pp. 243–65; C. Leitz, 'Nazi Germany's Intervention in the Spanish Civil War' in P. Preston and A.L. Mackenzie (eds), *The Republic Besieged: Civil War in Spain*. Edinburgh, 1996, pp. 53–85. By the same author, 'Nazi Germany and Francoist Spain, 1936–1945' in S. Balfour and P. Preston (eds), *Spain and the Great Powers in the Twentieth Century*. London, 1999, pp. 127–50.

8   On German intervention see the classic studies by R. Whealey, *Hitler and Spain: The Nazi Role in the Spanish Civil War*. Lexington, 1989. A more recent summary in S. Payne, *Franco and Hitler: Spain, Germany and World War Two*. New Haven, 2008. On the Italian case, see J. Coverdale, *Italian Intervention in the Spanish Civil War*. Princeton, 1975; B.R. Sullivan, 'Fascist Italy's Involvement in the Spanish Civil War', *Journal of Military History* vol. 59, no. 4, 1995, pp. 697–727.

9   Dispatch from the German ambassador in Rome, 18 December 1936. *Documents on German Foreign Policy, 1918–1945, Series D, Vol. III: Germany and the Spanish Civil War*. London, 1951, no. 157 (hereafter *DGFP* and number).

10 J. Sagnes and S. Caucanas (eds), *Les Français et la guerre d'Espagne*. Perpignan, 1990. D.W. Pike, *Les Français et la guerre d'Espagne*, Panis, PUF, 1975.

11 Quoted in G. Warner, 'France and Non-Intervention in Spain, July–August 1936', *International Affairs* vol. 38, no. 2 (1962), pp. 203–20; and Á. Viñas, 'Blum traicionó a la República', *Historia 16*, no. 24, 1978, p. 54.

12 Quoted in T. Jones, *A Diary with Letters, 1931–1950*. Oxford, 1954, p. 231. The author, friend and confidant of Stanley Baldwin, had been Secretary in the British Cabinet between 1916 and 1930; E. Moradiellos, *La perfidia de Albión: El gobierno británico y la guerra civil Española*. Madrid, 1996; and J. Edwards, *The British Government and the Spanish Civil War*. London, 1979.

13 Minute by Sir Samuel Hoare, 5 August 1936. The previous quotation is by Mr Jebb, 25 November 1936. Both quoted in E. Moradiellos, 'British Political Strategy in the Face of the Military Rising of 1936 in Spain', *Contemporary European History* vol. 1, no. 2 (1992), pp. 123–37 (quotations on pp. 128 and 130).

14 Testimony of André Blumel in Léon Blum, *Chef de gouvernament, 1936–1937*. Paris, 1967, p. 339.

15 Diary entry of 9 September 1937 regarding Azaña's interview with de Brouckère; Manuel Azaña, *Memorias de guerra, 1936–1939*. Barcelona, Grijalbo, 1996, p. 263.

16 Memo from the Chargé d'Affaires in London, 9 September 1936. *DGFP*, no. 79.

17 T. Powell, *México and the Spanish Civil War*. Alburquerque, 1981; D. Tierney, *FDR and the Spanish Civil War*. Durham, NC, 2007. R. Traina, *American Diplomacy and the Spanish Civil War*. Bloomington, 1968.

18   R. Stradling, 'Battleground of Reputations: Ireland and the Spanish Civil War' in P. Preston and
     A.L. Mackenzie (eds), *The Republic Besieged*, pp. 108–32; J. Tusell and G. García, *El catolicismo
     mundial y la guerra de España.* Madrid, 1993.
19   M. de Madariaga, *Los moros que trajo Franco: La intervención de tropas coloniales en la guerra
     civil Española.* Barcelona, 2002.
20   S. Weintraub, *The Last Great Cause: The Intellectuals and the Spanish Civil War.* New York,
     1968; V. Cunningham (ed.), *Spanish Front: Writers on the Spanish Civil War.* Oxford, 1986;
     Janet Pérez and W. Aycock (ed.), *The Spanish Civil War in Literature.* Lubbock, 1990.
21   Letter from 4 September 1936 quoted in F. Schauff, *La victoria frustrada: La Unión Soviética, la
     Internacional Comunista y la guerra civil Española.* Barcelona, 2008, p. 204.
22   Summary of Reports on the Civil War in Spain by Anatoly Nikonov, Deputy Chief of the GRU
     (Soviet Military Intelligence Mission) in Spain, 20 February 1937. Reproduced in R. Radosh,
     M. Habeck and G. Sevostianov (eds), *Spain Betrayed. The Soviet Union in the Spanish Civil War.*
     New Haven, 2001, doc. no. 33, p. 129.
23   G. Howson, *Arms for Spain: The Untold story of the Spanish Civil War.* London, 1998; Á.Viñas,
     El oro de Moscú. Barcelona, 1979.
24   Daniel Kowalsky, *Stalin and the Spanish Civil War*, New York, Columbia University Press, 2004.
25   Memorandum by Ginés Vidal (Director of the European Section, Spanish Foreign Office), 28
     January 1939. Archivo del Ministerio de Asuntos Exteriores (Madrid), serie Archivo Renovado,
     file 834, box 31. Reproduced in Moradiellos, *El reñidero de Europa*, p. 168.
26   Confidential remark made by Negrín to his colleague and confidant Juan Simeón Vidarte,
     Under-Secretary of the Home Office. Recalled in his memoirs: *Todos fuimos culpable.* Mexico
     City, 1973, pp. 764–5.
27   Telegram of the ambassador, 30 July 1937. *For the President: Personal and Secret Correspondence
     between Franklin D. Roosevelt and William C. Bullitt.* Boston, 1972, p. 222.
28   Memorandum, 3 November 1937. *Documents on British Foreign Policy, 1919–1939, Series 2, vol.
     XVII. Western Pact Negotiations: Outbreak of the Spanish Civil War.* London, 1979, n. 78.
29   Minute by Lord Cranborne, Parliamentary Under-Secretary of State at the Foreign Office, 21
     July 1937. FO 371/21295 W12237.
30   Report by Major E.C. Richards on Offensive Strategy in the Spanish Civil War, 25 November
     1938. FO 371/22631 W16269.
31   Dispatch from Ribbentrop (London) to Berlin, 8 December 1936. *DGFP*, no. 147. In the text,
     the Ambassador transmitted the content of his interview with the British Foreign Secretary.

Chapter 19

The Middle East and the Coming of War

T.G. Fraser

In the summer of 1942 German and Italian forces were positioned some sixty miles from Alexandria, threatening Cairo and the Suez Canal, and with them to overturn the entire Allied position in the region. So confident was he of such an outcome that Mussolini arrived in North Africa in anticipation of his triumphant entry into Cairo on a white horse, but General Sir Claude Auchinleck's spirited defence at El Alamein was to frustrate him. As war approached, the British were uncomfortably aware of how much their tenuous security depended on the stability of their position in the Middle East. In January 1939 the Chiefs of Staff reiterated earlier advice that they could not

> foresee the time when our defence forces will be strong enough to safeguard our territory, trade and vital interests against Germany, Italy, and Japan simultaneously ... If the balance were to be weighed against us even more heavily by the hostility of the Arab States of the Middle East, our position would be still more grave.

Egypt was central to Britain's lines of communication to India, the Far East and its African colonies. In Iraq, the air force guarded communications and protected 'our most important oil interests in Iraq and Iran'. The Imam of the Yemen had the potential to threaten Aden, while Saudi Arabia had enough power to 'threaten our land and oil lines of communication running through Transjordan and Iraq'. Palestine, the affairs of which had triggered their analysis, provided 'depth for the protection of the Suez Canal'.[1] Such considerations drove British policy in the Middle East region as the diplomatic situation in Europe deteriorated. The affairs of Egypt and Arab–Jewish conflict over Palestine lay at the heart of British concerns in the region.

From the sixteenth century onwards the predominantly Arab Middle East had been part of the Turkish Ottoman Empire, but with its defeat at the hands of the British in October 1918 that complex entity shattered. What emerged was an unstable Anglo-French *imperium*, which from the start was unloved and unwanted, except, for their own reasons, by the Jews of Palestine and the Christian Maronites of Lebanon. As war threatened in the late 1930s, the British, and to a lesser extent the French, were forced to confront the realities of the Middle Eastern policies they had adopted during the Great War and the subsequent peace settlement. The events of the late 1930s were essentially the *sequelae* of the decisions taken during, and just after, the previous war.

Faced with war against Turkey, the British enlisted the assistance of the forces of nascent Arab nationalism, focussed on Husayn, the Sharif of Mecca, and head of the Hashemite family. On 24 October 1915 the British High Commissioner in Cairo, Sir Henry McMahon, wrote to Husayn pledging recognition of Arab independence in return for support against the Turks. McMahon excluded certain districts to the west of Damascus, Homs, Hama and Aleppo, which, he claimed, were not purely Arab. In the late 1930s debate raged over whether this included Palestine, although Arabs saw no reason to question that it did not.[2] On that assumption, the Arab Revolt, led by Husayn's son Feisal, broke out on 5 June 1916. But the British were also working to a different agenda, which they were understandably at pains to conceal from their Arab allies, since it had nothing to do with Arab independence. Those at the head of affairs in London and Paris still thought in Imperial terms. The year of 1916 also saw the conclusion of the Sykes–Picot Agreement, which effectively planned to divide the Turkish territories between Britain and France, anticipating their Mandates for Iraq and Palestine and Syria and Lebanon at the 1920 San Remo Conference.[3]

The key British interest in the Middle East was Egypt, which was occupied by the British in 1882 and declared a British protectorate on the eve of the First World War. The key to Britain's trade in the region was the Suez Canal, which opened in 1869. It offered a quicker alternative than the Cape route to Britain's Imperial possessions in the east, to Australia and New Zealand, but, in particular, to India, the 'jewel in the crown' of the British Empire. More recently, a new concern had crept into British thinking on the region, with the navy's decision to change from coal to oil. The source of this new fuel was the Anglo-Persian Oil Company, formed in 1909, and effectively brought into British public ownership in 1914. Its facilities at Abadan were close to the Turkish port at Basra. It was this proximity that led the British into the Mesopotamian campaign, which experienced mixed fortunes until the final capture of Baghdad in 1918. Abadan's production increased dramatically between 1913 and 1918.[4] Control of the Middle East was vital to the kind of war Britain had waged and would certainly have to conduct again in the event of any future conflict.

The Sykes–Picot Agreement proved to be the prelude to the League of Nations Mandates over former Turkish territories, which were conferred on Britain and France at the San Remo Conference in April 1920. After much wrangling, Britain was given the Mandates for Palestine and Iraq, and the French those for Syria and Lebanon.[5] The French Mandates need not long detain us, except for their effect on Arab feelings. Neither country proved to be of economic value. By the 1930s their occupation was a strategic liability, diverting military resources from more vital areas. On 8 March 1920 Britain's wartime ally, Feisal, was proclaimed King of Syria, but in July he was unceremoniously evicted by General Henri Gouraud, the new French High Commissioner.

Arab discontent found particular expression in Palestine. Its focus was the pledge made by Foreign Secretary Arthur Balfour to the Zionists on 2 November

1917: that Britain viewed with favour the establishment of a 'National Home' for the Jews in Palestine. The Balfour Declaration was the result of complex negotiations, involving key British leaders, notably Balfour and David Lloyd George, with the British Zionist leader, the Russian-born biochemist Dr Chaim Weizmann. Such was Weizmann's talent for diplomacy that under his leadership the Zionists succeeded in having the terms of the Balfour Declaration written into the Mandate for Palestine, much to the discontent of the country's Arab majority, who felt doubly cheated of the independence that they believed had been promised to them.[6] It was an inauspicious start to Britain's new role in Middle Eastern affairs, the legacies of which were to extend over the next two decades, shaping British policies as war threatened again in the late 1930s.

One of the most remarkable features of the post-1918 period was the strength and speed with which Arab national sentiment asserted itself across the Middle East. As early as March 1919, widespread disturbances broke out in Egypt, suppressed by British forces, but which proved to be the prelude to three years of anti-British demonstrations and violence. In 1922 the British sought to 'square the circle' by conferring independence on Egypt, whilst retaining control of defence and the security of Imperial communications. This was, however, a unilateral British action, which the Egyptians did not recognize, a fact of which the British were uncomfortably aware.[7] Egyptian national sentiment did not diminish over the next decade – far from it. Attempts in 1928 and 1930 to negotiate a new treaty between the two countries foundered.

Iraq proved an even greater challenge. From the start, the new country was a potentially volatile construct of Shi'a Arabs in the south, a dominant Sunni Arab minority in the centre and Sunni Kurds in the north. The award of the Mandate to Britain provoked widespread revolt. Britain could sustain neither the cost nor the military effort, and in March 1921 the Colonial Secretary, Winston Churchill, decided to transfer power to Iraqi hands by offering the throne to Feisal. As a further gesture to the Hashemites, Feisal's brother, Abdullah, became Amir of Transjordan, which was separated from Palestine. A series of agreements followed, which culminated in Iraq's admission to the League of Nations in 1932, but since Britain retained military facilities, nationalist opinion was far from appeased. Even so, the country's importance grew dramatically once the potential of her oilfields was realized in the mid-1920s. Nor was Britain's connection with the Hashemites fated to prosper in the latter's heartland of the Arabian peninsula. Husayn's position had for some time been threatened by the rising power of Abd al Aziz Ibn Saud. By 1925, the latter had overthrown the Hashemites in the Hejaz, the kingdom of Saudi Arabia coming into being in 1932.[8] When war threatened in the late 1930s it was to Ibn Saud that the British looked to help sustain their position in the Arab world.

Palestine presented the British with their most intractable Middle Eastern problem in the inter-war period. Its importance rested almost entirely on the fact that it was the Holy Land. Jerusalem was a sacred city to the three great monotheistic religions, Judaism, Christianity and Islam, whose adherents all felt passionately about it. The stage was set for the increasingly bitter conflict between Arab and Jew, which was to become the overriding issue for the British in the Middle East as the prospect of war became ever more apparent in the late 1930s. What no one, Arab, Jew or Briton, could have foreseen in 1919 was the rise to power of Adolf Hitler, driven as he was by an obsessive anti-Semitism. How Britain would reconcile the rising political aspirations of the Arabs with the expectations of the Zionists for a National Home remained to be seen.

British prospects were dim from the start. Whilst the Palestinian Arabs shared the discontent felt elsewhere at the Anglo-French *imperium*, they had the particular grievance of the Balfour Declaration, which had offered to safeguard their civil and religious, but not political, rights. Simmering resentment broke surface on 4 April 1920 when demonstrations in Jerusalem ended in violence, leaving five Jews and four Arabs dead. Amongst the leaders was a young former Ottoman officer, Haj Amin al-Husayni, who was soon to assume a pivotal role in Palestinian affairs, especially as war approached, when he was appointed as Mufti of Jerusalem, something that was to haunt both the British and the Jews in the years to come.[9] Faced with unstable situation in Palestine, the British sought to appease the Arabs. By 1922 several things became clear. The extent of discontent in Egypt, Iraq and Palestine had greatly strained British military resources, forcing accommodations with Arab sentiment, which saw local rulers in place in Cairo, Baghdad and Amman. In Palestine, where the issues were more complex, the British had noticeably tempered the nature of their 1917 commitment to the Zionists. A pattern had emerged that was to be repeated in the late 1930s as the prospect of war threatened.

Finally, it must be acknowledged that Britain's Imperial woes were not confined to the Middle East and that her policies in the region contributed to unrest amongst a community whose concerns could only be ignored at their peril, namely, the Muslims of British India. Their fear was that the defeat of Turkey – to which Muslims of the Indian Army had contributed in fair measure – would lead to the loss of the world's remaining Islamic polity. The resulting disillusion amongst Indian Muslims led to the formation of the *Khilafat* movement, which combined pro-Turkish with pan-Islamic sentiment, and joined Mahatma Gandhi's non-co-operation campaign against British rule.[10] The extent to which the Indian Army relied on its ability to recruit and retain the loyalty of Punjabi Muslims meant that Middle Eastern issues were never far from the minds of the Imperial rulers in New Delhi and their political masters in London. Like the Royal Navy, the Indian Army was essential to Britain's position as a world power.

In the years after 1922 Britain's position in the Middle East stabilized after an initial period of turbulence. Even Palestine seemed to settle down, not least because Jewish settlement was sluggish for much of the 1920s. But in 1928 this situation changed abruptly as tensions between the two communities assumed a new dimension. The background was that political advances elsewhere in the Middle East meant that the Palestinian Arabs felt themselves to be at a disadvantage, but the immediate trigger was tension over long-standing agreements surrounding access to the Western Wall in Jerusalem. Disputes in 1928 escalated alarmingly the following year when widespread disturbances resulted in 133 Jews and 116 Arabs being killed, the latter mostly by the security forces. The result was a wide-ranging review of British policy, which culminated in a letter from Prime Minister Ramsay MacDonald on 13 February 1931, in which he reassured Weizmann that there would be no prohibition on Jewish immigration into Palestine.[11] Although neither man could possibly have realized it, this pledge was to assume critical importance for the Jews, since just two years later their position and future in Europe were to change irrevocably for the worse when Hitler assumed power in Germany.

The Nazi regime quickly set in train a policy of excluding Jews from German national life. On 1 April, a three-day boycott of Jewish businesses began, to be followed six days later by a law excluding Jews from the civil service, and so it went on, progressively barring Jews from university teaching, the press, cultural affairs and other areas where they had contributed so much to German life and learning. This phase of anti-Semitic activity culminated in the Nuremberg Laws of 1935, which instituted a rigid division between the *Reichsbuerger*, defined in the legislation as those who were of so-called German blood who were to have full citizenship, and the *Staatsangehoerige*, the Jews, who were not.[12] With anti-Semitism also endemic elsewhere in Central and Eastern Europe, it is hardly surprising that thousands of Jews looked to Palestine as the only means of escape from an increasingly hostile and threatening continent, especially as in the 1920s the Americans had closed their doors to mass immigration.

The result was to transform the nature of the proposed Jewish 'National Home' in Palestine. This may be seen in the surge in the Jewish population of Palestine to possibly over 400,000 by 1936.[13] Jews were still a minority in the total population, but the concept of a 'National Home' now had a new sense of viability and vitality. It witnessed, moreover, the flourishing in the Middle East of the culture of *Mitteleuropa*, most graphically illustrated by the arrival in 1936 of the Italian maestro Arturo Toscanini to conduct the seventy-piece Palestine Symphony Orchestra in a series of concerts largely featuring the works of Beethoven and Brahms, a poignant comment on Hitler's anti-Semitic policies.[14]

It was precisely these developments, which were giving hope to the Jews of Palestine and to the increasingly fearful Jews of Europe, which so alarmed the Arabs of Palestine, with consequences that were to produce problems for British policy in the Middle East as war approached. Evidence of this came in November 1935 when Arab political representatives approached the High Commissioner, Sir Arthur Wauchope.[15] On 25 April 1936, a body led by Haj Amin al-Husayni, soon known as the Arab Higher Committee, was formed to pursue a general strike which had begun a few days before. The Committee's most immediate purpose was to secure an end to Jewish immigration, but it also demanded the prohibition of the transfer of Arab land to Jews and the establishment of a National Government.[16]

Arab discontent in Palestine could not have come at a more difficult time for Britain. Hitler's eyes were firmly fixed on Europe and he seemingly had little desire to embarrass Britain overseas, at least before relations between the two countries deteriorated in 1938. It was not until March 1938 that the German profile in the Middle East began to assume a more threatening dimension with the launch of pro-Arab broadcasts. Then, in April 1939, Propaganda Minister Dr Joseph Goebbels visited Egypt in the course of a Mediterranean vacation.[17] But the intentions of Italy were much more immediate and potentially threatening. Signs of a changing attitude on Mussolini's part had come in March 1934 in a speech to the Fascist Party Assembly when he referred to the links, real and potential, between Italy and the Middle East. That same month, Radio Bari began Arabic broadcasts to the region.[18] Critically, in October 1935, Mussolini invaded Abyssinia, which his troops conquered the following May, provoking a major crisis in relations with Britain and France. The new Italian empire in north-east Africa presented a potential strategic threat to Britain's position in Egypt, the Sudan, and her lines of communication through the Red Sea. By 1936 the British were understandably deeply suspicious of Italian intentions in the region, as the Foreign Secretary, Anthony Eden, reported in June, at a sensitive time in the affairs of both Egypt and Palestine:

> Since the advent to power of Herr Hitler, and since the rearmament of Germany began to assume the rate and proportions with which it is now being carried on, His Majesty's Government have been mainly preoccupied by the continental ambitions of that country, the deferred threat implied by these to British interests and British territory, and the means by which this can be averted or met. In parallel they have been preoccupied by the aggressive nature of Japanese policy and the specific threats implicit therein to the British position in the eastern hemisphere. To these preoccupations the Italian conquest of Abyssinia has added a new and unexpected problem ...

Specifically, he alluded to 'the question of our oil supplies and to the importance to us of Moslem opinion in India'.[19] The following month, in the western Mediterranean the Spanish Civil War raised new problems, since the ultimately successful Nationalist forces were supported from Rome and Berlin. These developments set the context of British thinking about the Middle East throughout the next three years, a situation which worsened as Italian ambitions grew and Mussolini and Hitler nudged increasingly together.

Egypt was London's most immediate concern, although the affairs of Palestine were soon to eclipse it. The Egyptians continued to aspire to the removal of the remaining restrictions of the 1922 treaty, and in 1935 the United Front was calling for a new agreement with Britain. When the British failed to respond immediately, there was widespread rioting. Faced with the problematic intentions of Italy, Britain was forced to balance its need to placate Egyptian sentiment against the demands of Imperial security. Negotiations in the country were conducted between the Egyptian Premier, Mustafa al-Nahhas, and the

British High Commissioner, Sir Miles Lampson, with the Cabinet in London keeping a close eye on proceedings, strategic issues being at the forefront of their concerns. A clear indication of Britain's alarm over the nature of Mussolini's intentions was the decision in December 1935 to send substantial reinforcements to Egypt, including an infantry brigade, together with a battalion of light tanks, a company of medium tanks and a mechanized artillery brigade.[20]

As the negotiations got underway, the British were aware of just how much was at stake. While the treaty was to last for twenty years, and there was an anguished discussion over what would happen when it expired. The need to secure a settlement was more immediate than that, since 'an entire change had come over the situation since the draft treaties of 1928 and 1930 owing to the rise of Italy as a Mediterranean and North African Power'. As a result, the Cabinet was adamant 'that the retention of a British garrison on the Suez Canal and at or in the vicinity of Alexandria is essential'.[21] While the security of her position on the Canal had long been a British preoccupation, the emphasis on Alexandria was significant, both for its potential role as a naval base, although proper docking facilities did not yet exist, but crucially for its key position relative to the Libyan border. Its inclusion reflected the concern now being felt over Italian intentions, since the draft 1930 treaty had been willing to concede a withdrawal of British troops to the Canal Zone.[22]

While for the British these military provisions were of the essence, they were equally aware of the consequences of failure: 'Egypt was likely to be a turbulent and unreliable State, and that we could not afford to have.'[23] On 8 May 1936 Eden spelled out the implications of such an outcome:

> Failure to negotiate a treaty with Egypt, followed by disturbances in that country, their suppression by British force and the government of Egypt by His Majesty's Government by force and against the will of the Egyptian people, would be represented throughout the Arab Near East possibly as a sign of British bad faith, certainly as a proof of British Imperialism pursued at the expense of a weaker Mohametan country.[24]

Although negotiations proved tricky, the agreement was signed on 26 August 1936, by which time Britain was facing the even more acute problems of Palestine. Critically, however, the British had maintained what had become their key objective in the treaty negotiations, the retention of their crucial strategic and military interests in the western desert and the canal. As well as the right to retain troops at or near Alexandria for an eight-year period, all the facilities of Egypt were to be afforded the British in the event of war or international emergency. These provisions were to prove vital once Italy entered the war in 1940.[25]

As these negotiations progressed through the summer of 1936, they were shadowed by the deteriorating situation in Palestine. By the end of April, Wauchope was recommending the establishment of a Royal Commission as well as reinforcements from Egypt. The latter request was granted, but it carried worrying implications for Britain's position in the region, with the Cabinet noting that

> the Chief of the Imperial General Staff was somewhat perturbed at the effect of the course of events in Palestine on the situation in the Near East ... There was information that the Egyptians were in touch with Saudi Arabia, and the troubles in Palestine were another manifestation of a movement that might result in a serious Moslem outbreak.

In addition, the Cabinet was advised 'as to the possible reactions of the situation in Palestine on India, particularly if force had to be used'. Faced with a situation that 'was already very serious, as bad as in the disturbances of 1929', the Cabinet determined that policy was 'to secure a restoration of law and order in the mandated territory, after which some form of authoritative and independent Inquiry would have to be undertaken'.[26]

The Royal Commission, which was announced by the Secretary of State for Dominion Affairs, Malcolm MacDonald, on 7 August 1936, was, therefore, charged with investigating the causes of the disturbances in Palestine and making recommendations for the removal of the grievances of either Arabs or Jews. Chaired by Lord Peel, its most influential member turned out to be Reginald Coupland, Beit Professor of Imperial History at the University of Oxford, who had already made extensive studies of divided societies in the Empire and had been a keen student of the Irish settlement. The Royal Commission arrived in Jerusalem on 11 November 1936. In what turned out to be its crucial meetings on 23 December and then on 8 January 1937, Coupland presented Weizmann with the idea of two independent states. Two weeks later, at a personal meeting at Nahalal, the two men agreed that partition offered the best way forward, and then, when the Commission met at Helouan in Egypt to consider their findings, Coupland convinced his colleagues of its merits.[27]

The *Palestine Royal Commission Report*, signed on 22 June 1937, was both a masterly analysis of how the country had fared under the Mandate and a powerful piece of advocacy for what later generations would come to call a 'Two State Solution' through the mechanism of partition. The premise was that there were two communities in Palestine, one Asian in character, the other European, and that they had no sense of belonging to a single state. Only through partition could justice be done to the aspirations of each. The report offered in outline a scheme of partition in which the Jews would have a state on the coastal plain and in Galilee, that the British would retain Jerusalem with a land corridor to Jaffa, and that the Arab state would take in the rest of the country. That the proposed Jewish state would include a large Arab community, some 225,000 could be addressed through population exchange. Here, in summary, was the radical surgery being offered for Palestine, and it set the parameters of British policy over the next two years.[28]

Coupland's most important convert to the idea of partition was Weizmann, whose quick mind grasped that it offered the Jews the prospect of statehood at a time of their greatest need. The Zionist leader convinced the Colonial Secretary, William Ormsby-Gore, an old friend and ally since the days of the Balfour Declaration, that partition was the way forward.[29] Ormsby-Gore's advice assured the Cabinet that 'the best hope of a permanent solution, just to both parties and consonant with our obligations both to Jews and to Arabs, lies in the drastic and difficult operation of partition'.[30] On 30 June the Cabinet agreed to issue a statement endorsing the principle of partition, but with the critical caveat that they had to make enquiries about the details. Even so, two critical voices were heard – those of Eden, and the Marquess of Zetland, Secretary of State for India. While they did not deflect the Cabinet, their concerns were to grow appreciably in the months ahead.[31] Both men were already worried about Italy's intentions in the region.

In the following months doubts emerged about the Cabinet's wisdom in endorsing partition. In part, this reflected the idea's tepid reception by the Zionists, but, more seriously, its furious rejection by the Arabs. Weizmann's relations with the American Zionist leaders had long been poor, and the best that he could extract from the Zionist Congress in Zurich in August 1937 was a compromise resolution that rejected the Royal Commission's partition scheme, but authorized negotiations with the British to determine the exact nature of a Jewish state.[32] Then, on 11 September, an Arab National Conference at Bludan in Syria totally rejected partition.

These events coincided with a rising fear in influential British circles over Italian intentions. In March 1937 Mussolini paid an extensive visit to Libya, in the course of which he claimed to be the 'protector of Islam', and was presented with the 'Sword of Islam'. On 10 April a High Command for North Africa was announced, together with improved communications for Libya, and, most worrying of all, the formation of an Italian army corps in the colony. These developments posed a threat both to Egypt and the French territory of Tunisia.[33] September saw the Italian leader in Munich, Essen and Berlin, where Hitler went to extraordinary lengths to impress him with German power, beginning a courtship between the two countries that was consummated two months later when Italy joined the Anti-Comintern Pact. It comes, therefore, as no surprise that in October the Chiefs of Staff directed their local commanders in Egypt to 'examine detailed plans, based on the assumption of a single-handed war with Italy'. Their recommendations, which included the despatch of an anti-aircraft brigade and a fighter squadron, and the build-up of the defences of the key position of Mersa Matruh, including Egyptian troops, were hesitantly received in London. The Chiefs of Staff were not convinced that the new Italian forces were ready for offensive action. Recommending the fostering of good relations with Italy, they pointed to what they saw as the over-riding consideration: 'The despatch of any forces from this country must inevitably weaken our position vis-à-vis Germany, and we have always considered that we should take no action which would result in a diversion of our limited resources from our main objective, which is the security of this country against German aggression.'[34]

The best the British government could offer was to move Egyptian troops to Mersa Matruh and to create stores at strategic points.[35]

These realities set the stage for a reassessment of the government's commitment to partition. Perhaps sensing this, on 9 November 1937 Ormsby-Gore prepared a document in which he reiterated his belief that partition offered the best way forward, and that there should be no compromise with the Arab position. He now wanted to move forward with the appointment of a new commission that would work out on the ground the boundaries of the Arab and Jewish states. His arguments provoked a stiff response on the part of Eden. Buttressing his case with documents reflecting attitudes in Palestine, Egypt, Iraq and Saudi Arabia, he argued that 'we are now faced with solid and growing opposition from the majority of the native inhabitants of Palestine, and, what is much more serious, from the whole Arab world'. As far as Egypt was concerned, he pointed to the 'large Italian land and air forces on the western frontier', while 'Iraq is now a very important source of our oil supplies', all of which led him to the baleful conclusion that Palestine 'was now dominating every other question throughout the Middle East, and that our whole future relations with the Middle Eastern States depended almost exclusively on our handling of it. Our European adversaries have not been slow to seize on this fact.'[36]

When the Cabinet met to discuss the matter on 8 December 1937 it was immediately apparent how Chamberlain's mind was turning. It would, he argued, be 'premature' to announce that partition was 'too difficult', since it would lead them to be accused of 'having surrendered to threats and force'. But he pointed out that the proposed commission's work could take a year. Moreover, its terms of reference 'might be so worded that the Commission would not be debarred from saying that if partition was to take place, this or that solution was the best, but that in their view no workable scheme could be produced'. There was to be no forcible transfer of Arabs from the Jewish state. With such a steer, the Cabinet's course of action was clear, with Zetland chiming in to support Eden to the effect that if 'we were to announce that we were going to enforce partition, it would create a very difficult situation in India'. It was, then, decided that a commission would be appointed along the lines that Chamberlain had suggested, with the additional provision that 'if it was deemed necessary to inform the Commission that it was open to them to represent that no scheme of partition was likely to prove workable, this should be done by means of a personal communication to the Chairman'.[37]

The appointment of what was termed a technical commission was announced on 4 January 1938, and in March, under the chairmanship of Sir John Woodhead, it began its work. Its key task was to recommend boundaries for the two states, each being as homogenous and self-supporting as possible as possible. It left for Palestine on 21 April and its report was published on 9 November: not quite the year that Chamberlain had envisaged, but close enough.[38] As it did so, the long-standing pro-Zionist Ormsby-Gore was replaced at the Colonial Office by Malcolm MacDonald. Meanwhile, the international situation had changed unalterably with Hitler's annexation of Austria in March, accompanied as it was by brutalities against the country's Jews, and by his demands on Czechoslovakia, which brought Europe to the brink of war and which climaxed at Munich. As worries about the situation in Europe heightened, British defence planners warned that 'the goodwill of Ibn Saud and other Arab rulers is particularly important at this juncture, in view of the situation in Palestine'.[39]

As Woodhead's committee pursued its work, and the diplomatic situation in Europe grew more threatening, British leaders were reminded of the depth of Arab opposition to partition. In August, the Egyptian Prime Minister, Mahmoud Pasha, assured MacDonald that

> feeling in Egypt against our policy in Palestine was growing stronger and stronger, and that it was disturbing the friendly feeling towards Great Britain. He was very anxious about the situation, especially as he felt it would get worse. The critical attitude towards Great Britain was not confined to the public in Egypt. The same hostility was being roused in Iraq and Syria and elsewhere in Middle East. He had a talk with the Viceroy of India the other evening, when Lord Linlithgow told him that Moslem opinion in India was also becoming 'steadily more critical of our Palestine policy.[40]

These were not considerations that could easily be brushed aside. Even as the world's attention was focussed on central Europe, Middle Eastern issues intruded, with a concentration of the fleet at Alexandria as the result of information of the movement of Italian troops to Libya, and a warning by Zetland, that 'that Moslem opinion was becoming more and more exercised about the position in Palestine and we should probably require to retain in India all the troops which were now there'.[41]

Sticking carefully to his brief, Woodhead examined three possible versions of partition, none of which was found to be satisfactory. His report rejected sovereign independence in favour of a customs union; otherwise, the commission could not recommend the boundaries in question.[42] Britain was now released from her commitment to create a Jewish state through partition. The same night as the report's publication, *Kristallnacht* saw the murder of around one hundred Jews, thousands sent to concentration camps and the mass destruction of synagogues and Jewish businesses across Germany.[43] Even before then the government had confirmed that partition was no longer an option and that a conference would be held in London to decide the way forward.[44] The course of action they believed would best serve Britain's strategic interests as the international situation worsened soon emerged. It was simple: almost brutally so.

The conference was opened by Chamberlain on 7 February 1939, one week after Hitler's Reichstag speech in which he had ominously referred to the destruction of the Jews in Europe in the event of war.[45] It was a fruitless affair in which it is clear that the Jews never stood a chance, since the over-riding British consideration was strategic. On 18 January MacDonald warned his colleagues that 'the strength of feeling of the Arab public generally against our Palestine policy is making it more and more impossible for their rulers to maintain a pro-British attitude', and that 'the issue might easily become one in which in a crisis good Moslems were successfully called upon to wage a Holy War against us. The Arabs showed in the last war that they are not a people to be ignored.' While acknowledging the likliehood of a hostile reaction amongst American Jews over a total immigration ban, and the 'desperate frame of mind of the Jews', which, if immigration were stopped or 'reduced to a very low level', risked 'a violent outbreak of Jewish extremists in Palestine', his conclusion was clear, namely:

> Nevertheless, that we should be prepared to go a long way to meet the Arab repre-sentatives. We should be prepared to go as far as we reasonably can with a view either to reaching actual agreement with them, or, failing agreement, to so reducing their hostility that there is no longer a formidable risk of their joining our enemies in case of trouble.

His principal mechanism for securing Arab goodwill was to restrict immigration so that at the end of ten years the Jewish population would stand at forty per cent, or thirty-five if the Arabs did not agree the former figure. Either figure denied the Jews the prospect of statehood.[46]

These arguments were powerfully reinforced by Sir Thomas Inskip, the Minister for Co-ordination of Defence, who wished to place on record the views of the three service chiefs of the significance of the Palestine Conference for British positions in Egypt and the Middle East. Their conclusion was that 'if our future policy in relation to Palestine is such that it cannot be accepted by the Arab states as equitable, and is not a clear earnest of our intentions to maintain their friendship, these states who are already shaken in their belief in our good intentions will at last become alienated – if not actively hostile'. 'We have ample evidence', they argued, 'that nothing would be more welcome to the Totalitarian States than to see the disappearance of our predominant position in the eyes of the Moslem world. Germany in particular is already active in support of those subversive influences at present ranged against us.' Not surprisingly, the government agreed to endorse MacDonald's approach.[47]

The pace of events then quickened. On 15 March, as the Cabinet bleakly reviewed the imminent end of the conference, it received news of Hitler's takeover of what remained of Czechoslovakia. MacDonald reported Weizmann's conclusion that the proposals were a betrayal and that the Palestinian Arabs were likely also to reject them. Critically, however, he sensed that the Arab states felt that 'the terms had much to commend them'. When the conference ended two days later, the way was open for MacDonald to implement his policy. With Hitler's intentions clearly focussed on Poland, on 31 March, Chamberlain announced British support in the event of her independence being threatened. Since the security of Britain's position in the Middle East was now urgent, on 20 April Chamberlain told the Cabinet Committee on Palestine that 'we were now compelled to consider the Palestine problem mainly from the point of view of its effects on the international situation. It was of immense importance, as Lord Chatfield had pointed out, to have the Moslem world with us. If we must offend one side, let us offend the Jews rather than the Arabs.'[48]

The White Paper that was issued on 17 May did exactly that. In ten years' time Palestine was to be an independent state. On the critical issue of immigration, 75,000 Jews were to be allowed in over the next 5 years, any more being contingent on Arab agreement.[49] The Arab case had been met, even if the Arab Higher Committee could not see it that way. The Arab states were a different matter, since here the White Paper did exactly what was intended. British publicity used the White Paper to reinforce the support that key rulers, such as Transjordan's Abdullah, gave to the Allied cause throughout the war.[50] The White Paper reinforced what the British had earlier achieved in the 1936 negotiations with Egypt; namely, the use of key facilities in time of war, vital when Italy eventually came in on Hitler's side in 1940 and was then rescued the following year by the *Afrika Korps*. In the course of 1939, Britain steadily reinforced her Egyptian forces with troops from Palestine and India.[51] For the Jews, there was no rejoicing – quite the contrary. When the Zionist Congress met in Geneva from 16–24 August they were unanimous in their despair. The Nazi–Soviet Pact of 24 August stuck a knife not just in Poland, but into the heart of Europe's largest Jewish community.[52] What then happened is indelibly etched on what Europeans like to call their civilization. While the Jews had no alternative but to support Britain against Hitler, it was a far cry from 1917 and the British were not to be forgiven. As the Second World War approached, the affairs of Europe and the Middle East had become fatally intertwined. The legacies are with us still.

Notes

1   When I first began work on these topics, I was able to profit from the recollections of Sir John Martin, Secretary to the Peel Commission, and Professor L.F. Rushbrook Williams, Head of the Ministry of Information's Middle East section. I am grateful to The National Archives, Kew, London for permission to quote from the online Cabinet Conclusions (hereafter CC) and Cabinet Memoranda (hereafter CM) in their care. Cabinet Papers are © Crown Copyright. The Cabinet Conclusions (hereafter CAB23) may be found at: www.nationalarchives.gov. uk/cabinetpapers/cabinet-gov/cab23-interwar-conclusions.htm; and the Cabinet Memoranda (hereafter CAB24) at www.nationalarchives.gov.uk/cabinetpapers/cabinet-gov/cab24-interwar-memoranda.htm. Useful essay collections are: U. Dann (ed.), *The Great Powers in the Middle East 1919–1939*. New York/London/Tel Aviv, 1988; and M.J. Cohen and M. Kolinsky (eds), *Britain and the Middle East in the 1930s: Security Problems, 1935–39*. Basingstoke/London, 1992. I am grateful to Grace Fraser, Dr Leonie Murray and Professor Alan Sharp for improving my text, but any errors are entirely my own. The National Archives, Kew (hereafter NA), CAB24/282, CM, 'Cabinet: Strategic importance of Egypt and the Arab countries of the Middle East. Note by the Minister for Co-ordination of Defence', 16 January 1939, C.P.7 (39).

2   G. Antonius, *The Arab Awakening*. London, 1938; Florida, 2001, pp. 176–9.

3   T.G. Fraser, 'The Middle East: Partition and Reformation' in S. Dunn and T.G. Fraser (eds), *Europe and Ethnicity: The First World War and Contemporary Ethnic Conflict*. London and New York, 1996, pp. 158–76.

4   Sir A.T. Wilson, *Persia*. London, 1932, pp. 91–5.
5   A. Sharp, *The Versailles Settlement: Peacemaking after the First World War, 1919–1923*. Basingstoke, 2008, 2nd ed., p. 194.
6   T.G. Fraser, *Chaim Weizmann: The Zionist Dream*. London, 2009, ch. 6.
7   NA CAB24/259, CM, 'Egyptian Treaty: Memorandum by the Chairman of the Committee of Imperial Defence', 7 February 1936, C.P.25 (36).
8   Robert McNamara, *The Hashemites: The Dream of Arabia*. London, 2010, pp. 147, 149–52.
9   Fraser, *Weizmann*, pp. 98–9, p. 113.
10 L.F. Rushbrook Williams, *India in 1922–23*. Calcutta, 1923, pp. 253–4.
11 Fraser, *Weizmann*, pp. 125–30.
12 Lucy S. Dawidowicz, *The War Against the Jews*. New York, 1975, pp. 48–69.
13 T.G. Fraser, *Partition in Ireland, India and Palestine: Theory and Practice*. London and Basingstoke, 1984, p. 16; *Palestine Royal Commission Report*, Cmd. 5479, London, 1937, p. 113.
14 *Palestine Royal Commission Report*, pp. 113–17.
15 NA CAB 24/259, CM 'Palestine. Arab Grievances. Memorandum by the Secretary of State for the Colonies', 10 January 1936, C.P. 3(36). M.J. Cohen, *Palestine: Retreat from the Mandate. The Making of British Policy, 1936–45*. New York, 1978, p. 12. This provides a full account of the Mandate in this period.
16 *Palestine Royal Commission Report*, pp. 96–7.
17 T. Thacker, *Joseph Goebbels: Life and Death*. Basingstoke, 2009, p. 209; C.A. MacDonald, 'Radio Bari: Italian Wireless Propaganda in the Middle East and British Countermeasures 1934–8', *Middle Eastern Studies* 13, 1977, pp. 195–207.
18 Ibid, pp. 195–207.
19 NA CAB24/262, CM 'Problems Facing His Majesty's Government in the Mediterranean as a Result of the Italo-League Dispute, Memorandum by the Secretary of State for Foreign Affairs', 11 June 1936, C.P.165(36). See also Michael J. Cohen, 'British Strategy and the Palestine Question 1936–39', *Journal of Contemporary History*, volume 7, 3/4, 1972, pp. 157–83.
20 NA CAB23/82, CC, 'Egypt: Reinforcement of the Garrison', Cabinet 56 (35), 18 December 1935, p. 3.
21 NA CAB23/84, CC, 'The Anglo-Egyptian Treaty Negotiations: Present Position', Cabinet 31 (36), 29 April 1936, p. 6.
22 NA CAB24/259, CM, 'Egyptian Treaty: Memorandum by the Chairman of the Committee of Imperial Defence', 7 February 1936, C.P.25 (36).
23 NA CAB23/83, CC, 'Egypt: Proposed Treaty Negotiations', Cabinet 1 (36), 15 January 1936, p. 7.
24 NA CAB 24/262, CM, 'Anglo-Egyptian Treaty Conversations: Memorandum by the Secretary of State for Foreign Affairs', 8 May 1936, C.P.131 (36).
25 M.E. Yapp (ed.), *Politics and Diplomacy in Egypt: The Diaries of Sir Miles Lampson 1935–1937*. Oxford, 1997 is essential for an understanding of the British position. The 1936 Treaty is included as an Appendix.
26 NA CAB23/84, CC, 'Palestine: Establishment of a Legislative Council', Cabinet 36 (36), 13 May 1936, p. 6; NA CAB24/262, CM, 'Palestine: Memorandum by the Secretary of State for the Colonies', 11 May 1936, C.P.132 (36).
27 *Palestine Royal Commission Report*, pp. vi–xii; T.G. Fraser, 'Sir Reginald Coupland, the Round Table and the Problem of Divided Societies' in A. Bosco and A. May (eds), *The Round Table: The Empire/Commonwealth and British Foreign Policy*. London, 1997, pp. 407–19.
28 Fraser, *Partition in Ireland, India and Palestine*, ch. 6.
29 Ibid, pp. 133–7.
30 NA CAB24/270, CM, 'Report of Palestine Royal Commission: Memorandum by Secretary of State for the Colonies', 25 June 1937, C.P.166 (37).
31 NA CAB23/88, CC, 'Palestine: Report of the Royal Commission, 1936', Cabinet 27 (37), 30 June 1937, p. 3.
32 T.G. Fraser, 'A Crisis of Leadership: Weizmann and the Zionist Reactions to the Peel Commission's Proposals, 1937–8', *Journal of Contemporary History* 23, 4, 1988, pp. 657–80.
33 NA CAB 24/270, CM, 'Committee of Imperial Defence: Probability of War with Italy. Memorandum by the Secretary of State for Foreign Affairs', 15 June 1937, Committee of

Imperial Defence, 1332-B; Sir I. Kirkpatrick, *Mussolini: Study of a Demagogue*. London, 1964, p. 331.

34 NA CAB24/271, CM, 'Situation in the Mediterranean and Middle East: Note by the Minister for Co-Ordination of Defence', 19 October 1937, C.P.248 (37).

35 NA CAB 23/90, CC, 'Mediterranean and Middle East: Situation in Egypt', Cabinet 39 (37), 27 October 1937, p. 5.

36 NA CAB 24/272, CM, 'Policy in Palestine: Memorandum by the Secretary of State for the Colonies', 9 November 1937, C.P.269 (37); NA CAB 24/273, CP, 'Palestine: Memorandum by the Secretary of State for Foreign Affairs', 19 November 1937, C.P.281 (37).

37 NA CAB 23/90A, CC, 'Palestine: Government Policy', Cabinet 46 (37), 8 December 1937, p. 5.

38 *Palestine Partition Commission Report*, Cmd. 5854. London, 1938

39 NA CAB 24/278, CM, 'Mediterranean, Middle East and North Africa: Memorandum by the Minister for Co-ordination of Defence', 22 July 1938, C.P.178 (38).

40 NA CA 24/278, CM, 'Discussion on Palestine: Memorandum by the Secretary of State for the Colonies', 21 August 1938, C.P.190 (38).

41 NA CAB23/95, CC, 'The International Situation: Central Europe. Czechoslovakia. The Prime Minister's Visit to Herr Hitler', Cabinet 39 (38); NA CAB23/95, CC, 'The International Situation: Central Europe: Czechoslovakia. Further Defence Measures', Cabinet 41 (38), p. 3.

42 Fraser, *Partition in Ireland, India and Palestine*, pp. 146–8; *Palestine Partition Commission Report*, pp. 232–46.

43 I. Kershaw, *Hitler 1936–1945: Nemesis*. London, 2000, pp. 136–48.

44 D. Dilks (ed.), *The Diaries of Sir Alexander Cadogan O.M. 1938–1945*. London, 1971, p. 122.

45 C.R. Browning, *The Origins of the Final Solution: The Evolution of Nazi Jewish Policy 1939–1942*. Lincoln, NE and Jerusalem, 2004, p. 11.

46 NA CAB 24/282, CM, 'Palestine: Memorandum by the Secretary of State for the Colonies', 18 January 1939, C.P.4 (39).

47 NA CAB 24/282, CM, 'Cabinet: Strategic Importance of Egypt and the Arab Countries of the Middle East. Note by the Minister for the Co-ordination of Defence', 16 January 1939, C.P.7 (39); NA CAB 23/97, CC, 'Palestine', Cabinet 7 (39), 15 February 1939, p. 9.

48 NA CAB24/285, CM, 'Cabinet: Palestine. Draft Conclusions of Cabinet Committee', 21 April 1939, C.P.89 (39). Lord Chatfield was Minister for Co-ordination of Defence.

49 NA CAB 24/286, CM 24, 'Cabinet: Palestine. Memorandum by the Secretary of State for the Colonies, 12 May 1939, Palestine Statement of Policy', C.P.114 (39).

50 Personal information.

51 Paul Harris, 'Egypt: Defence Plans' in Cohen and Kolinsky (eds), *Britain and the Middle East in the 1930s*, p. 73.

52 Esco Foundation for Palestine, Inc., *Palestine: A Study of Jewish, Arab and British Policies*, vol. 2. New Haven, 1947, pp. 928–31.

Chapter 20

The 'Jewish Question' and its Impact on International Affairs, 1914–39

Mark Levene

Why should a relatively small, dispersed ethno-religious group have been such a critical factor in the origins of the Second World War? Without state, army, central authority – religious or otherwise – and with diverse social and cultural practices to the point where many would have actually contested that they were members of the same group, any 'realist' analysis would discount the significance of such an entity in *serious* international relations without further demur. We do not speak of the Jehovah's Witnesses as a factor in the origins of the war, even though we know that they were – in Nazi Germany – a persecuted group. Nor do we speak of the Roma in such terms and yet they suffered genocide too. We might, more narrowly, speak of the Catholic or Protestant factors in the rise of Nazism. But there is, significantly, no essay in this volume suggesting the churches were an element in the contest of forces leading to war.

Of course, we all have a ready answer as to why it was different when it came to the Jews. The answer is Hitler. His phobic obsession with the Jewish people projected them into the perilous limelight. 'No Hitler, no Holocaust,' the saying aptly goes. But that, in itself, begs the question: is one man's obsession really our first cause? If so, some of those histories of the Second World War, which in the not-so-distant past managed to avoid mention of the 'Final Solution' altogether, or simply had a footnote,[1] perhaps were not so obtuse.

The scholarly recognition of the centrality of the Holocaust in contemporary history is both salutary and necessary. However, the very fact that most of the historiography continues to treat it in essentially Germanocentric terms, reinforcing a sense of its singular, even aberrant nature, carries with it a tendency to narrow the contours of what is at stake. It will be argued here that while our subject has at its core a pathology – which in itself is bound to undermine standard treatments of how politics, including geo-politics, are supposed to operate – it was very far from a purely German one. It was both inherent in the socio-cultural make-up of European society and, with or without Hitler, had the potentiality in inter-war Europe to be a resurgent and destabilising force in both domestic relations and international affairs.

Judaism was as long embedded as Christianity on the European scene. It also happened to be father and mother to the latter religion. This is theologically significant of itself, not least as the early Christian sect's attempt to distance itself from its parentage included an increasingly passionate denunciation of the Jews as collectively culpable for the betrayal and death of their Jewish – subsequently deified – messianic leader. From the very beginning, Christianity was caught on the horns of its own dilemma. The Jews were the enemies of all that was virtuous and 'Christian' in humankind; the original and authentic enemies of the people. Yet they were at the same time the 'chosen' God bearers, the alleged legitimacy of Jesus as Christ being grounded in Old Testament prophecy, making them essential to the teleological process by which all humanity would arrive at the moment of general salvation.

None of this would have been of consequence if Christianity had not successfully allied itself with the late Roman Empire, setting itself on a path to European spiritual hegemony. The church felt constrained against the killing of Jews given their indispensability to the grand scheme of things, but if *they* had killed Christ they were clearly endowed not only with the most gut-wrenching malice but extraordinary, if not cosmic, powers to match. The only logical response was to either ensure that they were kept firmly at arm's length, a policy of Russian orthodoxy until the late eighteenth century, or under very tight control, as the Latin West increasingly determined through a slew of edicts denying Jews standard property, occupational or domicile rights. The paradox is that this situation may have actually benefited a medieval Jewish role as economic and administrative middleman: as Yuri Slezkine has put it, as a Mercurian class to a largely Apollonian, peasant-based European society.[2] If this spoke of the potentiality of co-existence it also carried further grounds for what in the Middle Ages became a deep vein of societal anti-Semitism. From the period of the Crusades through to the Reformation, European crisis saw its corollary in a profane litany of atrocities and expulsions against a people now clearly marked as economic as well as religious 'outsiders'.

The notion that the entire Jewish diaspora experience was of this 'lachrymose' variety has received some notable corrective in recent scholarship.[3] Logically, this history of victimhood should have had a firm line put under it by the monumental changes wrought through the advent and spread of a Western modernity. The emergence of secular polities, as led in revolutionary fashion by France, opened up the possibility that Jews could not only be divested of all the stigmas historically attached to them but embraced as full and equal fellow citizens. One expression of this sea-change was legal, with Jews being emancipated from previous legal restrictions in one nation state after another. Another was less tangible but arguably more far-reaching: a process of social acculturation and integration whereby they became 'like' other people to the point where difference became simply one of worshipping according to a different rite. The USA, with its enthusiasm for religious diversity, was notably ahead of Europe in this direction. At the other end of the spectrum, laggards such as Russia and Romania were expected, sooner or later, to fall in line behind the Western lead. The 1878 Treaty of Berlin was particularly significant for the way in which the Great Powers, abetted by a vocal Western Jewish lobby, sought to link international recognition of Balkan state sovereignty to a reciprocal granting of citizenship and religious freedom to all subject communities, Jews included.

The subsequent Romanian flouting of these obligations not only offers an important signpost to post-1919 'New Europe' resistance towards Western imposition of Jewish rights but also to a more general breakdown in the assumed liberal trajectory towards Gentile acceptance and toleration. Russia, with its significant Jewish population from the collapsed Polish–Lithuanian commonwealth of a century earlier, seemed to represent the acme of a state wilfully persecuting its Jews while turning a blind eye to popular, grass-roots pogroms. But if the gap between the position of the majority of Jews in eastern Europe and those more fortunate smaller numbers in the West was superficially explicable in terms of demographics, or problems of economic 'modernization', a rising tide of political anti-Semitism in France, Germany and even Britain suggested that something more was at issue. Much of the new antipathy was of a straightforward xenophobic nature as directed at the increasing flood of Jewish migrants from Russia and Romania heading west. Accusations of 'Jewish takeover', however, were as much directed at well-integrated but high-profile bankers and entrepreneurs as impoverished refugees. The anti-Semitic charge was that there was something intrinsically 'alien' *and* 'destructive' about the Jews, as bolstered by contemporary scientific and medical discourses.

Some of the more alert Jewish commentators on this darkening scene, especially in Russia, despaired of the assimilation project altogether and began preaching the need for a Jewish place of their own, perhaps in Palestine. Others turned increasingly towards revolutionary Marxism, the most obviously colour-blind of the ideologies proclaiming the imminence of a general human liberation. The important point for this consideration, however, is how Jewish responses to anti-Semitism helped fuel an emerging if very strange dialectic. Strange, because in no sense could one argue that Jews had the capability to offer a comparable counter-force to hostile elements in the European mainstream. After all, Jews remained everywhere a minority people dependent on the apparatus of state for their security and wellbeing. Equally, the nature of communal divisions actually intensified in response to the emerging crisis: a reality that meant that while the question 'What is to be done?' might be a prevalent one there was no unity among Jews locally, let alone globally, on what that ought to be. Jewish responses, whatever they were, were always amplified in the anti-Semitic mindset as evidence not just of ephemeral Jewish success but of some omniscient Jewish 'power'.[4] One might wish to dismiss these tendencies as the peculiar cultural by-products of societies attempting to curb their inner demons in the vortex of a rapidly engulfing modernity. 'The Jewish question', as it had come to be called, certainly wasn't going to bring civilization crashing down. But was it? The course of the Great War might seem to suggest otherwise.

'With "great Jewry" against us, there is no possible chance of getting the thing through – it means optimism in Berlin, dumps in London, unease in Paris.'[5] So wrote the British policymaker, Sir Mark Sykes in March 1916. At the time he was supposed to be negotiating an Allied carve-up of the Middle East, which makes his letter to the head of the British Foreign Office asserting that the Jews were the key to winning the 'thing' – the war – all the more astonishing. Yet Sykes was hardly alone. As the conflict ground on and the stakes grew ever higher, inter-Allied communications became fixated on the importance of 'winning' US Jewish finance on the one hand and 'calming' Russian Jewish revolutionary activity on the other. On the part of the Central Powers, conversely, a strategy for defeating the Allies had by spring 1917 narrowed down to getting Lenin and his 'Jewish' revolutionary entourage back into Russia, so bringing Petrograd into a separate peace.[6]

How could it be that a globally dispersed and internally fractious community of ten million souls had become seemingly a, if not *the*, critical card in the war's outcome? The answer has to be in some sense elusive, even enigmatic. It certainly had nothing to do with anything as tangible as demographic, economic or material assets. Nor ultimately was it very much to do with discrete Jewish actors, revolutionary or otherwise, except in the way that their existence fed a deep European psychological need to shift the blame for what was clearly becoming a *purposeless* slaughter on to some entirely different body. In this psychopathology of the First World War we have the essential origins of Jewish destruction in the Second. The Jews of 1914–18 resumed their historic role as scapegoats for the sins of the other Europeans, but with the dialectic of Jewish–gentile interactions now adding an exquisitely lethal twist.

The elements in European society who ought to have opposed the war, most obviously the mainstream socialist movements and the churches, were conspicuous by their failure. Most Jews in their public persona also went with the flow, proclaiming patriotic allegiance and fighting and dying for their respective countries. But a significant minority *were* outspoken. They rarely expressed their opposition *as Jews*. Most of those who did so were involved in ultra-radical parties, such as the Bolsheviks, though in Germany there were also Jewish figures within the Reichstag who were prominent within the 'peace party'. What is important for our purposes is that across Europe, among not just convinced anti-Semites but within large sections of mainstream elite opinion, the idea of opposition to the war became firmly associated with the Jews. As one post-war German detractor put it: 'Judaism and defeatism go together ... On that score, all proof either pro or con is pointless, even if 100,000 Jews died for their country.'[7]

To be sure, it could only happen by a series of steps that an accusation of anti-war dissent developed into the charge that Jews collectively (whether among the Allies or Central Powers) were actively disrupting the war effort, before culminating in the extraordinary self-exculpating slander that they had started the conflict for their own nefarious ends. By late 1918, press stories of a 'hidden hand' were as common in Britain as they were in Germany, including the story of 'authoritative' comment from a British military mission in Russia that the Tsar's assassination the previous summer was on the order of Jewish Bolsheviks.[8] Receptivity to the idea that there was an 'international Jewish conspiracy' to bring down European Christian civilization was already coalescing even before 'The Protocols of the Elders of Zion' – a pre-war Tsarist secret police fabrication – began to be informally circulated by White Russian émigrés among Allied personnel.[9]

But in a critical sense the Jewish 'plot' story had already impacted on high-level decision making a year earlier. Its clearest manifestation lay in the way Sykes' earlier angst had translated into a British government *idée fixe* of a synonymity between Jew and Bolshevik. The result in November 1917 was the Balfour declaration's support for a Jewish national home in Palestine.[10] The promoters of the Berlin scheme to defeat the Allies through the supposedly dispensable Bolshevik back door not only found their world crashing down around them a year on from the Soviet ascendancy but in a case of classic 'blow-back' with Bolshevik-style revolution exported to the streets of Berlin. It was hardly just the little Austrian corporal Adolf Hitler who was convinced that 'the Jew is to blame'.[11] What had taken place was not just a 'stab in the back' but a plan minutely conceived, orchestrated and directed by the Jews.

Seventy years on from the beginning of the Second World War, the sheer irrationality of what is described above will seem hard to countenance. Yet 'history' somehow has to convey how shaken European society was in the wake of the Armistice. If we accept that the atmosphere of that period was 'almost eschatological',[12] then the way in which the 'Protocols' became staple fare not just in Germany but through British and US quality press serializations, as well as in more popular pamphlet form, becomes less implausible. Yet if this tells us something of the degree to which paranoia took hold at 'home', we also have to remember how the situation in the east was altogether more destabilized and uncertain with the collapse of Austrian and Russian empires. The emotional intensity of German anti-Jewish vituperations in the wake of the failed Munich *Räterepublik* or Spartacist uprising can be seen as part of a broader pattern. Offered as definitive explanation for national humiliation or set-back, 'the Jewish-Bolshevik' – whether Bela Kun in Budapest, Leon Trotsky in Petrograd or Rosa Luxemburg in Berlin – now became the archetypal 'internationalist' enemy against which all nationalist movements in East–Central Europe were struggling for survival.

Crucially, high-level policy making at the Paris Peace Conference was certainly contaminated by this syndrome. The Western Allies in 1919 were already committed to the principle of national self-determination. But a more immediately urgent concern was to how to hold the line against the perceived spread of Bolshevism. For instance, the 'Big Three' were quite prepared to countenance Romanian action in support of Hungarian right-wing militia extirpation of Bela Kun, regardless of the infringement on Magyar sovereignty or the ensuing 'White terror', largely meted out against Jews. Moreover, with an eye to the longer term, they were also ready to offer additional military assistance and the green light for eastern expansion to anti-Bolshevik forces – the Poles in particular – who they reckoned as both protégés and sufficient to the task.[13] Throughout all this there is enough evidence from internal memoranda of senior Allied officialdom, more tellingly, from reports of informal conversations between the most high-ranking politicians and their aides[14] and finally from explicit statements by some Western leaders themselves to confirm that the evolving Allied policy towards Russia and the east carried a definite anti-Jewish subtext. Churchill – otherwise often seen as philosemitic – was among those at the time ready to publicly denounce 'destructive', 'atheistical', 'international Jews' as responsible for the mental and moral disease of bolshevism.[15]

But in the slippage towards this mindset, Allied leaders found themselves presented with a conundrum. No Western politician could be seen to be party to explicit anti-Jewish violence. Yet just as the Paris Peace Conference was getting into its stride in the spring of 1919, reports of exactly such violence in the east were flooding in. Paradoxically, these reports were not of the *worst* violence. Anti-Jewish atrocities, of a scale for which the term genocide would be appropriate, were at this time being committed in the Ukraine by a hotch-potch of forces nominally under the control of the failing Ukrainian Directory. Worse still would follow later in the year when Denikin's White Russian army was operating in the region.[16] And there was a further irony, too, in that Allied liaison officers working with Denikin's Siberian counterpart, Admiral Kolchak, were later shown to be complicit in recycling 'hate' material blaming Bolshevism on the Jews, which had emanated from OSVAG, Denikin's propaganda machine.[17] Yet throughout 1919 distant rumours of mass Jewish slaughter in the Ukraine had little by way of independent corroboration. Moreover, as the Allies aspired for (and indeed materially supported) a White victory against their 'Red' Bolshevik foe, they felt constrained from interfering in the fate of a region that the Whites were adamant was part of an 'indivisible' Russia.

Instead, where all eyes were fixed in spring 1919 was on a series of military massacres committed by Polish units, mostly operating in the contested eastern margins of their would-be state. These were widely reported and, later, closely investigated by US and British government-sponsored commissions of enquiry led by prominent Jewish figures.[18] Several hundred, all apparently non-combatant, Jews were found to have been killed in separate incidents. In each, sabotage or violent resistance to Polish authority linked to support for the Bolsheviks was the repeated Polish exculpation for what had occurred. Should we discern Allied sensitivity to Jewish protests back in Britain and the US as the goad to these commissions? Or alternatively, the repeated Allied warnings that continued violence of this nature might have deleterious repercussions on the provision of economic aid? Were these events, indeed, the catalyst to the Big Three deciding in early May to form a New States Committee (NSC) to consider how protection of minorities in the 'New Europe' was to be provided for under international aegis?

Logic suggested that the NSC was going to have to deal with more than simply the 'Jewish question'. The complex ethnographic mosaic of eastern

Europe posed the essential question: 'How was ethnic diversity to be squared with the creation of avowedly *nation*-states?' Yet what is so striking about the NSC deliberations is how they repeatedly turned back not to this bigger headache but rather to the Jewish one. There was a Jewish lobby in Paris, though these groups proved unable to speak with a single voice. Moreover, policy guidelines as laid down by the British Foreign Office *before* the Paris Peace Conference unequivocally stated that they were not to be drawn into any support for 'special' Jewish rights, 'particularly rights of cultural or educational autonomy', and that if Jewish spokesmen wished to pursue these issues it should be with the governments 'of their respective countries'.[19]

Yet these were *exactly* the issues the NSC negotiated with specific, 'moderate' Western Jewish lobbyists in Paris. These backroom discussions in turn gave to these figures – Lucien Wolf for (the Anglo-Jewish) Joint Foreign Committee (JFC) and Louis Marshall for the American Jewish Congress (AJC) – in particular an unprecedented influence that representatives of new states, or would-be states, were quick to interpret as meaning that they had had some special access to their own governments. The further consequence was that Wolf and Marshall found themselves repeatedly petitioned on matters of territorial disputes, long-term financial support and short-term food aid.[20]

The year of 1919 was, as a result, a unique moment in which the notion of Jewish diplomacy was elevated essentially on the back of a misconceived perception that Jews *qua* Jews had *once again* become a dangerously monolithic force on the world stage, and that if their desiderata were not met they would find ways of disrupting the peace. The ensuing Minorities Treaties, as hastily drafted by the NSC (more exactly the provisions for minority language educational autonomy), can be seen as an indirect concession to the most vocal eastern Jewish and US Jewish-supported, demands. Yet they were neither conferred with benign enthusiasm nor as part of some long-term Western agenda. On the contrary, the one thing that Allied interlocutors repeatedly emphasized was that this interpretation was 'completely inconsistent with the territorial sovereignty of the state'.[21] The only nationality to which Jews could belong in the 'new Europe' was the nationality of their respective state. Or as the League Minorities' Rapporteur pithily summarized in 1925, the treaties were 'to prepare the way ... for the establishment of a complete national unity'.[22]

What the Minorities framework actually underscored was the gaping void between the underlying issue of self-interest on the part of the West and that of their new state protégés in the East. All the Western Allies really wanted was a stable East that would not export masses of unwanted Jews to their shores. French post-war labour shortages moderated this prescript somewhat but without breaching the West's fundamental treaties' purpose to 'fix' *Ostjuden* and other minorities as *citizens* of their respective new states and so avoid any pretext for the sort of pre-1914 mass migration from Russia or Romania, where most Jews had remained citizenship-*less*. By handing over the supervision of the new framework to the League of Nations, the West further sought to manage its new system on the cheap. The US, of course, withdrew from the body of which President Wilson had been chief promoter. Britain and France, as its remaining guarantors, thereafter left Geneva to deal with infractions of the treaties as best it could and did little or nothing to strengthen the relevant instruments that would have enabled the League secretariat to respond to direct communal appeals for assistance. In short, once the immediate Bolshevik danger had passed, the West was willing to commit the 'Jewish question', as it saw it, to a consciously weak machinery in the extravagant hope that through eventual assimilation in the dominant cultures of the 'New Europe' the 'question' itself would go away.

Yet it was this very notion of *assimilation* that the new states overwhelmingly rejected. Other, Christian, minorities, in the course of time, might be duly integrated. Perhaps very limited numbers of Jews could be encompassed, too, within state homogenising programmes. But the notion that Jews as a whole were 'meltable'[23] into the general throng was considered by all Eastern state parties as both impossible *and* undesirable. Actual domestic policies in the 1920s may have varied. In Poland, under Marshal Pilsudski's *sanacja* regime, decorum was maintained largely through accepting that the Jews were separate and so – socially at least – leaving them alone. The avowedly more liberal Czechs, President Masaryk included, supported without reservation Jewish equality before the law, but were altogether more enthusiastic about Jews adopting an overtly Zionistic position, the clear inference being that the majority in due course would take themselves off to a *Jewish* Palestine.[24] The Czechs thereby offered a more honest insight into what implicitly all the Eastern states wanted: that the Jews be proclaimed as an internationally recognized 'national' entity: in other words, the exact opposite of Western diktat. Of course, it was the very principle of being dictated to as much as the substance that the new states equally railed against, most famously when they collectively staged their famous – if unsuccessful – diplomatic 'revolt' against the signing of the treaties in late May 1919. It was on this occasion that the Romanian leader, Bratianu, came closest to unsettling Allied composure when he reminded them that minority protection had been dropped from the general League covenant[25] – as adroit a way as any of the protégés telling their patrons that they were hypocrites who failed to practice what they preached.

And what of the supposedly 'protected' Jews themselves? Their situation was not simply one of being caught in a no man's land between a Western intention to keep them boxed in and an Eastern one to have them purged. Even under Tsarism, if one could not raise the money to get to the USA, one could always try one's luck within one of the emerging urban centres within the Western borderland sweep of Empire. If one was fortunate to live in neighbouring Austria-Hungary prospects for internal movement to a major city and there starting afresh were better still. Nor was the state in either case demanding one's *national* allegiance: a famously fervent Jewish loyalty to the Dual Monarchy was to the emperor, not to some notion of *sacre egoismo*. After 1918, borders, tariffs and new forms of taxation meant that an already precarious Jewish middleman role was faced with the potentiality of complete extinction. Worse, if one was one of the hundreds of thousands of Jews displaced as a result of war, one might find oneself not simply destitute but stateless to boot. There was no direct provision in the Minority Treaties for *staatenlos* Jews – another problem dumped on the League. Before Hitler or the depression, logic seemed to dictate that east European Jewish survival was firmly bound up with voluntary exit. Before that is, someone dared to repudiate the Minorities Treaties and forcibly eruct them. But with the West out of bounds, the USSR equally so, that only left Palestine. If more and more *Ostjuden* began gravitating towards Zionism in the inter-war period – in other words, towards an overt Jewish 'national' mimesis of the dominant European tendency – it was a testament not to the reality of Jewish power but quite the reverse.

If any one international leader held the notion of conspiratorial Jewish power as the fundamental cornerstone for his whole *Weltanschauung* it was Hitler. It was, he argued, the Jews who had brought Germany down in 1918; it was they who had to be avenged if Germany was take her rightful place as supreme Master of the World. Ultimately this vision of Manichaean struggle would be much more significant than its racial commentary, though when Hitler took over, in 1933, it was the sheer visceral hatred evident in his Storm Troopers' behaviour towards Jews on the German street that strongly registered in the Western media. Actually, the Nazi Jewish agenda was ill-defined. Even so, the idea that racial justification might be used in a modern 'civilized' state to roll back a religious community's civil rights, economically strangle them and, perhaps, force them out altogether, profoundly shocked Western sensibilities.

Tony Kushner has argued that it was this liberal viewpoint with its insistence on treating Jews as individuals, and thus otherwise as members of their respective host nations, which led to an ongoing Western non-comprehension of an ideology – more exactly a theodicy – which lumped them all together as a collective force for world evil.[26] Yet to what extent did this Western self-understanding hide its own more complex inner tension? We have already seen that the international Jewish power motif *did* play a significant role in Allied political deliberations, as it did in more overtly paranoid societal projection in the closing phase of the Great War. Though it clearly was dampened down in Britain as the country regained its post-victory poise, the tension between the liberal tendency to discriminate between 'good' and' bad' Jews (or 'assimilated' as opposed to 'foreign' ones), and the more problematic one to hold Jews close at hand responsible for the actions of those abroad, clearly began intruding, once again, into the new 1930s phase of crisis policy making.

Take, by way of example, a meeting at the Foreign Office in August 1934 between Neville Laski, one of the co-presidents of the thoroughly loyal JFC, and Sir Robert Vansittart, the Permanent Under-Secretary of State. It focused on growing Jewish efforts to develop an international boycott of German goods and businesses, as a response to Nazi persecution. The JFC, while it had petitioned the Foreign Office to intervene with Germany to restore Jewish citizen rights, was notable for its disavowal of the boycott movement, anxious that this would put British Jewry out of step with British government policy. But other more grass-roots, especially trade unionist-leaning Jewish groups in London's East End were active in the movement, an involvement that led London's Commissioner of Police, as early as April 1933, to order the Whitechapel police division to visit all Jewish shopkeepers in the locality and have boycott notices taken down. Clearly, the British government was anxious that the boycott might have the ability to harm British–German economic relations, with further political ramifications inferred from questions in Parliament, the answers to which suggested that the German government had lent on the British to staunch support for the campaign.

The discussion initiated by Vansittart, however, went much further than that. In extraordinarily undiplomatic language amounting to a dressing down of Laski, Vansittart vituperated against 'the aggressively flamboyant and narrow character of the anti-German propaganda carried on by certain Jewish quarters in America', citing the efforts of leading US Jewish lawyer Samuel Untermyer and adding that 'people were fed up' with him and 'tired of having "Jew" dinned in their ears'.[27] How far was this from the language of the Nazis? Clearly, Vansittart was speaking in private and he did not directly state that the JFC was responsible for the actions of other Jews in Britain. But then in a sense he did not have to. Whether the boycott was actually proving successful or not, here was a case where the British government was taking fright at the idea that a US-led collective Jewry somehow was capable of organising a global economic campaign to disrupt 'business as usual' very much in the same tenor as British ministers had made themselves fearful of another supposed US Jewish financial effort to sabotage the Allies in the Great War. But then any whiff of financial wheeler-dealing having underlying political motivation traceable back to some Jewish 'plutocratic' source was hardly the inter-war monopoly of the Nazis. In France, too, in 1934, the Stavisky affair became the occasion for a major Parisian riot against the alleged infiltration of Jewish corruption into government. And two years later when Leon Blum, France's first proudly Jewish, socialist party leader, took office as head of a Popular Front government it brought forth a veritable torrent of accusations that France had 'fallen under the yoke of a foreign nation' and would soon be plunged into war with Germany on behalf of the Marxists in Moscow.[28] The fact that within a year the great galaxy of leading Bolsheviks, who were of Jewish origin, were practically annihilated in Stalin's party purges would cut little ice with this sort of reasoning anymore than it would with the Nazis. But then back in Britain, government went to its own great efforts to row back from any notion that it might be being inveigled in a 'Jew's war', one late ministerial casualty being Leslie Hore-Belisha, Chamberlain's talented but 'so Jewish' Secretary of War.[29] What, of course, was odd in all this was that there was nothing that 'the Jews' were politically or economically able to do to dent the Nazi regime. But, then, when it came to the one issue in international politics in which the Jewish destiny under the Nazis had the capability to be truly destabilising– the issue of mass refugees – they had already proved themselves to be at complete cross-purposes.

Within months of the Minorities Treaties, the Balfour Declaration, the *other* poisoned fruit of European 'Jewish power' fantasies, was confirmed as British government policy. Yet the terms of Britain's Palestine Mandate seemed to stand in stark contrast to the Minorities framework. In facilitating Jewish immigration with the view of creating a Jewish national home in Palestine, the ultimate aim could be inferred as one not of fixing but rather divesting eastern Europe of its Jews, thus making the need for their diaspora protection redundant. However, not only was the Zionist project highly experimental, but it was never intended by the British to be the destination for more than a significant proportion of European Jewry. Not only was the issue of economic absorptive capacity central to a year-by-year quota system of tight immigrant access, but more paramount was the key caveat that it should not prejudice the rights of the other non-Jewish communities in Palestine – in other words the Arab majority.

Which is why the impact of Nazism proved so destructive not only in terms of Palestine itself but in the way it then looped back through reactive British decision making to become both a factor in the origins of war, and, in the process, helping to seal the European Jewish fate. The inexorable nature of this trajectory began in 1933 when the Nazis picked up on an ingenuous Zionist scheme to help encourage a failing, depression-bound, Palestine immigration by facilitating the export of German agro-industrial manufactures there; the sale, taken as the 'transfer' (*haʿavara*); to which Whitehall had demurred for fear of upsetting Berlin, of the immigrants' assets thus circumventing a German capital flight tax while at the Palestine end providing the necessary capital for them to be exempted from the standard quota requirements.[30] The benefits of such a scheme to the overall German economy were marginal. But as a method for both breaking the chimerical boycott and removing German Jews, the Nazi regime responded with enthusiasm.

While the Jewish world broke out in its most internecine of controversies over the way *haʿavara* wrecked both the principle and practice of boycott, its immediate results were quite tangible. Jewish migration to Palestine suddenly took on a dramatic surge, to the point where the 160,000 Jewish population in 1929 reached almost 400,000, or around a third of the Palestinian total, by 1937. Yet less than a quarter of the new immigrants were German Jews.[31] Even so, because of their economic weight and the stimulus they provided to land purchases, the Arabs for the first time recognized that their long-term hold on the country was in serious jeopardy. The result was revolt, the first 1936 phase alone sufficiently serious for a royal commission to propose partition of the Mandate into separate Jewish and Arab states.

Though the area of the proposed Jewish polity was a tiny 3,125 square miles and precipitated a further round of internal Jewish strife, this time specifically in Zionist ranks, its saving grace was that it offered to Zionism the opportunity to provide what had always been its primary objective – a safe haven for Jews, as determined by fellow Jews. In anticipation that *ha'avara*, or something like it, might have to be expanded in anticipation of a general Jewish evacuation from Germany,[32] the Peel recommendations were acknowledged as a life-line that the Zionist leadership duly accepted.

There was one obvious problem of implementation, namely the significant numbers of Arabs who would be displaced from the area of the Jewish state. Yet having been a party to the less-than-salubrious League-sponsored Lausanne Convention of 1923 in which some 650,000 Greeks and Turks were compulsorily 'exchanged' in the cause of national homogeneity, the abstract idea of vast population movements of *other* peoples' people did not seem to worry the British unduly.[33] The British incubus, rather, revolved around partition sparking off a much wider pan-Arab revolt, which the Chiefs of Staff, beset by problems of imperial overstretch, repeatedly warned could be catastrophic in the event of renewed war with Germany.[34] The course of events that had begun with Nazi support for *ha'avara* to which Whitehall had demurred for fear of upsetting Berlin[35] now took on a radically different turn. Partition was abandoned and, under the terms of the 1939 White Paper, only 75,000 new immigrants were to be allowed into Palestine over 5 years. With war imminent, Britain's commitment to the Jewish national enterprise thus seemed not simply to have been put on hold, but terminated in favour of majority Arab rule.

If this amounted to a closing vice on European Jewry, however, it was equally dependent on German actions as British reactions. The Nazis' preparations for war, heralded in 1936 with their Four-Year Plan, had its own much more radical Jewish subtext, which began to be fully implemented from summer 1938. Residual Jewish assets were consciously Aryanized to finance re-armament and the accordingly destitute German Jews encouraged to leave. This might take us into a different, albeit highly relevant, economic debate about the degree to which the several billion marks of expropriated Jewish wealth did, or did not, materially aid the Third Reich's drive to war. Jewish assets were clearly not nearly as fabulous as the Nazis had imagined. On the other hand, as Peter Hayes has argued, their five-per cent contribution to the national budget in Germany's final peacetime year may have represented the difference between acceleration or the opposite in German armaments production.[36] Putting this issue to one side, the relatively benign terms through which immigrants were able to recover a proportion of their assets under *ha'avara* should have now become inoperable. By the same token, the very notion that Germany might have still supported Palestine as the migrants' destination should also have ceased following the *Auswärtiges Amt*'s advice that a future Jewish state (as conceived by Peel) would constitute 'an additional ... power base for international Jewry, rather like the Vatican state for political Catholicism, or Moscow for the Comintern'.[37]

The contradictory nature of the polycratic state offers a somewhat more complex picture. *Ha'avara* in terms of capital transfers to Palestine (thanks to Jewish rather than German efforts) actually reached its high point in 1937–8, while as the front door on legal migration there was pushed tight, Heydrich's

SD became involved in a backdoor illegal route.[38] However, this should not distract us from the main new thrust of German policy. Beginning with the union with Austria in March 1938 (*Anschluss*), the regime accelerated mass Jewish expropriation and eviction. And as expectation of war rose, so too did the Nazis' *cantus firmus* of an internal Jewish security threat, dating back to the nightmare 1918 'stab-in-the-back' scenario. It was no accident that it was the SD that was given commission by Göring to ensure complete Jewish removal. Nor, as the storm clouds of conflict gathered, that he would tell fellow Nazis at the infamous post-*Kristallnacht* meeting on 12 November, that in that event 'we in Germany will first of all make sure of settling accounts with the Jews'.[39] Palestine may have been understood by Zionists as the Jewish refuge for exactly such an eventuality. But in the context of 1938–9 there could be no prospect of an orderly European Jewish retreat there. The 'Jewish question', as now rendered by the German refugee crisis, had moved on to new and entirely uncharted terrain.

Looked at through the perspective of the entire inter-war period what we can thus see in the Nazis' anti-Jewish onslaught is akin to an explosion ripping apart the Allied efforts to stabilize the Jewish position in Europe, besides putting out of action their emergency Palestinian safety-valve. Neither of these safeguards was primarily intended for German Jews, but for the great mass of their Eastern European counterparts. Nazi actions, however, had both direct and indirect knock-on effects in the 'New Europe'. Overt state-sponsored German violence became both goad to, and inspiration for, a rising crescendo of local grass-roots attacks on Jews, especially by Endeks in Poland and the Iron Guard in Romania. But it also posed the question to increasingly para-Fascist regimes in the East: 'If the Germans can turn the screws on their Jews with impunity, why can't we?' The Hungarian government of Bela Imredy was one that was clearly encouraged by the German example when it initiated efforts in late 1938 towards 'the supervision and liquidation of Jewish property without injury to production and national wealth'. Imredy's further call for a 'Europe-wide solution to the Jewish question'[40] was entirely consistent with what Romania and Poland, by then, were also actively promoting. Madagascar was the suggested destination for the majority of the Jews, regardless of all the evidence that this was preposterous.[41] Interestingly, others, such as the Serbian ultra-nationalist, Vaso Cubrilovic, read into the Nazi removal of their Jews a precedent for the eviction of other unwanted minorities. A world war would not break out, he argued, if what the Germans had done to them, Yugoslavia did to its Albanians.[42]

The problem with following the German example was that it could lead in entirely unpredictable directions. Poland, for instance, had repudiated its Minorities obligations without notable censure in 1934, but four years later its Denaturalisation Law, aimed at getting its retaliation in first against any Nazi attempt to return an estimated 50,000 German-domiciled Jews with Polish passports, rebounded when Germany began simply dumping large numbers of them on its border. What followed was like a chain reaction. The condition of the refugees rapidly deteriorated at the border crossing where neither Poles nor

Germans would take responsibility for them. The son of one benighted family, Hershel Grynspan, took out his frustrations by shooting a member of the German embassy staff. Goebbels saw in it the perfect pretext for a 'spontaneous demonstration' of popular outrage at Jewish perfidy: *Kristallnacht*.[43]

Adam Tooze has noted how closely the nationwide pogrom of 9 November was bound up with the Sudeten crisis, indeed how violent Nazi energy 'during the tension-filled summer of 1938 unloaded itself not in war, but an unprecedented assault on the Jewish population'.[44] But where in all this was the West? Were Britain or France just going to stand by and watch the spectacle of some 200,000 Jews cast into the wilderness? Was the US after nearly two decades of sitting on the sidelines finally going to come to the rescue? For a brief moment, in the spring of 1938, that seemed possible when President Roosevelt called for an international conference on the refugee crisis. It met at Evian, on the Franco-Swiss border, and at the President's initiative led to the formation the Intergovernmental Committee on Refugees (IGBR), seemingly in the process superseding the febrile efforts of the League. Yet if a desperate Jewry had some notion that this was going to be the occasion when the big powers would stand up to Hitler, they were to be sorely disappointed. Evian proved the occasion where all the nations present stood up and said they did not have room for any Jews, the US included. Worse, some, like the Australians and Canadians, took the opportunity to state that they did not very much like them anyway and did not want the problems they would bring. As the Zionist leader Chaim Weizmann acidly summarized, the world had become divided 'into two camps, one of countries expelling Jews, and the other of countries which did not admit them'.[45]

What tends to be forgotten is that Roosevelt was all along working to a proposition: that an economic deal could be struck with the Nazis providing for a mass European Jewish emigration, supported by sufficient funds. Thus, his intervention could be read as that of a great liberal (as well as prescient) leader not only prepared to break the mould by lending a helping hand to the Jews in their hour of need but admitting them into the American embrace, or finding them homes elsewhere. But while immigration restrictions were marginally eased in the US in the wake of Evian, as indeed in Britain, largely under public pressure, negotiating the *mass* Jewish release from the Nazis all revolved around money. More precisely, the so-called Rublee–Schacht negotiations were premised on the expectation that the 'rich' Jews of the USA and Britain could find a sum of at least 1.5 billion Reichsmarks as demanded by Berlin to secure a foreign currency loan against which the already sequestered assets of Germany Jewry would be nominally offset.[46]

Clearly, there were shades of *ha'avara* here, in which Schacht, Germany's one-time economic wizard, had played a critical role. The very fact that the ex-Economics Minister was brought back for this new project, with the direct authority of Hitler, suggests that the Nazis *were* in earnest. It was surely no coincidence that in January 1939 when the negotiations were meant to get into full swing Göring gave Heydrich a new mandate to form a central agency for Jewish emigration. But Berlin's anticipation (as in a sense Roosevelt's) was premised on the confabulated notion that 'Jewish high finance' could pluck any sum out of its bottomless hat. Putting aside the grotesque truth that the whole scheme was predicated on the idea of Western Jews ransoming German Jews in order to give the Nazis the wherewithal with which to continue their drive to war, the sums involved were vastly in excess of anything Jewish organizations could raise, and at a time when they were already severely overtaxed with immediate relief needs.[47]

No sooner had negotiations for mass exit began, moreover, than they started to unravel. US outrage at *Kristallnacht* was reflected in Roosevelt's own State of the Union address four days into 1939 in which the Nazi threat to US security and its core values of democracy and religious freedom were explicitly linked.[48] Hitler responded with his infamous speech on 30 January, in which he chillingly prophesied:

> if international Jewish financiers in and outside Europe should succeed in plunging the nations once again into a world war, then the result will not be the Bolshevisation of the earth and with it the victory of Jewry, but the annihilation of the Jewish race in Europe.[49]

The conventional wisdom treats these lines simply as evidence of Hitler's intention to commit the Holocaust. However, as Yehuda Bauer has emphasized, the Führer was actually demanding that the Jews should be settled outside Europe by international agreement. To be sure, the threat is blatant: if the West wouldn't act, the problem would be solved by other means.[50]

But then, *if* the West was already under the complete control of 'international Jewry' – the Bolsheviks included – at stake was not just whether Washington and London were intent on scuppering the Nazi demand to have the European Jews removed, preferably to some tropical reservation. The same would also be true of Hitler's 'just' demands in the East. From a Hitlerian perspective, the speech thus becomes one last desperate if shrill bid to keep the Schacht–Rublee negotiations on track and in so doing to break the Jewish stranglehold. In short, we have here the ultimate case of projection: one in which it is not Hitler who is preparing the groundwork for another world war but Christian civilization's oldest and greatest enemy.

Can we really countenance such projection as the *casus belli* for September 1939? It would certainly demand a very different way of looking at the origins of the war. Instead of travelling in separate compartments, the 'Jewish question' and geo-politics would have to be reconsidered through a broadly interconnected psycho-cultural as well as political prism. Yet we have already proposed that a precedent exists. In 1917, and again in 1919, European atavism broke on to centre stage in the notion that the Jews had the power to determine the course of the Great War and its aftermath. The great paradox was that by 1939 Hitler had stripped the pathology bare. The Jews as a collective entity had been shown to have neither physical let alone cosmic attributes. The evidence was for all to see in the summer of 1939 when the German ship, the *St Louis*, moved back and forth across the Atlantic with its forlorn cargo of unwanted refugees. Where was Jewish power now? The emergence of a Zionist body grandiloquently entitled the World Jewish Congress was a tribute only to the presumption. Barring its supporting role in an Anglo-French effort to sabotage Romanian efforts to move into the Axis sphere in early 1938, by way of invoking the Goga regime's violation of the Minorities Treaties,[51] its impact was precisely nil. Of course, in the increasingly surreal atmosphere in the run-up to war there were some bizarre schemes, such as that of Polish colonels to encourage a Polish–Jewish invasion of British Palestine, to which some desperate Jews (in this case extreme revisionist Zionists) were party.[52] Many Jewish representatives were present at Evian but all were cold-shouldered by the official delegates. Some months later, British Foreign Secretary Lord Halifax informed Laski that the Jewish question would not be affecting 'the British government's conduct of negotiations with the German government on matters involving peace or war'.[53]

Only the Nazis remained convinced that the Jews were the key. And in that discrepancy between Berlin's view and the rest, who had relegated them to an irrelevance, lay the trap into which Jews of Europe now fell.[54] Evian had already demonstrated that shorn of any pretext upon which they might 'perform with the others' the game of 'really serious, practical political affairs'[55] there could be no additional plea on humanitarian grounds. More than a year before the first shots had been fired, the West had abandoned its fellow protagonists in the creation of an Occidental civilization and in so doing sealed their continental fate. No wonder, seventy years on, mainstream Jewish views on Israel–Palestine remain so unyielding. The historians' role is certainly not to pardon. But if the saying that 'the Palestinians are the last victims of the Holocaust' is a true one, the Jews' own experience at the hands of their fellow Westerners may go some way to explaining it.

Notes

1   See H. Liddell Hart, *History of the Second World War*. London, 1970 for one notable example.
2   Y. Slezkine, *The Jewish Century*. Princeton, 2004.
3   Beginning, in fact, with S. Baron, 'Ghetto and Emancipation: Shall We Revise the Traditional View?' *The Menorah Journal* vol. xiv, no. 6 (1928), pp. 513–26.
4   See Count Lamsdorff, 'The Proposed Anti-Semitic Triple Alliance' in L. Wolf, *Notes on the Diplomatic History of the Jewish Question*. London, 1906, pp. 57–62 for a classic pre-1914 example.
5   See E. Kedourie, 'Sir Mark Sykes and Palestine, 1915–1916', *Middle Eastern Studies* vol 6 (1970), pp. 340–5 for the complete text.
6   See Z. Zeman and W. Scharlau, *The Merchant of Revolution: The Life of Alexander Israel Helfhand 'Parvus', 1867–1924*. London, 1965, ch. 10.

7   H. Bluher (1922), 'Secessio Judaica: Philosophical Foundations of the Historical Situation of Judaism and the Anti-Semitic Tradition', quoted in L. Poliakov, *History of Anti-Semitism* vol. iv: *Suicidal Europe 1870–1933*, tr. G. Klin. Oxford, 1985, pp. 324–5.

8   See Russia No.1, *A Collection of Reports on Bolshevism in Russia – Abridged Edition of Parliamentary Paper*. London, 1919.

9   N. Cohn, *Warrant for Genocide: The Myth of the Jewish World-Conspiracy and the Protocols of the Elders of Zion*. London, 1967.

10 M. Levene, 'The Balfour Declaration: A Case of Mistaken Identity', *English Historical Review* vol. cvii (1992), pp. 54–77.

11 Hitler speech 20 February 1920, quoted in W. Maser, *Hitler's Letters and Notes*, tr. A. Pomerans. London, 1974, p. 245.

12 R. Cecil, *The Myth of the Master Race: A Study in the Rise of German Ideology*. New York, 1972, p. 93.

13 A. Mayer, *Politics and Diplomacy of Peacemaking: Containment and Counterrevolution at Versailles, 1918–1919*. New York, 1967, pp. 296–308, 338–43.

14 National Archives, London (hereafter NA) FO 371/3904.529, Wyndham to FO 5 July 1919, Bevan to FO 1 September 1919.

15 W. Churchill, 'Zionism versus Bolshevism: A Struggle for the Soul of the Jewish People', *Illustrated Sunday Herald* 8 February 1920. S. Kadish, *Bolsheviks and British Jews: The Anglo-Jewish Community, Britain, and the Russian Revolution*. London, 1992, pp. 135–41 for a full interpretation.

16 E. Heifetz, *The Slaughter of the Jews in the Ukraine in 1919*. New York, 1921.

17 M. Levene, *War, Jews and the New Europe: The Diplomacy of Lucien Wolf, 1914–1919*. Oxford, 1992, pp. 243–6; Heifetz, *The Slaughter of the Jews*, pp. 14–27.

18 NA- FO371/3905/197853 for the Samuel report.

19 See Levene, *War, Jews and the New Europe*, pp. 209–10 for details.

20 Ibid., pp. 238–42.

21 H. Temperley, *A History of the Paris Peace Conference* vol. 5. London, 1921, p. 137. The section was written by the British NSC delegate, Sir James Headlam-Morley.

22 Quoted in C. Fink, *Defending the Rights of Others: The Great Powers, the Jews, and International Minority Protection, 1878–1938*. New York, 2004, p. 297.

23 Ibid., p. xvi.

24 H. Kieval, 'Masaryk and Czech Jewry, the Ambiguities of Friendship' in *idem., Languages of Community: The Jewish Experience in the Czech Lands*. Berkeley, 2000, pp. 198–216.

25 Fink, *Defending the Rights of Others*, pp. 232–5.

26 T. Kushner, *The Holocaust and the Liberal Imagination: A Social and Cultural History*. Oxford, 1994, esp. ch. 1.

27 S. Gerwitz, 'Anglo-Jewish Responses to Nazi Germany 1933–39: The Anti-Nazi Boycott and the Board of Deputies of British Jews', *Journal of Contemporary History* 26 (1991), pp. 267–8.

28 P. Hyman, *The Jews of Modern France*. Berkeley, 1998, pp. 147–8.

29 T. Kushner, *The Persistence of Prejudice: Antisemitism in British Society during the Second World War*. London, 1989, p. 12

30 F. Nicosia, *The Third Reich and the Palestine Question*. London, 1986, ch. 3 for details.

31 Ibid., pp. 100, 127.

32 Y. Bauer, *Jews for Sale? Nazi–Jewish Negotiations, 1933–1945*. New Haven, 1994, pp. 23–4 for the various projects emanating from Max Warburg.

33 M. Barutciski, 'Lausanne Revisited: Population Exchanges in International Law and Policy' in R. Hirschon (ed.), *Crossing the Aegean: An Appraisal of the 1923 Compulsory Population Exchange between Greece and Turkey: Studies in Forced Migration* vol. 12. New York, 2003, pp. 23–37 for close analysis.

34 L. Pratt, 'The Strategic Context, British Policy in the Mediterranean and Middle East, 1936-1939 in U. Dann (ed.), *The Great Powers in the Middle East Between 1919–1939*. New York, 1988, pp. 23–4.

35 G. Sheffer, 'Principle or Pragmatism: A Re-evaluation of British Politics towards Palestine in the 1930s' in Dann (ed.), *Great Powers*, p. 122.

36   P. Hayes, 'State Policy and Corporate Involvement, in the Holocaust' in M. Berenbaum and A. Peck, *The Holocaust and History: The Known, the Unknown, the Disputed and the Re-examined.* Bloomington, 1998, p. 208. Quoted in Nicosia, *The Third Reich*, p. 121. See also A. Tooze, *The Wages of Destruction.* London, 2007.

37   Quoted in Nicosia, *The Third Reich*, p. 121.

38   Bauer, *Jews for Sale?*, p.18.

39   Ibid., p. 36.

40   R. Zweig, *The Gold Train: The Destruction of the Jews and the Second World War's Most Terrible Robbery.* London, 2003, p. 16.

41   L. Yahil, 'Madagascar – Phantom of a Solution for the Jewish Question' in G. Mosse and B. Vago (eds), Jews *and Non-Jews in Eastern Europe.* Jerusalem, 1974, pp. 315–34.

42   H. Norris, 'Kosova and the Kosovans: Past, Present and Future as Seen Through Serb, Albanian and Muslim Eyes' in F. Carter and H. Norris (eds), *The Changing Shape of the Balkans.* Boulder, 1996, p. 15.

43   T. Maurer, 'The Background for Kristallnacht: The Expulsion of Polish Jews' in W. Pehle (ed.), *November 1938: From Kristallnacht to Genocide.* Oxford, 1991 for background.

44   Tooze, *The Wages of Destruction*, p. 274.

45   S. Adler Rudel, 'The Evian Conference and the Refugee Question', *Leo Baeck Year Book* 13 (1968), p. 236.

46   Tooze, *The Wages of Destruction*, p. 280.

47   Bauer, *Jews for Sale?*, ch. 2.

48   Tooze, *The Wages of Destruction*, p. 283.

49   M. Domarus (ed.), *Hitler, Reden und Proklamationen 1932–45* vol. 1. Wurzburg, 1962, p. 1058.

50   Bauer, *Jews for Sale?*, pp. 35–43 for close argument.

51   D. Vital, *A People Apart: A Political History of the Jews in Europe, 1789–1939.* Oxford, 1999, p. 859.

52   L. Weinbaum, *A Marriage of Convenience: The New Zionist Organisation and the Polish Government, 1936–1939.* Boulder, 1993, pp. 143–60.

53   Vital, *A People Apart*, pp. 885–6, 894–5.

54   S. Aronson, *Hitler, the Allies and the Jews.* Cambridge, 2004 for the thesis of the Holocaust as a multiple trap.

55   Vital, *A People Apart*, p. 896.

Chapter 21

The Sudeten Crisis of 1938: Beneš and Munich

Milan Hauner

In the life of Edvard Beneš (1884–1948), the second and fourth President of Czechoslovakia (1935–8 and 1945–8), Munich figures as the most traumatic moment. The ten years that remained in Beneš' life were his most dramatic. Among the four major charges levelled against Beneš by his critics were the Munich surrender, selling Czechoslovakia down the river to Stalin, opposition *vis-à-vis* Slovak autonomy and the expulsion of Sudeten Germans after 1945. The first charge affected Beneš most deeply. He admitted the traumatic impact of Munich several times while in exile, in the most startling way in August 1942 as the British government officially announced the annulment of the Munich *Diktat*: 'From September 1938, sleeping and waking, I was continuously thinking of this objective – to annul Munich and its consequences ... which for the last four years perhaps constituted the only aim of my life.'[1]

What is called the 'Events of Munich' were not merely the two conference days in the Bavarian capital from 29 to 30 September 1938 or the two weeks of dramatic events in the second half of September. Munich can be best understood as a tragedy in three acts,[2] starting with the abortive Sudeten uprising[3] and the departure of Lord Runciman[4] from Prague that resulted from Hitler's inflammatory speech at the Nazi Party Really at Nuremberg on 12 September: a 'curtain-raiser' opening the drama.[5] The first act was spectacularly accentuated by the announcement of the British Prime Minister's first flight to Germany to meet Hitler. As for the Czechoslovak President, he steadfastly refused to encounter the German dictator in person.[6] In doing so, Beneš made himself not only entirely dependent on the British and French mediators, but seriously limited his options. In the latter half of September he faced no more than three choices: war, plebiscite or transfer. Finding the plebiscite option unworkable since it would lead to complete disintegration of the multiethnic republic, Beneš was forced to select transfer, of which there were two variants: with or without territory. Finding the war option impossible for an isolated and abandoned Czechoslovakia, and finding the plebiscite unacceptable, Beneš had to accept the transfer of population with territory, i.e. a physical amputation of Czechoslovakia.

The first act of the Munich tragedy covered the week between 15 and 21 September, from the first meeting between Chamberlain and Hitler in Berchtesgaden, which ended with the Anglo-French plan and the subsequent resignation of the same government under pressure from the public. The second act began in Bad Godesberg on 22 September, during the second encounter between the British Prime Minister and the German dictator. In spite of Chamberlain's high expectations to settle the Czechoslovak crisis as quickly as possible, Hitler rejected the Anglo-French plan, based on ceding to Germany all Czechoslovak territory inhabited with more than fifty per cent German-speakers, and which the Czechoslovak government had accepted two days earlier under heavy pressure from London and Paris. Hitler now wanted territory where the Sudeten Germans no longer formed a majority, and which, if surrendered by Prague, would disrupt the main rail communications in Czechoslovakia. The new demands, known as the 'Godesberg Ultimatum', were rejected. Europe stood on the threshold of a general war. Reluctantly, the Western Powers proclaimed partial mobilization. France called up almost half a million reservists to strengthen the Maginot Line; Britain mobilized reservists for the Royal Navy. The Czechoslovak Government went a step further. Following French and British advice, they proclaimed general mobilization in the evening of 23 September. Forty Czech divisions would be ready in a few days to face the invaders. German troops, surrounding Czechoslovakia on three sides, were about the same strength, but better equipped. Germany possessed an overwhelming superiority in the air, Czechoslovakia its incomplete border fortifications.[7] Hitler had still not announced a general mobilization but was mounting an extremely noisy and effective propaganda campaign.[8] On the Czech side, however, spirits ran high in spite of the unreliability of ethnic minorities, especially the Sudeten Germans, many of whom did not answer the call up. During those five days and nights the Czechoslovaks stood on the threshold of war. From their point of view, it would have been a just war of defence against a Nazi invader, to be fought under optimal conditions, with France and Britain on their side, possibly even the Soviet Union as well, at least to act as a deterrent against Polish temptation to join Germany in the attack. Czech morale had never been better at any moment of the Sudeten Crisis. Under the new government, led by a one-eyed Czech hero of the First World War, General Jan Syrový, the humiliation of 21 September was quickly forgotten. It was also significant that the Czechoslovak mobilization was not disrupted by a German surprise attack. According to the witnesses closest to Beneš, his wife Hana and J. Smutný, both testified that the President had never been seen so content.

It was also during the night of 27–28 September that the French Premier Daladier worked on his radio address to incite the French people to do 'their duty' in the event of war, but which he never delivered.[9] However, no speech could force the French strategists to abandon their determination to sit the next war safely behind the protection of the Maginot Line – as it was to be demonstrated twelve months later when Germany attacked Poland. In order to be effective, French strategy required fundamental change with the effect of ordering French troops to get out of the concrete casemates of their under-ground fortification and cross the Rhine by seizing Freiburg, Karlsruhe and Saarbrücken on the first day of the war.[10] In spite of these shortcomings, the main figures on the chessboard seem to be displayed during the second act of the 'Munich Tragedy' in Czechoslovakia's favour.

Not even Beneš with his elaborate tactics of procrastination could have believed in September 1938 that the instruments of diplomacy could have saved Czechoslovakia's territorial integrity. The war option, paradoxically, would have been the only one left, which might have helped to restore Czechoslovakia, provided Germany could have been defeated. In 1938, however, neither the Foreign Office nor the Chiefs of Staff – together with the Chamberlain government the three pillars of British appeasement – believed that Germany could have been stopped by military means from invading and destroying Czechoslovakia. To restore Czechoslovakia, as it said in the Chiefs of Staff memorandum of 21 March, could 'only be achieved by the defeat of Germany and as the outcome of a prolonged struggle ... [in which] both Italy and Japan would seize the opportunity to further their ends, and that in consequence the problem we have to envisage is not that of a limited European War only, but of a World War', lasting many years and whose outcome would still be uncertain.[11] That view predominated in the official mind of the British government until Munich and beyond.

The third act of the tragedy opened on 29 September with the Munich Conference, which would serve at the same time as the dénouement. Ever since the first act of Berchtesgaden, Hitler had given away only very little, in anticipation that he would get it soon all back and add more to it. The conference abandoned the Godesberg Ultimatum in favour of the earlier Anglo-French plan of 19 September, whose terms were modified only slightly, offering Prague a few extra days for the evacuation of the Czech population from the Sudeten districts and the withdrawal of the Czech military before the *Wehrmacht* marched in.[12]

In describing Beneš' role of a memoirist–apologist, the dissident Czech historian Jan Tesař compared it to a chameleon-like transformation from participant to martyr, from culprit to victim.[13] This evolution went through multiple stages of re-editing under communist propaganda, which did not hesitate to attack Beneš while he was still alive as the protector of the Czech bourgeoisie, which had betrayed the nation to Hitler.[14] This transformation is detectable in Beneš' *War Memoirs*, of which the first volume, which carried the title *Mnichovské dny* [*Days of Munich*], was never published during his lifetime.[15] One can clearly discern a constant drive on Beneš' part to justify his behaviour by accusing the Western powers of treachery.

To his collaborators in London and to his radio audience, Beneš often promised to 'explain Munich and reveal all painful details' in the form of a report, presented after the end of the war in a suitable form, at the National Assembly. The longer version was incorporated in his *Memoirs*. Neither version, however, would reveal the promised painful details. In his 'Report to the Nation' of 28 October 1945 before the Parliament, Beneš apologized that he was still unable 'in view of certain international factors', as he put it, to reveal all necessary facts that should be made known. Nevertheless, he continued, 'I have got all evidence ready to be presented at a moment's notice when the situation becomes suitable or whenever asked by legitimate authorities.' Only then, Beneš concluded, '*I shall say the full and complete truth about the agonizing events as I saw and experienced them*.'[16] What Beneš meant by 'suitable moment' and 'legitimate authorities' has remained a real puzzle. There is no evidence that any of Beneš' colleagues advised against openness while discussing Munich; rather the opposite.[17]

It is difficult, for instance, to clarify, what went through Beneš' mind in the days immediately following Munich. He was forced to resign as President of Czechoslovakia on 5 October and spent the remaining days, prior to his sudden departure to England on 22 October, convalescing in consequence of an extreme physical and mental exhaustion.[18] But we also know that during the first days in England, while he worked on his slow recovery, Beneš was also working on an unknown version of his memoirs, now lost, assisted by his nephew, Bohuš Beneš, a junior diplomat at the Czechoslovak Legation in London, and by an English journalist, W.E. Hayter-Preston, who had already interviewed the President in Prague earlier in April and was now helping as editor under contract with the London publisher George Routledge & Sons. The memoirs, tentatively entitled *They Gave Us a Country*, were already advertised on the publishers' autumn list with sensational captions, which Beneš must have found distasteful, such as: 'Here you may learn, in the President's own words, what is the President's attitude to the fate of his country.'[19] The New York publisher A. Knopf, whom Routledge contracted to exploit the American market, proposed to serialize immediately the first portion of Beneš' manuscript before the second was even finished. Mrs Knopf argued that 'if we wait too long it will all be dead, and I believe things move more quickly here than they do in England and have a shorter life.'[20] While Routledge advised against serialization, because they rightly feared Beneš would not like that, Knopf, chasing the dollar, were still insisting on it.[21]

The final editing of the memoirs, with Beneš still convalescing, was suddenly interrupted for reasons not entirely clear. The publishers tried to persuade Beneš to add to the manuscript a 30,000-word supplement covering the recent September crisis. It is not apparent whether he agreed to do that, but from the confused correspondence it appears that Beneš was definitely upset by Knopf's insistence on newspaper serialization. The ensuing legal affair between Beneš and the publishers, who sued him for the breach of contract, had to be settled at two hearings of the Royal Court of Justice in December 1938 and January 1939. The Court decided in Beneš' favour and issued injunctions against the two defendants, Routledge and Preston, restraining them from publishing the book and from using in its subtitle the reference as 'being the work of, or authorized by, Dr. Beneš'.[22] Two weeks after the verdict Mr and Mrs Beneš, in the company of their nephew Bohuš, sailed to America.[23]

Beneš' last deliberation on the subject of Munich was in mid-November, after he had already encountered difficulties with the *They Gave Us a Country* project. He discussed Munich in the memorable long letter to 'a Czechoslovak politician in Prague'.[24] A politician of Beneš' calibre does not write a twenty-five-page-long letter to exchange frivolities, unless he wants to get a political message across. Beneš' detailed appraisal of his activities was of course written under the shadow of Munich, with the purpose of influencing his former collaborators in Prague. The matter was serious. Beneš felt he had to explain why he preferred surrender rather than war. In the first part of the letter he pledged 'never in the future to try to prove that anyone was guilty regarding the September events ... and accept fully accountability in situations where I was responsible'. He admits that, constitutionally, it should have been the government to take responsibility instead of him, but that it was him who in most cases acted. But he would have never acted without prior understanding and agreement with his colleagues in the government, he underlined.[25] Further, in the letter he mentions that he has been preparing his memoirs:

> and even if they will not be published immediately, I shall say everything as it really happened, without attacking or accusing anyone. I shall provide facts regarding internal as well as external affairs. Not in order to defend my policy – I regard it simply as my duty to elucidate this historically important period ... if war comes to Europe, to Germany, to Central Europe, or a break-up, or a revolution, or morass, etc.[26]

Will he be able to keep his word?

The other subject Beneš felt he had to explain to his domestic supporters was the war itself. Since July 1932, when he returned from the fruitless Disarmament Conference in Geneva, Beneš claimed that he realized that war in Europe was inevitable. Here he describes his message to the general staff: 'I am giving you four years,' he allegedly told them, 'the crisis will break out in 1936. By then, we must be ready.'[27] For a small country with limited resources, Czechoslovakia made a strenuous effort to re-arm, but four, not even six, years would be sufficient. Regarding her alliances, for which Beneš was directly responsible, the results were rather poor, except the problematic treaty with the Soviet Union, which looked good on paper, but could not be invoked without France marching first against Germany. To reach even a declaration of neutrality from Poland and Hungary did not seem achievable without substantial territorial concessions on the part of Czechoslovakia. Her military alliance with Romania and Yugoslavia, known as the Little Entente, had been originally designed against the restoration of the Habsburgs and was useless against a German threat.

In September 1938 Czechoslovakia's defences were put to a test. Her 40 divisions allied to 100 French would have been a real deterrent to Germany. When the French hesitated, Beneš refused to fight alone ('I shall not lead the nation to slaughterhouse'), nor could he rely, for complex political, ideological but also military reasons, on an isolated Soviet offer. But he was almost enthusiastic, as shown between September 23 and 28, to go to war with a firm guarantee of French and British help. On the other hand, should France and

Britain refuse to declare war on Germany, which everyone expected would be unleashed by a German invasion of Czechoslovakia, and very probably with Poland and Hungary joining in, Russia would merely send warplanes, and the whole world, not only German propaganda, would present the affair as the 'Second Spanish War'. 'To this', Beneš continues, 'we must add the question of our [Sudeten] Germans, our Slovaks, and the fear of being in coalition with Russia.'[28] Consequently, Beneš asked himself with a cool sense of logic: was it better to undergo the amputation but maintain the rest of the territory, or risk everything, including the loss of State? Was it better to choose openly an alliance with Russia alone and accept the consequences thereby implied, such as 'Bolshevization' all over the Central European region and the hostility of the West? Or retreat and consolidate, having been betrayed by allies and facing a vastly superior enemy, while keeping remnants of the State until the next settling of accounts with Germany, which had to come soon? Was there any chance of Soviet troops and warplanes coming to rescue of Czechoslovakia in spite of the absence of a common border and the hostile attitude of Poland and Romania, blocking the passage?

Although for reasons of propaganda Beneš praised publicly the Soviet readiness to help Czechoslovakia, military experts on both sides reached a negative conclusion. The short appearance of a Romanian document in the 1980s arose speculations that Bucharest in the end had agreed with the transit and overflight by the Red Army and Air Force in the last week of September 1938. They proved premature.[29] The document turned out to be fake. The ensuing debate, corroborated by additional research in East European archives in the process of opening after 1990, proved nevertheless stimulating[30] and was earmarked by the publication of Hugh Ragsdale's near-definitive study on the question of Soviet assistance to Czechoslovakia in the context of Soviet–Polish relations.[31]

For three years, Beneš kept his pledge not to comment on Munich. Readers found in his next book, *Democracy Today and Tomorrow*, scarcely any information on the Munich Conference.[32] Two years later, however, he finally broke his silence about Munich when he launched an offensive for the full recognition of his exile government in a manuscript entitled *The Fall and Rise of a Nation*. The Foreign Office strongly disapproved of his criticism of the British policy of appeasement and his interpretation of Munich as a national sacrifice. 'Everything I predicted has happened,' the over-confident Benes often said. That did not go well with the Foreign Office, which turned down Beneš' manuscript.[33]

The first draft of Beneš' *Memoirs* with the key chapter on Munich was completed in October 1943. In it, Beneš returns to the question of starting the European war in 1938 for the sake of Czechoslovakia that was willing to participate only as part of a 'Great Alliance', including the Soviet Union[34] and the United States, whose participations Beneš felt would be necessary to defeat Nazi Germany.[35] However, Beneš' claim of having [almost] always the right foresight and answer to approaching crises is echoed in his *Memoirs*, in which he refers to a certain 'Plan'.

He first announced the existence of such a plan in his radio broadcast of 22 September 1938, immediately after the government's capitulation to the Anglo-French ultimatum ('I have a plan for all seasons and will not be diverted by anything').[36] However, his abstract speech did not reveal any details of the 'Plan'. The speech was designed to calm down the angry Czech population, enraged because of the surrender of the Czechoslovak government.

It was only in the manuscript of his *Memoirs*, drafted several years later during the war in London, that Beneš revealed the details of his 'Plan', which he divided into three parts.

In the first part he discussed the war option with Germany, which he considered inevitable and bound to break out at any moment. Beneš himself wanted war *now*, i.e. in 1938, but France and Britain saw the situation differently:

> They preferred negotiations with Germany to their and our detriment. They forced us to make concessions which are murderous for us as well as them. If we had rejected them, we would have been completely abandoned by France and Britain and at once obliterated by Germany. Plain rejection of these painful concessions and an isolated Czech–German war would have created the worst possible situation for us.[37]

The second part of the plan involved refusing the war option. This left two remaining alternatives: the plebiscite and/or the transfer of Sudeten Germans.[38] In the event of negotiations failing and leading to the outbreak of war, France, Great Britain and the Soviet Union 'would support us'. There was no other way to keep the West 'on our side'. So 'we had to go in making concessions up to the very limit of our endurance, including self-sacrifice. In spite of this catastrophe, our nation must remain united and calm'. It was his intention, Beneš continued, to reach an agreement with the Poles, for the break-up of Czechoslovakia would mean the end of Poland as well. Beneš was predicting that if his plan of negotiations failed, the Czechs would suffer heavy territorial losses, but he felt a truncated state must be preserved. Beneš insisted, 'It is our duty – a terrible duty in the present difficult circumstances – to preserve the state, even deformed, at all cost until the moment when the next crisis with Germany arrives. Such crisis will certainly come and lead to general war, which will return to us everything what we shall lose now'. Henceforth, Beneš' endeavour for the remaining ten years of his life was dominated by the complex drive to clear his name . This strenuous effort has entered Czech historical writing under the term of the 'undoing of Munich' [*odčiňování Mnichova*].[39]

Beneš, though his hands were not soiled by touching Hitler's at any of the September 1938 conferences, must be seen, nevertheless, as one of the principal invisible participants. His undoing of his role in the Munich Agreement comprised two parts. One was official, which consisted of continuous criticism of the appeasers, especially at the Foreign Office and Quae d'Orsay, for the destruction of Czechoslovakia. Then, as soon as the international situation improved, Beneš would be able to concentrate on the restoration of Czechoslovakia with her pre-Munich borders.

The other repudiation efforts were discrete and covered three incidents, forcing Beneš to make unexpected turns, denials and reinterpretations as well as time-consuming ventures to re-write history, or simply to cover up the subject in deep silence. The first affair became known as the 'solicited ultimatum', originating in an alleged plot by the Czechoslovak Premier Milan Hodža, but with a tacit understanding of the rest of the government, the Army leadership and President Beneš, in response to the Anglo-French Plan, delivered on 19 September, of surrendering the majority German-speaking Sudeten districts of Czechoslovakia to Germany. The plot looked like a two-stage affair. During the first stage, the Czechoslovak government would vociferously reject the ultimatum as unacceptable in order to pacify the angry street mobs, while during the second phase the Western diplomats, returning in the dead of night with the enforced 'solicited ultimatum', left no option to the Czechoslovak government but to accept. The key disputed document was the despatch of the French Minister in Prague, Victor de Lacroix, of 20 September, which contained the phrase 'providing cover' to save the Czechoslovak government's reputation.[40] Beneš intuitively, without possessing any evidence, declared the text unreliable and tampered with by Georges Bonnet, the French Foreign Minister and evil ghost of Quai d'Orsay. The text of the auspicious telegram, however, could not remain secret too long. Within several weeks it was commented upon and appeared in the French press, and was reproduced at length later, upsetting Beneš enormously.[41] During the war he would devote a great deal of energy and dexterity to prove that the telegram had been tinkered with and must be treated a forgery, engaging even the poor de Lacroix to revoke the genuine version of his despatch and forcing Hodža in exile to re-write several times his affidavits.[42] Beneš' elaborate refutation of the 'solicited ultimatum' has been seriously weakened by the evidence now available in British and French archives.[43] The second affair concerned an alleged readiness by Beneš and Hodža to offer pieces of Czechoslovak territory to the Reich during several conversations they held with foreign diplomats prior to the Anglo-French plan of 19 September.[44]

The third incident involved the Nečas Mission. The irrefutable evidence associated with the Nečas Mission makes the need of continuous criticism of the previous two incidents irrelevant. It destroys the key portion of Beneš' argument against the 'solicited ultimatum' that he never offered a piece of Czechoslovak territory to Hitler prior to the delivery of the Anglo-French Plan. What was the Nečas Mission and why did Beneš decide to suppress its existence in his *Memoirs*? The Nečas Mission was an impromptu decision on the part of Beneš on 15 September in reaction to the news he received from London that Chamberlain was about to fly to Munich to meet Hitler. Beneš realized that Chamberlain was about to propose to Hitler territorial concessions to solve the Sudeten Crisis, which had reached a stalemate after the Henlein Party had rejected the so-called Fourth Plan. That plan contained maximal Czech concessions but was still based on maintaining the territorial integrity of Czechoslovakia. The Czech–German stalemate turned even worse after Hitler's inflammatory speech at the Nuremberg Nazi Party rally. This was followed by the Sudeten Germans, assisted from across the border from Nazi Germany, launching an uprising. The Czechoslovak authorities proclaimed martial law in the Sudetenland.[45] A complete deadlock added to the stalemate. For the first time, the Czechs had no domestic partner to negotiate about the Sudeten problem. Beneš and his government realized they would have to 'negotiate' with Hitler directly, which Beneš found impossible. Hence the only option left – save war – was to leave the negotiations completely in the hands of the Anglo-French mediators.

In order to try and thwart the Hitler–Chamberlain encounter Beneš had to devise a plausible counter-offer of territorial and other concessions to be offered to Hitler through French and British intermediaries, but subject to further transfer of between 1.5 and 2 million Sudeten Germans. Beneš hoped that despite the concessions he was prepared to give Hitler, Czechoslovakia as a whole would preserve her fortifications along the German border and that the economic cohesion of the country would be respected. Needless to say, the entire operation, which some historians call the 'Fifth Plan', was anti-constitutional and one would not find a single deputy of the Czechoslovak parliament ready to accept it. The carrier of Beneš' secret offer was Jaromír Nečas, a social democrat and Minister of Social Services in the Hodža government. In addition, he was also President Beneš' liaison with French Socialists, especially the former Prime Minister Léon Blum. Among the salient points of Beneš' instructions to Nečas were the following:

> Explain to our allies why a plebiscite would be absolutely impossible and impractical to conduct here ... Grant Germany so and so much thousands of square kilometres of territory ... not sure how much exactly: between 4000 and 6000 sq. km ... but [this must be] accompanied by the transfer of 1.5 to 2 Million Sudeten German in exchange ... while 'democrats, socialists and Jews,' would stay with us ... under no circumstance must it be know that all this came from me ... Not a word must be whispered to Osusky [Czechoslovak Minister in Paris]; request the same [discretion] from our French friends. Finally, destroy these notes.[46]

Nečas flew to Paris on 15 September. Two days later, he appeared in London, where the Anglo-French weekend conversation took place. Daladier tried to communicate the gist of Nečas' notes to Chamberlain during the lunch break, but to no avail. Having met Hitler for the first time on 15 September, Chamberlain was convinced that Hitler was not bluffing about invading Czechoslovakia. He thought he could help to prevent the outbreak of war by granting the Sudeten Germans the right to self-determination. Daladier, who did not like the plebiscite idea, disagreed and spent the rest of the meeting trying to persuade Chamberlain to change his mind.[47] He eventually succeeded and the Daladier–Chamberlain compromise, which replaced the idea of plebiscite with a direct transfer of population and territory, formed the basis of the ensuing Anglo-French proposal, sent to Prague on the following day, and which was at first rejected by the Czechoslovak government.

Thus Beneš' secret offer arrived too late to be taken seriously by either the French or the British, as Chamberlain had already offered Hitler a better deal in his first meeting: all Sudeten territory inhabited by more than fifty per cent German speakers.[48] Beneš' offer can be seen as a further elaboration of his subsequent suggestion to the French envoy de Lacroix, despatched to Paris on 17 September, that he was ready to relinquish territory to Germany, by referring obliquely to the Peace negotiations of 1919.[49] Thus, instead of improving Czechoslovakia's resolve to resist the Nazi threat, Beneš' secretive initiative to avoid war through compromise and half-baked concessions strengthened Chamberlain's and the Foreign Office's resolve to abandon Czechoslovakia by appeasing Hitler. France, willy-nilly, followed suit.

To re-evaluate the Nečas Mission is absolutely crucial for any updated inter-pretation of the dénouement of the Sudeten Crisis in its last dramatic stages leading to the Munich *Diktat*. Czech and Slovak historians, even after 1990, when they had full access to domestic and foreign archives, seem to be slow in fully appraising the consequences of the Nečas Mission during the final stage of the Sudeten Crisis.[50] Without the critical appraisal of the Nečas Mission and the subsequent fate of Beneš' original instructions, one would find it difficult if not impossible to explain why Beneš first delayed and then suppressed the publi-cation of the *Days of Munich*, the first volume of his wartime *Memoirs*. When later in the war he learned that Nečas did not destroy his original instructions from 15 September 1938, Beneš must have realized that his version of events in the *Days of Munich* could not hold ground if attacked by his communist and non-communist enemies.[51] Beneš' instructions to Nečas, in my view, did defini-tively contribute to Daladier's strange behaviour at Munich and his reluctance to defend Czechoslovakia's integrity by a declaration of war on Germany.[52]

Beneš' chief task in exile was to restore the Czechoslovak state in its pre-Munich borders. Having rejected the pro-Czechoslovak Slovaks (Hodža, Osuský) and anti-Nazi Germans (Jaksch) as partners, Beneš succeeded single-handed to pursue his vision, which even the hostile British Foreign Office reluctantly accepted over a three-year period during 1940–2. However, it is important to realize that the restoration of Czechoslovakia with her pre-Munich borders was not on Beneš' agenda during the first months following Munich, when he seemed to have accepted the truncated shape of Czecho-Slovakia, with the bulk of the Sudetenland outside its borders, and preached a radical geo-political relocation eastwards in order to attain a common border with the USSR.[53]

For three years, Beneš remained silent on Munich. In mid-1941, after the Soviet Union had been invaded by Germany, Beneš returned to the subject of Munich in his off-the-cuff conversations with his collaborators while he was working on his manuscript *The Fall and Rise*. To his archivist and 'ghost-writer' Jan Opočenský, he revealed that during the dramatic month of September 1938 he considered three options: either to risk war and die amidst his mobilized troops, or to commit suicide to shake up the West. In the end, he took the third option of going into exile in order 'bring the nation on the right side' of the war, which he believed must come soon.[54]

Perhaps no other British historian had been more intimately associated with the controversy over appeasement than the late A.J.P. Taylor. An opponent of Munich as a young Labour Party activist, he chose nevertheless to challenge the stultified anti-Munich attitude by notoriously defining Munich as 'a triumph for all that was best and most enlightened in British life; a triumph for those who had preached equal justice between peoples',[55] which can be interpreted in two ways: either as a revisionist defence of those who denounced the harshness and short-sightedness of Versailles, or as a sarcastic indictment of the British establishment at that time, enacted by its worst representative (Chamberlain). According to Taylor, Munich was not a triumph for Hitler at all.[56] As for Beneš, Taylor thought he emerged as the 'true victor of Munich in the long run'. As if he wanted to underline this conclusion in his inimitable way, Taylor liked to tell the following story (which I personally heard from him in 1976). During a visit in Prague in 1946 Taylor was taken by President Beneš to the window of his study at the castle to enjoy the magnificent view of the city. 'Look, isn't she beautiful [in the Czech language, Prague is, of course, a female], the only unspoiled city in central Europe, and all my doing.' When Taylor raised his eyebrows, Beneš added: 'By accepting the Munich settlement I saved Prague and my people from destruction.' At this point Taylor, showing his mischievous smile, added: 'I do not suggest that this was the lesson of Munich which a future historian should necessarily accept ...'[57] Indeed, we should not.

Notes

1   Beneš' radio address to home, 8 August 1942, after the British annulment of the Munich *Diktat*. Quoted from the critical edition: E. Beneš, *Paměti*, vol. 2, M. Hauner (ed.). Prague, 2007, pp. 194, 206–7; English ed., *Memoirs of Edvard Beneš: From Munich to New War and New Victory*, tr. Godfrey Lias. London, 1954, pp. 196, 209.

2   It was, of course, John W. Wheeler-Bennett who first called Munich a drama of three acts in his *Munich: Prologue to Tragedy*. London, 1948.

3   Most recently in D. Brandes, *Die Sudetendeutschen im Krisenjahr 1938*. Munich, 2008.

4   P. Vyšný, *The Runciman Mission to Czechoslovakia 1938*. London, 2003.

5   Term used by Wheeler-Bennett, *Munich*, p. 94.

6   To his biographer Beneš described Hitler as a 'vulgar and illiterate man, with no ability to reason', and whom he refused to see, despite several unofficial invitations. Beneš described himself as 'a human symbol of that democracy in Central Europe which Hitler loathed ... there could be no mental link between us'. When his friends allegedly urged him to see Hitler after the Austrian Crisis, Beneš threatened to put a hand grenade and a revolver in his pockets and use them on Hitler, 'if he shouts at me as he has shouted at Schuschnigg'. See C. Mackenzie, *Dr Beneš*. London, 1946, pp. 14–15.

7   Regarding the military balance between Germany and Czechoslovakia in September 1938, see Jonathan Zorach's excellent (unpublished) doctoral dissertation, *The Czechoslovak Army, 1918–1938* (1975); and such articles as his 'Czechoslovakia's Fortifications: Their Development

and Role in the 1938 Munich Crisis', *Militärgeschichtliche Mitteilungen* 2, 1976, pp. 81–94; M. Zgórniak, *Sytuacja militarna Europy w okresie kryzysu politycznego 1938r.*. Warsaw, 1979; *idem.*,'Forces armées Allemandes et Tchécoslovaques en 1938', *Revue de l'histoire de la 2e guerre mondiale*, April 1981, pp. 61–72; also M. Hauner,'Czechoslovakia as a Military Factor in British Considerations of 1938', *The Journal of Strategic Studies* 2 (1978), pp. 194–222.

8   E.g., Hitler's inflammatory speech in the Berlin Sport Palace on 26 September 1938.

9   E. du Réau, *Edouard Daladier 1884–1970*. Paris, 1993, pp. 271–3.

10   During the joint Anglo-French staff meeting on 26 September 1938 in London, General Maurice Gamelin declared that the French army, when fully mobilized (100 divisions), in view of facing only 8 German divisions along the Rhine, would advance immediately into Germany. See CAB 23/95, WO 106/5142.

11   'Military Implications of German Aggression Against Czechoslovakia'. C.O.S.698, CAB 27/627.

12   Wheeler-Bennett, *Munich*, pp. 171–82, 452–63.

13   J. Tesař, *Mnichovský komplex*. Prague, 2000.

14   In spite of the Beneš–Stalin agreement of December 1943, Beneš was viciously attacked in *Novoe Vremya*, 33, pp. 26–31. The article was promptly reprinted in Czech in the communist magazine *Tvorba*, 25 August 1948 – two weeks before Beneš died. For details see M. Hauner, 'Mnichov v díle Edvarda Beneše [Munich in the works of E.Beneš]' J. Němeček (ed.), *Mnichovská dohoda – Cesta k destrukci demokracie ve střední Evropě*. Prague, 2004, pp. 222–42.

15   The first draft was completed and circulated by Beneš in exile in the autumn of 1943 – but never published as long he lived. The first version was published by his former Chancellor Jaromír Smutný in London in 1955 (second ed. 1958). During the Prague Spring of 1968, an expanded edition of *Mnichovské dny* (ed. J. Soukup) was published for the first time in Prague, twenty years after the president's death. A critical edition of *Mnichovské dny* appeared finally in 2007 (ed. and commented on by M. Hauner) as volume 1 of a three-volume edition of Beneš' *War Memoirs*. See note 1.

16   Beneš' Report to the Nation, before the National Assembly, 28 October 1948, in Beneš, *Paměti*, vol. 3, doc.161, here pp. 587–8.

17   See my introduction to the origins of Beneš' *Memoirs*, discussion on the first draft, Beneš, *Paměti*, vol. 1, pp. 34–42.

18   As can be testified by his wife Hana's pocket calendar entries – the most reliable evidence to be found about Beneš' health. The National Museum Archives Prague, Hana Benešová papers, box 2.

19   Routledge Literary Archives, University of Reading. Personal interviews with witnesses. (hereafter RLA).

20   RLA – Mrs Knopf to Tom Murray Ragg, editor of Routledge, 19 October 1938.

21   Ibid. Mrs Knopf still failed to understand how deeply Beneš was offended. She would persist on serialization through scoop and wrote on 10 November 1938 to Tom Ragg, reminding him yet again about the thwarted serialization and the motivation that she 'did this in the hope that a serial publication would help the sale of the book and Benes' cause and possibly his pocket and incidentally yours and our own'.

22   *The Times* 21 January 1939.

23   Beneš was invited by the University of Chicago where he lectured until July 1939. In the US he did not have time to work on his memoirs. See Jan Opočenský, *Presidentův pobyt ve Spojených státech: Edvard Beneš a formování československého zahraničního odboje 1938–1939* [*The President's Sejourn in the US: E. Benes and the Formation of Resistance in Exile* ...], ed. and commented on by M. Hauner. Prague, 2000.

24   Ladislav Rašín (1900–45) was a radical nationalist who reproached Beneš in his letter of 7 November 1938 for not wanting war, for refusing to become Leonidas in defending the Bohemian Thermopile against German invasion. Rašín's letter and Beneš' response are published in Beneš, *Paměti*, vol. 3, doc. 85, pp. 271–85. For the English translation of Beneš' letter to Rašín, see 'Edvard Beneš' Undoing of Munich: A Message to a Czechoslovak Politician in Prague', *Journal of Contemporary History* vol. 38/4, pp. 563–77.

25   'Edvard Beneš' Undoing of Munich', p. 566.

26   Ibid.

27 Ibid., p. 571.
28 Ibid., pp. 573.
29 G. Weinberg, 'Munich after FiftyYears', *Foreign Affairs* vol. 67 (1988), pp. 176–7. The fraudulent document, fabricated by Ivan Pfaff (see below), was published in J. Hochman, *The Soviet Union and the Failure of Collective Security, 1934–1938*. Ithaca, 1984, pp. 194–201.
30 Two historians of Czech descent, Ivan Pfaff (*Die Sowjetunion und die Verteidigung der Tschechoslowakei 1934–1938*. Cologne, 1996, pp. 320, 363) and Igor Lukeš (*Czechoslovakia Between Stalin and Hitler*. Oxford, 1996, pp. 191, 198–201), have built their case on the intended Sovietization of Czechoslovakia in 1938, using as their main argument a conjured speech by Stalin's chief propagandist Andrei Zhdanov, allegedly delivered in Prague on 21 August 1938, and other fabricated evidence. No such visit by Zhdanov to Prague had ever taken place. My own critical analysis in English was published in *Kosmas* (*Czechoslovak and Central European Journal*), Fall 2004, pp. 46–63; *idem.*, 'The Quest for the Romanian Corridor: The Soviet Union, Romania and Czechoslovakia during the Sudeten Crisis of 1938' in F. Taubert (ed.), *Le Myth de Munich: 60 ans après* (Paris, Munich, 2002), pp. 39–77.
31 H. Ragsdale, *The Soviets, the Munich Crisis and the Coming of World War II*. Cambridge 2004.
32 Based on Beneš' university lectures at Chicago. Published by Macmillan in September 1939.
33 Published for the first time in 2004 as Edvard Beneš, *The Fall and Rise of a Nation: Czechoslovakia 1938–1941*, ed., annotated and introduced by M. Hauner. New York. East European Monographs.
34 Beneš, *Paměti*, vol. 1, pp. 373–84. Beneš' attitude to Russia has been analyzed in my article 'We Must Push Eastwards! The Challenges and Dilemmas of President Beneš after Munich', *Journal of Contemporary History* vol. 44 (4), October 2009, pp. 619–56.
35 Based on Beneš' account of his secret meeting with President F.D. Roosevelt, 28 May 1939. Beneš, *The Fall and Rise of a Narion*, pp. 133–41; Beneš, *Paměti*, vol. 2, pp. 86–93; Beneš, *Paměti*, vol. 3, docs101 and 109.
36 Beneš, *Paměti*, vol. 1, pp. 350–2.
37 Ibid. Here Beneš uses entire passages from his letter to Rašín (November 1938). See note 24 above.
38 Transfer opened two options: with or without territory. In 1938 it was Hitler who held the trump cards and demanded transfer with territory. After the reversal of fortunes in 1945, Beneš would insist on transfer *without* territory, i.e. physical expulsion of Sudeten Germans from their homes without compensation.
39 Ibid., p. 352.
40 *Documents diplomatiques Français 1932–1939* (DDF/2e/XI), 2e série, tom XI. Paris, 1977, doc. 232; Beneš, *Paměti*, vol. 3, doc. 57.
41 *Le Temps* 11 October 1938; *L'Europe Nouvelle* 29 October1938; *Gringoire* 19 December 1940.
42 Beneš' letter to de Lacroix, 20 January 1939, in Beneš, *Paměti*, vol. 3, doc. 87. De Lacroix complied but his testimony was dismissed in the post-war hearings conducted against the members of the Daladier government. See also the testimony of Léon Blum after the war in *Les Evenements survenus en France de 1933 à 1945: Rapports*, vol. I, p. 256. Hubert Ripka's vehement denial is devoid of evidence (H. Ripka, *Munich Before and After*. London, 1939, pp. 85–93. On the Beneš–Hodža relationship, see J. Kuklík and J. Němeček, *Hodža versus Beneš*. Prague, 1999, pp. 130–3, 180–1, 228–9.
43 DDF/2e/XI, no. 232; DBFP/3/II, nos 979, 981. Georges Bonnet, *Défense de la paix: De Washington au Quai d'Orsay*. Geneva, 1946, pp. 237–9, 247. Beneš and de Lacroix claimed that Bonnet had tampered with the text of his telegram of 20 September 1938 (*DDF* no.232). Textual comparison does not confirm this suspicion. Eduard Táborský, who worked with Beneš as his secretary during the war, thinks that Beneš' loquacity was the main cause of misunderstanding. Beneš used some historical parallels about considering territorial cessions during the Peace Conference of 1919 as he spoke to de Lacroix on 17 September 1938 (E. Taborsky, *President Edvard Beneš between East and West 1938–1948*. Stanford: 1981, p. 12.) .
44 Beneš, *Paměti*, vol. 3, docs. 65, 78. Hints at possibilities how to correct the Czechoslovak–German border in Germany's favour: DBFP/3/II, #884, 888; see also p. 519; and DDF/2e/XI, #232, 175, 180, 181.

45 To Hitler's and Goebbels' great anger, who wished that Henlein and Frank stayed in the Sudetenland with the rebels. See Goebbels' Diaries, *Die Tagebücher von Joseph Goebbels: Sämtliche Fragmente*. Munich, 1993–2004, vol. 1/6, pp. 93–113.

46 The secret Beneš' instructions to Minister J. Nečas of 15 September 1938 were published for the first time by J. Pachta and P. Reiman in *Příspěvky k dějinám KSČ*, vol. 1, 1957, pp. 104–33. The French translation is to be found in the Daladier Papers, *DDF/2ᵉ/XI*, no. 192; Beneš, Beneš, *Paměti*, vol. 3, #52. The authenticity of Beneš' instructions to Nečas has never been questioned. See also J. Zorach, 'The Nečas Mission during the Munich Crisis', *East Central Europe* 16 nos 1–2 (1989), pp. 53–70; D. Brandes, 'Eine verspätete tschechische Alternative zum Münchener Diktat', *Vierteljahreshefte für Zeitgeschichte* vol. 42/2 (1994), pp. 221–41.

47 Réau, *Edouard Daladier*, pp. 255–8; also *DDF/2e/XI*, doc.212. To the Czechoslovak minister in Paris, however, Daladier revealed a few more details after the Munich Conference. At the beginning, Daladier maintained, he was ready to defend Czechoslovakia if attacked by Germany, but not any more after he learned that President Beneš had come with proposals to cede territory to Germany together with one million or more of Sudeten Germans. When he mentioned this to Chamberlain, his immediate reaction was: if one million, why not two or even three, if this could bring about a definitive solution of the Sudeten problem?! Chamberlain insisted that even if Britain and France together went to war with Germany, they could not prevent the destruction and occupation of Czechoslovakia (see the COS memo, note 10 above). Only winning a global war could bring about the restoration of Czechoslovakia (Osuský to Beneš, 4 October 1938, in Beneš, *Paměti*, vol. 3, doc. 79).

48 For comparison, Chamberlain 'offered' Hitler much more (five times). In the final delimitations of the Munich settlement Germany acquired 29,000 square km of Czech territory with some 3.4 million inhabitants, of whom over 700,000 were of Czech nationality. See E. Táborský, *The Czechoslovak Cause*. London, 1944, p. 21.

49 Beneš, *Paměti*, vol. 2, doc.55. Osuský reproaches Benes that by talking about territorial concessions to de Lacroix as he did, he committed thereby an 'act of *suprême imprudence*'. At this stage Osusky still did not know about Beneš' secret instructions to Nečas that offered even more radical concessions.

50 See the restrained references to the Nečas Mission in the two main monographs by A. Klimek (*Velké dějiny zemí Koruny české*. Prague, 2002, vol. XIV, ch. VII, pp. 627–8) and J. Dejmek (*Edvard Beneš*, vol. 2. Prague, 2007, ch.18, pp. 146–50). The recent biographies of Beneš by Z. Zeman and A. Klimek (*The Life of Edvard Beneš 1884–1948*. Oxford, 1997; Czech version Prague, 2000) do not mention the Nečas Mission at all, although it is mentioned and analyzed in the main Slovak biography on Osuský (S. Michálek, *Diplomat Štefan Osuský 1889–1973*. Bratislava, 1999, pp. 97–9).

51 Anticipating death after his fourth heart attack, Nečas wrote in July 1943 from hospital an unusually candid letter to Beneš, a transcript of which has survived in the Osusky papers (Hoovers Institution Archives, Osusky collection, box 47). Nečas told Beneš that his wife had hidden the document, which would be delivered to him after the end of war. Since Nečas died in London in early 1945 and his wife perished in a concentration camp, Beneš felt free to suppress any mention of the Nečas affair in his *Memoirs*. However, without knowing for sure that the document had vanished, he decided, I would venture to speculate, to postpone the publication.

52 Daladier's contempt of Beneš, which appeared to be stronger than his hatred of Hitler, is the subject of an acclaimed recent fiction on the French Prime Minister: Georges-Marc Benamou, *Le fantôm de Munich* (Paris, 2007; Czech and English [US] translations in 2008). Absence of Czech sources, especially concerning Nečas and Osuský, is one of the main flaws of the book, exemplified by the grotesquely short chapter on Beneš (pp. 245–8).

53 See in detail M. Hauner, 'We Must Push Eastwards', note 34 above.

54 J. Čechurová et al (eds), *Válečné deníky Jana Opočenského*. Prague, 2001, p. 134.

55 A.J.P. Taylor, *The Origins of the Second World War*. London, 1967, pp. 234–5.

56 See F. Genoud (ed.), *The Testament of Adolf Hitler: The Hitler-Bormann Documents*. London, 1962, pp. 67, 95–7.

57 A.J.P. Taylor must have told this story to many people. But he was certainly not the only one who after the war witnessed Beneš' staged scene of martyrdom at the Prague Castle. See, e.g., Raymond Aron, *Mémoires* vol. 1. Paris, 1983, p. 262.

Chapter 22

Poland and the Origins of the Second World War

Piotr S. Wandycz

The Second World War began with an unprovoked German attack on Poland by air, sea and land on 1 September 1939. Ostensibly, the reason was the Polish rejection of Hitler's terms: annexation of Danzig and an extraterritorial highway through the 'Corridor'. On 17 September the Red Army, acting in collusion with Germany, marched into eastern Poland. Such historians as Mariusz Wołos and Sergei Sluch regard this fact as marking the entry of the USSR into the Second World War.[1]

The seventieth anniversary of the outbreak of the war intensified the discussion about its origins and the role played by Poland. New works appeared while older were scrutinized.[2] Writings stemming from political 'mythology' or 'historical revisionism', especially in Russia, hardly deserve mention.[3] It is worthwhile, however, to ponder a more balanced view of a Russian historian who wrote:

> All leading European powers bear to some extent the blame for the outbreak of the war. The major and greatest guilt should be assigned to the Hitlerite leadership of Germany which fervently strove to arrive at a military conflict. Both the Munich policy of the western powers and the non-aggression pact between Hitler and Stalin contributed to broaden the Nazi aggression.[4]

Starting with the Treaty of Versailles and its fulfilment or non-fulfilment by Britain, France and Germany in the 1920s and 1930s, going on to appeasement, the Czechoslovak crisis and the Ribbentrop–Molotov pact of 1939 with its secret protocol, we see Poland figuring prominently in all of them. Questions and interpretations vary regarding Poland's responsibility for the war. What were the options of Polish diplomacy in 1939? Was Danzig the real cause, as it was presented in some quarters then – the famous article by the French rightist politician Marcel Déat, '*Mourir pour Danzig*'[5] – and later? Was Great Britain also guilty? In 1939, on Warsaw's ruins, the Nazis put the sign 'England this is your work.'

The Treaty of Versailles has been subjected to various criticisms. John Maynard Keynes, the British economist, vilified the major peacemakers and denounced the clauses of the treaty.[6] In fact, Germany was not ruined and was to receive more Western aid than it ever paid in reparations. Nonetheless, the revisionist view has persisted. George Kennan claimed that the Second

World War resulted from 'the very silly, humiliating punitive peace imposed on Germany'.[7] More recently, Vladimir Putin, the Russian Premier, compared Versailles to a ticking bomb.

Years of painstaking research have produced a more balanced appraisal.[8] The editors of a major work on the subject concluded that 'scholars although remaining divided, now tend to view the treaty as the best compromise that the negotiators could have reached in the existing circumstances'.[9] According to Alan Sharp, 'The settlement was not perfect, it contained the potential seeds of future conflict, but also the potential for more hopeful future'.[10]

Most Germans considered the Treaty as a shameful *Diktat*. This was hardly surprising given Germany's wartime hegemonic designs as embodied in the treaties it had imposed on the vanquished Russia (Brest–Litovsk) or Romania (Bucharest). The Germans never felt that they had been defeated on the battlefield. Even harsh post-Second World War critics of Versailles such as Henry Kissinger admitted that 'having considered the pre-war world too confining, Germany was not likely to be satisfied with any terms available after defeat'.[11] Given this German attitude, Versailles was, as Jacques Bainville put it, '*Une paix trop douce pour ce qu'elle a de dur*'. It hurt Germany, but did not deprive it of means of re-emerging as a great power capable of seeking revenge and overthrowing the treaty.

This can be seen nowhere more clearly demonstrated than in the provisions regarding German–Polish borders. The Polish issue in Paris was important and controversial.[12] The Poles sought a settlement based partly on ethnographic and partly on strategic considerations.[13] The attitude of the 'Big Three' Allied leaders – Clemenceau (France), Lloyd George (Britain) and Wilson (USA) – toward Poland stemmed from their own peace programmes. For France, the key issue was guarding itself against a potentially more powerful Germany. Hence the slogan *securité d'abord*. Germany was to be hemmed in between France reaching the Rhine and its ally, a big Poland regaining the provinces once annexed by Prussia and having a secure access to the Baltic. East Prussia could be demilitarized, like the Rhineland.

Such terms, which the Allied experts did not consider unreasonable, stood no chance of being accepted by Wilson and Lloyd George. The US President was intent on basing peace on the principle of national self-determination (a very difficult concept to apply to the mixed East–Central European region) combined with a system of security achieved through the League of Nations. Imperfect arrangements could be resolved within the framework of the latter. Wilson blamed balance of power, secret diplomacy, alliances and rival blocs as responsible for the war. With open diplomacy, democracy would prevail and assure peace and stability. Although eulogized by the Poles as their protector during the war, Wilson had little knowledge of and no special sympathy for the Polish claims.[14]

British objectives as formulated by Lloyd George, and supported by such politicians as Marshal Jan Smuts, were to re-establish a stable Europe with

Germany eventually returning to its role of a continental power. Deprived of its colonies, its powerful navy, and burdened with increased reparations, Germany would no longer threaten Britain. Lloyd George believed a large Poland would strengthen France, and he preferred by far the Germans ('one of the most vigorous and powerful races of the world') to the Poles. The German leaders opposed every possible concession and every territorial claim to Poland and attempted to deprecate Polish civilization and capacity.[15] Lloyd George feared that Berlin would reject the treaty. Having satisfied British interests, Lloyd George was more than willing to sacrifice those of Poland. Eventually, with an unfulfilled promise of a British–American guarantee for France, he succeeded in making Clemenceau go along.[16]

The Polish–German borders as traced by Versailles and subsequently completed after plebiscites in Upper Silesia and southern districts of East Prussia fell short of adequate security considerations. Access to the Baltic Sea was restricted to a very narrow band of territory, which separated Germany from East Prussia. The Germans quickly called it 'the corridor' to stress its artificiality, although this had been old Polish land annexed by Prussia during Poland's partitions. The only harbour – Danzig (Gdańsk) – was made into a Free City with certain Polish commercial and maritime rights safeguarded. As set out in the treaty, the borders were hardly defensible. They also left some million Poles in Germany and several hundred thousand Germans in Poland. Poland could do nothing but accept them and thereafter oppose all German revisionist claims.

The peacemakers did not establish Poland's eastern borders, in view of the revolutionary chaos in Russia and the lack of a clear policy toward the Bolsheviks. Their preference was for a minimal strictly ethnic border, the so-called Curzon Line. It took a war between Poland and Red Russia in 1919–21, which ended with a compromise – the Treaty of Riga – to trace a frontier between the two countries. As regards the formerly Austrian Eastern Galicia, the peacemakers were reluctant about recognizing it as part of Poland, and did so tentatively. The Teschen (Cieszyn, Těšin) Silesia, which the Czechs seized in 1919, was denied to the Poles. The Polish eastern borders were finally recognized by the Allied Powers only in 1923.

The Polish Republic was from its beginnings exposed to the enmity of Germany and Soviet Russia. Their common ground was opposition to Versailles, which was regarded as unjust by the former and an imperialist peace by the latter. Seeking to evade military restrictions imposed on it by the Treaty, Germany found Russia a willing accomplice. The Treaty of Rapallo of 1922 symbolized the extent of German–Russian co-operation.

If Versailles *per se* could hardly be regarded as making the Second World War inevitable, the absence of a firm and consistent implementation process raised hopes in Germany for its non-fulfilment. Not only disagreements between France and Britain boded ill for the future – so did the absence of the USA from the League of Nations. Polish diplomacy had limited room of manoeuvre. Relying on Germany against Russia or vice versa was out of the question. The only option was a policy of non-alignment with either neighbour and alliances with France and the smaller neighbours in the region.[17] Thus, in 1921, a Franco-Polish treaty of alliance directed primarily against Germany was signed. In East Central Europe, however, only Romania was willing to become Poland's ally, chiefly against the Soviet Union. Czechoslovakia was adverse to a rapprochement with a Poland exposed to German and Russian enmity, not to mention the recent border dispute. Instead, Prague concentrated on building a regional bloc, dubbed the Little Entente, which was operative against much-weakened Hungary and Habsburg restoration, but not against a Great Power.

The inability of bringing Warsaw and Prague closer together weakened the French *barrière de l'est* viewed as a safeguard against Germany. The Skirmunt–Beneš pact signed in 1921 and encouraged by the French remained a dead letter. The efforts of Marshal Ferdinand Foch, the French war hero who visited Warsaw and Prague in 1923, resulted in a Franco-Czechoslovak alliance but without a military convention which figured in the Franco-Polish alliance. The efforts of the Chief of the Polish General Staff, Stanisław Haller, who visited Paris to discuss the modalities of possible joint military operations against Germany and also Russia, produced no concrete results.

After 1923, the political scene in France and in Europe changed drastically. French Premier Raymond Poincaré had favoured a hard line toward Germany. In January 1923 – acting against British wishes – the French forcibly reacted to the default of German reparations by entering the Ruhr. Berlin's response was passive resistance. The operation ended with a Pyrrhic victory. Opposed by the Anglo-Saxon powers, France was isolated. Even the Poles were worried lest the Ruhr occupation drive Germany into the Russian arms and lead to an armed conflict. Hence they adopted a cautious stand during the crisis.

In May 1924 the fall of the Poincaré cabinet opened the way for governments of the left, dominated by Aristide Briand. By applying financial pressure, the British and the Americans succeeded in having the question of reparations divorced from security. At the London Conference, a special commission chaired by an American Charles Dawes operated under the slogan 'Business, not politics'. Economic stabilization in Germany, following the collapse of the Mark, was to serve as a base for a working system of collective security. 'France put herself in the hands of the bankers and renounced her freedom of action.'[18] Under these circumstances, Paris began to have second thoughts about the value of its alliance with Poland, looked upon as a poor substitute for an agreement with Russia.[19]

Polish diplomacy had to redefine its policies and tactics. At the London Conference, Poland 'was left out in the cold' – so complained Polish Foreign Minister Aleksander Skrzyński (1922–3 and 1924–6), arguably the most outstanding Polish diplomat and theorist. Skrzyński formulated broad principles on which he based his foreign policy. He insisted that national objectives and interests ought to be in harmony with major trends of international society [20]

The chief objective was lasting peace, and there was no peace without justice, no justice without law, and law stemmed from the treaties. Hence Skrzyński enthusiastically supported the triple concept of arbitration, security and disarmament and the defunct Geneva Protocol. He believed that for Poland collective security was more important than alliances, not that he ignored the importance of military power. Poland, given its exposed position between Germany and Russia, was in need of special guarantees, and at no time would he even consider any territorial concessions.

At the beginning of 1925 Polish diplomacy had to confront a new problem – Gustav Stresemann's proposal of a Rhineland pact. Offering to recognize the territorial status quo in the West, Stresemann seemed to accept willingly the relevant provisions of Versailles – indeed his German critics accused him of *Erfüllungspolitik*. By satisfying the desire of France for security, but not extending guarantees to the Eastern allies, Stresemann strove to achieve a new European concert in which Germany would be a major partner. In vain Skrzyński argued that European peace was indivisible and security on the Rhine had to be complemented by security on the Vistula. French attempts to involve Great Britain in guarantees in the east failed, and Paris went along with the scheme at the Conference of Locarno in 1925.[21] The Poles had to be satisfied with an arbitration treaty with Germany and a new accord with France confirming the Franco-Polish alliance. The action under the latter, however, seemed to depend on the League.[22]

By making a distinction between guaranteed German–French–Belgian borders and the German–Polish frontier, Locarno raised the spectre of revisionism. True, the latter was temporarily put on a back burner, and Stresemann promised not to try to alter the borders by force.[23] Was Skrzyński right to opt for a 'strategy of active participation' rather than provoke a showdown with France and seek to torpedo the Conference? His efforts included even a visit to the United States, where the Minister vainly hoped to find support in the name of peace and democracy. There was no realistic alternative.

While the 'spirit of Locarno' prevailed, the next few years saw a gradual realization of Germany's plans to free itself from Versailles. Stresemann had joined Briand and Ramsay MacDonald, the British Prime Minister, as the third 'Locarnoite' and gained admission for Germany to the Council of the League of Nations. Poland had to be content with just a semi-permanent seat. Germany used the League forum to raise complaints about the treatment of the German minority in Poland, just as it seemed to use (although some historians disagree) the German–Polish customs war to weaken Poland's economy and make Warsaw more amenable to concessions concerning the 'corridor'. The Germans never missed any opportunity to argue to the British and the French that a normalization of German–Polish relations was not possible without a settlement of the 'corridor' and Upper Silesia.[24]

The British were not opposed to German revisionism provided it was not accomplished by force. In fact, they expected it, having no stake in Poland's territorial integrity. Briand thought that Poland could make some territorial concessions to Germany, using the machinery of the League. Both the French and the British showed interest in the German idea of Poland abandoning the 'corridor' to Germany in exchange for another corridor being created along the Niemen river to the Lithuanian port of Memel.[25] This was a wild idea.

Stresemann's other diplomatic cards included the Soviet Union, which regarded Locarno as an anti-Soviet combination. Thus in April 1926, shortly after Locarno, Germany signed the Berlin Treaty of Friendship and Neutrality with USSR. Paris was shocked, and not only Poland but also Czechoslovakia considered the treaty as contrary to Locarno. Berlin argued that this was not the case. As for Moscow, it manoeuvred between Berlin and Warsaw and Foreign Commissar Grigory Chicherin visited both capitals. Thereafter, the Soviet Union proposed a Russo-Polish non-aggression pact, but since Warsaw insisted on the inclusion of the Baltic States and Romania, the project was dropped.

For the next few years, Stresemann's first priority was a premature evacuation of the French-occupied Rhineland, which he called 'the rope of the strangler'. He argued that France no longer needed such a physical security guarantee and he was willing to offer in exchange a partial payment of reparations. Financial compensation was also broached in connection with some revision of the border with Poland. Paris and especially Warsaw were alarmed, particularly by the strategic implications of the evacuation.[26] French governing circles were divided whether to demand that Germany guarantee the Polish frontier, leave the issue in suspense, or hope for a deal between Stresemann and Marshal Józef Piłsudski, who in May 1926 seized power by a coup d'état.[27] A number of Polish–German technical agreements seemed to indicate that relations between Berlin and Warsaw were improving. In a conversation between Piłsudski and Stresemann in Geneva held in late 1927, both statesmen stressed that one should avoid new complications and regularize the mutual relations though negotiations without resorting to force. Much to Briand's disappointment Stresemann did not raise the border issue, viewing it inopportune at this juncture, but made several oblique references to it. Referring to a possible Polish–Russian non-aggression accord, he warned that should it go beyond the provisions of Versailles regarding Polish western frontiers, the border issue would be opened. Similarly, he asked about rumours of Poland's design on East Prussia, which Piłsudski emphatically denied.

Polish diplomacy, under Piłsudski, as the *de facto* master of Poland's destiny, continued the more or less moderate line of Skrzyński. Arguing that a premature evacuation of the Rhineland would render French military aid to Poland much more difficult, Warsaw sought a security gage. It could take the form of an Eastern Locarno, or a German–Polish pact of non-aggression, or a tripartite Franco-German–Polish treaty. The French government was not supportive and even failed to uphold the Polish project at the League of Nations of a general pact of non-aggression. Paris was determined not to harm in any way its relations with Berlin and Briand seemingly placed hopes on further decline of nationalism in Germany and the growth of a spirit of reconciliation.

Stresemann's death in 1929 marked an evolution, but not in the direction France expected. The evacuation of the Rhineland in 1930 was accompanied by an outburst of nationalist and revisionist passions. The Great Depression further radicalized Germany in a right-wing direction. Nevertheless, Briand and his associates viewed with equanimity a weakening of French ties to Poland. French, German and Belgian industrialists meeting in 1932 and 1933 expressed support for the idea of an exchange of the 'corridor' for Memel, to be followed by a Franco-German guarantee and even a military alliance. The French General Staff, however, still favoured close co-operation with Poland and tried to apply pressure on the government. But, as Soutou put it, the question was no longer what France could do for Poland, but what Poland could do for France.

Poland was virtually excluded from The Hague Conference in 1930: another blow to Polish interest and prestige.[28] Reassurances by Briand now sounded rather hollow.[29] The Polish Foreign Minister August Zaleski declared in the parliament that Poland had never opposed German strivings for friendship with France. He added that the Franco-Polish alliance would facilitate French rapprochement with Germany.[30] This was rather disingenuous. Briand never tried to re-establish the pre-Locarno balance of power in Europe, which had favoured Poland. As Soutou put it, for Briand, 'the security of France did not reside in the intangible respect for the treaties, but rather in an entente with Germany, even at the price of a certain weakening of the Treaty and of French leadership especially in Eastern Europe'.[31] A good example was provided by the attempts to water down the military alliance (mission of Marshal Franchet d'Esperey in 1927), which Piłsudski rejected.

As for Germany, the argument that Poland was an obstacle to the Locarno policies of European reconciliation and stabilization was propagandistic. Indeed, Peter Krüger is right to suggest that Poland was a touchstone which allowed to measure the extent to which Germany took seriously such policies. If under Stresemann the German–Polish border issue did not claim priority, this changed under the pressure of domestic developments – mainly growing chauvinism and revisionism.[32]

Marshal Piłsudski watched the developments in the Weimar Republic and was probing the possibility of direct dealings with Germany. In the autumn of 1930 Piłsudski supposedly sent an unofficial emissary, a Poznanian lawyer, to establish contact with Adolf Hitler. The message he passed through the Chief of Staff of S.A. Otto Wagener was roughly as follows.[33] As a nationalist, Piłsudski had followed with sympathy the movement of national awakening in Germany, but he knew well that nationalism is always accompanied by chauvinism. Referring to the German–Polish border, Piłsudski felt that even a great statesman could be submerged by the desire for revenge. The 'corridor' could be a potential cause of hostilities, but the Marshal hoped that it was possible to find a solution satisfactory to both nations. Once the Nazis gained power in Germany, a treaty of friendship and peace valid for ten years should be signed as quickly as possible, as Piłsudski was an old man. It could contain a secret clause providing that, within its time span, 'East Prussia would be reunited with Germany in such fashion as not to imperil Poland's free access to the Baltic Sea.'

This phrase and some of the other statements quoted verbatim raise serious doubts about its validity. After all, Wagener wrote about this conversation from memory several years later, and his account might have been coloured by later events.[34] It is hard to imagine that Piłsudski wanted to, or indeed was in a position to, cede any Polish territory.[35]

In spite of likely inaccuracies of Wagener's story, the episode itself was important. Hitler was impressed that the head of a foreign state approached him at this early stage of his career. His respect for Piłsudski, which he manifested several times later, was bound with the belief that the Marshal, had he lived, would have achieved a German–Polish reconciliation. This may well have well influenced Hitler's attitude toward Poland.[36] Hitler seems to have understood the significance of Danzig for the Poles. Piłsudski regarded it as a barometer of German–Polish relations and made it clear that he would not tolerate any infringement of Polish rights.[37] Thus in August 1932 Hitler rebuked the President of the Danzig Senate Hermann Rauschning, who urged that Berlin demand its return to the Reich. Hitler allegedly said that this would be an 'affront to Poland'.[38]

What were Hitler's views about Poland at that time?[39] His all-pervading racism, virulent anti-Semitism, contempt for the 'inferior' races like the Slavs and notions of a vast *Lebensraum* can be taken for granted, as was his conviction that Germany must be a world power or perish. Yet there is little about the Poles in *Mein Kampf*. Nonetheless, we find a curious remark that in the case of a war waged by Russia and Germany against the West, Russia would have to defeat the Polish state ('fully in French hands') to bring its troops to the Western front. Increasingly, Hitler saw Poland as a function of the German–Russian relationship, and raised the question: with Warsaw against Moscow or vice versa?[40]

Hitler's early references to Poland and the Poles were written in the context of such developments as the war with the Bolsheviks in 1920 and the plebiscite in Upper Silesia. He condemned Berlin's policies toward Poland during the First World War. The creation of a Polish state at that time he called 'the greatest crime committed against the German nation'.[41] Most of these early remarks about Poland were largely demagogic and did not differ from the virulent anti-Polish diatribes of German nationalists and revisionists. Even in February 1933, Hitler called the 'corridor' a 'hideous injustice' and demanded its return.[42]

After 1933, the international scene darkened. After gaining the right to equality of armaments and violating the disarmament clauses of Versailles, Germany left the League of Nations. Rumours began to circulate that Piłsudski had proposed to the French a preventive war against Germany. Hitler remarked that 'if France had capable statesmen it will attack us during the period of [our preparations], not itself but probably through its vassals in the east'.[43] While Piłsudski's alleged proposal was most likely little more than soundings in Paris and sabre rattling, it was taken seriously in Berlin.[44]

Piłsudski decided to engage in more active policies of bilateral character with both great neighbours. He believed Russia was a constant worry to Poland while Germany, temporarily too weak to wage war, would be a greater threat in the long run. Consequently, he tried to reassure Russia of his pacific intentions. One can assume that his statement to the Soviet envoy in 1926 that he would be a fool to think of a war against Russia was sincere.[45] In 1932 a treaty of non-aggression was signed between both states and it was followed by an exchange of visits and confidential conversations between high-ranking politicians.

Concentrating on Germany after Hitler's coming to power, Piłsudski played a subtle game in which he sought to reach a firm agreement with Berlin. Time was pressing as Germany was still weak and isolated. The German–Polish exchanges in 1933, surrounded by secrecy, went through several stages punctuated by the joint communiqués about the conversations between Hitler and the Polish Envoy Alfred Wysocki in May and Ambassador Józef Lipski in November 1933. Hitler agreed that mutual relations should be maintained in the framework of treaties and based on the exclusion of force. He also recognized the validity of the Polish argument that Germany's departure from Geneva created a security gap for Poland, which needed to be filled. Worried by these negotiations, Moscow proposed to Warsaw a joint guarantee of the Baltic States, and later it repeated the same offer to Berlin. It is likely that the purpose was to drive a wedge between Germany and Poland.[46]

On 26 January 1934 the Polish–German Declaration of Non-Aggression was signed. It stressed the desire for peace and good mutual relations and an engagement to seek solution to controversial problems without resorting to violence. Territorial issues were not mentioned. The Declaration produced a sensation in Europe and speculations about its objective and meaning were rife.[47] In the short run, the Declaration was clearly advantageous for both sides. It showed Hitler as a reasonable and peaceful leader while it left the door open for realization of future plans. The Führer expected Poland to become a junior partner (read satellite) of the Reich, assisting it in an ideologically motivated crusade for *Lebensraum*. Polish concessions to Germany would be compensated in the east. At this point, Hitler needed time to consolidate his power and achieve superiority of armaments. His immediate major goal was undermining the French system of alliances.

For Poland, the Declaration would bring respite from German revisionism, which under Hitler – seen as an Austrian and not Prussian – would shift to the south east of Europe. Piłsudski told his collaborators that he could guarantee such state of affairs for four years, which turned out to be a correct estimate.[48] A prominent Polish diplomat called the Declaration 'one of the greatest tactical successes which Polish diplomacy achieved during the twenty years period'.[49] It lessened the likelihood of a German–Soviet anti-Polish combination, showed that Poland could achieve on its own peaceful relations with Germany, emancipate itself from French tutelage, gain greater freedom of diplomatic manoeuvre and enhance its international standing. Poland, Piłsudski recalled, had been regarded as the 'centre of troubles'. Now it made an important contribution to peace, and the British government welcomed it. Did the Poles overestimate their own strength and position in Europe? Possibly.

Moscow suspected the existence of secret clauses, but seemed to be somewhat reassured by Foreign Minister Józef Beck's visit in February and the extension of the Soviet–Polish Non-Aggression Treaty for ten years.[50] The reaction in France was distinctly negative, although as two French historians have observed, the Declaration 'should not have been a surprise for Paris', and it was, in effect, logically included in accords of Locarno.[51]

In May 1935 Piłsudski died and Beck assumed the control of foreign affairs. A devotee of Piłsudski and a colonel in the army, Beck was highly intelligent and ambitious, conceited, and preoccupied with the prestige of his country. A German historian, Klaus Hildebrand, characterized Beck's policy as a 'mixture of cold calculation and overbearing pride'.[52] His favourite dictum was 'Nothing about us without us' and although he admitted that Poland was not a great power he insisted on self-respect and demanded that it be respected. The task of maintaining good relations with Germany without jeopardizing the alliance with France, while continuing the policy of balance between the two great neighbours, required a great deal of patience and tact, which Beck did not always display.[53] Did he really understand the nature of Nazism? He shared Piłsudski's low opinion of the League of Nations and dislike of the Czechs. His behaviour and style earned him the reputation of insincerity and untrustworthiness among foreign diplomats.[54] The French particularly disliked him and the French press did not hesitate to drag him through the mud. Not willing to suffer any slights from the French, Beck returned tit for tat. In these conditions, it was only human that Beck was flattered by the way he was always received in Berlin.

Some of the moves of Beck's diplomacy seemed to confirm the suspicion of his disregard of international norms and obligations, for instance, the speedy recognition of the Italian annexation of Ethiopia and of Manchukuo by Japan, or the unilateral suspension of the protection of National Minorities Treaty. Polish diplomacy seemed to go hand in hand with the Third Reich in torpedoing the Eastern Pact through which France wished to associate the Soviet Union more closely with collective security. Beck showed disdain for the Anglo-French–Italian accord, the so-called Stresa Front of 1935, which he rightly saw as nothing more than a façade. On the other hand, the Polish support for the vote censuring German violation of the disarmament clauses surprised those in the West who assumed that Warsaw would not dare to antagonize Berlin. Criticized as two-faced, Beck's diplomacy can be better understood in the context of his interpretation of the balance and his suspicion of multilateralism and what lay behind it. He was determined not to join pacts that could compromise Poland's independence and its vital interests. This appeared very clearly at the time of the supreme test: the German remilitarization of the Rhineland.

Under the pretext that the ratification in February 1936 of the French–Soviet alliance (which Warsaw had strongly opposed) was contrary to Locarno, Hitler denounced the latter and ordered the remilitarization of the Rhineland on 6 March 1936. The French reacted by verbal belligerence but in fact they were divided and looked up vainly to the British government for support. They complained of being isolated and deserted by its allies. Paradoxically, Locarno did not seem to create an obligation for Poland or Czechoslovakia to come to French assistance unless its territory was attacked. Beck made it clear to the French Ambassador that should it come to war Poland would fulfil its obligations as an ally. Knowing perfectly well that France would not resort to war, and unwilling gratuitously to antagonize Berlin, Beck inspired the publication of a communiqué in the semi-official *Iskra* which viewed sympathetically the German case. Accused of duplicity, his attitude made good sense. The alliance with France was to operate in case of war, but did not mean supporting every French move. The French thought otherwise, and engaged in intrigues to have Beck removed from his position.

Warsaw had no cause to regret the demise of Locarno. In fact it meant for Beck the possibility of restoring the Franco-Polish alliance to its original and firm mutual engagement. This may have been wishful thinking, for the Maginot Line and the law of 1935 (defence of homeland and empire) made it clear that France would fight only a defensive war – its military aid to Poland would be of highly dubious character.

After the remilitarization of the Rhineland, London with some support of Paris explored the possibility of a new Western Pact with security guarantees. Beck seized on the idea of adding an Eastern component comprising Germany–France–Poland. It was hardly a new idea, if we think of Skrzyński's similar efforts during the Locarno negotiations, and it stood no chance of realization. Similarly the somewhat imprecise 'Third Europe' project meant to strengthen Poland's international position through regional co-operation and Italian support – as a counterbalance to Germany – was hardly realistic.[55]

The policy of appeasement, with Britain in the lead, began to dominate the diplomatic scene in the late 1930s.[56] As always interested in rapprochement with London, Poland made overtures to the British. While attending the coronation of George VI in May 1937, Beck told the new British Prime Minister Neville Chamberlin that should Germany attack France or Belgium, Poland would come to their assistance. He repeated this statement at least twice later. The British were not interested. The Poles learned from Berlin that Halifax, the future British Foreign Secretary, told Hitler in November 1937 on an unofficial visit that London was not opposed to territorial changes in East Central Europe provided they were made peacefully.[57] The same month, Hitler had outlined his ideas on the international situation to a group of top generals and officials (the Hossbach memorandum), stressing the necessity of the *Lebensraum*. A conflict with Britain and France, these 'hate inspired antagonists of Germany', had to come: but when and how? Annexation of Austria and the destruction of Czechoslovakia were necessary prerequisites and their addition would strengthen the German economy and armed forces. In case of a German war with France, Poland with Russia in its rear would stay neutral as long as Germany was strong, but if the Germans suffered setbacks, Polish military action 'must be reckoned with'. The significance of the Hossbach memorandum is debatable. Hitler's ideas must be viewed within a changing international context. He was irresolute especially regarding German relations with Britain.

The *Anschluss* of Austria in March 1938 did not bring about a basic change in international relations. Beck made it known that Poland had no particular interest in the matter. But an almost-simultaneous Polish ultimatum to Lithuania demanding that the latter establish normal diplomatic relations with Poland created the impression of parallelism between the peremptory methods of Berlin and Warsaw.[58]

In the spring of 1938, the Czechoslovak crisis resulting from the escalating demands of the German minority in the Republic assumed international proportions. While Berlin was directing the separatist movement Britain attempted to mediate between President Edvard Beneš and the Sudeten leaders. The possibility of war loomed on the horizon.

Warsaw's demands that Polish minority receive the same concessions as the German minority as well as the frequent meetings with the Germans made Poland and Beck appear guilty of collusion with Hitler. Beck was not blind to the danger posed by complete Germany mastery of Czechoslovakia, but he correctly assumed that France would not assist its ally militarily, nor would Britain, bent on appeasement and the avoidance of war. Thus, Beck refused to join Western diplomatic demarches on behalf of beleaguered Czechoslovakia and expose Poland to German ire. On the contrary, the Polish diplomats were telling the Germans with some exaggeration that Berlin ought to appreciate Warsaw's policies of checkmating the USSR by preventing its help to Prague and thus contributing to peace. The Polish attitude toward the southern neighbour was certainly not in the best Polish tradition irrespective of the merits of Polish territorial claims. It is hardly true, however, that Warsaw's pressure on Prague contributed decisively to Beneš's capitulation. As for Beck's willingness to change completely his policy, should Britain and France declare war on Germany, it was most unlikely to become reality.[59]

At the Munich Conference on 29–30 September 1938 Britain, France, Italy and Germany granted all Hitler's demands and imposed them on Prague. Returning to London, Prime Minister Chamberlain declared that he brought 'peace with honour'.[60] As it turned out, peace would last only one more year, and possibly the best occasion to stop Hitler was lost. Warsaw was annoyed for being left out of the Munich conference. The ultimatum it addressed to Prague to cede the district of Teschen largely resulted from the fact that Beck did not want to have the dispute with Czechoslovakia arbitrated by the Great Powers.

The ultimatum earned Poland harsh criticism by international public opinion and contemptuous epithets. USSR viewed Munich as directed against it. As for Hitler, he was greatly displeased because he would have preferred to determine the fate of Czechoslovakia without the Western mediation and smash it militarily.[61]

During the last year of peace one can single out three main trends of Polish foreign policy.[62] Firstly, attempts to stabilize the relations with Germany through prolongation of the 1934 Non-Aggression accord, a declaration on borders similar to the German–Italian statement and a written confirmation of Hitler's assurances of 5 November 1937; secondly, continued overtures to London in view of a rapprochement; and thirdly, the already-mentioned somewhat vague plans for a 'Third Europe'.

The Führer's November utterance was very important. He said that no changes would occur in the legal–political situation of Danzig. The rights of the Polish population in the Free City would be respected, and Poland's rights in Danzig would not be violated. There would be no surprise action. He added, 'Danzig ist mit Polen verbunden'.[63] Now, after Munich, with Poland isolated and criticized in the West, Germany began to apply pressure on Warsaw. On 24 October 1938 Foreign Minister Joachim von Ribbentrop proposed a general settlement (Gesamtlösung) involving a guarantee of Poland's borders, providing Danzig went to Germany and an extraterritorial highway and railroad connecting Germany with East Prussia was built. Poland was asked to join the anti-Comintern pact to consult Berlin on matters of foreign policy.

During Beck's visit to Berchtesgaden on 5 January 1939 Hitler repeated the offer of guarantees of Polish borders provided a solution of the Danzig problem be found and the question of communications with East Prussia resolved. But the Chancellor promised that there would be no *faits accomplis*. Germany, he said, needed a strong Poland against Russia. Although Beck declared that there was no change in Hitler's policy toward Poland, he was for the first time somewhat pessimistic about the future.[64]

During the conversations with Hitler, Hermann Göring, Heinrich Himmler and Ribbentrop, who visited Poland, the Polish side expressed its willingness to consider various facilities for German transit and some form of German–Polish condominium in the Free City of Danzig. But giving up its sovereignty over part of Polish territory was out of the question. At a conference with President Ignacy Mościcki and other dignitaries held at the Warsaw castle around 10 January, Beck stated that if Germany insisted, the situation would be grave. Polish policy had to be firm. Any sign of irresolution would only lead to a downward path and subjection to Germany. Still, in his circular of 21 January he affirmed that there were no issues between the two countries that could not be settled through negotiations.[65] As for Hitler, he continued to believe that eventually Warsaw would agree to what he considered moderate demands. He saw it a junior partner in his long-range plans for war in the East and within his new European order. That was the real issue.[66]

The Munich Conference had been followed by German–British and German–French declarations on 30 September and 6 December 1938 respectively, asserting mutual determination to maintain peace. Hence when on 15 March 1939 Hitler proceeded to occupy Czechoslovakia in spite of his earlier assurances that he had no more territorial claims, this came as a blow to Chamberlain. According to some historians it marked the end of appeasement, while others see it as its continuation albeit in a changed form.[67]

Beck opined that Germany's recent moves (in former Czechoslovakia, the forcible annexation of Lithuanian Memel, and other activities in East Central Europe) 'have immeasurably increased, and at the same time, brought closer the threat of war'.[68] Informed of a tense conversation between Lipski and Ribbentrop, Beck said in his briefing that Germany has 'lost its calculability'.[69] On 4 April he told Lord Halifax, the British Foreign Secretary, that recent German policy 'has lost all moderation'.[70] In a sharp exchange with Ambassador Hans von Moltke, when the latter accused Warsaw of wishing to negotiate 'au bout des baïonnettes', Beck retorted 'C'est d'après votre système'.[71]

The French and British now came out with the idea of associating the Soviet Union in a joint action to restrain Germany. Beck opposed it on the grounds that it would be seen as provocative and depart from the Polish principle of equilibrium. The Foreign Minister stressed that he wanted good relations with the USSR and indeed they improved at this time. The first trade accord was signed in February.[72] The deputy Foreign Commissar Vladimir Potemkin said while visiting Warsaw in May that if Poland were attacked Soviets would adopt a friendly attitude.

True to his conviction that a bilateral approach was preferable to multilateralism, Beck responded positively when informed that Chamberlain would offer to guarantee Poland's independence in a speech on 31 March 1939. The Pole sought, however, to replace it later by mutual obligations, which eventually were embodied in a bilateral British–Polish agreement announced on 6 April 1939 and in written form in August. Historians differ in their interpretation of British motives and aims.[73] Did Britain want to divert the first German attack from the West to the East? It seems likely that the British intended the guarantee to bolster Poland in negotiating a compromise with Germany (and press Warsaw not to be intransigent) as well as to dissuade Hitler from resorting to force. The British–Polish alliance was meant to defer war rather than to prepare for it.[74]

Several writers criticized Beck for signing the alliance and thus precipitating the war, but as the Minister said later he was glad that he had signed the alliance and avoided 'lousy talks' with the Germans. Perhaps 'the outbreak of war would have been delayed, but it would come in the spring and we would be alone'.[75]

Did the guarantee make war inevitable? It certainly incensed Hitler, who proceeded to denounce the 1934 Declaration with Poland and the Naval Accord with Britain. On 11 April he authorized Fall Weiss – attack on Poland. But his various remarks showed that he was still unsure how to proceed. War for domination and *Lebensraum* was Hitler's constant aim but the moment to start it and how depended on a given situation.[76] Was a rapprochement with the Soviet Union an option? It had supporters in Berlin, although Hitler himself was somewhat doubtful.

Beck responded to Hitler on 5 May in a speech that reflected the national mood. The Poles, he said, wanted and deserved peace but 'peace ... has its price, high but definable. We in Poland do not recognize the conception of peace at any price. There is only one thing ... which is without price, and that is honour.'[77] It was obvious that Poland would fight if need be alone.

By and large, France played the second fiddle during the mounting crisis. It supported the British guarantee and participated in the negotiations with USSR.[78] The Soviet position and policies were of extreme importance and the Kremlin knew how to use them. Did the guarantee accelerate the process of Soviet–German rapprochement, which resulted in the Ribbentrop–Molotov pact of August 23?[79] Did Hitler see it as a green light for war, localized or general? It certainly greatly facilitated his final decision. Did Moscow sign the pact and the secret protocol (the existence of which the Russians admitted only in 1989), which included the partition of Poland, because the negotiations with the British and the French foundered on Warsaw's refusal to allow the Red Army to enter Polish territory?[80] A comparison of the timetable of Soviet simultaneous talks with the West and Germany does not bear it out. Moscow knew about the Polish stand already in the spring, but it raised the issue of passage as a pretext to break off the negotiations with Britain and France on 7 August. Was Stalin's main motive to gain time plus territorial expansion, which might have improved the Soviet military position, as his defenders allege? Did he fear a new Munich? Did he always favour the German option? Or, and this was presumably Stalin's main reason, he believed that the war between the West and Hitler would play in Soviet hands, exhaust both sides and allow the USSR to extend territorially and promote a revolution in Europe?[81]

The Polish diplomacy has been criticized for completely ignoring the possibility of a Nazi–Soviet accord.[82] This is only partly true, but one has to recognize that Beck erred in assuming that ideological chasm which separated Nazi Germany from Soviet Russia would not permit it. Was not Poland as a buffer preferable to a border with Germany? Would the Soviets risk a move against the West? But even if Warsaw had known that the Ribbentrop–Molotov pact was coming, it could not do anything about it.[83] Speculations on whether Poland could ally itself with USSR or capitulate to Hitler and join Nazi Germany in a war of conquest in the East are of counterfactual nature.[84] A Polish government that would have surrendered to Berlin – a de facto political suicide – would not have survived. Still, Beck's comments that the pact did not alter the situation seem odd.

German pressure on Poland increased. At a big rally in Danzig on 17 July, Goebbels demanded the return of the city to the Reich. The war of nerves continued. Nazi propaganda seeking to create an atmosphere of suspense and tension fanned feelings of animosity toward the Poles. Any anti-German demonstrations, incidents in Danzig or involving German minority in Poland were magnified. Thirsting for war, the Führer kept telling the Western diplomats that he wanted peace, but it sounded more and more hollow. As for German public opinion, it wanted Danzig and the 'Corridor', but did not want war. [85] The moves behind the scenes of British, German and Soviet diplomacy showed that each side tried to outwit the other, Moscow being in a position to choose the best bid.

Until the very last moment, Poland was willing to negotiate but not to send a special emissary with full powers. The browbeating of Czechoslovak president Emil Hácha was all too vivid in people's minds. Thus, the final German terms were broadcast as a communiqué (the sixteen points). They involved the annexation of Danzig, extraterritorial highway and railroad – in effect cutting Poland from the sea – and a plebiscite in the corridor. An emasculated Poland was to join the anti-Comintern pact and become de facto a vassal of the Third Reich. Hitler's private utterances made this perfectly clear. Still, Warsaw s deferring to Franco-British demands that it could not be accused of provocation delayed general mobilization.

On 1 September 1939 Germany struck without declaring war, using as a pretext a simulated coup on the radio station in Gleiwitz. While the battleship *Schleswig-Holstein* opened fire on the Polish garrison at Westerplatte, the *Luftwaffe* was reducing the little town of Wieluń to rubbles. After two days of vain efforts to persuade Germany to stop military operations, Britain and France declared war on the Third Reich.

Notes

1   See M. Wołos in S. Dębski and M. Narinski (eds), *Kryzys 1939 roku w Interpretacjach polskich i rosyjskich historyków*. Warszawa, 2009, p, 166.
2   See ch. 8 of P. Łossowski (ed.), *Historia Dyplomacji Polskiej*, vol. 4. Warszawa, 1995; and R. Wapiński, *Świadomość polityczna w Drugiej Rzeczypospolitej*. Łódź, 1989. M. Zacharias, 'Fakty, hipotezy, opinie, interpretacje', *Dzieje Najnowsze 1939*, vol. 41, no. 3 (2009), pp. 32–8. M. Kornat, *Polityka Równowagi 1934–1939: Polska między Wschodem a Zachodem*. Warszawa, 2007, short version 'The Policy of Equilibrium and Polish Bilateralism 1934–1939'. J. Micgiel and P S. Wandycz (eds). *Reflections on Polish Foreign Policy*. New York, 2007, pp. 47–88. A. Cienciala, *Poland and the Western Powers 1938–1939: A Study in the Interdependence of Eastern and Western Europe*. London, 1968; P. Wandycz, 'Poland between East and West' in G. Martel (ed.), *The Origins of the Second World War Reconsidered: The A.J.P. Taylor Debate After Twenty-Five Years*. Boston, 1986, pp. 187–209. H. Batowski, *Agonia pokoju początek wojny (sierpień-wrzesień 1939)*. Poznań, 1964. Polski Instytut Spraw Międzynarodowych, *Polskie Dokumenty Dyplomatyczne*. Warszawa, 2001 (hereafter PDD). Also *Polish Documents on Foreign Policy: 24 October 1938 to 30 September 1939*. Warsaw 2009 (hereafter PDFP).
3   Blaming Poland *re* plunging Europe in war combined with wild accusations of plotting against USSR especially by Beck.
4   Dashichev in Dębski and Narinski (eds), *Kryzys 1939*, p. 146.
5   *L'Oeuvre* 4 May 1939.
6   See E. Mantoux, *The Carthaginian Peace*. New York, 1952.
7   Cited in M. Boemke, G. Feldman and E. Glaser (eds), *The Treaty of Versailles: A Reassessment after Seventy-Five Years*. Washington, 1998, p. 3.

8   M. MacMillan, *Paris, 1919: Six Months that Changed the World.* New York, 2002, *passim*; or Z. Steiner, *The Lights that Failed: European International History 1919–1933.* Oxford, 2005, pp. 67–70; H. Butler, *The Lost Peace.* London, 1941.

9   See Boemke, Feldman and Glaser (eds), *The Treaty of Versailles*, p. 3.

10   A. Sharp, *The Versailles Settlement: Peacemaking in Paris, 1919.* Basingstoke, 1991, 2nd ed., 2008, p. 213.

11   Cited in Steiner, *The Lights that Failed*, p. 68.

12   Wandycz, 'The Polish Question' in *The Versailles Settlement*, pp. 313–35; K. Lundgreen-Nielsen, *The Polish Problem at the Paris Peace Conference: A Study of the Policies of the Great Powers and the Poles, 1918–1919.* Odensee, 1979; and T. Komarnicki, *Rebirth of the Polish Republic: A Study in the Diplomatic History of Europe, 1914–1920.* London, 1957.

13   They never claimed the historic borders of 1772, as sometimes erroneously asserted.

14   See B. Biskupski, 'The Origins of a Relationship: The United States and Poland 1914–1918', *The Polish Review* vol. 54, no.2 (2009), pp. 147–58.

15   H.V. Temperley (ed.), *A History of the Peace Conference of Paris.* London, 1920–4, vol. 2, p. 4.

16   On Franco-British exchanges, see P. Wandycz, *France and her Eastern Allies 1919–1925: French–Czechoslovak–Polish Relations from the Paris Peace Conference to Locarno.* Minneapolis, 1962, pp. 40–1.

17   Piłsudski spoke of two canons: first, a neutral stance *vis-à-vis* Germany and USSR so that they would be sure that Poland would not ally itself with one against the other, and alliances with France and Romania.

18   Bertrand de Jouvenel, cited in Wandycz, *France and her Eastern Allies*, p. 319.

19   See P. Wandycz, 'La Pologne face à la politique locarnienne de Briand'; P. Krüger, 'La Politique extérieure Allemande et les relations Franco-Polonaises (1918–1932); G-H. Soutou, L'alliance Franco-Polonaise (1925–1933): Ou comment s'en débarasser?' *Revue d'Histoire Diplomatique* nos. 2, 3, 4 (1981), pp. 237–348.

20   P. Wandycz, *Aleksander Skrzyński, Minister Spraw Zagranicznych II Rzeczypospolitej.* Warszawa, 2006, p. 32–50, 95, and his *Aleksander Skrzyński (1992–1931): Diplomate et philosophe: Nations, cultures et sociêtês d'Europe centrale au XIX et XX siècles. Mélanges offerts à Bernard Michel, sous la direction de Catherine Horel.* Paris, 2006, pp. 109–122. Also Marek Baumgart, 'Aleksander Skrzyński' in J. Pajewski (ed.), *Ministrowie Spraw Zagranicznych II Rzeczypospolitej.* Szczecin, 1992, pp. 135–50.

21   G. Johnson (ed), *Locarno Revisited: European Diplomacy 1920–1929.* London, 2004 is incredibly Anglocentric and narrow in its analysis and interpretation. It virtually ignores Polish and Eastern European aspects and repercussions in this period.

22   See Soutou, L'alliance Franco-Polonaise', p. 313.

23   See P. Krüger, 'Der Deutsch-Polnische Schiedsvertrg im Rahmmen der Deutschen Sicherheitsinitiative von 1925', *Historische Zeitschrift* vol. 230 (1986), pp. 577–612. Compare with Z.J. Gasiorowski, 'Stresemann and Poland after Locarno', *Journal of Central European Affairs* vol. 18 (1958), pp. 292–317.

24   As the Staatssekretär Carl von Schubert put it: Poland after being reduced politically at Locarno ought to be 'reduced militarily'. Cited in P. Wandycz, *The Twilight of French Eastern Alliances 1926–1936: French–Czechoslovak–Polish Relations from Locarno to the Remiliterization of the Rhineland.* Princeton, 1988, p. 20.

25   Ibid., p. 21; Soutou, 'L'alliance Franco-Polonaise', pp. 310–11.

26   According to the Treaty of Versailles the earliest date for the evacuation was 1935.

27   Philippe Berthelot of Quai d'Orsay suggested to the German Ambassador that Germany ought to negotiate with Piłsudski who '*ne serait pas éloigné de l'idée d'une entente avec l'Allemagne*'. Cited in Soutou, 'L'alliance Franco-Polonaise', p. 311.

28   The French did not object when the President of the Reichsbank Hjalmar Schacht spoke of the need to revise the German–Polish frontier.

29   He told Zaleski in the fall of 1928 that minor concessions to Germany were necessary to convince Britain that everything was done to avoid war, and have the British on the French side in case of war. See P. Wandycz, *Z Piłsudskim i Sikorskim: August Zaleski Minister Spraw Zagranicznych 1926–1932, 1939–1941.* Warszawa, 1999, p. 92.

30 Ibid., p. 94.

31 Soutou, 'L'alliance Franco-Polonaise', p. 348.

32 Krüger, 'Politique extèrieure Allemande', pp. 290–4.

33 H. Turner (ed.), *Hitler: Memoirs of a Confidant*. New Haven, 1985, pp. 49–50. German version: *Hitler aus nächster Nähe*. Frankfurt am Main, 1978.

34 P. Wandycz, 'Próba nawiązania przez Marszałka Piłsudskiego kontaktu z Hitlerem jesienią 1930 roku' in P. Wandycz, *Polska a zagranica*. Paryż, 1986, pp. 258–66.

35 Jerzy Krasuski's view that Piłsudski would not be opposed in principle to certain territorial concessions (*Stosunki polsko-niemieckie 1919–1931*. Poznań, 1995, p. 270) is not borne out by evidence. There are Piłsudski's statements to the contrary. See P. Wandycz, *United States and Poland*. Cambridge, MA, 1980, p. 214; B. Winid, *W Cieniu Kapitolu.Dyplomacja polska wobec Stanów Zjednoczonych Ameryki 1919–1939*. Warszawa, 1991, p. 160.

36 T. Szarota, 'Hitler o Piłsudskim oraz okupant wobec kultu Marszałka' in M. Andrzejewski (ed.), *Gdańsk-Gdynia-Europa-Stany Zjednoczone w XIX i XX wieku: Księga pamiątkowa dedykowana profesor Annie Cienciale*. Gdańsk, 2000.

37 In 1931 he ordered the destroyer *Wicher* to enter Danzig's harbour and open fire in case of an insult to the Polish flag.

38 Cited in Turner, *Hitler aus nächster Nähe*, p. 473.

39 Jerzy Borejsza, *Śmieszne sto milionów Słowian ... Wokół światopoglądu Adolfa Hitlera*, Warszawa, 2906.

40 *Mein Kampf* was for all practical purposes forbidden in Poland.

41 Borejsza, p. 98. The author cites several of Hitler's early speeches and articles.

42 *Sunday Express* 12 February 1933. After a violent Polish reaction, Berlin tried to downplay the interview.

43 Cited in G. Weinberg, *The Foreign Policy of Hitler's Germany: Diplomatic Revolution in Europe 1922–1936*. Chicago, 1970, p. 27.

44 See Wandycz, *The Twilight of French Eastern Alliances*, pp. 269–73.

45 See J. Borzęcki and P. Wandycz, 'Rozmowy Piłsudskiego z Wojkowem. Fragmenty Raportów', *Zeszyty Historyczne* no. 149 (2004), pp. 10–21.

46 See O. Ken, *Collective Security or Isolation? Soviet Foreign Policy and Poland 1930–1935*. St Peterburg, 1996, pp. 125–31.

47 The most recent: M. Wojciechowski (ed.), *Deklaracja polsko-niemiecka o niestosowaniu przemocy z dnia 26 stycznia 1934 r. z perspektywy Polski i Europy w siedemdziesiątą rocznicę podpisania*. Toruń, 2005. Texts in Polish and German.

48 K. Świtalski, *Diariusz 1914–1935*, A. Garlicki and R. Świątek (eds). Warszawa, 1992, pp. 660–61,

49 K. Morawski, 'Polityka zagraniczna Polski odrodzonej' in H. Paszkiewicz (ed.), *Polska i jej dorobek dziejowy*. London, 1956, vol. 2, p. 42.

50 See W. Materski (ed.), *Polityka zagraniczna Rosji i ZSRR*. Łódź, 1994, and his article in *Deklaracja*.

51 Soutou and Jouvenel. Wandycz, *The Twilight of French Eastern Alliances*, p. 335.

52 K. Hildebrand in Materski (ed.), *Deklaracja polsko-niemiecka*, p. 73.

53 Referring to the balance, Piłsudski said that we are sitting on two stools and cannot tell when we shall fall of one.

54 On Beck's personality and policies: R. Roberts, 'The Diplomacy of Colonel Beck', G. Craig and F. Gilbert (eds), *The Diplomats 1919–1939*. Princeton, 1958, pp. 579–614; the respective introductions to Beck's memoirs by A. Cienciala, *Polska polityka zagraniczna w latach 1926–1932* (should be 1932–9). Paris, 199l; and M. Wojciechowski, *Józef Beck, Ostatni Raport*. Warszawa, 1987. Compare M. Zacharias, 'Józef Beck i polityka równowagi', *Dzieje Najnowsze* vol. 2 (1988), pp. 2–37 and his polemics with S. Żerko in ibid., vol. 4 (2001), pp. 103–12 and vol. 4 (2003) pp. 137–55. D.C. Watt, whose knowledge of Polish affairs is minimal, calls Beck devious, arogant, incompetent, parochial and short-sighted, and repeats uncritically some of the slanderous gossip in *How War Came: The Immediate Origins of the Second World War (1938–1939)*. London, 1989, pp. 58–9. Compare P. Wandycz, 'Colonel Beck and the French: Roots of Animosity?', *International History Review* vol. 3, no. 1 (1981), pp. 115–27. See also Józef Łaptos, *Dyplomaci II w świetle raportów Quai d'Orsay*. Warszawa, 1993, *passim*.

55 M. Kornat, 'Realny projekt czy wizja ex-post? Koncepcja, Trzeciej Europy 1937–1938' in *idem.*, *Polityka Równowagi*, pp. 307–49. .

56 Appeasement was not a new invention: see P. Kennedy, *Strategy and Diplomacy 1870–1945*. London, 1983.

57 I thank Professor Cienciala for comments on my text.

58 Later Warsaw offered help to Lithuania to maintain its independence. See *PDFP*, p. 204.

59 An reappraisal of Beck's policy *vis-à-vis* Czechoslovakia by Cienciala is in *Polish Review* vol. 44, no. 2 (2009), pp. 243–62.

60 Repeating the words of Disraeli after the Congress of Berlin.

61 He vowed that he would not engage in similar dealings with such 'miserable worms' in the future. See *PDD* 1938, pp. 513, 521.

62 See documentation in *PDFP, passim.*

63 W. Jędrzejewicz (ed.), *Diplomat in Berlin 1933–1939: Papers and Memoirs of Józef Lipski Ambassador of Poland*. New York, 1962, pp. 303–4. Hitler told Beck during their first meeting in July 1935 that it would be a folly to drive Poland away from the Baltic.

64 Szembek, vol. 4, p. 467.

65 *PDFP*, s. 28–29. A reference to the conference is in Colonel Joseph Beck, *Dernier Rapport: Politique polonaise 1926–1939*. Neuchatel, p. 183. Also see Szembek, vol.4, pp. 467–8.

66 In May 1939 Hitler said: 'This is not the question of Danzig. For us the issue is the extension of the living space.' See M. Domarus, *Hitler, Reden und Proklamationen 1932–1945: Kommentiert von einem Deutschen Zeitgenossen*. Wiesbaden, 1973, B. II, T. 1, p. 1197. On another occasion, that he would have to be an idiot to get involved in a world war because of the 'lousy question of Danzig and the Corridor': M. Zacharias in *Dzieje Najnowsze* vol. 41, no. 3 (2009), p. 44. Also Żerko, 'Niemiecka polityka zagraniczna w przededniu II wojny światowej', Dębski and Narinski (eds), *Kryzys 1939*, pp. 85–123.

67 Dębski and Narinski (eds), *Kryzys 1939*, p. 270.

68 *PDFP*, p. 127.

69 Ibid., p. 137.

70 Ibid., p. 165.

71 Ibid., p. 150.

72 Once again the Poles ignored Göring's direct offer made in March of German–Polish military collaboration against the Soviets. See Jędrzejewicz, *Diplomat in Berlin*, p. 354.

73 See Cienciala, 'Rozważania nad dyplomacją polską i polityką brytyjską w 1939 r', *Kwartalnik Historyczny* no. 2 (2008), pp. 139–46.

74 The conversations between Polish, French and British general staffs in May proved of no practical value.

75 J. Szembek, *Diariusz, Wrzesień-Grudzień 1939*. Warszawa, 1989, p. 25.

76 Göring warned Hitler in late August 1939 of the risks of war. See M. Zacharias in *Dzieje Najnowsze* vol. 41, no. 3 (2009), p. 44.

77 *PDFP*, pp. 240–5.

78 See M. Gmurczyk-Wrońska, *Polska: niepotrzebny aliant Francji?* Warszawa, 2003; and M. Pasztor, 'Polityka francuska wobec Polski w latach 1936-1939', Tadeusz Kisielewski, red., *Droga ku wojnie: Polityka europejska i amerykańska w przededniu drugiej wojny światowej*. Bydgoszcz, 1999, pp. 54–83.

79 Adam Ulam argues in *Expansion and Coexistence: The History of Soviet Foreign Policy 1917–1967*. New York, 1968, p. 267 that paradoxically the guarantee profited USSR rather than Poland.

80 Some Western historians including D.C. Watt still tend to believe it. See *How War Came*. London, 1989, pp. 185–6.

81 M. Kornat, *Polska 1939 roku wobec Paktu Ribbentrop-Mołotow: Problem zbliżenia niemiecko-sowieckiego w polityce zagranicznej II Rzeczypospolitej*. Warszawa, 2002; A. Cienciala, 'The Nazi-Soviet Pact of August 23, 1939: When Did Stalin Decide to Align with Hitler, and Was Poland the Culprit?' in M. Biskupski (ed.), *Ideology, Politics and Diplomacy in East Central Europe*. Rochester, 2003, pp. 147–241; S. Dębski, *Między Berlinem a Moskwą: Stosunki niemiecko-sowieckie 1939–1941*. Warszawa, 2003. Viacheslav Dashichev deplores the consequences of the

pact for Russia and Europe while Mikhail Meltukhov defends the pact and places the blame for war on the British. See Dębski and Narinski (eds), *Kryzys 1939*, pp. 145–6 and 205.

82   *PDFP*, pp. 325–6, 329–30.

83   M. Kornat, 'Dyplomacja polska wobec paktu Ribbentropp-Mołotow z 23 sierpnia 1939 R.' in *Polityka Równowagi*, pp. 427–64.

84   Combined usually with condemnation of Beck's policy by among others: J. Łojek, *Agresja 17 września 1939: Studium aspektów politycznych*. Warszawa, 1990; P. Wieczorkiewicz, *Historia polityczna Polski 1935–1945*. Warszawa, 2005; or S. Cat-Mackiewicz, *Colonel Beck and his Policy*. London, 1944.

85   See I. Kershaw, *The 'Hitler Myth': Image and Reality in the Third Reich*. Oxford, 1987, p. 142.

Chapter 23

Poland, the 'Danzig Question' and the Outbreak of the Second World War

Anita J Prażmowska

On 31 March 1939 Neville Chamberlain announced to the Commons:

> in the event of action which clearly threatened Polish independence, and which the Polish Government accordingly consider it vital to resist with their national forces, His Majesty's Government would feel themselves bound at once to lend the Polish Government all support in their power.[1]

This commitment, a startling break with British foreign policy of dissociation from legal entanglements in European affairs, came on the background of rumours of an impending German move to incorporate the Free City of Danzig into Germany. This was a political gesture intended to forewarn Germany not to proceed with aggressive plans. The background to the British initiative was a localized conflict over the port city, which might have lead to a European war. By March 1939 the Danzig crisis was merely a reflection of the general state of tension that came to dominate European politics. The British guarantee to defend Poland was a last-ditch attempt to avert the war, even if it gave the appearance of Britain supporting a cause for which it had hitherto no sympathy.

The idea of a Free City had originated in the debates that took place during the Paris Peace talks in 1919. US President Woodrow Wilson stated that after the war Poland should have access to the sea in his fourteen-point declaration of US war aims. The Poles therefore requested the incorporation of the city and of East Prussia into the borders of the newly emerged Polish state. Lloyd George's opposition to Polish demands is well known, but less fully acknowledged is Wilson's lack of support for this request. Clemenceau, Wilson and Lloyd George, the three dominant personalities who determined the course of the debates, argued over a number of issues, and a compromise solution to the Danzig issue was advocated by the US delegation swayed the debate in favour of the Free City solution. Wilson finally suggested that the city and surrounding areas should become a Free City guaranteed by international agreements.[2] This turned out to be an uneasy compromise resented by Germany and Poland. League of Nations members were soon to find out that conflicts in the city would dominate League discussions and ultimately sour relations between the member states and the two claimants to the city.

The decision to appoint a High Commissioner whose role it was to mediate between the Free City and the Polish government proved unsatisfactory. From the outset the Poles contested their limited rights in the city. These disputes were made worse by genuine ambiguities and unresolved issues. The town and the areas included in the Free City comprised an area of 1,892 square kilometres. Ninety-five per cent of the community declared themselves to be German with only three per cent admitting to being Polish. The Free City was to be administered by an elected Senate, which was nearly entirely German too. Economically, the Free City created many areas for conflict. It had developed as an outlet for trade along the River Wisła, now entirely within the new Polish state, and its economic wellbeing depended on Polish trade. The Polish state was allowed to use the port facilities. This was in fact a defeat, as the Poles had hoped to secure the ownership of the port and to obtain a military base. In the late 1920, as a result of economic conflicts with Germany and anxious about the consequence of the German economic blockade, the Polish state built a new port in the town of Gdynia. The result of this was a slump in trade passing through Danzig.

Polish thinking on the issue of access to the sea and on the Danzig question was never consistent and went through various stages. In the first place, strategic rather than economic factors played a role. Access to the sea was seen as a vital element of any plans for a future war against Germany or the Soviet Union. It was assumed that France, Poland's military ally, would send aid to Poland via the Baltic.[3] In 1927 Polish irritation with the League was reciprocated by the League High Commissioner, who tried to reduce the extent of the League's intervention in Poland's relations with the city. The Polish government's method of dealing with these problems was to open direct talks with the Senate, thus bypassing the League. In 1927 this policy looked likely to succeed when a centre-left coalition won a majority in the Senate.[4]

Yet the Polish government consistently viewed difficulties in its dealings with the Senate of the Free City through the prism of its relations with Germany. The League's interventions were interpreted as favouring Germany. This was not always the case, but the Piłsudski regime, which came to power in 1926, assumed that the League was always hostile to Polish interests. This brief period of constructive relations came to an end when the Nazi Party became increasingly active in the Free City. Stresemann's policy had been that of maintaining Germany's claim to the Free City, but not to press this demand, and instead to seek partial accommodation with the Polish government. This, it was hoped, would lead to the return of Danzig to Germany, with Poland being granted its own port within Danzig.[5]

The economic situation in Danzig had always been difficult, but during the early 1930 the consequences of the world economic crisis became acute. The Danziger's response was to blame the Poles for having rerouted trade to Gdynia.[6] This led a rise of support for the local Nazi party. The local German community was angry at the Poles' ability to undermine the city's economy, but they were not prepared to approve any agreements with the Polish government. The Nazi leadership in Berlin exploited the economic situation and the nationalist frustration. Goebbels was sent to Danzig to restructure the local Nazi party organization and to initiate an aggressive campaign. He was successful.[7] The Danzig Nazi organization grew rapidly, securing seats in the elected assembly and entering into coalition agreement with the right-wing parties. Attacks on Polish prerogatives in the city and the port were challenged repeatedly. The Polish government and the Senate contrived to arrange incidents to highlight their respective grievances. Count Manfredo Gravina, an Italian who was the League representative in the City during this period, supported German claims and fanned the difficult situation by showing open hostility to Polish arguments.[8]

In October 1933 the League appointed a new High Commissioner, Sean Lester, a Catholic and citizen of the Irish Republic. He was given the task of finding a way of defusing the tension and in particular of negotiating with the Poles. Unfortunately, Józef Beck, the Polish Minister for Foreign Affairs, assumed Lester represented British interests and did nothing to collaborate with the latter's efforts to block the growth of Nazi power in the city. Beck's preoccupation with asserting Polish authority and in particular his deep resentment that Poland was not accorded the status of a Great Power blinded him to the fact that Germany, and not France and Britain, were Poland's biggest enemies. Lester attempted to use the League's authority to prevent the Nazis from taking over the Senate of the Free City. His arrival coincided with a new line in Poland's foreign policy caused by the government decision to establish a dialogue with the German government. This was preceded by probes about the Danzig issue. First Polish approaches to Hitler gave immediate results. In the run-up to the opening of talks on the non-aggression agreement Hitler declared that he was 'against any action directed against Polish rights and legal interest in the Free City of Danzig'.[9] The signing of the non-aggression declaration meant that the issue of Danzig became a touchstone of good relations. The Poles turned the full force of their irritation against the League, perceiving its presence in the city to be an obstacle to the further improvement of relations with Germany. German withdrawal from the League of Nations and the signing of the non-aggression declaration was followed by a decrease in anti-Polish propaganda. This gave rise to optimism in Warsaw. Although the Nazi leadership in Berlin repeatedly assured the Polish government that Germany had no intention of claiming Danzig, continuing Nazi outrages in the city and the persistent state of tension suggested that the matter was far from resolved.[10]

It was unfortunate that the Polish government concluded that the best way forward was to continue building stronger links with Germany, while trying to reduce – what Beck considered to be – the League's irksome interference in Danzig. In February 1937 the League appointed Carl Burckhardt, a Swiss national, to act as the new High Commissioner. By then Lester had admitted that he had failed in upholding the democratic principles in the city and that the local Nazis through violence and intimidation had secured absolute control over the Senate. Poland had played an important role in that process by refusing to support Lester when he condemned the Nazis. Lester had asked the Polish government to give support to the German parties that opposed the Nazis, but the government ignored his pleas.[11] When Burckhardt arrived in Danzig he was left in no doubt that the Poles wanted to see the League withdrawn from the area. The Polish President made it clear to him that Poland and Germany shared a common objective of destroying the Soviet Union. Beck likewise emphasized to Burckhardt that he did not wish to see the League interfering in Poland's relations with the Free City because he was convinced that he was capable of resolving all problems in direct dealings with Berlin.[12] Such a degree of Polish approval for German objectives signalled to the League representatives that the Poles would do nothing to support its role in the city.[13] Polish foreign policy now moved toward developing closer relations with Germany to the exclusion of outside arbitration. With hindsight, it is obvious that Beck was excessively confident of his ability to negotiate with the German government from what he perceived to be a position of strength. His conviction that the Danzig Nazis were controlled by the party in Germany was not unfounded, but he did not consider the possibility that Berlin would not use its influence on the Danzig party to curb violent attacks on Polish rights and citizens. Thus Beck consistently overlooked information from the Polish Commissioner General in Danzig, who sought to alert him to the fact that by destroying democratic rights in the city the Nazis were changing the political landscape to the point that no civil rights were guaranteed. In 1936 Kazimierz Papée, the Polish Commissioner in Danzig, reported that all but Nazi trade unions were banned and race laws were being introduced, limiting the rights of professionals and traders to pursue any activities in the city without first obtaining a licence from the Senate, which was wholly Nazi.[14] The Commissioner furthermore reported on the extent of Berlin's control over the Danzig Nazis. While this in principle reassured Beck of the rightness of his approach to the Danzig problem, the Polish Commissioner warned that the activities of the Danzig Nazis appeared to go beyond matters relating to the Free City. He reported that they were disseminating anti-Polish propaganda and seeking to encourage anti-Polish feelings within the German communities living within Poland's borders.[15]

At this stage attempts were made by Britain to limit the League's involvement in the Free City because conflicts there had the capacity to impact negatively on Britain's policy of appeasing Nazi Germany. In January 1937 the League agreed to limit its involvement in conflicts between the Polish state and the Danzig Senate and to confine its role to that of acting as an observer.[16] This decision proved difficult to maintain as the Danzig Senate's progressive introduction of Para-Nuremberg laws caused an international outcry. From the beginning of 1938, Jewish lawyers and doctors were prevented from practising in Danzig. This in turn required the representatives of the three countries that dealt with Danzig matters in the League to respond. Britain, France and Sweden would have preferred to ignore these developments, but this proved difficult due to the strength of outcry from the Jewish communities in the Britain and the US. Danzig Jews also sought to leave the city and requested visas, which caused the British Foreign Office anxiety about the numbers of Jews likely to arrive in the UK. The Polish representative in Danzig had cautioned his government about the implications of the Danzig situation on Poland's standing in Europe.[17] At this point, the Polish government became once more anxious that the League should still remain responsible for the city. By then Berlin's role in reining in and unleashing the Danzig Nazis was fully recognized.[18] Meanwhile, Beck continued to object to the League's presence in the Free City, implying that it was an obstacle to Poland resolving all outstanding problems through direct dealings with Berlin. Whereas in reality when the Polish government realized that the League had postponed making a decision on withdrawing the High Commissioner, Beck tried to cover all options. While he publicly attacked British and French interference in Danzig, he attempted to increase Poland's standing through direct negotiations with Berlin. This very same policy was being pursued by Hitler's regime. In January 1938, during a meeting with Beck, Hitler reassured the Polish Minister for Foreign Affairs that he did not want to change the situation in Danzig. By stressing that he attached importance to the maintenance of good relations with Poland, Hitler assured Beck that the Danzig issue would not be allowed to impact negatively on relations between the two states. Hitler told Beck that this commitment was 'binding irrespective of the fate of the League'.[19]

The background to Poland's apparent dependence on direct negotiations with Hitler was the fact that British and French policies appeared to focus on developing good relations with Germany. While the two viewed the Danzig issue as an obstacle to the constructive pursuit of their appeasement of Germany they were effectively pushing Poland in the direction of strengthening its ties with Germany. During the tense early months of 1938, Burckhardt left the Poles in no doubt that if the situation in Danzig was to become untenable the British and the French would withdraw the League from the city.[20] This message was confirmed in London. When in July 1938 the Danzig Gauleiter Albert Foster visited London the Foreign Office confirmed that he was left in no doubt that 'the British Government would view with pleasure the possibility of Poland and Germany reaching an agreement over Danzig'. The only condition was that the cloak of legality should be retained.[21] Both leaks from Burckhardt and information from London fanned Beck's suspicion that the Danzig issue would be used by the European powers as part of negotiations to improve relations with Germany, where a willingness to withdraw the League from Danzig would be offered as a gesture of good will irrespective of the consequences of such actions on Polish rights in the city.

The Czechoslovak crisis of 1938 appeared to offer the Poles an opportunity to obtain reassurances from Germany. Unfortunately, in spite of close co-operation between the two states in the propaganda war waged against Czechoslovakia, Poland failed to secure the most important objective, namely, the establishment of Polish authority in areas between the Soviet Union and Germany. The Poles anticipated that the Western powers would object to German plans for the dismemberment of Czechoslovakia. As it turned out, Chamberlain took the lead in defusing the crisis. The German government's claims that it was merely representing the interests of the persecuted German community in Czechoslovakia were accepted as legitimate. The Poles had their own reasons for supporting German policies. They hoped to regain control of the Teschen region grabbed by the Czechs in 1919. In the long term, they hoped to weaken the Czechoslovak state by encouraging Slovak independence and the breakaway of Ruthenia, which they hoped would be incorporated into Hungary, forming a common border with Poland. Beck's desire to profit from what he firmly believed to be German need for Polish co-operation and approval of its policies towards Czechoslovakia went even further. His *chief de cabinet* recorded that Beck discussed the matter with President Sławoj-Składkowski and Śmigły-Rydz, the Minister of Defence. The latter suggested that Poland's willingness to see Czechoslovakia weakened and dismembered should only be offered in return for guarantees in Danzig.[22] When Poland was not invited to the Munich Conference, its irrelevance to Germany was starkly manifested.

The sense of unease that haunted the Poles as the Czechoslovak crisis unfolded intensified when Britain became closely involved. So anxious was Beck about the implications of Western approval for German actions in Eastern Europe that immediately after Chamberlain's first visit to Hitler on 15 September he instructed Józef Lipski, Polish diplomat and Ambassador to Germany, to seek a meeting with Hitler. Clearly affected by the atmosphere created by the meeting with the British Prime Minister, Hitler refused to engage in a conversation on the Danzig issue.[23] Acting on Beck's further instruction, Lipski requested a separate meeting with Joachim Ribbentrop, the German Minister for Foreign Affairs. The meeting, which took place on 24 October 1938, marked a new stage in Polish–German relations. The Poles were left in no doubt that Germany's success in the destruction of the Czechoslovak state and the realization that Britain and France would do little to protect the status quo in Eastern Europe lay at the root of Ribbentrop's determination to put relations with Poland on to a new footing. Lipski was treated to a comprehensive review of relations. Whereas Germany was willing to extend the Polish–German non-aggression agreement for another twenty-five years, Ribbentrop suggested that the Free City of Danzig should be in due course incorporated into the Third Reich and that an extra-territorial link through the Polish-held territories should be built thus linking the city with West Prussia. There was no disguising the fact that Germany was moving towards treating Poland as a subordinate state and not a partner. The most obvious indication of this important change of policy and tone lay in the boldness with which Ribbentrop put forward demands relating to the Free City.[24]

The first Polish response to these new German demands reflected bewilderment at the new state of affairs. Beck instructed Lipski to reassure Ribbentrop that Poland would seek a mutually acceptable solution to the Danzig problem.

He further maintained that the League was the source of all problems, as he described its role as having 'far reaching prerogatives ... but not able to fulfil its task in a manner beneficial to the Free City and to Polish interests ...'[25] While Berlin did not for the time being press its demands, the Poles were left to consider the implications of the initial suggestion. Beck's response was to review the whole of Polish–German relations, an analysis from which he drew some comfort. Although Germany's actions in fomenting anti-Polish sentiments among the Ukrainian population had been noted, new violent attacks on Polish property and nationals in Danzig could not be overlooked. By the Vienna Award of 1 November 1938 Germany had granted Hungary Czech territories. German domination of areas that Poland up to now considered to be its sphere of influence was thus confirmed. Hungary and Romania, two states on which Beck had hoped to base his plans for a Polish-dominated Central European bloc, moved towards closer relations with Germany. As firmly as Beck and his advisers clung to the conviction that Germany had to retain Polish goodwill, realities suggested otherwise.[26]

In January 1939 Beck made two foreign trips. The first was to Germany where, he held talks with Hitler and Ribbentrop. From them he heard that while the Danzig issue could be postponed, in the long term Germany expected Poland to agree to its incorporation into the Reich. Hitler stressed that good relations with Poland still mattered to Germany and assured Beck that Germany would agree to the incorporation of Ruthenia into Hungary. Though the interview seemed friendly, the statement that Danzig would finally have to return to Germany was worrying. Beck chose to believe that this was not a demand or even a warning, but a game of bluff. Furthermore, he chose to believe that by resolutely rejecting Hitler's demands he had made an impact on the German leader.[27] The other trip was to France, where Beck's ostensibly private sojourn was ignored by French politicians. French disinterest only confirmed to Beck that Poland would have to face Germany on its own. His response was, more firmly than before, to focus on Danzig as a barometer of the state of relations with Berlin. If Germany demanded the incorporation of the city into Germany, this would suggest that Hitler wanted a confrontation and not an accommodation with Poland.

On his return to Poland, Beck instigated a major review of Polish foreign policy. It was decided to pursue two lines of policy in relation to Germany: one of firmness and the other of reasonable accommodation. While rejecting the demand that Danzig should be restored to Germany, a number of compromises were to be offered. At this stage Beck still thought in terms of demanding that the League protection should be withdrawn from Danzig hoping that this might satisfy Hitler. Believing that the Germans resented the League's presence as much as he did, Beck hoped to replace the League guarantees of the city's status with direct guarantees from Germany.[28]

During the month following the signing of the Munich Treaty, while the precise implications of German recent actions remained unclear, all European governments looked for some indication of what were Germany's next objectives. France and Britain sought further clarification as to what Germany really wanted to do. Unfortunately for Beck, Polish complicity in the break-up of Czechoslovakia had made a negative impression on the French and British ministers, notwithstanding their own active involvement in forcing the Czechs to accept the loss of the Sudeten region. The result was that, anticipating German actions in Danzig, both governments signalled their desire to see the League withdrawn from the city. Edward Raczyński, the Polish Ambassador to London, was only too well aware of the Foreign Office's anger at Beck's public rebuff of British requests that Poland should not press its demands to Teschen at the height of the autumn crisis in Czechoslovakia. He was not surprised when on 9 December 1938 he was informed that the British government would seek the withdrawal of League protection from the city by 16 January.[29] Beck protested and finally succeeded in persuading the League Rapporteurs to postpone this decision. By then he had come to the conclusion that he needed the League to remain in the city, at least until he was certain that the German leadership would not make a unilateral decision on the matter. We know that his desire to offer Germany some concession over travel links between the city and West Prussia went hand in hand with a determination to remove the bad impression his previous actions had created on the British. On 23 December 1938 Sir Howard Kennard, British Ambassador to Warsaw, reported that Beck informed him that he wanted to strengthen relations between the Polish and British navies. Under this inauspicious request lay an attempt to set aside previous misunderstandings.[30]

The last two weeks of March 1939 abounded in rumours and threats of possible German action. On 12 March Hitler decided to destroy what remained of Czechoslovakia and occupied Bohemia and Moravia on 15 March. Two days later, Viorel Tilea, the Romanian Minister to London, informed the Foreign Office that Germany had demanded the monopoly of Romanian oil production. This was a worrying piece of information, as access to oil would allow Germany to wage war without fear of an economic blockade. This coming on the heels of naked German aggression against Czechoslovakia mobilized the British Cabinet to consider the possibility of German demands going beyond merely redressing grievances. The Cabinet's first response was to agree that Germany, through its continuing demands in Eastern Europe, posed a threat to British interests. It was decided that the views of all East European and Balkan states were to be solicited. By 20 March plans were narrowed down to seeking some form of co-operation between Britain, France, the Soviet Union and Poland.[31] In the meantime, rumours – which the Poles refused to deny or confirm – suggested that Germany was putting pressure on Poland for the return of Danzig. Both the French and British ministers found themselves in a dilemma. Until now they would have wanted the Poles and Germans to resolve their differences and to reach an accommodation on the city. Both Western European democracies feared that Poland would resist with its full military force and this would lead to a European war, not least of all because France would be obliged to take action against Germany.[32]

The British and French governments were right in their concern about Polish–German relations. The Poles, mindful of the way the Czechoslovak government lost control over its own affairs when it accepted British mediation in the summer of 1938, would not divulge details of recent Polish–German talks. Nevertheless, it was generally presumed that the two countries were either discussing or disagreeing over Danzig. In reality, the matter was much more serious. The Poles had already felt slighted by lack of German support when they expected to be invited to the Munich Conference. The First Vienna Award marginalized the Poles and also made clear that Germany was determined to act as a broker in regional disputes. The Poles had not been informed by Germany of its proposed action in relation to Czechoslovakia in March. Beck had in the long term hoped to see Slovakia separate from the Czechs. He had hoped that this would lead to the creation of a Slovak state, which would be wholly dependent on Poland, but the Slovak protectorate came under German control. In the Baltic, events unfolded quickly and unexpectedly. On 20 March 1939 Ribbentrop demanded that the port city of Memel should be ceded to Germany. The Lithuanian government had no alternative but to agree. German control over the Baltic coast was thus extended. Hence, when Ribbentrop put to the Polish Government a demand that Danzig should be restored to Germany, Beck saw this request as an ultimatum. To the military regime that had ruled Poland since 1926, the issue of access to the sea was a matter of prestige as well as economic and strategic convenience. Beck in particular had stressed the importance of Poland being a maritime power. In his attempts to form a Central European bloc of countries independent of Germany and the Soviet Union, he went out of his way to develop relations with Sweden and Finland. The expansion of German domination of the Baltic coast clearly rendered these and all strategic plans irrelevant but in the long term also raised questions as to why Germany was pursuing these policies.

On 21 March Ribbentrop held a meeting with Lipski. Ribbentrop's opening sentence was ominous, as he stated that he intended to 'discuss German–Polish relations in their entirety'. Ribbentrop proposed that Danzig should be incorporated into the Third Reich. Poland should also agree to Germany building an extra territorial rail and road link between Danzig and West Prussia. In return, Germany was prepared to offer guarantees that Poland's control of the Poznań region would not be challenged. Germany would also guarantee Poland's frontiers.[33] As if to reinforce the point that Poland was subservient to Germany, Ribbentrop made references to the fact that Germany had not opposed the emergence of an independent Poland. He also reminded the Polish ambassador that Polish and Hungarian demands to Czechoslovak territories had been approved by Germany. Lipski felt that the request, though couched in polite form, was in reality an ultimatum.[34] The proposal that Ribbentrop had put to the Poles went to the very heart of relations with Poland, which had been since 1934 based on the assumption that the controversial question of the Free City of Danzig was a reflection of the state of relations between the two states.

By coincidence, the British Ambassador to Warsaw communicated an equally important proposition to the Polish government. The Foreign Office believed that Germany was preparing to challenge Poland on the Danzig issue and the proposal made by Kennard followed on the heels of the earlier enquiry communicated to all East European states about their possible response to German aggression. Kennard put to Beck a startling proposal that Britain would be willing to sign a bilateral agreement with Poland as a result of which both would act jointly on the Danzig issue. In Halifax's formulation, 'if the Danzig question should develop in such a way as to involve a threat to Polish independence then this would be a matter of gravest concern to ourselves'.[35] An interesting condition for the conclusion of this agreement was that the French government should not be informed of this agreement.

The British proposal to Poland has to be seen in the context of the fast-evolving situation. The British declared intention to enter into a bilateral agreement with Poland should neither be seen as an expression of a commitment to act if Germany tried to annex the Free City nor was it the outcome of a carefully considered change in British foreign policy. In March, the rapidly evolving situation in Europe caused the British Cabinet and in particular Chamberlain unease. It was agreed that there was a need for action to signal to Germany the unacceptability of its policies, hence the initial badly thought out approaches to the Soviet Union and other East European states. This was nevertheless quickly qualified when the implications of Soviet participation in any anti-German declaration were considered.[36] The initiative to approach the Poles with a new proposal was made on the background of rumours that Germany was likely to act. The prospect of a war breaking out over Danzig compelled Chamberlain to enter into direct talks with Poland. The purpose of the initiative was not to reassure the Poles that they would be guaranteed aid were they to take action. On the contrary, the bilateral agreement was a way of making sure that German expansion was halted, but that the Poles did not precipitate a war.[37] As Beck evaluated the usefulness of the British offer to his dual approach to relations with Germany, he saw both merits and demerits in it. He continued in his determination to resolve all problems in Poland's relations with Germany by means of direct talks, but the British offer held out the prospect of aid and finance, which Poland's rulers were loath to reject. Thus, Beck offered a cautious but encouraging response mirrored by a continued stubborn unwillingness to share any information as to the substance of talks with the Germans.[38]

When the final decision was made by the British Cabinet to offer Poland a guarantee to support it if there was a threat to its independence, this was done in the heat of the moment. Although the opinions of the military chiefs and of their French counterparts had been sought, the information provided by both was not used to evaluate the likely success of such a gesture on the events unfolding in Danzig and on thinking in Warsaw. A badly thought out declaration made by Chamberlain was not a genuine commitment to defend Poland but an attempt to forestall another act of aggression by Germany. Rumours rather than facts lay at the root of the decision to make a public declaration of support to the Poles. This is surprising, since the British Consul in Danzig sent regular reports to the Foreign Office outlining the way the Danzig Nazis reduced the Senate's functions. These nevertheless never made it to the Cabinet discussions.[39]

Only a day after Chamberlain made the declaration to the House of Commons serious doubts were raised as to whether this indeed meant that Britain would fight in defence of Poland and in particular to maintain the status of the Free City of Danzig. Both the full wording of the declaration and the editorial of *The Times* suggested that the decision as to whether Polish security was threatened and thus whether the British obligation was invoked would rest in British hands. As we know, during the months following the declaration, neither the Danzig Nazis nor Germany proceeded to take action to change to status of the city. The British Embassy in Berlin was a source of information on the state of play, suggesting frequently the imminence of German aggression.[40] F.M. Shepherd, Acting British Consul-General in Danzig, likewise continued to warn that the Danzig Nazis were remilitarizing the city in preparation for conflict with Polish troops.[41] Danzig remained a constant source of tension in Europe. It was nevertheless a particular source of anxiety to the British government on account of the recently publicly declared determination to aid Poland in the defence of its territory but also because the Polish government remained steadfastly resolute in its policy of keeping the British out of the picture.

During the months preceding the German invasion of Poland the British Foreign Office debated a possibility that would have placed the government in a particular quandary. What would have been the British government's legal obligation if the Danzig Senate voted for the Free City to join Germany? In principle the British, like all member states of the League of Nations, would have been obliged to take action against an aggressor state, but a voluntary *Anschluss* was something quite different. Any action to prevent this happening would have been not only legally dubious, but unlikely to receive public support. As rumours of an imminent vote in the Senate persisted, Halifax grappled with the predicament the Foreign Office faced. He informed the Cabinet that he had warned British ambassadors in Warsaw, Berlin and Rome to prepare for such a possibility. Kennard in Warsaw was asked to hold a meeting with Beck and to try and persuade him that in the event of this happening Poland should not take military action and should instead confine its response to a milder form of diplomatic disapproval, namely economic and diplomatic pressure.[42] As the Foreign Office reasoned, it was for the time being important to prevent Poland from seeing the likely Senate vote for the incorporation into Germany as action indicative of German aggressive intensions. British diplomatic representatives abroad did not address the Danzig problem in their dealings with German representatives, in line with the policy of trying not to attach undue importance to the emerging flashpoint.

This manner of approaching the Danzig crisis inevitably led to the Foreign Office viewing likely Polish action as threatening European peace. The underlying British thinking was that the Danzig Nazis would not act on their own and would be guided by Berlin. The most important task therefore became to persuade Beck that were the situation in Danzig to escalate, Poland should not view this as aggression, and that Beck should be prevailed upon not to take action without prior consultation with Britain.[43] A diplomatic tug-of-war ensued with the Foreign Office trying to bind the Poles to allow the British government to assume responsibility for reducing the state of tension in Danzig. Since the Polish government would divulge neither the state of relations with Germany nor their own thinking on the subject, British efforts failed. This left the British politicians in a permanent state of anxiety.

Kennard in Warsaw had his time cut out, for he knew Beck and the Polish military regime well enough to realize that any attempt to bind them to comply with British requests not to view German actions in relation to Danzig as significant were doomed. In any case, most British diplomatic representatives in east and south-east European states knew that Britain's standing had been damaged by its complicity in the break-up of Czechoslovakia in the autumn of 1938 and the lack of response to German actions against Czechoslovakia in March 1939. Not surprisingly, Beck's response to Kennard was to ask what Britain proposed to do in the event of German aggression, but a clear answer was not forthcoming.[44]

Throughout April and May 1939 British and French Chiefs of Staff met to discuss joint action. One important item on the agenda of these meetings was the question of the eastern front. It was quickly apparent that such a front was no more than a figure of speech, as neither France nor Britain proposed to actually fight Germany, little more to deploy troops and resources east of Germany. While the Poles were not privy to the ongoing Franco-British staff talks they were aware of the lack of preparation to support Poland on the eastern front. In Paris a Polish delegation continued discussions on a military convention to the Franco–Polish alliance, whereas a British staff mission arrived in Warsaw on 23 May only to inform the Poles that Britain had no plans to aid the Poles in the event of a war with Germany.[45] The consequence of these exchanges were visible as the Poles continued in their determination not to inform the British as to whether they were holding talks with the Germans and on what they would do if the Danzig Nazis took action. A policy of brinkmanship was being played by the Poles, who not only deeply resented the fact that Britain and France were conducting talks with the Soviet Union, but also were stalling on the completion of the agreement with Poland. The inconclusive financial talks cast a further shadow over Polish–British relations. The Treasury's reluctance to release any funds to Poland was accompanied by attempts to force the Polish government to review a contract awarded to a French rather than to a British electricity company to install an electricity grid in Poland.[46]

While the British government still grappled with the dilemma of whether to support the Poles or to use all means available to try and rein them in, the situation in Danzig rapidly escalated. By August, the Polish and German governments operated on the assumption that war was inevitable. Leaders of the Polish military regime tried by various means to secure further French and British military commitments and supplies in anticipation of the impending conflict. When these were still not forthcoming they surprisingly acted on the assumption that neither Western democracy would in reality afford to lose Poland as an ally. In these circumstances, Danzig became the fulcrum upon which Anglo-Polish relations came to be unsteadily balanced. This explains why the Danzig issue was the subject of Cabinet discussions in July and August. The full extent of the dilemma faced by British policy makers was articulated by Halifax at a Cabinet meeting on 2 August. During a debate on German long-term objectives he stated that Danzig should not be seen as a reason to go to war, but if a threat to Polish security arose from Danzig then Britain would honour its obligation to support Poland.[47]

At the beginning of August, the Polish government and the Senate were once more in conflict. Since May, Polish customs inspectors had been under constant attack, which made their job impossible. This allowed the Nazis to militarize Danzig to the point that it became a fortress. In August, the Senate informed the Poles that it would no longer recognize Polish customs guards.[48] This led the Poles to warn the Senate that it was acting outside its jurisdiction. Beck also took an opportunity to attack Burckhardt for supposedly dissemi-nating false information about the city.[49] The German government intervened only to be informed by the Polish government that it had no right to make representations on behalf of the Danzig Senate. When the Poles had decided to confront the Danzig authorities they did not seek British advice, but merely informed the Foreign Office of the crisis after the fact. The Poles threatened to bomb Danzig from the sea and the Senate backed down. The Foreign Office was appalled to hear how close the two had come to a military conflict. The Danzig issue continued to be a bone of contention between the Polish and German government with Britain desperately trying to wrestle from the Poles an agreement not to proceed without British approval. While Beck belligerently refused to do so, the British government sought means of ascertaining whether indeed Danzig was merely a pretext for a conflict with Poland or a difficulty that could be resolved with a modicum of good will.

The British Cabinet chose to believe that the latter was the case, whereas the Poles increasingly acted on the assumption that war with Germany was likely to break out in the near future. To the Poles the Danzig crisis, like reports of tension on the Polish–German border in Silesia and German claims that Poland was mistreating the German minority were seen as signs of a German propa-ganda campaign, which inevitably preceded an outright attack.

In the end, it was the Poles who were correct. On 23 August the Danzig Senate voted for the city to return to the Reich. The Danzig Gauleiter Albert Forster was appointed Head of the Danzig state. These actions contravened the League charter and in principle should have been a matter for the League. Instead the British and French government spoke of negotiations and used their diplomatic offices to try and persuade Beck to appoint a negotiator or at least to accept the appointment of a suitable person to negotiate between the Polish and German government. Events nevertheless fast overtook these efforts for on 1 September the German battleship *Schleswig-Holstein* attacked the Polish fort and ammunition dump of Westerplatte on the tip of the Hel peninsula. Danzig was officially incorporated into Germany on that day. Burckhardt, who was in the city, was instructed to leave immediately. Wholesale attacks on Polish property and citizens completed the picture.

On 1 September 1939 developments taking place in Danzig were of little consequence as on the same day, in the early hours of the morning, Germany initiated a military attack on Poland. In the end the war did not start because of Danzig, though the city had always been a reliable barometer of relations between the two states.

Notes

1   House of Commons Debate 345, 31 March 1939, cols 2421–2.

2   A. Cienciala, 'The Battle for Danzig and the Polish Corridor at the Paris Peace Conference of 1919' in P. Latawski (ed.), *The Reconstruction of Poland, 1914–1921.* Houdsmill, 1992, pp. 81–4.

3   A.J. Prażmowska, 'The Role of Danzig in Polish–German Relations on the Eve of the Second World War' in J. Hiden and T. Lane (eds), *The Baltic and the Outbreak of the Second World War.* Cambridge, 1992, pp. 76–7.

4   S. Mikos, *Wolne miasto Gdańsk a Liga Narodów 1920–1939.* Gdańsk, 1979, pp. 144–5.

5   C.M. Kimmich, *The Free City: Danzig and German Foreign Policy, 1919–1934.* New Haven, 1968, pp. 104–5.

6   H. Levine, *Hitler's Free City: A History of the Nazi Party in Danzig, 1925–39.* Chicago, 1973, p. 37.

7   P. McNamara, *Sean Lester, Poland and the Nazi Takeover of Danzig.* Dublin, 2009, pp. 26–7.

8   Ibid., p. 28.

9   W. Jędrzejewicz (ed.), *Diplomat in Berlin 1933–1934: Papers and Memoirs of Josef Lipski, Ambassador of Poland.* New York,1969, pp. 73–4.

10   C. Gdańsk, *National Identity in the Polish–German Borderlands.* London, 1990, pp. 122–3.

11   McNamara, *Sean Lester*, pp. 224–7.

12   Ibid., p. 48.

13   C. Burckhardt, *Moja Misja w Gdańsku 1937–1939.* Warszawa, 1979, p. 46.

14   Polish Institute and Sikorski Museum (henceforth PISM) A12, 881, 14 January 1936 and 4 February 1937.

15   PISM A12, 881, 30 December 1937.

16   Mikos, *Wolne Miasto Gdańsk a Liga Narodów*, pp. 322–3.

17   Archives of the Free City of Danzig, Gdańsk (henceforth AG), 259/931, 24 May 1938.

18   PISM, A12, 881/2, 30 December 1937.

19   Jędrzejewicz (ed.), *Diplomat in Berlin 1933-1934*, p. 334.

20   AG, 259/931, 27 May 1938.

21   AG, 259/931, 22 June 1938.

22   J. Zarański (ed.), *Diariusz i Teki Jana Szembeka, 1938–1939*, vol. 4. London, 1952, 12 March 1938.

23   Jędrzejewicz (ed.), *Diplomat in Berlin 1933–1934*, pp. 406–7.

24   A.J. Prażmowska, 'Poland's Foreign Policy: September 1938–September 1939', *Historical Journal* vol. 29 no. 4 (1986), p. 854.

25   Official Documents Concerning Polish–German and Polish–Soviet Relations 1933–1939, also known as The Polish While Book, Poland, 1940, no. 44, pp. 47–8.

26 Zarański (ed.) *Diariusz i Teki Jana Szembeka*, 7 December 1938.
27 Josef Beck, *Final Report*. New York, 1957, pp. 171–2.
28 J. Łubieński, 'Ostatnie negocjacje w sprawie Gdańska. Wyjątki z pamiętnika', Dziennik Polski i Dziennik Żołnierza, 3 December 1953.
29 PISM A12, 53/21 9 December 1939.
30 National Archives, London (henceforth NA), FO 371 23129, C27/27/35, 23 December 1938.
31 NA CAB 23/98, Cabinet 13/39, 20 March 1939.
32 A.J. Prażmowska, *Britain, Poland and the Eastern Front, 1939*. Cambridge, 1986, pp. 42–5.
33 The Polish White Book, no. 61, pp. 61–3.
34 Zarański (ed.) *Diariusz i Teki Jana Szembeka*, 23 March 1939, pp. 562–8.
35 NA FO371, C4086/3356/18, 24 March 1939.
36 Prażmowska, *Britain, Poland and the Eastern Front*, pp. 44–5.
37 Ibid., p. 52.
38 Ibid., p. 53.
39 NA FO371, 23133, c3822/93/55, 22 March 1939.
40 Documents on British Foreign Policy (henceforth DBFP), 3rd series, vol. v, no. 163, pp. 199–220.
41 NA FO 371 23022, C9973/54/18, 14 July 1939.
42 NA CAB 23/99, Cabinet 27/39, 20 May 1939.
43 DBFP, vol. v, no. 442, pp. 492–3, 10 May 1939.
44 DBFP, vol. v, no. 459, pp. 636 and 690.
45 Prażmowska, *Britain, Poland and the Eastern Front*, pp. 94–7.
46 NA, FO371, 23146, C10029/1110/55, 12 July 1939.
47 NA CAB 23/100, Cabinet 40 (39), 2 August 1939.
48 Levine, *Hitler's Free City*, pp. 151–2.
49 PISM A.12 53/25, 1 August 1939.

Chapter 24

Stalin and the Outbreak of the Second World War

Geoffrey Roberts

For Joseph Stalin the Second World War started long before Germany invaded Poland in September 1939. It began, the Soviet dictator said, when Japan invaded China in July 1937. 'A new imperialist war is already in its second year,' he told delegates to the eighteenth party congress in March 1939:

> a war waged over a huge territory stretching from Shanghai to Gibraltar and involving over five hundred million people. The map of Europe, Africa and Asia is being forcibly re-drawn. The entire post-war system, the so-called regime of peace, has been shaken to its foundations.

Stalin viewed this 'new imperialist war' as a re-run of the First World War – a renewal of the struggle between the great capitalist powers to divide up the spoils of the world. On one side were the 'non-aggressive, democratic' states of Britain, France and the United States who defended the status quo; on the other a bloc of aggressor states – Imperial Japan, Nazi Germany and Fascist Italy – all seeking to overturn the boundaries set by the peace settlement of 1919. Stalin traced the inception of this inter-imperialist struggle to Japan's invasion of Manchuria in 1931 and Italy's invasion of Abyssinia in 1935. These events were followed by German and Italian military intervention in the Spanish Civil War in 1936 and in 1938 by Hitler's seizure of Austria and the Sudeten region of Czechoslovakia.

Japan's expansion into Manchuria and China had already led to a series of border clashes with the Soviet Union. In June 1937, Soviet and Japanese gunboats contested control of the Amur River, while at Lake Khasan in summer 1938, a battle erupted between the Soviet Far Eastern Army and the Japanese Kwantung Army over the occupation of strategic highpoints on the border between Korea, Manchuria and the USSR. The Soviet Union and Japan were destined to clash again at Khalkhin-Gol on the Mongolian–Manchurian border in summer 1939 when General Georgii Zhukov encircled and defeated a 75,000-strong Japanese army – an operation that launched his reputation as a daring military commander. Even so, the Soviets did not consider Japan to be the main threat to peace or to Soviet security. The 1938 Soviet war plan identified Germany as the chief enemy and allocated 140 divisions and 10,000 tanks to the defence of the USSR's western borders. In the Far East, the Red Army's projected deployment against Japan was only a third of that strength. As the authors of the Soviet war plan noted, Japan had been weakened by its war of attrition in China and would only pose a significant threat to the Soviet Union, if it were to ally with Germany. The key to safeguarding Soviet security lay in Europe and in neutralizing the threat posed by Nazi Germany.[1]

The high priority accorded to the German threat was signalled in Stalin's speech to the eighteenth party congress. This was not because of overwhelming German power, argued Stalin, since the combined strength of Britain, France and the United States was far greater than that of Germany. Hitler had succeeded in Spain, Austria and the Sudetenland because the western states had pursued a 'policy of non-intervention'. This was not simply passive appeasement but an active policy to encourage the Germans and the Japanese to expand towards the Soviet Union:

> In the policy of non-intervention is revealed a striving, a desire ... not to hinder Japan, say, from involving itself in a war with China, or, better still, with the Soviet Union; not to hinder Germany, say, from entangling itself in European affairs, from involving itself in a war with the Soviet Union, allowing the participants to sink deeply into the mire of war ... and then when they have become weak enough, to appear on the scene with fresh strength ... to dictate conditions to the enfeebled belligerents.

Stalin concluded with his much-quoted warning that the Soviet Union would not be 'drawn into conflicts by warmongers who are accustomed to have others pull the chestnuts out of the fire for them'. A literal translation of the Russian phrase Stalin used captures his meaning much better: 'to rake the fire with somebody else's hands' (zagrebat' zhar chuzhimi rukami). In other words, the Soviet Union was not going to be dragged into doing the Western states' fighting for them.[2]

Stalin's view that the Second World War had, in effect, begun two years before and his belief in a Western conspiracy to provoke a Soviet–German war are key to understanding his actions during the crisis that led to the outbreak of war in 1939. Stalin's suspicions of the West were rooted in contemporary communist ideology, in particular, the fundamentalist belief in the existence of an explicit capitalist conspiracy to overthrow the Soviet socialist system. As he often stated, the stronger the Soviet system became the more threatening it was to capitalism and the more hostility it aroused from its class enemies. This outlook had its origins in the Russian Civil War of 1918–20 when the Americans, British and French actively supported the Bolsheviks' opponents and almost succeeded in strangling the Soviet regime at birth. Twenty years later Stalin was confident he could defend the USSR from another such capitalist onslaught but he was determined that, when the inevitable war came, it would be fought on terms favourable to the Soviet Union.

Equally important in Stalin's calculations was his negative assessment of Anglo-French appeasement of Hitler – the policy of pacification (politika umirotvoreniya), as the Soviets liked to call it. When Hitler came to power in 1933 it was possible for the Soviets to continue the so-called 'Rapallo relationship' with Germany, notwithstanding the anti-communist character of the Nazis' domestic regime. The Rapallo treaty signed in 1922 had re-established relations between the two states. Soviet Russia and Weimar Germany developed a productive political, economic and military partnership. Trade between the two states grew exponentially and the Soviets helped the Germans to evade the military restrictions of Versailles by providing facilities for training and weapons development. In 1926 Moscow and Berlin signed a Treaty of Friendship and Neutrality. In 1931 that treaty was prolonged for a further five years. Hitler ratified this protocol in March 1933, but it soon became apparent that he was intent on pursuing an anti-Soviet foreign policy. Soviet–German trade collapsed, military co-operation was curtailed and there was no let up in the anti-Bolshevik rhetoric of the Nazis. In June 1933 Alfred Hugenberg, the German Economics Minister, submitted a memorandum to a World Economic Conference that seemed to suggest Germany would, as Hitler had advocated in *Mein Kampf*, seek *Lebensraum* (living space) in Russia. 'The Hugenberg Memorandum shows us', wrote Deputy Foreign Commissar Nikolai Krestinsky, 'that the present government ... has not given up the foreign policy ideas which the national Socialists developed in theory and actively worked for in all the years of their struggle for power. The German government is prepared to participate in a military coalition against us, is prepared to expand its military power for war with us.'[3] These fears were reinforced further in October 1933 when Germany withdrew from international disarmament negotiations and the League of Nations. It was clear Hitler intended to challenge the entire peace settlement and would rearm Germany in order to do so.

The Soviet response to these developments was to embrace the policy of collective security; broadly a strategy to pursue bilateral and multilateral defence alliances whose aim was to contain the Nazi threat to the European order.[4] By the end of 1933, a significant détente in Franco-Soviet relations had developed. In December of that year Foreign Commissar Maxim Litvinov promulgated a new Soviet foreign policy doctrine. Previously the Soviets had sought peaceful co-existence with all states and had stood aloof from inter-capitalist quarrels. Now Litvinov's view was that

> it can scarcely be doubted that in the present international situation no war, wherever it may break out, can be localised and no country can be certain that it will not be drawn into the war once it has begun. The Soviet Union therefore is interested not only in its own peaceful relations with other states, but in the maintenance of peace generally.

Litvinov's doctrine of the 'indivisibility of peace' was underlined by Stalin at the seventeenth party congress in January 1934 when he defended Soviet détente with France on the grounds that 'if the interests of the USSR demand rapprochement with one country or another which is not interested in disturbing the peace, we adopt this course without hesitation'.[5]

It was partly at France's behest that the USSR joined the League of Nations – an organization that the Soviets had previously scorned as a 'capitalist club' responsible for carving up the globe – in February 1934. Membership facilitated Soviet participation in discussions about a collective security agreement in Eastern Europe to guarantee existing borders and to pledge mutual defence in the event of external aggression. These negotiations were commonly called the 'Eastern Locarno' negotiations – a reference to the Locarno Pact of 1925 that had established a similar set of collective security arrangements in Western Europe. Germany had been a signatory of the Locarno Treaty and was a participant in the Eastern Locarno negotiations but Berlin's proposal was for a multilateral non-aggression treaty rather than a system of collective security.

Stalin signalled the importance he attached to the Eastern Locarno negotiations by granting an audience to Anthony Eden when the British Foreign Affairs Minister visited Moscow in March 1935. In the 1930s Stalin rarely agreed to meet visiting foreign politicians unless they were communists. He told Eden the problem with the German counter-proposal for a non-aggression pact was that Germany could not be trusted to stick to its international agreements. Only a binding mutual security agreement could guarantee peace and security in Eastern Europe. To illustrate his point Stalin delivered the following homily on collective security:

> There are here in this room six people, imagine that between ourselves there is a pact of mutual assistance and imagine that, for example, Comrade Maisky [the Soviet Ambassador to London] wanted to attack one of us – what would happen? We would all join forces to beat Comrade Maisky ... It is the same with the countries of Eastern Europe.[6]

The negotiations for an Eastern Locarno failed because of German (and Polish) objections but in May 1935 the Soviets succeeded in concluding a mutual assistance pact with France and with France's ally, Czechoslovakia. Hopes were also high in Moscow that a similar alliance could be secured with Great Britain. However, mid-1935 proved to have been the pinnacle of the Soviet campaign for collective security. Discussions with the British went nowhere. The pacts with France and Czechoslovakia failed to develop into a workable military alliance. In October 1935, Mussolini invaded Abyssinia and the Soviets were not impressed by the League of Nations' failure to impose effective sanctions on Italy. Then in March 1936 Britain and France remained passive in response to Hitler's remilitarization of the Rhineland. Even more damaging to Soviet collective security policy aspirations were the diplomatic complications of the Spanish Civil War.

Not long after the start of the civil war in July 1936, Britain and France set up the international Non-Intervention Committee, designed to stop external military aid to either Spain's Republican government or to the military mutiny led by General Franco and his fascist supporters. The USSR joined the committee and pledged to refrain from aiding Republican Spain, but only if Germany and Italy also adhered to the non-intervention agreement. Since the Germans and Italians continued to supply Franco this was reason enough for the Soviets to support the Republican side. Some 2,000 Soviet military advisers served in Spain while the Communist International (Comintern) organized 40,000-strong International Brigades to fight alongside the Spanish Republicans. The USSR supplied hundreds of tanks and planes to the Republican government, albeit at a price. Among the strongest Soviet supporters of aid to Spain was Stalin, in contrast to Litvinov, who, as a diplomat, placed greater priority on maintaining good relations with Britain and France.

The British and French wanted to stop the Spanish Civil War from escalating into an international conflict. They were also mindful of the need to maintain good relations with Germany and Italy to secure a wide-ranging re-negotiation of the Versailles peace settlement – the key goal of Anglo-French appeasement of Hitler and Mussolini. To the Soviets, however, their non-intervention policy appeared to be yet another rejection of collective security while making concessions to fascist aggression. Even Litvinov was disappointed by British and French policy and in 1936–7 he gave a number of speeches mocking them and denouncing the ineffectiveness of the non-intervention agreement.[7]

The Spanish Civil War also prompted a further deterioration in Soviet relations with Nazi Germany. After the Franco-Soviet pact was signed in May 1935 Moscow's relations with Berlin had hit a new low amid German accusations that the Soviets were pursuing a policy of encircling Germany, much as Russia had done before the First World War. This allegation was broadly accurate, but Stalin was careful not to burn all his bridges to Berlin. He restrained Litvinov's anti-Nazi tendencies somewhat and was receptive to German overtures about an expansion of trade relations. When those German overtures became more overtly political, Stalin responded, in January 1937, with a proposal to hold negotiations on improving relations. Just as the Soviets identified divisions in Anglo-French ruling circles about appeasement they perceived economic and political interests within the Nazi power bloc that favoured an eastern orientation in German foreign policy. They also believed the German overtures were a sign of the weakness and fragility of Hitler's regime. In the event, nothing came of these discussions, and Soviet–German relations resumed at the distance set by the clash over Spain and by Germany's signature of the Anti-Comintern Pact in November 1936. Ostensibly an anti-communist agreement, the pact was in fact a German–Japanese alliance directed against the USSR.[8]

The next episode in the sorry story of the Soviets' search for collective security was the Czechoslovakian crisis of 1938. The curtain-raiser was the German takeover of Austria in March. Moscow responded by calling for international discussions on measures to check further German aggression, in particular the threat posed by Hitler's nationalist ambitions to Czechoslovakia. Under the terms of the Soviet–Czechoslovak pact of May 1935, the USSR was pledged to aid Czechoslovakia. But Soviet aid was linked to France fulfilling its mutual assistance obligations first. Throughout the Czech crisis, therefore, Soviet policy had a singular refrain: France should fulfil its obligations to Czechoslovakia and so too would the Soviet Union. At the same time, the Soviets did not believe the crisis would result in a major war. They believed that if, with their support, France backed Czechoslovakia, Hitler would retreat from his demand for the Sudetenland. Alternatively, and more likely, Czechoslovakia would be betrayed to Germany by France (and Britain). In that scenario the Soviets did not rule out aiding Czechoslovakia unilaterally if the country resisted Hitler, but such aid would be limited and would fall short of an all-out declaration of war on Germany. Stalin was determined not to be dragged into a Soviet–German war while Britain and France stood on the sidelines, but he was prepared to take some risks.[9]

How far Stalin was prepared to go was never tested. Czech President Benes decided not to fight but to accept the Munich agreement. Under its terms the Sudetenland was annexed to Germany. In return, Hitler guaranteed the sovereignty of the rest of Czechoslovakia. The Soviets were outraged by their exclusion from the Munich negotiations and denounced the agreement as a betrayal not only of Czechoslovakia but of the general interests of peace. As Vyacheslav Molotov, the Soviet Premier, put it in his speech to the Supreme Soviet in November 1938:

> The fascist and so-called democratic powers of Europe came together at Munich and the victory over Czechoslovakia was complete ... The French and English governments sacrificed not only Czechoslovakia, but their own interests as well for the sake of an agreement with the aggressors ... The bargain between the fascist governments and the governments of the so-called democratic countries, far from lessening the danger of the outbreak of the second imperialist war, has on the contrary added fuel to the flames. The aggressive European countries have worked out future plans not only for carving up the map of Europe again, but also for a new sharing out of colonies.[10]

Munich was a mortal blow to the policy of collective security and all but ended Soviet hopes for an alliance with Britain and France against Hitler. But Moscow did not retreat into complete isolation. Instead, Stalin bided his time and awaited events. As Stalin said in his speech to the eighteenth party congress, while the Western appeasers might wish for a Soviet–German war, the course of Hitler's future expansion might be in their direction: 'It might be thought that areas of Czechoslovakia were given to the Germans at the price of a commitment to begin a war with the Soviet Union but the Germans are refusing to pay the bill and sending it away.'

The opportunity to revive Soviet collective security policy came five days after Stalin's speech. On 15 March 1939 Hitler occupied Prague and declared the Czech lands of Bohemia and Moravia to be a German protectorate. The dismemberment of Czechoslovakia was complete. Hitler's actions convinced British and French policymakers to abandon appeasement and seek a united front with the Soviet Union. On 18 March the British asked the Soviets what they would do in the event of an attack on Romania – seen as next in line for a German takeover. Litvinov responded by proposing the immediate convening of a conference of the representatives of the USSR, Britain, France, Poland and Romania. London thought that such a conference would be premature and proposed instead a declaration by Britain, France, Poland and the USSR on the integrity and independence of states in east and south-east Europe. The Soviets agreed to sign the declaration, but Litvinov doubted Britain and France had really abandoned appeasement. On 19 March he wrote to Ivan Maisky, his ambassador in London:

> The Czechoslovak events seem to have aroused public opinion in England and France ... Nonetheless, if in the immediate future Hitler does not commit any new acts of expansion and perhaps even makes a new peace gesture, Chamberlain and Daladier [the British and French premiers] will again start defending the Munich line ... The mood built up in government circles in favour of cooperation with the USSR cannot therefore be considered a lasting one. Even if the Czechoslovak events and the ultimatum to Rumania have somewhat alarmed Chamberlain and Daladier ... they fit in completely with their favourite concept of Germany's movement to the East.[11]

Litvinov's suspicions were further aroused by the British and French decision to drop the joint declaration with the Soviets and to issue, on 31 March 1939, a guarantee of Poland's independence – a guarantee later extended to include Romania and Greece. The Soviets were not impressed by the Anglo-French guarantees, on which they had not been consulted. In the event of war, the USSR would be in the front line of German aggression. The British and French knew they needed the USSR's support to defend Poland, Romania and Greece and they pressed the Soviets for such a commitment. Moscow's response was delivered on 17 April 1939 when Litvinov summoned Seeds, the British Ambassador, from the theatre and presented him with an eight-point plan for a triple alliance between Great Britain, France and the USSR:

1 The conclusion of a mutual assistance pact between the three states.
2 Anglo-Soviet French guarantees of all the east European states bordering the USSR, not just Poland, Romania and Greece.
3 An agreement on military commitments in the event of war.
4 A British announcement that their guarantee of Poland was directed against Germany, not the USSR.
5 A declaration that the Romanian–Polish treaty of alliance was directed against all states or else be revoked as directed against the USSR.
6 In the event of war no peace negotiations except by common consent.
7 Simultaneous signature of a political pact and a military convention.
8 Joint negotiations with Turkey for a mutual assistance agreement in the Balkans and the Near East.[12]

The triple alliance proposal set out the Soviet terms for an alliance with Britain and France against Germany. Above all, the Soviets wanted to secure a war-fighting alliance. Unlike in 1938, they did not believe Hitler could be stopped short of all-out war. It was no longer a question of collective security to deter Hitler from war but collective defence to fight the Germans when the time came. The Anglo-French response to the Soviets' triple alliance proposal was, to say the least, desultory. The French reiterated the proposal for the Soviet Union to underwrite the Anglo-French guarantees of Poland, Romania and Greece. Pressed by Moscow, the French agreed to a degree of reciprocity, but their redrafted proposal fell far short of the all-embracing system of security guarantees required by the Soviets. The British did not hurry to reply at all. The failure of the triple alliance proposal to make any real headway was fatal for Litvinov's position as People's Commissar for Foreign Affairs. On 3 May he was relieved of his job and replaced by Molotov.

Litvinov's removal from office provoked speculation about a change in Soviet foreign policy, a contemporary speculation subsequently taken up by many historians.[13] Typically, it has been suggested that Litvinov was sacked because he was a strong supporter of the triple alliance proposal and as a prelude to an about-turn in Soviet policy in favour of an alliance with Germany. But Litvinov was not particularly enthusiastic about the triple alliance and his replacement by Molotov was not followed by any change in Soviet policy towards Germany. It seems likely that Stalin replaced Litvinov because he was disappointed with the results of his Foreign Commissar's negotiations with the British and French. Stalin had decided to take direct charge of discussions about the triple alliance and no one was closer politically and personally to Stalin than Molotov. Their relationship dated back to the 1920s when Molotov was Stalin's chief lieutenant in the power struggle following Lenin's death. In 1930 Stalin made Molotov his Prime Minister, in which capacity he played an important role in foreign as well as domestic policy making. Stalin's and Molotov's views and attitudes on international affairs were closely aligned. As Stalin's appointment diary shows, the two men saw each other on an almost daily basis.[14] In short, Molotov could be relied upon to do exactly what Stalin wanted. Molotov also proved to be a very effective negotiator. William Strang, a British Foreign Office official who was sent to Moscow to help Seeds with the triple alliance negotiations, summed up their course as follows:

> The history of the negotiations is the story of how the British government were driven step by step, under stress of Soviet argument, under pressure from Parliament and the press and public opinion polls, under advice from the Ambassador at Moscow, and under persuasion from the French, to move towards the Soviet position. One by one they yielded points to the Russians. In the end they gave the Russians the main part of what they asked for. Everything in the essential structure of the draft agreement represented a concession to the Russians.[15]

Molotov's first meeting with Seeds was on 8 May 1939. The British Ambassador brought unwelcome news. Like the French, the British wanted a public declaration from the Soviets that they would support Britain and France in the event of hostilities arising from the Anglo-French guarantees to Poland and Romania.[16] This was completely unacceptable to Moscow: the whole point of the triple alliance proposal was to create a system of reciprocal security guarantees under which Soviet obligations to the British and French would be balanced by those to the USSR (i.e. Anglo-French support for Soviet action in defence of the Baltic States against German aggression). 'As you see, the English and French are demanding of us unilateral and gratuitous assistance with no intention of rendering us equivalent assistance,' Molotov cabled his ambassadors in London and Paris.[17]

On 14 May the Soviets responded to the British proposal with an *aide-mémoir* reiterating their triple alliance proposal.[18] On 27 May the British and French submitted to Molotov the text of a draft mutual assistance pact. It was limited in scope, its system of guarantees restricted to those states wanting to be guaranteed (thus excluding the Baltic States). But London and Paris had conceded Moscow's essential demands for a formal triple alliance and a system of reciprocal guarantees. To the amazement of Seeds and Jean Payart, the French diplomatic representative, Molotov immediately and angrily rejected the proposal. It did not contain, Molotov argued, any plan for the organization of effective defence against aggression, offered no indication of serious intent on the part of Britain and France, and proposed consultation rather than immediate assistance in the event of hostilities. The problem was that the mutual assistance envisaged in the Anglo-French draft was tied to League of Nations procedures. That, said Molotov, would transform the pact into 'a mere scrap of paper' because 'in the event of aggression mutual assistance will not be rendered immediately ... but only after deliberations in the League of Nations, with no one knowing what the results of such deliberations would be'. Payart and Seeds assured Molotov that the reference to the League of Nations was just a matter of public relations, but he remained implacable.[19]

On 31 May Molotov reported on the international situation to the Supreme Soviet – his first such speech since becoming People's Commissar for Foreign Affairs. His theme was a familiar one: the Anglo-French appeasement of aggressive states had encouraged their appetite for expansion, the prime example being the Munich agreement, which had led to the destruction of Czechoslovakia. Molotov noted recent changes in British and French foreign policy but said that 'at present it is impossible to say whether these countries have a sincere desire to abandon the policy of non-intervention, the policy of non-resistance to further aggression'. Molotov also revealed details of the recent diplomatic exchanges with London and Paris, making it clear that any mutual assistance pact would have to be based on equal and reciprocal obligations.[20]

The Soviet response to the Anglo-French draft pact was formally set out in a counter-draft on 2 June. The proposed mutual assistance treaty should give effect to League of Nations' principles, said the Soviet draft, but its operation would not be tied to League procedures, and Latvia, Estonia and Finland were named as countries the Soviets wanted guaranteed.[21] The catch, from the British and French point of view, was that the three Baltic States – fearing the Soviets as much as they did the Germans – did not want to be guaranteed by Moscow. But their rejection of a Soviet guarantee was of no importance to Molotov, who argued that the general interests of peace and the specific security needs of the USSR should override any Baltic objections. On 10 June Molotov instructed Maisky:

> To avoid misunderstandings we consider it necessary to make clear that the question of the three Baltic States is a question without whose satisfactory solution it would be impossible to bring the negotiations to a conclusion. We feel that without guaranteeing the security of the northwestern borders of the USSR by providing for decisive counter-action ... against any direct or indirect attack by an aggressor on Estonia, Latvia or Finland it will be impossible to satisfy public opinion in the Soviet Union ... this is not a question of technical formulas but one of agreeing on the substance of the question, after which it will not be difficult to find a suitable formula.[22]

On 15 June the British and French presented another document. It proposed that in the case of threats to states that did not want to be guaranteed the triple alliance partners would consult with each other and decide if there was 'a menace to security' that merited the implementation of mutual assistance obligations.[23] This proposal was immediately rejected by the Soviets on the grounds that the security guarantees were automatic in the case of states the British and French wanted guaranteed but subject to consultation in the case of states the USSR wanted guaranteed. If the British and French were unwilling to impose a guarantee on the Baltic States, said the Soviet *aide-mémoir*, then the whole issue of guarantees should be dropped and the triple alliance would only operate in the event of direct attacks on the three signatories.[24] That same day Molotov cabled Maisky and Yakov Suritz, Soviet Ambassador in Paris:

> The French and the English are putting the USSR in a humiliating and unequal position, something which under no circumstances would we accept ... We feel that the English and French want to conclude a treaty with us which would be advantageous to them and disadvantageous to us, that is, they do not want a serious treaty based on the principle of reciprocity and equality of obligations. It is clear we shall not accept such a treaty.[25]

Molotov's threat to take the issue of security guarantees off the negotiating table was a very effective tactic. For the British and French the whole point of the triple alliance was to gain Soviet support for their guarantees to Romania and especially Poland, a state under immediate threat from Hitler because of the dispute over control of the port of Danzig. By 1 July, the British and French had agreed to the Soviet position on the question of guarantees, on condition the list of countries guaranteed was not published but contained in a secret protocol.[26] This was acceptable to the Soviets, but a much larger problem was now looming. Integral to the Soviet triple alliance proposal was agreement on a military convention detailing the terms of practical military co-operation between the three states. Stalin was expecting to fight a war with Hitler in the very near future so he wanted clarity about what support he could expect from Britain and France. For this reason the Soviets insisted on the military and political treaties comprising the triple alliance being signed simultaneously. London and Paris, on the other hand, thought Hitler could be deterred from war by a political treaty followed by negotiations for a military convention. At a meeting with Seeds and Paul-Emile Naggier (the new French Ambassador) on 17 July Molotov made it clear this was unacceptable.[27] In a telegram to Maisky and Suritz later that day Molotov's anger about the prolonged, tedious and frustrating negotiations came to the fore:

> We are insisting that a military pact is an inseparable part of a military–political agreement ... and categorically reject the Anglo-French proposal that we should first agree on the 'political' part of the treaty and only then turn to the question of a military agreement. This dishonest Anglo-French proposal splits up what should be a single treaty into two separate treaties and contradicts our basic proposal to conclude the whole treaty simultaneously, including its military part, which is actually the most important and political part of the treaty. You understand that if the overall agreement does not include as an integral part an absolutely concrete military agreement, the treaty will be nothing but an empty declaration and this is something we cannot accept. Only crooks and cheats such as the negotiators on the Anglo-French side have shown themselves to be all this time could pretend that our demands for the conclusion of a political and military agreement are something new in the negotiations ... It seems nothing will come of the endless negotiations. Then they will have no one but themselves to blame.[28]

Again, London and Paris gave way. On 23 July Seeds and Naggier told Molotov that the Soviet proposal had been accepted. Molotov seemed very pleased and suggested Moscow as the venue for military discussions, to start immediately: 'The mere fact that the military conversations were starting would have a much greater effect in the world than any announcement about the political articles. It would be a powerful demonstration on the part of the three governments.'[29]

The military talks opened in Moscow on 12 August. The crunch came quickly when on 14 August the head of the Soviet delegation, Defence Commissar Marshal Kliment Voroshilov, posed the following question to the British and French delegation: would the Red Army be allowed to cross into Poland and Romania in the event of German aggression? The Anglo-French negotiators responded that when war came the Poles and the Romanians would surely invite the Red Army in. This was not satisfactory to the Soviets, who wanted to know in advance if their transit would be allowable. When it was suggested they should ask the Poles and Romanians for advance consent, Voroshilov replied that Poland and Romania were the allies of Britain and France and the subject of Anglo-French security guarantees, so it was up to London and Paris to obtain the permission. Talks continued while the British and French delegates consulted their governments but on 17 August Voroshilov proposed an adjournment until the receipt of an answer to this question. When the meeting resumed on 21 August the British and French had nothing definite to report and the talks were adjourned *sine die*, never to resume.[30]

The military talks collapsed because the British and French failed to satisfy Moscow on the question of the Red Army's right of passage across Poland and Romania. This was no side concern, but a vital strategic issue for the Soviets, not least because the Red Army's operational plans called for an advance into Poland and Romania in the event of war with Germany.[31] But that was only one facet of the failure of the triple alliance negotiations. The negotiations also failed because by summer 1939 Stalin had an alternative. By the time the Anglo-French military delegation arrived in Moscow, Molotov was already engaged in negotiations with Germany. Doubting the triple alliance negotiations would produce a satisfactory outcome, the Soviets had decided at the end of July 1939 to hedge their bets by seeing what Berlin had to offer.

The Germans had been trying to woo the Soviets since the beginning of the triple alliance negotiations.[32] Their motive – to avert the triple alliance – was self-evident and the German overtures were not at first taken seriously in Moscow. When Schulenburg, the German Ambassador in Moscow, made an approach on 20 May about re-opening trade talks, Molotov told him that he had

> the impression that the German government was playing some sort of game instead of conducting business-like economic negotiations; and that for such a game it should have looked for its partner in another country and not the government of the USSR ... We had come to the conclusion that for the success of the economic negotiations it was necessary to create a corresponding political basis.

Molotov further noted in his report to Stalin that

> throughout the whole conversation it was evident that for the ambassador my statement was most unexpected ... The ambassador strove for a more concrete explanation of the political basis that my statement had in mind but I avoided giving a concrete answer to this question.[33]

Schulenburg did not meet Molotov again until 28 June. The ambassador reminded Molotov of what had been said at their previous meeting about the political basis of Soviet–German relations. Germany, Schulenburg told Molotov, wanted not only to normalize relations with the Soviet Union, but to improve them. As proof of this he pointed to the restrained tone of the German press in relation to the USSR and to Germany's recent non-aggression pacts with Latvia and Estonia. He also reassured Molotov that Germany had no 'Napoleonic' plans in relation to the USSR. Molotov responded that the Soviet Union was interested in the normalization and improvement in relations with all countries, including Germany, but he wanted know how Berlin proposed to improve relations with the USSR. Since Schulenburg had nothing specific to propose, the conversation ended on an indeterminate note.[34]

The next major development came at the end of July when Georgii Astakhov, the Soviet diplomatic representative in Berlin, reported to Molotov on two conversations with Karl Schnurre, a German diplomat who specialized in economics and had been involved in past discussions about Soviet–German trade:

> Germany is prepared to discuss and come to an understanding with us on the questions that both sides are interested in, and to give all the security guarantees we would require from them … To my question about how confident he was that his words reflected the mood and intention of higher circles, Schnurre said that he spoke on the direct instructions of Ribbentrop [the German Foreign Minister] … Naturally, we didn't give Schnurre any hopes, limiting ourselves to general noises and promising to bring the talks to your attention.[35]

Two days later, on 29 July, Molotov sent Astakhov his reply:

> Political relations between the USSR and German may improve, of course, with an improvement in economic relations. In this regard Schnurre is, generally speaking, right. But only the Germans can say concretely how political relations should improve. Until recently the Germans did nothing but curse the USSR, did not want any improvement in political relations and refused to participate in any conferences with the USSR. If the Germans are now sincerely changing course and really want to improve political relations with the USSR, they are obliged to state what this improvement represents in concrete terms … The matter depends entirely on the Germans. We would, of course, welcome any improvement in political relations between the two countries.[36]

On 2 August the Germans made yet another approach when Foreign Minister Ribbentrop told Astakhov 'that there are no contradictions between our countries from the Black Sea to the Baltic. On all problems it is possible to reach agreement.'[37] The next day Schulenburg met Molotov and proposed an improvement in Soviet–German relations in three stages: firstly, the conclusion of an economic agreement; secondly, better press relations; and thirdly, the development of cultural and scientific cooperation. Schulenburg stressed, too, that there were no conflicts of interest between Germany and the USSR in the Baltic and that Berlin had no plans that ran counter to Soviet interests in Poland. Molotov's response was mixed: he welcomed the German desire for an improvement in relations but cast doubt on the sincerity and durability of the apparent shift in German foreign policy. Schulenburg's conclusion from the meeting was 'my overall impression is that the Soviet Government is at present determined to sign with England and France if they fulfill all Soviet wishes ... it will ... take a considerable effort on our part to cause the Soviet Government to swing about'.[38]

By the time Schulenburg next met Molotov on 15 August, the Anglo-Soviet–French military negotiations were already in progress. At the meeting Molotov asked the ambassador about the German government's attitude toward a non-aggression treaty between the two countries.[39] Two days later they met again. Molotov handed Schulenburg a formal written proposal for a non-aggression pact, together with a 'special protocol'. The ambassador pressed for Ribbentrop to be invited to Moscow for face-to-face negotiations, but Molotov refused to set a date.[40] At a further meeting on 19 August, Molotov made it clear that before Ribbentrop came to Moscow it had to be certain that an agreement would be reached, especially in relation to the special protocol. The meeting ended at 3.00 p.m. but at 4.30 p.m. Schulenburg was summoned back to the Kremlin and told by Molotov that Ribbentrop could come to Moscow on 26–27 August.[41] According to Stalin's appointments diary Molotov saw Stalin just before his meeting with Schulenburg and again after the second meeting, so the authorization for Ribbentrop's visit must have been cleared by Stalin on the telephone. But the date set by the Soviets was not soon enough for the Germans and on 21 August Schulenburg handed Molotov an urgent personal letter from Hitler to Stalin requesting that Ribbentrop be received on 22 August. 'The tension between Germany and Poland has become intolerable. Polish demeanour toward a great power is such that a crisis may arise any day,' Hitler wrote to Stalin. Two hours later Molotov delivered Stalin's positive reply to Schulenburg.[42]

Ribbentrop duly arrived in Moscow on 23 August. Stalin did most of the talking for the Soviet side at the meeting he and Molotov had with Ribbentrop, a pattern to be repeated in countless encounters to come with foreign diplomats. The outcome was the signature of a Soviet–German non-aggression treaty in which the two states pledged neutrality in the event of the other becoming involved in a war with a third party. Appended to the public treaty was a 'secret additional protocol' delineating future Soviet and German spheres of influence in Eastern Europe. With agreement sealed, Stalin proposed a toast to the health of Hitler and Molotov a toast to Stalin in recognition of the role his speech to the eighteenth party congress had played in bringing about a political reversal in relations with Germany. As Ribbentrop was leaving, Stalin told him that he could guarantee on his word of honour that the Soviet Union would not betray its new partner.[43]

The conclusion of the Nazi–Soviet pact signalled a new, neutralist course for Soviet foreign policy. What that meant was explained by Molotov in his speech to the Supreme Soviet on 31 August 1939. He began by explaining why the triple alliance negotiations had failed: Poland, encouraged by Britain, had rejected proposed Soviet military assistance, which meant it was not possible to arrive at a suitable military agreement. Following the failure of the military negotiations with Britain and France, said Molotov, the USSR decided to conclude a non-aggression pact with Germany. Explaining how it was possible for the Soviet Union to sign a non-aggression treaty with the anti-communist Nazi state, Molotov told his audience that 'the art of politics does not consist in increasing the number of one's country's enemies. On the contrary, the art of politics in this sphere is to reduce the number of such enemies and make the enemies of yesterday good neighbours, maintaining peaceable relations one with the other.' In conclusion Molotov stressed that both the Soviet pact with Germany and the triple alliance negotiations, unsuccessful though they were, showed that no important international questions could be decided without the participation of the USSR.[44]

Germany invaded Poland on 1 September 1939. On 17 September the Red Army invaded Poland from the east. This dual invasion was presaged in the secret additional protocol to the Nazi–Soviet pact:

> In the event of a territorial and political rearrangement of the areas belonging to the Polish state the spheres of influence of Germany and the USSR shall be bounded approximately by the line of the rivers Narew, Vistula and San. The question of whether the interests of both parties make desirable the maintenance of an independent Polish state and how such a state should be bounded can only be definitely determined in the course of further political developments.[45]

But this agreement was not a clear-cut advance decision to invade and partition Poland – Stalin was far too cautious for that. How he acted in relation to Poland would depend on the course of the German–Polish war and on the reaction of Britain and France. In the event, Poland collapsed surprisingly quickly, and the British and French, although declaring war on Germany, showed no inclination to become militarily involved in operations in the east. In such circumstances it was safe for the USSR to occupy by force its sphere of influence in Eastern Poland, which Ribbentrop began badgering Stalin to do from early September.[46]

The Soviet invasion was announced in a radio broadcast by Molotov, who claimed the Red Army was intervening in Eastern Poland to safeguard the Ukrainians and Belorussians who lived there.[47] This rationale was not as fanciful as it might seem. The Polish territories occupied by the Red Army consisted mainly of the western regions of the Ukraine and Belorussia, which lay east of the so-called 'Curzon Line' – the ethnographic frontier between Russia and Poland drawn up by a commission of the Paris Peace Conference in 1919. The actual border, however, had been determined by Poland's victory in the Russo-Polish war of 1919–20 and under the 1921 Treaty of Riga the Soviets were forced to cede Western Belorussia and Western Ukraine to Poland. But they were never reconciled to the permanent loss of those territories. The Soviet invasion of Eastern Poland embodied, therefore, patriotic–nationalist aspirations as well as the geopolitical logic of keeping the Germans out of Western Belorussia and Western Ukraine.

One politician who welcomed the Soviet invasion of Poland was Winston Churchill, who said in a radio broadcast on 1 October that 'we could have wished that the Russian armies should be standing on their present line as the friends and allies of Poland instead of as invaders. But that the Russian armies should stand on this line was clearly necessary for the safety of Russia against the Nazi menace.'[48] Of course, at this time Churchill still hoped that the Soviet Union could be weaned off neutrality and enticed into co-operation against Hitler. Stalin, however, had decided to ally himself with Hitler for the time being. At the end of September Ribbentrop returned to Moscow to negotiate a German–Soviet Boundary and Friendship Treaty that would settle the demarcation line between the two states in Poland. Following talks between Ribbentrop, Stalin and Molotov, the Soviet Union and Germany published a joint declaration on 28 September calling for an end to the war and blaming the Western powers for continuing hostilities.[49]

Molotov took up the theme of Anglo-French culpability for the war in his speech to the Supreme Soviet on 31 October 1939:

> In the past few months such concepts as 'aggression' and 'aggressor' have acquired new concrete connotation, new meaning. It is not hard to understand that we can no longer employ these concepts in the sense we did, say, three or four months ago. Today, as far as the European great powers are concerned, Germany is in the position of a state which is striving for the earliest termination of war and for peace, while Britain and France ... are in favour of continuing the war and are opposed to the conclusion of peace.

In his August speech Molotov had announced the Soviet Union's dealignment in European international politics. Now he specified the USSR's realignment alongside Germany, albeit as political collaborator not military ally:

> Since the conclusion of the Soviet–German non-aggression pact on 23 August an end has been put to the abnormal relations that have existed between the Soviet Union and Germany for a number of years. Instead of the enmity ... we now have a rapprochement and the establishment of friendly relations .... Relations between Germany and other western European bourgeois states have in the past two decades been determined primarily by Germany's efforts to break the fetters of the Versailles treaty ... This it was which in the long run led to the present war in Europe. The relations between the Soviet Union and Germany were based on a different foundation which had nothing whatever in common with perpetuating the post-war Versailles system. We have always held that a strong Germany is an indispensable condition for a durable peace in Europe.[50]

These were precisely the terms in which Soviet Russia had justified the Rapallo relationship with Germany. Stalin and Molotov proposed to revive the intensive political, economic and military co-operation with Germany that had existed in the 1920s. That relationship had disintegrated when Hitler came to power, but Stalin and Molotov never viewed the nature of the Nazi regime as an insurmountable obstacle to good relations. As the Soviets were fond of saying, the USSR stood for peaceful co-existence with all states, irrespective of their internal regime. Relations with Hitler had broken down because of his foreign policy, not his political ideology. Whether Hitler would revert to an anti-Soviet foreign policy remained an open question. Meanwhile, Stalin and Molotov did not rule out the possibility of long-term co-existence, even an alliance, with Nazi Germany. As Stalin told Ribbentrop on 27 September: 'Soviet foreign policy has always been based on the belief in the possibility of cooperation between Germany and the Soviet Union ... Hence it is with a clear conscience that the Soviet government begins the revival of collaboration with Germany. This collaboration represents a power that all other combinations must give way to.'[51]

Stalin has often been accused of being responsible for triggering the outbreak of the Second World War by signing a pact with Hitler that gave the Nazi dictator the confidence to attack Poland and risk a war with Britain and France. But that was not Stalin's analysis of the situation. He was convinced that war was inevitable so the issue was not how to deter Hitler's aggression, but whether to fight alongside Poland, Britain and France or to remain neutral. Stalin was sceptical about British and French intentions. He doubted the two powers were serious about wanting a triple alliance and suspected their goal was to trap the Soviet Union into fighting a war alone against Germany. He later told Churchill that he 'had the impression that the talks were insincere and only for the purpose of intimidating Hitler, with whom the Western Powers would later come to terms'.[52] Stalin said much the same thing to his closest confidants. 'We preferred agreements with the so-called democratic countries and therefore conducted negotiations,' he told the Comintern leader, Georgi Dimitrov, on 7 September 1939. 'But the English and the French wanted us for farmhands and at no cost.' In the same conversation with Dimitrov Stalin revealed another aspect of the calculation that led him to conclude a deal with Hitler:

> A war is on between two groups of capitalist countries ... for the redivision of the world, for the domination of the world! We see nothing wrong in their having a good hard fight and weakening each other. It would be fine if at the hands of Germany the position of the richest capitalist countries (especially England) was shaken. Hitler, without understanding it or desiring it, is shaking and undermining the capitalist system ... We can manoeuvre, pit one side against the other to set them fighting with each other as fiercely as possible. The non-aggression pact is to a certain degree helping Germany. Next time we'll urge on the other side.[53]

Some commentators have linked this statement to his speech to the eighteenth party congress and concluded that Stalin conspired to provoke a new world war in 1939 in order to precipitate a new wave of revolutionary upheavals in Europe – as had happened as result of the First World War, including, of course, the Bolshevik seizure of power in 1917. Some historians also cite a speech Stalin supposedly made to the Politburo on 19 August 1939 in which he reviewed the prospects for the 'Sovietization' of Europe as a result of a war that he intended to provoke and then prolong by signing the Nazi–Soviet pact. But that conclusion is false because the alleged speech is a forgery that first made its appearance in the French press in November 1939 as a piece of propaganda designed to discredit Stalin and to sow discord in Soviet–German relations.[54]

Far from plotting to provoke war in 1939, Stalin feared a major military conflict would revive the anti-capitalist coalition that had almost succeeded in toppling the Bolsheviks from power during the Russian Civil War. That was why he gambled on a pact with Hitler. While it was not a guarantee of peace and security, it did seem to offer the best chance of keeping the Soviet Union out of the coming war. Like everyone else, Stalin expected that if Britain and France did declare war on Germany as a result of their guarantees to Poland there would be a prolonged war of attrition, allowing the Soviet Union time to strengthen its defences. That assumption, however, proved to be a fundamental miscalculation. The Nazi–Soviet pact paid dividends for Stalin in the short term but only at the cost of substantially strengthening the Soviets' future enemy. Soviet neutrality helped Hitler to triumph over France as well as Poland and paved the way for German military hegemony in Europe. It became the springboard for Hitler's invasion of the Soviet Union in June 1941 that propelled the German armies all the way to Leningrad, Moscow and Stalingrad. Eventually, the Soviets were able to stabilize their defences and to counter-attack, but the cost was catastrophic. It is impossible to say whether the Soviet Union would have fared any better had Stalin decided to risk an early attack by standing up to Hitler in 1939.

Notes

1   *1941 God*, vol 2. Moscow, 1998, pp. 557–71.
2   I. Stalin, *Voprosy Leninizma*. Moscow, 1952, 11th ed., pp. 603–14. English translations of Stalin's speech may be found on the internet.
3   Cited by I.F. Maksimychev, *Diplomatiya Mira protiv Diplomatiya Voiny*. Moscow, 1981, p. 42.
4   On Soviet collective security policy see G. Roberts, *The Unholy Alliance: Stalin's Pact with Hitler*. London, 1989; J. Haslam, *The Soviet Union and the Struggle for Collective Security in Europe, 1933–1939*. London, 1984; J. Hochman, *The Soviet Union and the Failure of Collective Security in Europe, 1934–1938*. New York, 1984; S. Pons, *Stalin and the Inevitable War, 1936–1941*. London, 2002; and S. Dullin, *Des Hommes D'Influences: Les ambassadeurs de Staline en Europe, 1930–1939*. Paris 2001.
5   J. Degras (ed.), *Soviet Documents on Foreign Policy*, vol. 3, 1933–41. Oxford, 1953, pp. 51, 70.
6   *Dokumenty Vneshnei Politiki SSSR* vol. 18. Moscow, 1970, doc. 148.
7   On Soviet foreign policy and the Spanish Civil War see G. Roberts, 'Soviet Foreign Policy and the Spanish Civil War, 1936–1939' in C. Leitz (ed.), *Spain in an International Context*. New York, 1999; D.T. Cattell, *Soviet Diplomacy and the Spanish Civil War*. Berkeley 1957; E.H. Carr,

The Comintern and the Spanish Civil War. London, 1984; S.G. Payne, *The Spanish Civil War, the Soviet Union and Communism*. New Haven, 2004; and D. Kowalsky, *Stalin and the Spanish Civil War*. Columbia, 2004.

8 On Soviet–German relations in the 1930s see G. Roberts, *The Soviet Union and the Origins of the Second World War*. London, 1995, ch. 3.

9 On Soviet policy during the Czechoslovakian crisis see J. Haslam, 'The Soviet Union and the Czechoslovakian Crisis of 1938', *Journal of Contemporary History* vol. 14 (July 1979), pp. 441–61; I. Lukes, 'Did Stalin Desire War in 1938?, *Diplomacy and Statecraft* vol. 2, no. 1 (March 1991), pp. 3–53; Z. Steiner, 'The Soviet Commissariat of Foreign Affairs and the Czechoslovakian Crisis in 1938', *The Historical Journal*, vol. 42, no. 3 (1999), pp. 751–79; H. Ragsdale, *The Soviets, the Munich Crisis, and the Coming of World War II*. New York, 2004; and M.J. Carley, 'Only the USSR has Clean Hands: The Soviet Perspective on the Failure of Collective Security and the Collapse of Czechoslovakia, 1934–1938', *Diplomacy and Statecraft* vol. 21, no. 2 (2010), pp. 202–25.

10 Degras, *Soviet Documents on Foreign Policy*, pp. 309–11.

11 *Soviet Peace Efforts on the eve of World War II* (hereafter *SPE*). Moscow, 1973, doc. 167.

12 Ibid., doc. 239.

13 On discussions of Litvinov's dismissal see: G. Roberts, 'The Fall of Litvinov: A Revisionist View', *Journal of Contemporary History* vol. 27 (1992), pp. 639–57; A. Resis, 'The Fall of Litvinov: Harbinger of the German–Soviet Non-Aggression Pact', *Europe–Asia Studies* vol. 52, no.1 (2000), pp. 33–56.

14 *Na Prieme u Stalina*. Moscow, 2008.

15 W. Strang, 'The Moscow Negotiations 1939' in D. Dilkes (ed.), *Retreat from Power*, vol.1. London, 1981. On the triple alliance negotiations see M.J. Carley, *1939: The Alliance That Never Was and the Coming of World War II*. Chicago, 1999' and G. Roberts, 'The Alliance That Failed: Moscow and the Triple Alliance Negotiations, 1939', *European History Quarterly* vol. 26, no. 3 (1996), pp. 383–414.

16 *SPE* docs 278, 279.

17 Ibid., doc. 280.

18 Ibid., doc. 291.

19 Ibid., docs 311, 312.

20 Ibid., doc. 314.

21 Ibid., doc. 315.

22 Ibid., doc. 323.

23 Ibid., doc. 329.

24 Ibid., doc. 330.

25 Ibid., doc. 331.

26 Ibid., doc. 357.

27 *Documents on British Foreign Policy* (hereafter *DBFP*), 2nd series, vol. 6, doc. 338; *Documents Diplomatiques Francais* (hereafter *DDF*), 2nd series, vol. 17, docs. 223–4.

28 *SPE* doc. 376.

29 *DBFP* vol.7, pp. 115–20; *DDF*, vol.17, doc. 282.

30 The Soviet records of the military talks may be found in *SPE* docs 411, 412, 413, 415, 417, 425, 429 and 437.

31 *1941 God*, vol. 2, pp. 557–71.

32 See Roberts, *The Soviet Union and the Origins of the Second World War*, ch. 5.

33 *God Krizisa, 1938–1939*, vol. 1. Moscow, 1990, doc. 362.

34 Ibid., doc. 442.

35 Cited by S.A. Gorlov, 'Sovetsko-Germanskii Dialog Nakanune Pakta Molotova-Ribbentrop 1939g', *Novaya i Noveishaya Istoriya* no.4 (1993), p. 22.

36 *God Krizisa*, doc. 511.

37 Ibid., doc. 523.

38 *Nazi–Soviet Relations*. New York, 1948 (hereafter *NSR*), pp. 39–41.

39 Ibid., pp. 52–7; *Dokumenty Vneshnei Politiki 1939 God* (hereafter *DVP 1939*), vol. 1. Moscow, 1992, doc. 556.

40   *God Krizisa*, doc. 570; *NSR*, pp. 59–61.
41   *God Krizisa*, doc. 572; *NSR*, pp. 59–61.
42   *God Krizisa*, docs 582–3; *NSR*, pp. 66–9.
43   *NSR*, pp. 72–8.
44   Degras (ed.), *Soviet Documents on Foreign Policy*, pp. 361–71.
45   *NSR*, p. 78.
46   Ibid., p. 86.
47   Degras (ed.), *Soviet Documents on Foreign Policy*, pp. 374–6.
48   Cited in G. Roberts, *Stalin's Wars: From World War to Cold War, 1939–1953*. London, 2006, p. 38.
49   *NSR*, p. 108.
50   Degras (ed.), *Soviet Documents on Foreign Policy*, pp. 388–92.
51   *DVP 1939*, vol. 2, p. 609.
52   Remarks recorded by Churchill's interpreter Major A.H. Birse at a meeting in Moscow in August 1942: Harriman Papers, Library of Congress Manuscript Division, Chronological File 14–15 August 1942, container 162.
53   I. Banac (ed.), *The Diary of Georgi Dimitrov*. New Haven, 2003, pp. 115–16.
54   See Roberts, *Stalin's Wars*, p. 35.

Chapter 25

American Isolationism and the Coming of the Second World War

Manfred Jonas

In the summer of 1935 the US Congress responded to the prospect of a new war in Europe with a neutrality act. This was the high water mark of US isolationism. That policy originated in the late eighteenth century when the US wanted to protect its still fragile independence by extricating itself from the clutches of a Europe dominated by Britain, France and Spain, the maritime powers who had long controlled the Americas. The United States owed its existence at least in part to the rivalry among those powers. France, after all, had provided decisive military support to Britain's North American colonies after 1778, mainly as a way of striking back at the British, to whom it had surrendered its own North American colonies just fifteen years earlier. Alliance with France, however, made it virtually impossible for the new nation to settle its problems either with Britain, whose recognition of American independence was half-hearted at best, or with Spain, which controlled both the mouth of the Mississippi River, crucial to trade from America's interior, and Florida into which the new Americans were moving.

When the French Revolution appeared to give the relationship an ideological basis as well and when Britain and France went to war with each other in 1793, a US–French alliance became a distinct liability. In 1794 the US Congress passed its first ever neutrality act. This was an assertion of independence in defence of America's commercial and territorial interests. It did not seek to cut the country off from world affairs or keep the US out of all wars. In his farewell address in 1796, President George Washington provided the rationale for this policy when he asserted that 'Europe has a set of primary interests which to us have none or a very remote relation', but urged his countrymen to take advantage of their 'detached and distant situation' while extending commercial relations with other nations as far as possible.

In his first inaugural Presidential address in 1801 Thomas Jefferson, ever the phrase-maker, added peace and honest friendship with all nations to the list of the country's foreign policy aims but concentrated, as he was to do during his presidency, on an independent policy that promoted and protected American commerce with all nations, while entering into 'entangling alliances with none'.[1] By the end of his presidency, Jefferson had gone a considerable way toward assuring the permanence of the United States. He successfully defended US commerce, displayed military prowess in a war against the Barbary pirates and virtually doubled the size of the country with the purchase of Louisiana from Napoleon – a deal only made possible by the existing rivalries among Great Britain, France and Spain. These rivalries continued to challenge America's independence and to threaten its trade. The Royal Navy harassed US shipping, impressed American sailors and confiscated American goods in transit to France. This culminated in war between 1812 and 1814. By any rational measure, the United States lost that war, but, given Britain's other problems, was able to gain peace terms that led to disarmament on the Great Lakes, clarified commercial relations and settled much of the northern boundary of the Louisiana Purchase. For the first time, dealings with the British took on the character of negotiations between equals.

The Napoleonic Wars not only changed the balance of power but also the relationship of the United States to Europe. Spain's subjugation by Napoleon encouraged successful revolutions in its American colonies and assured her continuing imperial decline. In 1818 the US exploited Spanish weakness by acquiring what had been Spanish Florida and laying claim to northern California, where Russia and Britain already maintained outposts. In 1821 rumours that the Hoy Alliance, led by Russia, might seek to restore its colonies to Spain caused US President James Monroe to announce what later became known as 'The Monroe Doctrine'. On 2 December 1823 he declared before Congress that the American continents 'are henceforth not to be considered as subjects for future colonization by any European powers' and the US would regard any attempt to extend 'their system' to the western hemisphere 'as dangerous to our peace and safety'.[2] He rejected a British proposal for a joint statement opposing the return of its colonies to Spain in favour of this independent, unilateral action. When no effort was ever made to restore her American colonies to Spain, the wisdom of a policy of independence seemed confirmed. Russia even withdrew its small colonial settlement in California and set the southern boundary of its colony of Alaska north of anything ever claimed by the United States. Diplomatic relations were quickly established with the new countries in Latin America and continental expansion under the banner of 'manifest destiny' became a matter largely outside the realm of foreign policy.

The United States sympathized with the European revolutions of 1830 and 1848, but offered no assistance to the revolutionaries. In his annual message to Congress of 2 December 1845 President James Knox Polk reaffirmed Monroe's 'doctrine' in an effort to keep Great Britain and France out of Texas, and then proceeded to admit Texas to the American union. The United States negotiated with Great Britain over the division of the Oregon Territory and then fought a war with Mexico that involved no European power even indirectly in order to acquire California. The US tried to buy Cuba from Spain in the 1850s and was instrumental in bringing Japan into full contact with the world at large. The country's major concern was no longer maintenance of its independence, which seemed assured, but of internal unity, which was not.

The bitter four-year American Civil War that preserved that unity did not alter the tenor of the nation's policy with Europe. Quite to the contrary, non-interference in purely European matters seemed an excellent example to set while trying to prevent various European powers from taking sides in the war in America. Thus, on 11 May 1863, Secretary of State William H. Seward rejected an invitation to join France, Great Britain and Austria in an attempt to persuade Russia to modify its designs on Poland by citing Washington's afore-mentioned farewell address. He applauded America's successful resistance to 'seductions from what, superficially viewed, seemed a course of isolation and indifference' and he praised the policy of 'nonintervention, straight, absolute, and peculiar as it may seem to other nations',[3] and vigorously reasserted the Monroe Doctrine in an effort to end French schemes for control of Mexico.

After the Civil War, the United States entered a period of rapid growth, and this led to greater involvement in world affairs. By 1884 the US had not only joined the International Red Cross but also sent a delegation to the Berlin Conference dealing with the problems of the Congo Free State. The growth of American trade and the build-up of a modern navy led to the acquisition of trading rights and coaling stations not only in the Pacific, but in Africa and along the Persian Gulf as well. The United States now wanted – and obtained – a pledge from the powers for an 'open door' so that its goods could enter the Congo on fair terms. On taking office in 1885, President Grover Cleveland opposed that agreement on the basis it could possibly become an entangling alliance.[4]

Yet the process of US involvement in international affairs accelerated. In 1888, the United States hosted the first international conference of its own, the Washington Conference on Samoa, and it regularly took part in international conferences for the remainder of the nineteenth century. It sent delegates to the First International Peace Conference at The Hague in 1899, among them Captain Alfred Thayer Mahan, whose book *The Influence of Sea Power* on *History: 1660–1783* had provided a blueprint for America's rise to world power and influenced the growth of German and Japanese naval expansion as well. At that conference, the US delegates supported the creation of the Permanent Court of International Arbitration, but signed the convention establishing the tribunal only with this reservation:

> Nothing contained in this convention shall be so construed as to require the United States of America to depart from its traditional policy of not intruding upon, interfering with, or entangling itself in the political questions or policy or internal administration of any foreign State; nor shall anything contained in the said Convention be construed to imply a relinquishment by the United States of America of its traditional attitude toward purely American questions.[5]

By this time, Great Britain had effectively accepted the Monroe Doctrine by submitting a long-standing boundary dispute with Venezuela to international arbitration. In taking note of that, Secretary of State Richard Olney asserted that

the United States is practically sovereign on this continent, and its fiat is law upon
the subjects to which it confines its interposition ... because, in addition to all other
grounds, its infinite resources combined with its isolated position render it master of
the situation and practically invulnerable as against any and all other powers.[6]

Where Monroe had acted sixty years earlier from recognition of US weakness,
Olney now spoke from a perception of obvious strength.

By the late nineteenth century The United States had built a sizeable navy,
gone to war with Spain, acquired Puerto Rico, Hawaii and the Philippines and
become a considerable power in the Far East. In direct consequence, Britain
in March 1898 proposed a joint effort to insure equal commercial opportunity
in China. The British Ambassador in Washington was promptly informed
that any joint action would be inconsistent with the traditional policy of the
United States. Instead, Secretary of State John Hay prepared his own so-called
Open Door notes to the powers the following January asking them, in effect,
to provide 'a fair field and no favour' in the competition for trade in the Far
East.[7] Like President Monroe, he rejected joint action with Britain in favour
of independent action. Within a year, the US contributed to an international
military force for the first time when 5,000 US troops from the Philippines
helped to put down the Boxer Rebellion in China.

After becoming President in 1901, Theodore Roosevelt increased American
involvement in world affairs still further. He personally began to play an
ever-larger role on the world stage. He made America's new military might
visible to everyone by sending the battle fleet around the world in 1907. He
vastly expanded the scope of the Monroe Doctrine by proclaiming that it was
the nation's duty to exercise 'an international police power' in the countries
below the Rio Grande.[8] He also sought to maintain the open door in Asia by
negotiating an end to the 1904–5 Russo-Japanese War with a treaty concluded
in Portsmouth, New Hampshire and agreed to participate in the Algeciras
Conference in 1907–8, where he attempted to maintain an open trade policy
in Morocco against French demands for a trade monopoly. Roosevelt hugely
enjoyed playing an active role in world politics and believed that his various
interventions, whether as arbitrator, conciliator or policeman, were of great
benefit to the United States. Like the US Senate which, after some persuasion,
ratified the Algeciras treaty in 1908, he was, however, 'without purpose to
depart from the traditional American foreign policy'.[9]

Six years later, President Woodrow Wilson responded to the outbreak of war
in Europe as Washington had in 1793 with a declaration of neutrality and an
appeal to the American people to be 'impartial in thought as well as in action'.
Wilson ran for re-election in 1916 under the slogan 'He kept us out of war.'
He had not changed his thinking when in his note to all of the powers of 22
January 1917 he called for a peace without victory to be maintained by a League
of Nations. When Wilson took the United States into war against Germany and
those allied with her on 2 April 1917 he stressed that it was a unilateral act in

defence of America's commercial and maritime rights. It was almost as an after-thought that he added the much quoted phrase 'the world must be made safe for democracy'. Wilson waited until the overthrow of the Tsar brought democracy temporarily to Russia before asking Congress to declare war, and the US entered no formal alliance, but participated in the war as an 'associated power'.

The entry of the United States tipped the stalemated war in Western Europe in favour of Britain and France, and Wilson soon emerged as spokesman for the shape of the post-war world. The German government sent its request for an armistice to the US President and it was Wilson who laid down the conditions that had to be met. At the top of the list was regime change in Germany and amongst its allies. By the time the armistice was signed on 11 November 1918 the Kaiser was in exile in Holland and Germany had become a Republic.

When Wilson left for Versailles on 4 December he was hailed as a world hero, a supreme peace maker, and the saviour of mankind. He was triumphantly received by the populace in all the Allied capitals he visited. The increasing involvement of the United States in international affairs was now apparently complete. The USA had emerged as a world leader and now had the oppor-tunity to shape the new world order that followed Germany's defeat. For a brief moment it seemed possible that a nation that had become rich and powerful enough so that it no longer needed to fear being forced into actions that contra-vened its interests could go far to reshape the world in its own image. Franklin D. Roosevelt was to have considerable success in doing so a quarter century later.

Yet Woodrow Wilson never got the chance to try. The treaty the US President brought back from Versailles and asked the Senate to ratify was in many ways a flawed document. Wilson had fought with only very modest success against too punitive a treaty and had been forced to make many compromises in order to win acceptance for what he regarded as the essential element among his Fourteen Points: a general association of nations affording mutual guarantees of political independence and territorial integrity to great and small states alike. Those compromises affected self-determination, boundaries, reparations and other largely European matters and could be seen as setting this country squarely on the path to permanent entanglement in European affairs. So, of course, did the security treaty Wilson signed at Versailles, which guaranteed France's border with Germany. When the Senate failed to ratify the treaty and thereby rejected membership in the League of Nations the word isolationism entered the political vocabulary to characterize America's traditional foreign policy.[10]

It would be wrong to think, however, that refusal to join the League did anything to isolate the United States from Europe or the world. Quite the contrary: the US was richer and stronger than ever and much of Europe was in a trough of economic depression and political instability. Such a situation required greater international involvement than ever to make the world into a place in which America could continue to prosper. Secretary of State Charles

Evans Hughes and President Herbert Hoover worked hard during the 1920s to achieve that goal while co-operating with the League, up to a point. Their policy of involvement without actual commitment is visible in various initiatives taken during the 1920s such as the Dawes and Young Plans on German reparations, the limitation of naval armaments and the maintenance of the open door in the Far East. It was on display in 1926 when the Senate approved adherence to the World Court, but only with the unacceptable reservation 'that the court shall not ... without the consent of the United States, entertain any request for an advisory opinion touching any dispute or question in which the United States has or claims an interest'.[11]

Another graphic illustration of US involvement in the new world order that emerged at Paris was the Kellogg–Briand Pact. The French Foreign Minister Artistide Briand was looking for a security guarantee from the United States. So on the tenth anniversary of US entry into the World War he proposed a treaty to outlaw war between the two countries. Secretary of State Frank B. Kellogg rejected the idea of any commitment to a European power for the usual reasons, but under pressure from the domestic peace lobby he turned Briand's idea into a multi-national pact to outlaw war as an instrument of national policy. It was ultimately signed by seventy-seven nations. This Pact of Paris was a pious piece of paper that contained no enforcement provisions. Still, the Senate ratified it only after receiving assurances that the United States retained the right not to enforce the treaty against violators.

Kellogg won the Nobel Peace Prize for this in 1929 just as the collapse of the New York stock market triggered a world-wide depression. But Hoover remained as convinced as ever that America had no need for collective arrangements. '[We] are more free from the haunting fear of attack than any other people in the world,' he reassured the Daughters of the American Revolution in an Armistice Day address. While acknowledging US responsibility to work for world peace, he asserted that it could 'only be fulfilled to its fullest measure by maintaining the fullest independence', and in particular by 'independence from any combination pledged to the use of force to maintain peace'.[12] It was a restatement of the traditional isolationist position.

By the time Japanese armies invaded Manchuria in September 1931 the Great Depression was approaching its nadir and foreign relations were receiving little attention in the United States. Though we now tend to regard the Manchurian crisis as a prelude to the Second World War, that was by no means clear at the time. Japan's action clearly violated the Kellogg–Briand Pact and the Nine-Power Treaty of 1922 to both of which the United States was a party, and the US responded by condemning the Japanese action and by a adopting a policy of non-recognition.

Shortly after China brought the Mukden Incident before the League, Hoover reminded his cabinet in a memo that '[we] are not parties to the League of Nations, the covenant of which has also been violated ... We should co-operate with the rest of the world', and 'we should do so as long as that cooperation remains in the field of moral pressures'.[13] When the League Council discussed Japan's actions in October, the United States agreed to send Prentiss Gilbert, its Consul at Geneva, to attend the meetings, but only to discuss the possible application of the Kellogg–Briand Pact. When the League attempted to draw Gilbert into a more general discussion, Stimson instructed him to cease attending meetings, and only reluctantly agreed, after a telephone call from British Foreign Secretary Lord Reading, to let him go to one more open and one more secret session as an observer at a seat away from the conference table. When it turned out that there were no seats away from the table and when Briand added his plea that Gilbert should nevertheless remain, Stimson reluctantly agreed 'to let him go on sitting at the damned table' on condition that he 'keep his mouth shut'.[14] When Japan completed its conquest of Manchuria before the League had taken any action, Stimson announced that the United States 'does not intend to recognize any situation treaty or agreement which may be brought about by means contrary to the covenants and obligations of the Pact of Paris of April 27, 1928, to which treaty both China and Japan, as well as the United States, are parties'. Stimson's doctrine of non-recognition was, as Sir John T. Pratt pointed out, 'a peculiarly American technique, the fruit of American isolationism'.[15]

When Japan responded with an attack on Shanghai on 28 January 1932, the United States sent troops and naval vessels there and persuaded Britain, France and Italy to join in asking Japan to stop the fighting and to enter into negotiations with China in the presence of neutral observers. Japan refused this offer of mediation on 4 February and the United States took no further action. Neither did the League of Nations, which limited itself to condemning Japan's action, withholding recognition from Manchukuo and calling for Japanese withdrawal from China. A day later Stimson expressed the United States' support of the League while still 'reserving for itself independence of judgment with regard to method and scope'. Six months earlier, in accepting his party's nomination for a second term, Hoover had told the convention delegates: 'We shall … consult with other nations in times of emergency to promote world peace. We shall enter no agreement committing us to any future course of action or which shall call for the use of force to preserve peace.'[16]

In the election 1932, questions of foreign policy played no role of any kind. The new President, Franklin D. Roosevelt, entered office in March 1933 without intent to alter the line espoused by Hoover. His inaugural address made only the briefest reference to non-domestic matters, and that referred to the policy of the 'good neighbour', a term first used by Secretary of State Henry Clay in the 1820s to describe the relationship between the United States and the new countries of Latin America under the Monroe Doctrine. Roosevelt gave support to the Geneva Conference on Arms Limitation to which the United States had sent delegates in 1932 and, in discussions with Britain's Prime Minister Ramsay MacDonald and French Premier Eduard Herriot in Washington in April, the US agreed not undercut collective actions against aggressors. When the American delegate spoke at Geneva on 22 May however, he expressed America's willingness to consult with others in case of a threat to peace, but promised not to oppose undercut collective action against a designated aggressor only 'if we concur in the judgment rendered'. On 29 May 1934 he added for purposes of clarification that the United States would not 'participate in European political negotiations and settlements and will not make any commitment whatever to use its armed forces for the settlement of any dispute anywhere'.[17] Hoover's policy of involvement without commitment thus clearly remained in force.

The near collapse of the American economy in the early 1930s brought domestic issues to the fore and led to a general re-examination of America's involvement with the world. The US withdrawal from the London Economic Conference in the summer of 1933 was an indication that the United States intended to pursue an independent course in the world financial crisis. In April 1934, the Johnson Act prohibiting loans to nations in default on debts stemming from the First World War reflected unhappiness with America's earlier involvement in 'Europe's wars'. Implementing the 'Good Neighbour' Policy, on the other hand, promised to stimulate American trade without requiring commitments in Europe. This became the favoured path for overcoming the economic crisis at home. Roosevelt sent reciprocal trade bills to Congress in March of 1934, convinced that full recovery could not be achieved without the restoration of America's shrunken trade. Soon after the passage of this legislation, the Export–Import Bank was set up to facilitate that commerce. Secretary of State Cordell Hull was to negotiate twenty-one reciprocal trade agreements covering three-fifths of American exports and imports before the outbreak of war in Europe. The recognition of the Soviet Union in November 1933 and the passage three months later of the Tydings–McDuffie Act that promised independence to the Philippines within ten years were similarly prompted, at least in part, by the need to revive commerce to offset the effects of the Depression by reducing, if anything, America's international involvement.

Yet developments in Europe that increasingly threatened world peace and order became more difficult to ignore. A split developed between those who saw this as a reason for reducing America's world involvement still further and now adopted the label of isolationist and for the remainder of the decade did battle with the more Wilsonian supporters of the traditional policy who became increasingly concerned about the threat itself. As international crises grew more dangerous during the late 1930s, the battle over isolationism took centre stage. The often-heated rhetoric of this debate sometimes obscured the fact that the two sides shared the same tradition and differed with regard to the desirable extent of world involvement but were in full agreement on the matter of commitment. For the isolationists, a greater degree of separation from the concerns of Europe seemed necessary. 'I believe', Senator William E. Borah of Idaho explained to the Council of Foreign Relations,

> in the foreign policy which offers peace to all nations, trade and commerce with all
> nations, honest friendship with all nations, political commitments, express or implied

with none … In matters of trade and commerce we have never been isolationists and never will be. In matters of finance, unfortunately, we have never been isolationists and never will be. But in all matters political, in all commitments of any nature or kind which encroach in the slightest upon the free and unembarrassed action of our people, or which circumscribe their discretion and judgment, we have been free, we have been independent, we have been isolationists.

A fellow isolationist, Senator Hiram Johnson of California, voted against American adherence to the World Court 1935, insisting that joining would be another attempt 'to meddle and muddle … in those controversies that Europe has and that Europe never will be rid of' and warning that 'going into the Court will ultimately mean going into the League of Nations'.[18]

The Nye Committee that the Senate set up in 1934 to determine whether bankers and munitions-makers had led the United States into the First World War was headed by an isolationist. It concluded that future wars could best be avoided not by co-operative efforts to maintain peace, but by neutrality legislation that would curb the dangerous proclivities of vested interests. On 17 April 1934 Secretary of State Cordell Hull – who was not an isolationist – set up a high-level departmental committee to begin a study of the question of neutrality legislation. That committee turned for advice to Charles Warren, a leading American authority on international law, who obliged with a lengthy memorandum entitled 'Some Problems in the Maintenance and Enforcement of the Neutrality of the United States.' The Warren memorandum called for an impartial arms embargo on all belligerents, the limitation of arms shipments to neutrals, a ban on American travel on belligerent vessels and the restriction of contraband trade with belligerents to pre-war levels.[19] In substance, Warren's proposals differed only slightly from those ultimately developed by the Nye Committee. Roosevelt expressed strong interest in these proposals and asked the State Department to prepare neutrality legislation for submission to Congress. While the State Department was still wrestling with this problem, he met with the Nye Committee on 19 March 1935 and asked it to consider the entire neutrality question with a view to submitting legislation.

The Neutrality Act of 31 August 1935 was loudly applauded by isolationists, but it was passed by very large majorities in both houses of Congress and promptly signed by a President who was clearly no isolationist. He would have preferred more flexible legislation, but had no more intention than did the isolationists of departing from America's traditional policy. That was still the case the following year when the law was extended. A further restriction was added to the mandatory Neutrality Act of 1937, which became law on 31 May.

Only a month after the 1935 Neutrality Act became law, Italy invaded Ethiopia. The US responded by issuing its required neutrality proclamation prohibiting the export of arms, ammunition and implements of war to both belligerents and forbidding Americans to travel on belligerent vessels. The League of Nation branded Italy as the aggressor and began imposing sanctions on 11 October 1935. In subsequent communications with the British and Italian ambassadors Hull made it clear that American actions with regard to the Italo-Abyssinian War were 'developed under our own separate, independent course and initiative and without the slightest relationship to sanctions or any other movements of other nations or peace agencies at Geneva'.[20] Those actions amounted to trying to stay as far out of the picture as possible.

The State Department had first learned of Mussolini's designs on Abyssinia (modern-day Ethiopia) in September 1934. Coming shortly on the heels of Germany's withdrawal from the Geneva Disarmament Conference and from the League of Nations itself, Italy's preparation for war in Africa made peace in Europe all the more precarious. When Ethiopia brought the matter formally to the League in June 1935 it received a chilly reception, since Britain and France were still trying to keep Mussolini on their side rather than Hitler's. On 3 July an increasingly desperate Emperor Haile Selassie asked the US to help prevent war from breaking out in contravention of the Kellogg–Briand Pact. Hull's reply indicating support for the pact but no intention to invoke it produced a headline in the *New York Times* that read 'President Rejects Ethiopia's Appeal for Peace Effort'. An even more desperate move by the Emperor to give the US a direct economic stake by granting an oil concession to a subsidiary of the Standard Vacuum Oil Company only led the State Department to call in the officers of the company and persuade them to terminate the concession.[21]

Germany's remilitarization of the Rhineland in March 1936 added to tensions in Europe and effectively ended the League's effort to impose sanctions on Italy in favour of a policy of appeasement designed to keep Mussolini in counterbalance to Hitler. When the Spanish Civil War erupted on 17 July, Germany and Italy offered military support to Franco at once while paying lip-service to Britain's policy of non-intervention. The United States sought to insure its own non-involvement by imposing an arms embargo on Spain. Though Roosevelt preferred a discretionary embargo, he acquiesced in the mandatory one Congress approved early in 1937 with only a single dissenting vote, once again demonstrating the US determination to keep its distance from European wars. When fighting broke out in China on 7 July and turned into full-scale war by mid-August, Roosevelt did not invoke the neutrality act in this undeclared war because he believed that would hurt China far more than Japan, but he felt compelled to address the world situation once more. In his so-called 'quarantine speech' of 5 October he bemoaned the fact that 'the security of 90 percent of the population of the world is being jeopardized by the remaining 10 percent', who are responsible for the present 'reign of terror and international lawlessness', and for the first time warned publicly that 'if those things come to pass in other parts of the world let no one imagine that America will escape, that it may expect mercy, that this Western Hemisphere will not be attacked'. He had no suggestion as to what the United States might actually do, and repeated references to the Kellogg–Briand Pact and Nine-Power Treaty suggested no change in US policy was imminent.[22] But the idea that the United States and all the Americas were in danger effectively changed the nature of the discourse.

Though the speech was prompted by renewed war in the Far East, Roosevelt was certain that the main threat to world peace came from Nazi Germany and that the development of the airplane into a lethal long-distance weapon made it a threat to the United States. A week later he told the press that he planned to ask Congress for an additional $500,000,000 in defence funds at once and shortly thereafter asked Assistant Secretary of the Army Louis Johnson to work out plans for a substantial expansion of the American air force. He further suggested that the production of military aircraft be raised from 2,600 to 15,000 per year. At the same time, he approved a French mission to the United States to discuss purchases of planes and the construction of aircraft plants in Canada.[23] In May, he had signed the Naval Expansion Act of 1938, which provided for a two-ocean navy and had put an operational Atlantic squadron in place by September.

If Hitler's bellicosity and Germany's rapid remilitarization had created that threat, the annexation of Austria to the Reich in March 1938 heightened it, particularly when it was soon followed by the first threats against Czechoslovakia and, not long thereafter, by Mussolini's seizure of Albania. These events moved Roosevelt to renewed attempts to ease tensions. He called the Evian Conference of thirty-two nations, which met in July to discuss the issue of Jewish refugees fleeing from Nazi Germany and revived an earlier plan to involve nine small powers with the United States in an effort to lend support to Britain's attempt to reach a practical understanding with Germany. As Hitler continued to threaten Czechoslovakia, Roosevelt sent him a message urging continued negotiations, to which Hitler replied with a tirade about self-determination and the rights of the Sudeten-Germans. Roosevelt now suggested that a conference of all interested parties be called if the negotiations broke down. 'The Government of the United States', said Roosevelt, 'has no political involvements in Europe and will assume no obligations in the conduct of present negotiations.'[24] When the Munich Agreement was concluded on 30 September and Britain's Prime Minister Neville Chamberlain announced it meant 'peace for our time' Roosevelt sent him a congratulatory telegram.

But Roosevelt had serious second thoughts almost immediately. Appalled by what he learned of Hitler's behaviour at Munich – by his announcement on 9 October that Germany's western fortifications would be strengthened and by anti-Jewish violence in Germany on 8–9 November – he became convinced that the Führer could not be appeased but needed to be stopped. He sought yet another $500,000,000 for defence spending in December 1938 and spoke of the need for an American air force of 10,000 aircraft with the capability to build 20,000 more each year. 'For the first time since the Holy Alliance of 1818', he told a meeting of his defence chiefs, the United States 'faced the possibility of an attack on the Atlantic side of both the Northern and Southern hemispheres.'[25]

Hitler, of course, broke the Munich Agreement when he marched his troops into Czechoslovakia in March 1939. Stalin, now certain that the Munich settlement was intended to clear the way for Germany to move eastward, began to rearm the Soviet Union and, to gain both time and breathing room for that, entered into the negotiations that by August resulted in the Molotov–Ribbentrop Pact. France, appalled both by Hitler's breach of the accord, also reached the conclusion that the Führer could not be appeased and began to re-arm in earnest. In January, the French government sent a purchasing mission to the United States, which ordered 1,000 aircraft for July delivery. At a meeting with the Senate Military Affairs Committee, Roosevelt cited that sale as contributing significantly to America's defence. He did not actually say that America's frontier lay on the Rhine, but he clearly conveyed his belief that a well-armed France was necessary to the defence of the United States.

The growing perception that the Atlantic could soon become more of a bridge than a barrier undermined one of the basic assumptions that had underlain America's traditional foreign policy. If the US could be attacked from Europe, it was no longer in 'the detached and distant situation' Washington had posited and Europe's problems no longer had 'none or a very remote relation'. That was particularly true when these wars were likely to have world-wide dimensions. In the 1930s US foreign policy was still composed of three distinct segments: the traditional non-entanglement policy with respect to Europe; a Latin American policy that had metamorphosed into the Good Neighbour Policy; and the Open Door policy primarily for East Asia, but for Africa and the Middle East as well. By the middle of the decade these areas became more closely linked.

Hitler's actions seemed to be part of a global threat to the United States and as the hopes for successful appeasement waned American policy became primarily one for avoiding not just a European but a global war. In East Asia that meant continued support for China and a determined effort to prevent the establishment of Japan's Greater East Asia Co-Prosperity Sphere. In Latin America, it meant countering Fascist influence by supporting Pan-American co-operation, and in Europe it meant continuing attempts to dissuade Hitler and Mussolini from their expansionist courses and providing all possible support for Britain and France to build up their deterrent strength. When Hitler seized Czechoslovakia and a portion of Lithuania for good measure and Mussolini invaded Albania, the State Department condemned both actions as 'wanton lawlessness'. On 14 April 1939 Roosevelt sent a new message to the dictators asking for formal pledges that thirty-one specified countries not be attacked for the next ten years in return for American agreement to participate in a world conference. At the same time, he sought legislation to replace the mandatory arms embargo with a cash-and-carry provision that clearly favoured the democracies. No formal reply to Roosevelt's message was ever received, but Hitler was clearly angered by it.[26] In a speech to the Reichstag on 28 April Hitler declared the Anglo-German naval agreement and the non-aggression pact with Poland null and void and he derided Roosevelt's message line by line.

When Germany invaded Poland on 1 September 1939 the European war the United States had made serious efforts to prevent was underway. In a fireside chat that evening, Roosevelt told a shocked nation that when 'peace has been broken anywhere, the peace of all countries is in danger' and announced: 'This nation will remain a neutral nation, but I cannot ask that every American remain neutral in thought as well. Even a neutral ... cannot be asked to close his mind or his conscience.'[27] In issuing a neutrality proclamation and invoking the Neutrality Act on 5 September, he had no intention of departing from a foreign policy that had always been unilaterally determined and designed to protect and defend the interests of the United States. But Roosevelt was convinced that Hitler and Germany posed a direct threat to the US and enabling Britain and France to win their war provided the country's best means of defence. He had also learned from experience. Wilson had taken the country to war in 1917 to uphold neutral rights and make the world safe for democracy and had wound up negotiating with European nations at Versailles about essentially European issues. Roosevelt wished to avoid even the appearance of entanglement as he sought, in effect, to enlist the European democracies in the effort to make the world safe for the United States. Within a week of invoking the neutrality act he wrote directly to Prime Minister Chamberlain and to Winston Churchill, the new First Lord of the Admiralty, inviting both 'to keep me in touch personally with anything you want me to know about'.[28]

The success of Germany's *Blitzkrieg* in Poland prompted Roosevelt to move immediately and decisively on the matter of neutrality revision. On 21 September he told a joint special session of Congress that he wanted to return to neutrality based squarely on international law. That had been the policy of the United States since its earliest days, he maintained, and had been departed from only twice, disastrously during the Jefferson Administration when the Embargo and the Non-Intercourse Acts had led to economic ruin and to the war of 1812 and again with the Neutrality Acts of 1935–7, which he now very much regretted signing. With isolationist sentiment undermined by recent events, Congress responded favourably, and by 4 November had replaced the arms embargo with a cash-and-carry provision favourable to the Western Allies. Chamberlain sent a note of congratulation and thanks. The isolationists, afraid that a commitment to all-out aid would inevitably lead to war, placed their reliance for keeping the United States secure on an impregnable defence.

In his State of the Union message on 3 January 1940, Roosevelt repeated his intention of keeping the country out of the war, though he pointed out the 'vast difference between keeping out of war and pretending that this war is none of our business'. He found a way to provide aid to Finland after the Soviet Union invaded and made three attempts to explore the possibilities for making peace. He asked James D. Mooney, a General Motors executive with high-level contacts in Germany, to inquire if there were interest in Berlin in settling the conflict, possibly with himself serving as moderator. He invited forty-six neutral nations to consider exchanging views on a post-war order for the purpose of helping achieve it. Most significantly, he sent Under-Secretary of State Sumner Welles to Rome, Berlin, Paris and London to learn the views of the four governments on the possibilities of concluding a just peace. On 2 March, the day after Welles had been received by the Führer and well before he had completed his mission, Hitler issued the order for the attacks on Denmark and Norway.

From the American perspective, the 'real war' that began on 9 April 1940 with those attacks turned the world upside down. The swift German conquest of France and much of the rest of Western Europe in a matter of weeks, followed by Italy's entry into the war and its drive across North Africa, as well as the Battle of Britain, broadcast almost nightly into American homes, had a profound effect on public opinion in United States. Great Britain was left fighting virtually alone and all of Churchill's determination and bravado could not hide the fact Hitler was on the verge of winning the war.

The mounting sense of insecurity that these events produced in the United States turned the promise of aid into *de facto* alliance with Britain as soon as Roosevelt became convinced that Britain would not surrender. It prompted his decision to seek an unprecedented third term in office and, more tellingly, influenced the Republicans not to nominate an isolationist to oppose him, but Wendell Willkie, a party newcomer who strongly supported all-out aid to Britain.

The Committee to Defend America by Aiding the Allies, a bi-partisan political action group, had already been formed in May to win public support for the policy of providing aid to Britain and France. In his first message to Roosevelt after becoming Prime Minister, Churchill asked for 'the loan of forty or fifty of your older destroyers' and some assurance that 'when we can pay no more, you will give us the stuff all the same'.[29] The destroyers were not really lent, but were traded to Britain on 2 September in return for assurance that 'in the event that the waters of Great Britain become untenable for British ships of war, the latter would not be turned over to the Germans or sunk but would be sent to other parts of the Empire for continued defence' and for the use of Newfoundland, Bermuda, the Bahamas, Jamaica, St Lucia, Trinidad and British Guiana as sites for US air and naval bases in the event of an attack on the Western hemisphere.[30] That deal so obviously strengthened America's defensive capabilities that the military Chiefs of Staff could give their required approval in good conscience. Churchill recognized its inequity, but desperately needed the destroyers, and took comfort in the hope that at least it moved the US closer to entering the war. The possibility that it indeed did so prompted the formation of the America First Committee, which quickly became the leading isolationist pressure group. For Roosevelt, the deal was simply part of his effort to defend the country without actually going to war. On 14 September the US passed its first peacetime selective service act, which was intended to build its relatively small armed forces into a credible deterrent.

After Roosevelt's landslide election victory in November 1940 he gave his view of the situation to the American people in a broadcast fireside chat he called 'a talk on national security'. 'Never before', the President pointed out,

> has our American civilization been in such danger as now. For on September 27, 1940
> ... three powerful nations [Germany, Italy and Japan], two in Europe and one in Asia,

joined themselves together in the threat that if the United States of America interfered with or blocked the expansion program of these three nations ... they would unite in ultimate action against the United States ... The oceans that once protected us no longer provided defense when aircraft could fly from the British Isles to New England and back without refueling ...

he explained, and he called for an all-out effort to increase the production of ships, aircraft and other materials of war. 'We are planning our own defense,' he concluded,

and in its vast scale we must integrate the war needs of Britain and the other free nations which are resisting aggression. This is not a matter of sentiment or of controversial personal opinion. It is a matter of realistic, practical military policy ... We must be the great arsenal of democracy.

Twelve days later, the lend-lease bill was introduced in Congress as House Resolution 1776. Its passage on 11 March 1941 was the commitment that the United States had avoided since 1793. It produced a *de facto* alliance not simply with Britain, but with any country with which Germany was or would be at war. Roosevelt reaffirmed that commitment and that alliance on 27 May 1941 when he issued a proclamation of unlimited national emergency and, in a radio address before the ambassadors and ministers from all Western Hemisphere countries, including a Canada already at war with Germany, spelled out the danger faced by the Americas. Invoking the spirit of the signers of the US Declaration of Independence – as had the number given the lend-lease resolution – he declared: 'We will not accept a Hitler-dominated world. And we will not accept a world, like the post-war world of the 1920s, in which the seeds of Hitlerism can again be planted and allowed to grow.' Accordingly, when Germany invaded the Soviet Union on 22 June, aid was offered to the USSR on the same terms already extended to Britain. Before war's end, over 50 billion Dollars (some 700 billion in today's currency) were expended on lend-lease. Ninety-five per cent of that amount went to Great Britain, the Soviet Union, France and China, the four nations who, together with the United States, were to determine the shape of the post-war world and to serve as the permanent members of the Security Council of the United Nations.

The commitment to aid any country at war with the Axis was intended to defend the nation against a perceived threat and to lay the groundwork for a post-war order based on American values. It included no promises, secret or otherwise, that might have been perceived as even potentially entangling. Roosevelt made this clear when he met Churchill aboard an American warship at anchor off Newfoundland in early August. He showed little interest in the details of the aid commitment the British Prime Minister sought to discuss but insisted Churchill publicly accept the Atlantic Charter, his informal blueprint for the post-war world order he hoped to create.

The implementation of lend-lease soon led to a series of actions designed to assure the delivery of supplies, actions that included enlarging the security zone in the North Atlantic, casting a security net over Greenland and the Azores, landing American troops in Iceland in July and, in time, engaging in a miniature undeclared naval war against German U-boats in the Atlantic. In the Pacific, it led to renewed efforts to revive the Open Door. When Japan moved further into French Indo-China in July, the United States froze Japanese assets under its control and imposed an embargo on oil exports. Military aid to Chinese forces fighting the Japanese was stepped up. Though Prince Konoye, Japan's Prime Minister, sought a meeting with Roosevelt to discuss the crisis in September and a special envoy was sent to Washington in early November, the United States insisted that Japanese forces quit all Chinese and Indo-Chinese territory and pledge an open door in Asia before any top-level meeting could be held.

Japan's unmistakable rejection of these conditions came on 7 December 1941 with the attack on the home base of the US Fleet at Pearl Harbor. At the White House that evening, Secretary of War Stimson suggested that America respond with a declaration of war not only against Japan but against Germany as well. Roosevelt, who always regarded Hitler as the chief enemy, but was committed to avoiding war, was not ready to do so. Hitler, who had long restrained his admirals, now decided, however, that 'Germany, Italy and Japan will jointly wage the war forced upon them by the United States of America and England.' 'How one defeats America', the Nazi leader told Japan's ambassador, '[I do] not know yet.'[31] On 9 December German submarine commanders received orders to begin immediate attacks on American ships and on the following day the German chargé in Washington was instructed to deliver a declaration of war on 11 December. The United States was now fully engaged in the war it had committed itself to win – but not to fight – nine months before. The foreign policy George Washington had inaugurated in 1793 had been fully outgrown.

Notes

1   Washington did not regard this as a permanent policy, but rather as an 'endeavor to gain time to our country to settle and mature its yet recent institutions, and to progress without interruption to that degree of strength and consistency, which is necessary to give it, humanly speaking, the command of its own fortunes'. J.D. Richardson (ed.), *Messages and Papers of the Presidents*. Washington, 1896, vol. 1, p. 209.
2   The essential elements of what later came to be called the Monroe Doctrine are in Richardson (ed.), *Messages and Papers of the Presidents*, vol. 2, pp. 218–19.
3   See H. Blinn, 'Seward and the Polish Rebellion of 1863', *American Historical Review* XLV (1940), pp. 828–33.
4   J. Fry, 'Jon Tyler Morgan's Southern Expansionism', *Diplomatic History* 9 (Fall 1985), pp. 329–46 puts America's new-found interest in Africa in context.
5   In J. Scott, *The Hague Peace Conferences of 1899 and 1907*. Baltimore, 1909, vol. 2.
6   US Department of State, *Foreign Relations of the United States, 1895*, vol. 1, p. 558.

7   Ibid. *1899*, pp. 128–42.

8   US Congress, *Congressional Record*, 58th Cong., 3rd session, p. 19.

9   W. Malloy, *Treaties, Conventions, International Acts*, 4 vols. 1910, vol. 2, p. 2183.

10 Standard American dictionaries did not include the term until 1922. The 1933 supplement to the *OED* lists an article in the *Glasgow Herald* of 21 April 1921 as its first political use. Scholarly recognition came in 1924 with J. Rippy and A. Debo, *The Historical Background of the American Policy of Isolation*. Northampton, MA, 1924.

11 *Congressional Record* 67 (1926), p. 2306

12 W. Myers (ed.), *The State Papers and Other Public Writings of Herbert Hoover*. New York, 1934, vo. 1, pp. 234–5.

13 H. Hoover, *The Memoirs of Herbert Hoover: The Cabinet and the Presidency, 1920–1933*. New York, 1952, pp. 368–70.

14 Stimson to Gilbert, 19 October 1931, telephone call of same date Reading to Stimson, and telephone conversation Stimson to C. Dawes. *Foreign Relations, 1931*, vol. 3, pp. 248, 259–60, 248–58.

15 *Foreign Relations, 1931*, vol. 3, pp. 7–8; B. Wallace, 'International Affairs: How the United States Led the League in 1931', *American Political Science Review* XXXIX (1945), p. 113; J. Pratt, *War and Politics in China*. London, 1943, p. 226.

16 D.F. Fleming, *The United States and World Organization, 1920–1933*. New York, 1938, p. 452; *State Papers of Herbert Hoover* vol. 2, p. 260. See also W.W. Willoughby, *The Sino-Japanese Controversy and the League of Nations*. Baltimore, 1936, pp. 500–1.

17 US State Department, *Peace and War: United States Foreign Policy, 1931–1943*. Washington, 1943, pp. 8–12, 188–9.

18 *Congressional Record*, 73rd Cong., 2nd session, pp. 315–17; *Congressional Record*, 74th Cong., 1st session (1935), p. 773.

19 A copy of the Warren Memorandum is in File 811.04418/28, State Department Papers, National Archives.

20 Hull Memorandum, 2 December 1935, *Foreign Relations, 1935*, vol. 1, pp. 866–9.

21 Hull to George, 5 July 1935, in ibid., pp. 723–4. See also B. Harris Jr, *The United States and the Italo-Ethiopian Crisis*. Stanford, 1964, pp. 38–42.

22 *Papers Relating to the Foreign Relations of the United States: Japan, 1931–1941*. Washington, 1943, vol. 1, pp. 384–6.

23 Complete *Presidential Press Conferences of Franklin D. Roosevelt* (25 vols. in 12; New York, 1972), XII, pp. 155–8.

24 Hitler to Roosevelt, 26 September 1938; Wilbur J. Carr to Hull, 28 September 1938; Roosevelt to Hitler, 27 September 1938, in *Foreign Relations, 1938*, vol. 1, pp. 673, 689, 685.

25 J. Blum, *From the Morgenthau Diaries: Years of Urgency, 1938–1941*. Boston, 1965, pp. 46–9.

26 Welles statement, 17 March 1939, and Hull statement, 8 April 1939, in US State Department, *Peace and War*, pp. 454–5. Note on Goering–Duce Conversation, 16 April 1939, in *Akten zur deutschen auswärtigen Politik* (Baden-Baden, 1956), D, 6:215.

27 Roosevelt's address was published in *Peace and War*, pp. 483–5.

28 Roosevelt to Churchill, 11 September 1939, in F. Loewenheim, H. Langley and M. Jonas (eds), *Roosevelt and Churchill: Their Secret Wartime Correspondence* New York, 1975, p. 89. To Chamberlain he also said that he hoped and believed that the arms embargo would be repealed within a month.

29 Churchill to Roosevelt, 15 May 1940, in ibid., pp. 92–3.

30 These terms were first communicated in Roosevelt to Churchill of 13 August 1941 in ibid., pp. 108–9.

31 Ribbentrop to Embassy in Italy, 5 December 1941, and to Embassy in Japan, 8 December 1941, in *Documents on German Foreign Policy, 1919–1945*. Washington, 1949–66, series D, 13, pp. 958, 983; Minutes of Hitler–Oshima meeting in Andreas Hillgruber (ed.), *Staatsmänner und Diplomaten bei Hitler*. Frankfurt, 1967, vol. 2, p. 41.

Chapter 26

A Pivotal Power:
The United States and the International System of the Inter-War Period

Patrick O. Cohrs

Seeking to shed new light on the wider origins of the Second World War, this chapter will re-appraise two central questions. What was the United States' role in the international system of the inter-war period? And what part did US policy play in the pre-history of the twentieth century's second global cataclysm?

The view that following the Senate's rejection of the Versailles treaty the United States became more or less completely isolationist, above all in the crucial realm of international security, was originally prevalent after 1945. More recent studies have acknowledged some US influence on international developments, but they have tended to confine it to the sphere of 'economic diplomacy', especially in Europe. More importantly, there has not been any consensus in the long-standing debate over what made the American quest for international stability between the two world wars ultimately futile.[1] Liberal critics of US policy after Wilson have argued that by failing to support the League it decisively weakened efforts to fortify peace through collective security and binding standards of international law.[2] By contrast, influential 'realist' studies have claimed that by failing to extend post-war security guarantees, especially to France, US decision makers undermined not only the Versailles system but also any prospects of establishing a balance of power against Germany's allegedly inevitable turn to aggressive revisionism. Similar claims have been advanced regarding America's failure to contain Japan's aggressive advances in China, especially since the Manchurian crisis of 1931.[3]

The following analysis aims to advance a different interpretation of the pivotal yet also distinctly constrained role of the United States in the inter-war period's embattled international system. While examining the extent and consequences of America's *relative* isolationism after 1919 it seeks to explain the impact – and failure – of aspirations that in fact prefigured those of the post-Second World War era: to reform the unstable Versailles system and to extend an 'American peace' in Europe, on which this chapter will focus, yet also in the Far East. Both positively and negatively, the pursuits of American policy-makers between 1919 and 1941 were formative for redefining the United States' relations with the world in the twentieth century. Exploring their endeavours can elucidate a momentous re-orientation and learning process. The critical challenge for US decision makers ever since the Great War was to learn how to exercise *and legitimate* a liberal American hegemony. More profoundly, a '*Pax Americana*' was only sustainable if the United States took the lead, not in unilaterally extending an informal 'American empire' while eschewing international commitments, but in co-operating with other powers to establish new ground-rules of international politics, security and economics.[4]

Re-appraising the question why neither a constructive US hegemony nor a legitimate international order emerged in the inter-war period can also broaden our understanding of the developments and crises that ultimately led to the Second World War. To this end, the chapter will examine a process of adjustment and reorientation that fundamentally altered America's global role. Broadly speaking, this process, which progressed and regressed between the early 1920s and the world crises of the 1930s, comprised four stages. In its first two stages, it culminated in two quests to reform international order after Versailles. First came the attempt of the pre-eminent US Secretary of State of this crucial decade, Charles E. Hughes, to establish – under the isolationist constraints of the Republican 'New Era' – a transatlantic 'community of ideals, interests, and purposes' and a new peace system in the Far East. Then, in the latter 1920s, followed a second bid, dominated by the influential Commerce Secretary and Later President Herbert Hoover, to expand a more non-committal and predominantly economic 'American peace'. The third stage of America's re-orientation process was reached when Hoover saw no alternative to reverting to an ever more unilateral course in the vain hope of mastering the unprecedented shockwaves of the Great Depression. The fourth and final stage of this process began with Roosevelt's quest to overcome the depression and embark on a fundamental reform of the American capitalist republic through the New Deal. It was only then that the real shift to a more or less unmitigated American isolationism occurred and Roosevelt felt compelled to disengage from world politics. As a consequence, the United States withdrew from any meaningful international commitments in Europe and East Asia. Arguably, Roosevelt's underlying aim was to create the preconditions for a renewed and more powerful international engagement of the United States, which then proved decisive during and after the Second World War. But America's withdrawal in the crisis-ridden 1930s contributed significantly to creating the constellation that led to the abyss of 1939.

There is no doubt that the Great War had destroyed all prospects of re-establishing the Eurocentric – and war-prone – international system of the Imperialist era. At the same time, the war had turned the United States into the new 'world creditor', particularly of its wartime allies Britain and France, and made it the predominant financial and economic power, with Wall Street replacing the City of London as the hub of the international financial system. But the post-war international constellation confronted US decision makers with an unprecedented challenge in the sphere of international politics. In short, they had to devise policies that accorded with the new power America wielded, and gain international legitimacy for their aspirations. At the same time, they faced a critical domestic challenge. Here, they had to legitimate any international engagement, let alone commitments, they considered necessary. And they had to do so against strong counter-currents of isolationism that manifested themselves – in the 1920s and overwhelmingly in the 1930s – not only in US public opinion but also, and crucially, in Congress.

Wilson's failure to gain the Senate's endorsement of the Versailles treaty ended his quest for an 'American peace'. Unquestionably, his defeat weakened both the League and the Versailles system severely. But it did not signify the end of US attempts to transform the international system. Although on different terms, this quest was continued under his successors in the 1920s and 1930s.

The original post-war constellation created an antagonism between an isolated Germany, which might eventually pursue an assertive revisionism to cast off Versailles, against an apprehensive France that sought ever more assertive ways to contain the looming German threat. Having lost the Anglo-American alliance guarantee of 1919 the preponderant French Premier of the 1920s, Raymond Poincaré, eventually felt compelled to go beyond the status quo of 1919 in order to bolster French security. In an attempt to gain control over strategic German resources, especially in the Ruhr area, he not only brought Weimar Germany to the brink of disintegration. He also provoked the crucial crisis of the post-war years, the Ruhr crisis of 1923. It led to the emergence of a new, though as yet unconsolidated, Euro-Atlantic international system in the mid-1920s.

Unlike the Versailles system, which in fact aggravated European post-war calamities, the system of London and Locarno, forged in the aftermath of the Ruhr conflict, created the essential framework for Europe's political and economic reconstruction. At the same time, it laid the groundwork for the stabilization and international integration of a democratic Germany, also furnishing the foundations of a new though as yet far-from-consolidated security architecture indispensable to this end. More precisely, what emerged as the (unfinished) Euro-Atlantic peace order of the 1920s was founded through the first and formative strategic bargains of the post-First World War era, the London reparations settlement of 1924 and the Locarno security pact of 1925. These settlements achieved what had proved impossible at Versailles: they inaugurated principles and ground rules through which the only realistic path towards a sustainable post-war order could be opened up – principles and ground rules that could underpin balanced *and reciprocal* agreements forged with, not against, the representatives of the embattled Weimar Republic.[5]

To understand how the essentially transatlantic system of London and Locarno was built, and why it ultimately collapsed, requires a re-appraisal of what became the second US quest to establish a '*Pax Americana*' after the Great War. This quest was pursued by two protagonists who each pursued their own in many ways post-Wilsonian yet also distinct visions of international order: the aforementioned secretary of state Hughes, who seized the reins of

US diplomacy in 1921, and the increasingly influential Commerce Secretary Hoover, who from 1929 directed American policy from the White House. As noted, both had to operate in a predominantly isolationist environment. Undeniably, the 1920s saw the emergence of many new internationalist and pacifist pressure groups, including the influential 'outlawry of war' movement. Yet Republican policymakers clearly perceived as predominant those forces that desired to return to an – elusive – isolationist 'normalcy' after the Great War.[6]

In response to the Ruhr conflict Hughes initiated a marked reorientation of Republican post-war policy *vis-à-vis* Europe. Transcending narrowly defined economic diplomacy, he advanced his own doctrine, declaring that its guiding principles would be 'Independence', which did not signify 'isolation', and 'Co-operation', which did not extend to 'alliances and political entanglements'. On these premises, Hughes aspired to foster not the unilateral expansion of a commercial empire but a new 'peace system': an international 'community' of ideals and interests in which the American government acted as an informal but consistently committed arbiter.[7] Its nucleus was to comprise the United States, the states of Western Europe and, crucially, Weimar Germany. The more long-term challenge was to extend such a fledgling community towards Eastern Europe. More generally, Hughes pursued a regional approach to international order. He sought to establish viable regional peace systems, notably in Europe and the Far East, that could become building blocks of a stable global order. Hughes had thus taken the lead in creating the Washington system of 1922, which established the first global naval arms-control regime and a 'Magna Carta' protecting China's integrity. It should be stressed that the Washington accords could not yet settle a tenable East Asian status quo. They were forged in a transition period in which long-standing European and American claims, Japan's interests and the rivalling aspirations of Chinese nationalists and communists, eventually advanced by Chiang Kai-shek and Mao, were hardly reconcilable. But the Washington system nonetheless marked an important advance. It stabilized a complex constellation for nearly a decade, and it had the potential of paving the way for a post-imperial order in East Asia. By including Japan, it also began to strengthen exponents of a new liberal and Western-orientated course in Tokyo like the subsequent foreign minister Shidehara Kijuro and the later premier Hamaguchi Osachi.[8]

In Hughes' view, initiating a Washington process in Europe was no less imperative. And he indeed found a way to do so, and to foster 'effective international co-operation', by promoting the 'depoliticization' and 'rational' settlement of the Ruhr conflict through the so co-called Hughes plan, which he had proposed in December 1922. It gave rise to the formative Dawes plan of 1924. Joining forces with the first British Labour government under Ramsay MacDonald and Anglo-American financiers, Hughes was instrumental in transforming the Dawes plan into a complex but overall legitimate political agreement at the London reparations conference.[9]

The London settlement of August 1924 was greeted in Europe as no less than the dawning of an 'American peace'. It did not yet resolve the dispute over

German reparations that had burdened post-war politics. Crucially, however, it was the first agreement negotiated between the victors and the vanquished of the war. And it finally created an instrument for settling the most acute post-Versailles problem: reparations. Taking into account its 'actual capacity to pay', the Dawes scheme lowered Germany's annual obligations, and it led to the initial 800-million Goldmark loan to Germany that a syndicate headed by the House of J.P. Morgan and Co arranged in October 1924. The Dawes regime thus initiated an asymmetric cycle of financial stabilization: Germany mainly relied on US capital to pay reparations to France and Britain, and the latter – both debtors of the United States after 1918 – could in turn use reparations funds to meet their obligations *vis-à-vis* Washington, although France would only ratify the Mellon–Bérenger debt settlement in July 1929. It is worth underscoring that a massive crisis of the reparations and debt regime was not inevitable. Under the circumstances, the settlement of 1924 offered the best possible framework for consolidating Weimar Germany. It set Europe on a path of pacification in the 'golden' latter 1920s. But it had to be sustained.[10]

The second pillar of what would evolve into an unfinished transatlantic peace order was the security pact of Locarno, signed in October 1925. The Locarno accords not only enshrined Germany's acceptance of the post-war status quo on its western borders and, through separate arbitration treaties, Berlin's commitment to peaceful change in Eastern Europe. More precisely, the German government committed itself, against tangible domestic opposition, to seeking changes of Germany's borders with Poland and Czechoslovakia, which had been imposed on the vanquished at Versailles, only by peaceful means. Even more significantly, Locarno also laid the foundations for the emergence of a new European concert whose core comprised Britain, France and the Weimar Republic. It is critical to understand, however, that only the transatlantic advances of 1924 had created the necessary and essential preconditions for a success of the Locarno process – and that US support for the pact had a significant part in its success.[11] The American government was still not prepared to countenance any direct strategic commitments in Europe. Instead, the State Department emphasized that the responsibility for creating a new European security framework lay squarely with the European powers. Viewing the Locarno pact as an important step in this direction, the Coolidge administration and leading Wall Street bankers thus brought America's financial and political influence to bear on its behalf. At the same time, the Locarno approach had the virtue of relieving Washington of any official obligations that neither the Senate nor the American electorate would have sanctioned.[12]

As noted, 'realist' studies have criticized Washington's myopic 'dollar diplomacy' and alleged disregard for America's long-term security interests during this seminal period. And they have claimed that their net-effect was to prepare the ground for Nazi Germany's subsequent assault on international order.[13] But neither the eventual failure of US post-war policy nor the disintegration of the transatlantic system of London and Locarno were unavoidable.

What occurred between 1930 and 1932, and what Hitler completed thereafter, was *not* the inevitable consequence of misdirected US pursuits of peaceful change. Rather, US policymakers failed because they did not fulfil the United States' new hegemonic responsibilities in consolidating the advances of London and Locarno. Above all, they did not sustain previous efforts to stabilize the newly republican Germany and to promote its international integration. Both hinged on further strategic agreements with those who, like the German foreign minister Gustav Stresemann, struggled to pursue peaceful change and a *rapprochement* with the Western powers.[14] Instead of promoting such agreements, Republican policy reverted to disengagement. Essentially, the successes of the mid-1920s led leading actors like Hoover and Hughes' successors Frank Kellogg and Henry Stimson to conclude that they had already taken decisive steps towards reforming the Versailles system and that Europe's further stabilization would not require the American government to make any more binding commitments. This placed severe limits on the prospect of transforming the settlements of the mid-1920s into a more permanent peace order.

Washington thus retreated to a largely economic pursuit of international stability, which came to be dominated by Hoover's aspiration to promote his own version of 'American peace'. In contrast to the Republican majority in Congress, the Commerce Secretary and future President was never an isolationist who focused on safeguarding narrowly conceived national interests. Though insisting on a high degree of US 'self-sufficiency', he was not oblivious of the growing transatlantic interdependence, not just in the sphere of high finance. Keen to expand US commercial predominance *and* what he regarded as salutary American practices, Hoover in fact came to pursue an ambitious agenda. He became the most influential proponent of economic diplomacy: an economically underpinned, and politically aloof, approach to international relations. Consequently, he interpreted the reparations settlement of 1924 not as a *caesura* in international politics but as the result of America's economic expertise.[15]

What subsequently gained ground in Washington was Hoover's assertive claim that the time had come to establish a different kind of '*pax Americana*', which finally replaced the defunct Eurocentric world order of the nineteenth century. Hoover conceived of it as a system of liberal–capitalist states – under the *informal* hegemony of the United States – that regulated their interests mainly through peaceful economic competition and the transnational co-operation of financial elites. In Hoover's projection, such a system would allow the American government largely to stay aloof from international politics.[16] It would mainly employ private or semi-official agents like the architect of the Dawes regime, Owen Young, and the aforementioned reparations agent Parker Gilbert. More generally, Hoover believed that such agents could effectively promote the wider process of 'rational' economic and political modernization he advocated. In his judgement, such US-style modernization would be the most effective way of consolidating the Weimar Republic, and it would foster European stability without requiring serious efforts to countenance European debt-relief or to reduce US tariff barriers, which the Fordney–McCumber Act of 1922 had raised steeply. In short, the progressive modernism of America's Republican 'New Era' was to set an example for all of Europe.[17] Though less confident about the prospects of Europe's long-term pacification, Kellogg and Stimson essentially supported Hoover's overall orientation. Both concluded that Washington's promotion of the Dawes scheme and the Locarno pact had marked the essential limits of official US intervention in post-war Europe.[18]

Against this background it is hardly surprising that there was no real prospect of widening the nascent European concert of 1925 into a more robust Euro-Atlantic security system. This became most obvious during the negotiations over the Kellogg–Briand Pact. In the spring of 1927, the French foreign minister Aristide Briand proposed to Washington a bilateral pact of perpetual peace, committing both nations to 'the renunciation of war as an instrument of national policy'.[19] Briand's initiative propelled an intricate process of transatlantic negotiations that resulted in an unprecedented though ultimately ineffectual treaty. Pressed by the American 'war outlawry' movement, a champion of which was his political mentor, the overall isolationist Republican Senator William Borah of Idaho, Kellogg essentially steered this process in accordance with US interests and self-imposed strategic constraints. In the end, the Coolidge administration did not conclude not bilateral 'defensive treaty' with Paris that would have committed the United States to Europe's post-war status quo. Rather, on 27 August 1928 it joined Britain, France and Germany as well as Poland, Czechoslovakia and Japan in signing a general war-renunciation pact, which was also underwritten by numerous other states (eventually including the Soviet Union). Yet what became known as the Kellogg–Briand Pact lacked any international mechanisms to enforce the treaty's core provisions or to impose sanctions against those who departed from the pledge to renounce war as a means of international politics.[20]

More consequentially still, the Hoover administration decided to abstain from any political steering role in making of the Young plan and the negotiations that led to the most significant Euro-Atlantic settlement before the Great Depression: the comprehensive though not yet final reparations agreement forged at the first Hague conference in August 1929. The compromise thrashed out at The Hague – by the Locarno powers, yet without any American participants – also settled the most critical facet of the cardinal Rhineland question that had divided France and Germany. It was agreed that the Franco-Belgian occupation was to be terminated by June 1930, significantly prior to the Versailles treaty's 1935 deadline. In retrospect, however, this settlement not only came too late to pre-empt the subsequent demise of international order. It also was also less substantial than it could have been. And the limitations of US policies, notably those of the newly inaugurated Hoover administration, had a significant bearing on this outcome, with ultimately disastrous consequences for the fledgling post-war order of the 1920s.[21]

Undoubtedly, US decision makers opted for disengagement in part because they did not want to be involved in political negotiations that could raise the spectre of debt relief. Yet their aloofness was also motivated by more fundamental considerations. Particularly, Hoover adhered to his conviction that a reliance on outmoded European diplomacy was part of the problem, not the solution. And he also adhered to his creed that a genuine solution to the reparations dispute, and Europe's wider post-war problems, had to be founded solely upon 'economic ground', without undue regard for 'political considerations'. Precisely because they championed progressive aloofness on these terms, US decision makers saw no need for what their European counterparts, especially Stresemann and Briand, deemed critical for advancing European stabilization: further comprehensive settlements that comprised both financial and political components.[22]

The Young plan, whose adoption was the other central result of The Hague, was more than short-lived compromise dominated by the narrow financial interests of the reparations creditors Britain and France – and their American creditor. It provided Weimar Germany with an urgently needed, if imperfect, framework of financial and political certainty. Terminating the control regime of the Dawes plan, the Young settlement also paved the way for the creation of what could potentially become the hub of a more crisis-proof global financial system: the Bank for International Settlements. But the first Hague conference did not produce what would have been most imperative to ensure the post-war order's further consolidation: a more fundamental reform of the Dawes regime that essentially turned it into a more solid framework not only for controlling the cycle of US loans, German reparations and British and French debt payments but also, and crucially, for regulating Europe's further financial *and* *political* stabilization. Washington's refusal to underpin the Young settlement through effective political commitments had crucial repercussions. The Bank for International Settlements could only become an ephemeral precursor of the World Bank. The Young regime remained an equally limited and ephemeral precursor of the Bretton Woods system. Thus, a critical opportunity was missed to strengthen the international system of the inter-war period before the Great Depression. Above all, it was missed by an American administration unable, and unwilling, to fulfil its hegemonic responsibilities.

The escalation of the World Economic Crisis after 1929 turned into a vicious spiral of successive crises that international policymakers could ultimately no longer control. While the power of European states to contain the crisis was highly constrained, the Hoover administration's responses to what became a rapid deterioration process came late, and they proved insufficient to prevent the disintegration of the nascent 'American peace' of the 1920s. Once the Great Depression overshadowed everything else, the United States lacked the means to forestall the demise of international order. Above all, US decision makers had ever fewer incentives or sanction powers at their disposal to counter, let alone reverse, the disintegration of the Weimar Republic and Japan's eventual turn to militaristic authoritarianism. It is important to understand, however, that the world crisis of the early 1930s did not prove that the system of London and Locarno was inherently flawed and that the advances made since 1923 had in fact prepared the ground for the calamities that engulfed Europe and the world after 1929.

The underlying causes of the Great Depression have to be sought in the financial and economic realm. Of critical import was the failure of the Republican post-war administrations to institute tighter control mechanisms to restrain Wall Street hyper-speculation during the 'roaring twenties'. Equally critical were the deficiencies of the supposedly self-regulating gold-standard system that had been reconstituted after 1918 and the asymmetric trade system of the post-war decade. Here, the double standards of US foreign economic policy even increased imbalances between 1919 and 1929. That the protectionist Smoot–Hawley Act was passed only months after 'Black Friday' while the Hoover administration still pursued 'open door' policies abroad only underscored these double standards.[23] More broadly, the unwillingness of US political and financial decision makers to foster a more robust architecture of international politics and finance bore a significant share of the responsibility for the fact that the Wall Street Crash could eventually escalate into a full-blown world crisis in 1931.

Once the Great Depression reached its peak, its debilitating effect on internal politics – and national economies – made it ever harder for governments on all sides to pursue international co-operation. Not least because they had failed to develop the system of London and Locarno further, in co-operation with the European powers, Hoover and Stimson now found it all the harder to cope with the greatest challenge to global stability after 1919. The United States' behaviour in fact accelerated a fundamental reversal towards 'self-help' policies that finally corroded the international system of the 1920s. The world financial and trade system dissolved into protectionist blocs and closed national spheres of influence. What spelled even more disastrous consequences was that a 'renationalization' process also affected international politics. Dissolving the European concert, it also rendered the Hoover administration's belated and limited crisis-management attempts futile.

What proved most consequential in the early 1930s was that US policymakers had been unwilling to persuade Congress to consolidate the Young regime through political guarantees, bail-out provisions and crisis-reaction mechanisms. By 1931 it was too late for any decisive initiative to cut through the Gordian knots of post-war debt and reparations politics. On 20 June 1931 Hoover proclaimed a one-year moratorium on all 'intergovernmental debts' and reparations.[24] Yet the moratorium could not rescue the Young regime. Because the Hoover administration still dreaded concessions to its debtors, it had no part in the decisive Lausanne conference convened in the summer of 1932. Thus it had to register from afar that Britain and France not only renounced their reparations claims *vis-à-vis* Germany but also effectively abandoned any further debt payments to the United States.

Earlier, the Hoover administration had also finally abandoned its maxim of non-entanglement in Europe's political affairs. Yet its efforts to spur pacific though in fact drastic changes in the post-war status quo – at a time of acute crisis – proved ineffectual. In short, both Hoover and Stimson now concluded that it was high time to address what they considered legitimate German grievances. They sought to induce France to moderate its reparations claims, pursue substantial disarmament and finally accept a revision of the Polish–German frontier, all to moderate the increasingly assertive policies of the Brüning government. American efforts to this end culminated in talks with the French premier Pierre Laval in Washington in the autumn of 1931.[25] But these initiatives never amounted to a consistent strategy. They were still constrained by Hoover's reluctance to make the case for wider strategic commitments to rescue the Euro-Atlantic post-war order. When the final Geneva Disarmament Conference began its proceedings in February 1932, the Hoover administration had reverted to strict non-engagement, distancing itself from any League-based efforts to establish a general arms-limitation regime.[26] The subsequent failure of the Geneva conference all but completed the disintegration of the system of London and Locarno. This process and the parallel dissolution of the Weimar republic would ultimately allow Hitler to launch his assault on global order.

The most striking instance of the United States' inability to uphold international order in the depression era of course occurred not in Europe but after the Japanese invasion of Manchuria in September 1931, which led to the establishment of the puppet regime of Manchukuo in February 1932. The Hoover administration not only refused to participate in international sanctions or embargos against Japan, but also refrained from any forceful protests against Japan's violation of the Washington system's nine-power treaty, which formally protected China's integrity. Washington's response was ultimately restricted to the Stimson Doctrine. It stipulated that the United States would not recognize either the Manchukuo regime or any further forcible changes of the East Asian status quo. Stimson himself had earlier advocated a firmer policy. But Hoover was not prepared to countenance any military or economic measures to enforce the new doctrine, not least because he feared Congressional opposition. The Hoover administration's reaction to the Manchurian crisis underscored to what extent America's progressive aloofness had undercut any prospects of preserving international order in the maelstrom of the depression years. The crisis also sealed the fate of the Washington system. Despite the naval compromise of the 1930 London conference, this cornerstone of the nascent 'American peace' of the 1920s had already been corroded by the underlying conflict between the Anglo-American powers and the aggressive aims of the Japanese military, which gained an ever more dominant influence on Japan's international policies.

When Roosevelt entered the White House in March 1933, just over one month after Hitler had been appointed *Reichskanzler* in Berlin, he had one clear priority. He intended to use the mandate of his election victory in November

1932 to concentrate on a national rather than an international policy of renewal: the aspiration to reinvigorate and profoundly reform the American republic 'from within', through what became known as the New Deal. Arguably, even if he had desired to do so, Roosevelt would neither have had the international leverage nor the critical domestic backing to direct common international efforts to prevent a further deterioration of the European and global situation. The political consequences of the World Economic Crisis were too immense, the domestic constraints they imposed too severe. In the mid-1930s, the Senate's expanding neutrality legislation and the ever more entrenched isolationism of a majority of Americans underscored that the Roosevelt administration was not in a position to effect a major reorientation of US foreign policy, a reorientation that could have prevented the descent to the Second World War. Notably, Roosevelt did not have any mandate to offer credible strategic support to Britain and France, strengthening their resolve to resist Hitler instead of 'appeasing' the German dictator until it was too late to contain him. As in the case of Japan, the decisive opening for integrating a German republic rather than an increasingly assertive dictatorship in a new international order had existed in the 1920s. It did not re-appear in the 1930s.

In the early phases of the New Deal, the Roosevelt administration essentially withdrew from any leadership role in the spheres of international politics and finance. Most notoriously, Roosevelt refused to prop up the ailing British pound when this issue came to a head during the 1933 London economic conference. He thus sealed the fate of the already brittle monetary system of the inter-war period. More generally, Roosevelt essentially came to opt for national, often unilateral approaches to all major issues from financial stabilization to disarmament. Seeking to bring about a self-reliant recovery, he aspired to no less than a progressive modernization of the American model of liberal–capitalist democracy, replacing the *laissez faire* paradigm of the 1920s. Through the New Deal the federal government acquired a newly central role in regulating the US economy and safeguarding the welfare of American citizens, particularly through social and job-creation programmes like the Tennessee Valley Authority. While the economic success of the New Deal remains in dispute, its long-term international significance seems beyond doubt. It not only salvaged the fundamentals of America's hence more regulated capitalist republic in a decade in which this 'model' appeared to be in decline *vis-à-vis* more authoritarian systems, including the Soviet Union. It also fulfilled Roosevelt's underlying hope: the transformative revitalization of its state and society in the 1930s created the preconditions for the success of America's unprecedented mobilization and war effort that enabled it to prevail over the Axis powers in the 1940s.

But while authoritarian forces appeared to triumph in the 1930s the United States turned inward. It was now, rather than after Wilson's defeat, that it turned its back on Europe and the international system. The Roosevelt administration did not actively abet the expansionism of the Hitler regime, let alone Imperial

Japan, but its inability to pursue a more active global engagement, which was essentially due to towering domestic constraints, contributed significantly to the rapid deterioration of what even before 1929 had been an unconsolidated international system. This created a growing strategic vacuum in which Hitler, Mussolini and the leaders of the Kwantung Army in China and their political allies in Tokyo could operate – and undermine all the international standards and rules that had been painstakingly established in the 1920s.

Even under the constraints of the 1930s, however, the Roosevelt administration never adopted a course of complete isolationism. It recognized the Soviet Union in 1933, for example. In some respects, Roosevelt and his Secretary of State, Cordell Hull, also began to define their own, though necessarily restrained, version of an 'American peace' – aspirations for a *Pax Americana* in the Western hemisphere and for an 'economic peace' on American terms. Firstly, Roosevelt placed the United States' relations with the countries of Latin America on new foundations. Through what became known as his 'Good Neighbour' policy he signalled a clear break with previous US imperialism, seeking to foster instead an essentially post-imperial peace order in the Western hemisphere. In his conception, a new 'inter-American peace' was to serve as an exemplary model for global order. It challenged German, Italian and Japanese conceptions of imperialism and autarky, yet also British and French ambitions to preserve their overseas empires. In his inaugural address on 4 March 1933 Roosevelt demonstratively dedicated his presidency to 'the policy of the good neighbor'. He sought to cultivate an ideology of 'Pan-Americanism', based on 'equality and fraternity'.[27] At the inter-American Montevideo conference in December 1933 Hull officially underwrote the new maxim of non-interference in the internal or external affairs of Latin American states.

Of long-term significance was also the thrust of the Roosevelt administration's foreign economic policy. In short, it sought to build on US 'Open Door' maxims in an effort to reverse the underlying trend of the depression era: the fragmentation of the world into closed and hostile economic blocs. US aspirations to liberalize world trade were primarily directed against German and Japanese attempts to consolidate 'autarkic' spheres of influence. Yet they also challenged the protectionist imperial-preference system that Britain and its Dominions had established at Ottawa in 1931. A consistent liberal policy of course also called for a reversal of Congressional protectionism. But this would only be achieved after the Second World War. After 1933, Hull became the champion of a new American doctrine of 'peace through free trade'. Echoing Cobdenite liberalism in mid-nineteenth-century Britain, he espoused the maxim that 'freer commerce made for peace and unfair trade made for war', which he had first formulated as an ardent supporter of Wilson.[28] As Secretary of State, Hull fought for a reciprocal trade law, which was then passed in 1934. By 1939 he had managed to weave a network of trade and tariff-reduction agreements with Britain and fifteen other countries.[29] But Hull and likeminded policy makers like Dean Acheson, then Under-Secretary of the Treasury, had more far-reaching ambitions. They sought to create a liberal economic world order on American terms. In 1938 Acheson outlined the measures he considered imperative: the elimination of tariff barriers; the removal of any 'exclusive or preferential trade arrangements'; and the creation of 'a broader market for goods made under decent standards'. No less important, though, was the establishment of a new 'stable international monetary system'.[30] Eventually, these aspirations would give rise to the Bretton Woods system.

Yet while the first contours of a new economic 'American peace' thus appeared as the United States emerged from the depression, US foreign and strategic policy *vis-à-vis* Europe and East Asia became profoundly isolationist. Why? The question how far Roosevelt was fundamentally constrained by overwhelming isolationist tendencies in US domestic politics remains controversial.[31] It would be erroneous to conclude that he actively promoted such tendencies to concentrate on his New Deal agenda. As noted, his underlying aim became to create the domestic conditions for America's return to a more decisive international role. Like Wilson, he saw himself as a steward and tutor. To guide the American people in domestic and foreign affairs was to become a key component of his famous 'fireside chats', the radio broadcasts he would continue until the final stages of the Second World War. But it was and remained a hallmark of his foreign policy in the 1930s that he only acted once he could be assured of as broad a popular consensus as possible regarding any step he contemplated. And there is little doubt over how pronounced the overall turn to unmitigated isolationism was both in the US Senate and the wider American public. This indeed placed tangible checks on Roosevelt's room to manoeuvre.

Most importantly, urged on by a Senate Select Committee headed by the Republican Senator Gerald Nye from North Dakota, Congress passed a series of ever more restrictive Neutrality Laws between 1935 and 1939, chief among them the Neutrality Act of 1937. But the majority of its supporters only represented a groundswell of isolationist sentiment which exceeded that of the 1920s.[32] This sentiment became particularly entrenched but was by no means confined to the mid-western heartland of small-town America that had found its champions in Nye and the then still staunchly isolationist Senator Arthur Vandenberg from Michigan. It was sharpened by influential 'America First' papers like the *Chicago Tribune*. Support for 'impartial neutrality' also came from the Federal Council of Churches and influential anti-war groups like the National Council for the Prevention of War, the National Peace Conference and the Women's League for Peace and Freedom. Only a minority of conservative and progressive internationalists, notably those grouped around the League of Nations Union and the Carnegie Endowment for International Peace, continued to stress the need to strengthen international co-operation. But for the time being they were prophets in the wilderness. By the mid-1930s, the notion that, pushed by the interests of East Coast high finance and arms manufacturers, the Wilson administration had dragged the United States into an unnecessary war in 1917 had become very widespread. In 1934 the publication of the influential book

Merchants of Death by H.C. Engelbrecht and F.C. Hanighen had heightened popular suspicions of this kind and increased support for a more unequivocal neutrality policy. The Nye committee inquired into the dealings and interests of weapons manufacturers and major New York banking firms like J.P. Morgan for whose interests the American people had allegedly made sacrifices in the trenches of the Great War. To prevent a recurrence of such a scenario the Nye committee made recommendations that led to the first neutrality law of 1935. Setting the precedent for all subsequent legislation, whose impact can hardly be understated, it banned Americans from travelling to war zones; it prohibited any American loans to belligerents; and above all it imposed an impartial arms embargo, which barred not only aggressors but also their victims from obtaining American weapons. The aim of the Neutrality Act of 1937 was to make these laws permanent.

But even under the Neutrality Laws the United States did not pursue a strictly isolationist policy. Roosevelt eventually managed to modify Congressional restraints, arguing that they could benefit an aggressor that had built up 'vast armies, navies, and storehouses of war' while denying support to its victims. The President adopted a plan by his adviser Bernard Baruch who had proposed that trade with belligerents should be conducted on the basis of the 'cash-and-carry' principle. Following the outbreak of war in Europe he in September 1939 proposed an amendment under which a formally neutral United States could sell arms and goods to any country, on the provision that the buyers collected their purchases and paid for them in cash straightaway.[33] In practice, as he knew well, this would allow the United States to aid the maritime power Britain as well as France against Nazi Germany. Congress passed the amended Neutrality Act in November 1939. The end of American 'neutrality' would precede the attack on Pearl Harbor. It came with the Lend-Lease Act of March 1941, which authorized the American government to sell, lend or give war materials to friendly nations.

The inner-American controversies over the meaning and extent of 'neutrality' had been raging against a background of rising political tension and acute crisis in Europe and East Asia. The United States remained aloof when in July 1937 the Kwantung Army provoked the second Sino-Japanese war in which, abetted by the authoritarian government in Tokyo, the Japanese military sought to widen its dominion against Chinese nationalist forces under Chiang Kai-shek. In Europe, the same attitude prevailed when Hitler began to unhinge the international order of the 1920s, remilitarized the Rhineland, brought Austria 'home to the Reich' in 1938 and subsequently sought to reclaim the Sudeten area, allegedly to protect the local German minority.[34] This has given rise to the thesis that Roosevelt became a 'silent accomplice' of Hitler and those who destroyed global order in the latter 1930s and that he even pursued his own version of 'appeasement', particularly towards Nazi Germany, which gave Hitler the opening to wage war.[35] But these interpretations seem misleading. In the final analysis, Roosevelt did not join the British premier Neville Chamberlain in adopting a policy of 'appeasement' that actively sought to accommodate Hitler's demands on the assumption that this would avert war. Rather, he ultimately pursued a policy of temporization that aimed to pre-empt an escalation of the European situation and restrain Hitler through general but insubstantial US peace initiatives. The underlying rationale of this policy was to gain time to prepare the ground for a major reorientation from isolationist 'neutrality' towards war-preparedness and the capacity to aid and possibly lead a coalition of states against the authoritarian challengers of the 1930s should this become unavoidable. Roosevelt's main challenge in this context remained a domestic one: to legitimate such a reorientation and to build a bipartisan coalition of support.

Also from an American perspective a fundamental distinction has to be made between the pacification policies of the 1920s and 'appeasement' after 1933. The former sought to address core problems and inequities of the original Versailles system, and thus also to allay German grievances. But they did so through mutually agreed rules for the settlement of international disputes, on the premise of committing democratically elected German leaders to international rules *and obligations* under the system of London and Locarno. The latter, though pursued for understandable reasons in the grim constellation, was an ultimately misguided and futile series of attempts to 'appease' a dictator who never had any intention of respecting international agreements and seized on long-standing German grievances to advance his own, qualitatively different agenda of aggressive expansionism, which contravened anything resembling a legitimate international order. *Vis-à-vis* Hitler, the incentives of a mutually beneficial interdependence that US policy makers had offered after 1919 were meaningless. All major concessions the United States could potentially press for from afar – on the Sudeten question or the 'Polish Corridor' – would not only have been morally reprehensible. They also would have failed to pacify the Nazi regime. Giving in to unilateral German demands was bound to whet the Nazi appetite for more. On the other hand, the cardinal American problem was that Roosevelt did not have the political leeway or military means (yet) to pursue an effective policy of containment – a policy that strengthened the political will and ability of Britain and France to pursue the strategy that Winston Churchill advocated in 1938: to put a 'lid' of moral and political isolation on the Hitler regime to provoke its implosion.[36]

Roosevelt did not intend to drag the United States into a European war, though he considered it increasingly likely. He only deemed an actual intervention unavoidable in the spring of 1941. But since the mid-1930s he regarded it as one of his main tasks to loosen the shackles of isolationism. He realized that in the face of the rising authoritarian threats, and the new technological power they too commanded, the United States could no longer afford to rely on its relative hemispheric insulation: it had to assume a global security posture. To achieve this, Roosevelt had to effect a profound change of domestic attitudes towards America's international role and responsibilities. Yet he remained highly cautious and at times ambivalent, sending different signals to different audiences. The most famous example of Roosevelt's early public efforts to alert the American public was his 'quarantine speech' of October 1937. He warned that 'the present reign of terror and lawlessness' threatened 'the very foundations of civilization', and thus all 'peace-loving nations must make a concerted effort' to oppose such forces, and there was no escape either for the United States into 'mere isolation or neutrality'. Rather, America had to join forces with others to stem 'the epidemic of world lawlessness' through a 'quarantine'. But Roosevelt remained vague about what such a 'quarantine' would entail. The only exception was his proposal that America join the other powers of the Washington Nine-Power Treaty of 1922 in denouncing Japanese aggression and re-asserting China's integrity. Yet this was to no avail.[37]

While hardening his rhetoric Roosevelt also temporarily contemplated – furtively – an American role in the peaceful settlement of European disputes. He did so, as noted, to restrain rather than appease Hitler: to commit him to a negotiating process that would at least postpone a further escalation of the Old World's crisis while the United States was still politically and militarily unprepared. For a time, Roosevelt thus entertained the idea of making the United States the arbiter of European peace efforts. This was first proposed by his key adviser, the Under-Secretary of State Sumner Welles, in 1937. The Welles plan stipulated that Washington should call a general peace conference to forge an international agreement on what he called 'fundamental norms' and 'standards of international conduct'. Outlining a new regime of guarantees for equal access to raw materials, Welles also proposed a new Washington conference of the major powers, this time to promote general disarmament. Essentially, Welles sought to revive US approaches of the 1920s to deal with a dictator who disdained consensual methods of peaceful change. He had earlier advised Roosevelt to support Hitler's colonial claims and to consider promoting certain 'European adjustments', notably regarding the 'Polish Corridor' and the Sudeten area, to salvage European peace. Roosevelt sounded out the British government on Welles' proposals at the beginning of 1938. Eden favoured the scheme, but Chamberlain and Halifax dismissed it as unrealistic. In Washington, Hull registered his staunch opposition to what he deemed an 'illogical' and fatuous scheme. Eventually, Roosevelt distanced himself from it as well.[38]

Once the Sudeten crisis had escalated Roosevelt renewed his overtures. He went so far as to send a 'peace message' to the four powers involved in the dispute – Nazi Germany, Czechoslovakia, Britain and France – urging them on 26 September to seek a 'pacific settlement' of their controversies. On 19 September he had held out the vague possibility of holding a world conference 'for the purpose of reorganizing all unsatisfactory frontiers on rational lines', only to discard it later.[39] And he had dispatched Welles to renew the – futile – proposal for a peace conference not just to address the Sudeten question but also to approach a wider European agreement. Despite these overtures, Roosevelt never desired to be the chief architect of European appeasement. He only took initiatives once his main aim had become to postpone the outbreak of war in Central Europe. Secretly, Roosevelt had actually encouraged Chamberlain and the French Premier Édouard Daladier to take a firm stand against Hitler's pressure, and he above all urged both governments to prepare for a defensive war. He told Britain's Ambassador Lindsay that while he would be delighted if Chamberlain's appeasement strategy bore fruit he basically did not believe it was workable: putting pressure on the Czechoslovak government to acquiesce in Hitler's demands would only lead to further German ultimatums, particularly for a return of the 'Polish Corridor'.[40] Yet America's international influence was distinctly limited at this critical juncture. Roosevelt had nothing to offer to back a firm Anglo-French policy. He could provide neither troops nor loans or other incentives to this end. So he finally backed Chamberlain's course and praised the British premier when he infamously claimed to have salvaged 'peace for our time' at the Munich conference on 29 September 1938. Roosevelt expressed his hope that the Munich settlement would dampen further German aspirations in continental Europe. But he essentially viewed it as a reprieve – an agreement that gave the West European democracies, and the United States, some breathing space to re-arm and take a firmer stance in the future.[41] Hitler would dash such hopes when occupying the remaining parts of Czechoslovakia in the spring of 1939.

In the aftermath of Munich, Roosevelt told a conference assembling the heads of US military and civilian defence in mid-November 1938 that 'the recrudescence of German power at Munich had completely reoriented our own international relations' and confronted the United States with a historic threat: 'for the first time since the Holy Alliance of 1818' it faced 'the possibility of an attack on the Atlantic side in both the Northern and the Southern Hemispheres'. To respond to this threat, he demanded above all the rapid expansion of American air power.[42] But the Roosevelt administration's foreign policy remained a tightrope walk. Not even the outbreak of the Second World War allowed Roosevelt to set a new course. It was *not* a watershed for America's role in the world. On the one hand, the president insisted on numerous occasions that he was not moving his country towards intervention. On the other, he sought to pave the way – *vis-à-vis* Congress and the American public – for more effective aid to Britain and France and for an active policy of war-preparedness. During Europe's 'Phoney War' Roosevelt contemplated proposing peace talks with the aim of averting a defeat of Britain and France and a constellation in which Nazi Germany and the Soviet Union would dominate the bulk of the Eurasian land mass. In February 1940, he sent Welles on another peace mission to Berlin, Rome, Paris and London. Predictably, though, Welles' talks with Hitler and his Foreign Minister Ribbentrop proved fruitless.

After Nazi Germany's *Blitzkrieg* victory over France, Roosevelt redoubled his efforts to loosen the constraints of America's neutrality policy and to steer both Congressional and public opinion in the direction of a war-preparedness. He strove to broaden public support for his course at a time when Congressional opposition to involvement remained strong and the newly introduced Gallup Polls showed that in the summer of 1940 sixty-one per cent of Americans still thought the United States should stay out of the conflict. Such attitudes were hardened by the isolationist America First Committee, founded in September 1940, whose most prominent spokesman was Charles Lindbergh. Yet Roosevelt could count on the support of the internationalist Committee to Defend America by Aiding the Allies, formed in May 1940. He now pressed for stepped-up armament programmes and the re-introduction of the draft, then implemented through the Selective Training and Service Act.

Following his re-election, Roosevelt announced in his famous 'fireside chat' on 29 December 1940 that the United States must act as 'the great arsenal of democracy' against the axis powers.[43] Having authorized the destroyers-for-bases deal in August, he had already embarked on a policy of *de facto* making the US Britain's 'arsenal', aiding Britain short of breaching neutrality legislation, while the Battle of Britain was approaching its climax. On 6 January 1941 the President told Congress that the United States could not accept 'a dictator's peace'. Instead, he proclaimed US allegiance to a different 'world order': 'the moral order' of the 'Four Freedoms', premised on the freedom of speech and expression, freedom of worship, freedom from want and freedom from fear, which he sought to achieve through 'a world-wide reduction of armaments'. To advance towards this order, and to defend the security of the western democracies, he asked Congress for authority and funds to supply 'in ever increasing numbers, ships, planes, tanks, guns' to 'those nations which are now in actual war with aggressor nations'. He thereby vindicated the seminal Lend-Lease Programme, which would be passed with a substantial Congressional majority.[44] Roosevelt thus made clear that the United States would not seek a peace of accommodation with Hitler Germany or Imperial Japan. In a wider context, it became clear by the summer of 1941 that the threat both regimes posed, for the first time, to the United States' hemispheric security had been critical for creating a new geo-political and domestic constellation: a constellation in which Roosevelt could eventually oversee the transformation of America's role from an originally passive, isolationist power to the pivotal power of the Second World War. But only the Japanese assault on Pearl Harbor precipitated the decisive shift.

Pearl Harbor marked a fundamental *caesura*. It not only led to America's entry into the war but also spurred a momentous transformation. The United States, which had become the international system's potential hegemon after 1918 but reverted to isolationist aloofness after the Great Depression, would emerge as the pivotal power after 1945. Building on Wilsonian maxims, yet also searching for more 'realistic' ways to realize them, Roosevelt came to envisage a universal and integrative post-war order, though he would insist that, as the world's principal new powers, the 'Four Policemen' – the United States, the Soviet Union, Britain and China – had to form a kind of world directorate to oversee the establishment of this order. During their Placentia Bay summit in August 1941, he and Churchill had mapped out its general principles. The system of the Atlantic Charter was essentially premised on the 'Four Freedoms' and can in fact be seen as the blueprint for a new 'American peace'. More profoundly, what occurred after 1941 can be seen as the culmination of a drawn-out learning and reorientation process. It led the United States to assume a hegemonic role and unprecedented international commitments in the international system that came to be built after the Second World War, not only in the United Nations – and, eventually, America's post-war alliance systems in Europe and East Asia – but also in the new international economic order of Bretton Woods.

Notes

1　See M. Hogan (ed.), *Paths to Power*. Cambridge, 2000, pp. 168–267; M. Leffler, *The Elusive Quest*. Chapel Hill, 1979.
2　See S. Pedersen, 'Back to the League of Nations', *American Historical Review* 112/4 (October 2007), pp. 1091–117.
3　See H. Morgenthau, *Politics among Nations* 4th ed. New York, 1967, pp. 20–40; and for an overview A. Iriye, *The Origins of the Second World War in Asia and the Pacific*. New York, 1987.
4　This builds on P. Schroeder, 'The Mirage of Empire versus the Promise of Hegemony' in P. Schroeder, *Systems, Stability, and Statecraft*. New York, 2004, pp. 298–300. See also M. Hunt, *American Ascendancy*. Chapel Hill, 2007, pp. 70–114.
5　See P.O. Cohrs, *The Unfinished Peace after World War I*. Cambridge, 2006, pp. 129ff., 201 ff. Cf. Z. Steiner, *The Lights That Failed*. Oxford, 2005, pp. 240ff., 387ff.
6　See D. Kennedy, *Freedom from Fear*. Oxford, 1999, pp. 385–9.
7　Hughes addresses, 4 September and 30 November 1923, in C.E. Hughes, *The Pathway of Peace*. New York, 1925, p. 8; Hughes memorandum, 1 July 1924, cited in after S.F. Bemis (ed.), *The American Secretaries of State and Their Diplomacy*, vol. X. New York, 1928, p. 369.
8　See Hughes address, 29 December 1922, in Hughes, *The Pathway of Peace*, pp. 32ff.; A. Iriye, *After Imperialism*. Cambridge, MA, 1965.
9　Hughes address, 29 December 1922, in Hughes, *The Pathway of Peace*, pp. 50–3; Hughes memorandum, 18 December 1922, *Hughes Papers*, Library of Congress.
10　See Cohrs, *The Unfinished Peace after World War I*, pp. 154–86.
11　Ibid., pp. 237–58.
12　Kellogg to Coolidge, 8 November 1925, *Kellogg Papers*, Minnesota Historical Society, St Paul; Strong memorandum, 11 July 1925, *Strong Papers*, Federal Reserve Bank Archives, New York.
13　See S. Schuker, *The End of French Predominance in Europe*. Chapel Hill, 1976, pp. 385–93.
14　See P. Krüger, *Die Außenpolitik der Republik von Weimar*. Darmstadt, 1985, pp. 372–506.
15　Hoover address, 14 December 1924, box 75, Hoover Papers, Hoover Presidential Library, West Branch, Iowa.
16　Ibid.
17　See Hoover address, 'The Future of our Foreign Trade', New York, 16 March 1926, Washington, DC, 1926.
18　See Kellogg to Coolidge, 7 October 1924, *Kellogg Papers*; Stimson to Hoover, 8 June 1929, NA RG 59 462.00 R296/2941/1/2.
19　Briand statement, 6 April 1927; Kellogg to Herrick, 11 June 1927, papers relating to the *Foreign Relations of the United States* 1927, vol. II, pp. 611–14 (hereafter *FRUS*).
20　Kellogg memorandum, January 1928, *Kellogg Papers*, roll 27. The Soviet Union acceded to the pact in 1929.
21　See Cohrs, *The Unfinished Peace after World War I*, pp. 531–71.

22 Hoover address, 14 December 1924; 'Memorandum on War Debt Settlements', 1927, Hoover Papers, Commerce Department, boxes 75, 365.

23 See C. Kindleberger, *The World in Depression, 1929–39*. Berkeley, 1973, pp. 95ff., 291–308.

24 See H. Hoover, *Memoirs* vol. II. London, 1952, p. 70; Stimson diary, 15 and 18 June 1931, Stimson Papers, Sterling Library, New Haven.

25 Stimson diary, 30 September 1931. See also ibid., 30 July 1931, vol. XVII, nos 169–73, Stimson Papers; Hoover, *Memoirs*, vol. II, pp. 88–9.

26 Stimson diary, vol. XVII, no. 183, July 1931, Stimson Papers; *FRUS 1931*, vol. I, pp. 501–4.

27 Roosevelt inaugural address, 4 March 1933, and speech to Pan-American Union, 12 April 1933; F.D. Roosevelt, *Roosevelt's Foreign Policy*. New York, 1942, pp. 3–5.

28 C. Hull, *The Memoirs of Cordell Hull*. New York, 1948, vol. I, pp. 100–1.

29 R. Dallek, *Franklin D. Roosevelt and American Foreign Policy, 1932–1945*. Oxford, 1995, pp. 84–93.

30 Quoted after D. Hendrickson, *Union, Nation, or Empire*. Lawrence, 2009, p. 363.

31 See S. Casey, *Cautious Crusade*. Oxford, 2001, pp. 3–45.

32 See M. Jonas, *Isolationism in America, 1935–1941*. New York, 1966.

33 Roosevelt speech, 21 September 1939, US Department of State, *Peace and War: United States Foreign Policy, 1931–1943*. Washington, 1943, pp. 485–7.

34 Official US reactions to Mussolini's attack on Ethiopia in 1935 and the Spanish Civil War were no different. See Dallek, *Franklin D. Roosevelt and American Foreign Policy*, pp. 101–28.

35 See A. Offner, *American Appeasement*. Cambridge, MA, 1969, pp. 276–80; F.W. Marks, *Wind over Sand*. Athens, GA, 1988, pp. 136–45.

36 See Churchill broadcast, 16 October 1938, in M. Gilbert, *Winston S. Churchill*, vol. 5, Companion Volume. London, 1982, III, pp. 1216-27.

37 Roosevelt address, 5 October 1937; 'Fireside Chat', 12 October 1937, Roosevelt, *Roosevelt's Foreign Policy*, pp. 129–32, 132–3; *FRUS* 1937, vol. I, pp. 665–70.

38 See Welles to Roosevelt, 26 October 1937, Roosevelt Papers, PSF, box 23, Roosevelt Presidential Library, Hyde Park, New York; Eden memorandum, 21 January 1938, FO 954, vol. 29, British National Archives, Kew; Hull, *The Memoirs of Cordell Hull*, vol. I, pp. 546–8.

39 Roosevelt message, 26 September 1938, Roosevelt, *Roosevelt's Foreign Policy*, pp. 148–9; [memorandum of conversation Roosevelt–Lindsay, 19 September 1938], *Documents on British Foreign Policy, 1919–1939*, series III, vol. VII. London, 1954, pp. 627–9.

40 *Documents on British Foreign Policy*, series III, vol. VII, pp. 627–9.

41 Roosevelt to King, 11 October 1938, in E. Roosevelt (ed.), *F.D.R.: His Personal Letters* (New York, 1947–50), vol. IV, p. 816; to Phillips, 17 October 1938, Roosevelt Papers, PSF: Hull, *The Memoirs of Cordell Hull*, vol. I, pp. 593–5. Cf. Dallek, *Franklin D. Roosevelt and American Foreign Policy*, pp. 162–72; and B. Farnham, *Roosevelt and the Munich Crisis*. Princeton, 1997, pp. 91–137.

42 Oliphant memorandum of White House meeting, 14 November 1938, Morgenthau Diary 150: 338, Roosevelt Presidential Library.

43 US Department of State, *Peace and War*, pp. 598–607.

44 Roosevelt message, 6 January 1941, Roosevelt, *Roosevelt's Foreign Policy*, pp. 318–24.

Chapter 27

Japanese Foreign Policy and the Outbreak of the Asia-Pacific War: the Search for a Modus Vivendi in US–Japanese Relations after July 1941

Haruo Iguchi

As part of America's attempts to mount economic pressures on Japan to end its aggression against China, the US government revoked its bilateral trade treaty with Japan which expired in January 1940. This agreement safeguarded Japan's purchases of war-related materials in the United States, but two significant factors contributed to Japan's ability to soften the impact of this legislation. Firstly, Japan's Yokohama Specie Bank created secret bank accounts in the United States. Secondly, Japan's Mitsui Trading Company circumvented American tariff barriers on textiles and silk. This postponed the Japanese bankruptcy predicted by many government analysts in the US in their numerous reports on Japan's economic vulnerability. Only after the passage of the Lend-Lease Act did the American stance against Japan become much tougher. In the first months of 1941 the United States transformed a patchwork of export restrictions into full-blooded financial warfare overseen by truculent anti-Axis lawyers determined to show Japan no mercy.[1]

A leading member of this group was Dean Acheson, appointed by President Franklin D. Roosevelt in January 1941 as Assistant Secretary of State for Economic Affairs. He worked closely with the Treasury Department whose Secretary, Henry Morgenthau, had led the administration since its start in aiding China, a stance that strengthened further after the outbreak of the Sino-Japanese War in July 1937. Acheson aligned himself in 1940 with those Americans who supported aiding Britain even at the risk of war with the Axis and he supported Lend Lease, as did Morgenthau, who helped China secure war materials after the passage of that law in March 1941.[2]

Japan did not declare war on China in July 1937 because a formal state of war would trigger America's Neutrality Act and prevent Japan from purchasing war supplies there. Japan disguised its aggressions in China as earlier in Manchuria with the establishment of puppet regimes rather than formal military occupation or military government.[3] On 18 January Prime Minister Fumimaro Konoye declared that Japan was no longer going to deal with the Chiang Kai-shek regime, a decision that Shinichi Kitaoka, Professor of Japanese political history, describes as 'one of the greatest blunders in the entire history of the Showa period'.[4]

The Japanese Empire from 1937 to 1941 depended heavily on American capital, strategic materials and technology for its aggressions in Asia. The Japanese government, the puppet regime of Manchukuo and its ruler, the Kwantung Army, supported the industrialist Yoshisuke Ayukawa's decision to centre his conglomerate consisting of heavy and chemical industries there and to attract foreign capital, especially from the US.[5] A staff member at the American consulate in Mukden, Manchuria, John Paton Davies, observed that for 'Manchukuo' to become Japan's industrial base serving Japan's expansionism in China, Ayukawa needed American and British investments to fulfil the puppet regime's ambitious five-year plan for boosting its heavy and chemical industries. On 24 December 1937, Davies told Naoki Hoshino, a senior Japanese bureaucrat in 'Manchukuo', that this required the Kwantung Army to relax economic controls and permit foreign investments but he doubted this would happen.[6] Furthermore, if Japan and its puppet regime, 'Manchukuo', pressed the US to adhere to their decision in December 1937 to relinquish extraterritorial rights in Manchuria, this could lead to America's complete denial of dealing with 'Manchukuo' on an unofficial basis, an issue to be addressed when discussing the possibility of modus vivendi in late November 1941.

Japan's drive for autarky never addressed the fundamental issue of how to become independent from American oil. The US supplied about eighty per cent of Japan's energy requirements. The remainder came from the Dutch East Indies (Indonesia). According to Miller, 'In the twenty-first century, it is hard to imagine how overwhelmingly the United States dominated the global petroleum industry; the US supplied 63 per cent of the global supply of crude oil and consumed about the same percentage.' Japanese policy makers therefore pursued diplomatic talks with the United States to avoid war in order to secure oil.[7]

Most scholars agree that Japan's decision to send troops from northern Indochina to southern Indochina started the clock ticking for war with the United States. Akira Iriye argues that the point of no return in US–Japanese relations was American President Franklin D. Roosevelt and British Prime Minister Winston Churchill's decision to contain Japan's northward and southward thrust taken during the Argentia Conference on 9 August.[8] From early 1941 until then, the two countries had been discussing solutions for a rapprochement with Japan. The two big stumbling blocks were the Tripartite alliance, which Japan formed with Germany and Italy in September 1940, and the Sino-Japanese War. Lend Lease, approved by Congress in March 1941, authorized military aid not only to Britain, but later to China after 6 May and the Soviet Union after 22 June. During the first summit between Roosevelt and Churchill they not only agreed on the Atlantic Charter but also to provide aid to Stalin and to prevent Japan's expansion toward south-east Asia.

Could war between Japan and the United States after the summer of 1941 still have been postponed?[9] Continued debates have centred on whether the Hull Note, handed to the two Japanese ambassadors in Washington, DC,

Kichisaburo Nomura and Saburo Kurusu, on 26 November 26, might have delayed war. This argument was actually nullified by Churchill's and Chiang Kai-shek's opposition to appeasing Japan and by Japan's desperation for oil and inability to contain the mounting pressure for war against the US Britain and Holland. Even had Japan been willing to postpone the surprise attack on Pearl Harbor and negotiate troop withdrawal from China and Indochina in exchange for oil, the US stance on 'Manchukuo' had hardened during 1940–1. The Japanese military, deluded by optimistic information from the Germanophile Ambassador in Berlin, General Hiroshi Oshima, discounted the possibility that the Soviets might reverse the German offensives against Moscow in the week before the attack on Pearl Harbor. Tokyo was focused on going to war, while Japanese diplomats in Washington, who undoubtedly read more realistic American news reports about the Russian campaign, were still frantically trying to prevent it.[10]

Japan's advance into northern Indochina in September 1940 was met by increased American economic sanctions. Japan had justified coercing Vichy France to accept the stationing of Japanese troops there as necessary for its military operations against the Chungking government led by Chiang Kai-shek, but the Americans, British and Dutch were convinced that Japan would use southern Indochina to attack their colonial possessions in Southeast Asia to plunder their resources. Japan ignored Roosevelt's 28 July proposal to Kichisaburo Nomura, Japanese Ambassador to the United States, for creating a neutral Indochina and equal access to resources there in exchange for withdrawal of Japanese troops from Indochina; on that day Japanese troops moved into southern Indochina. Secretary of State Cordell Hull became embittered when months of talks with Nomura produced only further Japanese expansionism. Roosevelt in addition to freezing all Japanese assets in the United States on 25 July, introduced an oil embargo on 1 August. Britain immediately followed suit. In August Roosevelt and Churchill issued a stern warning to Japan. Churchill wanted an ultimatum to protect Britain's flow of much-needed resources from its colonies in south-east Asia, but Roosevelt toned down the statement.[11]

The full-scale American economic sanctions, which Japanese civilian and military leaders had not anticipated, had unintended but severe consequences for both countries. Under Secretary of State Sumner Welles, who shared top American military officials' anxiety about avoiding war with Japan at least until American forces in the Pacific had enough capability to defend themselves, advised caution. He suggested that Roosevelt allow pending export licenses for oil to Japan to be honoured and in a few weeks permit licensing of oil exports to Japan subject to the 1935–6 quota. Roosevelt agreed, but hotter heads in the administration such as Morgenthau, Acheson, State Department Adviser on Far Eastern Affairs Stanley Hornbeck and Interior Secretary of State Harold Ickes prevailed.

Hull thought oil sales to Japan would continue on a case-by-case basis even with these embargoes, but overzealous sub-cabinet-level officers in the State and Treasury Departments made no such exceptions. Hull did not become aware of this situation for weeks after the United States, Great Britain and the Dutch froze Japanese bank accounts and refused to sell oil and other strategic raw materials to Japan. Roosevelt's role remains uncertain. Miller writes: 'An absence of evidence prevents an undisputed conclusion as to whether Roosevelt accepted the unconditional freeze of Japan's dollars because it was thrust upon him or because it was the policy he desired.'[12]

Miwa has examined whether the decision to freeze Japanese assets and impose a complete halt to American supply of oil to Japan left the Roosevelt administration little diplomatic leeway. He analyses the diplomatic attempts to find loopholes in the financial freeze by Sadao Iguchi, Counsellor in the Japanese Embassy, whom Acheson described as 'indefatigable',[13] and by Tsutomu Nishiyama, the Japanese Financial Commissioner and a former board member of the Yokohama Specie Bank. He endorses Miller's view that Acheson, Morgenthau and his staff rather than Roosevelt and Hull insisted on the tough policies that provoked Japan to use force to secure strategic raw materials in south-east Asia.[14]

Japanese policymakers in November 1941 concluded their synthetic fuel project in Manchuria was a 'pipe dream' supplying only a tiny portion of Japan's energy requirements. American policymakers should have been aware of this. The State Department knew of Japan's failures to establish synthetic fuel and other industries to achieve 'self-sufficiency' from Manchurian consular reports. In October 1941, U. Alexis Johnson, the post-war American Ambassador to Japan, reported from Mukden that Japan's synthetic fuel project was making little progress.[15] American diplomats had an excellent grasp of Japan's failures to boost Manchuria as its independent industrial base from 1937 to 1941.[16]

With no oil forthcoming from Manchuria, Japan tried to secure oil supplies from the Dutch East Indies through diplomacy and threats of force. From September 1940 to the time of American freezing of Japanese assets Japan negotiated with Dutch officials in Batavia for oil and other strategic raw materials. During much of that time, from December 1940 to June 1941, Sadao Iguchi's father-in-law, Kenkichi Yoshizawa, a veteran China Hand who had served as Foreign Minister under his father-in-law, Prime Minister Tsuyoshi Inukai, was representing Japan in negotiating with Dutch authorities in Batavia. (Inukai, who was one of the key sponsors assisting Sun Yat-sen during his exile in Japan, was assassinated during his premiership by naval officers while trying to purge Army officers responsible for the Manchuria Incident and to seek a compromise with China: the Inukai cabinet marked an end to nurture of parliamentary democracy during the pre-war period.)[17]

After the outbreak of war between Germany and the USSR on 22 June 1941 American concerns about Japanese intentions increased. Foreign Minister Matsuoka advocated that Japan attack the Soviet Union but Konoye dissolved the cabinet to remove him. American policy makers wanted to stop Japan's northward and southward expansion to enable the Soviets to concentrate on fighting the Germans and to deny Japanese control over strategic raw materials in south-east Asia. Until they were convinced the USSR would survive they sought to buy time to contain Japan. On 1 December Germany made a last desperate attempt to capture Moscow. On 5 December, in temperatures that plummeted to minus 30 degrees Celsius, the Soviets launched a successful counteroffensive.[18]

Konoye's cabinet collapsed in mid-October when Roosevelt rebuffed his overtures for a summit. Senator Elbert D. Thomas, a Democrat from Utah who had lived in Japan with wife as a Mormon missionary from 1907 to 1912 and was fluent in Japanese. sensed that this meant war. Hideki Tojo, War Minister and the war hawk in the Konoye cabinet, formed a new cabinet on 18 October. Lord Keeper of the Privy Seal Kido recommended Tojo to Emperor Hirohito, who wanted to avoid war with the United States and Britain, because he was loyal to the Emperor and could counter any opposition should a compromise be reached between America and Japan, but America remained deeply suspicious of the new government's intentions.[19]

The fundamental issue throughout 1941 was that Japan would not accede to Hull's four principles: territorial integrity, non-interference in the internal affairs of other countries, equal economic opportunity and change in order through peaceful means. Hull made this a precondition of bilateral talks and negotiations in the spring (the John Doe Associates), the summer (Konoye's attempt for a summit with Roosevelt) and in November–December 1941.[20] America insisted on the Open Door principle in dealing with Japan in 1941. Ambassador Nomura's choice of Raoul E. Desvernine, a noted anti-Roosevelt figure, as his adviser was unwise, but most of Japan's influential American contacts were right-wing Republicans and it proved impossible to recruit a Democrat with the ear of the President. Furthermore, the Japanese Consulate General in New York City ran a propaganda operation which further alienated the American government. In spring 1941, when diplomat Hidenari Terasaki arrived in Washington, one of his aims was to influence American isolationists, and he made contacts with O.K. Armstrong, a leading American Firster.

Desvernine was close to Herbert C. Hoover, the former US President known for his antagonistic relations with Roosevelt since the 1932 Presidential election. Hoover shared the non-interventionist outlook voiced by America's largest voluntary political organization, the America First Committee. Desvernine, when President of Crucible Steel, evinced strong interest in conducting business with Ayukawa's economic interests in Manchuria. Hoover advised Desvernine and Ambassador Nomura's colleague, Japanese Financial Commissioner Tsutomu Nishiyama in New York City. Ambassador Kurusu's eleventh-hour contact with Bernard Baruch was made possible by Desvernine acting upon Hoover's advice. Roosevelt remained suspicious of Japanese motives but permitted Baruch to have a dialogue with Kurusu and Nomura.[21]

American deciphering of Japanese diplomatic codes via MAGIC meant Roosevelt and Hull knew that the 5 November 1941 Imperial Conference had decided on a break in relations with America if no compromise was reached by 25 November, a date which was later revised to 29 November in a cable sent from Tokyo to Ambassador Nomura on 22 November (Tokyo time).[22] Because Tokyo did not inform Ambassador Nomura that Japan was going to war by early December, American officials did not grasp that date. They were, however, much more aware than the two Japanese ambassadors that war was imminent after 1 December from their readings of Japanese diplomatic cables between Tokyo and Berlin.

Foreign Minister Shigenori Togo sent Saburo Kurusu to assist Ambassador Nomura. Hull knew there were two plans for a compromise with the United States. Both included withdrawal of troops from Indochina in exchange for lifting the oil embargo and the financial freeze. Proposal A, which demanded American acquiescence in a Japanese-led order in Asia; (e.g., withdrawal of Japanese troops from China within 2 years except North China and other specified areas for 25 years and the suspension of the U.S. aids to China) and Proposal B, which was a stop-gap measure that did not address fundamental issues dividing the two countries such as shelving the China question but demanded resumption of trade between Japan and the United States, including a specific quantity of oil to be supplied from the US. When Nomura submitted Proposal A to him on 7 November, Hull promptly rejected it, as did Roosevelt on 10 November. Roosevelt told Nomura that Japan must withdraw troops from Indochina and China. Plan A was clearly dead, so Plan B was cabled to Nomura shortly before Kurusu's arrival in Washington on 17 November. Togo indicated that this was Japan's final proposal and if no compromise could be reached based upon it, the bilateral diplomatic talks could be ruptured. Because Nomura thought it essential to offer a more clear-cut commitment to withdraw troops from Indochina so that Hull would not reject Plan B, when he saw the Secretary of State on 18 November, he proposed, without securing prior approval from the Foreign Minister, a status quo ante to return the bilateral relations back to the situation prior to Japan's advance into southern Indochina. Hull was willing to listen to this idea since he was very aware that top American military officials wanted to postpone armed conflict with Japan until spring 1942 to build sufficient forces in the Pacific. When Togo received Nomura's report, he was enraged by Nomura's premature leakage of Japan's ultimate compromise to commit full removal of armed forces from Southern Indochina to Northern Indochina and ordered him to submit Proposal B (embodying an abstract intention to withdraw from Indochina), which he did to Hull on 20 November. Hull said he would consider the matter within his government and with the British, Chinese, Dutch and Australian ambassadors.[23]

On 26 November, the same day that Japanese Naval Task force left Hitokappu Bay, Kuriles, for Pearl Harbor, the crisis between US and Japan deepened when Hull, with Roosevelt's approval, handed a stern note to the two Japanese ambassadors in Washington demanding that Japan withdraw all military and police forces from China, sign six power non-aggression agreements (with, America, Britain., Holland, China and Thailand), confirm the neutrality of Indochina, allow equal economic access to Indochina, recognize Chiang Kai-shek's regime, deny military, political or economic aid to other regimes in China, and not fulfil its obligations under the Tripartite pact with Germany and Italy. In return, America would resume bilateral trade, remove the financial freeze on Japanese assets in the US and negotiate a bilateral reciprocal free trade treaty. Japan could decipher coded American diplomatic cables, and believed that a modus vivendi was likely to be presented to the two Japanese ambassadors. Government officials in Japan, including Tojo and Togo, based this interpretation on their reading of American diplomatic cables reaching Ambassador Grew in Tokyo. On 30 November, Togo cabled Nomura to protest the sudden American shift in negotiating posture as evidenced by the 'Hull Note'.[24] Japan's disappointment was based on their last minute's hope that the U.S. could accept Japan's Proposal B with modification of limiting the provisional accord of modus vivendi for three months to be renewable by agreement. However, Roosevelt and Hull did not make any promise during their conversations with Nomura and Kurusu that the U.S. Government agreed to shelve the China issue and give a free hand to Japan. The essence of the Hull Note was the U.S. package of modus vivendi with the Japanese commitment of total withdrawal from China to restore peace in East Asia. To this firm U.S. demand, the Japanese Army could not agree.

Upon hearing this, Senator Thomas warned that a war against Japan could not easily be won, attracting wide press criticism. On 26 November Nomura and Kurusu advised that an exchange of telegrams between President Franklin Roosevelt and Emperor Hirohito outlining their mutual desire to avoid war might ease the growing tension. Kurusu originally got this idea after hearing a rumour that some quarters in Washington had suggested Roosevelt send a telegram of goodwill to Emperor Hirohito in October 1941 to avert the downfall of the Konoye cabinet. When he reached Washington in November, Kurusu learned from his subordinate Hidenari Terasaki that such an idea was still being suggested by influential men like Thomas and Reverend E. Stanley Jones. On 3 December Jones met Roosevelt and, based on his meeting with Terasaki, urged the President to send a telegram to Emperor Hirohito emphasizing the need for maintaining peace in the Pacific.

On 1 December the Japanese Government decided to go to war against the US, UK and Holland. MAGIC revealed the contents of Togo's three cables in response to Oshima's 29 November telegram from Berlin. Oshima wrote that Hitler and Ribbentrop were eager for an immediate Japanese attack on the US and that Germany would then declare war on America. Ribbentrop, disguising Germany's faltering military situation near Moscow, informed Oshima that Germany expected victory against the Soviet Union in 1942. In response, Togo argued that Japan could not accept the Hull Note's demand for dismantling the Tripartite Pact. Since August 1941 Japan had been trying to reassure the US government that the Tripartite Pact did not oblige Japan automatically to declare war on the US and Japan could exercise independent judgment on war participation under the Pact.

In cable 985 Togo instructed Oshima secretly to inform Hitler and Ribbentrop that Japan's diplomacy with the US 'now stand[s] ruptured' and 'there is extreme danger that war may suddenly break out between the Anglo-Saxon nations and Japan through some clash of arms ... and the time of the breaking out of this war may come quicker than anyone dreams'. In cable 986 Togo told Oshima to inform the two German leaders that Japan's priority was expanding southward, but if the Soviet Union decided to strengthen further its ties to America and Britain Japan would consider intervention there. Togo did not send these cables to the two Japanese ambassadors in the US. These and other cables translated by MAGIC were also not sent to the top American army and navy commanders in Hawaii, which later led to the argument that had they been provided with that information they would have judged that there was not any hope of a diplomatic solution.[25]

Roosevelt, who read the MAGIC intercepts, was naturally suspicious about Japanese intentions. The two Japanese diplomats were completely unaware of the imminence of war between the two countries. All they knew was that 29 November was the deadline for a compromise with the US. On 28 November MAGIC intercepted a cable from Togo to the two ambassadors informing them that 'the negotiations will be de facto ruptured. This is inevitable.' However, he added, 'I do not wish you to give the impression that the negotiations are broken off'.[26]

According to Henry Morgenthau's diary entry of 3 December 1941, Roosevelt told Morgenthau 'he had the Japanese running around like a lot of wet hens'. After, he asked them the question (on 2 December through Under-Secretary of State Sumner Welles) as to why they were sending so many military, naval and air forces into Indo-China. Roosevelt thought 'the Japanese [were] doing everything they can to stall until they are ready'. In the meantime, he was 'talking with the English about war plans as to when and where the USA and Great Britain should strike'.[27] Baruch's conferences with Kurusu at the former's residence in the Mayfair Hotel on 3 December had Roosevelt's full consent. Baruch 'dictated a full report of the conversations to the President – including a request that Mr Roosevelt send a personal appeal direct to Emperor Hirohito'. Both men were well aware of the grim situation and Kurusu agreed with Baruch's warning that in the event of a war between the two countries Japan 'will be completely crushed by the US because of its industrial might'.[28] Baruch later denied he had made a 'suggestion for a one-billion dollar loan to Japan' as a means of avoiding war.[29] Kurusu claimed this was discussed during the meeting.[30] According to Kurusu, Baruch told him that he was worried about the slow progress in America's military preparedness programme and saw no reason for Japan and the US to go into war. Like many other American policymakers, Baruch was concerned primarily with developments in the European theatre. In the Far East, he saw an underlying insecurity in the psyche of the Japanese military since their loss to the Soviet Army at Nomohan in 1939. They discovered their limit through that battle and felt nervous about it. In order to remove the 'inferiority complex' of the Japanese military, Baruch argued that Roosevelt's 'arsenal of democracy' idea should be applied to Japan in a way that would help build Japan's industries and boost its production. Baruch suggested to Kurusu that America should lend $1 billion to Japan for its industrial development.[31] After his meeting with the Japanese diplomats, Baruch 'immediately telephoned General Watson, who came over with a White House stenographer to whom [he] dictated a summary of [his] conversations with Kurusu'. According to Kurusu, after their meeting on 3 December Baruch sensed a positive reaction from the President and he told Kurusu that he and the President were planning to meet for the second time regarding this matter on 10 December.[32]

Nomura cabled Togo on the morning of 6 December about the progress he and Kurusu had made in their attempts to continue diplomacy. In Nomura's cable 1272, he discusses Initiatives A and B, which seem to have been carried out by Baruch. Initiative A referred to the 4 December lunch between Roosevelt and Nomura's and Kurusu's 'operative'. The operative had argued that Roosevelt should act as an intermediary in the Sino-Japanese War to avoid a US–Japan war. Initiative B was Nomura's and Kurusu's attempt to formulate a new proposal to the US to persuade Hull to present it as a new American initiative. The two ambassadors stressed that Hull might seem dogmatic but people well acquainted with him told them he could 'be quite flexible' in the actual application of principles.[33]

Yet Togo ignored this cable. The two Japanese ambassadors' suggestion of an exchange of cables between Roosevelt and Hirohito had upset him. Tojo, Togo, Navy Minister Shimada and Lord Keeper Kido agreed the scheme was impossible, as they feared a rebellion if Japan was seen to be giving in to the 'Hull Note' demands.[34]

At 6.00 p.m. on 6 December Roosevelt received information that the Japanese were about to wage war. Roosevelt sent his cable to Hirohito urging peace to Ambassador Grew to ensure the message would not be held up in the Foreign Ministry. Roosevelt instructed Hull to send the message by grey code to save time even at the risk of having the message intercepted. The message arrived at noon in Tokyo, but the cable was automatically delayed for ten hours. Grew knew such a message was coming because he had heard about it on the daily San Francisco radio broadcast, but he did not receive the coded triple-priority message until 10.30 p.m. and the telegram reached Emperor Hirohito after the attack at Pearl Harbor had begun.[35] Upon their return to Japan in 1942, Nomura and Kurusu learned from Tojo that he felt Japan probably would not have started the war had the 6 December cable from the President been sent a few days earlier and had the Hull Note been a little more conciliatory.[36] Tojo's comment, however, should be understood in the context of Japan's increasing military disadvantage after its defeat at Midway.

After Pearl Harbor, although Hoover publicly called for unity to carry out the war effort, he remained critical of Roosevelt's policy toward Japan.[37] Meanwhile, Desvernine ran into trouble with the American government after Pearl Harbor, when the Justice Department considered prosecuting him because of his involvement in the clandestine effort at the eleventh hour. This charge was dropped when Baruch told Attorney General Francis Biddle that 'he would appear as the first witness for the defense'.[38]

Kurusu wrote to Ayukawa on 6 September 1946 that he was 'filled with deep emotion' when he compared Japan's

> numerous economic difficulties up ahead with [his] negotiation with Bernard Baruch over a billion-dollar loan to Japan [right before Pearl Harbor], a subject matter having close relations with [Ayukawa's] activities before the war; [Kurusu] really regret[ted] the fact that that one-in-a-million opportunity slipped through [his] hands [because of Pearl Harbor].[39]

Roosevelt and his cabinet, at their meeting on 7 November, were confident that the American public would support America going to war if Japan attacked British or Dutch possessions in south-east Asia. On the afternoon of 1 December Roosevelt assured the British Ambassador Lord Halifax that America would fight in such an eventuality. Yet it remained uncertain whether US public opinion would support war. This dilemma was solved by Japan's attack on Pearl Harbor, which Roosevelt called a day that 'shall live in infamy'. Although Hitler and Ribbentrop told Ambassador Oshima that Germany would go to war with Japan if the latter attacked the United States the Tripartite Alliance did not require the three powers to declare war on the US unless the latter first attacked one of them. On 11 December Hitler did Roosevelt a favour by declaring war on the US, allowing the President to make the destruction of Hitler's regime the first objective in America's war aims.[40]

Yet we must consider whether in late November a modus vivendi avoiding war with Japan was possible. On the morning of 26 November the Japanese government cabled its embassy in Washington demanding oil, including aviation gasoline. The Hull Note was handed to the two Japanese ambassadors in the afternoon. The American draft modus vivendi offered much less that Japan demanded, prohibited the sale of aviation gasoline and allowed oil only for civilian usage. On this basis the odds against an agreement seemed overwhelming. Furthermore, the Americans considered renewing the selling of oil on a monthly basis for up to three months.[41] As Herbert Feis pointed out in his book on Pearl Harbor in 1950:

> If possible disputes over troop movements on both sides after a truce agreement did not bring the truce to a quick end, arguments over oil would have done so. Very different notions existed in Tokyo and Washington as to what was expected under the phrase, 'a required quantity of oil [in Japan's Proposal B].' The Japanese Government ... wanted four million tons a year from the United States and one million tons a year from the Indies. The American Government would not have agreed to supply anything like such quantities, which were enough to keep Japanese reserves intact.[42]

Could the two Japanese ambassadors have continued talks with the United States based on the Hull Note? For example, what about 'Manchukuo'? Ambassador Yoshijiro Umezu (later Chief of Staff) cabled from 'Manchukuo' to the Foreign Ministry in Tokyo to enquire whether Hull's proposal included Manchuria. He apparently received no reply. The Hull Note did not demand that Japan relinquish the South Manchuria Railway, so even if the United States demanded a reversion to the position before the Manchuria Incident, that would not have meant Japan giving up the railroad or its right to militarily protect it. American officials may have entertained the idea of recognizing 'Manchukuo' in drafting a modus vivendi that was never presented. The US, which, until 1939 had applied a watered-down version of the Open Door principle to Manchuria, now shifted to a rigid application of it.[43] Hull's Note set no specific deadline for Japanese troop withdrawals from China. Despite Tojo's persistent opposition to troop withdrawal from China, there might have been some room for an agreement on a withdrawal timetable. Against this is the fact that Japan had set up puppet regimes in China and had refused to talk to the Chungking government since January 1938. Once they received the Hull Note, even those Japanese leaders who had deep misgivings about war against Britain and America could not overcome vociferous voices in the Japanese military arguing for war. Former Ambassador to the United Kingdom and post-war Prime Minister Shigeru Yoshida told Togo that he should not interpret the Hull Note as a de facto ultimatum because Yoshida believed it could be a basis for negotiation as prefaced in the Hull Note. Kido's 29 November diary entry indicated that voices for moderation around the Imperial Throne could not contain the louder voices urging war. Those Japanese leaders who had deep misgivings about going to war against America and Britain dared not resist because of the memory of bloody assassinations that followed a 26 February 1936 coup attempt. As Emperor Hirohito recalled in his monologue recorded by his staff in spring 1946, he could not oppose the decision to go to war because anyone who opposed would be killed and a much more violent regime installed in the aftermath of a bloody coup.[44]

In October 2004 the Japanese Foreign Ministry (hereafter the Ministry) published the original documents of Japan's Final Memorandum (hereafter the Memo) submitted to the US on Sunday 7 December 1941. The *New York Times* had reported already on 9 December 1999 Takeo Iguchi's discovery of the original draft in a file of the Diplomatic Records Office of the Ministry. The documents reveal that the Ministry intended to use a standard version of ultimatum by concluding that 'we are forced to terminate the negotiations … and that your government shall be held responsible for all the consequences that may arise in the future'. However, the last phrase hinting at use of force against the US was eliminated under the pressure from the military in the final text of 5 December. Article I of the Hague Convention required the prior delivery of an ultimatum in clear wording. The final notice to the US was too equivocal to satisfy such requirements. Confidential military documents proved that

Japanese army and navy Chiefs of Staff pressed the Ministry not to issue any notice before the attack since it might jeopardize their surprise operations. Togo insisted on prior notice and Japan submitted the following Memo to terminate the negotiations: 'The Japanese Government regrets to have to notify hereby the American Government in view of the attitude of the American Government it cannot but consider that it is impossible to reach an agreement through further negotiations.'[45]

Japanese envoys in Washington met Hull a little after 2.00 p.m on Sunday 7 December 1941, forty minutes after the attack in Pearl Harbor. Tokyo's instructions had been to deliver the Memo at 1:00 p.m., a mere half an hour before the attack. Roosevelt denounced Japan's method: 'the US was suddenly and deliberately attacked while negotiations were continuing and a Japanese reply to the message of the United States contained no threat nor hint of war or armed attack'.[46] To defend Japan's position of attacking the US without a prior ultimatum, it was later argued that since Japan was suffering from economic sanctions it had a right to save itself from economic extinction and a war of self-defence obviated an obligation to issue an ultimatum. The following entry of 29 November 1941 in the 'Confidential War Diary' of the Army General Staff should also be noted: 'The US has not made any preparation for war. A sudden attack on the US is to be consummated more successfully than German blitzkrieg on the USSR.'

Would the half-hour prior notice intended by the Japanese government have satisfied the contemporary international legal requirements? At the Far Eastern Military Tribunal, it was pointed out that relevant provisions of the Hague Convention were technically defective since they did not specify a precise length of time required for a prior notice and that Japan had taken advantage of this legal loophole. Japanese lawyers further argued that prior notice was in effect delivered since the US had already decoded and read the text of Japanese Memo before the attack. An important reference about the timing of delivery of the Memo is found in the 'Records of Discussions' written by the Japanese army's Chief of Staff, General Sugiyama. At the meeting of the Japanese government and Supreme Military Command on 4 December, Togo proposed that, in order to submit the final notice to the US to terminate negotiations in lieu of an ultimatum, a text of the Memo should be sent from Tokyo to the Embassy in Washington on 5 December so that its decoding could be completed on 6 December. The military insisted the Memo should be further delayed by one day to ensure a successful naval operation. Sugiyama recorded in his entry of 6 December that it should be sent to the Embassy at 4.00 a.m. on 7 December (Japanese Standard Time) and its submission to the US Government was set at 3.00 a.m. on 8 December (Japanese Standard Time). However, what actually happened was that the dispatch of the Memo was not completed by 4 a.m. and the concluding part of the Memo was sent twelve hours later at 4.00 p.m. This delayed dispatch of the last part of the Memo critically handicapped the final typing of the whole text by the Embassy on Saturday 6 December making impossible the delivery of the Memo on Sunday 7 December at 1.00 p.m., just before the surprise attack.

The causes of delay were multiple: a combination of top-level decision making, military pressures on timing to safeguard the secrecy of the attack and the communication processes for transmitting coded text from the Ministry by way of the Tokyo Central Telegram Office to the US. Japan confused its own embassy in Washington about its intentions and this contributed to the problems of 7 December. Since Tokyo meticulously planned to inform the US State Department at 1.00 p.m., barely half an hour before the Pearl Harbor attack, they should have taken every care to ensure efficient and accurate handlings by the Embassy for decoding and finalizing the Memo to enable its punctual delivery. Indeed the whole text, including the final conclusion of the Memo and all corrections, should have arrived by the afternoon of Saturday 6 December at the latest, as decided in Tokyo on 4 December.

The deciphering of Roosevelt's message to the Emperor may have caused a change in the communication schedule between Tokyo and Washington. This theory would attenuate those who were culpable in withholding the cabling of the final part of the Memo for twelve hours, although they should not be exonerated for their wilful interference in the communications of the heads of states. There is also documentary evidence that reveals that tampering with urgent cables by lowering their level of urgency might have occurred. For example, the instruction cable for presenting the Memo at 1.00 p.m. was designated in the Ministry's original document as 'most urgent', requiring the delivery to the Embassy at any time, even at the latest hour, but in the corresponding MAGIC intercepted cable it reads 'urgent – very important'. An urgent-designated cable is sent to the Embassy not after mid-night but in the first morning delivery whereas one marked as 'very/extremely urgent' should be delivered late at night. Kameyama, who headed the Ministry's Telegram Section, had a muddled explanation of the confused designation and the delayed corrections of cables at the Far Eastern Military Tribunal and in his posthumous papers. Some cover-ups and distortions of events surrounding Pearl Harbor diplomacy were made after the war perhaps to save the honour of their organizations or save themselves. It serves no purpose to distort historical facts or bury controversy. Each nation wishes to write its own history with pride and dignity, but they should avoid a trap of national fanaticism, dogma and cover-ups.[47]

On 6 December 1941 President Roosevelt sent a telegram addressed to the Japanese Emperor and expressed in general terms his wish to maintain peace in the Pacific. The American Ambassador in Tokyo, Joseph Grew, was supposed to receive that cable but because of a deliberate delay in the handling of this cable in the Tokyo Central Postal Office Ambassador Grew did not receive the message in a way that would have permitted him to have an audience with Emperor Hirohito before the Japanese surprise attack on Pearl Harbor.[48] During the war, Senator Thomas argued that there was 'pretty good evidence that he was not even allowed to receive the [cable] sent to him by President Roosevelt just before Pearl Harbor, at least until war broke out, and it was too late'.[49]

When considering Japan's exorbitant proposal for oil, Miwa may be right about the likelihood of diplomatic failure even if a modus vivendi had been chosen by both parties as the starting point for the final talks just before Pearl Harbor.[50] By mid-January 1942 Marshall Georgi Zhukov's Soviet forces had pushed the Germans back to where they had commenced Operation Typhoon two months earlier, but Japan at the time was preoccupied with its military successes and operations in south-east Asia. Soviet spy Richard Sorge's spy ring in Japan had succeeded in finding out through its member Hotsumi Ozaki that the Japanese government had decided on a southern advance. This pivotal information was cabled to Moscow in early October and led to the redeployment on 12 October of 4 million troops 1,000 planes and 1,000 tanks westward across Siberia to defend Moscow – a critical component in Stalin's success in holding the Soviet capital and beginning to turn the tide in the European war.[51]

Japan, unlike Germany, was not a mortal threat to the United States. Even if enough B17s were deployed in the Philippines and elsewhere in the Pacific to deter Japanese attack, they had serious flaws because they were ineffective in bombing naval ships. The Open Door in China was not a vital interest for the United States either. The United States, however, could not accept Japanese domination of the Asia-Pacific region. A compromise with Japan in late November could have resulted in the breakup of the coalition that Roosevelt had worked on to contain the Japanese as observed by China's appeal to Roosevelt and Churchill not to compromise and the luke-warm or reluctant attitude of Britain, Australia and Holland to compromise on modus vivendi.[52]

Yet there remains that lingering and nagging question: what if Japan and the US had decided to postpone war for three months? This counterfactual recurred during the Cold War and post-Cold War years and has not been fully answered.[53]

Notes

1 E. Miller, *Bankrupting the Enemy: The US Financial Siege of Japan before Pearl Harbor.* Annapolis, 2007, p. 108.

2 M. Chadwin, *The Warhawks: American Interventionists before Pearl Harbor.* New York, 1968, pp. v–vi, 22, 28–9, 45, 58–60, 78–9, 87–9, 113–14, 120–3, 134–41, 154–9, 175.

3 Y. Kato, *Mosaku suru Senkyuhyakusanjyu nendai: Nichibei Kankei to Rikugun Chyukenso.* Tokyo, 1993, pp. 67–79.

4 S. Kitaoka, *Nihon no Rekishi 5: Seito kara Gunbu e.* Tokyo, 1999, pp. 298–9.

5 H. Iguchi, *Unfinished Business: Ayukawa Yoshisuke and US–Japan Relations, 1937–1953.* Cambridge, MA, 2003.

6 J.P. Davies Jr to N.T. Johnson, American Ambassador, Peiping, 4 January 1938, 'China: Mukden Consul General Records, 1938, 631-800', Box 19, RECORD GROUP 84, College Park, MD; J. Davies Jr to Secretary of State Hull, 'Manchurian Heavy Industries Company and American Investments Therein', 4 January 1938, pp. 16–17. 'China: Mukden Consul General Records', 1938, pp. 631-800, Box 19, RECORD GROUP 84, College Park, MD.

7 Miller, *Bankrupting the Enemy*, p. 157.

8 A. Iriye, *Origins of the Second World War in Asia and the Pacific.* New York, 1987.

9 N. Saul, *Friends or Foe? The United States and Russia, 1921–1941*. Kansas, 2006, pp. 382–3; W. Cohen, *America's Response to China: A History of Sino-American Relations* 4th ed. New York, 2000, pp. 124–5.

10 On the other hand, at the time of Foreign Minister Yosuke Matsuoka's pursuit of a Neutrality Pact with the USSR, the Japanese government ignored Ambassador Oshima's warnings on 18 April, 4 and 6 June that Germany was planning to attack the Soviet Union. Oshiama's June cables stated that Adolf Hitler and Foreign Minister Joachim von Ribbentrop informed him of such a plan; Oshima's April cable was ignored by Japanese top civilian and military officials.

11 T. Wilson, *The First Summit: Roosevelt and Churchill at Placentia Bay, 1941*. Kansas, 1991, pp. 136–8; H, Feis, *The Road to Pearl Harbor*. Princeton, 1950, pp. 255–8.

12 On export licensing, see Miller, *Bankrupting the Enemy*, pp. 198, 200. M. Miwa, *Taiheiyo senso to Sekiyu*. Tokyo, 2004, ch. 2.

13 D. Acheson, *Present at the Creation: My Years in the State Department*. New York, 1969, p. 27.

14 Sadao Iguchi was my grandfather and was Japan's Vice Minister for Foreign Affairs in Japan's signing of the San Francisco Peace Treaty and the bilateral security treaty. Acheson, of course, was then the American Secretary of State.

15 Krentz to Secretary of State, 11 October 1941, U. Alexis Johnson, 'Manchuria Financial Report: June–September, 1941', 'China: Mukden Consul General Records, 1941', 850-861.3 Box 37, RECORD GROUP 84, College Park, MD.

16 H. Iguchi, 'Zai Manshu Beikoku Ryojikan to Nicchu Senso, 1937–1941' ('American Consulates in Manchuria and the Sino-Japanese War, 1937-1941' in *The Journal of Military History* vol. 45, no. 3 (December 2009), pp. 4–28.

17 T. Sakai, *Taisho Democracy Taisei no Hokai: Naisei to Gaiko*. Tokyo, 1993; C. Wilbur, *Sun Yat-Sen: Frustrated Patriot*. New York, 1976.

18 W. Heinrichs, 'The Russian Factor in Japanese–American Relations' in H. Conroy and H. Wray (eds), *Pearl Harbor Reexamined: Prologue to the Pacific War*. Honolulu, 1990.

19 16 October 1941 entry of the diary kept by Thomas's wife in Box 4 of the Elbert Thomas Papers; H. Iguchi, 'Senator Elbert D. Thomas and Japan', *Journal of American and Canadian Studies* no. 25 (2007), pp. 77–105. See also: Congress of the United States, *Investigation of the Pearl Harbor Attack: Report of the Joint Committee on the Investigation of the Pearl Harbor Attack*. Washington, 1946, p. 28.

20 Iriye, *Origins of the Second World War in Asia and the Pacific*, chs 4–6.

21 Iguchi, *Unfinished Business*, pp. 144–70. Miller provides in detail the role played by Raoul Desvernine. Roger B. Jeans, *Terasaki Hidenari, Pearl Harbor and Occupied Japan*, Lantham, 2009, 33–4.

22 Feis, *The Road to Pearl Harbor*, pp. 313, 326.

23 Ibid., pp. 303–25.

24 Gaimusho (Ministry of Foreign Affairs) (ed.), *Nihon Gaiko Bunsho Nichibei Kosho 1941nen Ge*. Tokyo, 1990, p. 212. Ken Kotani, *Nihon no Intelligence; Naze Joho ga Ikasarenainoka*, Tokyo, 2007, pp. 178–81.

25 Congress, *Investigation of the Pearl Harbor Attack*, pp. 179, 200, 204–5, 409–10. The Japanese texts of these cables are in Gaimusho (Ministry of Foreign Affairs) (ed.), *Nihon Gaiko Bunsho Nichibei Kosho 1941ne*, pp. 208–11. With regard to the Tripartite Pact, see T. Iguchi, *Demystifying Pearl Harbor: A New Perspective from Japan* tr. D. Noble. Tokyo, 2010, p. 102.

26 Iguchi, *Demystifying Pearl Harbor*, p. 102.

27 J. Blum, *Roosevelt and Morgenthau: A Revision and Condensation of From the Morgenthau Diaries*. Boston, 1970, p. 420.

28 'Japan Pair "Didn't Know": Envoys Still Maintain Pearl Harbor Surprise' and 'Pre-Pearl Harbor Confabs Said Held with FDR Consent', *The Pacific Stars and Stripes*, 7 December 1951, Microfiche Number 136.1, Ayukawa Yoshisuke Papers. .

29 'Pre-Pearl Harbor Confabs Said Held with FDR Consent'.

30 Kurusu, *Nichibeigaiko Hiwa*. Tokyo, 1952, p. 170.

31 The $1 billion episode is also mentioned in Kurusu Saburo to Ayukawa Yoshisuke, 6 September 1946, Microfiche Number 511.1, and Kurusu to Prime Minister Yoshida Shigeru, 22 November 1951, Microfiche Number 136.1, Ayukawa Yoshisuke Papers. Kurusu's letter to Yoshida

mentions that Baruch had thought providing $10 billion to Japan would calm the 'inferiority complex' of the Japanese military.

32 B. Baruch, *Baruch: The Public Years*. New York, 1960, pp. 28–91; and Kurusu, *Nichibeigaiko Hiwa*, pp. 168–70, 179. Kurusu states in his memoir the talks between the two took place on 30 November but the Morgenthau Diary and a cable from Nomura to Tokyo indicate the meeting occurred in December.

33 Iguchi, *Demystifying Pearl Harbor*, p. 226.

34 S. Togo, *The Cause of War*. New York, 1956, pp. 165–6.

35 For Roosevelt's decision to send the message and its subsequent delayed delivery, see J. Toland, *The Rising Sun: The Decline and Fall of the Japanese Empire*. New York, 1970, pp. 193–4, 199; and C. Hull, *The Memoirs of Cordell Hull: Volume II*. New York, 1948, pp. 1091–4.

36 Kurusu, *Nichibeigaiko Hiwa*, p. 160.

37 J. Doenecke, 'Anti-Interventionism of Herbert Hoover', *Journal of Liberterian Studies* 8 (summer 1987), pp. 319–20.

38 Transcript, Payson J. Treat Oral History Interview, 19 September 1967, p. 15, 21 August Memo, Herbert C. Hoover Presidential Library.

39 Microfiche Number 136.2, Ayukawa Yoshisuke Papers.

40 R. Esthus, 'President Roosevelt's Commitment to Britain to Intervene in a Pacific War', *Mississippi Valley History Review* (June 1963), pp. 34–8.

41 26 November 1941, Cable No. 833 (translated by MAGIC on 26 November 1941), US Department of State, *The 'MAGIC' Background of Pearl Harbor* vol. 4. Washington, 1977, A-92. During a meeting on 1 November in which Proposal B was discussed, the draft version of Proposal B showed that Japan would demand one million tons of aviation gasoline a year. Miwa, *Taiheiyo senso to Sekiyu*, 119. See also the text of the American modus vivendi in Congress, *Investigation of the Pearl Harbor Attack*, p. 36.

42 Feis, *The Road to Pearl Harbor*, p. 311.

43 Iguchi, *Demystifying Pearl Harbor*, p. 136.

44 6 September, 29, 30 November, 1 December, Koichi Kido, *Kido Koichi Nikki* (Kido Koichi Diary). Tokyo, 1966; Kanryo Sato, *Dai Toa Senso Kaikoroku*. Tokyo, 1985, p. 158 (regarding 6 September).

45 H. French, 'Pearl Harbor Truly a Sneak Attack, Papers Show', *New York Times* 9 December 1999. See sugiyama Memo in note 47.

46 Hull, *The Memoirs of Cordell Hull*, p. 1095.

47 Iguchi, *Demystifying Pearl Harbor*, chapters 17–23. Gunjishi Gakkai '(Military History Association), eds., *Daihonei Rikugunbu Rikungunbu Senso Shidohan Kimitsu Senso Nisshi, Kinseisha*, 1998; Sanbo Honbu (Imperial Army General Staff), *Sugiyama Memo: daihonei Seif Renraku Kaigi to Nikki, Volume 1, Hara Shobo, 1989, 535–38, 563–67*.

48 Iguchi, *Unfinished Business*, 169.

49 See the transcript of 14 July 1945 broadcast by the National Broadcasting Company, p. 5, '1945 Aug. 18 Japan after Surrender', Box 78, Thomas papers.

50 Miller, *Bankrupting the Enemy*, p. 240.

51 Sorge and the members of his spy ring were arrested on 18 October. Sorge analyzed that the Japanese government had decided not to attack the Soviet Union on 2 July and it was not going to do so until the spring of 1942 at the earliest. For details, see C. Johnson, *An Instance of Treason: Ozaki Hotsumi and the Sorge Spy Ring*. Stanford, 1990,

52 J. Donecke and M. Stoler, *Debating Franklin D. Roosevelt's Foreign Policy*. Lantham, 2005, pp. 144–5. With regards to the flaws in the capability of the B17s, see M. Schaller, *Douglas MacArthur: The Far Eastern General*. New York, 1989, p. 50.

53 B. Russett, *No Clear And Present Danger: A Skeptical View Of The United States Entry Into World War II*. Boulder, 2010. Originally published by Harper & Row in 1972.

Chapter 28

Economics and the Origins of the Second World War

Richard J. Overy

There is a very obvious sense in which the Second World War was regarded as a war about economics. In 1939 a great many, perhaps the majority, on the left in Europe assumed that the war was an 'imperialist war' provoked by a crisis of capitalism. The left-wing publisher Victor Gollancz, reflecting on the nature of the war in a book published in 1942, described a process of simple economic competition:

> The capitalists of one country, supported by their government, want to seize or exploit in one form or another a particular piece of territory: the capitalists of another country may want the same piece of territory: and if they both want it greedily enough, war will result ...'[1]

These were insights first brought out by the British economist J.A. Hobson before the First World War, and famously given systematic treatment in Lenin's *Imperialism: The Highest Stage of Capitalism*, published in 1917 in Zürich and republished regularly during the 1920s and 1930s. [2] In 1938 an updated edition containing new data was published claiming to show that there had been seventy-five wars since 1918 occasioned by the capitalist order, of which no fewer than eleven were directed at the Soviet Union.[3] These are views that are now given almost no serious attention by historians when discussing the origins of the war in 1939. 'Capitalists' in most European states seem to have preferred peace to war. Even Gollancz admitted that the orthodox explanation did not work very well for 1939. He preferred to explain the origin of war not as an issue of simple economics but of an urge to 'power', in which the capitalist elite acted as the orchestrator of all the many social, political and ideological sources of the desire to project that power violently outwards.[4]

Marxist analysis of the existing international economy in the 1930s appeared nevertheless to be describing some kind of reality and it is important not to dismiss entirely the view that protecting or extending markets or seeking secure sources of raw material were not important elements of economic policy-making before 1939. What remains more problematic is the assumption that 'capitalists', a word never very clearly defined in pre-war discourse, played a leading role in creating the conditions for war and in promoting its declaration. Recent historiography has tended to argue a rather different case – that economic elites (both financial and industrial) in the major European states generally favoured appeasement as a means of avoiding war. Any conflict on the scale of 1914–18 was regarded as a calamity for economies that were trying to claw their way back from the economic recession and whose elites had memories of the disruptive aftermath of the last war. This was no less true of industrial and banking circles in Germany, which proved just as willing to discuss issues of market sharing and technical collaboration with their opposite numbers in Britain and France. The negotiation, for example, which finally produced an Anglo-German Coal Agreement on 28 January 1939, was conducted by the British Mining Association and the Rhenish–Westphalian Coal Syndicate. While both sides operated with the knowledge and support of their respective governments, the effort to agree on the relative size of coal exports was something welcomed by the two sets of mine owners on straightforward commercial grounds. It is significant that delegations from the Federation of British Industry and Reichsgruppe Industrie then followed up this agreement with a more general commitment to collaboration in order to avoid 'destructive competition', expressed in the Düsseldorf Agreement signed on 14 March 1939. This agreement was reached the day before German troops entered Prague, an event that created the circumstances that undid the Munich Settlement and alienated the British and French governments from Hitler, a fact that suggests there was a substantial gap between what businessmen were hoping for and what politicians (in this case Hitler and his entourage) were actually planning.[5]

The same interest in economic collaboration was also evident in France in the year following the Munich agreement. French businessmen visited Germany in late 1938 and 1939 and were impressed by the industrial boom they witnessed and by the idea that the entrepreneurial elite was incorporated into the whole state structure through the various economic groups and associations, capable, it was thought, of exercising an influence denied to the economic elite in France. There was strong pressure from industrial groups, particularly in the iron-producing region of Lorraine, for direct co-operation with German business along the lines sought by British interests. On 1 March 1939 the industries involved set up the *Association française d'intérêts permanents en Allemagne* and invited German representatives to Paris to discuss collaboration between different industrial branches.[6] German economic interests seem to have been less interested in collaboration with France than with Britain and the occupation of Prague did lead to a limitation, though not a cessation, of discussions between the two sides. In this case, too, international politics obtruded into international economic relations. The evidence suggests that left to themselves business elites would have preferred to find ways of reaching bilateral or multilateral market-share or price agreements. Even the German chemical giant IG Farben, which profited substantially from its integration into the production programmes of the Second Four-Year Plan in Germany, was happy to reach marketing agreements with the British-based Imperial Chemical Industries and the American Standard Oil and Dupont corporations, an enthusiasm that was fully reciprocated.[7] These surviving exchanges made commercial sense to industry whatever the political situation prevailing at the time.

In the 1930s, with the onset of rearmament, many businesses wanted to be able to make money out of lucrative state contracts for high-cost military equipment. At the same time they hoped that armaments would have a natural deterrent effect and would not result in a disruptive and destructive war. Naive or self-interested as this view may have been, it was a paradox of the growing reliance on state orders and of the diversion of investment funds to industries that profited from the military build-up. The nature of this paradox was explained by the President of the German Reichsbank, Walter Funk, in a conversation with the governor of the Bank of England, Montagu Norman, in Basle in March 1939:

> [Funk] did not wish the tug-of-war in armaments between England and Germany to go on without limit. Nor did he think that it would do so ... Meanwhile Funk hoped that the tug-of-war would go on. The activity in armaments was making Germany prosperous, not the reverse. Moreover, the more arms the two countries got, the stronger they became; and the stronger they became, the greater the hope of avoiding war.[8]

Funk may have been disingenuous in his remarks, but it was widely understood in the West as well that armaments created an artificial economic boom whose advantages were difficult to argue against, but which at the same time expanded the risk of conflict. The economist G.D.H. Cole, writing in 1939, argued that there would be recession in Britain 'but for the intensity of the rearmament campaign', but regretted the fact that rearmament provoked endless war scares.[9]

For most businesses, however, there were limits to the extent to which they could influence government policy or popular politics. Much of the economic ambition expressed in public political discourse in the 1930s was shaped by political circumstances and driven by political and military interests and did not necessarily coincide with capitalist expectations or preferences. In 1934, Gustav Krupp, one of the principal beneficiaries of German rearmament, complained to a Swiss visitor, 'Believe me, we are worse off here than the natives in Timbuctoo.'[10] The concept of the 'primacy of politics' has sometimes been used as a way to exculpate economic elites from responsibility for major political choices – war, territorial expansion – but it was a familiar concept for businessmen in the 1930s who were unused to direct political intervention and found themselves poorly prepared to contest it. The same Gustav Krupp who complained about economic policy in 1934 observed in a speech that same year that 'primacy always belongs to politics', but did not see this as something businessmen could do very much about.[11] It is perhaps more useful to see it as a way of describing how governments could and did pursue policies that failed to coincide with the perceived long-term interests of economic elites, even though these elites were usually able to adjust their interests profitably to the prevailing political reality, as they did in Germany and Japan when the economic New Order was established in Europe and Asia in the early 1940s. Ironically, the same companies that rearmed and went to war in the years 1939 to 1945 were instrumental in shaping economic co-operation in the changed political climate of the 1950s.

The principal issue of political economy in the 1930s was the division between what came to be called the 'have' or 'have-not' powers, or what the Italian dictator Benito Mussolini liked to call the 'proletarians' and the 'pluto-crats'. This was a crude characterization derived from the uneven distribution of economic resources and opportunities among the major powers and the different effects of the world economic crisis of 1929–33 that resulted from this imbalance. The 'have-not' powers were defined by their self-conscious sense that they had lost out in the scramble for empire and lacked a sufficient domestic resource base to compensate for that lack. Germany, Italy and Japan counted themselves among their number. Britain, France and the United States were regarded as the plutocratic powers, despite the damaging effects of the recession also experienced in the West.

This distinction was already articulated in the 1920s, most famously in Hans Grimm's best-selling novel *Volk ohne Raum* [*A People Without Space*], which argued that all Germany's economic and political problems would be solved by creating a larger area for the German people. But the political resent-ments it generated were ameliorated by the upswing in the world economy between 1924 and 1928 and the effort to re-establish a workable international economy after the disruptions of the Great War.[12] The sense of being 'have-not' powers was exacerbated by the breakdown of the multi-lateral commodity and currency system in the economic recession and the emergence for the following decade of neo-mercantilist policies designed to beggar neighbours and protect the homeland. A statistical memorandum prepared in Germany for the delegation to the World Economic Conference in 1933 described German financial obligations to the West as 'tribute', designed to leave Germany perma-nently impoverished and economically victimized.[13] Germany, Japan and Italy might well have coped with the recession and accepted efforts to reintegrate with the wider world economy if it had not been for the self-interest of the richer powers, Britain in particular, in reinforcing the shift towards unilat-eralism in order to protect domestic economic and political interests. The fragmentation of the world economy, exposed clearly in the failure of the World Economic Conference of June 1933, exacerbated the vulnerability of the less-well-endowed states and promoted radical political solutions to economic disadvantage.[14]

The three 'have-not' states shared some common economic ambitions, which derived from their perception of economic disadvantage and the means necessary to overcome it. They were all three profoundly affected by the prevailing concept of empire as a source of economic strength as well as a key to political prestige. This extended not only to the idea that the British and French Empires shielded the two metropolitan states from the full blast of economic crisis, but to the belief that control over additional territory and population gave easy access to raw materials and markets. The growing share of imperial imports and exports in British and French trade in the 1930s lent weight to this argument, but its roots were really to be found in the nineteenth century when Germany, Italy and Japan were latecomers in the imperial race and made to feel as such by the established empires. By the 1930s empire was a declining asset, and it is ironic that at precisely the point where empire was no longer easily defensible or defended, three major states decided that empire was the solution to their problems. All three expressed imperial ambitions in terms of an economic 'new order' in order to make it seem that their imperialism was not simply a return to the pre-1914 world. The idea of a 'new order', which was the name given to the German and Japanese economic spheres in the early 1940s, and adopted by all three states when they signed the Tri-Partite Pact in September 1940, was a deliberate rejection of the liberal economic tradition of the nineteenth century, which, like political counterpart, was deemed to be derelict by the 1930s. The sense that liberal economics did not work was hardly confined to the three 'have-not' states, but it was only in Germany, Italy and Japan that active efforts were made to adopt an alternative economic concept of self-sufficient or 'autarkic' blocs and to embark on rearmament programmes whose purpose was to create and protect the larger imperial space thought to be a necessary pre-condition for economic wellbeing.[15]

The first of the 'have not' states to embark on a programme of territorial expansion was Japan. The Japanese economy expanded rapidly in the years before the recession of 1929 based on increasing levels of industrialization and the export of cheaply produced consumer goods. This was necessary to fund Japan's high dependence on imported foodstuffs and mineral products. The recession undermined Japan's international position because trade was hit heavily by the introduction of tariff restrictions in Western markets. One way of reacting to Japan's economic vulnerability was to increase the self-sufficiency of Japan's imperial area, which included Korea and Formosa. Food self-sufficiency in the empire expanded during the 1020s and by 1930–5 Korea and Formosa (now Taiwan) supplied between them ninety-five per cent of Japan's staple food imports. Higher-value staple foodstuffs were also expanded in Japan itself to mitigate any danger of blockade in the event of war. A five-year plan in 1932 saw an increase of forty per cent in the sown wheat area in Japan; the output of marine products expanded rapidly in the 1930s, rising from 3 million tons in 1926 to around 4.2 million tons in 1938. [16] The food situation was finally secured by the acquisition of the northern Chinese province of Manchuria following the 'Mukden Incident' in September 1931.

The relationship between territorial expansion and economic vulnerability was well understood in leading Japanese circles in the 1920s. Navy leaders feared Japan's heavy dependence on overseas supplies of fuel oil and from the

1920s began a systematic policy of storing and stockpiling fuel supplies. The Japanese Army invested heavily in the 1920s in production in Manchuria, which supplied one-fifth of Japanese annual iron supply. In 1925 a 20-year plan was drawn up to develop 5,500 miles of railways in the region to help promote Japanese exports to Manchuria and to move mineral and food supplies to the coast for shipping to Japan.[17] The dangers posed by the local Chinese warlord Zhang Xueliang to Japanese control of the South Manchurian Railway, a trading lifeline in the region, encouraged the local Japanese garrison 'Kwantung' army to launch a coup on 18 September 1931 and to take large parts of Manchuria under Japanese control. The subsequent creation of the puppet state of Manchukuo in 1932 as nominally independent masked the reality that northern China was now included in Japan's self-sufficient imperial area. In 1935 a five-year plan for agricultural procurement was drawn up for Manchuria and by 1939 the sown area in the region for major staple products had increased by forty per cent. Much of the increased output was destined for Japan, whose food supplies were met entirely from the trading bloc of Korea, Taiwan and Manchuria. The new territories in China also consumed food imports from the rest of the Japanese Empire and in 1938 it proved necessary to control wheat imports into Manchuria to safeguard Japanese consumption.[18] Manchuria became an important area for industrial development and between 1931 and 1935 some 700 million yen were invested to expand output of energy and raw material resources. Of these one of the most important was the possible exploitation of oil reserves and the development of synthetic oil output based on processing shale. Western oil firms were excluded from carrying out oil exploration in the area, but the search for oil proved disappointing and Japan remained heavily dependent on American supplies.[19] Between 1937 and 1941 actual production of synthetic oil was only eight per cent of what was planned.[20]

During the 1930s the Japanese government sought to exclude Western economic interests from its own territorial bloc. In 1934 the so-called 'Amau Doctrine' was announced, warning the West that China and East Asia should now be regarded as Japan's economic sphere of interest. In 1933 the Great Asia Association was founded in Japan and campaigned for a new economic order in Asia under Japanese domination in which a large self-sufficient region would supply minerals, fuel and foodstuffs to the Japanese heartland, which would in turn supply heavy industrial and manufactured products to the outlying regions. This formed what came to be called during the Second World War the 'Co-Prosperity Sphere'.[21] The armed forces in Japan recognized that to maintain the new area of economic empire it would be necessary to increase the size of the military. In their new view of the world, self-sufficiency and security went hand in hand, although there were regular arguments between military and civilian leaders in the 1930s about how to balance economic and military demands effectively. The 'Fundamental Principles of National Policy' agreed in August 1936 looked to develop Manchuria economically and to expand the output of armaments and basic industries as rapidly as possible.[22] The war with

China that broke out in July 1937 increased the urgency of both programmes and introduced a crop of legislation to expand production of oil, iron, and steel and to control strategic trade. Military expenditure as a proportion of net domestic product rose from 6.3 per cent in 1935 to 23 per cent in 1938, by which time it constituted 92 per cent of Japanese central government expenditure.[23] It was funded largely by extensive deficit financing and an expansionary fiscal policy and could not be sustained indefinitely. Japanese leaders in the late 1930s faced a profound dilemma: to build the autarkic bloc and the economic new order required a possible war for key resources – principally the oil and minerals of south-east Asia – but war could only be effectively waged if Japan possessed a self-sufficient economic base. This was the same dilemma faced by Italy and Germany.

Italy's territorial ambitions in the 1930s reflected a similar perception, already elaborated in the 1920s, that the international economic order, sustained by the capital and trading needs of the major Western powers, was no longer viable and would have to be transcended by some kind of new economic order which could turn Italy into one of the great powers. Italy, like Japan, was underdeveloped industrially and heavily dependent on key imports of minerals and fuel. Italy, too, had a high dependence on food imports and an agricultural base in which it was difficult to expand production substantially. In 1936 fifty-two per cent of Italy's workforce was still on the land and only one-quarter in industry.[24] In the 1920s the Italian Fascist government encouraged investment in hydro-electric schemes and the expansion of grain production to compensate for a persistently unfavourable balance-of-trade but only after the recession had undermined the markets Italy depended on for exports and reduced the international tourist trade did the regime move towards a more active policy of controlled trade and strategies of self-sufficiency. The efforts to raise domestic agricultural output had much more limited success than in Japan, while Italy's small colonial empire could offer little compensation. It proved possible to reduce Italy's import dependence on foodstuffs, which fell from 24.1 per cent of imports in 1926–30 to 14.3 per cent in 1938–40 (including a fall in the volume of wheat imports of 75 per cent over the same period), but it was difficult to expand domestic food production, which rose by only 7 per cent between 1926–30 and 1940.[25] The only solution was to limit domestic consumption, which was done principally through controls over trade, distribution and currency transactions.

In Italy the move towards a comprehensive policy of autarky was bound up with the regime's plans for territorial expansion. The opening moves to control the free flow of trade and payments came in early 1934 as the armed forces began to prepare for the invasion of Abyssinia (Ethiopia) in October the following year. The resulting conflict was, as Giorgio Rochat has argued, predominantly a product of Fascist Italy's imperial and political ambitions but it was also fuelled by the expectation that the area would yield important sources of mineral wealth (including oil) and food supply.[26] In the aftermath of the recession and the changed complexion of the world economy Italy, it was argued, needed its *spazio vitale* (living space). In 1932, Foreign Minister Dino Grandi argued that an extension of the empire in Africa was essential as a place to send Italy's surplus population and a source of raw materials, and although Mussolini seems to have been more attracted to the possible prestige of the operation, its underlying rationale was to try to create a larger territorial empire to make Italy the centre of a new regional economic area and to reduce reliance on distant markets and uncertain imports. This strategy was reinforced by the invasion and occupation of Ethiopia between October 1935 and May 1936, when Italy was subject to economic sanctions by the League of Nations. The ending of sanctions on 4 July 1936 proved too late to turn Mussolini away from a policy of economic controls and autarky, which began with a decree in November 1935 and was completed with the appointment of Felice Guarneri in November 1937 to ministerial rank, responsible for controlling trade and exchange, limiting luxury consumption, prohibiting the export of strategically necessary goods, limiting all inessential imports and 'the empowering of the economic resources of the nation'. Mussolini announced the change in strategy at a meeting of the Corporations on 23 March 1936 when he called for the highest possible measure of national economic independence to counter the 'eternal undervaluing' of Italy by the western liberal states.[27]

In this instance too the securing of living space and the establishment of an imperial region required increased security against the possible threat posed by the more prosperous Western states, which had vital interests in the Mediterranean theatre. In Italy's case there were few opportunities for conquest that would supply secure sources of vital strategic materials (and ironically the large reserves of oil in Libya remained hidden beneath the recently conquered desert) and so the strengthening of the armed forces and the preparation of the economy for possible war had to be undertaken largely from Italy's own domestic resources. In 1936 and 1937 every branch of the Italian productive economy had to produce an autarkic plan to be completed at some point in 1940 or 1941. Between 1937 and 1940 the value of Italian trade fell by just over one-third, while the output of many major sectors expanded substantially between 1936 and 1941. Electricity generation expanded by 48 per cent, exceeding the plan; iron-ore output grew 35 per cent, aluminium production by 200 per cent, magnesium by 500 per cent, and so on. But the plans were difficult to fulfil, and the spectacular increases came in products where the initial output was generally very low. Out of thirty-two raw materials and metals, only eleven reached the targets set four years before.[28] The resource problems that Italy faced were made worse by the almost permanent military activity undertaken by the regime, first in Ethiopia, then from 1936 to 1939 fighting with the Nationalists in Spain, finally the occupation of Albania in late March 1939. These actions forced the Italian armed services to maintain a high annual military budget, 4.7 billion lire in 1934–5, 14.4 billion in 1938–9 and 27 billion for 1939–40, before Italy had even joined in the Second World War.[29] This explanation was not necessarily turned into large quantities of additional equipment, as it was for states not actually at war. Military aircraft production was 1,768 in 1936, but was still only 1,750 in 1939. Nor did the autarkic plans supply what was really needed for Italy's armed forces, above all the supply of oil, which was also Japan's principal weakness. In 1940 Italy still needed to import almost all her fuel oil supplies, which explains why the later campaigns in North Africa, directed towards the British-controlled oil reserves of the Middle East, were so central to Italian strategy.

The German search for living space (*Lebensraum*) and pursuit of a self-sufficient economic region was altogether more dangerous for the international order than the ambitions of either Italy or Japan. Germany was a major industrial power with the capacity to produce vanguard technologies and extensive, though incomplete, supplies of the major resources needed to sustain a war economy. Moreover, in Silesia and Alsace-Lorraine there were substantial additional resources that had been territory in the German Empire before the Versailles settlement removed them, which all German nationalists wanted to see returned. Beyond these border regions were smaller and weaker states in Central and Eastern Europe that held large resources of raw materials, food supply and oil (Romania and Hungary) and were temptingly within easy reach of German political influence or military action. The idea of a large economic area, dominated by Germany, went back to before 1914 and was revived in the 1920s as a possible solution to Germany's weak bargaining position with the West. After the recession, which hit Germany more heavily than either Italy or Japan, the appointment of Hitler brought to power a politician who saw Germany's future in terms of building through armed force a large territorial empire, replete with adequate economic resources. The creation of a large economic area (*Grossraumswirtschaft*) was designed to free Germany from any threat of blockade and to ensure that the international marketplace could no longer determine German fortunes: 'the ultimate decision as to the outcome of the world market', wrote Hitler in 1928 in his 'second book', 'will lie in power'.[30] This neo-mercantilist view of the economy was reinforced by circumstances: by the time Hitler came to power, German trade was a fraction of what it had been in 1929 and Germany was cut off from prospects of heavy foreign capital investment, which had helped to shield the economy in the mid-1920s from the pressures of the world economy. Hitler seems to have instinctively disliked the abstract economics of trade flows and international capital accounts but he understood the physical possession of territory and resources, and this could only be secured by military action.

Successful warfare itself was regarded as a function of economic strength. A German official at the Statistical Office summed up this relationship on the eve of war in 1939: 'A modern war can no more be fought without a highly developed, efficient national economy than without a well-trained and well-equipped armed forces'.[31] This was a natural response to the alleged failure of the German home front in the Great War. In the 1920s senior German military leaders explored the implications of the relationship between successful economic preparation and mobilization and the possible war of the future.[32] Their conclusions fitted closely with Hitler's perception that only effective economic preparation, or 'economic rearmament', would make it possible to wage war and that this would mean a strategy of economic self-sufficiency since Germany was almost certain to be cut off from secure supplies of vital materials once a major war had broken out. The result in Germany in the 1930s was a similar paradox to the one facing Japan: Germany needed an autarkic economic bloc to guarantee all the necessary resources to fight a total war, but would have to risk a war in order to secure it. To reduce the level of risk, Hitler was the driving force behind a rapid rearmament programme from 1933 onwards, which was designed to intimidate any power likely to impede the creation of a larger economic region. The armed forces were happy for Hitler to privilege the military, but were less confident that the risk of war with the West should be run in order to supply a secure economic foundation.

The paradox facing Germany in the 1930s was resolved in Hitler's mind by the launch in October 1936 of the Second Four-Year Plan, which like the Japanese and Italian five-year plans was designed to create a self-sufficient base in Germany to face the prospect of a major war in the 1940s.[33] The purpose of the plan was to create the conditions that would make it possible to create a strong and secure Germany, as Hitler made clear in the memorandum he wrote in August 1936 to launch the new economic strategy: 'The nation does not live for the economy ... it is finance and economy, economic leaders and theories, which all owe unqualified service in this struggle for the self assertion of our nation.'[34] The Four-Year Plan was part of a wider net of controls over imports and exports and currency flows (set up in the September 1934 New Plan) and over the pattern of domestic capital formation and price and wage fixing, all of which was designed to protect large-scale and expensive rearmament from the damaging effect of market forces. But at the heart of the Plan was the same issue of physical expansion of resources confronted in Japan and Italy. In the German case the success of the planning was more marked, partly because German science was better able to supply the technical breakthroughs needed to provide effective industrial substitutes – oil from coal through the process of hydrogenation, and synthetic textiles and rubber. By 1939 Germany was between 80 and 100 per cent self-sufficient in a range of major foodstuffs. Stocks of essential grains and fats were increased so that by August 1939 there were 6.2 million tons of stored grains and 487,000 tons of fats. Coal and lignite output (the latter the raw material for producing oil from coal) increased by 31 per cent and 41 per cent respectively between 1937 and 1940; domestic iron ore by 127 per cent.[35]

These latter figures could be achieved only by expanding Germany territorially. On 5 November 1937, in a meeting recorded by his adjutant Friedrich Hossbach, Hitler announced that side by side with efforts for self-sufficiency and rearmament, it was necessary to find additional 'living space' for Germany's cramped population. This, he said, 'could only be solved by means of force', and his immediate targets were Austria and Czechoslovakia.[36] Hitler achieved both union with Austria in March 1938 and the internationally guaranteed transfer of the Sudetenland in October that year, and the occupation of Bohemia and Moravia in March 1939 without a war, but certainly by exploiting force. These were areas for which it was possible to make a political case for their incorporation, particularly Austria, but the arrival almost immediately of officials from the Four-Year Plan to integrate raw material and machinery production into German programmes shows the extent to which economic motives played an important part. Austria supplied iron ore and engineering capacity; the Sudetenland was rich in lignite (a major synthetic fuel plant was subsequently constructed at Brüx) and a range of other mineral products; Bohemia and Moravia brought iron, coal and the huge Skoda armaments works, whose shares were eventually controlled by the state-funded *Reichswerke Hermann Göring*, first established as a holding company for the autarkic activities of the Four-Year Plan in 1937.[37] Trade agreements with Romania, Yugoslavia and Hungary also tied these economies closely to the German economic sphere and provided a more secure source of foodstuffs and raw materials, particularly oil.[38] The rapid expansion of German military output between 1938 and 1941 was based partly on the early establishment of this larger Central European economic area. By 1938–9 German military spending as a proportion of the net national product was 17.2 per cent, the following year 30 per cent. Already in 1938–9 direct spending on the armed forces was 64 per cent of government revenue.[39]

The important point in any discussion of the role of the 'have-not' states in the background to the Second World War is to distinguish clearly between economic *ambitions* and economic *causes*. That all three states embarked on these programmes in the wake of the failure of economic multilateralism and free-market mechanisms was not accidental. Karl Blessing, a deputy at the German Central Bank, and its future director in the 1960s, explained in an address in August 1937 that the German shift to autarky was the fault of Britain, France and the United States for failing to sustain a free market: 'if she did not do it [economic isolation] she would be bound to go under in the event of war'.[40] The search for a new economic order, linked to the creation of new economic blocs, organized on neo-mercantilist lines represented a set of economic aims which might or might not have led to war. All three states engaged in aggression in the process of trying to achieve a reorientation of the global economy, and until 1939 managed to achieve this without a major war against the Western powers. All three realized that to secure and protect the new regional blocs it would be necessary to achieve higher levels of direct military spending and military output which could either act to deter other states from intervening or be used to shield the new areas from attack. This was a strategy of great risk, and its ultimate result was to provoke other states into a competitive arms race and the abandonment of any further effort to re-establish a workable world economy or to pursue a multi-lateral political solution. Economic ambitions therefore made major war more likely and conditioned its probable nature and extent, but did not necessarily cause war as such.

The search for living space, economic blocs and enhanced military security did not take place in a vacuum and other states were forced to react to what was perceived to be an increasingly co-ordinated programme to subvert the existing order. This was certainly the view of the Soviet Union, whose survival as the only example of socialist economics appeared to be threatened directly in the 1930s by at least two of the three revisionist states – Japan and Germany. Both saw war with the Soviet Union as a possibility, perhaps a necessity, at some time in the future, but only German leaders thought about the possibility that Soviet territory might supply the ideal living space to free Germany entirely from dependence on the wider world economy.

For Soviet leaders the economic picture was confused, because Leninism–Marxism posited the idea that the major imperialist states, Britain and France, were likely to pose the greater threat. From at least 1931 Stalin and the Soviet leadership began to warn publicly about the possibility of a new war and at the annual Communist Party Congress on 26 January 1934 Stalin gave a shrewd analysis of the implications of the current crisis:

> The intensified struggle for foreign markets, the disappearance of the last vestiges of free trade, prohibitive tariffs, trade war, currency war, dumping, and many other analogous measures which demonstrate extreme nationalism in economic policy have made the relations among the various countries extremely strained, have prepared the ground for military conflicts, and have put war on the order of the day as a means for a new redivision of the world.[41]

The search for security against this threat first led the Soviet Union to champion the ideal of collective security following admission to the League of Nations in September 1934, but eventually, after the evident bankruptcy of the League, to reach non-aggression pacts with Germany in August 1939 and then Japan in March 1941. But the principal response was to redirect the economic modernization drive begun in the late 1920s towards military goals. Defence expenditure was 1.8 billion roubles in 1931 but 14.8 billion in 1936, and reached 40 billion in 1939. From the Third Five-Year Plan, launched in 1937, resources serving the military came to dominate the economy. Around twenty per cent of industrial investment went into military production.[42] Like Germany, Italy and Japan the Soviet Union saw an intimate relationship between domestic economic development and future security, though the Soviet Union was rich enough in resources to be able to develop autarkic policies without foreign expansion.[43] The priority in Moscow was at all costs to avoid being dragged into a capitalist war, but at the same time to develop an economic base and military presence strong enough to safeguard the Soviet Union if it was the victim of aggression.

The more interesting case is the reaction of Britain and France. The ambitions of the three 'have not' states threatened the global economic interests of the two richest European powers. Although both paid lip service after the recession to the idea of re-establishing a multilateral system of trade and exchange, and a lowering of barriers to international revival, fears of further economic crisis and domestic political unrest pushed them towards a more self-sufficient economics. Declining trade ratios were compensated for by redirecting trade to empire markets and signing in bilateral agreements on payments and trade outlike as empire. Neither Britain nor France was as self-consciously autarkic as the three 'have-not' powers, but they did increase the proportion of empire self-sufficiency. British trade with the empire increased to almost half of all trade by 1938, while investment in the empire was fifty-nine per cent of all overseas investment in 1930. France increased trade with its colonies to a third of all exports by 1936 and by 1940 forty-five per cent of French investment was in empire areas. The French view of *'le salut par l'empire'*, which took on added significance as Europe approached war in 1939, was the mirror image of the imperial ambitions of the three aggressor states.[44] The complaints of the 'have-not' states that the economic advantage derived from territorial empires was unevenly distributed was certainly not without foundation. A report to the Bank of England on German activity in the Balkans in October 1938 pointed out that 'The British Empire is like a Fortnum and Mason's store as compared with Germany's local grocer's shop.'[45]

The priority for both Britain and France was to protect the empire and to preserve their economic stability, but above all to avoid war, which would be likely to undermine both objectives, and could happen in one of any three theatres – Europe, the Mediterranean or Eastern Asia. It would be wrong not to see an economic conception at the heart of Western strategy in the 1930s as well, linked closely to wider political and security interests. When Neville Chamberlain became British Prime Minister in May 1937 he set out to try to arrive at what he called a 'Grand Settlement' in international affairs, which amounted to trying to find ways in which economic concessions could be used to buy the international goodwill of 'have-not' states, Germany in particular. 'Might not a great improvement in Germany's economic situation', he asked rhetorically, 'result in her being quieter and less interested in political adventures?'[46] This was a question that might have been asked before Hitler came to power, when more could have been done to prevent German resentment taking a political form. The idea of what Anthony Eden, Chamberlain's first Foreign Secretary, called 'economic appeasement' faced major hurdles when Britain, and more reluctantly the French 'Popular Front' government, tried to explore the possibility of buying German compliance in 1937 and 1938. Eden crucially recognized the danger of allowing Germany to disengage entirely from what remained of the Western economic order:

> But there are many who say that economic appeasement provides the key to our diffi-
> culties, and it is certain that with most of our political problems there is an economic
> problem inextricably intertwined ... what is a serious danger is that Germany is moving

away from the economic system of Western Europe into an idiosyncrasy of attitude not unlike that of Soviet Russia ... It is therefore of urgent importance to restore Germany to her normal place in the Western European system.[47]

It was this belief that prompted British and French politicians to find an offer for Germany that might be sufficiently tempting to restrain German revisionism, and so create the conditions for a restoration of the liberal economic order, including perhaps Italy and Japan as well. It was also a view that won widespread popular support among the British public, many of whom regarded economic conflicts as the root cause of international stability. In November 1937 a major petition was delivered to Chamberlain calling for an international commission to adjudicate issues on 'access to raw materials and world markets, colonial development and the problem of surplus populations'. These, the petition continued, 'are so frequently at the root of the unrest and rivalry among nations'.[48]

The precise negotiations over what might be offered to Germany were triggered by an approach from the German Economics Minister, Hjalmar Schacht, in August 1936, when he suggested that the return of some of Germany's former colonies in Africa might be a suitable concession. The associated idea that the return of Togoland or Cameroon or even Tanganyika might solve Germany's problems of access to raw materials and excess population could not be taken seriously, since German trade with its colonies before 1914 was less than 0.5 per cent of all German trade, and British negotiators remained sceptical of 'the customary lecture about colonies and raw materials', as one of them put it.[49] It was nevertheless seen as a gesture of goodwill that might be accompanied by economic concessions on tariffs and quotas and a possible long-term loan to ease Germany's shortages of foreign currency. The precondition for any serious negotiation on this basis was always that Germany should first give firm guarantees of good behaviour, even though it was difficult to see what form such guarantees might take. Even Schacht, who was regarded as a moderate force in German politics, would not be drawn on the question of what Germany might offer in return.[50]

The prospect of some form of economic concession as a means to recreate a functioning European or world-wide economic order was always doomed to failure. In the first place, Germany did not want to accept reintegration on Western terms. A Bank of England official observed in September 1936 that it was not surprising that Germany had chosen the path of autarky 'when the Germans feel themselves tightly enclosed by a ring of foreign nations which, they think, wish to alter the course of events in Germany'.[51] German leaders did not want to accept a return to a freer economy precisely because they believed the wider world economy had been responsible for the German economic crisis in the first place. Even Schacht was unwilling to countenance a major loan, which it was felt would tie Germany, like reparations, to the financial interests of the West. The British and French negotiators also came to realize that Schacht was a fading force in German politics following Hermann Göring's appointment to head the Four-Year Plan. 'He is not prepared to drive a motor car', ran a report of a visit to Schacht in September 1937, 'in which he holds the steering-wheel, while Göring and his friends have the brakes and the accelerator.'[52] Schacht was forced to resign in November 1937 because of his lukewarm attitude to further rearmament and his continued and unauthorized contacts with Western leaders. There were, moreover, substantial difficulties on the side of Britain and France when it came to considering seriously the transfer of colonial territory. Martin Thomas has argued that the French war ministry and navy were strongly opposed to giving Germany any of the former West African colonies on the assumption that they would be used for military purposes, since they had no real commercial value. The French Ministry of the Marine elaborated fantastic images of a joint German and Italian pincer attack against British and French African colonies, supported by possible Japanese incursions.[53] These fantasies caused less anxiety in London, but even Chamberlain wondered whether it would not be better to give Germany someone else's colonies – French or Portuguese – rather than British.

It is striking when looking at Western discussions about the way in which a world economy might be reconstructed how little it was accepted that the richer economies would have to make real concessions or exercise a firm international leadership in order to secure it. There was a growing fatalism in the West, including the United States, about the impossibility of finding a means to stabilize and reintegrate the world economy, which produced exactly the effect the West hoped to avoid. This was evident, for example, in the approach to Japan. Montagu Norman, writing to the former President of the Japanese Central Bank in May 1937, agreed with his complaint that the absence of a stable currency system based on gold (which had largely been abandoned during the recession) was a major factor limiting a return to an international economy: 'there is little doubt that, since the abandonment of the gold standard as we knew it, a framework in which the economy of each country operated has been lost.'[54] But a few months later Norman wrote to the Governor of the Bank of New Zealand, Leslie Lefeaux, about the irresponsible way in which Japan had reacted to an economic situation largely of the West's making:

> And now Japan publicly proclaims her adherence to the gospel of the 'have-nots', which has hitherto been preached by Italy and Germany, we have the spectacle of powers, whose international gospel professes to be the repelling of Communism adopting in world affairs an attitude essentially similar to that of the Communist in domestic matters.[55]

There was little acceptance that this was a situation brought about as much by British, French and American failure to sustain a workable world economy in the first place or to make serious efforts to reconstruct it during the decade that followed. The British economist Henry Clay, writing in 1937 about Germany's political preference for self-sufficiency, complained of 'the feeling of schism in what used to be one cultured community' without acknowledging what made such a schism possible.[56]

The chief reaction of Britain and France to the breakdown of the international order was to rearm as well. From 1936 both states embarked on major programmes of military expansion to enable them to protect their territorial interests abroad and to safeguard the metropolitan area. By 1939 military spending in Britain constituted twenty-two per cent of the net national product, in France twenty-three per cent. These were not programmes just designed to protect Western economic interests, since the country at whom the preparations were chiefly directed, Germany, was regarded not only as a major political and security threat, but as a state dedicated to destroying the values of Western civilization. But the direct effect of a shift towards rearmament as the solution in 1937 and 1938 exacerbated economic conditions on world markets by forcing Britain and France to invest more in the domestic economy rather than abroad and to compete for strategic materials and foodstuffs for immediate use or for stockpiling. The effect of Western rearmament was to create just the conditions for heightened economic rivalry that the West had wanted to avoid. As prices rose during 1938 and 1939, and export growth slowed, Britain and France faced inflationary pressures that the controlled economies of the 'have-not' states could limit more effectively. As Talbot Imlay has shown, short-term issues of political economy pushed Britain and France rapidly towards a situation in which a war in the near future became an economic necessity unless the decision to confront or deter the aggressors was to be finally abandoned.[57]

What role did these many economic issues play in the outbreak of world war in September 1939? There is little argument that economic ambitions and fears played an important part in shaping the international crisis of the 1930s, but this leaves open the question of whether economic considerations explain the timing and scale of conflict too. In the case of Italy and Japan the case can be made more easily. Italian leaders recognized that in 1939 Italy simply lacked the economic capacity, after years of warfare, to embark on a major conflict with the Western states. Mussolini's decision to avoid honouring his treaty obligations, delivered to Hitler on 25 August 1939, was veiled by presenting the Germans with an exaggerated list of material requirements before war could be contemplated. The later decision to enter the war shortly before the defeat of France was opportunistic, in the hope that it might provide, among other things, economic advantages. In Japan's case, too, the final acceptance that war with the West was strategically necessary, taken in the autumn of 1941, had a clear economic motive behind it, since without the resources of south-east Asia and facing a tighter blockade of vital materials from the United States, Japan could not sustain its war effort.

In neither the Italian nor the Japanese case was it likely that they would have sought a war with the West had it not been for the onset of the German war with Britain and France. The real test of the economic argument lies with the extent to which Hitler's decision for war was governed by economic factors. It has often been suggested that Hitler's Germany opted for a general war in 1939 because the economic strains caused by large-scale rearmament in a controlled economy could no longer be supported, and that a war against Britain and France ostensibly over the issue of German claims against Poland was a choice dictated by imminent economic or social crisis. This thesis was suggested in the 1960s by Tim Mason and subsequently elaborated in his analysis of a German domestic crisis in 1939 caused by internal pressure from the workforce to raise wages in a context of full employment. Mason argued that this resulted in an 'escape into war' to avoid the political implications of social protest and a second 'stab-in-the back'.[58] The thesis has recently been revived in a rather different form by Adam Tooze, who has argued that a combination of unresolved balance-of-payments problems, rising inflationary pressures and the need to exploit a temporary lead in armaments pushed Hitler to opt for a general war. 'Hitler's decision to unleash a European war', Tooze has argued, was a case of 'better sooner than later'.[59]

This is an argument largely based on circumstantial speculation rather than hard evidence and it begs two important questions: first, was there an economic crisis of sufficient difficulty in 1939 to justify launching war against the West? Second, were Hitler's strategic calculations evidently governed by economic considerations? The first issue is certainly open to interpretation since the German economy, in trying to undertake large-scale self-sufficiency and an exceptional level of military preparation, did face potential economic strains. These were not disguised from Hitler by the government ministers and officials who had to cope with the economic implications of state spending on arms. The Finance Minister, Count Schwerin von Krosigk, sent Hitler a memorandum in September 1938 warning of the dangers of inflation and the popular fears of economic crisis that this might generate.[60] Hjalmar Schacht and his Central Bank directors sent a memorandum to Hitler in January 1939 painting a bleak picture of a 'currency and financial situation at danger point'. Schacht was sacked two weeks later.[61] A month before the outbreak of war, the state secretary in the Economics Ministry, Friedrich Landfried, wrote to his opposite number in the Finance Ministry about the dangerous situation emerging as consumers were frustrated by the absence of sufficient consumer goods and the preference given to rearmament.[62]

Domestic economic pressures had existed throughout the period from 1933 when Hitler was first in power, but the regime had created ways of controlling or neutralizing them by imposing ever-tighter state controls and a strategy of state economic management. In the context of a comprehensive framework of economic steering, German recovery and rearmament were easier to achieve than was the case for either Britain or France in the 1930s. The response of the regime in 1939 was to continue to find positive ways of ensuring that the goal of state-sponsored remilitarization could continue until the point when the economic restructuring and the military build-up had reached the point when large-scale war could be contemplated. Rather than wait to be overtaken by a tide of crisis, Hitler and his officials worked to prevent or contain the more serious economic consequences of Hitler's strategy. Schacht was replaced by Walter Funk, a member of Göring's circle and already Minister of Economics. On the day of his appointment, 19 January 1939, Hitler sent Funk a letter detailing his responsibilities: to maintain price and wage stability, protect the currency, to expand private investment in public projects and to instil National Socialist principles into the activities of the central bank.[63] Funk, with the assistance of the state secretary in the Finance Ministry, Fritz Reinhardt, set out to try to resolve the short-term financial pressures. The result was the introduction of the so-called 'New Finance Plan', which became law on 26 April 1939, and was designed to cope with the large number of public contracts and major construction plans occasioned not just by rearmament but by house building, the remodelling of German cities and motorway building. The plan was to introduce payment partly with tax certificates, redeemable later with a substantial remission of future tax payments. Extra tax incentives were given to firms that could show that they were expanding their export earnings, while increases in income tax were to be imposed on high earners.[64]

Other efforts were made in 1939 to limit the problems. The Finance Ministry required all government departments to make substantial savings by rationalizing their activities and stripping out redundant labour.[65] The Four-Year Plan leadership set out a series of measures in the spring of 1939 designed to ensure that trade and currency reserves could be sustained in 1939 by reducing freight and shipping costs, simplifying the bureaucratic demands on traders and undertaking active negotiations with Germany's trading partners to simplify and speed up transactions.[66] Even those who complained of the difficulties were keen to find solutions rather than simply voice their fears. Von Krosigk recommended a propaganda campaign aimed at the German public to allay their fears of inflation and to instil confidence in the currency. Landfried recommended in July 1939 that the financial pressures be removed by encouraging ordinary Germans to save rather than spend, with the promise of future benefits. If they kept their savings invested for five years, they would be given substantial tax concessions.[67] It is interesting to observe that both von Krosigk and Landfried argued that time was on Germany's side, not against it. These policies and plans did not solve all Germany's economic problems, but they demonstrate the way in which economic officials in Germany were capable of reacting creatively to issues that emerged within the context of a controlled economy, as they did after 1939 when it proved possible to switch to a large-scale war economy, ration consumption effectively and avoid inflation. When a director of the German Central Bank, Emil Puhl, met British officials in Basle in June 1939, he explained to his counterparts that individual well-being was no longer the aim of German economics, which was pioneering for the world a new system of 'collective well-being' based on central economic controls that would allow Germany to enter 'smoothly on a new and more hopeful phase'.[68] Hitler, it was reported a month later, was impervious to economic 'misgiving'.[69]

The second and more compelling argument against the idea that economic crisis pushed Hitler to wage a general war is the large body of evidence to show that he did not want a war with the West in 1939. His initial hope that Poland would voluntarily enter the German political sphere on German terms was frustrated by March 1939 and led Hitler to plan his war on Poland. His view, expressed on 23 May 1939, that 'The task is to isolate Poland ... It must not come to a simultaneous confrontation with the West' might be taken as an attempt to persuade anxious generals that war was worth risking, knowing that war with the West would result, but that reading would make no sense of all the subsequent statements Hitler made about preferring local war to general war and his frustrated efforts to drive a wedge between Britain and France to ensure that any danger disappeared, nor of the widely anticipated collapse of Western firmness once a non-aggression pact was secured with the Soviet Union.[70] Almost all the existing evidence suggests that Hitler's aims in 1939 were driven by political and military calculations, not least his desire to wage a short and successful war of conquest as the Japanese and Italians had done earlier in the decade. There were, of course, economic motives as well in the conquest of more 'living space' and the acquisition of Polish labour, food and raw material resources. German businesses that had lost properties in the transfer of Upper Silesia to Polish rule in 1920 were hopeful of having them restored.[71] In Poland too the Four-Year Plan and the *Reichswerke* were poised to take immediate advantage of new resources and did so days after the arrival of German forces. The war against Poland fitted into the general ambition to create a 'Large Area Economy'. But there is only circumstantial evidence that Hitler used this opportunity deliberately to be able to strike at France and Britain because he believed in August 1939 that the economy would not stand it if he did not. After general war had broken out, Hitler still counted on Britain and France backing away from real conflict.

The idea of a general war driven by economic calculation credits Hitler with too much understanding of economic reality. Much of the economic advice he was given was ignored (and in some cases suppressed before he could even read it) and was almost certainly poorly understood by a leader whose grasp of economics was rudimentary beyond the idea of stealing the things that Germany needed. Moreover, the argument for economic causes fails to engage with the absence of any real planning for a war against the West in the summer of 1939. If Hitler had wanted war with Britain and France he could simply have declared it. Yet there were compelling arguments against a general war, not least economic ones. War against Britain and France gave no guarantees – and might well have been lost had the West concerted a more effective strategy – and it immediately created economic isolation and blockade, the loss of much of the German merchant fleet, an end to credit lines from British Empire sources and a dangerous reliance on a narrow range of oil resources. A meeting in November 1939 in the Economics Ministry highlighted the sudden difficulties Germany was faced with: 'We are practically cut off from overseas, so strong restraint must be practised.'[72] The quick victory in 1940 masked the dangers that Germany faced by the emergency economic conditions imposed by war in the West, and was certainly not planned. The coming of war with the West in 1939 accelerated Germany's economic problems and offered few solutions.

A much better case for timing can be constructed for Britain and France, and for a number of reasons. In the first place the two Western states hoped to be able to deter Hitler in 1939 from further territorial expansion, which after the occupation of Prague they were not prepared any longer to tolerate. Though faced with conflicting evidence, there was sufficient intelligence information throughout the summer crisis to reinforce the assumption that Germany would not risk war, either because Hitler would perceive that the economic balance between Germany and the West was unfavourable to him or because the economy was in serious difficulties and would be unhinged by a major war. This interpretation was not only applied to Germany, but in general to the 'have-not' powers, who, it was suggested, 'would be unable to wage a protracted struggle'.[73] This was certainly true of Italy, whose economic problems after years of warfare were rightly expected to inhibit Mussolini from joining a war at Hitler's side. But it had a particular force in the German case, partly because ever since the failure of economic appeasement it was assumed that the German economy remained vulnerable to crisis, and partly through mere wishful thinking. The German resistance also had regular contacts with the West and insisted that German economic and social conditions were such that a policy of firmness would pay dividends. It was perhaps possible, as Lord Halifax, Eden's successor as Foreign Minister, explained, that domestic problems might well push 'the mad dictator to insane adventures', but the consensus was that economic weaknesses would persuade even Hitler that a major war was too risky. French decision makers in particular built up an image of German economic vulnerability in 1939 to suggest 'the possibility of a moral and physical collapse'.[74]

If Hitler could not be deterred, the two Western states also realized that they would have to wage war now rather than later or risk economic and social problems of their own. This 'matter of timing', as George Peden has called it, was much more pressing in the West than it was in Germany, where public opinion was unable to express any anxieties about rearmament and the economy (and news) were both closely controlled.[75] In Britain and France the public cost of high military spending was evident in rapidly falling gold reserves (British gold fell from £800 million in spring 1938 to £460 million at the outbreak of war), the declining value of the pound and the franc and a high balance-of-payments deficit, which for Britain reached £70 million in 1939. So pressed was the British economy by summer 1939 that when the Polish government made reasonable requests for financial aid or export credits to help with military preparation against Germany, the British Chancellor of the Exchequer told Chamberlain that any help was 'really impossible' given Britain's own weakened state.[76] Instead of the £60 million credit asked for, Poland got the promise of £8 million shortly before the outbreak of war, and was unable to redeem it. The Governor of the Bank of England warned the Chancellor, Sir John Simon, in late July 1939 that by the autumn British gold resources would be inadequate to meet liabilities: 'we are assuring a financial catastrophe', he concluded.[77]

There were also potential problems from the workforce, which, despite rising employment and increased overtime, were not likely to be enthusiastic in the medium term about military spending crowding out spending on welfare or amenities. Having opted for a policy of rearmament in the hope that it would provide security and inhibit aggression, the West faced the reality that they were the ones vulnerable to the dangerous effects of the very policy designed to produce an end to crisis. The only way this circle could be squared was to remain firm at all costs, willing to wage a major war if it came, but hopeful until the last moment that Hitler would back down. Britain and France, not Germany, were the ones caught in a vicious economic circle.

The third factor linked to economic calculation lay in the kind of war Britain and France planned to wage. This was based almost entirely on calculations that the German economy was so economically vulnerable that sooner or later it would collapse and Germany would sue for peace as it had done in 1918. The staff talks begun between Britain and France in March 1939 took as the starting point the idea that Germany would be exposed to economic blockade while British and French forces, massed behind the Maginot defences, would wait until German internal conditions were ripe before mounting their own invasion.[78] They planned for a three-year war, but hoped it might end much sooner. The important point was the fact that the 'have-not' states' perception of their own economic weaknesses also pushed Britain and France towards an essentially economic conception of future warfare. In addition to blockade, the RAF planned to mount bombing attacks against German industrial targets, starting with the cities of the Ruhr–Rhineland industrial region.[79] The whole purpose of the planning and organization for a bombing campaign carried out since 1937 was to attack Germany's Achilles' heel. Rather than have to face the German army in the field, British forces hoped to be able to shortcut any war by applying military economic pressure.

This explains the attraction to the Western states of two economic warfare operations which were planned in the winter of 1939–40: the first was to occupy the Swedish iron ore mines in an operation codenamed 'Avonmouth'; the second was to launch pre-emptive air strikes against the Soviet oilfields around Baku and Grosny to cut Germany off from supplies of oil agreed under the German–Soviet Trade Treaty of August 1939.[80] This second plan, which originated in Paris, was taken up enthusiastically in London where it was felt that destroying Soviet oil would not only 'prove disastrous for Germany' but would have the added bonus of provoking 'the complete collapse of the war potential of the USSR' as well.[81] Much of this was operational fantasy, but it shows the extent to which Allied thinking about modern war was coloured exceptionally by the new discourse of 'total war', which saw conflict in terms of weakening the home economy rather than defeating the enemy armed forces. Misplaced confidence in German economic vulnerability persisted over five years of heavy bombardment of German cities, without preventing the German economy from continuing to produce increased quantities of armaments.

The belief that the possession of adequate material resources, territory and population determined national wellbeing, guaranteed independence and made it possible to wage war effectively now seems very much a product of a particular age. Since 1945 a (usually) buoyant world trading economy has rendered obsolete the idea that territory and raw materials – 'living-space'– guarantees economic prosperity. Germany and the Japanese Empire both declined in size but became economic superpowers. Britain lost an empire and used up most of its raw material resources, but is still among the economic top ten. But in the inter-war years, when poverty was more widespread and an international trade and payments system difficult to sustain, a crude Malthusian view of political survival made it seem that possession of additional material resources or territory was the only real security. In this sense the Marxist interpretation of war in the 1930s was not so wrong, since war was clearly directed at securing markets and resources and limiting or denying the access of other states, and these things could only be achieved by war. Manchuria, Ethiopia, Czechoslovakia and Poland were all swallowed up in the 1930s because they supplied additional resources, whatever the political or prestige motives that also accompanied their conquest. Britain and France reluctantly joined the arms race to protect their economic and political interests, and thought of waging war in military–economic terms – reducing the enemy's economic power as the principal means of weakening his military capability. Of course ideology also mattered, and political differences, which derived from the different perspectives that the 'have' and 'have-not' states brought to bear. Immediate political ambitions almost certainly brought Germany to attack Poland on 1 September 1939, while a mixture of ideological concerns for the future of the West and a sense that war could not be postponed easily without grave political risk led Britain and France to declare war on Germany two days later. Yet it is interesting to observe that one of the two British MPs who spoke out against the declaration of war on the morning of 3 September did so because in his view the war was 'a hard, soulless, grinding materialist struggle for human gain'.[82]

Notes

1   V. Gollancz, *Shall Our Children Live or Die?* London, 1942, p. 18.

2   For a discussion of its provenance see R. J. Overy, *The Morbid Age: Britain Between the Wars.* London, 2009, pp. 189–91. There were plenty of books by Marxists in the 1930s arguing the same case. See, for example, A. Hutt, *This Final Crisis.* London, 1935; or E. Wilkinson and E. Conze, *Why War? A Handbook for Those Who Will Take Part in the Second World War.* London, 1934.

3   E. Varga and L. Mendelsohn (eds), *New Data for V. I. Lenin's 'Imperialism, the Highest Stage of Capitalism'.* London, 1938, pp. 264–6.

4   Gollancz, *Shall Our Children Live or Die?*, pp. 20–1.
5   S. Newton *Profits of Peace: The Political Economy of Anglo-German Appeasement*. Oxford, 1996, pp. 97–101. See too N. Forbes 'London Banks, the German Standstill Agreements and "Economic Appeasement" in the 1930s', *Economic History Review* 2nd series, 40 (1987), pp. 571–87; R.F. Holland 'The Federation of British Industries and the International Economy', *Economic History Review* 2nd series, 34 (1981), pp. 294–8.
6   A. Lacroix-Riz, *Le Choix de la Défaite: les élites françaises dans les années 1930*. Paris, 2007, pp. 467–8.
7   C. Higham, *Trading with the Enemy*. London, 1983, pp. 36–8, 220; Lacroix-Riz, *Le Choix de la Défaite*, pp. 469–74.
8   Bank of England Archive, London, OV34 vol. 9, conversation between Montagu Norman and Walter Funk at Basle, 13 March 1939, p. 2.
9   G.D.H. Cole, 'Britain's Economic Policies and World Affairs' in A. Forbath (ed.), *Europe into the Abyss*. London, 1939, pp. 55, 58–9. See too the arguments in F. Allen, *Can Capitalism Last?* London, 1937; G.D.H. Cole, *Economic Prospects: 1938 and After*. London, 1938.
10 F. Somary, *The Raven of Zürich: The Memoirs of Felix Somary*. London, 1986, p. 175
11 Krupp Archive, K-A(L), Reden ab 7 Juli 1933, speech of 10 January 1934, p. 13. See R.J. Overy, *War and Economy in the Third Reich*. Oxford, 1994, 'Primacy always belongs to Politics: Gustav Krupp and the Third Reich', pp. 119–43.
12 H. Grimm, *Volk ohne Raum*. Munich, 1926
13 Bundesarchiv-Berlin (BAB), R7/3401, 'Deutschland unter dem Versailler Vertrag', Economics Ministry memorandum, 27 April 1933, p. 3.
14 See P. Clavin, *The Failure of Economic Diplomacy: Britain, Germany, France and the United States, 1931–36*. London, 1996 esp. chs 6–7.
15 On the decline of *laissez faire* in Britain see F. Trentmann, *Free Trade Nation: Commerce, Consumption and Civil Society in Modern Britain*. Oxford, 2008, pp. 348–61.
16 B.F. Johnston, *Japanese Food Management in World War II*. Stanford, 1953, pp. 26–7, 32, 50–1.
17 Y. Matsusaka, *The Making of Japanese Manchuria, 1904–1932*. Cambridge, MA, 2001, pp. 354–69
18 Johnston, *Japanese Food Management*, pp. 63–7.
19 R. Goralski and R.W. Freeburg, *Oil and War*. New York, 1987, pp. 92–3.
20 M.A. Barnhart *Japan Prepares for Total War: The Search for Economic Security 1919–1941*. New York, 1987, p. 146.
21 See Hosoya Chihiro, 'Britain and the United States in Japan's View of the International System' in I. Nish (ed.), *Anglo-Japanese Alienation 1919–1952*. Cambridge, MA, 1982, pp. 58–60.
22 M.A. Barnhart 'Japan's Economic Security and the Origins of the Pacific War', *Journal of Strategic Studies* 4 (1981), pp. 112–14.
23 H.T. Patrick, 'The Economic Muddle of the 1920s' in J.W. Morley (ed.), *Dilemmas of Growth in Pre-War Japan*. Princeton, 1971, pp. 250–1.
24 R. Petrie, *Von der Autarkie zum Wirtschaftswunder: Wirtschaftspolitik und industrieller Wandel in Italien 1935–1963*. Tübingen, 2001, pp. 11–12.
25 A. Nützenadel, *Landwirtschaft, Staat und Autarkie: Agrarpolitik im faschistischen Italien (1922–1943)*. Tübingen, 1997, pp. 392–5.
26 G. Rochat, *Le guerre italiane 1935–1943: Dall'impero d'Etiopia alla disfatta*. Turin, 2005, pp. 15–26; see too J. Gooch, *Mussolini and his Generals: The Armed Forces and Fascist Foreign Policy, 1922–1940*. Cambridge, 2007, pp. 239–51.
27 Cited in Petri, *Autarkie zum Wirtschaftswunder*, p. 35.
28 This and other figures from ibid., pp. 130–42.
29 R. Mallett, *The Italian Navy and Fascist Expansionism1935–1940*. London, 1998, p. 60.
30 *Hitler's Secret Book*, intro. T. Taylor. New York, 1961, p. 99.
31 BAB, R3102/3005, Reich Statistical Office memorandum 'Wehrwirtschaftliche Planung' (n.d. but early 1939).
32 See J. Maiolo, *Cry Havoc: The Arms Race and the Second World War 1931–1941*. London 2010, pp. 39–45.
33 On the Four-Year Plan see R.J. Overy 'The Four-Year Plan' in T. Gourvish (ed.), *European Yearbook of Business History, number 3*. Aldershot, 2000, pp. 87–106.

34 W. Treue, 'Hitlers Denkschrift zum Vierjahresplan, 1936', *Vierteljahreshefte für Zeitgeschichte* 3 (1955), p. 206.

35 Bundesarchiv, Berlin, R26 I/18 'Ergebnisse der Vierjahresplan-Arbeit', spring 1942, pp. 9, 20–2.

36 'Minutes of the Conference in the Reich Chancellery, 5 November 1937' in *Documents on German Foreign Policy: Series D, Vol. 1* (HMSO, 1949), pp. 29–39.

37 For details of the takeover of resources see R.J. Overy, 'The Reichswerke "Hermann Göring"' in *War and Economy in the Third Reich*, pp. 146–55. On the immediate plans for mobilising the economic resources of the Sudetenland see BAB, R26/IV/4, Four-Year Plan directors' meeting, 3 October 1938, 'Ergebnis der Besprechung über die Eingliederung Sudetendeutschlands in die reichsdeutsche Wirtschaft', chaired by Göring.

38 See on this D. Kaiser, *Economic Diplomacy and the Origins of the Second World War*. Princeton, 1980, ch. 10.

39 BAB, R2/21908, Finance Ministry memorandum, 'Zusammenstellung der Gesamteinnahmen des Reiches sowie der Ausgaben für Rüstungszwecke', 26 April 1939.

40 Bank of England, OV34/86, 'Germany wants neither Inflation nor Isolation', address on 24 August 1937 (translated from *Staatsbank*, 29 August 1937).

41 Report by Stalin to the seventeenth Congress of the CPSU, 26 January 1934 in J. Degras (ed.), *Soviet Documents on Foreign Policy*, 3 vols. Oxford, 1951–3, vol. 3, pp. 65–8.

42 R.W. Davies and M. Harrison, 'Defence Spending and Defence Industries in the 1930s' in J. Barber and M. Harrison (eds), *The Soviet Defence-Industry Complex from Stalin to Khrushchev*. London, 2000, pp. 73, 87–8.

43 On the nature of Soviet economic planning see L. Samuelson, 'Mikhail Tukhachevsky and War-Economic Planning: Reconsiderations on the Pre-War Soviet Military Build-up', *Journal of Slavic Military Studies* 9 (1996), pp. 804–47.

44 M. Thomas, 'Economic Conditions and the Limits to Mobilization in the French Empire, 1936-1939', *The Historical Journal* 48 (2005), pp. 473–5.

45 Bank of England, OV34, vol. 9, memorandum for Otto Niemeyer, 25 October 1938, p. 5.

46 Cited in S. Newman, *March 1939: The British Guarantee to Poland*. Oxford, 1976, p. 41.

47 Cited in B-J. Wendt, 'Economic Appeasement – a Crisis Strategy' in W. Mommsen and L. Kettenacker (eds), *The Fascist Challenge and the Policy of Appeasement*. London, 1983, p. 164. The memorandum by Eden was for the Imperial Conference, May 1937.

48 University of Liverpool special collections, Caradog Jones papers, D48/5/1, Petition to His Majesty's Government, draft 6 January 1937.

49 Bank of England, OV34/85, note by Cobbold, 13 November 1936.

50 On this see M. Thomas, *Britain, France and Appeasement: Anglo-French Relations in the Popular Front Era*. Oxford, 1996, pp. 115–22.

51 Bank of England archive, file S. 89 (1), memorandum by C. Gunston, 'Germany's Economic Troubles', 21 September 1936, p. 3.

52 Bank of England, memorandum by Gunston 'visit to Berlin September 1937', p. 2.

53 Thomas, *Britain, France and Appeasement*, pp. 128–33.

54 Bank of England, Governor's Letters, G3/204, Montagu Norman to Eigo Fukai, 10 May 1937.

55 Ibid., Montagu Norman to Leslie Lefeaux, 13 October 1937.

56 Bank of England, OV34, vol. 7, Henry Clay to Gunston, 11 February 1937.

57 See the discussion in T. Imlay, *Facing the Second World War: Strategy, Politics and Economics in Britain and France, 1938–1940*. Oxford, 2003, esp. chs 5–6.

58 For the full discussion of the thesis see T.W. Mason, 'Some Origins of the Second World War', *Past and Present* no. 29 (1964), pp. 67–87; idem., 'Innere Krise und Angriffskrieg' in F. Forstmeier and H-E. Volkmann (eds), *Wirtschaft und Rüstung am Vorabend des Zweiten Weltkrieges*. Düsseldorf, 1975, pp. 158–88. See also R. J. Overy, 'Germany, "Domestic Crisis" and War in 1939', *Past and Present* no. 116 (1987), pp. 138–68.

59 A. Tooze, *The Wages of Destruction: The Making and Breaking of the Nazi Economy*. London, 2006, p. 322. There is also a third argument, suggested by Götz Aly in *Hitler's Beneficiaries: How the Nazis Bought the German People*. London, 2008 that Germany's whole war effort from 1939

was simply a form of state-sponsored robbery to make the German people better off through opportunities for plunder. This thesis has not won wide acceptance.

60 BAB, R2/24266, von Krosigk Handakten, letter from von Krosigk to Hitler 1 September 1938.

61 BAB, R43 II/234, Schacht and Reichsbank Directorate to Hitler 7 January 1939, p. 1; telegram from Hitler to Schacht, 19 January 1939; chancellery communiqué, 19 January 1939.

62 BAB, R43 II/790, Landfriied to Fritz Reinhardt 11 July 1939, pp. 1–2.

63 BAB, R43 II/234, Draft letter from Hitler to Funk 19 January 1939.

64 BAB, R2501/3485, 'Der Neuen Finanzplan', Ausführungen des Staatssekretärs Reinhardt 24 March 1939; Reichsbank memorandum 'Die Durchführungsverordnung zum Neuen Finanzplan', 28 April 1939.

65 BAB, R2/21908, Finance Ministry press announcement, 3 April 1939, 'Budget Plans for 1939'.

66 BAB, R26 IV/vorl.51, report from Paul Körner to the Four-Year Plan General Council, 31 March 1939, pp. 8–14.

67 BAB, R43 II/790, Landfried to Reinhardt, 11 July 1939, pp. 2–6: 'Through this the economy would finally thanks to the savings of consumers be put in the position again to supply them at a later date on an increased scale.'

68 Bank of England, OV34 vol. 9, Note of a Conversation with Dr Puhl at Basle, 12 June 1939.

69 Ibid., 'Germany: Financial Position', 21 July 1939.

70 *Akten zur Deutschen auswärtigen Politik*, Serie D, Band vi. Baden-Baden, 1956, p. 479. On Hitler's desire for a small war see R.J. Overy, 'Germany and the Munich Crisis: A Mutilated Victory?' *Diplomacy and Statecraft* 10 (1999), pp. 191–215.

71 See Overy, *War and Economy*, pp. 111–12. More recently see H. Wixforth and J. Bähr, 'Die Expansion im besetzten Europa' in H. Wixforth et al., *Der Flick-Konzern im Dritten Reich*. Munich, 2008, pp. 400–14.

72 BAB, R7/3005, minutes of conference in the Economics Ministry on trade questions, 24 November 1939. p. 1.

73 Bank of England, OV 34 vol. 9, memorandum, 23 May 1939, p. 6.

74 Cited in P. Jackson, *France and the Nazi Menace: Intelligence and Policy-Making, 1933–39*. Oxford, 2000, p. 357. The comment was made by Alexis Léger at the French Foreign Office on 31 August 1939. See too F.H. Hinsley et al., *British Intelligence in the Second World War: Volume 1*. London, 1979, pp. 67–9.

75 G. Peden, 'A Matter of Timing: The Economic Background to British Foreign Policy, 1938–39', *History* 69 (1984), pp. 15–28.

76 The National Archives, Kew, London (henceforth TNA) PREM 1/357, memorandum for the Prime Minister from Sir John Simon, 15 May 1939.

77 Bank of England, G3/206, Montagu Norman to Simon, 24 July 1939.

78 TNA, AIR 9/105, chiefs of staff 'British Strategical Memorandum', 20 March 1939; see too M. Alexander and W.J. Philpott, 'The Entente Cordiale and the Next War: Anglo-French Views on Future Military Co-operation, 1928–1939', *Intelligence and National Security* 13 (1998), pp. 68–76.

79 See, for example, TNA, AIR 9/79 Air Ministry plans division, 'Note on the Relative Merits of Oil and Power as Objectives for Air Attack', 16 October 1939: 'The ultimate aim of the OIL and RUHR plans is identical – the collapse of Germany through shortages of essential war materials' (p. 8).

80 On the oil plan see C.O. Richardson, 'French Plans for Allied Attacks on the Caucasus Oilfields, January–April 1940', *French Historical Studies* 8 (1973).

81 TNA, AIR 9/138, Plan M.A.6, 'Appreciation of the Attack on the Russian Oil Industry', 2 April 1940, pp. 1–2.

82 *Parliamentary Debates*, vol. 351, col. 298, 3 September 1939. The MP in question was the independent socialist John McGovern.

Chapter 29

Historians at War

Anthony Adamthwaite

The Second World War rumbles on. 'Two world wars and one world cup' rings out when England's youth meets Germany's. At ceremonies marking the war's seventieth anniversary in 2009, Russian Prime Minister Vladimir Putin condemned the Nazi–Soviet non-aggression pact as 'immoral', comparing it to the Munich agreement.[1] Books pour forth. Faced with the tightly packed shelves, even aficionados might be tempted to echo Clement Attlee's rebuke to Harold Laski's criticism of party policy in 1945: 'a period of silence ... would be welcome'.[2] Do we really need more books? Very much so. True, publications keep historians in business, but there remain compelling reasons for writing about the causes of the war. Key features of the war – genocide, nuclear weapons, ethnic cleansing and the targeting of civilians – impact heavily on the twenty-first century. Recent trends make a fresh look at the historiography both timely and necessary. Research has illuminated not only immediate war origins but the whole inter-war landscape, giving us a much more nuanced sense of the era. And the return of biography and narrative that fell out of fashion in the 1970s and 1980s has greatly added to our understanding. The debate has entered a post-revisionist phase with the focus on stock taking and finding common ground rather than making revisionist and counter-revisionist challenges.

Publications are copious on the experience and conduct of war, slight on causes. Why the imbalance? Partly it's a process of catching up – because earlier writing focused on origins, partly the complexity of origins defies easy synthesis. Views vary on when the war began as well as on the relationship between the European and Asian-Pacific conflicts. What's more, the expanding frontier of evidence under the thirty-year rule inevitably draws researchers to other topics. When A.J.P. Taylor's *The Origins of the Second World War* came out in 1961, only the captured German archives were accessible. Easing archive access in Britain and France generated a spate of books in the 1970s and 1980s. However, as post-1945 material became available researchers gravitated towards the Cold War. Moreover, the emergence of the Holocaust as the dominating theme in discussions of the war pushed the primary question – 'How did we get into the war?'– into the background.

The popular stereotype of war origins was that of a wicked Hitler plotting a war of conquest, opposed at the eleventh hour by timorous democracies that had whetted his appetite by shameful surrenders. The classic statement of this view was the book *Guilty Men* (1940). Leading historians like Sir John Wheeler-Bennett and Sir Lewis Namier endorsed the morality play theme.[3] Surprisingly, young historians like Martin Gilbert, Richard Gott and Keith Robbins, who might have challenged orthodox views, simply recycled them.[4]

Why did the morality play interpretation have such an easy ride? Quite simply, the available evidence supported it. Germany's collapse yielded hundreds of tons of state documents reaching back to Bismarck. Allied teams quickly screened Third Reich files in order to prepare a prosecution case for the Nuremberg war crimes trials. After the First World War Germany had won the document wars by rushing out in six years (1922–7) forty volumes of an edited official collection, *Die Grosse Politik*[5] – an amazing achievement by any standard. Determined not to be outsmarted this time round the Allies promptly published trial documents, together with selections from German foreign ministry papers.[6] The inaccessibility of allied records buttressed the received version. Whitehall's wartime decision to publish Foreign Office papers for 1919–39 prioritized the years 1938–9, thereby furnishing fresh evidence for the failure of appeasement.[7] Completing the project took almost forty years. As a result, the hinterland of British policy remained for long patchily documented.[8]

Although the thirty-year rule opened large swathes of inter-war records, much remained hidden. The obsessive secrecy of government and society beggars belief. UK state intelligence agencies routinely denied their existence. Occasionally, humour broke through. While the headquarters of MI5 was temporarily at Wormwood Scrubs in 1939, the bus conductor would shout, 'All change for MI5.' Papers were locked away indefinitely until the Public Records Act of 1958 created a fifty-year rule. As late as 1954, Foreign Secretary Anthony Eden refused a request from a prominent Tory backbencher for access to Foreign Office papers about the Entente Cordiale of 1904.[9] Nearly thirty years went by before the Enigma secret entered the public domain in Britain. Citizens waited decades for official histories of major episodes of the nation's history – wartime intelligence, European policy, the Falklands War and MI5.[10] Whitehall, in BBC *Yes Minister* mode, invited historian M.R.D. Foot to write the first history of the wartime Special Operations Executive and then proceeded to set up an obstacle course to deter him.[11] The Waldegrave initiative on Open Government (1993) began a further liberalization of access. At the time of writing a twenty-year rule has replaced thirty – although full implementation might take ten years.

Cold War ideology buttressed the standard version of war origins. Former premier and foreign secretary Sir Anthony Eden described the theme of his memoirs as 'the lessons of the thirties and their application to the fifties'.[12] Cold warriors twinned Hitler and Stalin, and proscribed appeasement as cowardice and surrender. On major issues like post-war planning, the Truman Doctrine and the decisions to intervene in Korea and Vietnam, policy makers insisted that containment, not appeasement, offered the only realistic and honourable strategy. During the Cuban missile crisis, the media denounced Adlai Stevenson, US Ambassador to the United Nations, as an appeaser who 'wanted a Munich'.[13] The academy did its bit. Political scientists merged Nazism and Communism in a totalitarian model.[14] Nor did historians protest the Cold War straitjacket. In 1949 the President of the American Historical Association pontificated on 'the social responsibilities of the historian', asserting that 'total war, whether it be hot or cold, enlists everyone the historian is no freer from this obligation than the physicist'.[15] The loyalty oath imposed by University of California Regents in 1949–50 enforced campus repression. Britain had its own witch-hunt. Marxist historian Eric Hobsbawm recalled: 'for those not already in academic posts before the cold-war blacklisting began in the spring of 1948, the chances of university teaching were to be virtually zero for the next ten years.'[16]

British wartime myth also reinforced orthodoxy. The politics of the 1940s and 1950s shaped discussion of war origins. *Guilty Men* was prefaced by Churchill's words: 'the use of recriminating about the past is to enforce effective action at the present'. Resisting Hitler revived pride in Britishness. Lawrence Olivier's *Henry V*, premiered in November 1944, captured the triumphalist mood. Skilful editing deleted inconvenient textual references to domestic strife, massacres of French prisoners and usurpation. On VE-Day, *The Times* spoke of Britain and its empire commonwealth defending civilization alone and for longer than its allies. In resisting tyranny, the nation had recovered its traditional grandeur, confirming the values of democracy, patriotism and discipline. God had protected his people. Past and present achievements – parliamentary democracy, empire, industrial leadership, victory over Nazism – fused to give a sense of uniqueness. From this perspective, the international retreats of the 1930s became aberrations, the consequence of ineptitude.

The deep conservatism and insularity of British academic culture inhibited revisionist thinking. Historians nowadays live in the 'small world' described by novelist David Lodge. They travel the globe from one conference to the next and they can communicate via the World Wide Web. Sixty years ago, historians travelled rarely and knew little about one another. To be sure, specialists kept abreast of international scholarship, but the ever-burgeoning cyberspace networks of research institutes, conferences, colloquia, workshops and journals that promote reassessment and revision did not exist. When in 1961 Pierre Renouvin invited A.J.P. Taylor to lecture at the Sorbonne, it was a very special event – 'the first such invitation to an English historian since the war'.[17] A majority of the profession cold-shouldered both the new history represented by the French Annales School and contemporary history, insisting on the need to wait for the documents. The French school had its converts: Hugh Trevor Roper led a small group who tried 'to bring English historical studies out of their backwater' by establishing an English version.[18] The extent of indifference to recent history can be gauged from the response to a conference call by a senior French academic, Henri Michel, doyen of resistance historians. In 1959 he circulated everyone teaching history or politics in British universities, inviting them to a conference in Liege on European resistance. Only M.R.D. Foot responded.[19] Prejudice against recent history influenced appointments: 'In the ten years between 1951 and 1960 the number of new academic appointments in Britain ... to which persons whose main work lay in the field of contemporary history were appointed ... could be counted on the fingers of one hand'.[20] The British experience was not read in a global frame. The Oxford History syllabus of the early 1950s stopped in 1914, barely acknowledging the world beyond Europe except under the rubric 'Expansion of Europe' ruled. Few of the public knew much about recent European history and contemporary affairs. Russianist E.H. Carr believed that the 'serious study of Soviet history and institutions has been almost entirely neglected in Great Britain'.[21] Research and teaching privileged the origins of the war of 1914, with Munich and appeasement sidelined as too recent for scholarly study. When Taylor tried to bridge the divide between the academy and public, colleagues dismissed him as a charlatan who cheapened the discipline by making himself rich through journalism. Philosophers reacted similarly. Mary Warnock's fellow dons disapproved of her broadcasting on the BBC's *Third Programme*: 'the very idea of popularizing one's academic subject was anathema'.[22]

American historian J.H. Hexter, a specialist in Tudor and seventeenth-century England, once observed that the profession could be divided into lumpers and splitters. The lumpers have certainly left their mark on debates about twentieth-century Europe. The years 1914–45 are often described as a thirty-years war, and the period 1919–39 as a European civil war. One historian has referred to the Europe of these years as a 'Dark Continent'.[23] How the past is sliced up, sorted and labelled obviously shapes our understanding. Donald Cameron Watt wrote of an ideological civil war raging across the length and breadth of the continent: 'To very many people who lived through the years of the 1930s what seemed to be in train was not the approach of another war between states, but the preliminary stages of a civil war between the forces of oligarchy, aristocracy, authoritarianism, fascism and those of popular democracy, socialism, revolution.'[24] The rise of paramilitary leagues, imbued with a goal of revolution, and wielding violence against opponents, had produced by the mid-1930s 'in most countries of Europe a dissolution of the normal social and political process into civil disorder or civil strife'.[25] Militarization as a result of the First World War, it is alleged, dissolved the idea of a common European society, engendering violence and political extremism.

On closer inspection the notion of a European civil war is not as helpful as it might at first appear. By 1922, the Irish, Finnish and Russian civil wars had all ended. Mussolini and Hitler both came to power without large-scale violence. It is not true that by the mid-1930s most European countries faced the threat of civil dissolution or disorder. French right-wingers clashing with police in the Stavisky riots of 6 February 1934, Mosleyites and Communists battling in London's East End did not make a revolution. Diversity and complexity characterize inter-war Europe. The neat binary categorizations of democrats versus fascists projected by contemporary propaganda are misleading. What is remarkable is just how much stability and modernization the two major democracies enjoyed through the inter-war years, as indeed did Scandinavian and Benelux countries and large parts of independent Central and Eastern Europe. Describing Europe of this time as a 'Dark Continent' obscures much that was hopeful and progressive.

But what about Spain and France in the mid-1930s? Surely the Spanish war and the paroxysms of the French Popular Front confirm a European civil war? The stereotype of everyone fighting for the left or right is misleading. There were four Spains in 1936–9, not two: as well as Republicans and Nationalists there were the would-be mediators, and those like Salvador de Madriaga who opted out of the conflict.[26] To these might be added a fourth Spain of reluctant conscripts, the 'forest people' of Javier Cercas's *Soldados de Salamina* (2001) who arranged informal truces and fraternizations and who deserted as quickly as possible.[27] Spain's neutrality in the war of 1914–18 shielded it from mainline European tensions. Whatever the influence of wider European concerns, Spain's peculiarities – peripheral nationalism, anarchism, the land problem, the weakness of the state, the role of the military and the effects of colonial warfare in Morocco – weighed most in the breakdown that led to civil war.

The danger of civil war in France was more apparent than real. 'Before any foreign war,' Blum wrote to his wife in 1942, 'France would have had civil war, with precious little chance of victory for the Republic.'[28] At the time, however, Blum did not voice this fear publicly. Nor did diplomatic observers signal concern about the risk. While some of the governing elite may have feared civil war, there is no hard evidence that it posed an immediate and significant threat. Notwithstanding a lot of shouting and marching, society possessed considerable resilience. Only two serious episodes disturbed public order – the Stavisky riots and the Clichy incident in March 1937, when police fire killed six demonstrators. To be sure, as Orwell's train to Irun steamed through the French countryside, peasants working in the fields turned and gave the anti-Fascist salute, but as a gesture of solidarity, not a call to revolution. In the Czech crisis of September 1938, when opinion fiercely argued the pros and cons of defending France's ally, the Daladier government calmly mobilized a million reservists without protest or incident. Admittedly some of the French officer corps favoured Franco and castigated Republicans as 'Reds', but since the Dreyfus Affair at the turn of the century the army had doggedly avoided intervention in politics. There is no firm evidence of military plots against the regime and no reason to think that the general staff would have intervened *pronunciamento* style in a domestic emergency.[29]

At first glance, lumping together the two world wars seems common sense. Philip Bell calls it 'a powerful thesis, resting on much solid evidence and strong internal logic'.[30] After all, Germany's bid for power provides a strong thread of continuity. Marshall Foch's condemnation of Versailles as a twenty-year truce testified to the Allied supremo's bitterness and disappointment. Stefan Zweig's *The World of Yesterday* (1942) evokes the feeling shared by so many contemporaries of a world shattered by the war of 1914. However, the thirty-years war interpretation – outwardly so plausible – does not pass close scrutiny. Certainly the Great War left a fractured world, but not necessarily a doomed one. Responses to the wreckage depended on generations and vantage points. To someone like Zweig, who reached maturity well before 1914, the losses must have seemed irretrievable; for others, however, peace promised a fresh start – the chance to achieve the reconciliation and disarmament that had eluded the old world. To be sure, German ambitions drove both conflicts, but they were not identical in 1914 and 1939. Hitler's racist genocidal mission was a new phenomenon. True, Hitler shared Kaiser Wilhelm II's aim of making Germany Number One in Europe, but he also contemplated a bid for world power. From a philosophical standpoint, the thirty-years war idea implies a determinism that denies the intrinsic contingency of events. If Europe's history ran on tramlines, what agency did decision makers, ideologies and economic forces have? And why stop with a thirty-year span? Why not settle for Philip Bobbitt's long seventy-six-year epochal war (1914–90): 'the war that began in 1914 must properly be seen as having continued until 1990'.[31] The trouble with catchall explanations is that, like original sin, they appear to explain a lot but in fact explain little. They do not tell us why an international war started in Europe in 1939 rather than 1936 or 1945. Moreover, the thirty-year concept, as well as being overly deterministic, does not square with the evidence of renewal and stabilization in the 1920s. Zara Steiner's magisterial overview of the decade, *The Lights That Failed* (2005), argues compellingly that the 1920s constituted a new beginning in international relations, not just marking time on the road to a second war.

Sometimes the gap between scholarly and popular understanding appears alarmingly wide. Divergent readings of the Paris peace settlement are a case in point. While a time lag between reassessments and standard views is normal, it's remarkable how after decades of growing academic consensus Versailles is still popularly perceived as a punitive peace that caused the Second World War. Give a dog a bad name! Perhaps scholars are to blame for writing too much for each other. Happily, Margaret MacMillan's *Peacemaking 1919: Six Months that Changed the World* (2001) successfully reached out to academic and general readers alike, hopefully dispelling lingering misperceptions. A flawed settlement yes, but all things considered a considerable achievement. The negative consequences of peacemaking flowed not so much from the treaties as the disarray of the victors. Clemenceau reminded parliamentary colleagues: 'the treaty will be what you make it'.[32] Recent scholarship points up not only the importance of evaluating Versailles in the context of multiple constraints but as part of a much larger and longer process lasting until the Treaty of Lausanne of 1923, and arguably until Locarno in 1925. By the mid-1920s a real sense of stabilization and promise for the future was palpable. While older narratives highlighted America's withdrawal from Europe, Patrick Cohrs makes a strong case for an effective Anglo-American partnership in bringing about European stabilization.[33] To be sure, fragility marked post-Locarno stabilization, but this reflected the newness of the international system. Leaders faced a steep learning curve in devising and testing new rules of transnational co-operation. Although the economic tsunami of 1929 swamped the system, the initiatives taken offered valuable lessons for post-1945 European construction.

Historians differ widely on the usefulness of the thirty-year war thesis as an explanatory tool, but there is no denying the havoc caused by the world economic crisis – arguably more decisive than the legacy of the Paris peace settlement. It devastated the domestic and international landscape, creating the conditions for the rise of extremist political movements and the likelihood of war. 'No single factor', writes Richard Overy, 'was more important in explaining the breakdown of the diplomatic system in the 1930s than the world economic crisis.'[34] Economic historians still question the causes of the crash, but there is agreement on its effects. By pulling the plug on the international economy and exacerbating social conflict within states, the depression undermined the territorial status quo. Mass misery and unemployment brought political upheaval, which in turn hobbled international co-operation. Protectionism and beggar-my-neighbour policies destroyed trust and confidence. As well as facilitating Adolf Hitler's rise to power, the crash provided neighbouring states with cogent reasons for conciliating him. Deflation and the fear of aftershocks delayed rearmament. For a while the survival of capitalism appeared in question.

Marxist historians fitted the Great Depression into an economic explanation of the Second World War that became the authorized version of Soviet historiography. With capitalism on the skids, piranha-like imperialist powers fought each other for markets, resources and territory – much as Lenin had diagnosed the war of 1914. But the interpretation never became part of mainstream debates. The pragmatism of most historians resisted thesis-driven history whether Marxist or of the Spengler–Toynbee variety. Like the thirty-years war idea, the Marxist interpretation is a catchall that tells us next to nothing about the specificity of 1939–41. That said, two strands of the economic interpretation concerning Nazi Germany achieved some plausibility. Firstly, Tim Mason argued that the Third Reich's economic troubles drove Hitler into a war for plunder.[35] Secondly, big business allegedly ran Hitler, paying him and calling the tune. These claims won't wash. Adam Tooze's investigation of the German economy refutes the idea of a domestic economic crisis in 1938–9. As for big business, it certainly bankrolled Hitler at times but the analyses, of Ian Kershaw and Richard Evans suggest a partnership, with Hitler as senior partner in the driving seat.[36]

Hitler's victory in the battle of the books is undeniable. Nazism in all its shapes and forms is still sexy and hogs the Amazon listings. By 2000 the score totalled 37,000 publications on the history of Nazi Germany – 12,000 since 1995.[37] In 2005 a school watchdog warned of the Hitlerization of UK history teaching.[38] Outgoing German ambassador Thomas Matussek complained of the nation's obsession with Nazism.[39] Down the years the question of Germany's responsibility for the war of 1939, together with the pros and cons of Western appeasement, has consistently topped the debate. In 1945 Germany's responsibility went unquestioned, as did the continuity of its ambitions. Academic writing, notably Rohan Butler's *The Roots of National Socialism* (1941) and A.J.P. Taylor's *The Course of German History* (1945) indicated a one-way street from Frederick the Great to Hitler. 'German thought and German practice', wrote Butler, 'have for the last century and a half been undermining the civilization of the West ... civilization is confronted face to face with barbarism'.[40]

Can we speak of substantive continuity of German goals from 1914–45? If Hitler had not existed would others have taken his place? It is now generally agreed that despite obvious continuities – winning empire in Eastern Europe and European hegemony – the discontinuities count for more. In effect, the Third Reich concocted a new menu. Fired with a racial and ideological brew, it reached out for much more than Wilhelmine Germany. Although social darwinism and nationalism fuelled Imperial Germany's expansionism, elites accepted the international system. Nazism, however, as Hitler insisted in 1936, was a 'doctrine of conflict'. Violence was of its essence – internal terror, external conquest and genocide. There was no intention of working with the international community. Totalitarian diplomacy established a continuity between peace and war where 'subversion, propaganda, diplomatic and economic pressure, war of nerves, threat of war, localized war and general war itself all merged into a single spectrum'.[41] Recent writing re-emphasizes the driving force of ideology for racial policy and territorial expansion. Ideology furnished the ultimate aim of world domination based on the rule of an Aryan master race. Imperial Germany Germanized non-Germans but did not murder them. The Third Reich made anti-Semitism an official state doctrine for the first time in modern history. Adam Tooze argues persuasively that Hitler targeted the United States as Germany's principal enemy because of its economic might and as the centre of world Jewry. How did Hitler set about achieving his agenda? Was he master of the house? In 1945, the beginnings of the two world wars were perceived differently. The disaster of 1914 seemed more accident than design – in Lloyd George's words, the nations 'slithered' into war. But 1939, by contrast, appeared to be the outcome of premeditated aggression.[42] With the Cold War at full blast, it suited the Western democracies and Germans to demonize Hitler, shuffling off responsibility for events onto leader and henchmen. Germans described the Nazi period as 'the unconquered past' – far too recent and traumatic for stocktaking. In search of a loyal and willing Federal Republic, the West found it convenient to magnify the role of Hitler and his minions.

Taylor's claim that Hitler, far from making plans for war, had seized opportunities provided by others triggered the first phase of the debate on origins: was Hitler a planner or opportunist? Hugh Trevor-Roper, Regius Professor of Modern History at Oxford University, author of *The Last Days of Hitler* (1947), staunchly defended the planner thesis. The murky academic politics of Trevor-Roper's appointment to the Regius Chair spiced up the tussle with Taylor.[43] The underlying assumption of the planner-versus-opportunist discussion was of a monolithic Nazi state, allowing Hitler full power of decision. By the 1970s research revealed a different picture of the Third Reich – a jungle of opposing power centres and warring barons. As a result, a new phase of discussion opened: intentionalists versus structuralists. Intentionalists asserted the primacy of Hitler's ideas and intentions; structuralists insisted on the decisive dynamic of competing interest groups and personalities. Hitler, according to Hans Mommsen, was 'in all questions which needed the adoption of a fundamental and definitive position, a weak dictator'.[44] Fortunately, there is a consensus on the Third Reich's racial and foreign policies. Until quite recently the missing link in the historiography was the lack of a comprehensive and authoritative economic history. Now we have what are likely to be definitive works on the economy, Hitler and the workings of the state. Whatever the battle lines in some areas of domestic policy in the Third Reich, Hitler commanded foreign policy decisions. He had an agenda and an itinerary, which he pursued opportunistically. Research since the 1990s has successfully reinserted the centrality of economics, ideology and Hitler's leadership. His commitment to war from 1933, responsibility for its outbreak in 1939 and the widening of the conflict in 1941 stands firm. He was master of the house. What kind of wars did he envisage? It seems clear that as well as local wars he wanted a big one – a reckoning with Stalin, Churchill and Roosevelt.

The jury is still out on France's responsibility for the decisions that led to war. Until the 1970s French policy in the inter-war years was a Cinderella subject. Standard accounts treated Marianne as an also-ran, in tow to Britannia. In fact, the Third Republic was a pivotal player in international affairs, and its military collapse dramatically transformed Europe and world politics. Resisting Hitler's bid for Czechoslovakia in 1938 might well have prevented the outbreak of European war in September 1939, and a victory in 1940 would have ended the war before it became global, thereby preserving Europe's primacy. 'We are ten times better informed on the Second World War and its aftermath', wrote historian René Rémond in 1957, 'than on the end of the Third Republic.'[45] Nevertheless, historians fought shy of engaging with the French story, partly because of closed archives, partly because the state prioritized research on the Resistance, and partly because the events of the late 1930s seemed an open-and-shut case. An ailing Republic, without a powerful continental ally and militarily outclassed by Germany, suffered a series of major diplomatic reverses culminating in defeat and occupation. The French, like the British, blamed a wicked Hitler, indulged for too long by fearful democracies. However, there was a sting in the tail. Rather than excoriating their 'guilty men', the French blamed perfidious Albion for inventing appeasement. 'The Munich Agreement', declared a former ambassador to Nazi Germany, 'was the logical consequence of the policy practiced by Britain and France, but principally inspired by Britain.'[46] Novelist Francois Mauriac went much further. 'The British', wrote Mauriac, were 'responsible, in large part, for the conflict of 1939'.[47] No Gallic counterparts of A.J.P. Taylor disturbed French historiography. Taylor's emphasis on the shared responsibility of London and Paris for the coming of war proved unwelcome. When he personally gave copies of *Origins* to Pierre Renouvin and Maurice Baumont, luminaries of French diplomatic history, 'neither of them acknowledged my gift or spoke to me again'.[48]

The shock and humiliation of 1940 framed perceptions of war origins. Recovery of national pride depended in part on finding scapegoats. Resentments over Britain's conduct before, during and after the Battle of France determined attitudes. At home 'guilty men' abounded: Munichois, Vichyites and collaborators. However, pursuing all of them was neither practical nor desirable. Restoring post-Liberation confidence and cohesion required a resistance myth of a self-liberating citizenry united against the German occupier. The Provisional Government of 1944–6 exercised considerable prudence in purging elites. Enough blood had flowed – about 9, 000 summary executions took place before General de Gaulle's government imposed its authority. A general hue and cry would have contradicted the newly minted myth of a united nation. As De Gaulle put it: 'France doesn't need to look too closely at who did what during the Second World War, France needs to assert her thousand year continuity'.[49]

Declassification under the thirty-year rule breathed new life into the study of inter-war policy. A stream of path-breaking books from French, British and North American historians overturned orthodox views and established fresh narratives. Yet the reasons for the failure of French diplomacy to prevent war and for the subsequent debacle remain controversial. Robert Young's *France and the Origins of the Second World War* (1996) sought to rehabilitate the governing elite, arguing that the retreats and defeats reflected not moral or political incapacity but genuine doubts and uncertainties. In brief, the complexities, constraints and challenges overwhelmed well-intentioned leaders. Recourse to ambivalence and indecision was both understandable and unavoidable. They did the best they could: 'contradiction or ambivalence is inherent in the human condition ... the trick ... is neither to inculpate nor exonerate. It is to explain.'[50] True, historians should not rush to judgement. Yet, can explanation be separated from assessment of responsibility? Eschewing judgement leaves us with little more than a truism, namely that the French wrestled with dilemmas common to decision makers everywhere. Demonstrably, ambiguity and uncertainty belong to the human condition. But why did the French perform so miserably in the 1930s and succeed so well after 1945? Why do some countries get their act together while others fail?

Understandably, the trauma of 1940 made the politics and diplomacy of the 1930s seem like a one-way street to Vichy. But, in the light of what we know today about the Battle of France, it makes sense to disentangle the political and military stories. 1940 was primarily a military disaster, not the inexorable outcome of a terminally sick state and society. Moreover, it was an Allied disaster, product of a shaky Franco-British alliance and divided counsels. Nevertheless, far from being a foregone conclusion, Germany's victory, as Ernest May argues, was a risky gamble that might easily have gone wrong.[51] While not everyone accepts May's thesis on 1940, it serves as a reminder of the chanciness and openness of events. Individuals could and did make decisive differences. In 1938, Foreign Minister Georges Bonnet's dogged fight to keep France out of war influenced the outcome of the Munich crisis. French historians blamed the 'English governess' for their country's misfortunes.[52] But French appeasement was as much a homegrown product as its British counterpart. As well as detestation of war and fear of Germany it reflected a genuine desire for Franco-German reconciliation and a European settlement. The social dimension mattered a lot. Blum in 1936–7 and Daladier in 1938–9 sought international détente to help stabilize domestic turbulence. British tutelage was deliberately fostered to shield France from the consequences of disengagement from central and Eastern Europe. Publicly, decision makers solicited British commitments for France's allies; privately, they invited a lead. Ministers, far from being reluctant recruits in a London-inspired enterprise, were committed to concili-ation. They cherished the illusion of economic agreements with Fascist dictators leading to political rapprochement. Yet alternatives to appeasement existed. Consider the robust revival of French policy in the spring of 1939: instead of taking orders from the English governess, Paris demanded conscription and guarantees for Romania – and got them. More's the pity firmness came too late: 'the French have not been clever at taking their opportunities with us' observed Ralph Wigram, head of the central department of the Foreign Office. On one occasion he sent his wife to Paris, ostensibly on a shopping trip, in reality to convey privately to a French delegation what they should ask for in London.[53]

Taylor argued that the outbreak of war had 'little to do with Hitler' and the 'vital question' was why Britain and France failed to resist Germany before 1939.[54] Taylor's argument heralded a long-running debate on appeasement. From the late 1960s the benefit of public and private archives spawned articles and monographs. Revisionists sought to rehabilitate Prime Minister Neville Chamberlain. Appeasement, it was stressed, far from being a diplomacy of fear and cowardice, represented a realistic search for détente, propelled by wide public support, deep detestation of war and the conviction that Germany had genuine grievances. Although London and Paris had launched large rearmament programs, their immediate military and economic weaknesses combined with the triple threat from Germany, Italy and Japan left no alter-native but conciliation. 'Hope for the best and prepare for the worst' is how one leading revisionist epitomized the process.[55] In short, the only practical policy was the one pursued.

In the 1990s post-revisionists headed by R.A.C. Parker counter-attacked in force. Parker suggested that Chamberlain neglected alternative options such as accelerating rearmament, giving a clear pledge to France and seeking the support of the Soviet Union. Instead, the search for agreement with Hitler 'strengthened both Hitler's ambitions and his internal authority'. Moreover after March 1938, Parker contended, enough support in parliament and country might have been mobilized for a strong alliance with France and a strategy of containing Germany within a League framework. Sadly, the government 'rejected effective deterrence', thereby losing any hope 'of preventing the Second World War'.[56]

Was Hitler deterrable? Did practical alternatives to appeasement exist? Some points merit further discussion. Revisionists have not fully addressed a fundamental criticism of appeasement, namely that it ignored the ideological irrationality of Nazism and Fascism. British and French leaders assumed Hitler and Mussolini were sensible, rational men who would keep their word. 'I have the impression that here was a man who could be relied upon when he had given his word,' wrote Chamberlain after meeting Hitler. 'Hitler', he told colleagues, 'would not deliberately deceive a man whom he respected ... he had now established an influence over Herr Hitler'.[57] Secondly, it is now clear that the Chamberlain cabinet pursued appeasement with obstinate single-mindedness and ruthlessness. The management of public opinion is a case in point. In 1938, before Munich, a sizeable minority opposed conciliating Germany. Robust news management restricted and suppressed inconvenient information and opinion. The same ministerial single-mindedness applied to the exploration of alternatives might have produced effective outcomes. If British and French opinion was more fluid than generally recognized, so too was the international situation. 'The outstanding feature' of the international situation, minuted Eden in late 1937, was 'its extreme fluidity'.[58] That Hitler wanted war from 1933 does not mean he could not have been stopped. Opportunism and flexibility characterized his approach. Unprepared for a major conflict, he might well have hesitated in the face of a strong Anglo-French front in 1937–8.

If London and Paris had opted for deterrence from 1938, could they have counted on Moscow? Russia was the joker in the pack. A veritable mountain of evidence and analysis surrounds British, French and German intentions. Much of the commentary now wears a distinctly faded look. The fire has now gone out of the old polemics. Not so the history of Russia's involvement. It still sparkles with unresolved controversy. Russia's importance as a player is incontestable. The Nazi–Soviet non-aggression pact of August 1939 rendered the coming of war inevitable. Without it, Hitler would have hesitated to invade Poland and risk a two-front war. Two questions are very much alive. Could Russia have been corralled into an Anglo-French containment front before Munich? What chances of successful co-operation remained after October 1938?

Russia's role remains problematical because compared to the sources for the other great powers we know virtually nothing about Joseph Stalin's inner thinking. Yet his grip on policy was quite firm. Unsurprisingly, for lack of hard evidence historians have advanced a variety of interpretations. During the Cold War Soviet historians stressed Stalin's commitment to collective security as the main foreign policy goal in the 1930s. The manifest failure of this policy forced Stalin to turn to Germany and conclude a non-aggression pact. By contrast, some Western historians emphasized the 'war-revolution' concept as the main motor, insisting that Stalin's pursuit of collective security was really a device to provoke a new world war and a revolutionary situation, affording Soviet Communism a second chance to champion world revolution. Others suggest that Stalin's main interest lay in restoring the German–Soviet Rapallo relationship of the 1920s when the two states had co-operated politically and militarily. None of these readings withstands close scrutiny. Geoffrey Roberts offers the most cogent recent interpretation of Stalin's concerns on the eve of war.[59] Security came first for the Soviet ruler. The last thing he wanted was a major conflict. Ever present was the fear of a great capitalist coalition aimed at smashing the Soviet Union. In the mid-1930s the search for collective security through the League, Popular Fronts, and co-operation with Britain and France, seemed the most promising path. The Anglo-French response to the Spanish Civil War and the Czech crisis deepened Stalin's distrust of the democracies. Was an Anglo-Franco-Soviet alliance still possible after Munich? Doubtful, to say the least. When France's ambassador tried to explain his country's Munich diplomacy, Potemkin, Deputy Commissar for Foreign Affairs, responded: 'My poor friend, what have you done? For us I see no other outcome than a fourth partition of Poland.'[60]

Benito Mussolini's hefty blows to collective security and the status quo brought European war closer: invading Ethiopia in 1935, enabling Franco's victory in Spain, facilitating the Munich agreement on Czechoslovakia, attacking Albania in April 1939 and helping Hitler to finish off France in June 1940. Quite an achievement for a courtesy great power without real clout. Scholars differ sharply on the motives and nature of fascist policy. More than enough documentation exists for several interpretations. Pride of place goes to the *Duce*'s collected works – all forty-four volumes, together with Renzo De Felice's eight-volume biography. The problem is what to make of it all. The chameleon-like quality of leader and movement makes it hard to find coherence and consistency. Ernest Hemingway, as a journalist in Rome, attended Mussolini's first press conference. When reporters entered, the *Duce* sat at his desk apparently reading intently before raising his head to greet them. Hemingway edged forward to see the book. It was a French–English dictionary – turned upside down.

Chaplin's *Great Dictator* (1940) captured the comic elements of the Rome–Berlin Axis. In the same vein, Anglophone historians of the 1950s and 1960s treated Mussolini as light relief after the terrible nastiness of Hitler and Stalin. True, differences existed: considerably less internal repression (though not in Africa); much dysfunctionalty, especially in the army and police; a strong church and monarchy; and roller-coaster relations with Hitler. Denis Mack Smith considered Mussolini an opportunist living 'in cloud cuckoo land', improvising foreign policy 'almost daily'.[61] In contrast Italian historians, notably Renzo De Felice, viewed Mussolini and his regime much more sympathetically, asserting that he wanted to avoid war and stressing the continuity of Fascist diplomacy with that of Italy's pre-1914 governments. According to De Felice, Mussolini, like his Liberal predecessors, exploited his country's nominal great power status by playing a balancing role among heavyweights in order to gain empire and leverage. In particular, he sought France's recognition of Italy as a great power with an African empire. For De Felice, Mussolini was a benign dictator: 'mean spirited, if you will, but far from the cold fanaticism and the ferocious determination of a Hitler, of a Stalin, or of a Churchill'.[62] Was Mussolini therefore little more than a fence sitter who, failing to get what he wanted from London and Paris, fell into Hitler's embrace? De Felice would not accept this verdict but conceded that a new ideological Mussolini emerged in the 1930s.

The dominant voice, however, in the debate is MacGregor Knox.[63] In his view, Mussolini was from the beginning a programmatic dictator, ideologically wired and intent on war. He aimed at making Italy a truly great power by breaking the British and French hold on the Mediterranean and North Africa. The prerequisite was alliance with Germany. The interpretation is forcefully presented but not entirely persuasive. Showman and supreme opportunist, or war hungry revolutionary ideologue? Mussolini is best seen as a mix of conflicting tendencies. Increasingly drawn to Germany after 1935, he wanted the best of both worlds – ideological solidarity with Hitler while retaining autonomy and benefits for Italy. Thus he brokered a deal at Munich because he did not want to go to war and attempted to do the same in September 1939. In 1940 he waited for the assurance of France's defeat before jackal-like moving in for the spoils.

In December 1941 the Asian-Pacific conflict and the European war fused. Predictably, a huge literature encrusts the origins of the Asian-Pacific conflagration. In 1996 Michael A. Barnhart called for a new synthesis and pointed to the signs of an emerging consensus on the causes of the Asian-Pacific war.[64] The consensus is only partly realized, and a synthesis is yet to be written. The complexity of the issues and the number of players has inhibited the writing of a grand narrative. Britain, China, France, Japan, the United States and the Soviet Union all played parts. Another difficulty is the relative opacity of Japanese–American decision making. Then, as today in Washington DC, several power centres vied for a decisive say in policy making. Franklin D. Roosevelt kept his cards close to his chest and behaved at times quite deviously. Japan had a dual diplomacy: two policies pursued at the same time, one by the army/navy and one by the cabinet. Given a weak foreign ministry, the lead power centres were army/navy. Bitter policy divisions prevailed in government agencies.

Orthodox views on the origins of the Second World War in mid-twentieth century America assumed innocence and benevolence abroad. A wise Uncle Sam had for a second time rescued Europeans from the mess they had made. American advice in the approach to war had not been heeded. Japan had planned and unleashed a sneak attack at Pearl Harbor on an innocent bystander. Revisionists quickly challenged assumptions of victimhood and innocence. Paul Schroeder writing as early as 1958 declared that the Pacific War was 'unnecessary and avoidable'.[65] Roosevelt's 'excessive moralism' and desire to join the European war had caused him to ratchet up the Tokyo–Washington quarrel.

Arnold Offner argued that the United States had pursued a parallel appeasement in Europe: 'the United States was itself a revisionist power in Europe, pursuing an independently formulated policy of appeasement which was incompatible with those of Britain and France'.[66] In reply, Roosevelt's defenders argued that the president's efforts to organize resistance were frustrated by Chamberlain's pursuit of a bilateral Anglo-German approach. Support for the view that by 1938–9 Roosevelt definitely wanted to stop Hitler comes from Dominic Tierney.[67] He contends that Roosevelt's desire to help the Spanish Republic led him to break with isolationist opinion and a 'Fortress America' attitude. According to Tierney, in the spring of 1938, Roosevelt secretly devised a scheme to bypass Congress by providing covert aid to Spanish republicans.

David Lodge's Professor Morris Zapp in *Changing Places* has the ambition to kill Jane Austen forever as a subject of criticism and research by dealing with all and every subject that could possibly arise out of reading her. For Austen, this has a ring of possibility. For war origins, it's too fanciful for words. Readers expecting certainties and closure may be disappointed by this tour of changing interpretations. To many interesting questions there are not and never will be any genuine answers. While we cannot look forward to treasure troves of intimate Hitler and Stalin diaries, polemic and publications will not dry up. The debate is endless. All history is contemporary history. The twenty-first century will have different perspectives on the mega quake of 1939–45.

What of future research trajectories? *Triumph of the Dark*, Zara Steiner's synoptic sequel to *The Lights That Fail*ed, poses a slew of questions that will help frame a fresh agenda.[68] Mental maps and prosopography promise a rewarding methodology for international history. Several major topics have yet to be intensively addressed. High on the list is a study of the 1930s British Foreign Office, together with transnational analyses of foreign policy making elites. One striking gap in the literature is the lack of an in-depth look at British public opinion in the 1930s. Intelligence material presents another new challenge. The large releases in recent years have still to be incorporated into the literature.[69] One growth area in the historiography has been the investigation of German-based businesses in the Nazi period. The relationship between foreign policy and business in the democracies deserves similar scrutiny. Missing too is an analysis of the ideological mobilization of ordinary Germans and Italians. The theme crops up in many texts, but focused enquiries remain to be written.

Final reflections. One hazard of long-running debates is amnesia – of two kinds. As Oliver Sacks discovered in his own field, important books on the same theme can quickly sink into oblivion.[70] The moral perhaps is that we should always go first to the older histories. Secondly, and more alarmingly, some authors – doubtless unwittingly – appear to encourage the forgetting of key episodes. Judging from recent overviews, the Spanish Civil War, arguably of decisive significance for the outbreak of European war, seems to be slipping off the radar.[71] Yet Spain is the pre-war crisis with the fastest growing literature. An obvious conclusion from reviewing the historiography is that international historians must reach out beyond academia and narrow sub-groups to a wider audience. Taylor's *Origins*, though long outdated, still remains in print. New history writing should strive for the same accessibility. Since the 1950s the changing debate has greatly enriched our understanding of war origins. An appreciation of the subtleties, ambiguities and complexities of the time has replaced the overly simplistic binary categorizations like planner/opportunist, appeasers/anti-appeasers that held scholars captive in the 1960s and 1970s. While there is still much we don't know, we are certainly wiser than the German commandant of an Allied POW camp who prided himself on his command of English. Suspecting an escape plan, he summoned the prisoners together, and seeking to overawe them declared: 'You think I know damn nothing. Well, I know damn all.'

Notes

 1   http://news.bbc.co.uk/today/hi/today/newsid_8239000/8239491.stm.
 2   A. Bullock, *Ernest Bevin: Foreign Secretary*. Oxford, 1985, pp. 70–1.
 3   J. Wheeler-Bennett, *Munich: Prologue to Tragedy*. London, 1948; L. Namier, *Conflicts: Studies in Contemporary History*. London, 1942; *idem., Diplomatic Prelude, 1938–1939*. London, 1948.
 4   M. Gilbert and R. Gott, *The Appeasers*. London, 1963; M. Gilbert, *The Roots of Appeasement*. London, 1966; K. Robbins, *Munich 1938*. London, 1968.
 5   *Die grosse politik der europaischen kabinette 1871–1914: Sammlung der diplomatischen akten des Auswartiges amtes*. Germany, Auswartiges Amt, Berlin 1922–7. The first volume of France's rival series *Documents diplomatiques Français 1871–1914* appeared in 1929, the last in 1959!
 6   *Nazi conspiracy and Aggression*. Office of the United States Chief of Counsel for Prosecution of Axis Criminality, USGPO, Washington, 1946, vols 1–8; *Nazi Conspiracy and Aggression: Opinion and Judgment of the International Military Tribunal*. USGPO, Washington, 1947; *Nazi Conspiracy and Aggression: Supplement*. Office of United States Chief of Counsel for Prosecution of Axis Criminality, USGPO, Washington, 1947–8; *Documents on German Foreign Policy, 1918–1945* Series D (1937–45), London, 1949–64.
 7   U. Bialer, 'Telling the Truth to the People: Britain's Decision to Publish the Diplomatic Papers of the Inter-War Period', *Historical Journal* 26, 2, pp. 349–67.
 8   *Documents on British Foreign Policy, 1919–1939* (hereafter *DBFP*), 3rd series (1938–9). London, 1949–55, 10 vols; *DBFP, 1919–1925* 1st series. London, 1947–86; *DBFP, 1929–1938* 2nd series. London, 1947–84; *DBFP* series 1A (1925–29). London, 1966–75.
 9   E. Boyle Mss, Brotherton Library Special Collections, University of Leeds, MS 660/24058.
10   F.H. Hinsley et al., *British Intelligence in the Second World War: Its Influence on Strategy and Operations*, 5 vols. London, 1979–90; A. Milward, *The United Kingdom and the European Community, vol. 1: The Rise and Fall of a National Strategy 1945–1963*. London, 2002; L. Freedman, *The Official History of the Falklands Campaign*. London, 2005, vols 1–2; C. Andrew, *Defence of the Realm: An Authorized History of MI5*. London, 2009.
11   M.R.D. Foot, *Memories of an SOE Historian*. London, 2008, pp. 134–9.
12   Foreword, *The Memoirs of Sir Anthony Eden vol. 2: Facing the Dictators*. London, 1960
13   D. Tierney et al., *Failing to Win Perceptions of Victory and Defeat in International Relations*. Cambridge Mass, 2006, p. 120.
14   Z. Brzezinski and C. Friedrich, *Totalitarian Dictatorship and Autocracy*. Cambridge MS, 1956.
15   W.A. Speck, *TLS*, 15 November 1996, p. 33.
16   Ibid. For E.H. Carr's difficulty in securing a post see Jonathan Haslam, *The Vices of Integrity*. London, 1999.
17   A.J.P. Taylor, *A Personal History*. London, 1984 ed., p. 306.

18   Trevor-Roper letter 28 May 1955, Richard Davenport-Hines (ed.), *Letters from Oxford: Hugh Trevor-Roper to Bernard Berenson*. London, 2006, p. 171.
19   Foot, *Memories of an SOE Historian*, p. 129.
20   D.C. Watt, 'Contemporary History: Problems and Perspectives', *Journal of the Society of Archivists* (October 1969), p. 512.
21   Haslam, *The Vices of Integrity*, p. 121.
22   M. Warnock, *A Memoir: People and Places*. London, 2000, p. 115.
23   M. Mazower, *The Dark Continent: Europe's Twentieth Century*. London, 1998.
24   D.C. Watt, *Too Serious a Business*. London, 1975.
25   Ibid., p. 15.
26   P. Preston, *Comrades!: Portraits from the Spanish Civil War*. London, 1999; *idem., Doves of War: Four Women of Spain*. London, 2002.
27   For the myth of mass militancy see M. Seidman, *Republic of Egos: A Social History of the Spanish Civil War*. Madison, 2003.
28   C. Audry, *Leon Blum ou la politique du juste*. Paris, 1955, pp. 126–7.
29   For the French officer corps and military responses to Spain see M. Alexander, 'Soldiers and Socialists: The French Officer Corps and Leftist Governments, 1935–7' in M. Alexander and H. Graham (eds), *The French and Spanish Popular Fronts Comparative Perspectives*. Cambridge, 1989, pp. 62–78; P. Jackson, 'French Strategy and the Spanish Civil War' in C. Leitz and D. Dunthorn (eds), *Spain in an International Context 1936–1959*. New York, 1999, pp. 55–79.
30   P.M.H. Bell, *The Origins of the Second World War in Europe*. London, 2007, 3rd ed., p. 32.
31   P. Bobbitt, *The Shield of Achilles: War, Peace and the Course of History*. London, 2003, p. 571.
32   A. Adamthwaite, *Grandeur and Misery: France's Bid for Power in Europe 1914–1940*. London, 1995, p. 63.
33   P.O. Cohrs, *The Unfinished Peace after World War I: America, Britain and the Stabilization of Europe, 1919–1932*. New York, 2006.
34   Cited F. McDonough, *The Origins of the First and Second World Wars*. Cambridge, 1997, p. 103.
35   T. Mason and R.J. Overy, 'Debate: Germany, "Domestic Crisis" and War in 1939' in P. Finney (ed), *The Origins of the Second World War*. London, 1997, pp. 90–112.
36   A. Tooze, *The Wages of Destruction: The Making and Breaking of the Nazi Economy*. New York, 2006; I. Kershaw, *Hitler, 1889–1936: Hubris*. New York, 1999, *Hitler, 1936–1945: Nemesis*. New York, 2000; R.J. Evans, *The Coming of the Third Reich*. New York, 2004, *The Third Reich in Power*. New York, 2005, *The Third Reich at War*. New York, 2009.
37   Evans, *The Coming of the Third Reich*, p. xvi.
38   Annual Report: Qualifications and Curriculum Authority (QCA), *The Times* 22 December 2005, p. 4.
39   http://news.bbc.co.uk/2/hi/uk_news/education/4553782.stm.
40   R. Butler, *The Roots of National Socialism*. London, 1941, pp. 196–7.
41   J. Stern, *Hitler, the Fuhrer and the People*. London, 1975, p. 216.
42   E.M. Robertson (ed.), *The Origins of the Second World War: Historical Interpretations*. London, 1971, p .4.
43   A.J.P. Taylor, 'How to Quote: Exercises for Beginners'; H.R. Trevor-Roper, 'A Reply' in Robertson, *The Origins of the Second World War*, pp. 100–2.
44   I. Kershaw, *The Nazi Dictatorship: Problems and Perspectives of Interpretation*. London, 2000, p. 70, n. 5.
45   R. Remond, 'Plaidoyer pour une histoire délaissée. La fin de la IIIe République', *Revue Francaise de science politique* 7 (1957), p. 257.
46   A. Francois-Poncet, *Souvenir d'une ambassade a Berlin*. Paris, 1946, p. 314.
47   F. Mauriac, *Memoires politiques*. Paris, 1967, p. 292.
48   Taylor, *A Personal History*, p. 306.
49   'Memory of evil, enticement to good: An interview with Tzvetan Todorov', http://www.eurozine.com/articles/2005-08-19-todorov-en.html.
50   R. Young, *France and the Origins of the Second World War*. London, 1996, p. 150.
51   E. May, *Strange Victory: Hitler's Conquest of France*. New York, 2000.

52 F. Bedarida, 'La gouvernante anglaise' in R. Remond and J. Bourdin (eds), *Edouard Daladier, chef de gouvernement (Avril 1938–September 1939)*. Paris, 1977, pp. 228–40.

53 V. Lawford, *Bound for Diplomacy*. London, 1963, pp. 267–8.

54 A.J.P. Taylor, *The Origins of the Second World War*. London, 1961, p. 9.

55 See D. Dilks, '"We Must Hope for the Best and Prepare for the Worst": The Prime Minister, the Cabinet and Hitler's Germany 1937–9', *Proceedings of the British Academy* (1987).

56 Cited in R. Henig, *The Origins of the Second World War 1933–1941*. London, 2001, p. 91. The two essential starting points for the post-revisionist position are: R.A.C. Parker, *Chamberlain and Appeasement*. London 1993; F. McDonough, *Neville Chamberlain: Appeasement and the British Road to War*. Manchester, 1998.

57 A. Adamthwaite, *The Making of the Second World War*. London, 1977, pp. 62–3.

58 Ibid., p. 95.

59 G. Roberts. *Stalin's Wars: From World War to Cold War, 1939–1953*. New Haven, 2006, p. 7.

60 A. Adamthwaite, *France and the Coming of the Second World War*. London, 1977, p. 264.

61 McDonough, *The Origins of the Second World War*, p. 98.

62 M. Knox, 'In the Duce's Defence', *TLS* 26 February 1999.

63 M. Knox, *Mussolini Unleashed: 1939–1941*. New York, 1982, *To the Threshold of Power 1922/33: Origins and Dynamics of the Fascist and National Socialist Dictatorships*. New York, 2007.

64 M. Barnhart, 'The Origins of the Second World War in Asia and the Pacific: Synthesis Impossible?', *Diplomatic History* 20, 2 (1996), pp. 241–60.

65 McDonough, *The Origins of the Second World War*, p. 109.

66 Henig, *The Origins of the Second World War*, p. 100.

67 D. Tierney, *FDR and the Spanish Civil War*. Durham NC, 2007.

68 Z. Steiner, *Triumph of the Dark: European International History 1933–1939*. Oxford, 2010.

69 J.R. Ferris, '"Now that the Milk is Spilt": Appeasement and the Archive on Intelligence', *Diplomacy and Statecraft* 19, 3 (2008), pp. 527–65.

70 O. Sacks, *A Leg to Stand On*. London, 1984.

71 M. Mazower, *Dark Continent: Europe's Twentieth Century*. (London 1998) has only a few scattered one-liners; R. Vinen's *A History in Fragments: Europe in the Twentieth Century*. London, 2000 lives up to its name by providing only fragmentary references.

Index of Persons

Printed in Great Britain
by Amazon.co.uk, Ltd.,
Marston Gate.